The Two Horizons New Testament Commentary

Joel B. Green and Max Turner, *General Editors*

Two features distinguish THE TWO HORIZONS NEW TESTAMENT COMMENTARY series: theological exegesis and theological reflection.

Exegesis since the Reformation era and especially in the past two hundred years emphasized careful attention to philology, grammar, syntax, and concerns of a historical nature. More recently, commentary has expanded to include social-scientific, political, or canonical questions and more.

Without slighting the significance of those sorts of questions, scholars in THE TWO HORIZONS NEW TESTAMENT COMMENTARY locate their primary interests on theological readings of texts, past and present. The result is a paragraph-by-paragraph engagement with the text that is deliberately theological in focus.

Theological reflection in THE TWO HORIZONS NEW TESTAMENT COMMENTARY takes many forms, including locating each New Testament book in relation to the whole of Scripture — asking what the biblical book contributes to biblical theology — and in conversation with constructive theology of today. How commentators engage in the work of theological reflection will differ from book to book, depending on their particular theological tradition and how they perceive the work of biblical theology and theological hermeneutics. This heterogeneity derives as well from the relative infancy of the project of theological interpretation of Scripture in modern times and from the challenge of grappling with a book's message in Greco-Roman antiquity, in the canon of Scripture and history of interpretation, and for life in the admittedly diverse Western world at the beginning of the twenty-first century.

THE TWO HORIZONS NEW TESTAMENT COMMENTARY is written primarily for students, pastors, and other Christian leaders seeking to engage in theological interpretation of Scripture.

1 and 2 Timothy and Titus

Robert W. Wall

with Richard B. Steele

William B. Eerdmans Publishing Company
Grand Rapids, Michigan / Cambridge, U.K.

© 2012 Robert W. Wall
Case Studies © 2012 Richard B. Steele
All rights reserved

Published 2012 by
Wm. B. Eerdmans Publishing Co.
2140 Oak Industrial Drive N.E., Grand Rapids, Michigan 49505 /
P.O. Box 163, Cambridge CB3 9PU U.K.

Library of Congress Cataloging-in-Publication Data

Wall, Robert W.
    1 and 2 Timothy and Titus / Robert W. Wall with Richard B. Steele.
        p.   cm.   — (The Two Horizons New Testament commentary)
    Includes bibliographical references and indexes.
    ISBN 978-0-8028-2562-9 (pbk.: alk. paper)
    1. Bible. N.T. Pastoral Epistles — Commentaries.
    I. Steele, Richard B., 1952-   II. Title.

BS2735.53.W35   2012
227'.83077 — dc23

                                                              2012035587

www.eerdmans.com

Contents

Preface	ix
Abbreviations	xiii
Introduction	1
A Canonical Approach to the Pastoral Epistles	2
Texts as "Treasures in Earthen Vessels"	2
The Pauline Authorship of the Pastoral Epistles	4
The Occasion of the Pastoral Epistles as Apostolic Letters of Succession	7
The Literary Form of the Pastoral Epistles as Letters of Succession	9
The Social World of Paul's Urban Congregations	11
The Canonization of the Pauline Letter Collection	15
The Formation of the Pauline Collection	16
The Final Form of the Pauline Collection	24
The Theological Contribution of the Pastoral Epistles to the Pauline Canon	27
The Hermeneutical Role of the Pastoral Epistles within the Pauline Canon	34
Reading the Pastoral Epistles with the Acts of the Apostles	36
The Rule of Faith in Theological Interpretation	40
Three Cases in Point	44

Contents

Bibliography	46
Commentaries on the Pastoral Epistles	46
Other Works on the Pastoral Epistles	47
Works on Canonical and Rule of Faith Interpretation	52
1 TIMOTHY	**55**
1:1-2 Paul Greets Timothy	57
1:3-11 The Aim and Manner of Christian Instruction	61
1:12-17 Paul Thanks God	70
1:18-20 Paul Repeats His Charge to Timothy	75
2:1-7 Instructions regarding Congregational Worship	78
2:8–3:1a Worship Practices of Christian Men and Women	85
3:1b-7 Profiles in Leadership: Household Administrator	98
3:8-13 Profiles in Leadership: Household Servants	107
3:14–4:7a Profiles in Leadership: The Household of God	110
4:7b-16 Paul Charges Timothy to Serve Only Christ	120
5:1-16 Caring for Widows	126
5:17-25 Care of Elderly Men	131
6:1-2a The Conduct of Christian Slaves	136
6:2b-10 False Teachers	139
6:11-16 Charge to Remain Faithful to Christ Jesus	143
6:17-19 Final Instructions for the Congregation's Wealthy Communicants	148
6:20-21 Concluding Benediction	151
A Rule of Faith Reading of 1 Timothy	154
The Creator God	154
Christ Jesus the Lord	163
The Community of the Spirit	169
Christian Existence and Discipleship	186
Consummation in a New Creation	195

CASE STUDY: JOHN WESLEY AND THE EARLY METHODIST SOCIETIES	201
2 TIMOTHY	**215**
1:1-2 Paul Greets Timothy	216
1:3-7 Paul Thanks God for Timothy	218
1:8-14 Unashamed of a Sacred Calling	225
1:15-18 The Example of Onesiphorus	231
2:1-3a A Faithful Succession	235
2:3b-7 Three Examples of Suffering	238
2:8-13 Suffering as a Resurrection Practice	241
2:14-26 True and False Teachers	248
3:1-9 The Last Days	259
3:10–4:5 Prepared for Every Good Work	263
EXCURSUS: THE SEPTUAGINT AS THE CHRISTIAN OLD TESTAMENT?	271
4:6-8 Paul's Death Is at Hand	281
4:9-22 Final Instructions, Greetings, and Benediction	283
A Rule of Faith Reading of 2 Timothy	289
The Creator God	289
Christ Jesus the Lord	293
The Community of the Spirit	299
Christian Existence and Discipleship	304
EXCURSUS: THE ROLE OF SCRIPTURE IN THE FORMATION OF A FAITHFUL CHURCH	310
Consummation in a New Creation	315
CASE STUDY: JOHN WILLIAM FLETCHER: JOHN WESLEY'S DESIGNATED SUCCESSOR	319
TITUS	**331**
1:1-4 Paul Greets Titus	334
1:5-9 A Qualified Elder	339

1:10–2:1 A Defiled Opposition	342
2:2-10 A Healthy Household	346
2:11-14 Salvation's Appearance	352
2:15–3:8c Salvation's Bath	357
Excursus: The Canonical Effect of Titus 3:5b-6	367
3:8d-15 Final Instructions, Greetings, and Benediction	370
A Rule of Faith Reading of Titus	**374**
The Creator God	374
Christ Jesus the Lord	378
The Community of the Spirit	381
Christian Existence and Discipleship	384
Consummation in a New Creation	388
Case Study: Phoebe Palmer and the Wesleyan Holiness Movement	**390**
Index of Authors	402
Index of Subjects	406
Index of Scripture References	410

Preface

In an edgy *Provocation*, "Kill the Commentators," Søren Kierkegaard famously said with biting irony that "Christian scholarship is the Church's prodigious invention to defend itself against the Bible, to ensure that we can continue to be good Christians without the Bible coming too close. Dreadful it is to fall into the hands of the living God. Yes, it is even dreadful to be alone with the New Testament."[1] The collection of Pauline Pastorals, 1-2 Timothy and Titus, is among those biblical writings that have suffered from bad press and neglect because of the "invention" of modern Christian scholarship. The academy's verdict, now axiomatic, is that their authorship (not by Paul) and social location (long after Paul's death) have rendered them useless for scholars interested in questing after the "real" Paul and his theological center. Furthermore, their reinterpretation of Paul for a later patriarchal "household of God" might seem to make their instruction irrelevant for congregations of postmodern readers.

Despite an array of famous (and even important) one-liners found in these letters, the staple of catechism classes for centuries, there are also "texts of terror" that have been used or abused to push sisters and brothers to the harsh margins of a community called to instantiate God's love in the world. 1 Tim 2:9-15 is such a text, especially when received with its history of patriarchal interpretation that has denied God's call of gifted women to Christian ministry or has restricted them to domestic chores. In a similar way, the catalog of credentials for church leadership in 1 Timothy 3, even though presented as a guideline, has been prescribed in an artless manner to exclude mature believers from using their talents to secure the congregation's spiritual and so-

---

1. Søren Kierkegard, *Provocations: Spiritual Writings of Søren Kierkegaard* (ed. C. E. Moore; Farmington, PA: Plough, 2002), 201.

cial well-being. And the sentiment that the role of slaves is to benefit their masters (1 Tim 6:1-2), even when contextualized by the social world of ancient Roman culture, sounds an embarrassing note in today's world, alert to the horrors of human trafficking. No wonder many modern Christians, who like the author of these letters seek to adapt the gospel to culturally acceptable patterns of behavior, find these instructions offensive. Within more conservative communions where these letters are on the approved reading list, their instruction is typically applied only selectively to defend a congregation's countervailing orthodoxy or social practices against liberal religion, which advances women clergy too quickly or has been too soft on perceived heresy and modernity's moral relativism.

Rick Steele and I rather suggest that whether or not the Pastorals are paraded and practiced in a Christian congregation or studied in our scholarly guilds is less the result of a verdict about their authorship or current hip-factor, and more the result of a theology of the Bible as the church's Scripture. We approach these letters, as the faithful reader does every other writing the church receives in its biblical canon, as *sacred* texts, made so by the continuing inspiration of God's Spirit and put to use under the Spirit's direction as a means of grace to grow Christian faith and a vital piety. We agree that our various Bible practices may confidently target holy ends — deeper communion with God and loving fellowship with others — not on the conditions that a text's attributed author is confirmed by historians or that its original meaning can be reconstructed by the tools of modern criticism, but on the belief that God's Spirit sanctifies and uses these same texts to lead Jesus' followers into truth about God's providential way of ordering the world.

This commentary has unfolded over many years of teaching these texts, with the help and prodding of many colleagues and students. I gladly admit my debt to them all. Besides several classes of students who have studied these texts with me, I have benefited from several superb commentaries published by scholars more learned and skilled than I. Those by John Calvin, Jouette Bassler (1996), Luke Johnson (1996, 2001), Howard Marshall (1999), Raymond Collins (2002), and Phil Towner (2006) have been of particular value. In addition, the working bibliography of this book credits an array of other conversation partners whose collective work has been of inestimable importance in guiding my own (sometimes idiosyncratic!) reading of and reflection on these letters. I should note that the reader will find everywhere the keen influence of Brevard Childs and James Sanders, whose important work and, in the case of Jim Sanders, friendship, have made a profound impression on my thinking about an interpretive approach to Scripture as a canon of sacred texts whose history of formation and literary form intend to guide how a faith community uses its instruction in search of theological understanding.

The careful reader will also note the influence of Steve Fowl and Joel Green, both friends and collaborators of many years, who have shaped my thinking about a theology of Scripture that coheres to Spirit-led performances within a community of faithful readers. The busy design of this commentary, which integrates a canonical approach to exegesis and a theological reading constrained by Tertullian's articulation of the apostolic Rule of Faith and is grounded in stories of Christian movements and those who led them, is a testimony to Steve and Joel's insistence that Scripture must be firmly located in ecclesial soil and envisage an equal commitment to its role in forming Christian beliefs and virtue. To this interpretive community of patience and truth-telling should be added my wonderful colleagues at Seattle Pacific University, especially those in Scripture: Sara Koenig, Jack Levison, Bo Lim, David Nienhuis, and Frank Spina. Finally, I note a special debt of gratitude to the hard work of Steve Perisho, our librarian extraordinaire, and Bill Horst, my graduate assistant, whose help especially in tracking down sources and fashioning indexes has been invaluable. They are simply the best!

Rick Steele and I have been friends and colleagues at Seattle Pacific University for many years; it has been a special blessing to work on this project together. He is a brilliant classroom teacher — among the best I have ever observed — whose skill at storytelling and relating Christian theology to real events and people is reflected in three case studies spread through this commentary. They are not only superb scholarly productions, but they reflect a deep sensitivity for teaching Scripture in ways that enliven faithful practice.

Finally, there is hardly another in our circle who is more generous with his time as a scholar and exemplary in his care of friendships than Eugene E. Lemcio. He is the very personification of the faithful servant profiled in these letters! Perhaps no one has benefited more from his graciousness than I have. From the moment I arrived on our campus many years ago — Gene was among those who met Carla and me to help unload a large vanload of furniture into our new home in Seattle — he has mentored and encouraged me in both my academic calling and Christian discipleship. He edited drafts of my work, offering countless suggestions for improvement before sending it off for publication. We talked over meals about teaching Scripture to our students in ways that framed their questions and formed their faithfulness to God. He is the very best conversation partner one can imagine — careful, honest, curious, humble, always wanting the very best

Preface

of and for the other. It is a very great pleasure to dedicate this book to him on the occasion of his retirement from our faculty as an extraordinary professor of New Testament.

Robert W. Wall
Lent, 2012

Abbreviations

AB	Anchor Bible
ABC	African Bible Commentary
ABD	*Anchor Bible Dictionary*
ACNT	Augsburg Commentaries on the New Testament
AnBib	Analecta biblica
ANTC	Abingdon New Testament Commentaries
AUSS	*Andrews University Seminary Studies*
AYBRL	Anchor Yale Bible Reference Library
BAG	Bauer, W., W. F. Arndt, and F. W. Gingrich. *A Greek-English Lexicon of the New Testament and Other Early Christian Literature.* 4th ed. Chicago: University of Chicago Press, 1957.
BBR	*Bulletin for Biblical Research*
BibInt	*Biblical Interpretation*
BJRL	*Bulletin of the John Rylands Library*
BNTC	Black's New Testament Commentaries
BT	*The Bible Translator*
ChBib	*The Church's Bible*
CBQ	*Catholic Bible Quarterly*
CC	Continental Commentaries
CCR	Cambridge Companions to Religion
CGLP	Coptic Gnostic Library Project
CGTC	Cambridge Greek Testament Commentary
CH	*Church History*
COS	Church of the Saviour
CPR	*Continental Philosophy Review*
DPL	*Dictionary of Paul and His Letters*
DTIB	*Dictionary for Theological Interpretation of the Bible.* Edited by Kevin J. Vanhoozer, Craig G. Bartholomew, Daniel J. Treier, and N. T. Wright. London: SPCK, 2005.

Abbreviations

EC	Epworth Commentaries
EQ	*Evangelical Quarterly*
ExpTim	*Expository Times*
FRLANT	Forschungen zur Religion und Literatur des Alten und Neuen Testaments
GBS	Guides to Biblical Scholarship
GNS	Good New Studies
HBT	*Horizons in Biblical Theology*
HNT	Handbuch zum Neuen Testament
HR	*History of Religions*
HTR	Harvard Theological Review
HUT	Hermeneutische Untersuchungen zur Theologie
IBS	*Irish Biblical Studies*
ICC	International Critical Commentary
Int	*Interpretation*
IJST	*International Journal of Systematic Theology*
JAAR	*Journal of the American Academy of Religion*
JBL	*Journal of Biblical Literature*
JHC	*Journal of Higher Criticism*
JRelS	*Journal of Religious Studies*
JSNT	*Journal for the Study of the New Testament*
JSNTSup	Supplemental Volume to Journal for the Study of the New Testament
JSOT	*Journal for the Study of the Old Testament*
JTI	*Journal for Theological Interpretation*
JTS	*Journal of Theological Studies*
KPG	Knox Preaching Guides
LN	*Greek-English Lexicon of the New Testament: Based on Semantic Domains*. Edited by J. P. Louw and E. A. Nida, 2d ed. New York: United Bible Societies, 1989.
LNTS	Library of New Testament Studies
LOTS	Library of Hebrew Bible/Old Testament Studies
LTP	*Laval théologique et philosophique*
MNTC	Moffatt New Testament Commentary
MNTS	McMaster New Testament Studies
ms(s).	manuscript(s)
MS	Mediaeval Studies
MT	Masoretic Text
NCB	New Century Bible
NewCB	New Clarendon Bible
NIB	New Interpreter's Bible
NIBC	New International Biblical Commentary

NICNT	New International Commentary on the New Testament
NIGTC	New International Greek Testament Commentary
NovT	*Novum Testamentum*
NovTSup	Novum Testamentum Supplements
NPNF	Nicene and Post-Nicene Fathers
NTC	New Testament in Context
NTG	New Testament Guides
NTL	New Testament Library
NTM	New Testament Monographs
NTOA	Novum Testamentum et Orbis Antiquus
NTS	*New Testament Studies*
NTT	New Testament Theology
OHS	Basil of Caesarea, *On the Holy Spirit*
OTL	Old Testament Library
PE	*Pro Ecclesia*
PNTC	Penguin New Testament Commentary
PRSt	*Perspectives in Religious Studies*
PWS	Pietist and Wesleyan Studies
RB	*Revue biblique*
ResQ	*Restoration Quarterly*
RNT	Regensburger Neues Testament
SB	H. Strack and P. Billerbeck, *Kommentar zum Neuen Testament aus Talmud und Midrasch*. 6 vols. Munich: Beck, 1922-61.
SBJT	*Southern Baptist Journal of Theology*
SBL	Society of Biblical Literature
SBLDS	Society of Biblical Literature Dissertation Series
SBLSBS	Society of Biblical Literature Sources for Biblical Study
SD	Studies and Documents
SE	*Studia evangelica*
SJT	*Scottish Journal of Theology*
SNTSMS	Society for New Testament Studies Monograph Series
SNTSU	Studien zum Neuen Testament und seiner Umwelt
SNTW	Studies of the New Testament and Its World
St	*Studium*
StBL	Studies in Biblical Literature
StPtr	Studia Patristica
TDNT	*Theological Dictionary of the New Testament.* Edited by G. Kittel and G. Friedrich. Grand Rapids: Eerdmans, 1964-76.
TNTC	Tyndale New Testament Commentaries
TrinJ	*Trinity Journal*
THNTC	Two Horizons New Testament Commentary
TynBul	*Tyndale Bulletin*

Abbreviations

UBSHS	United Bible Society Handbook Series
VC	*Vigilae christianae*
WBC	Word Biblical Commentary
WJF	Fletcher, John William. *The Works of the Rev. John Fletcher, Late Vicar of Madeley.* 4 vols. New York: Carlton and Lanahan, 1854.
WJW	*Works of John Wesley.* Edited by Albert C. Outler et al. Nashville: Abingdon, 1984-.
WJW-Jackson	*Works of John Wesley.* Edited by Thomas Jackson. 3rd ed. reprint, Peabody: Hendrickson, 1984.
WTJ	*Wesleyan Theological Journal*
WUNT	Wissenschaftliche Untersuchungen zum Neuen Testament
ZNW	*Zeitschrift für die neutestamentliche Wissenschaft und die Kunde der älteren Kirche*

Introduction

Joel Green's invitation to contribute a commentary on the Pauline collection of "Pastoral Epistles" to this series has given me an opportunity to continue exploring features of a canonical approach to theological interpretation. I had already begun to question the historical-critical assessment of the Pastoral Epistles when the invitation came, not so much because of disagreements with the now axiomatic verdict of their deutero-Pauline authorship and post-Pauline social location, but because the practical effect of this negative judgment of their "authenticity" has had a de-canonizing effect on their current readers. In the minds of many, if the Pastoral Epistles were authored by nameless pseudepigraphers who only selectively remembered and reinterpreted Paul's apostolic legacy for a post-Pauline setting in which a de-apocalypticized, politically domesticated, and patriarchal "household of God" had become the ecclesial norm, then their instruction, which was designed for a more repressive time and another kind of faith community, seems irrelevant for readers shaped by a postmodern *Zeitgeist*.

The practices and orienting concerns of theological interpretation cohere to a theology of the Bible as the church's Scripture. The reception and uses of Scripture at its ecclesial address, indexed by the hermeneutics of the canonical process and the final literary form of its canonical product, are of a piece with what the one, holy, catholic, and apostolic church confesses about itself. There is no Christian Scripture apart from the church, and so a theological reading of Scripture will generally be interested in the interpenetrating relationships of different texts within the one biblical canon, in the holy effects an interpretation has on its faithful readers, in the catholic reach of its application to different Christian communities in different time-zones, and in its coherence to what the apostles witnessed and proclaimed of the incarnate One. Quite apart from and in no way in competition with an interpreter's linguistic acuity or historical-critical fluency, theological interpretation emphasizes how the church practices and performs its Scripture to form its spiritual wisdom and to guide the lives of its members with God and one another.[1]

A Canonical Approach to the Pastoral Epistles[2]

Texts as "Treasures in Earthen Vessels"

A persistent objection to the canonical approach is that it refuses to read biblical texts as historically shaped. But this is not the case: no one who approaches a text by the light of its textual setting within the biblical canon or its canonical performances as Scripture doubts for a moment that such a text must also be approached as a human production with full awareness of the particular socio-historical forces at work during the long history of its composition and canonization. In fact, on the rare occasion that biblical writers reflect on what they are doing, they do not characterize their writing as a magical performance or divine dictation but as an occasional and conventional literary act, addressed to real people and read aloud to particular congregations (e.g., Luke 1:1-4; Eph 3:3-4; 1 Tim 4:13; Rev 1:1-4).

Canonical exegesis is characterized by an interest in this human, historical element. Like the apostolicity of Paul's gospel, the apostolicity of the text requires the interpreter to regard it as a "treasure in earthen vessels" (2 Cor 4:7). All the factors that shaped the earliest literary history of individual biblical compositions at their diverse points of ancient origins — language, date and location, religious experience, and spiritual crisis or social struggle — should also inform the exegete's understanding of what the text actually says, even if written and first read and heard for reasons that differ from why it is subsequently received by a later generation of readers/hearers as Scripture. The aim of faithful exegesis is not to hunt down "the" normative meaning of a text based on what the author or first readers intended. It is, rather, to address a text's lack of clarity as a major cause of its misuse or non-use among its present interpreters. The goal of critical exegesis is to build a consensus

---

1. For a recent description of the orienting concerns of a canonical approach to theological interpretation, see my discussion in *Biblical Hermeneutics: Five Views* (ed. S. Porter and B. Stovell; Downers Grove: InterVarsity, 2012).

2. See my general introduction to this interpretive strategy, "Canonical Context and Canonical Conversations," in *Between Two Horizons: Spanning New Testament Studies and Systematic Theology* (ed. Joel B. Green and Max Turner; Grand Rapids: Eerdmans, 1999), 165-82. The exegetical portions of this commentary attempt to illustrate this interpretive strategy as set out in this essay.

within a community of readers, agreeing on what a text plainly says ideally in anticipation of its various performances as a sacred text.[3]

Exegesis that clarifies what a text plainly says should also aim at restoring to full volume the voice of every biblical witness. The endgame of this critical work is the recovery of the whole sense or "tenor" of Scripture, which is vocalized as a chorus of its various witnesses to God's word. To presume the simultaneity between every part of the whole, without then adequately discerning the plain sense of each in turn, not only shortchanges the diversity of the whole but undermines the integral nature of Scripture, thus distorting its full witness to God.[4] If the penultimate aim of hard-nosed exegesis is to expose the theological plurality of Scripture, its ultimate purpose is "to put the text back together in a way that makes it available in the present and in its (biblical) entirety — not merely in the past and in the form of historically contextualized fragments."[5] In this sense, then, exegesis of the literal or plain sense of Scripture is foundational for scriptural interpretation, but has value only in relationship to a more holistic end.[6]

The linguistic priority of the exegetical task does expose the inherent elasticity of words and their grammatical relationships. Further changes in the perception of a text's meaning may result from new evidence and different exegetical strategies and from interpreters shaped by diverse social and theological locations. In fact, neutrality toward texts as human productions requires such changes in meaning to be made. Our experience with biblical texts in particular, layered into the history of their interpretation, cautions the exegete not to absolutize a particular textual meaning. Building a critical consensus regarding what a text plainly says is never a static process and requires the more careful and current thinking of an entire community gathered to work toward this common end. Nonetheless, this text is canonical for a particular religious community. Exegesis intended to bring greater clarity to the Bible must then be aimed by the community's teachers at more practical

---

3. Although we disagree about the ends of exegesis, J. Barton's *The Nature of Biblical Criticism* (Louisville: Westminster John Knox, 2007) is in my mind the best available discussion of this crucial point.

4. The work of M. Bakhtin has been especially helpful in reimagining how the theological diversity of Scripture's multiple witnesses requires a clear definition of each and creative reflection on how it interacts and continues to influence every other witness. In drawing on this point, most critics cite Bakhtin's discussion of the nature "polyphony" in *Problems of Dostoevsky's Poetics* (Minneapolis: University of Minnesota Press, 1984).

5. Jon D. Levenson, *The Hebrew Bible, the Old Testament, and Historical Criticism* (Louisville: Westminster John Knox, 1993), 79.

6. Esp. Brevard S. Childs, *Biblical Theology of Old and New Testaments* (Minneapolis: Fortress, 1992), 719-27.

Introduction

ends: knowing more precisely what to believe and how to behave as God's people must.

Fortunately, several commentaries on the Pastorals have been recently published that do excellent work in locating these letters in their ancient social worlds. I stand on the shoulders of their authors to see my way clear on these historical-critical matters.[7] The following discussions of the standard topics of modern historical prolegomena are glossed by the interests of canonical exegesis. In my view, the modern quest of the historical Paul and a version of textual meaning predicated on authorial intent have largely been guided by a myth of originality that assumed a text's normative meaning is brought to clarity by a rigorous assessment of its author's social and literary worlds. However the interpreter reconstructs the text's "original" meaning by the tools of critical exegesis comes to serve as the regulatory norm that measures the validity of any subsequent meaning, especially to protect the text's author from his self-serving interpreters.[8]

But while the historian is also interested in clarifying the plain sense of the text and in constraining self-serving uses of it, such interests hardly secure the text's theological value for today's reader. Therefore, my discussions of the standard questions of introduction intend to make us more alert to what the Pastoral Epistles actually teach as textual treasures in earthen vessels.[9]

The Pauline Authorship of the Pastoral Epistles[10]

This commentary names the author of the Pastoral Epistles "Paul." Such an attribution is not secured by historical analysis, since the hard evidence nec-

---

7. The reader is encouraged to consult especially the commentaries of Jouette M. Bassler, I. Howard Marshall, William D. Mounce, Philip Towner, Raymond F. Collins, Luke Timothy Johnson, Samuel Ngewa, and George W. Knight. Several important monographs noted in following footnotes develop more thoroughly important thematic and background matters. A fluent primer by Mark Harding, *What Are They Saying about the Pastoral Epistles?* (New York: Paulist, 2001), is a good portal into these introductory matters, though now somewhat dated.

8. This is the essential conclusion of Robert Morgan, "Made in Germany: Towards an Anglican Appropriation of an Originally Lutheran Genre," in *Aufgabe und Durchführung einer Theologie des Neuen Testaments* (ed. Cilliers Breytenbach and Jorg Frey; WUNT 205; Tübingen: Mohr Siebeck, 2007), 85-112.

9. See Stephen E. Fowl, *Theological Interpretation of Scripture* (Eugene: Wipf and Stock, 2009), esp. 13-53.

10. My construction of and response to this historical concern are set out in brief in an exchange with Stanley E. Porter; see his "Pauline Authorship and the Pastoral Epistles: Implications for Canon," *BBR* 5 (1995): 105-23, and my response, "Pauline Authorship and the Pastoral

essary to do so is much too sparse and uncertain. The Paul who addresses every reader of these letters is not the historical Paul, but the "canonical" Paul, whose continuing importance as Christ's apostle frames the church's use of his biblical letters in every age.

Even so, the historian's quest of the real author of the Pastoral Epistles remains important to their reception within the modern academy: did the historical Paul participate in writing the Pastoral Epistles as attributed, or did someone else do so under his name long after his passing and probably without his permission? And if the evidence points us in this direction, did the author do so to deceive, or to assume a sacred duty to continue writing in the spirit of the departed apostle? It has become axiomatic for modern criticism to deny Pauline authorship of 1 Timothy on historical grounds, and in most cases also of 2 Timothy and Titus.

Without repeating the arguments on every side of this ongoing debate, let me simply sketch the evidence typically used by those who contend the Pastoral Epistles are not written by Paul and are therefore "inauthentic," "deutero-Pauline," or "fictive," or given other similar rubrics that effectively set them outside the Pauline corpus: (1) use of vocabulary different from that of the genuine letters; (2) images of a more developed (= post-Pauline) church structure (e.g., 1 Tim 3:1-16; Tit 1:3-7); (3) routine appeal to traditions about Paul as an exemplary person worthy to be imitated (e.g., 1 Tim 1:12-17; 2 Tim 3:11-14) or to formulas of his teaching as the congregation's theological norm (e.g., 1 Tim 2:3-7; Tit 2:11-14; 3:3-7; cf. the "faithful sayings" of 1 Tim 1:15; 2 Tim 1:9; 2:11-13), which many contend are intended to preserve the blessed memory of a now-deceased Paul; (4) the imprecise description of Paul's opponents, suggesting that they are fictionalized and used for rhetorical ends; (5) teaching or practices inconsistent with what we know from the genuine letters; and (6) a "sociology of domesticity" that points to a later time period when earliest Christianity's apocalyptic gospel and practices were replaced by a concern for long-term social stability and political respectability (e.g., 1 Tim 2:8-15; 6:1-2).

This body of evidence generally fails to convince me. The diversity evident within the Pauline collection at every level makes it difficult to nail down any single letter as non-Pauline on the grounds that it is different from the rest.[11] Additionally, Paul may have followed ancient convention and writ-

---

Epistles: A Response to S. E. Porter," *BBR* 5 (1995): 125-28. What follows offers a more pointed discussion of a canonical approach to this question.

11. By and large, I accept Porter's trenchant rebuttal of this historical criticism and his counterargument in "Pauline Authorship." The issue I have with this methodological interest lies not here but in his epistemic assumption, also modernist, that authorship equates with apostolicity.

ten letters with the aid of secretaries or even co-authors: the collaborative nature of literary productions in antiquity may help explain the Pastorals' different vocabulary and distinctive literary character within the Pauline letter corpus. Every Pauline letter is linguistically, theologically, and sociologically inconsistent with every other Pauline letter due to variations of secretary/editors/co-authors, audience, occasion, and Paul's own developing theological understanding.[12] This is true even within the Pastoral Epistles collection, where differences among them in language, purpose, and theological emphasis can be easily detected and will be explained in a brief introduction to each.

Suffice it to say that from the historian's perspective that, if the historian's Paul did not participate in writing the Pastoral Epistles, if "Timothy" and "Titus" are fictional recipients of letters Paul did not write, if these letters' dates of composition came long after the apostle's death, if they were written for a church that did not know Paul in person, if the opponents and problems mentioned in the letters are merely tropes that reimagine Paul's legacy for a later day, then the world behind the text that frames its exegesis would necessarily be cast in different ways than if it could be determined that Paul did actively participate in their production. In my mind, however, these speculations of who is responsible for the canonical letters (i.e., the letters in their final form) are largely irrelevant considerations when deciding a text's canonicity. Moreover, the argument, often heard among conservatives, that a fictive letter would have been skunked out as a deception and rejected as canonical in antiquity strikes me as an anachronism, since what determines a literary fiction or a "real" author is itself subject to modern historical-critical criteria.[13]

---

12. See Hermann Patsch's study of the reception of F. Schleiermacher's initial and highly controversial essay that first challenged Pauline authorship of 1 Timothy: "The Fear of Deutero-Paulinism: The Reception of Friedrich Schleiermacher's 'Critical Open Letter' concerning 1 Timothy," *Journal of Higher Criticism* 6 (1999): 3-31. Schleiermacher's argument was based almost entirely on his assessment of "non-Pauline phrases and a host of *hapax legomena* that provided the decisive evidence against Pauline authorship." Sharply negative reactions also came from those scholars who shared Schleiermacher's grammatical-historical interests in the text (esp. M. J. H. Beckhaus) and who used the same approach to argue the same might be said of any Pauline letter. That is, the principal argument against Schleiermacher challenged the very existence of a Pauline linguistic standard by which to measure the authenticity of any "Pauline text."

13. The most able of these "deception" arguments is presented by T. L. Wilder, *Pseudonymity, the New Testament, and Deception: An Inquiry into Intention and Reception* (Lanham: University Press of America, 2004). The essential argument goes something like this: if an author other than Paul wrote a letter as a substitute for the real thing, then his intention was to deceive others and on this moral basis the church's reception of what had been written would have been subverted by the imposter who had written it.

Introduction

In this regard, the most striking feature of modernity's quest of the real author of biblical texts is the tacit connection made (at least since the Reformation) between the text's author and a letter's apostolicity. The modern marginalization of the Pastoral Epistles on the basis of their inauthenticity is rooted in what A. Lincoln calls an "authorial fallacy."[14] According to this fallacy, the criterion of a text's apostolicity is based on whether modern historical reconstructions "prove" a real apostle had a hand in the production of the text. A critical orthodoxy based on the "assured results" of leading scholars on this point often predetermines a judgment about a text's usefulness or continuing authority. In fact, L. T. Johnson implies that increasingly an *idola theatri* is in play as the principal reason the Pastoral Epistles are marginalized within the academic guild, where scholars sometimes accept the verdict of critical orthodoxy without careful examination.[15]

The apostolicity of a biblical text is recognized by the church, not by modern historical constructions, but from its effects when it is used. Most of the biblical compositions are anonymous or come with attributions that are difficult to nail down on historical grounds. Judgments about apostolicity are therefore mostly intuitive rather than critical and are based on track records of practical use by Christians as a means of divine grace. The church's treasuring of these earthen vessels is not blindly given but predicated on hard evidence of a practical kind.

The Occasion of the Pastoral Epistles as Apostolic Letters of Succession

Even though recent commentaries have offered elaborate reconstructions of the circumstances that occasioned the writing of each of the Pastoral Epistles, most contend that the instructions and exhortation found in them respond in some way to early opponents of Pauline Christianity. While several opponents are named in these letters, the passing references to them hardly explain the letters as a whole. Not only is the opponents' profile thinly drawn, the letters' instruction is practical, personal, and not very concerned to correct the bad theology of Paul's opponents.

Put simply, the occasion of these letters is better understood as a response to the crisis of Paul's departure (cf. 1 Tim 1:3; Tit 1:5) and the effects his absence may have on his unproven associates and their fledging households

---

14. Andrew T. Lincoln, *Ephesians* (WBC; Dallas: Word, 1990), lxxii-lxxiii.
15. Luke T. Johnson, *The First and Second Letters to Timothy: A New Translation with Introduction and Commentary* (New York: Doubleday, 2001), pp. 52-54.

of believers in hard places. The variegated instructions, theological formulas, and pastoral admonitions in these letters are apropos of the succession of a Pauline apostolate to the ever-next generation of his tradents who must struggle afresh to get their religious bearings in the absence of their charismatic and experienced leader. Indeed, false teachers and teachings pose a real threat to apostolic succession because their correction must be executed by the church's leaders when Paul is no longer available in person to deal with their various needs.

The reading of the Pastoral Epistles, then, constructs what Charles Taylor has called a "social imaginary" of what an apostolic succession might look like on the ground.[16] That is, Paul's instructions to his successors Timothy and Titus define a set of normative practices and beliefs, both congregational and individual, that help every generation after Paul imagine how an apostolic succession should take place in a post-apostolic setting. Simply put, these letters help their intended readers — Paul's successors — imagine for themselves the root concern of any succession: what would Paul do were he here among us today? In helping to guide an apostolic succession, reading these letters forges an intuition of how a sacred household should be organized practically and theologically and what it ought to anticipate as the material effects of being organized thus.

In this way the interpreter's move from the particularity of an ancient (or authored) text to the more universal meaning of a canonical (or church's) text may be facilitated. For example, while the particular catalog of virtues found in 1 Timothy 3 profiles the sort of person best able to serve a congregation according to Paul's world, readers today can read the same catalog not as a checklist of leadership but to help cultivate a sense of who can best lead them in their own historical moment. In fact, the church's reception of the three letters to complete the Pauline canon for the not insignificant reason of providing "church orders" (according to the Muratorian Canon) suggests an ongoing performance: the instruction of these letters forms and guides local congregations of Paul's tradents in every age and place, who then safeguard the canonical goods of his apostolate to help people reimagine Paul from one generation to the next.[17]

---

16. I first learned of Charles Taylor and this idea of a "social imaginary" in a private conversation with L. D. Russ, who helped me understand its value for describing the effect of a congregation's Bible practices. Taylor's concept of a shared understanding of our political or social surroundings is fully articulated in his *A Secular Age* (Cambridge: Harvard University Press, 2007).

17. In explaining why the Pastoral Epistles were chosen as the first commentary of the African Bible Commentary, Samuel Ngewa says the concern of the letters is the same as that of the

Introduction

The Literary Form of the Pastoral Epistles as Letters of Succession

Since the genre of sacred literature is a carrier of theological freight, it is an important element of theological interpretation: a composition is shaped by theology, but its literary expression also shapes the reception of that theology by its readers. In this regard, whatever occasions the writing of a letter also determines the form of written response. While the Pastoral Epistles are correspondence like other Pauline letters, they are written in response to a particular theological crisis when the leader departs and his work must be succeeded and continued by others. Letters of succession are paraenetic: they instruct, exhort, and present examples and models to imitate (cf. Acts 20:17-35). But in doing so they target a particular crisis occasioned by any succession of leadership, made even more critical in this case because the leader is an apostle who has been providentially given a word from God for this moment of salvation history (see the comment on Tit 1:1-3). This is an apostolic succession, and its sacred deposit must be safeguarded for the next generation (see the comment on 2 Tim 1:13-14 and 2:1-2).[18] Significantly, this species of letter also facilitates the role the Pastoral Epistles perform within the Pauline canon.

Of course, letters took many forms in the ancient world. Most were written communication to bridge the distance between two parties. Oratory was an important social convention of Paul's world, and letters were the literary expression of speech. Among the various kinds of letters preserved from the ancient world, perhaps the most common is private correspondence, similar in function and form to the Pastoral Epistles. We now possess literally thousands of ancient papyrus letters, stored in museums across the world, which reflect a variety of transactions but follow a standard literary pattern: an opening greeting, the main body, and a concluding benediction.

Of the various functions performed by private letters, the Pastoral Epistles are letters of "instruction and order" — although the instructions contained in 1 Timothy and Titus are to order a congregation while those given in 2 Timothy are more personal and seek to order Timothy's life after the model exemplified by Paul. While there are few exact parallels to the Pastoral Epistles from the ancient literary world, they do bear a striking family resemblance to

---

series: to focus on the church leaders and pastors of a new movement (the Association of Evangelicals in Africa) who need to "examine themselves in light of Scripture to lead the people of God in a way that conforms to Scripture." *1 and 2 Timothy and Titus* (ABC; Grand Rapids: Zondervan, 2009), xix.

18. See Johnson's important discussion of literary form, especially the connection between form and function in *1-2 Timothy*, 93-97.

9

those letters of antiquity still in our possession. The paraenesis of 1 Timothy and Titus is roughly the same as a kind of administrative instruction found in letters we possess and so allows the exegete to make general observations about the literary form of these letters (see below).

Letters of antiquity began with formal greetings so that the recipient would know the sender immediately upon unrolling the scroll. Paul's letters generally followed this well-known script: "Sender to recipient, greetings." In personal letters such as the Pastoral Epistles, this formula was amplified to highlight the nature of the relationship between sender and recipient; this in turn clarified the expected response of the letter's recipient to its instructions. In the case of the Pastoral Epistles, Paul's address underwrites his personal relations with Timothy and Titus and his spiritual authority as well. Especially when the NT reader has the Paul of Acts in mind, Paul's identification of himself as an "apostle of Christ Jesus" posits the religious importance of his mission and message for the future of the church, which Timothy and Titus are now delegated by him to organize in Ephesus and Crete.

The main body of a personal letter takes up the business at hand. (In this sense, it functions much like a sermon in a worship service.) Differences of emphasis and vocabulary that the careful reader notes from one Pauline letter to another reflect the range of controversies and crises that Paul considers and seeks to resolve in the main body of his various letters. Advice is given, instruction rendered, commands made, doctrine corrected, and false teachers rebuked according to Paul's understanding of Scripture's roles within the faith community (cf. 2 Tim 3:16b). The purpose of the main body of a personal letter follows this strategy, but ostensibly with a particular person rather than a congregation in view. The subject matter of 1 Timothy and Titus is primarily concerned with conveying instructions that would order congregational life in pagan places — not unlike the early second-century *Didache* as well as other Christian writings written across the next several centuries for a developing, expanding missionary church. The main body of 2 Timothy is quite different, with a heightened sense of Paul's passing and of the importance of Timothy's role to carry on Paul's legacy to the next generation — a kind of literary "last will and testament" of the revered apostle.

The concluding words of a Pauline letter, including the Pastorals, include many elements. While always a blessing of some kind is found, miscellaneous greetings, exhortations, itineraries, summaries of concern, and other personal reminders are included as well. What this suggests about the Pastoral Epistles is that they were not intended by Paul as "private" letters but for a wider readership beyond Timothy and Titus.

The more personal tone and themes of 2 Timothy suggest a professional

Introduction

relationship between a mentor and apprentice that seems to require equal measure of encouragement with a firm reminder of the important mission at hand. This observation is important for understanding the particular literary genre of 1 Timothy as a private letter (see above) and underscores the astute observation of L. T. Johnson that 2 Timothy is written in the manner of a *personal paraenetic letter*, not as a farewell brief but as — I would call it — a succession letter. Likewise, 1 Timothy and Titus are in the manner of *mandata principis* — that is, official letters from a superior to an administrative associate for use at a specific location, which mix instruction (probably read publicly) with personal exhortation (probably kept private).[19] These literary observations explain not only the occasion of the Pastoral Epistles but also their continuing role for a church that does its work in the absence of the apostle and is charged, as Timothy was, to safeguard the Pauline apostolate for the next generation.

The Social World of Paul's Urban Congregations

The corpus of Paul's canonical letters, which is introduced and framed within its canonical setting by his story in Acts, indicates that those converted to Christianity by his urban mission came from a variety of cultural backgrounds, reflecting the makeup of the Roman cities in which Paul had his greatest successes. In particular, recent scholarship has demonstrated that the Pastoral Epistles share much with Greco-Roman philosophy and ethics, both academic and popular, in both subject matter (e.g., virtuous life, truth claims and falsehood, moral practices, household, and so on) and literary form (e.g., proverbs, paraenesis, biography, lists, biographic models, epigrams, and so on).[20]

No shift in the social world of earliest Christianity is more remarkable than the movement from the Palestinian and rural setting of the "Jesus movement" to the Roman and urban setting of Paul's missionary church. And no study of earliest Christianity is more crucial to a critical reading of the Pastoral Epistles than an honest assessment of the "collision" between Paul's missionary practices and those cultural norms that shaped the Greco-Roman world.[21]

---

19. See Johnson, *First and Second Letters to Timothy*, 97.

20. Drawing this landscape, however inconclusively, remains the singular contribution of M. Dibelius and H. Conzelmann's influential commentary, *The Pastoral Epistles: A Commentary on the Pastoral Epistles* (Hermeneia; Philadelphia: Fortress, 1972), and more recently is elaborated in a series of important articles by A. J. Malherbe.

21. Richard Horsley (see in particular Horsley, ed., *Paul and Empire: Religion and Power in Roman Imperial Society* [Harrisburg: Trinity, 1997]) has led recent Pauline scholarship in

Introduction

At a surface level, the Pastoral Epistles reflect considerable contact with the cultural horizons of the Roman cities of the day. To a large degree, L. T. Johnson's reconstruction of the ways of being religious in the Greco-Roman world corresponds with the nature of social interactions and conflicts mapped by the Pastoral Epistles.[22] Each of the four modes of religious practice he notes, especially within Judaism and then earliest Christianity — participation in divine benefits, moral transformation, transcendence of the world through religious experience and confession, and "household" practices that promote sociopolitical stability — is thematic of Paul's instructions to Timothy and Titus. Moreover, there is considerable ambivalence, if not real conflict, that recognizes the decisive and non-adaptive character of his apostolate and vocation: he suffers as a Roman criminal because of the gospel he proclaims, and he fully expects that his successors will experience a similar outsider status (see the comments on 2 Tim 2:8-13). Ironically, the Pastoral Epistles are deeply concerned about the redemption of outsiders — those who live outside the sacred household — while recognizing that Christian confession and practice are inherently marginal. In any case, the Pastoral Epistles are case studies of Christianity's apocalypse into a foreign world, complete with instructions that are formative of a confessing community — "God's household" — struggling to "lead a quiet and peaceful life in full godliness and holiness" (1 Tim 2:2b) as members of another, very different household.

The cities of Paul's mission, including Ephesus (mentioned in 1 and 2 Timothy) and Nicopolis in Greece (mentioned in Tit 3:12), were typically important commercial centers of the empire, cosmopolitan in social makeup, and conveniently located for travel by land and sea. Most cities were divided into ethnic neighborhoods, each with its own public places. Especially important was the large Diaspora Jewish population, which normally settled into urban enclaves, each identified by its synagogue (or "voluntary organization"). Otherwise, most Roman cities tolerated a diversity of religious cults devoted to the worship of local deities, deities of the Greek pantheon, "mystery" (or "new age") religions, and the Roman Caesar.

The family household is the principal metaphor of the church in the Pastoral Epistles in part because it was the social context for much of Paul's

---

mapping the difficult terrain between an emergent Pauline Christianity and the dominant imperial cult and ideology.

22. Luke T. Johnson, *Among the Gentiles: Greco-Roman Religion and Christianity* (AYBRL; New Haven: Yale University Press, 2009), esp. 111-41. See also C. Kavin Rowe, *World Upside Down: Reading Acts in a Greco-Roman Age* (Oxford: Oxford University Press, 2009).

missionary activities. Roman households were mostly larger "compounds" which combined shops, living accommodations, gathering places with play yards for children. As a Pharisee, Paul was bi-vocational, working to support his mission by day and teaching interested people by night. His missionary strategy and congregational gatherings, alluded to throughout the Pastoral Epistles and in Acts, were easily adapted to this household structure. Further, households were often large and always inclusive communities: each member held certain responsibilities, and their relationships to others were predicated on these roles. The patterns of this political structure were also easily adapted to the congregational life. The "Christianization" of the Roman household curtailed any potential for internal conflict, even between household congregations in the same city, while also commending the gospel to outsiders who might measure its truth on the basis of Christian conduct. In part, this recognition explains Paul's abiding concern for virtuous character in his description of those who make up the Christian household/congregation.

At the same time, the household is a social institution shaped by a particular social hierarchy. The head of the house was typically the father or another older male, and indications of gender, social class, and rank are noted everywhere in the Pastoral Epistles. For example, even though aspiring to the same virtuous persona, the poor widow occupies a different place in the Christian household (1 Tim 5:1-16) than does the married woman of means (2:9-15), and the instructions Paul gives to each reflect their very different social status. From Acts one is able to discern a broad range of social groups represented in a Pauline congregation, reflecting the diversity in the cities, including a substantial middle class. Paul's great "Magna Carta" of Gal 3:28 (cf. Col 3:11) is really a descriptive statement about the mixed membership of a congregation, perhaps asserted with the more revolutionary subtext that "in Christ" these different groups, cut along social, gender, ethnic, and geographic lines, are able to achieve an uncommon solidarity because of the presence of divine grace.

The long-standing discussion of the household codes of Pauline paraenesis (and of the NT in general), besides drawing obvious parallels with the management scheme of Roman households (and the Greek philosophical tradition that shaped it), has been mostly concerned with the role they perform within the Christian writings in which they appear, whether to improve relations with non-believers or to organize the internal relations of believers. Rather than a microcosm of the empire, however, the Christian congregation is presented as a "household of God, the church of the living God" (1 Tim 3:15) and as such as a microcosm of "God's way of stewarding the world" (1:4). Hardly a trope of social domestication as some insist, the ecclesial household shaped by this divine pattern challenges the world and changes the world. There is hardly a more powerful image of this than the distinctive epiphany passages of the Pastoral Epistles, according to which God's grace and friendship erupt into the world in order to rescue the world from sin and purify a people for good works (so Tit 2:11-14). The household trope, then, implies neither an inoffensive assimilation into the pagan world nor a prophetic resistance to it. Rather, the Pastoral Epistles presume a particular cultural setting in which the family household is the meeting place where people encounter God and are re-created or transformed into a family that belongs to God (1 Tim 3:15).

Additionally, the theological commitments of the Pauline gospel are sometimes juxtaposed with images of imperial Rome to create a deep sense of the church's counterculture. For example, the church is instructed to pray for its civil rulers (1 Tim 2:2) while at the same time confessing its allegiance to one God (vv. 3-4), who mediates humanity's salvation through one Messiah (vv. 5-6) and the instruction of a single apostle (v. 7). While the church is certainly not seditious, it is plainly intolerant of any claim of the emperor's singular role or right to save and teach the world. Paul reminds Timothy of Jesus' "good confession" before Pilate (6:13), who personified Rome's occupation of the Holy Land, as apropos of the kind of faithfulness demanded by "God, the blessed and only Ruler, the King of kings and Lord of lords" (v. 15). Roman culture is engaged by a "good confession" of a divine who rules over Rome's Caesar. It should come as no surprise that Paul speaks of the costly effect of doing so in 2 Timothy — a letter in which his personal suffering is recalled more poignantly than in any other Pauline letter.

Diaspora Jews such as Paul typically settled in neighborhoods in which the synagogue was a central gathering point of religious and social life — probably in the common area of a Jewish household rather than a distinct building. Christianity began as a messianic movement within Second Temple Judaism and was thoroughly Jewish in its core theological beliefs, ethical behavior, religious and exegetical practices, liturgy, and social patterns. While the church gradually separated itself from the synagogue, primarily over controversies related to the conditions for initiating repentant pagans into Christian fellowship, both remained intimately related in the world of the NT. The level of their discourse (and disputation!) is keenly reflected in the Pastoral Epistles, in which the false teachers appear to be Jews, perhaps Christians, who contest certain Pauline beliefs and perhaps even the manner by which converts are folded into the faith. These are intramural conflicts, probably arising within the same household of believers, which had as much to do with the social identity or structures of a congregation belonging to the God of Israel as with religious practices or theological beliefs.

Introduction

Finally, it seems clear not only from Paul's autobiographical statements in his letters but also from his story as narrated in Acts that his missionary organization included several colleagues to whom he delegated important responsibilities (Phil 4:2-3). Paul preferred to engage in the work of ministry in person (Rom 1:10-11), no doubt believing that his apostolic gifts mediated God's grace in powerful and distinctive ways (v. 5). His missionary associates, such as Timothy and Titus, were faithful substitutes for his apostolic persona when he went missing for the hard work of preaching the gospel or establishing a congregation of converts to the Christian faith (1 Cor 4:16-17; 16:10-11; 1 Thess 3:2). In this sense, then, the instructions and charges a departed Paul gives to Timothy and Titus to establish Christian congregations or correct his opponents in Ephesus and Crete reflect a strategy and theological curriculum he would have used had he been there to engage in this ministry himself.

The Canonization of the Pauline Letter Collection[23]

The effect of forming whole collections of individual writings for a single biblical canon creates a literary aesthetic that is substantively and functionally different from what corpora scholars invent according to their historical reconstructions of authorship and social location. For example, the various corpora of "authentic" letters used to fashion a critical Pauline theology typically differ in shape and substance from the thirteen-letter Pauline corpus fashioned and fixed during the church's canonizing process. The theological priority of reading Scripture's Pauline witness at its ecclesial address compels the interpreter to shift an interest in an author's intentions in writing to the church's intentions in canonizing it. In this sense, the canonical approach drills down on a *second* point of origin that follows the postbiblical history of an authored text, written for a particular audience, to the church's recognition and reception of it as canonical for all subsequent Christians.

The deep logic of this shift of interest from a text's point of composition to its point of canonization, with its various ancillary claims of canonical rather than authorial intent and textual meaning, follows the epistemol-

---

23. What follows revises my chapter in *The Pauline Canon* (ed. S. Porter; Leiden: Brill, 2004), 22-44. See also in the same volume James W. Aageson, "The Pastoral Epistles, Apostolic Authority, and the Development of the Pauline Scriptures," 5-26, and Stanley E. Porter's trenchant essay on the various proposals of the formation of the Pauline canon, "When and How Was the Pauline Corpus Compiled? An Assessment of Theories," 95-127. I have been helped along in this case study, even if in a somewhat different direction, by Aageson's excellent monograph, *Paul, the Pastoral Epistles, and the Early Church* (Peabody: Hendrickson, 2008).

ogy of modernity's defense of a text's "original meaning." Any reasonable definition of historical-critical orthodoxy can be reappropriated for defining the interpretive contingency of a text's canonization, except now the readers of a *canonical* text (rather than an authored one) are located differently both in relationship to their social worlds and in relationship to the biblical text. In fact, we may know more about the circumstances of a text's canonization than we do of its composition, making it an even more practical critical measure than the reconstruction of an authorial original in protecting the sanctity of the text from interpretive abuse. But the primary warrant for making this move is, of course, meta-theological: indexing a biblical text's "original meaning" to the church's initial reception of a text as Scripture illumines it within its canonical context, which is how any faithful reader should receive it as a means of grace. Even so, according to H. Gamble's assessment, the "early history of Paul's letters and the process by which they were collected are very obscure."[24]

The Formation of the Pauline Collection

Most modern efforts at reconstructing the pre-canonical reception history of the Pauline corpus are concentrated by the following four moments:

1. The Pauline biography found in the Pastoral Epistles, whenever composed and by whomever, suggests that a canonical collection of his writings was a logical if also likely next step following his death. The memories of his apostolic persona and mission along with the summaries (or "faithful sayings") of his message leave no doubt of Paul's God-given authority and his lasting importance to the church, especially in contrast to his various rivals. In fact, one argument against the Pauline authorship of the Pastoral Epistles is the rather immodest picture of a canonical Paul that is drawn by this biography of him: Paul is a Christian saint and martyr whose unrivaled authority in the church insinuates the truth claims of his gospel and life as moral exemplar as the norm for all who believe. The memory of his piety and preaching has become the norm of a truly Christian life and witness.

In most letters, Paul routinely writes that he intends to make an apostolic "house-call" on the letter's recipients, presumably to check whether his instructions have been followed. As R. Funk argued, the rhetorical function of a tacit warning of an imminent official visit is to intensify the importance of the letter itself, which in this case supplies an inferior but effective substi-

---

24. H. Y. Gamble, *The New Testament Canon* (GBS; Philadelphia: Fortress, 1985), 36.

tute for Paul's persona and the edifying charisms he conveys within the faith community.²⁵ Sharply put, the letter represents the "spirit" of the prophetic Paul, which communicates the word of the Lord in his personal absence. If so, then Paul himself offers support for the canonical perception that the NT collection of Pauline letters is an effective medium for continuing the true "spirit" of Paul's witness to God's gospel in the post-Pauline church.

2. The emergence of the Pauline letter collection, perhaps already by the end of the first century and perhaps put into circulation by the apostle himself, carries immediate value as the substitute for the personal presence of the now departed Paul. We should not be surprised, then, by the first actual reference to a collection of Pauline writings, with the implication that it is regarded as Scripture, in 2 Pet 3:16. Here a collection of Pauline writings serves the church as a Christian appendix to the Jewish Scriptures.²⁶ This shows us that a collection of Pauline letters had been put into "catholic" circulation "according to the wisdom given him" (2 Pet 3:15b; cf. 2 Tim 3:15) and that it was found to be not only difficult to understand but also susceptible to distortion by false teachers. The importance of this witness to the earliest reception of the Pauline canon should not be minimized by modern criticism's suspicions of 2 Peter. In fact, I think it offers us the essential clue that explains the late arrival of the Pastoral Epistles to complete the extant ten-letter Pauline corpus (see below).

D. Trobisch speculates that an earlier edition of this Pauline collection was actually fashioned and put into play by Paul himself. He bases his hypothesis on the contemporary convention of other teachers of important schools, such as Seneca and Cicero, who gathered their writings into collections for future students. This prospect is even more likely if we place Paul, the missionary-teacher, in an urban (and thus well-educated) church and recognize that his letters are informed by the practices and rhetorical conventions of teachers. Trobisch suggests Paul's "authorized recension" included only Romans, 1 and 2 Corinthians, and Galatians.²⁷ After Paul's death, his most influential colleagues (Timothy or Onesimus?) added a "posthumous collection" to Paul's volume, which they perhaps edited and expanded as encyclicals to meet the needs of a wider audience, and published them together

---

25. Robert W. Funk, "The Apostolic Parousia: Form and Significance," in *Christian History and Interpretation: Essays in Honor of J. Knox* (ed. William Reuben Farmer, C. F. D. Moule, and Richard R. Niebuhr; Cambridge: Cambridge University Press, 1967), 249-68.

26. F. F. Bruce, "Some Thoughts on the Beginning of the New Testament Canon," *BJRL* 65 (1983): 38-39.

27. David Trobisch, *Paul's Letter Collection* (Minneapolis: Fortress, 1994), 55-96. But see Porter's criticisms of Trobisch's thesis and evidence in *The Pauline Canon*.

Introduction

as his "collected letters," with Ephesians serving as the collection's theological introduction (following the well-known thesis of E. Goodspeed followed notably by J. Knox). The practical aim of this expanded collection was to make available to subsequent generations Paul's best thinking in response to a wide range of theological and ecclesiastical issues. Trobisch includes all thirteen letters in this collection. While I agree for theological reasons that all thirteen Pauline letters are required to cultivate a fully Pauline understanding of Scripture's witness to the gospel (see below), Trobisch's historical basis for doing so is lacking. The evidence from the second century shows rather the widespread circulation within Pauline circles of a ten-letter collection, but not yet of the canonical edition of thirteen letters.

Trobisch's essential hypothesis finds partial support in J. Barton's thesis that the frequency of quotation is tacit evidence of a letter's importance in the church and even its canonicity. When considering this citational evidence from the early second century, then, the letters Trobisch includes in Paul's own collection are the very ones cited much more frequently than his other letters combined.[28] Even if an early second-century date is accepted for the formation of this early form of the Pauline canon, Barton fails to account for the curious silence of Justin Martyr, who never quotes from a known Pauline letter. Moreover, the more robust portrait of an authoritative Paul found in Acts (even though as a prophet like Jesus and not as a letter writer) does not come on board until the end of the second century, when two versions of Acts were put back into circulation. Yet, at the very least, the studies of Trobisch and Barton are highly suggestive of a Pauline collection mentioned in 2 Pet 3:15-16 and perhaps even alluded to in 2 Tim 3:14-17, where Paul speaks of his own teaching (v. 14) as having the same influence as Israel's Scripture in Timothy's spiritual formation.

3. What recent studies have made clear is that Paul's letters were received as canonical as a collection of select letters rather than as individual letters one at a time.[29] The first known collector of a Pauline corpus was Marcion (160 C.E.). Given the prior history of the Pauline corpus to this point, Marcion's Pauline collection was likely an edited collocation of one popular version already in wide circulation.[30] Marcion collected and used Paul, however, with clear theological intent, since his theology was predicated on Pauline theol-

---

28. John Barton, *Holy Writings, Sacred Text: The Canon in Early Christianity* (Louisville: Westminster John Knox, 1997), 14-24.

29. Cf. A. Lindemann, "Die Sammlung der Paulusbriefe im 1 und 2 Jahrhundert," in *The Biblical Canons* (ed. J. M. Auwers and H. J. Jonge; BETL 153; Leuven: Leuven University Press, 2003), 321-51.

30. Gamble, *New Testament Canon*, 41.

ogy.³¹ Often in sharp contrast to emergent catholic Christianity, which did not pay much attention to Paul, Marcion's innovation was to vest an extant Pauline collection with normative authority for Christian formation: that is, the Pauline corpus was no longer "Scripture" (as in 2 Peter) but *"canon."*³² This move was to push the catholic church in the direction of a Christian Bible of its own, perhaps sooner than would have been the case otherwise.

Most critics of Marcion, both ancient (e.g., Irenaeus, Tertullian) and modern (e.g., Harnack), infer from his canon list that he intentionally excluded the Pastoral Epistles as canonical for his faith community (see below). If so, his reasons for doing so remain obscure to most scholars, myself included, unless he recognized his own beliefs in the profile of the opponents whom Paul roundly attacks in these letters!³³ I, with a growing number of scholars, doubt that Marcion or Valentinus and their followers knew the Pastoral Epistles. In any case, the Beatty manuscript (P^{46}) from the end of the second century follows Marcion's list, suggesting that his ten-letter edition of Paul did not diverge from the corpus of Pauline letters generally in circulation at the time.

Almost certainly Marcion's use of this Pauline collection as Scripture for the formation of a non-catholic version of Christianity triggered several countermeasures by the church's principal theologians. Ironically, one of these countermeasures was to promote the purchase of Paul's gospel and piety for catholic consumption! That Marcion, perceived a heretic, would stipulate a Christian Bible for his faith community provoked Tertullian, his fiercest opponent and learned defender of catholic faith, to respond and offer his own version of a Pauline collection, which included the Pastoral Epistles, with

---

31. I find James A. Sanders's comment highly suggestive: the rich theological diversity found in the final form of the NT may well reflect the canonizing community's response to Marcion's exclusivist and hegemonic use of Paul. *Canon and Community* (GBS; Philadelphia: Fortress, 1984), 37. I suspect Marcionism is what Christianity looks like when using the Pauline letters as its "canon within the canon."

32. In distinguishing between a text's canonical and scriptural authority, I follow the lead of Charles Wood, *The Formation of Christian Understanding* (Philadelphia: Westminster, 1981), 82-105. On the one hand, the community's "Scripture" transmits formative traditions, important in learning the faith; on the other hand, a biblical "canon" more narrowly norms the community's beliefs and practices. During the canonical process, many sacred texts used as (and even called) "Scripture" by the church catholic (including many Christian and Jewish apocryphal texts) were not finally included in the biblical canon because they did not perform well in assessing and delimiting an emergent catholic faith and witness. The stakes are much higher for the performance of canonical texts.

33. As J. Knox famously speculates in his *Marcion and the New Testament: An Essay in the Early History of the Canon* (Chicago: University of Chicago Press, 1942).

Marcion's alleged omissions restored and the Book of Acts serving as its narrative and biographical introduction.

A second line of evidence is provided by the ground-breaking work of I. Dunderberg on the Valentinian school. Although the target of Irenaeus and frequently cited as an example of so-called "Gnosticism," Dunderberg locates Valentinus, and especially his moral teaching, *within* a fluid Pauline tradition of the second and third centuries. That is, Valentinianism is a Pauline insider rather than sub-apostolic (i.e., Gnostic) school of thought. What is interesting about Dunderberg's study is the repeated note he sounds that nowhere in the Valentinian literature is found a clear allusion to the Pastoral Epistles. On the one hand, the memory and apostolate of Paul are clearly contested from several fronts during the latter half of the second century; yet, on the other hand, all rivals for the true soul of the Pauline legacy look for and secure the real Paul in the ten-letter Pauline corpus.

4. This line of evidence brings us to the moment the Pastoral Epistles were added to an extant ten-letter corpus to complete its canonical edition. Alas, the precise moment of the church's earliest reception of the Pastoral Epistles as a collection is unknown, but here is the evidence with which we work: P^{32} is a codex that contains the ten-letter Pauline corpus apart from 2 Thessalonians (missing but probably originally present) and the Pastoral Epistles.[34] The earliest papyrus evidence of the Pastoral Epistles is P^{46}, a codex dating roughly from the early third century that includes a fragment of Titus. Still other early papyri including a collection of Paul's letters do not mention the Pastoral Epistles. While the *Biblia Patristica* catalogs many apparent allusions to the Pastoral Epistles from the second century, most clearly from Polycarp (ca. 120), scholars are divided over whether they allude to the Pauline texts or to oral tradition. Even if this evidence, if accepted, indicates a likely date of composition in the first century, it does not by itself indicate the more crucial date of canonization, which most scholars place at the end of the second century. While the apostolicity of the letters was attested quite early, then, their catholicity was not.[35] Only by maintaining a distinction between

---

34. However, see Philip H. Towner, *The Letters to Timothy and Titus* (NICNT; Grand Rapids: Eerdmans, 2006), 6-7.

35. Eusebius observed that the catholicity of a sacred text was the decisive requirement for its recognition as canonical. In this regard, several writings that ultimately were included in the biblical canon were initially disputed, not because of theological error or doubts about apostolic origin but because of the limited scope of their use within the catholic church. The argument presented here does not require Pauline authorship of the Pastoral Epistles; neither does it require that a case be made for "canon pseudepigraphy," according to which a biblical document was composed to complete a canonical collection. While this is perhaps the case for James

Introduction

dates of composition and canonization can one explain the broad circulation of the ten-letter Pauline corpus apart from the Pastoral Epistles throughout most of the second century.

The plausible conclusion is that the Pastoral Epistles were known as a collection and used throughout the second century, but only with limited circulation (principally among groups of the Pauline mainstream). Again, the church's reception of the Pastoral Epistles collection as canonical must be distinguished not by questions of authorship but by the scope of the church's use. Marcion, for example, evidently published and circulated the ten-letter Pauline corpus, based on commonplace practice among Christians of his era, but does not seem to know the Pastoral Epistles.

In addition, J. Kovacs's study of the contest between Valentinus and Clement over the Pauline legacy has substantially narrowed the gap between these two Pauline interpreters,[36] while I. Dunderberg has sought to retrieve the Valentinians from the Gnostic hinterland and place them among the Paulinists vying over the legacy of the canonical Paul.[37] Their work further illustrates my point because, like Marcion, Valentinus used the ten-letter Pauline corpus to support his teaching without a single reference to the Pastorals. Dunderberg explains this silence by saying that "there is no evidence that the author of the *Gospel of Truth* would have known [the Pastorals]."[38] Again, the

---

or even for 2 Peter, it is not necessarily the case for the Pastoral Epistles, which are attested earlier. It is a "category mistake" of biblical scholars who consistently assume that apostolicity, and specifically a book's apostolic authorship, carries with it automatic acceptance as canonical. This is simply not so any more than canonical status would not be granted to an anonymous text. Routinely, even if they are not always aware of it, scholars date the composition of a text differently than they date its reception as Scripture and its date of canonization. Acts is an example of this, since most scholars date its composition much earlier than its first known use as Scripture by Irenaeus in 175 c.e. Without attempting to explain the unexplainable — namely, the long period of silence between the composition of a text and its canonization — I simply want to claim there are two different dates of hermeneutical promise which must be studied and mined with different sets of orienting concerns. In the case of the canonical approach to biblical interpretation, a text's *second* point of origin, when it is recognized as sacred and included in the biblical canon for Christian formation, is of primary concern.

36. Kovacs has published a series of important articles on this topic, which are now layered into her superb commentary on 1 Corinthians for *1 Corinthians Interpreted by Early Christian Commentators* (The Church's Bible; Grand Rapids: Eerdmans, 2005). A précis for a forthcoming book on this debate was presented to the Nordic NT Conference in Joensuu, Finland, June, 2010 — "Contending for the Legacy of Paul: Clement of Alexandria and the Valentinian Gnostics."

37. Ismo Dunderberg, *Beyond Gnosticism* (New York: Columbia University Press, 2008), 1-31.

38. Cf. Ismo Dunderberg, "The Reception of Paul in Valentinianism" (paper presented at

real problem with the Pastorals has less to do with their Pauline authorship and more to do with their limited use among Paulinists of the second century.

This suggests, in any case, that the Pastoral Epistles may have been added to complete the Pauline corpus in a way that settles this intramural debate among rival Christian groups over the identity of the canonical Paul.[39] The effect of forming a whole collection, then, is to form a coherent witness to Paul's persona and proclamation as exemplary of Christian faith for the whole church. And within this canonical setting, the Pastoral Epistles are appropriated as hermeneutical writings whose new role is to guide readers of the Pauline corpus to a right understanding of Paul's legacy as "teacher of the nations."

Two more ideas from earliest Christianity's polemic against Marcion may illumine this point. In concluding his discourse against Marcion (*Against Marcion* 5.21), Tertullian seems to suggest that Marcion knew the three Pastoral Epistles but rejected them *(quod ad Timotheum duas et unam ad Titum de ecclesiastico statu compositesrecusauerit)* because they are brief and written to individuals. Not only this, but to Marcion's religious detriment the Pastoral Epistles treat "ecclesiastical discipline," among the very elements which Marcion was lacking. Tertullian thus implies that Marcion is heretical *because* his Pauline canon is incomplete. While anyone can easily point out the flaw in Tertullian's argument by noting that Marcion included Philemon, his intuition about an incomplete Pauline canon appears right.

J. Quinn further appeals to this text in Tertullian to supply patristic evidence for a collection of three Pastoral Epistles at the time of Marcion and Valentinus.[40] Accordingly, the subsequent Muratorian fragment[41] envisages distinctions already widely understood within the ancient church between

---

the SNTS annual meeting, Berlin, July 2010), 3. In private conversations Dunderberg suggested to me that, had Valentinus known the Pastoral Epistles, he would surely have made use of them, especially the sayings about sin and the moral catalogs.

39. There is no patristic evidence that any of the Pastoral Epistles circulated independently of the other two. The problem of the similarity of 1 Timothy and Titus — why include Titus with 1 and 2 Timothy when 1 and 2 Timothy together have an integrity all their own — is perhaps best understood by the aesthetic principle since "three is a satisfactory and symbolic number, implying a true collection." So Richard I. Pervo, *The Making of Paul: Constructions of the Apostle in Early Christianity* (Minneapolis: Fortress, 2010), 84.

40. Jerome D. Quinn, "P46 — The Pauline Canon," *CBQ* 36 (1974): 381-84.

41. The list's date and provenance are notoriously contested, especially since Albert C. Sundberg made a case for a fourth-century date and a provenance in the Eastern (not Roman) church: "Canon Muratori: A Fourth-Century List," in *HTR* 66 (1973): 1-41, and more recently defended by Geoffrey M. Hahneman, *The Muratorian Fragment and the Development of the Canon* (Oxford: Oxford University Press, 1992).

Introduction

the nine congregational letters (plus Philemon) and these three briefer letters written to individuals about church order. Thus, the Muratorian fragment commends two discrete Pauline collections, adding that the authority of the second three-letter collection is based on their effective performance "for the ordering of ecclesiastical discipline."[42]

This phrase, which also suggests a theological function of the Pastoral Epistles, and the final shape of this list, which combines the ten-letter corpus with the Pastorals, are remarkable innovations — especially when compared to other contemporary lists of extant Pauline letters that do not include the Pastoral Epistles. The Muratorian fragment's assessment of the Pauline corpus almost surely reflects anti-mainstream politics, not in a petty way but to correct the broader consensus in the emergent catholic church. In fact, it seems highly unlikely, as Tertullian suggests, that Marcion and Valentinus rejected this second collection for the same facile reasons that would have logically prompted them to exclude Philemon as well. Nor is there any evident reason for excluding them on theological grounds. In fact, as C. Nielson rightly argues, the Pastoral Epistles display many of the characteristics of the church from which Marcion emerged and theological beliefs with which he would have agreed.[43] Given the fluid nature of the canonical process, it therefore seems more likely that Marcion did not exclude this second collection for due cause and more probably simply did not know about these writings — and we can only wonder why.

What we can observe, then, is a phenomenon of collection-building as a type of evolutionary mechanism. New external threats present by the mid-second century and on the horizon, a change of audiences, and new internal

---

42. I am reading the three Pastoral Epistles together not because of evidence retrieved by modern criticism but because of another imperative gleaned from the formation of the Pauline canon for the emerging NT canon. Indeed, the differences among the letters encourage their study at discrete points of origin, but my interest is in cues by the canonical process during which the three were recognized as Scripture and added to the Pauline canon as an integral collection of three. Their canonical occasion is the same, and the similarities among them (e.g., individual addressees, churchly themes, literary form and conventions, common occasion) compel the reading of them together as "Pastoral Epistles." See Donelson, who argues that rival Christianities were dominant in the church when the Pastoral Epistles were written, not the canonical Paul and his tradents. Lewis R. Donelson, *Pseudepigraphy and Ethical Argument in the Pastoral Epistles* (HUT 22; Tübingen: J. C. B. Mohr, 1986).

43. Charles M. Nielson, "Scripture in the Pastoral Epistles," *PRSt* 7 (1980): 4-23. In my mind, had he known the Pastoral Epistles, Marcion would almost certainly have used them to secure his teaching, especially about Christ. For example, it seems inconceivable, based on the little we actually know of his teaching, that Marcion would not have used 1 Tim 3:16 or Tit 2:11-14 or any of the five "canonical sayings" of the Pastoral Epistles, had he known them.

pressures facing an expanding religious movement all forge a different ecclesial environment than Paul's original mission. So the collection of his letters must be adapted in order for his apostolate to survive. Put positively, subsequent readers of Paul of about the time the Pauline canon reached its final canonical form, such as Irenaeus and especially Tertullian, found the sweep of its concerns readily adaptable to this new environment. When the dust finally settled on the Marcionite controversy at the dawning of the third century, so pivotal in the formation of the NT canon, the theologians of the early church had not only given us the very idea of a Christian biblical canon but also formed its Pauline corpus, which now included the Pastoral Epistles. It is important to read them today in this ancient light.

The Final Form of the Pauline Collection

In his neglected 1955 monograph, *The Formation of the Pauline Corpus of Letters*, C. Leslie Mitton already signals a shift of interest in Pauline letters as separate literary entities to a consideration of them as a whole collection.[44] While overly optimistic that a scholarly consensus had emerged in settling the various historical-critical problems of individual Pauline writings, he rightly points out that consideration of the literary whole necessarily concentrates on a range of different problems, mostly indeterminate and unsettled: Why were these individual letters preserved together into a corpus? When and where did this formative process take place? By whom, by what process, and according to what criteria did the Pauline canon reach its final thirteen-letter form? The nature of these questions presumes the historian's hard work in sifting through the available evidence, most of it indirect, to reconstruct the canonical process.

While the formation of the Pauline canon is profitably studied as a historical phenomenon — what might be termed a "canonization from below" — it should also be mined for what this process implies for Bible practices in an ecclesial setting. Most scholars of canonization are not interested in explaining the choices made in forming the biblical canon theologically as a process of spiritual discernment led by the Holy Spirit — a "canonization from above." A canonical approach is interested in a careful reconstruction of the canonical process as a deep reservoir of important interpretive clues for using Scripture to inform the witness and form the faith of today's church.

---

44. C. Leslie Mitton, *The Formation of the Pauline Corpus of Letters* (London: Epworth, 1955).

Introduction

The church's discernment of the Spirit's leading role in the production of the biblical canon is not predicated on the identity of a text's author but on its effect in forming a congregation that is wise for salvation and mature for good works.

Most modern constructions of the canonical process follow individual books through their earliest history, whether in the West or East and whether evinced in manuscripts, in allusions and citations in early Christian writings, or in canon lists. While useful in helping track the sociology and theology that attend the canonical process in antiquity, this kind of work largely ignores the phenomenology of the process itself: almost every individual book entered the biblical canon as an integral member of a whole collection (e.g., Torah, Psalter, Book of the Twelve, Fourfold Gospel, Pauline collection, Catholic Epistle collection, etc.). The final redaction of a collection, therefore, evinces an aesthetic that is maximally effective for performing the authorized roles of a biblical canon. In Pauline idiom, these roles include making believers wise for salvation and bringing them to maturity to perform the good works of God (see the comments below on 2 Tim 3:15-17). If a reader recognizes this theological dimension of the Bible's formation, instantiated in its final literary form, then the phenomena of canonization, and in particular the "canonical shaping" of discrete collections of biblical books and their placement within the final form of the biblical canon, can be mined for interpretive prompts that continue to guide how these texts are faithfully used as the church's Scripture.

In this sense, I contend that the final literary form of the biblical canon is a work of aesthetic excellence. That is, the formation of a canonical collection or even of the biblical canon as a whole concluded and its final shape fixed at the moment the church recognized that a *particular* literary shape of a collection or the canon had sufficient aesthetic excellence to function effectively as Scripture. While certainly related to what the church affirms about the Bible's authority and holiness, its formation into a textual analog of the apostolic Rule of Faith is the end-result of a vast repertoire of choices spiritual leaders observed being made when gathering individual texts into discrete collections and then putting these collections together to form a single biblical canon.

But this observation begs a more practical question that is more to the present point: *What prompted the church to make those editorial decisions that put collections of individual sacred writings together into a particular shape and size?* Even if we are to believe these decisions merely recognize the Spirit's will, A. Harnack observed that, a century before the church discerned which way the wind was blowing, its various canon lists and manuscript traditions

Introduction

evinced multiple different possible shapes and sizes of this canon of sacred texts. This debate continues into our own day, whether to set aside the very idea of a biblical canon or to open it up to additional texts. The tenor of this debate begs the question why the church settled on the biblical canon it did and in particular on a thirteen-letter Pauline collection that includes these three Pastoral Epistles. Why this canonical shape and not some other?

How an object is formed and how its parts work together as a whole for a purpose are decisive in whether it will be received and used. Thus N. Wolterstorff advances a functional and activist conception of aesthetic excellence:[45] a work of public art should be shaped and sized in a way that makes it accessible for changing audiences, constantly performing in ways that inspire them to do good work or to live more virtuously as a result.

In applying Wolterstorff's definition of aesthetic excellence to the final literary form of the biblical canon, I would argue that in addition to a deep sense of the Bible's completeness and coherence as a trusted witness to the word and ways of God,[46] the Bible's shape may be appraised as an artifact of aesthetic excellence, with the following implications.

First, the church discerned when the Bible had been shaped into the particular literary form that would most effectively enable the Spirit to use it in forming a holy people who know and serve God. Each collection of texts was received into the canon on the basis of a résumé of ecclesial performances that would commend its future productivity according to the purposes of God. The church's decisions were in this sense rational and based on solid evidence that a given text was already widely used for congregational teaching, reproof, and correcting and training believers into the way of God. Scripture is a beautiful thing because it performs its public roles well.

Second, the biblical canon possesses inherent literary properties that draw readers to its wisdom or into its narrative world as advice or a story of higher quality. Are there norms of excellence that may be applied to the biblical canon that might help clarify the church's choice as one based upon its aesthetic as well as religious excellence? Indeed so. For example, the Bible's diverse parts are noteworthy because of their rich texture. As a literary genre,

---

47. See Nicholas Wolterstorff, *Art in Action* (Grand Rapids: Eerdmans, 1980), esp. his proposal of a distinctively "Christian aesthetic," 65-174. Wolterstorff is therefore not primarily interested in whether art can be used as a source of Christian theology or as an auxiliary of divine revelation, although I take it he would allow that great art which deals with themes central to the Christian faith might better function in drawing people to God.

46. So, e.g., Christopher Seitz allows that the final literary form of the canonical text "bears the fullest witness to all that God has said and handed on within the community of faith," *DTIB* 102.

the biblical canon is a collection of collections made up of artfully told stories, memorable lyrics, vivid poetry, exacting law codes, all of which direct us to ultimate meaning. Yet these diverse and discrete parts are nicely fitted together into whole collections and then into a single biblical canon whose internal unity of theological and moral content renders a more coherent — and perhaps for this reason compelling — word about God. Moreover, the effects of reading Scripture in the company of the Spirit and the worshiping community enable the reader to experience God's holy presence, and the joy and peace, the conviction and judgment elicited by the divine word.

Finally, like an artist who changes the wording of a poem or a line in a painting because it makes the poem better or the painting's image more arresting, we might allow that the indwelling Spirit forms a community's capacity to recognize what bits in what form are necessary in constructing a single biblical canon that is most effective in accomplishing its holy purposes. The church's decisions in forming the collections of the biblical canon, if they are directed by the Holy Spirit, will effectively help accomplish God's redemptive desires for the world. In other words, if a loving God has created us for loving communion with God and each other, then the church's production of Scripture in its present canonical form and so the church's practices of Scripture — its careful exegesis, its theological interpretation, its vibrant proclamation — must target this same holy end.

The Theological Contribution of the Pastoral Epistles to the Pauline Canon

In what way does the addition of the Pastoral Epistles to complete the Pauline collection also complete its apostolic witness? Here we will consider three important themes that are emphasized in the Pastoral Epistles and that reconceive the Pauline apostolate as important for the future of the church.

The Church as the "Household of God"

Even a cursory reading of the Pastoral Epistles within the Pauline canon witnesses to a different conception of the church. For example, "church," *ekklēsia* (ἐκκλησία), used often in the other Pauline letters, is used only three times in the Pastoral Epistles, all in 1 Timothy (3:5, 15; 5:16) and perhaps a later Pauline gloss on its earlier use. The distinction is not between a voluntary organization — "church" — and a more structured "household," since both identify a congregation of believers. Nonetheless, noting the Muratorian Canon's claim that these letters are "for the ordering of ecclesiastical discipline," von Campenhausen famously concluded the Pastoral Epistles envisage a church structure and male authority, a more domesticated social organism that replaced the more free-wheeling charisms of the church's apostolic leadership.[47] This analysis seems to draw support in part from the evident shift in the Pastoral Epistles from the charismatic community of 1 Corinthians, where the church is a community of "kindred spirits" who live and worship together as the "body of Christ" under the aegis of the Spirit, who gives believers "spiritual gifts" to empower their congregational ministries and "spiritual fruit" to empower their corporate solidarity (this "body" idea is elaborated especially in Ephesians and Colossians).

But von Campenhausen's highly influential analysis of the Pastoral Epistles' idea of the church is overdetermined. As Johnson rightly notes, we do not find in the Pastoral Epistles what we would expect if von Campenhausen (and many others who follow his lead) were right: an elaborate hierarchy more like later ecclesiastical models of "official" Christianity, details of a leader's roles and responsibilities, and a theological defense for such church orders. We find nothing in these letters that suggests the creation of a new organizational structure. Rather what we find is a congregation fashioned after a household (cf. Gal 6:1-10), more like the synagogue structure of Diaspora Judaism[48] or the Greco-Roman *collegia* — both social models familiar to Paul.[49] 1 Timothy and Titus, the two Pastoral Epistles most interested in church order, are more interested in the moral character and spiritual maturity of congregational leaders than in rigid requirements or job descriptions. In fact, the titles used for these leadership posts are probably terms for common household positions, supervisor ("bishop") and household servant ("deacon"), rather than formal ecclesiastical titles. In any case, they are used elsewhere in the Pauline corpus (Rom 16:1; Phil 1:1) and are hardly unique to the Pastorals.

My intent in questioning the current critical conclusion about the Pastoral notion of an institutionalized "church" is to shift the connotation of "church discipline" from a concern for social structure to the practices of and relations

---

47. Hans von Campenhausen, *Ecclesiastical Authority and Spiritual Power in the Church of the First Three Centuries* (Peabody: Hendrickson, 1997), 106-23.

48. Philip Towner's conjecture that the catchphrases "people of God" or "church of God" used in the Pastoral Epistles echo OT teaching that asserts that Israel belongs to God, central to the social identity of the Diaspora synagogue, seems relevant here; see his *The Goal of Our Instruction* (JSNTSup 34; Sheffield: Sheffield Academic, 1989). That is, the distinctive idiom for the church in the Pastoral Epistles reflects a synagogal social identity and by implication also a synagogal social structure.

49. Luke T. Johnson, *Letters to Paul's Delegates* (NTC; Valley Forge: Trinity, 1996), 14-16.

Introduction

within a "household of God" (1 Tim 3:15). The Pastoral Epistles are primarily concerned with the protocol and importance of Christian formation: the congregation functions as a household of believers who receive the apostolic word and practice its truth in an orderly, caring manner.[50] This is a missionary church, steadfastly on guard against all manner of opposition to maintain the word's theological purity, since its members' salvation from sin depends on it.

"Teaching" words, διδασκαλία/διδάσκαλος/διδάσκω *(didaskalia/didaskalos/didaskō)*, are used far more here than anywhere else in the NT. A Pauline congregation is formed by "healthy" (i.e., Pauline) teaching (1 Tim 1:10-11, etc.).[51] Theological formulas are scattered throughout, sometimes introduced as "faithful sayings," and supply the curriculum for authorized instructors of the Pauline school such as Timothy and Titus. The theological substance of this curriculum coheres to a Pauline rule of faith,[52] even seeking to extend its formative significance for a setting where Paul has departed by vesting the core claims of his gospel and the memory of his missionary practices with a different language and additional layers of meaning.[53]

Paul's successors are enabled to teach, remind, and transmit to others the goods of his apostolate by the Spirit's "special" gift (so 1 Tim 4:14; 2 Tim 1:6). Even von Campenhausen must admit that the authority of the "teaching office" in the Pastoral Epistles is established more in terms of Paul's prophetic authority than in terms associated with an "office" established by a religious institution.[54] That is, the gifted teacher — including Paul's immediate successors — is not granted authority by ecclesial review of their character and academic credentials but is set apart by apostolic appointment (2 Tim 1:6) and prophetic utterance (1 Tim 4:14). The teacher is not one who holds an ecclesiastical office but is more like the prophet of God who

---

50. See Frances M. Young, *The Theology of the Pastoral Epistles* (NTT; Cambridge: Cambridge University Press, 1994), 79-85.

51. Consideration of the entire semantic subdomain for teaching (LN §§33.224-50) would extend and deepen this impression enormously: there is a keener emphasis in the Pastoral Epistles on the activities and substance of Christian teaching, along with the moral character of the "apt teacher," than anywhere else in Scripture.

52. I take it this is what Jouette M. Bassler means when she calls the Pastoral Epistles' theological argot "mundane." *1 Timothy, 2 Timothy, Titus* (ANTC; Nashville: Abingdon, 1996), 31-34.

53. Cf. Brevard Childs, *The New Testament as Canon: An Introduction* (Philadelphia: Fortress, 1984), 387-95; *The Church's Guide for Reading Paul: The Canonical Shaping of the Pauline Corpus* (Grand Rapids: Eerdmans, 2008), 69-74.

54. Hans von Campenhausen, *Ecclesiastical Authority*, 116; although von Campenhausen remains true to his larger polemic and thinks this move back toward a genuinely Pauline idea is fictional.

carries God's word to instruct God's people under the Spirit's anointing — the Spirit of "power and love and self-control" rather than of "timidity" (2 Tim 1:7; cf. 1 Cor 2:13).

The only title given the pastors Titus and Timothy is "man of God," which trades on its use for OT prophets, carriers of God's word to God's people (see the comments on 2 Tim 3:14–4:4). Otherwise the duties and practices given them by Paul are apropos of delegated leadership: they teach and preach Paul's gospel as a word of truth and instruct congregations founded by Paul's missionary endeavor, and they safeguard the memories and practices of the Pauline apostolate and pass it on to other tradents. Timothy is called "the pillar and foundation of the truth" (1 Tim 3:15) and so must practice and parade this truth (4:13) according to his ordination (v. 14). He is held responsible for the congregation's salvation (v. 16). In fact, the political structure of the "household of God" vests considerable authority in the successor of the apostolate, not in the form of a church office but because of Paul's hands-on ordination (2 Tim 1:6-7), precisely because the word of God the "man of God" carries into ministry is none other than the word disclosed to Paul "in due time *(kairos)*" (see the comment on Tit 1:3).

The Pastoral Epistles' teaching about the church interprets and completes Pauline ecclesiology but does not move it in a different direction: "the ecclesiology of the Pastoral Epistles (is) akin to that of Paul."[55] They imagine the church as a "household" belonging to God, shaped by teachers of the Pauline word, and thus clarify the church's vocation, introduced and elaborated in other Pauline letters, for a setting in which the powers of Paul's apostolic persona are absent. Timothy and Titus are the successors of the Pauline apostolate who must absorb the instructions given them in these letters to establish a protocol and working principles and rules, much like those found in a "household," that will effectively transmit Paul's theological and personal legacy into the ever-changing next generation of his spiritual progeny (2 Tim 2:2). Only then will the church be able to extend his witness to God's gospel to the ends of the earth.

The Test of the Real Christian: Performance of "Good Works"

A. Malherbe has located the keen emphasis on moral formation found in the Pastoral Epistles in the intellectual culture of the wider Greco-Roman world.[56]

---

55. Marshall, *Pastoral Epistles*, 521.
56. Among several important studies on this topic, see especially *Paul and the Popular Philosophers* (Philadelphia: Fortress, 1989).

The various catalogs of virtues found here identify Christian faith with the competent person, one who is moderate, modest, self-controlled, and a good citizen whose conscience protects him against imprudent conduct. In essence, the interplay between moral character and theological confession found in the Pastoral Epistles underscores the fundamental structure of Pauline thought: "there is an indissoluble connection between beliefs and behavior," between Pauline orthodoxy and social orthopraxis.[57] Conversely, where this connection appears broken, where moral chaos is found, this is evidence of opposition to the core claims of Paul's gospel. Thus, for every virtue list there is a contrasting vice list, and the two together delineate the real difference between embodied truth and falsehood. This is also consistent with both Jewish theology and Greco-Roman moral philosophy. There is also clear continuity between the evangelical purpose of Paul's mission and this "indissoluble connection" between "healthy (i.e., Pauline) doctrine" and virtuous character (so 1 Tim 1:8-11).

Given this fundamental continuity, there are still distinctive emphases in the Pastoral Epistles that round off the Pauline profile of the believer's lifestyle. The distinctives of the Pastorals' paraenesis within Pauline paraenesis are best explained by the keen interest in teaching described above. Sharply restated, the Pastorals define moral character in terms of that species of faithful disciple who can teach "healthy doctrine" to others who make up a "household of God" dedicated to Christian instruction.

Yet two features of this profile of the "apt teacher" stand out and supply a moral standard for all faithful disciples: "godliness" (εὐσέβεια, *eusebeia*, 1 Tim 2:2; 3:16; 4:7, 8; 6:3, 5, 6, 11; 2 Tim 3:5; Tit 1:1) and "good (ἀγαθός/καλός, *agathos/kalos*) work(s) (ἔργον, *ergon*, 1 Tim 2:10; 3:1; 5:10, 25; 6:18; 2 Tim 2:21; 3:17; Tit 2:7, 14; 3:1, 8, 14), catchwords critical to the Pastoral Epistles' "special" language. The implicit consistency between the believer's internal (spiritual) character (εὐσέβεια, *eusebeia*) and the character of the believer's external (public) life (ἔργα ἀγαθά, *erga agatha*) subverts any attempt to internalize and privatize Christian formation — again, no doubt, in service of the community's missionary vocation. Godly believers produce good works as the concrete demonstration of the gospel's truth, because of the "indissoluble connection" in Pauline Christianity between beliefs and behavior.

The idea of "good works" in the Pastoral Epistles, so pivotal to how they portray the Christian life, defines those moral habits that result from the work of God's grace. "Good works" characterize the life, brought to maturity by Bible practices (2 Tim 3:16b), that accords with God's will and is therefore

---

57. Bassler, *1 Timothy, 2 Timothy, Titus*, 34.

pleasing to God (v. 17). In fact, the paraenetic contrast between evil and good works which typically frames the Pauline polemic against false teachers (who perform evil works) also illustrates the public effect of God's salvation-creating grace in the true believer's life (cf. Rom 12:1). This idea, then, is not only theologically considered but also the *necessary* evidence of the gospel truth that Paul and his successors preach. No matter the apparent agreements between these "good works" with contemporary secular philosophy, they are deeply grounded and reflective of what stands at the center of Paul's thought world: the sinner who believes the gospel is initiated into a new life with God, whose grace transforms the believer from doing evil to doing good.

This stress on "good works" in the Pastoral Epistles as the effective moral yield of receiving God's grace brings out in bold relief a point that is made elsewhere in the Pauline canon, most effectively in Rom 12:1; 2 Cor 9:8; and Eph 2:8-10. The net result is to correct what I think is a dangerous tendency of the (especially) Protestant misreading of Paul, which demonizes good works as somehow subversive of the sinner's dependency on Christ's death for salvation. Further, the Pastoral Epistles' stress on the formation of a "godly" character as the distinguishing mark of the faithful believer, who is then morally competent to perform "good works," corrects another tendency of that misreading of Paul, namely, the emphasis on teaching a saving orthodoxy to the exclusion of any instruction in a practical divinity that embodies confessed truth in the hard work of Christian charity and virtue. In this regard, too, the emphasis of the Pastoral Epistles, intensified by the addition of the Catholic Epistles collection, brings a necessary balance to the church's appropriation of the Pauline canon.

The Pastoral Epistles' Portrait of the Canonical Paul

A final illustration is the expanded résumé of the apostle Paul found in these letters. Even though it is commonplace these days to suggest that the Pastoral Epistles convey a portrait of Paul, mostly to serve as an apologia in support of his legitimacy as an exemplar and apostle, at the moment when the Pastoral Epistles were added to complete the Pauline canon toward the end of the second century this orienting concern was instantiated in a heated debate over Paul's real legacy. The portrait of Paul in the Pastoral Epistles was intended to secure a particular portrait of the canonical Paul for subsequent generations of believers.

This characterization can be gathered under different rubrics. For example, from these materials one might sketch a biography of Paul that includes his experience of conversion (1 Tim 1:12-16), his apostolic calling

(1 Tim 1:12-16; 2 Tim 1:8-12; Tit 1:1-3), his reception of God's word at a *kairos* moment in salvation's history (Tit 1:3; cf. 1 Tim 1:10-11), and on this basis his distinctive appointment by the risen Christ as teacher of the nations (1 Tim 2:7; cf. Acts 13:47). This biography is extended to include exemplary missionary experiences (e.g., 2 Tim 3:10-13) and the names of personal opponents and supporters (1 Tim 1:20; 2 Tim 1:15-18; 2:17; 4:9-21; Tit 3:12-14). This is an extraordinary example of the canonical Paul since the eternal destiny of real (i.e., named) individuals is related to their personal relations with Paul — not unlike the frightened sailors on the ship in stormy seas narrated in Acts 27: safe haven finally is located wherever Paul is! The memory of this Paul regards the security and continuity of his apostolate.

There is nowhere a more expansive definition of the Pauline apostolate and its religious purchase for the church than Tit 1:1-3. In the equally lengthy greeting that begins Romans and so the Pauline corpus, Paul, while addressing the Romans, is also concerned to set out the core beliefs of his gospel, which is preached to empower the salvation of the nations. But in Titus the core concerns regard the importance of Paul himself for the salvation of God's elect. Here it is not the risen Christ that sets out the terms of the gospel, as in Romans, but God's word delivered directly to Paul at a καιρός ἴδιος *(kairos idios)*. On this basis a "knowledge of the truth" is delivered to fashion the faith of God's elect so that God's promise to them, made in ages past, might now be fulfilled. Paul is now front and center in the outworking of God's promised salvation.

This evocative greeting agrees with the claim, nowhere else made in the Pauline canon, that Paul was appointed "a teacher of the true faith to the nations" (1 Tim 2:7). What he taught is compressed into canonical sayings spread across the Pastoral Epistles (1 Tim 1:15; 2:15–3:1a; 4:9; 2 Tim 2:11-13; Tit 3:4-8) as well as in dense theological formulas (e.g., 1 Tim 3:16). These texts are not so much useful for catechism as they are the kind of sound-bites that summon the community's teachers to a curriculum for instruction organized around these big ideas.

Even more crucially, this portrait and its various bits underwrite the importance of the Pauline apostolate that is now passed on to others to safeguard, with the Spirit's help, and transmit to still other teachers (1 Tim 6:20; 2 Tim 1:13-14; 2:1-2). There is a peculiar eschatology that emerges in these letters that is linked to the apostle Paul and that concerns the eternal destiny not only of certain individuals but also of the (especially Gentile) church. Even as Jesus is concerned about what choices his disciples will make in his absence, since these choices concern eternal life, Paul is similarly concerned in these letters that the believers follow his example and instruction.

Introduction

The Hermeneutical Role of the Pastoral Epistles within the Pauline Canon

At the point of canonization, when the Pastoral Epistles were added to an extant ten-letter collection to complete the Pauline canon, the legacy of Paul's apostolate was still up for grabs. There was no agreed upon "canonical Paul" yet in play within the church catholic. Marcion v. Tertullian, Valentinus v. Irenaeus were intramural battles over Paul that took place along a broad trajectory throughout the second century (and perhaps continue into the twenty-first!).

R. Pervo's study of the second-century ferment and foment along this trajectory, while contested at several points, nonetheless raises important questions for a theological reading of the Pastoral Epistles. For example, even though most interpreters routinely discuss the relationship between the apocryphal *Acts of Paul and Thecla* and the Pastoral Epistles, especially in connection with particular people mentioned or common themes, Pervo aims their relationship at the reception of an authoritative Paul, which by 175 C.E. had become "a rather murky and frothy pool" of competing ideas and images.[58] The author of *Paul and Thecla* is the broker of a particular reading of an apocalyptic, ascetic Paul and as such is highly critical of rival readings, including the one envisaged by the canonical Paul of the Pastoral Epistles. In fact, according to Pervo, the most obvious thematic disagreements between *Paul and Thecla* and the Pastoral Epistles — over household life (i.e., marriage, women, celibacy, child-raising), spiritual gifts, and political authority for example — suggest that the narrator of *Paul and Thecla* seeks to discredit the Pastorals' version of the Pauline apostolate and its succession to the next generation and beyond.

The canonization of the Pastoral Epistles reflects the triumph of a particular way of remembering Paul and teaching the goods of his apostolate to others that confirms the trustworthiness of his portrait in the canonical Acts (see below). The church not only found the apocryphal Paul unreliable, but its verdict in favor of the Pastorals' Paul also suggests that the apostolate of the apocryphal Paul cannot be trusted for Christian formation. Simply put, *at the point of their canonization the Pastoral Epistles formed an intellectual rejoinder to competing interpretations of the Pauline apostolate in a way that fixed a normative understanding of his memory and message according to which the Pauline corpus is read.*

---

58. R. Pervo, "To Have and to Have Not: Receptions of Paul in the *Acts of Paul*" (paper presented at the annual meeting of SNTS, Berlin, July, 2010), 13; *The Making of Paul: Constructions of the Apostle in Early Christianity* (Minneapolis: Fortress, 2010).

2 Pet 3:15-16 remains, especially when glossed by 2 Tim 3:14-17, a pivotal text for understanding the continuing role of the Pastoral Epistles in the Pauline corpus. Depending on the date of this text, it seems likely that its valorization of the Pauline corpus, which 2 Peter claims is a fount of spiritual "wisdom" (v. 15), shares the same effect as Israel's Scripture, which conveys "wisdom" necessary for salvation (2 Tim 3:15). But 2 Peter also indicates that Paul's letters' lack of clarity opens them up to potential abuse by the very teachers it castigates. This passing reference of a Pauline collection hints at a hermeneutical crisis that might threaten the future of the community.[59]

The addition of the Pastoral Epistles collection to the extant Pauline corpus subsequent to the cautionary note sounded in 2 Peter may therefore be understood as a response to such a crisis. Not only does its portrait of a canonical Paul (see above) respond decisively to the battle over Paul's legacy within Pauline Christianity, the canonical sayings and the theological formulas that fashion a Pauline rule of faith, along with the instructions about personal and congregational practices that illustrate how the rule is applied, are spread across its pages to commend a particular version of Pauline Christianity that chooses sides — I would argue at the Holy Spirit's bidding — in a challenging and contested succession.

The hermeneutical props alluded to in the Pastoral Epistles are what one should expect in a collection that helps a community respond to the intellectual crisis provoked by disagreements over the canonical Paul. For example, opponents are sometimes named, with clear allusions made to other Pauline letters in which a contested belief (e.g., resurrection) is set out in a way that agrees with the Pastoral Epistles (see the comments on 1 Tim 1:18-20 and 2 Tim 2:8-20). Other allusions to antecedent Pauline letters seek to clarify practices unique to Paul's apostolic office from those that are normative of Christians (see 1 Tim 5:18-19). In part, one of the hermeneutical props of the Pastoral Epistles is to help Pauline tradents distinguish the unique apostolic practices of Paul (e.g., 1 Tim 1:20) from the "pattern of healthy teachings" (2 Tim 1:13) that are received from Paul but then passed on to others (so 2 Tim 2:1-2). Such a distinction may well include restrictions about marriage and celibacy, which an ascetic, apocalyptic Paul may well have advanced in his lifetime (1 Corinthians 7) but which have been lifted for a post-Pauline community. Vivid memories of Paul's conversion (see 1 Tim 1:12-17) and body of work are scattered

---

59. In a similar way, Margaret M. Mitchell proposes that Paul's Corinthian correspondence marks the origins of Christian hermeneutics made necessary by the "confusion and even alienation" generated by his earlier letters when their instructions were not adequately explained. *Paul, the Corinthians and the Birth of Christian Hermeneutics* (New York: Cambridge University Press, 2010), 5-6.

across these letters that exemplify what is expected of his successors (see 2 Tim 2:1-7; 3:10-14). The canonical sayings (1 Tim 1:15; 2:15–3:1a; 4:8-9; 2 Tim 2:11-13; Tit 3:4-8a) and other important theological formulas or syntheses (e.g., 1 Tim 2:3-7; 3:16; Tit 2:11-14; 3:4-8) fashion a Pauline rule of faith, which continues to regulate how the community should adapt Paul's gospel to everyday life.[60] These same theological agreements, which focus on the pattern of God's redemption of everyone, also guide the community's use of Israel's Scripture for wisdom of salvation (so 2 Tim 3:15). A controversial example of this prop is found in 1 Tim 2:13-15a, where Paul's biblical Eve instantiates the redemptive plan of Israel's God set out in vv. 3-6 and proclaimed to the nations by Paul (v. 7). Still other memorable aphorisms are found throughout the Pastoral Epistles which aid the church to this day in the catechism of new believers.

Rather than approaching the Pastoral Epistles as a marginal collection of biblical letters, whether because they are addressed to individuals rather than to congregations, because of authorship doubts or a late date of composition, or because certain instructions seem offensive to contemporary sensibilities, we should read them within their present canonical setting as of indispensable importance in guiding faithful readers of the Pauline corpus as a distinctive apostolic witness to God's gospel.[61]

Reading the Pastoral Epistles with the Acts of the Apostles

The differences between Acts and the letters that follow in the canon are obvious. For example, the Paul of Acts is sometimes at odds with Paul's own self-understanding or missionary agenda evinced in the Pauline letters. Nor does Luke characterize Paul as a letter-writer or quote extensively from any of Paul's letters.[62] Reading Acts at the point of its canonization according to the

---

60. Even though targeting a different thesis than mine, the fascinating argument of Mark M. Yarbrough, *Paul's Utilization of Preformed Traditions in 1 Timothy: An Evaluation of the Apostle's Literary, Rhetorical, and Theological Tactics* (LNTS 417; New York: Clark, 2009) is suggestive of the letter's hermeneutical value, since many of the traditions he identifies distill and clarify materials congregational leaders may have used in worship and catechesis for Christian theological formation. In fact, well-known verses from the Pastoral Epistles help fund Christian liturgies of worship and ordination to this day.

61. Aageson, *Paul, the Pastoral Epistles, and the Early Church*, argues that the Pauline canon includes multiple layers from multiple Pauline authors that envisage an emerging Pauline tradition and church. I largely agree with this conclusion, but I understand the role of the Pastoral Epistles within the Pauline corpus differently — as more decisive for a canonical (i.e., ongoing, catholic, apostolic) reading of the final form of the Pauline corpus.

62. But see Steve Walton, *Leadership and Lifestyle: The Portrait of Paul in the Miletus*

church's intentions for its biblical canon, however, would seem to compel a less adversarial relationship between the Paul of Acts and the epistolary Paul.[63]

The potential gains of this approach to Paul may be illustrated when considering the textual "seam" that weaves together the final snapshot in Acts of Paul in Rome (see 28:17-31) and the opening words of Paul to the Romans, which taken together introduce biblical readers to a missionary-minded apostle who is "eager to proclaim the gospel to you also who are in Rome" (Rom 1:15).[64] The interplay between the endings of Acts and Romans underwrites the orienting concern of a *canonical* Paul, who is not found in a secluded study writing dense Christian theology but on the city streets or in a rented apartment relating the Christian gospel to life in practical and persuasive ways. In this regard, among the most important roles a canonical Acts performs is to introduce the Bible's readers to the authors of the NT letters. While the historical reliability of these portraits is contested, they convey a sense of moral and religious authority and thus cultivate a high regard for the truth and importance of these letters for the formation of faithful readers. The optimistic narrative of Christianity's expansion into pagan territory in Acts is directed to use not as a historical resource but as a theological source that contributes to the church's ongoing understanding of its vocation and identity.

Speech and 1 Thessalonians (SNTSMS 108; Cambridge: Cambridge University Press, 2000), who challenges this consensus by noting several allusions to a likely proto-Pauline canon. For a comprehensive listing and analysis of the intertextual echoes of the Pauline letters in Acts, see David Wenham, "Acts and the Pauline Corpus II: The Evidence of Parallels," in *The Book of Acts in Its Ancient Literary Setting* (ed. Bruce W. Winter and Andrew D. Clarke; Grand Rapids: Eerdmans, 1993), 215-58.

63. The relationships between the Paul of Acts and the epistolary Paul and between the historian's construction of the real Paul and his legacy within early Christianity have been a storm center of NT studies since F. C. Baur; see W. Ward Gasque, *A History of the Interpretation of the Acts of the Apostles* (Peabody: Hendrickson, 1989), 21-106. Christopher N. Mount's recent study begins to rethink this earliest history of Acts within the bounds of a canonical process that relates the narrative of Paul in Acts to the origins of Pauline Christianity and of a canonical Paul late in the second century (rather than in the second or third generation as Baur and others argue); *Pauline Christianity: Luke-Acts and the Legacy of Paul* (NovTSup 104; Leiden: Brill, 2002). If Mount is correct, the initial reception and use of Acts as Scripture by Irenaeus and then Tertullian is critical to the church's canonization of Acts. See Robert W. Wall, "A Canonical Approach to the Unity of Acts and Luke's Gospel," in *Rethinking the Reception and Unity of Luke-Acts* (ed. Andrew F. Gregory and Christopher K. Rowe; Columbia: University of South Carolina Press, 2010), 172-91.

64. See Robert W. Wall, "Romans 1:1-15: An Introduction to the Pauline Corpus of the New Testament," in *The New Testament as Canon* (ed. Robert W. Wall and Eugene E. Lemcio; JSNTSup 76; Sheffield: JSOT, 1992), 142-60.

Introduction

Acts also cultivates a sense of the relationships among the letter writers and thus provides a distinctive angle into the literary relationships between the Pauline letters and the Pillars' letters. Similarities and dissimilarities in emphasis and theological conception between the two letter collections may actually correspond to the manner by which Acts tells of reports from the different missions and of the theological convictions and social conventions required by each (e.g., Acts 2:42-47; 9:15-16; 11:1-18; 12:17; 15:1-29; 21:17-26). The relationships between James and Paul or between Peter and James as depicted at strategic moments in Acts are generally collaborative rather than adversarial and frame the interpreter's approach to their biblical writings as essentially complementary in both meaning and function, though certainly not uniform and sometimes in conflict. If the critical consensus dating Acts to the late first century is accepted, which makes it roughly contemporaneous with the earliest pre-canonical stage in the formation of the NT,[65] then it is likely that its collection of portraits of early Christian leaders provides an important explanatory model for assessing the relationship between (and even within) the two emergent collections of canonical letters. The form and function of these Christian writings and their relationship to each other is another articulation of the early church's "sense" of the more collaborative relationships among their authors and interpretative traditions, which is, then, reflected in Acts. For example, if Peter and John are partners in Acts, then we should expect to find their written traditions connected in an emergent Christian Bible and their intracanonical relations representing the church's perception of their theological coherence. Likewise, the more difficult although finally collegial relationship between the James and Paul as narrated in Acts 15 and (especially) 21 may well envisage their partnership in ecclesial formation in a manner that Protestant interpretation has sometimes subverted. The church that claims continuity with the first apostles by means of Acts tolerates a rich pluralism even as the apostles do within Luke's narrative world, although not without controversy and confusion.

---

65. David Trobisch, *Die Endredaktion des Neuen Testaments. Eine Untersuchung zur Entstehung der christlichen Bibel* (NTOA 31; Göttingen: Vandenhoeck und Ruprecht, 1996). But now see the recent studies of Richard I. Pervo and Joseph B. Tyson, both published in 2006, which date the earliest version of Acts to the early second century, and of Strange, who follows Cadbury and Lake in dating the canonical version of Acts to the late second century. But none of these reconstructions, even if accurate, undermine my essential claim. Richard I. Pervo, *Dating Acts: Between the Evangelists and the Apologists* (Santa Rosa: Polebridge, 2006); Joseph B. Tyson, *Marcion and Luke-Acts: A Defining Struggle* (Columbia: University of South Carolina Press, 2006); W. A. Strange, *The Problem of the Text of Acts* (SNTSMS 71; Cambridge: Cambridge University Press, 1992).

The story of Paul in the second half of Acts particularly confirms the importance of God's appointment of Paul as a prophetic carrier of God's word and points readers forward to the Pauline letters. The stories of Paul's urban missions in the great Roman cities of his day — Philippi, Thessalonica, Corinth, Ephesus, and Rome — prepare the NT's readers for the letters. Although the intracanonical relationship between Acts and the Pauline letters is laden with historical questions, this commentary will continue to ask what these stories of Paul's mission in Acts might contribute to our reading of Paul's letters today as his legacy passes to his living readers. My interpretive interest in this relationship is both rhetorical and theological. At a rhetorical level great narratives such as Acts have the capacity to evoke powerful impressions that influence how we approach related, more discursive literature such as the Pauline letters. Acts tells us something of the canonical Paul's persona, his circumstances, his vocation and religious motives that enable the interpreter of his letters to fill in their gaps imaginatively and in agreement with Pauline tradition. His speech to the Ephesian elders at Miletus (Acts 20:17-35) makes clear the importance of his personal example, his message, and his mission to the nations. In him God has vested extraordinary charisma and Paul's faithfulness has exploited it to set out the future of the church. But this is precisely the crisis envisaged in the Pastoral Epistles: this exemplary, authoritative Paul of Acts is not in Ephesus with Timothy or in Crete with Titus, and yet they must continue the apostle's legacy without him.

Yet Acts is not only an evocative narrative, it is a theological narrative that gives its own witness to God's gospel: the interpreter's interest in the relationship between Acts and the Pauline letters is motivated also by theological understanding. While the Jewish cast of Luke's narrative of Paul and his mission has long been recognized as a critical problem when contrasted to the essentially Gentile cast of the Pauline letters, in combination they envisage the very prophetic protocol that Acts sponsors. In particular, the founding of different congregations is according to Acts at its roots a Jewish enterprise: it begins in the synagogue with Jewish and Gentile converts attached to the synagogue. Even when Paul is forced to leave the synagogue to maintain the Christian character of his urban mission, he does not leave behind the congregation's Jewish practices or constituency (e.g., see 18:5-8). Even though by the time Paul writes letters to these congregations the communicants are primarily Gentile (e.g., 1 and 2 Corinthians), the future of their communion is predicated on their Jewish origins — the very point that Acts illumines by its narrative emphasis. The connection between Acts and the Pauline letters suggests, then, that "to the Jew first, then the Greek" is an ecclesial calculus every bit as much as it is a soteriological protocol.

Introduction

But how does Acts illumine the theological contribution *each* letter makes to a full understanding of Paul's *biblical* testimony or his ongoing spiritual authority in the life of the ongoing church catholic? Does Acts contribute to our understanding of Paul's opponents, who may have subverted his testimony and authority in the life of the church then and still today? While I am convinced that a more precise historical understanding will make the interpreter more aware of these theological concerns, it is these "canonical" interests in the stories of Paul in Acts that this commentary will seek to cultivate.

The Rule of Faith in Theological Interpretation[66]

Distinct from but in cooperation with the standard rules of biblical criticism, the Rule of Faith constrains what an interpreter may or may not retrieve from a biblical text for the community's theological instruction. This strategy is predicated on the assumption that Scripture is by nature and practice a hermeneutical book and on the observation that the reception and shaping of both canon and creed were regulated and read from the beginning as analogical of the apostolic Rule of Faith. In this way the apostolicity of the church is safeguarded by the apostolicity of the Bible, whose practices are constrained by an interpreter's attentiveness to the content and grammar of the apostolic Rule. On the basis of this circularity, then, the Rule of Faith should not only regulate the interpreter's critical retrieval of theological goods from the sacred text, it should also supply an apt grammar of theological agreements that arranges those goods into a coherent and unified articulation of God's word across the diverse witnesses that comprise the biblical canon.

In introducing a recent issue of *International Journal of Systematic Theology* devoted to various hermeneutical theories of theological interpretation of Scripture, J. Webster editorializes that "the most fruitful way of engaging in theological interpretation of Scripture is to do it," further suggesting that "especially academic conventions change more often by subversion than by high theory."[67] Whether my Rule of Faith reading of the Pastoral Epistles is finally subversive or even upgrades the academy's business as usual, this commentary seeks to test this interpretive strategy: Does the application of the apos-

---

66. See my introduction to this second interpretive strategy, "The Rule of Faith in Theological Hermeneutics," in *Between Two Horizons: Spanning New Testament Studies and Systematic Theology* (ed. Joel B. Green and Max Turner; Grand Rapids: Eerdmans, 1999), 88-107. The "theological horizons" that follow the exegetical portions of this commentary seek to illustrate this interpretive practice.

67. John Webster, "Editorial," *IJST* 12 (2010): 116.

tolic Rule of Faith (in this case as formulated by Tertullian) help guide the interpreter's reading of these three letters as the word of God?

In retrospect I found this task a difficult even if a rewarding experience. The difficulty lay not in its novelty, although I am not aware of another commentary that uses the Rule of Faith in this way from which to learn the hermeneutical ropes. Even though the importance of the Rule of Faith to chasten biblical criticism is now frequently mentioned, one does not find actual performances of this interpretive practice applied to biblical texts. The primary reason I found this strategy difficult, however, is that its application is more intuitive than formal, a rule of thumb more than a rule to follow. By this I am referring not to a kind of theological intuition that is generally accepted as a property of theological interpretation but to an epistemic property cultivated over time within particular faith communities by worship and moral practice, by the catechesis of their membership, by good sermons heard and ecumenical creeds confessed, by Christian hymns sung together, and so on. Stephen Fowl contends that interpretive virtues and aims that are brought to Scripture are shaped in advance by the spiritual habits and ecclesial practices of faithful communities in which the strong readers actively participate. What goods are readily recognized in biblical texts as theologically promising, whether to afflict the comfortable or comfort the afflicted, are mostly determined by our spiritual affections shaped within communities of practice.[68] That is, the apprehension and application of the apostolic Rule in interpretation tends to be informal and intuitive. The hearing of God's word in Scripture is shaped by worship and reading rather than by the more formal application of a critical tool to mine a biblical text for meaning.

Additionally, I continue to find it difficult to separate exegesis from theological interpretation — at least in the manner recently called for by J. Barton.[69] While Barton's definition of biblical criticism as a primarily linguistic exercise is admirable and certainly improves on the hegemony of historical criticism within the academic guild, his concern that theological interpretation of Scripture runs the risk of eisegesis is unnecessary if theological interpretation is rooted in a careful reading of the text. After all, one can hardly fault the exegetical chops of Brevard Childs, whom Barton singles out as exemplary of this kind of risk!

R. W. Jenson argues that the *regula fidei* was a "communal linguistic

---

68. Stephen E. Fowl's programmatic essay is *Engaging Scripture: A Model for Theological Interpretation* (Malden: Blackwell, 1998). But now see his *Theological Interpretation of Scripture*.
69. Barton, *Biblical Criticism*, 137-86.

Introduction

awareness of the faith delivered to the apostles" and was no text at all.⁷⁰ Although I am not satisfied with his fuller discussion of this point, it may help explain why the application of an apostolic grammar to sacred texts is more intuitive than a formal intellectual exercise. In Jenson's mind, the Rule of Faith is "adduced," and, when it was articulated in the ancient church, its theological agreements were expressed in various ways and not in a single form. Even though I would contend that both canon and creed are analogs of this same *regula fidei* and observe that the formation of each unfolds along parallel tracks into the fifth century, Jenson observes that those patristic articulations of "the faith delivered to the apostles" became increasingly complex and creedal in expression in a way that the distinction between creed and Rule of Faith became blurred over time.

In any case, this initial attempt at a theological reading cued by the apostolic Rule of Faith trades on Tertullian's bold expression of this Rule in *Prescription against Heretics* 13. The salutary result made the theological goods of the Pastoral Epistles more evident and helped organize and nuance these goods into a coherent commentary, able to enter into conversation with other Pauline and canonical texts whose theological materials may be organized in a similar fashion. Here, then, are the core beliefs that set out Tertullian's theological grammar, which I have followed in this commentary:

1. *The Creator God:* "There is only one God, and he is none other than the Creator of the world, who produced all things out of nothing through his own Word, first of all sent forth."
2. *Christ Jesus the Lord:* "This Word is called his Son, and, under the name of God, was seen 'in diverse manners' by the patriarchs, heard at all times in the prophets, at last brought down by the Spirit and power of the Father into the Virgin Mary, was made flesh in her womb, and, being born of her, went forth as Jesus Christ; thenceforth he preached the new law and the new promise of the kingdom of heaven, worked miracles, and having been crucified, rose again the third day. Having ascended into the heavens, he sat at the right hand of the Father."
3. *The Community of the Spirit:* "Christ sent instead of himself the power of the Holy Spirit to lead such as believe."⁷¹

---

70. Robert W. Jenson argues that the *regula fidei* was a "communal linguistic awareness of the faith delivered to the apostles" and was no text at all. *Canon and Creed* (Louisville: Westminster John Knox, 2010), 14-18. Although I am not satisfied with this description, it may explain my sense that the application of an apostolic grammar to texts is more intuitive than formal.

71. The idiom of "church" is not used. Rather, the sense in Tertullian's writings is more local and congregational in force. This follows Paul, whose ecclesiology hardly ever prescribes be-

4. *Christian Existence and Discipleship.* "In putting on our flesh, Christ made it his own; and in making it his own, he made it sinless . . . because in that same human flesh he lived without sin" (*On the Flesh of Christ* 16).
5. *Consummation in a New Creation:* "Christ will come with glory to take the saints to the enjoyment of everlasting life and of the heavenly promises, and to condemn the wicked to everlasting fire, after the resurrection of both these classes shall have happened, together with the restoration of their flesh."

The decision to use Tertullian's "communal linguistic awareness of the faith delivered to the apostles" rather than another was based on two substantial reasons. First, the narrative that secures his theological grammar is Trinitarian, thereby placing it more firmly on a trajectory beyond Irenaeus's precedent in a way that aims us toward Nicaea. Second, Tertullian's articulation of the apostolic Rule more adequately reflects the version in play when the Pauline collection reached its final canonical form toward the end of the second century. He seems prescient of the importance in the relationship between the Pauline and the Pillars' apostolates, which is instantiated in a canonical process that eventually adds a Pillars' collection of seven so-called "Catholic Epistles" to a Pauline canon, recognizing, we should presume, the effect of doing so on a church whose theology is mostly shaped by its Pauline witness. In this sense, Tertullian's Rule may well facilitate a conversation between these two disparate but complementary letter collections — a prospect that lies outside the range of this commentary.[72] One should add in passing that the church's early apologists, who were also the principal architects of the idea of a Christian biblical canon, did not separate their Bible practices from their confession of the Rule of Faith. Tertullian himself assumed that the absence of this apostolic deposit — whether canon or creed — in a congregation would inevitably lead to heresy. Central to the Pastoral Epistles is this same idea that the "pattern of healthy teaching" is safeguarded by the "good tradition" (2 Tim 1:13-14).

---

lief in a "catholic" church (although perhaps so in Ephesians). Certainly in the Pastoral Epistles as elsewhere in the Pauline canon the focus is on a local congregation of believers and individuals or individual subgroups within it. For this reason I prefer the rubric "community" over "church."

72. See Robert W. Wall and David Nienhuis, *Reading the Catholic Epistles as a Canonical Collection* (Grand Rapids: Eerdmans, forthcoming).

Introduction

Three Cases in Point

Frances Young has famously said that "theology is always earthed in a context."[73] This commentary takes as axiomatic the claim that the Bible can and should be read *theologically* as the church's sacred Scripture. That is, the Bible can and should be used by local congregations of believers as a primary source of knowledge about the nature and saving activity of the triune God. While read with critical tools and ecumenical creeds, a canon of sacred texts is best read as the timeless auxiliary of the Holy Spirit, who guides and governs every "household of God" at any time and in every place.

To make this point stick, Richard B. Steele has constructed a case study to conclude the commentary on each letter. 1 Timothy concludes with a study of "John Wesley and the Methodist Societies," 2 Timothy with a study of "John William Fletcher: John Wesley's Designated Successor," and Titus with a study of "Phoebe Palmer and the Wesleyan Holiness Movement." Each tells the story of the succession of prominent Methodist leaders and the vibrant Christian communities they served. Each instantiates key themes of the Pastoral Epistles in memorable ways. Each testifies to how Christian communities should conduct themselves in times when unsettling changes are taking place in both parochial life and the wider world. Each illustrates themes that reverberate throughout the Pastoral Epistles. We believe this case study approach to theological interpretation will make more concrete the reflections on the letters guided by the apostolic Rule of Faith.

But these are also historical studies that help readers "earth" the Pastoral Epistles into the life of other Christian communities in our own day and for their own world. This is so because they provide illustrations of what these sacred letters instruct: what Paul calls the "household of God" (οἶκος θεοῦ, *oikos theou*) can and must embody what he describes as "God's way of ordering reality" (οἰκονομία θεοῦ, *oikonomia theou* — not only in its teaching and preaching, but in its liturgy and prayer life, in its fellowship and polity, and in its public witness. Accordingly, those who read the Pastoral Epistles in their ecclesial context are bound to hear resonances of other Christian communities that faithfully follow its instructions.

Moreover, just as Paul's letters to Timothy and Titus concern themselves, among other things, with the question of how his own imminent death will affect his two protégés and their respective communities, so these cases illustrate the problems associated with changes that take place over time in the leadership and mission of dedicated Christian communities. For this rea-

---

73. Young, *Pastoral Letters*, 1.

son, the issue of how the theological goods and moral practices of a particular religious tradition are maintained and adapted over time is made explicit in the Wesley-to-Fletcher-to-Palmer sequence.

Steele has tried to give us something more than extended "sermon illustrations" or formulaic hagiographies. That is, he has tried to tell each story on its own terms without trivializing it by distilling some spiritual "point" or moral "lesson" from it. These episodes of Christian history supply insight into the Pastoral Epistles, and vice versa.

Bibliography

Commentaries on the Pastoral Epistles

Arichea, Daniel C., and Howard A. Hatton. *Paul's Letters to Timothy and Titus.* UBSHS. New York: United Bible Societies, 1995.
Barrett, C. K. *The Pastoral Epistles.* NewCB. Oxford: Oxford University Press, 1963.
Bassler, Jouette M. *1 Timothy, 2 Timothy, Titus.* ANTC. Nashville: Abingdon, 1996.
Bernhard, J. H. *The Pastoral Epistles.* CGTC. Cambridge: Cambridge University Press, 1899.
Brox, Norbert. *Die Pastoralbriefe.* RNT. Regensburg: Pustet, 1963.
Calvin, John. *The Second Epistle of Paul the Apostle to the Corinthians and the Epistles to Timothy, Titus and Philemon.* Grand Rapids: Eerdmans, 1964.
Chrysostom, St. John. *The Homilies of St. John Chrysostom, Archbishop of Constantinople, on the Epistles of St. Paul the Apostle to Timothy, Titus, and Philemon.* Translated by J. Tweedy. Oxford: Parker/London: Rivington, 1853.
Collins, Raymond F. *1 and 2 Timothy and Titus: A Commentary.* NTL. Louisville: Westminster John Knox, 2002.
Davies, Margaret. *The Pastoral Epistles.* EC. London: Epworth, 1996.
Dibelius, Martin. *Die Pastoralbriefe.* 4th ed. revised by Hans Conzelmann. HNT 13. Tübingen: Mohr Siebeck, 1955.
Dibelius, Martin, and Hans Conzelmann. *The Pastoral Epistles: A Commentary on the Pastoral Epistles.* Hermeneia. Philadelphia: Fortress, 1972.
Easton, Burton Scott. *The Pastoral Epistles.* London: SCM, 1947.
Ellicott, C. J. *Commentary on the Pastoral Epistles.* London: Longmans, 1861, 1883.
Fee, Gordon D. *1 and 2 Timothy, Titus.* NIBC. Peabody: Hendrickson, 1988.
Fiore, Benjamin, and Daniel J. Harrington. *The Pastoral Epistles: First Timothy, Second Timothy, Titus.* Rev. ed. Collegeville: Liturgical, 2007.
Guthrie, Donald. *The Pastoral Epistles.* TNTC. London: Tyndale, 1990.
Hanson, Anthony T. *The Pastoral Epistles: Based on the Revised Standard Version.* NCB. Grand Rapids: Eerdmans, 1982.
Hendriksen, William. *New Testament Commentary: Exposition of the Pastoral Epistles.* London: Banner of Truth, 1959.
Houlden, John L. *The Pastoral Epistles.* PNTC. London: SCM, 1989.

Hultgren, Arland J. *I-II Timothy, Titus*. ACNT. Minneapolis: Augsburg, 1984.
Johnson, Luke T. *The Pastoral Epistles*. KPG. Atlanta: John Knox, 1987.
———. *Letters to Paul's Delegates: 1 Timothy, 2 Timothy, Titus*. NTC. Valley Forge: Trinity, 1996.
———. *The First and Second Letters to Timothy: A New Translation with Introduction and Commentary*. New York: Doubleday, 2001.
Karris, Robert J. *The New Testament Message — The Pastoral Epistles*. Dublin: Veritas, 1979.
Kelly, J. N. D. *A Commentary on the Pastoral Epistles*. BNTC. London: Black, 1963.
Knight, George W. *The Pastoral Epistles: A Commentary on the Greek Text*. NIGTC. Grand Rapids: Eerdmans, 1992.
Lock, Walter. *The Pastoral Epistles*. ICC. Edinburgh: Clark, 1924, 1952.
Marshall, I. Howard, and Philip P. Towner. *A Critical and Exegetical Commentary on the Pastoral Epistles*. ICC. Edinburgh: Clark, 1999.
Martin, Ralph P. "1, 2 Timothy and Titus." Pages 1237-44 in *Harper's Bible Commentary*. Edited by James L. Mays. San Francisco: Harper and Row, 1988.
Mounce, William D. *Pastoral Epistles*. WBC. Nashville: Nelson, 2000.
Ngewa, Samuel. *1 and 2 Timothy and Titus*. ABC. Grand Rapids: Zondervan, 2009.
Parry, R. St. John. *The Pastoral Epistles*. Cambridge: Cambridge University Press, 1920.
Quinn, Jerome D. *The Letter to Titus*. AB 35. Garden City: Doubleday, 1990.
Quinn, Jerome D., and William C. Wacker. *The First and Second Letters to Timothy: A New Translation with Notes and Commentary*. Grand Rapids: Eerdmans, 2000.
Scott, Ernest Findlay. *The Pastoral Epistles*. MNTC. London: Hodder and Stoughton, 1963.
Simpson, Edmund Kidley. *The Pastoral Epistles: The Greek Text with Introduction and Commentary*. London: Tyndale, 1954.
Stott, John R. W. *Guard the Gospel: The Message of 2 Timothy*. Leicester: Inter-Varsity, 1994.
Towner, Philip H. *1-2 Timothy and Titus*. Downers Grove: InterVarsity, 1994.
———. *The Letters to Timothy and Titus*. NICNT. Grand Rapids: Eerdmans, 2006.
Twomey, Jay. *The Pastoral Epistles through the Centuries*. Chichester: Wiley-Blackwell, 2009.
Witherington, Ben, III. *Letters and Homilies for Hellenized Christians: A Socio-Rhetorical Commentary on Titus, 1-2 Timothy and 1-3 John*. Vol. 1. Downers Grove: InterVarsity, 2006.

Other Works on the Pastoral Epistles

Aageson, James W. *Paul, the Pastoral Epistles, and the Early Church*. Peabody: Hendrickson, 2008.
———. "The Pastoral Epistles, Apostolic Authority, and the Development of the Pauline Scriptures." Pages 5-26 in *The Pauline Canon*. Vol. 1. Edited by Stanley E. Porter. Leiden: Brill, 2004.
Allan, J. A. "The 'in Christ' Formula in the Pastoral Epistles." *NTS* 10 (1963): 115-21.
Bassler, Jouette M. "The Widow's Tale: A Fresh Look at 1 Tim 5:3-16." *JBL* 103 (1984): 23-41.
Belleville, Linda L. "Teaching and Usurping Authority: 1 Timothy 2:11-15." Pages 205-23 in *Discovering Biblical Equality*. Edited by Ronald W. Pierce and Rebecca Merrill Groothuis. Downers Grove: InterVarsity, 2004.

Blackburn, Barry L. "The Identity of the 'Women' in 1 Timothy 3.11." Pages 301-19 in *Essays on Women in Earliest Christianity*. Vol. 1. Edited by Carroll D. Osburn. Joplin: College, 1993.
Campbell, R. Alastair. "'Do the Work of an Evangelist.'" *EQ* 64 (1992): 117-29.
———. *The Elders: Seniority within Earliest Christianity*. SNTW. Edinburgh: Clark, 1994.
———. "Identifying the Faithful Sayings in the Pastoral Epistles." *JSNT* 54 (1994): 73-86.
———. "Καὶ μάλιστα οἰκείων — A New Look at 1 Timothy 5:8." *NTS* 41 (1995): 157-60.
Childs, Brevard S. *The Church's Guide for Reading Paul: The Canonical Shaping of the Pauline Corpus*. Grand Rapids: Eerdmans, 2008.
Collins, Raymond F. "The Image of Paul in the Pastorals." *LTP* 31 (1975): 147-73.
———. *Letters That Paul Did Not Write: The Epistle to the Hebrews and the Pauline Pseudepigrapha*. GNS 28. Wilmington: Glazier, 1988.
D'Angelo, Mary R. "*Eusebeia*: Roman Imperial Family Values and the Sexual Politics of 4 Maccabees and the PE." *BibInt* 11 (2003): 139-65.
Davies, Margaret. *The Pastoral Epistles*. NTG. Sheffield: Sheffield Academic Press, 1996.
Donelson, Lewis R. *Pseudepigraphy and Ethical Argument in the Pastoral Epistles*. HUT 22. Tübingen: Mohr, 1986.
———. *Colossians, Ephesians, 1 and 2 Timothy, and Titus*. Louisville: Westminster John Knox, 1996.
Duff, Jeremy. "P[46] and the Pastorals: A Misleading Consensus?" *NTS* 44 (1998): 578-90.
Ellingworth, Paul. "The 'True Saying' in 1 Timothy 3,1." *BT* 31 (1980): 443-45.
Elliott, J. K. *The Greek Text of the Epistles to Timothy and Titus*. SD 36. Salt Lake City: University of Utah Press, 1968.
Fiore, Benjamin. *The Function of Personal Example in the Socratic and Pastoral Epistles*. AnBib 105. Rome: Pontifical Biblical Institute, 1986.
Fitzmyer, Joseph A. "The Structured Ministry of the Church in the Pastoral Epistles." *CBQ* 66 (2004): 582-96.
Fuller, J. W. "Of Elders and Triads in 1 Timothy 5:19-25." *NTS* 29 (1983): 258-63.
Goodwin, Mark J. "The Pauline Background of the Living God as Interpretive Context for 1 Timothy 4.10." *JSNT* 61 (1996): 65-85.
Grayston, K., and G. Herdan. "The Authorship of the Pastoral Epistles in the Light of Statistical Linguistics." *NTS* 6 (1959-60): 1-15.
Gundry, Robert H. "The Form, Meaning, and Background of the Hymn Quoted in 1 Timothy 3:16." Pages 203-22 in *Apostolic History and the Gospel: Biblical and Historical Essays Presented to F. F. Bruce on His 60th Birthday*. Edited by W. Ward Gasque and Ralph P. Martin. Exeter: Paternoster, 1970.
Hanson, Anthony Tyrrell. *Studies in the Pastoral Epistles*. London: SPCK, 1968.
Harding, Mark. *Tradition and Rhetoric in the Pastoral Epistles*. StBL 3. New York: Peter Lang, 1998.
———. *What Are They Saying about the Pastoral Epistles?* New York: Paulist Press, 2001.
Harris, Murray J. "Titus 2:13 and the Deity of Christ." Pages 262-77 in *Pauline Studies: Essays Presented to Professor F. F. Bruce on His 70th Birthday*. Edited by F. F. Bruce, Donald A. Hagner, and Murray J. Harris. Grand Rapids: Eerdmans, 1980.
Harrison, P. N. *The Problem of the Pastoral Epistles*. Oxford: Oxford University Press, 1921.
Haykin, Michael A. G. "The Fading Vision? The Spirit and Freedom in the Pastoral Epistles." *EQ* 57 (1985): 291-305.

Holmes, J. M. *Text in a Whirlwind: A Critique of Four Exegetical Devices at 1 Timothy 2.12-15*. JSNTSup 196. Sheffield: Sheffield Academic, 2000.

Hultgren, A. J. "The Pastoral Epistles." Pages 151-53 in *The Cambridge Companion to St. Paul*. Edited by James D. G. Dunn. Cambridge: Cambridge University Press, 2003.

Johnson, Luke T. "II Timothy and the Polemic against False Teachers: A Reexamination." *JRelS* 6-7 (1978): 1-26.

———. *Letters to Paul's Delegates*. NTC. Valley Forge, PA: Trinity Press, 1996.

———. "*Oikonomia Theou*: The Theological Voice of 1 Timothy from the Perspective of Pauline Authorship." *HBT* 21 (1999): 87-104.

Karris, Robert J. "The Background and Significance of the Polemic of the Pastoral Epistles." *JBL* 92.4 (1973): 549-64.

———. "The Function and *Sitz im Leben* of the Paraenetic Elements in the Pastoral Epistles." Ph.D. diss., Harvard University, 1971.

Kidd, Reggie M. "Titus as *Apologia*: Grace for Liars, Beasts and Bellies." *HBT* 21 (1999): 185-209.

———. *Wealth and Beneficence in the Pastoral Epistles*. SBLDS 122. Atlanta: Scholars, 1990.

Knight, George W., III. *The Faithful Sayings in the Pastoral Letters*. Kampen: J. H. Kok, 1968.

———. "ΑΥΘΕΝΤΕΩ in Reference to Women in 1 Timothy 2.12." *NTS* 30 (1984): 143-57.

Köstenberger, Andreas J. "A Complex Sentence: The Syntax of 1 Timothy 2:12." Pages 53-84 in *Women in the Church: An Analysis and Application of 1 Timothy 2:9-15*. 2nd ed. Edited by Andreas J. Köstenberger and Thomas R. Schreiner. Grand Rapids: Baker, 2005.

Köstenberger, Andreas J., and Thomas R. Schreiner. *Women in the Church: An Analysis and Application of 1 Timothy 2:9-15*. 2nd ed. Edited by Andreas J. Köstenberger and Thomas R. Schreiner. Grand Rapids: Baker, 2005.

Kroeger, Richard Clark, and Catherine Clark Kroeger. *I Suffer Not a Woman: Rethinking 1 Timothy 2:12 in Light of Ancient Evidence*. Grand Rapids: Baker, 1992.

Lane, William L. "1 Tim iv.1-3: An Instance of Over-Realized Eschatology?" *NTS* 11 (1964-65): 164-67.

Lau, Andrew Y. *Manifest in Flesh: The Epiphany Christology of the Pastoral Epistles*. WUNT 2.86. Tübingen: J. C. B. Mohr, 1996.

MacDonald, Dennis R. *The Legend and the Apostle: The Battle for Paul in Story and Canon*. Philadelphia: Westminster, 1983.

MacDonald, M. Y. *The Pauline Churches: A Socio-Historical Study of Institutionalization in the Pauline and Deutero-Pauline Writings*. SNTSMS 57. Cambridge: Cambridge University Press, 1988.

Malherbe, Abraham J. "Medical Imagery in the Pastoral Epistles." Pages 19-35 in *Texts and Testaments: Critical Essays on the Bible and Early Church Fathers*. Edited by W. Eugene March. San Antonio: Trinity University Press, 1980.

———. "'In Season and out of Season': 2 Timothy 4:2." *JBL* 103 (1982): 23-41.

———. "Godliness, Self-Sufficiency, Greed, and the Enjoyment of Wealth: 1 Timothy 6:3-19." *NovT* 52 (2010): 376-405.

Marshall, I. Howard. "Faith and Works in the Pastoral Epistles." *SNTSU* 9 (1984): 203-18.

———. "The Christology of the Pastoral Epistles." *SNTSU* 13 (1988): 157-77.

———. "Salvation, Grace, and Works in the Later Writings in the Pauline Corpus." *NTS* 42 (1996): 339-58.

———. "Brothers Embracing Sisters." *BT* 55 (2004): 303-10.
Martin, Ralph P. *New Testament Foundations: A Guide for Christian Students*, vol. 2: *The Acts, the Letters, the Apocalypse*. Rev. ed. Grand Rapids: Eerdmans, 1986.
McEleney, Neil J. "The Vice Lists in the Pastoral Epistles." *CBQ* 36 (1974): 203-19.
Meier, John P. "*Presbyteros* in the Pastoral Epistles." *CBQ* 35 (1973): 323-45.
Merk, Otto. "Glaube und Tat in den Pastoralbriefen." *ZNW* 66 (1975): 91-102.
Miller, James D. *The Pastoral Letters as Composite Documents*. SNTSMS 93. Cambridge: Cambridge University Press, 1997.
Mott, Stephen Charles. "Greek Ethics and Christian Conversion: The Philonic Background of Ti. II,1.14 and II,3-7." *NovT* 20 (1978): 22-48.
Moule, C. F. D. "The Problem of the Pastoral Epistles: A Reappraisal." Pages 113-32 in *Essays in New Testament Interpretation*. Cambridge: Cambridge University Press, 1982. Originally in *BJRL* 47 (1965): 430-52.
Murphy-O'Connor, Jerome. "2 Timothy Contrasted with 1 Timothy and Titus." *RB* 98 (1991): 403-18.
Neumann, Kenneth J. *The Authenticity of the Pauline Epistles in the Light of Stylostatistical Analysis*. Atlanta: Scholars, 1990.
Niebuhr, Karl-Wilhelm, and Robert W. Wall. *The Catholic Epistles and Apostolic Tradition*. Waco: Baylor University Press, 2009.
Nielson, Charles Merritt. "Scripture in the Pastoral Epistles." *PRSt* 7 (1980): 4-23.
Osburn, C. "ΑΥΘΕΝΤΕΩ (1 Timothy 2:12)." *ResQ* 25 (1982): 1-12.
Padgett, Alan. "Wealthy Women at Ephesus: 1 Tim 2:8-15 in Social Context." *Int* 41 (1987): 19-31.
Page, Sydney. "Marital Expectations of Church Leaders in the Pastoral Epistles." *JSNT* 50 (1993): 105-20.
Patsch, Hermann. "The Fear of Deutero-Paulinism: The Reception of Friedrich Schleiermacher's 'Critical Open Letter' concerning 1 Timothy." *JHC* 6.1 (1999): 3-31.
Payne, Philip Burton. "Libertarian Women in Ephesus: A Response to Douglas J. Moo's Article, '1 Timothy 2:11-15: Meaning and Significance.'" *TrinJ* 2 (1981): 169-97.
———. "1 Tim 2.12 and the Use of *oude* to Combine Two Elements to Express a Single Idea." *NTS* 54 (2008): 235-53.
Pervo, Richard I. *The Making of Paul: Constructions of the Apostle in Early Christianity*. Minneapolis: Fortress, 2010.
Petersen, William L. "Can ΑΡΣΕΝΟΚΟΙΤΑΙ Be Translated by 'Homosexuals'? (1 Cor 6:9; 1 Tim 1:10." *VC* 40 (1986): 187-91.
Porter, Stanley E. "What Does it Mean to Be 'Saved by Childbirth' (1 Timothy 2.15)?" *JSNT* 49 (1993): 87-105.
———. "Pauline Authorship and the Pastoral Epistles: Implications for Canon." *BBR* 5 (1995): 105-23.
Prior, Michael. *Paul the Letter Writer and the Second Letter to Timothy*. JSNTSup 23. Sheffield: JSOT, 1989.
Quinn, Jerome D. "The Last Volume of Luke: The Relation of Luke-Acts to the Pastoral Epistles." Pages 62-75 in *Perspectives on Luke-Acts*. Ed. Charles H. Talbert. Edinburgh: Clark, 1978.
———. "The Holy Spirit in the Pastoral Epistles." Pages 35-68 in *Sin, Salvation, and the Spirit*. Edited by D. Durken. Collegeville, MN: Liturgical Press, 1979.

———. "Paul's Last Captivity." Pages 289-99 in *Studia Biblica 3*. Edited by Elizabeth A. Livingstone. JSNTSup 3. Sheffield: Sheffield Academic, 1979.

Robinson, T. A. "Grayston and Herdan's 'C' Quantity Formula and the Authorship of the Pastoral Epistles." *NTS* 30 (1984): 282-88.

Scholer, D. M. "Women's Adornment: Some Historical and Hermeneutical Observations on the New Testament Passages." *Daughters of Sarah* 6.1 (1980): 3-6.

Schwarz, Roland. *Bürgerliches Christentum im Neuen Testament? Eine Studie zu Ethik, Amt und Recht in den Pastoralbriefen*. Klosterneuburg: Österreichisches Katholisches Bibelwerk, 1983.

Skeat, T. C. "'Especially the Parchments': A Note on 2 Tim 4.13." *JTS* 30 (1979): 173-77.

Stettler, Hanna. *Die Christologie der Pastoralbriefe*. WUNT 2:105. Tübingen: Mohr Siebeck, 1998.

Thiselton, Anthony C. "The Logical Role of the Liar Paradox in Titus 1:12, 13: A Dissent from the Commentaries in the Light of Philosophical and Logical Analysis." *BibInt* 2 (1994): 207-33.

Towner, Philip H. "The Present Age in the Eschatology of the Pastoral Epistles." *NTS* 32 (1986): 427-48.

———. "Gnosis and Realized Eschatology in Ephesus (of the Pastoral Epistles) and the Corinthian Enthusiasm." *JSNT* 31 (1987): 95-124.

———. "Structure and Meaning in Titus 3:1-8." Unpublished paper, 1994.

———. "Pauline Theology or Pauline Tradition in the Pastoral Epistles: The Question of Method." *TynBul* 46.2 (1995): 27-314.

———. "Can Slaves Be Their Masters' Benefactors? 1 Timothy 6:1-2a in Literary, Cultural and Theological Context." *Current Trends in Scripture Translation* 182/183 (1997): 43-50.

———. "The Portrait of Paul and the Theology of 2 Timothy: The Closing Chapter of the Pauline Story." *HBT* 21.2 (1999): 151-70.

———. "The Function of the Public Reading of Scripture in 1 Tim 4:13 and in the Biblical Tradition." *SBJT* 7 (2003): 44-54.

———. "Christology in the Letters to Timothy and Titus." Pages 219-44 in *Contours of Christology in the New Testament*. Edited by Richard N. Longenecker. MNTS 7. Grand Rapids: Eerdmans, 2005.

———. "The Old Testament in the Letters to Timothy and Titus." Pages 891-918 in *Commentary on the Use of the Old Testament in the New Testament*. Edited by G. K. Beale and D. A. Carson. Grand Rapids: Baker, 2007.

Verner, David C. *The Household of God: The Social World of the Pastoral Epistles*. SBLDS 71. Chico, CA: Scholars, 1983.

Viviano, Benedict Thomas. "The Genre of Matt. 1–2: Light from 1 Tim 1:4." *RB* 97 (1990): 31-53.

Wall, Robert W. "Pauline Authorship and the Pastoral Epistles: A Response to S. E. Porter." *BBR* 5 (1995): 125-28.

———. "The Function of the Pastoral Letters within the Pauline Canon of the New Testament: A Canonical Approach." Pages 27-44 in *The Pauline Canon*. Vol. 1. Edited by Stanley E. Porter. Leiden: Brill, 2004.

———. "1 Timothy 2:9-15 Reconsidered (Again!)." *BBR* 14.1 (2004): 81-103.

Westerholm, Stephen. "The Law and the 'Just Man' (1 Tim 1,3-11)." *St* 36 (1982): 79-95.

Wilson, S. G. *Luke and the Pastoral Epistles*. London: SPCK, 1979.
Winter, Bruce W. "*Providentia* for the Widows of 1 Timothy 5.3-16." *TynBul* 39 (1988): 83-99.
Wire, Antoinette Clark. *The Corinthian Women Prophets: A Reconstruction through Paul's Rhetoric*. Minneapolis: Fortress, 1990.
Witherington, Ben, III. *Letters and Homilies for Hellenized Christians*, vol. 1: *A Socio-Rhetorical Commentary on Titus, 1-2 Timothy and 1-3 John*. Downers Grove: InterVarsity, 2006.
Wolter, Michael. *Die Pastoralbriefe als Paulustradition*. FRLANT 146. Göttingen: Vandenhoeck und Ruprecht, 1988.
Wright, D. F. "Homosexuals or Prostitutes: The Meaning of ΑΡΣΕΝΟΚΟΙΤΑΙ (1 Cor 6:9; 1 Tim 1:10)." *VC* 38 (1984): 125-53.
———. "Translating ΑΡΣΕΝΟΚΟΙΤΑΙ (1 Cor 6:9; 1 Tim 1:10)." *VC* 41 (1987): 396-98.
Yarbrough, Mark M. *Paul's Utilization of Preformed Traditions in 1 Timothy: An Evaluation of the Apostle's Literary, Rhetorical, and Theological Tactics*. LNTS 417. New York: Clark, 2009.
Young, Frances M. *The Theology of the Pastoral Letters*. Cambridge: Cambridge University Press, 1994.
Zamfir, Korinna, and Joseph Verheyden. "Text-critical and Intertextual Remarks on 1 Tim 2:8-10." *NovT* 50.4 (2008): 376-406.

Works on Canonical and Rule of Faith Interpretation

Abraham, William J. *Canon and Criterion in Christian Theology*. Oxford: Clarendon, 1998.
———. *Canonical Theism*. Grand Rapids: Eerdmans, 2008.
Adam, A. K. M. *What Is Postmodern Biblical Criticism?* Minneapolis: Fortress, 1995.
Barton, John. *Holy Writings, Sacred Text: The Canon in Early Christianity*. Louisville: Westminster John Knox, 1997.
———. *The Cambridge Companion to Biblical Interpretation*. Cambridge: Cambridge University Press, 1998.
———. *The Nature of Biblical Criticism*. Louisville: Westminster John Knox, 2007.
Bleich, David. *The Double Perspective: Language, Literacy, and Social Relations*. New York: Oxford University Press, 1988.
Crites, S. "The Narrative Quality of Experience." *JAAR* 39 (1971): 291-311.
Fowl, Stephen E. *Engaging Scripture: A Model for Theological Interpretation*. Malden, MA: Blackwell, 1998.
———. *Theological Interpretation of Scripture*. CC. Eugene: Wipf and Stock, 2009.
Gorman, Michael J. *Elements of Biblical Exegesis: A Basic Guide for Students and Ministers*. Rev. and exp. ed. Peabody, MA: Hendrickson, 2001.
Holland, Norman Norwood. *The Dynamics of Literary Response*. New York: Oxford University Press, 1968.
———. *5 Readers Reading*. New Haven, CT: Yale University Press, 1975.
Jenson, Robert W. "The Religious Power of Scripture." *SJT* 52 (1999): 89-105.
———. *Canon and Creed*. Louisville: Westminster John Knox Press, 2010.
Johnson, Luke T. *Scripture and Discernment*. Nashville: Abingdon, 1996.

Malherbe, Abraham J. *Canon and Criterion in Christian Theology.* Oxford: Clarendon, 1998.
McDonald, Lee Martin. *The Formation of the Christian Biblical Canon.* Rev and exp. ed. Peabody: Hendrickson, 1995.
Meade, David G. *Pseudonymity and Canon: An Investigation into the Relationship of Authorship and Authority in Jewish and Earliest Christian Tradition.* WUNT 39. Tübingen: Mohr, 1986.
Metzger, Bruce M. *The Canon of the New Testament: Its Origin, Development, and Significance.* Oxford: Clarendon, 1987.
Mitchell, Margaret M. *Paul, the Corinthians and the Birth of Christian Hermeneutics.* New York: Cambridge University Press, 2010.
Moxness, Halvor. "Honor and Shame." Pages 19-40 in *The Social Sciences and New Testament Interpretation.* Edited by Richard L. Rohrbaugh. Peabody, MA: Hendrickson, 1996.
Patzia, Arthur G. *The Making of the New Testament: Origin, Collection, Text, and Canon.* Downers Grove: InterVarsity, 1995.
Sanders, James A. *Canon and Community: A Guide to Canonical Criticism.* GBS. Philadelphia: Fortress, 1984.
Seitz, Christopher. "Canonical Approach." Pages 100-102 in *DTIB.* London: SPCK, 2005.
Treier, Daniel J. "Scripture, Unity of." *DTIB.*
Trobisch, David. *Die Endredaktion des Neuen Testaments. Eine Untersuchung zur Entstehung der Christlichen Bibel.* NTOA 31. Göttingen: Vandenhoeck und Ruprecht, 1996.
Vanhoozer, Kevin J. "Scripture and Tradition." Pages 149-69 in *The Cambridge Companion to Postmodern Theology.* Edited by Kevin J. Vanhoozer. CCR. Cambridge: Cambridge University Press, 2003.
Wall, Robert W. "Canonical Context and Canonical Conversations." Pages 165-82 in *Between Two Horizons: Spanning New Testament Studies and Systematic Theology.* Edited by Joel B. Green and Max Turner. Grand Rapids: Eerdmans, 1999.
———. "The Rule of Faith in Theological Hermeneutics." Pages 88-107 in *Between Two Horizons: Spanning New Testament Studies and Systematic Theology.* Edited by Joel B. Green and Max Turner. Grand Rapids: Eerdmans, 1999.
———. "A Canonical Approach to the Unity of Acts and Luke's Gospel." Pages 172-91 in *Rethinking the Reception and Unity of Luke-Acts.* Edited by Andrew F. Gregory and Christopher K. Rowe. Columbia, S.C.: University of South Carolina Press, 2010.
Watson, Francis. *Paul and the Hermeneutics of Faith.* London: Clark, 2004.
Webster, John. *Holy Scripture: A Dogmatic Sketch.* Cambridge: Cambridge University Press, 2003.
Wood, Charles M. *The Formation of Christian Understanding: An Essay in Theological Hermeneutics.* Philadelphia: Westminster, 1981.

1 Timothy

The theological crisis that occasions 1 Timothy is set out early in the letter (1:3): Paul's personal absence from Ephesus, and so also the absence of his apostolic charisms, intensifies the threat of heterodox teaching and of the congregation's accommodation of Greco-Roman culture. After all, these threats would seem much less prominent were the apostle on site distinguishing false teaching from the word of truth or hard at work guiding the formation of Christians whose life is shaped by his instruction (vv. 4-5). Paul's absence occasions an epistemic crisis when knowledge of the truth, even if mediated by his delegated leaders, is less certain, less clear-cut, and more vulnerable to competing claims and challenges (cf. Phil 1:12-18).

The situation is not unlike that facing the disciples of Jesus when he announces his departure (John 13:33; 14:1-4). The disciples also perceive his departure as an epistemic crisis, poignantly posed by Thomas: "How can we know the way?" (14:5). Jesus' response to him is instructive: on the one hand, he famously maintains his unique authority as the only way to God (v. 6) while promising his disciples the Spirit, who will continue to mediate his truth to them in his absence. In this letter, Paul's instructions to Timothy function as a medium of his personal presence: Timothy knows something of how Paul would have handled things were Paul with him.

The introduction of Timothy in Acts 16:1-5 supplies the canonical context of this letter's address. The reader knows from Acts that Timothy is the child of a mixed marriage in the Diaspora. Evidently his non-Jewish father shaped his religious identification, since he was not yet circumcised. For this reason Paul circumcises him, not only to restore his mother's Jewish identity but to personify in Timothy the restored Israel that now includes repentant Jews and Gentiles (cf. Acts 15:13-29; 1 Tim 2:7).[1]

---

1. Robert W. Wall, "Acts," in *The New Interpreter's Bible* (Nashville: Abingdon, 2001), 10:213-23.

On this basis, we may imagine that the conflict between Jewish and pagan religious backgrounds, which personifies Timothy's religious upbringing, contextualizes the disputations he might have in Ephesus with those who pretend to be "teachers of the Law." While Paul vigorously chastises them (1:6-7), it is left to Timothy to correct them as a restored Jew (v. 3).

The Timothy of Acts then accompanies Paul on a European mission that eventually takes him to Ephesus (Acts 18:5; 19:22). He again is mentioned as a member of Paul's entourage when leaving Ephesus some months later for Macedonia (20:4). Although Acts does not tell us Timothy's full story, it does provide readers with a few biographical details that locate him on Paul's missionary team that evangelized Roman Ephesus, when, the reader now assumes, he became familiar with the city's cultural currents and people. Within this narrative setting, then, Timothy is easily recognized as a good choice to conduct Paul's business in his absence: he is the ideal tradent and successor to Paul there.

Instructed to continue Paul's work in his absence, Timothy personifies the faithful recipient of the Pauline legacy. Of course, Paul is irreplaceable: it is to him that the glorious gospel of God has been entrusted (1 Tim 1:10-11; 2 Tim 1:11; Tit 1:3), and he alone is the appointed teacher of truth to the nations (1 Tim 2:7).[2] In this sense, the prospect of his departure, whether to another place (1 Tim 1:3; Tit 1:5) or in death (2 Tim 4:6), occasions an epistemic crisis. Timothy is asked to organize a Christian congregation in a pagan place and safeguard the Pauline tradition for the next generation, tasks Paul himself was appointed to complete. The apostle's perceived ambivalence about Timothy's readiness to succeed him, most clearly implied by 2 Tim 1:6-7, may well reflect a Thomas-like puzzlement: How can a successor know the way when the one granted spiritual authority to put the nations to rights goes missing? The problems facing the intended readers of 1 Timothy in a post-Pauline setting are best understood when a person of particular spiritual authority goes missing.

The letter's recipient is made alert to what is at stake by an opening that recalls Rom 1:1-15, itself glossed in canonical setting by the ending of Acts, which depicts a faithful Paul continuing his prophetic ministry in Rome while facing an uncertain future (Acts 28:17-31).[3] What seems especially apropos in recalling the opening of Romans is its mention of Paul's absence (Rom

---

2. Notably, other apostles are not named when Paul is addressing Timothy and Titus as in other Pauline letters.

3. See Robert W. Wall, "Romans 1:1-15: An Introduction to the Pauline Corpus of the New Testament," in *The New Testament as Canon* (ed. Robert W. Wall and Eugene E. Lemcio; JSNTSup 76; Sheffield: JSOT, 1992), 142-60.

1:10), which prevents him from personally imparting his gospel and apostolic charism (v. 5) to believers there, which makes them more vulnerable to evil's corrupting force (v. 11). Paul wrote Romans for the same reason that he now writes 1 Timothy: as an epistolary substitute for his personal presence to provide pastoral encouragement and apostolic instruction to guide believers during his absence from them.[4] In fact, Paul's expansive self-identification in those opening words of Romans raises a haunting question for the reader of 1 Timothy: Given Paul's apostolic presence and performances, how will the church have a future without him? 1 Timothy offers readers a different response to this crisis than offered by Romans: rather than presenting readers the content of his gospel, Paul gives Timothy instructions in the organization, moral and professional practices, and working relationships that guide those responsible for forming Christian congregations into God's household (3:15).[5]

1:1-2 Paul Greets Timothy

¹From Paul, an apostle of Christ Jesus by the command of God our Savior and Christ Jesus our hope, ²to Timothy, genuine son in faith: Grace, mercy, and peace from God the Father and Christ Jesus our Lord.

1 Timothy begins in a manner typical of other Pauline letters and according to the literary conventions of antiquity: the sender greets the letter's intended recipient (see also 2 Tim 1:1-2; Tit 1:1-4).[6] While expected in a letter, such a salutation has an important rhetorical role: to frame the posture of sender to recipient for one reading the correspondence that follows. In antiquity as today, what one says in greeting another forges first impressions that shape the future of their communication. For example, Paul identifies himself as "an apostle of Christ Jesus by the command of God," which clearly establishes his

---

4. Cf. Robert W. Funk, "The Apostolic Parousia: Form and Significance," in *Christian History and Interpretation: Essays in Honor of J. Knox* (ed. William Reuben Farmer, C. F. D. Moule, and Richard R. Niebuhr; Cambridge: Cambridge University Press, 1967), 249-68.

5. Luke T. Johnson interprets these instructions (and those of Titus) as apostolic mandates *(mandata principis)* for those delegated with the responsibility of imitating Paul's exemplary persona and missionary practices in his absence. Johnson, *The Pastoral Epistles* (KPG; Atlanta: John Knox, 1987), 94-97.

6. The standard introduction to the literary conventions and practices of letter writing in antiquity is David Edward Aune, *The New Testament in Its Literary Environment* (Philadelphia: Westminster, 1987), especially 158-82.

spiritual authority over Timothy and assumes that Timothy will comply with what he is instructed to do in this letter. Paul's address of Timothy as his "genuine son" softens what might otherwise seem like an authoritarian stance, so that Timothy's adherence to Paul's written instruction might be prompted by the more intimate relationship they share (cf. 2 Tim 1:2; Tit 1:4).

The precise nature of Paul's stipulated authority as "an apostle of Christ Jesus" has long been debated among scholars.[7] At the very least, we should agree that Paul's own understanding of apostleship is different from that of Acts, which limits the apostolate to associates of the historical Jesus (Acts 1:21-22). If we define apostleship by the letter's own terms, especially by its Pauline biography, apostleship is funded by memories of a particular ministry, by the core beliefs of a specific gospel, and by the virtuous life of its exemplar. More critically, it is the risen Christ himself who "placed Paul into service" (1 Tim 1:12) as a "preacher and apostle" (2:7) of "the glorious gospel of the blessed God" (1:11). While this less political definition of apostleship may be attributed to 1 Timothy's occasion and genre, it does cohere with the résumé of the Paul of Acts, whose importance for the future of the church derives from his conversion to Jesus, his prophetic calling (Acts 9:15-16), and his exemplary career as a prophet like Jesus (20:18-35), rather than from any special status granted him by some ecclesial authority (cf. Gal 1:1, 11-12) based on personal association with the historical Jesus. Indeed, not only is the authorization of the Pauline apostolate predicated on different grounds than that of the Jerusalem Pillars, who were with Jesus from the beginning, but the deep logic of the Pauline gospel is underwritten by the narrative of Paul's conversion experience and his missionary vocation rather than by his acquaintance with the Incarnate Word (cf. 1 John 1:1-4).

If we are to understand Timothy as the ideal tradent of the Pauline apostolate, the effect on the continuing reception of this letter is to conceive of apostolicity as a body of goods transferable to others. Even though Paul is absent, his gospel and the memory of his ministry are passed on from Timothy to still others (see 6:21; cf. 2 Tim 2:2; Acts 20:17-35). And this idea of apostolicity guides a particular way of reading the canonical collection. If the biblical memory of Paul's gospel and way of life is not a thing of the past but exemplary of a living tradition with a catholic scope that is passed on from one generation of believers to the next no matter the time zone, then it is appropriate

---

7. The debate is less over the technical meaning of ἀπόστολος *(apostolos)*, "one sent out," and generally concerns the prophetic ministry of the word; see K. H. Rengstorf, *TDNT* 1:407-47. The debate is over the precise nature of Paul's apostolic authority, which evidently was disputed even in his lifetime (cf. 1 Cor 9:1).

for contemporary readers to identify with Timothy: in some sense "Timothy" and "Titus" are tropes for the faithful tradent who receives and passes on the Pauline apostolate to those who are his "genuine child(ren) in the faith."[8]

While exceptional within the Pauline canon (cf. Phil 3:20; Eph 5:3), the repeated reference to God as "our Savior" (1 Tim 1:1; 2:3; 4:10; Tit 1:3; 2:10; 3:4) confesses a central Jewish belief that would have also been readily understood in the Greco-Roman world, where both deities and important leaders (e.g., rulers and military generals) were called "saviors." They were judged "saviors" not only because they rescued people from calamity but also because they were sources of benefaction that enhanced the lives of their subjects. Significantly, this title used in the letter's address anticipates the letter's central theological claim that "God our Savior desires all to be saved" (2:4) and that God's desired salvation benefits every sinner who is delivered through the messianic work of Jesus from death for eternal life (1:15-16; cf. 2:5-6).

Parallel to this designation of God as Savior, Jesus is personified as "our hope," a Christological confession without parallel in the Pauline canon (cf. Col 1:27). The grammatical parallel between these opening phrases about God and Jesus implies that the divine command that legitimizes Pauline apostleship is given by both in unison and with mutual support (cf. 1 John 1:3). Moreover, this same parallel combines salvation and hope as logically inclusive expectations of the Pauline tradent: if God's purpose is creation's redemption, then the messianic work of Christ Jesus supplies a realistic hope that God's purpose will be fully realized (so 2:3-6). The letter to Titus elaborates this very point in two powerful theological formulas, arguing that God's epiphany indicates that God is both the source and object of humanity's hope (see the comments on Tit 2:11-14; 3:4-8).

Although no clear motive exists why the Pastoral Epistles typically place "Christ" before "Jesus," the rhetorical effect is to give priority to the church's claims about Jesus as the messianic broker of God's promised salvation. The congregation's hope in the coming triumph of God our Savior is therefore framed by Christ's personal history, not only during his first coming (1:15; 2:5-6) but at his second coming as well (4:10; 5:5; 6:17). Mention of these critical Christological moments at the beginning and ending of the letter forms a rhetorical *inclusio* that supplies the motive of a congregation's ready compliance to the instructions passed on to them by the canonical Paul.

The letter's intended recipient is Timothy (1:2a; but see 6:21b), who represents the apostolate to others in Paul's absence (cf. 2 Tim 2:2). The commu-

---

8. See Brevard S. Childs, *The Church's Guide for Reading Paul: The Canonical Shaping of the Pauline Corpus* (Grand Rapids: Eerdmans, 2008), 96-97.

nicative intent of the epithet, "genuine son," not only expresses Paul's affection for Timothy but also the expectation that one who is truly a son will imitate his father to help maintain the family's honor and status within society.[9] Aristotle observed that children naturally learn to become adults by imitating their parents (*Poetics* 1448). According to Jaeger's now famous study of *paideia* in early Greek civilization, the role of imitation was central to the general pattern of a person's learning and cultivated a person's symbolic universe.[10] Framed by this historical perspective, the rhetorical relationship between author and audience may be understood as mimetic: Paul is Timothy's role model, whose character and sacred practices are learned firsthand. This mentoring relationship is the presumed subtext of the Pastoral Epistles' extensive use of biography (e.g., 1 Tim 1:12-17) and personal memory (e.g., 2 Tim 3:10-15), and extends also to the practical instructions given to the "son" to imitate so as to preserve the work the "father" has begun (2 Tim 2:2).

This thickened understanding of the letter's address may guide readers to approach the letter's paraenesis as curricular; its literary conventions such as biography, exhortation, reminder, and moral instruction purpose to teach the "craft" of apostolic ministry to the "son" as his successor so that he will be able to continue the family's work of organizing and shaping the faith and witness of Christian congregations with due diligence and skill. Moreover, since the letter is written without a normal "thanksgiving," which typically introduces the letter's occasion (but see 1:12-17), Paul's opening salutation rather than a prayerful thanksgiving hints at this special relationship with Timothy as the letter's occasion. Indeed, the subsequent text that notes Paul's departure from Ephesus in effect marks the beginning of a succession of his apostolate (see below on 1:3).

In usual Pauline fashion, the letter's salutation (1:2b) combines the traditional greeting between Gentiles, "grace," with that of Jews, "peace." This interpenetration of two worlds, characteristic of the catholic scope of God's salvation, is also instantiated in Timothy's DNA. In this way, the addition of "mercy" to Paul's greeting probably introduces an important theological theme of his correspondence with Timothy more than it is a response to a particular theological crisis facing Timothy's congregation.

---

9. Cf. Benjamin Fiore, *The Function of Personal Example in the Socratic and Pastoral Epistles* (AnBib 105; Rome: Pontifical Biblical Institute, 1986), 35-38. This address, when compared to 2 Timothy's "dear child" (2 Tim 1:2), may reflect a different epistolary genre or occasion. For example, the use of "genuine" to qualify Timothy's sonship may signal the problem with "inauthentic" teaching, which provides an important subtext of the instructions that follow.

10. Werner W. Jaeger, *Paideia: The Ideals of Greek Culture*, vols. 1-3 (trans. Gilbert Highet; New York: Oxford University Press, 1945).

1:3-11 The Aim and Manner of Christian Instruction

³As I requested you to do when leaving for Macedonia: stay longer in Ephesus so that you may instruct certain individuals not to teach divergent doctrine ⁴or to pay attention to myths and unending genealogies. Their teaching only encourages idle speculation rather than faithfulness to God's way of ordering the world. ⁵The aim of instruction is loving relationships that come from a pure heart, a good conscience, and earnest faith. ⁶Some have rejected this and have turned to fruitless discussion, ⁷wanting to be Torah teachers without understanding either what they are saying or what they are claiming. ⁸We know, for example, that the law is good if used lawfully. ⁹We understand a law is not for an innocent person but for the lawless and rebellious, godless and sinners, unholy and profane, for those who commit patricide and matricide, for murderers, ¹⁰sexually unfaithful, homosexuals, slave dealers, liars, perjurers, and anyone else who acts contrary to healthy teaching, ¹¹which agrees with the glorious gospel of the blessed God that has been entrusted to me.

The typical pattern of a Pauline letter would lead the reader to expect a thankful note sounded following the salutation (see below on 1:12-17); instead we find the letter's occasion made clear: Paul's departure from Ephesus requires that Timothy stay behind to organize a Christian congregation in his absence. Although we are not told why Paul should instruct his protégé to do what may seem obvious to others, the charge to correct certain rivals regarding both the substance (vv. 3-5) and pedagogy (vv. 6-7) of their "divergent doctrine" does seem to make Timothy's work more urgent if not also more difficult in Paul's absence. The extended footnote about the law (vv. 8-10), especially when its performance "agrees with the glorious gospel of the blessed God" (v. 11), may indicate something of the "divergent doctrine" promoted in Ephesus.

Paul rarely identifies his rivals by name (cf. 1:19-20; 2 Tim 2:16-18) and typically substitutes symbol for substance when discussing what they teach (cf. 1 Tim 4:1-4; Tit 1:10-12; 3:9-11).[11] But, whatever they teach, it seems that these faceless individuals do not represent the Pauline apostolate and may even exert a negative influence within the congregation in Ephesus. Paul's

---

11. See Ben Witherington's balanced summary of scholarly conjecture about the identity and teaching of these opponents in *A Socio-Rhetorical Commentary on Titus, 1-2 Timothy and 1-3 John* (Letters and Homilies for Hellenized Christians 1; Downers Grove: InterVarsity, 2006), 341-47. He follows J. L. Sumney's method for identifying opponents in Pauline letters, even though Sumney uses 2 Corinthians for illustration and does not include the Pastoral Epistles in his analysis. Jerry L. Sumney, *Identifying Paul's Opponents* (JSNTSup 40; Sheffield: JSOT, 1990).

entreaty for Timothy to stay put in Ephesus to instruct them makes little sense otherwise.

But the theological crisis that occasions this letter is not the presence of these rival teachers, as most commentators insist, but the apostle's departure from Ephesus and the implicit threat to his gospel precipitated by his personal absence (cf. Rom 1:10-11). The difficult tasks of forming a fledging Christian congregation in a pagan place are left to Timothy. While the mention of rivals may sound an alert, the real need is to prepare Timothy for the business at hand. The relative lack of attention given to these false teachers, beyond this opening riff, and the kind of instructions and practical advice that follow indicate that the letter's real aim is to guide Paul's successor in forming a healthy Christian congregation according to the "glorious gospel of God" entrusted to the apostle Paul.

The setting of this hard work is Ephesus, a cultural and religious center of the ancient world and the capital city of Roman Asia — among the empire's most prosperous regions. In due time, Ephesus would also become the headquarters of the missionary organization founded by Paul and perhaps also the place where the Pauline collection was formed — not an insignificant prompt, then, given the subsequent role of the Timothy correspondence within the canonical form of this epistolary collection.[12]

"In Ephesus" also cues the reader's interest in the story of Paul's mission in that city according to Acts 19, where the city is depicted as rife with religious conflict, provoked mostly by Paul's identity as a Jewish teacher, whether in the neighborhood synagogue or town square. Despite a mission that embraced both Jews and Gentiles (19:10, 17), his departure from the synagogue (v. 9) and the conflict over his Jewish identity (v. 34) form an intertext with Paul's significant self-reference as a teacher of the Gentiles (see the comment below on 1 Tim 2:7). A mission that began among the Jews of Ephesus had spread across the metropolis to become a Christian movement among repentant pagans whose religious background was non-Jewish and Hellenistic in their religious customs and sensibilities. The fact that the internal structure of the household church is Jewish coheres with the story of the canonical Paul in Acts, whose public mission as "light to the nations" is notably Jewish in content and public manners.[13]

Moreover, the passing mention of Paul's "departure for Macedonia" re-

---

12. For the importance of Ephesus in the formation of the NT canon, see Eugene E. Lemcio's study, "Ephesus and the New Testament Canon," in Robert W. Wall and Eugene E. Lemcio, *The New Testament as Canon* (JSNTSup 76; Sheffield: JSOT, 1992), 335-60.

13. Cf. Scot McKnight, *A Light among the Gentiles: Jewish Missionary Activity in the Second Temple Period* (Minneapolis: Fortress, 1991).

calls the narrative of Acts 19–20 and the repeated forays Paul made with Timothy from Ephesus into Macedonia (cf. 19:21-22; 20:1-6). More importantly, Timothy is among those who heard Paul's succession speech in Acts 20:18-35, and the loud echoes of that crucial speech now frame the theological crisis to which the Timothy correspondence responds and the role it now performs in the Pauline canon: how will the legacy of Paul's apostolate survive his departure? This correspondence supplies the exhortation and instruction of the departed apostle, which now directs the formation of the community left behind as custodian of his apostolic witness to God's gospel and missionary vocation for the next generation of believers.

The hortatory παρακαλέω (*parakaleō*, "request," 1:3) is used here to make a request but with a note of irony since all such requests come from an "apostle of Christ Jesus" (v. 1) without thought of noncompliance. Paul gives instructions with the air of command. Yet the apodosis of this initial and programmatic request is lacking, with the rhetorical effect — perhaps purposeful — of elevating the importance of Paul's departure: a succession has taken place in Ephesus, and Timothy is now left on his own with only written instruction from his mentor-apostle to conduct the mission's business at hand.

The purpose clause states what congregational business Timothy is left to conduct: to "instruct certain individuals" (cf. v. 3). The meaning of παραγγέλλω (*parangellō*, "instruct") was quite elastic, and its use here has been variously translated. The preference of most commentators is "command," following its sense elsewhere in the Pauline corpus when the apostle's instruction delineates a congregation's rule of faith and life (e.g., 1 Cor 11:17; 1 Thess 4:11; 2 Thess 2:4-12). But the verb's use again in v. 5, where it sets out the aim of a congregation's instruction, marks out a semantic field that does not convey strong-armed correction of non-Pauline doctrine but rather catechesis of an entire congregation that would include these "certain individuals." In this sense, Timothy's instruction of the gospel entrusted to Paul would not only define the terms of true religion but would expose its fault-lines in a more priestly fashion.

While the precise identity of these teachers is indeterminate (and should not really matter to the reader), the text plainly says their instruction is funded by "divergent doctrines" and their pedagogy specializes in *pilpul* — those meaningless exegetical practices that conclude without spiritual benefit. Paul's dismissal of a religious curriculum that specializes in "myths and unending genealogies" (v. 4a) is similar to concerns expressed by his two contemporaries, Plutarch and Philo, both of whom described myths as "useless fabrications" (Plutarch, *De Defectu Oraculorum* 46) and "mistakes" that follow from inconclusive arguments (Philo, *De Congressu* 53). The added adjective, "unending," is a trope for the futility of targeting biblical genealogy (cf. Tit 1:14; 3:9) rather than Paul's gospel (cf. 1 Tim 4:7; 2 Tim 4:4; Tit 1:14) as the source of a congregation's religious instruction. He later demonizes an ascetic lifestyle warranted by these "different doctrines" that sets aside certain social conventions (e.g., marriage, foods, table fellowship) as inherently deleterious to life with a holy God (see 4:1-5).

The teachers are called νομοδιδάσκαλοι *(nomodidaskaloi)*, "Torah teachers" (1:7). Although the meaning and use of νόμος *(nomos)* are notoriously fluid in the NT (and in the whole Hellenistic literary world), the compound *nomodidaskaloi* is used by Luke more narrowly and clearly of Jewish interpreters of the biblical Torah (Acts 5:34), targeting in particular the interpretive practices of the Pharisees (Luke 5:17). The issue between Jesus and other Jewish teachers was the use to which the Torah is put, whether to save or to condemn. In fact, Paul appeals to every part of the law and the prophets to align his missional motives with God's promised salvation (cf. 2:4-6). We can reasonably assume, then, that his objection to these teachers does not concern the continuing importance of Torah for a Christian congregation (so 1:8a; cf. Rom 7:7-12), but rather their improper use of the Torah when they substitute "myths . . . and idle speculation" for fidelity to "healthy teaching, which agrees with the glorious gospel of the blessed God" (1:10b-11a), since by preaching this "glorious gospel" one learns the truth that "Jesus Christ came into the world to save sinners" (1:15).

Religious instruction is a practical matter, and the manner and consequence of what one teaches is one viable measurement of theological perspicuity. For this reason, the reader is made alert by Paul's use of μὴ . . . μηδέ *(mē . . . mēde)* to construct a pair of prohibited practices: "do not teach . . . do not pay attention." The teacher responsible for safeguarding the Pauline canon must combine gospel norms with a pedagogy that pays attention to a congregation's spiritual life and ethical choices. It is not incidental to the message of this letter, especially when read within the context of a worshiping community, that the summaries of Pauline dogma — canonical sayings that express the core beliefs of the "glorious gospel" entrusted to an apostolate — are illustrated by personal example and defined by paraenetic discourse. Christian instruction that sounds a Pauline note is a practical divinity. Yet the tradent is hardly a religious fundamentalist who makes a clean break from those considered heterodox. In fact, Timothy's more redemptive strategy should be to engage those who disagree with his gospel "so that they may learn not to blaspheme" (1:20).

Even though it is the target of Paul's instruction, the precise meaning of οἰκονομία θεοῦ *(oikonomia theou)*, which is translated above as "God's way of ordering the world," is notoriously difficult to pin down.¹⁴ The meaning of *oikonomia* doubtless follows from its root, οἶκος (*oikos*, "house"), and is generally thought to refer to the mundane routines of managing a household. Perhaps one hears resonances of a similar phrase, θεοῦ οἰκονόμος (*theou oikonomos*), which Paul uses in Tit 1:7 of the congregation's ἐπίσκοπος (*episkopos*) or "administrator" (see 1 Tim 3:1-7) and in Gal 4:1-2 of the heir's relationship to his "trustees" (so NASB, οἰκονόμοι, *oikonomoi*) as analogical of Christian conversion. The catchphrase *oikonomia theou* is probably rooted in this same typological soil and envisages a kind of divine trusteeship by which the triune God manages the outworking of salvation's history within the ongoing community of faith.

According to Hellenistic thought at least as early as Aristotle, the efficiently managed household, whether political (1 Tim 2:2), religious (3:15), or familial (5:1-2), follows time-tested patterns that effectively order the workload of important groups. In this social world, then, one could expect little upward or downward mobility. The status quo was a reflection of the natural order, so that one's status was predetermined by fate or family inheritance. This same concept extended to the moral compass of the individual, according to which the virtue of self-control was cultivated to subdue personal ambitions, whether to benefit the common good or that of particular voluntary organizations (cf. 1 Tim 3:6-7; Acts 19:23-40).

The later reference to the church as "God's household" (οἶκος θεοῦ, *oikos theou*, 3:15) suggests that *theou* in *oikonomia theou* is a subjective genitive: that is, the Creator is the manager of creation. "In faith" (ἐν πίστει, *en pistei*), then, affirms the believer's trust in God's providential care of the world. The reader now understands that the continuation of Paul's mission following his departure is of a piece with God's overall management of the world (see the comment on Tit 1:1-3).

Moreover, the letter's wide-ranging instructions are formative of the church's existence in the world as God's household, and as such make it a public microcosm of the *oikonomia theou*. Ancillary of this role, the "gospel of the blessed God" (1:11) is the curriculum of a Christian congregation's catechesis into God's way of stewarding the world. Almost certainly this is the leading edge of Timothy's ministry in Paul's absence and suggests that the Pauline metaphor for the church, "God's household," is a significant political

---

14. Our translation and understanding trades on Luke Johnson's programmatic discussion of the catchphrase, which he considers thematic in the letter: *1-2 Timothy*, 147-54; see also his "*Oikonomia Theou*: The Theological Voice of 1 Timothy from the Perspective of Pauline Authorship," *HBT* 21 (1999): 87-104, especially 95-104.

trope of a pattern of public life that is ultimately subversive of Roman rule. The images of suffering and imprisonment in 2 Timothy make clear that Rome and Christianity subscribe to opposite household visions.

God's household vision aims at "loving relationships" (ἀγάπη, *agapē*, 1:5a); whether people love one another is a test of their theological orthodoxy (so also 1 John 4:7-8). In Pauline thought, *agapē* is not an abstract rule of life but the principal characteristic of a congregation's life together, formed in the company of the indwelling Spirit (Gal 5:16-26). As such, love for neighbor is a marker of the congregation's life in Christ (Rom 5:5; 8:35; 13:9). Well known in the history of interpreting this feature of Pauline ethics is its implicit contradiction of the teaching of Jesus, who made loving God "the first and greatest commandment" (Matt 22:38). Matthew's Gospel places that commandment in a context similar to this letter's, in an argument between Jesus and Torah teachers over the meaning of the law and the prophets (cf. Matt 22:34-40; 1 Tim 1:7). In fact, Aquinas (among others) interpreted *agapē* more broadly as loving relationships with both God and neighbor to reconcile this purported conflict over the love command between Jesus and Paul.

The triad of religious virtues — "pure heart, good conscience, earnest faith" (1:5b) — are marks of the congregation whose moral competence cultivates loving relations. This triad is a unique formulation of Christian existence within the NT, and its Hellenistic resonance may well reflect the Pauline mission to the nations.[15] In any case, the integration of inward affections and outward practices is central to a Pauline definition of the Christian life and follows the pattern of Jesus' moral instruction exemplified by the Sermon on the Mount (Matt 5:17-48; 6:1-21). In fact, Paul doubtlessly agrees with other Christian readers of Israel's Scripture that observing the command of Torah is the moral marker of a covenant-keeping community, not to displace the singular importance of the Christ event in God's redemptive plan, but as an essential expression of God's victory over sin.[16]

---

15. Collins calls attention to the mixture of tropes, which draws from Judaism (heart), Christianity (faith), and secular Hellenistic culture (conscience) to draft an "interpretive triad" of religious life. By making "good conscience" the pivotal member of the triad, it is especially apropos for those struggling to adapt their Christian faith to their Hellenistic culture. Raymond F. Collins, *1 and 2 Timothy and Titus: A Commentary* (NTL; Louisville: Westminster John Knox, 2002), 28.

16. In this sense, surely the criticism of a Christian theological interpretation of the Hebrew Bible raised by Gershom M. H. Ratheiser, *Mitzvoth Ethics and the Jewish Bible: The End of Old Testament Theology* (LOTS 460; New York: Clark, 2007) is misplaced. While his charge is true that a Christological rereading of Tanakh is implicitly (and necessarily) supersessionist,

The first quality is a "pure heart" and is central to the execution of the moral life (cf. 2 Tim 2:22; Acts 15:5-11). According to Jewish psychology, the "heart" is the epicenter of human existence — emotions, affections, motives, that which determines what one sees and how one acts. According to the OT prophets, the human heart is what drives the outward expressions of one's personality; the community follows the inclinations of its collective heart according to the exhortation of the *Shemaʿ* to love God with "your whole heart" (Deut 6:4-5). Moreover, the Jewish purity laws, which the Paul of Acts (and his mission) observed following his conversion to Christ (Acts 21:21-26), maintained covenant fellowship with God by whom one's inward motives and affections were constantly cleansed of deceit and self-centeredness. Of course, the question of purity is central to the discussion and decision of the earlier Jerusalem Council, which was prompted by the repentant Pharisees' question about purity and table fellowship (Acts 15:4-21). Acts (and perhaps 1 Timothy) was probably written around the time *1 Clement* 41.1 connected a "pure heart" with the practices of Christian worship — with prayer, sharing goods, fellowship, and Scripture reading (see 1 Tim 4:7b-13).

Even if the believer has cultivated a "pure heart" with affections inclined toward God, the pivotal element of this triad is the "good conscience," which is central to a Hellenistic conception of the moral life, which influenced Diaspora Judaism's (and so Paul's) moral catechesis. Even though it is not mentioned in the OT, Philo can list the "good conscience" among his *Special Laws* (1.203) as the internal spiritual capacity to discern God's will with the intention of obeying it. Of course, if the *telos* of God's providential care of creation is loving relationships, the spiritual affections that incline one toward another in friendship result from the believer's "pure heart" and "good conscience." In this sense, these inward moral qualities, forged within a congregation by Pauline instruction, are requisite for the congregation's public witness as well as its social solidarity.

The final element of this triad is an "earnest faith," which adds a distinctively Christian dimension to the sort of person from whom loving relationships is a real possibility. Different connotations have been made of Paul's use of "faith" in the Pastoral Epistles, but its repetition here (vv. 2, 4, and 5) seems to imply a single-minded affirmation of God's way of ordering reality (so v. 4b). Whether this is personified by faithful actions or profession of beliefs,

---

which the NT itself suggests (see Acts 17:1-5), it does not follow that Christian interpreters have failed to pick up the importance of the moral life ("*mitzvoth* ethics") as an identity marker of a covenant community's loyalty to its God. See, e.g., Walther Eichrodt, *Theology of the Old Testament* (OTL; Philadelphia: Westminster, 1961), 1:70-177.

the force of this virtue is to embrace vigorously and rigorously the gospel truth disclosed by God in Christ Jesus.[17] Augustine writes that "if our faith involves no lie, then we do not love that which is not to be loved, and living justly, we hope for that which will in no way deceive our hope" (*On Christian Doctrine* 1.40-44).

In the Pastoral Epistles, what conforms to "the glorious gospel of the blessed God" (1:11) in life and doctrine is considered theologically "healthy" (1:10: ὑγιαινούσῃ, *hygiainousē*) — a Greek medical term that provides an apt metaphor of a functional sense of Christian instruction developed in the Pastoral Epistles (cf. 1 Tim 6:3; 2 Tim 1:13; 4:3; Tit 1:9, 13; 2:1-2).[18] This adjective evokes the image of a vital congregation shaped by Pauline instruction and would have struck a responsive chord among ancient readers familiar with its use in moral discourse: good instruction is the moral foundation of all healthy relationships. Maximus of Tyre wrote a century after Paul that "truth and healthy understanding and morality and knowledge of the law and right cannot be acquired in any other way than by actually doing them, just as one can never learn the craft of shoemaking unless one actually works at it" (*Discourses* 16.3).

Sandwiched between these assertions about Christian instruction and its instructors is Paul's reflection on the Torah in 1:8-11. As here (v. 8), so in Romans (7:12) Paul admits that Torah, revealed by God on Mount Sinai, is inherently "good." Rightly used, it is an important resource in understanding God's gospel. Pauline paraenesis, including this letter's, typically includes catalogs of vices and virtues shaped by the particular occasion but built with standard literary conventions of ancient moral handbooks, both Jewish and secular. Some of these lists contain only the deadliest of vices or by contrast the cardinal virtues, while other lists — especially Jewish — are more exhaustive. For example, Philo's famous list in the *Sacrifices of Abel and Cain* contains 146 vices to avoid in a right relationship with God, several of which are peculiar to his Alexandrian social setting. The rhetorical use of such lists,

---

17. Protestant interpreters since Calvin have struggled with this verse precisely because it seems to suggest a subordinate role for faith and even because it seems to displace a theological orthodoxy in which believers place their confidence for a moral orthopraxy of "loving relationships"; cf. John Calvin, *The Second Epistle of Paul the Apostle to the Corinthians and the Epistles to Timothy, Titus and Philemon* (Grand Rapids: Eerdmans, 1964), 191-92. Their struggle is misplaced when it is realized that this passage's contention is that love is the *telos* of Christian instruction only as the moral effect (and therefore religious test) of "healthy doctrine" — a central Pauline belief.

18. See Abraham J. Malherbe, *Paul and the Popular Philosophers* (Minneapolis: Fortress, 1989), 121-36.

whether long or short, is to create memorable mental impressions or even draft rough caricatures of the reprobate (vice) or productive (virtue) life. The effect in this regard is cumulative, and few scholars give any importance to perceived differences among the different lists.

Following Jewish literary practice, however, Paul typically constructs each moral catalog with a particular situation or audience in mind, often ranking the most relevant vice or virtue first. The general impression made by this particular vice list (vv. 9-10) is to draft the profile of one who is the opposite of the virtuous person capable of entering into and sustaining loving relationships. The "lawful" use of the rule of law is to define clearly the behavior of the "lawless and rebellious" as "contrary to healthy teaching" (v. 10), which is the basis of their repentance from sin and spiritual restoration (cf. vv. 12-16). Unlike its improper use by the opponents who engage in "fruitless discussion" (v. 6), then, this proper use of Torah is of a piece with the general aim of Christian instruction set out in v. 5; but, rather than the "innocent person," it targets the "lawless and rebellious."

Paul's list of paired vices appropriately follows the canonical shape of the Decalogue, which brings together in two interpenetrating "tables" those patterns of behaviors that embody a community's love for God and neighbor. In this particular catalog, the first three pairs of vices subvert a congregation's devotion to God. The first pair, "lawless and rebellious" (v. 9), introduces deviant behavior contrary to allegiance to God's ways and probably implicates those opponents whose "doctrines of demons" are contrary to the Creator's good intentions (4:1-5). The fourth pair, "patricide and matricide," introduces vices contrary to a love for neighbor. Moreover, if "God's way of stewarding the world" aims people toward a particular quality of life, then the villainous manner of discourse cast by this catalog illustrates social chaos: households of any kind, especially the household of God, cannot survive these egregious misbehaviors. The backdrop of each, of course, is the Torah, which not only condemns each of these malefactions but treats them as serious subversions of the community's identity as a people belonging exclusively to God.

Perhaps special comment is needed regarding the pairing of πόρνοι *(pornoi)* and ἀρσενοκοίται *(arsenokoitai)*, which I have translated "sexually unfaithful" and "homosexuals." In today's climate of sexual politics, it is common to find linguistic studies of *arsenokoitai* that locate its use in an ancient Roman setting and keep it there rather than moving it into the present on the basis of its epistolary or canonical setting. Together with its companion *pornoi*, which is forbidden by the Decalogue (Exod 20:14; cf. Lev 18:22; 20:13), it sets out the broad impress of God's sense of order in sexual relationships. While one might reasonably argue that the word's homosexual referent in its

Roman setting is different from what male homosexuality might imply in a twenty-first-century middle-class setting, the plain sense within its canonical setting is that homosexuality is at odds with God's preference for mutually caring heterosexual relationships. Exegesis alone does not settle what is at stake in the current discussion about homosexuality within the church, where Scripture is treasured. This is a complex interpretive matter that concerns what the church actually does with the plain sense of Scripture's teaching about human sexuality, especially in light of the fourfold Gospel's portrait of Jesus' generosity toward sinners and outsiders, which leads one to accept those who practice what Scripture condemns.[19]

Finally, I note that the public vitality of a community was already widely used as a standard by which the content of its instruction was measured. Homer (*Iliad* 8.524), Plato (*Republic* 9.584e), Philo (*Abraham* 223), and especially Epictetus (*Discourses* 1.11.28; 2.15.2; 3.9.2-5) taught that particular kinds of words were inherently "healthy" while others sickened a people. In keeping with this general sentiment, Paul writes that the gospel entrusted to him consists of "healthy teaching" and accords with God's very own gospel (1:10-11). This is the calculus that underwrites the instruction of a canonical Paul: the spiritual health of a Christian congregation and its leadership is the salutary effect of the orthodoxy of its instruction. His is a practical divinity, always expressed in terms that connect the proclamation of truth with how truth performs in real life. For this reason, the loving relations that are God's purpose for people spring forth from an interior life shaped by healthy doctrine. An "unlawful" use of the law (v. 8) is that brittle kind of legalism that substitutes a rigorous doing of the law's letter for a robust dependence on divine grace.

1:12-17 Paul Thanks God

[12]I thank Christ Jesus our Lord, who has strengthened me and considered me faithful, appointing me to a ministry [13]even though I was an ex-blasphemer and persecutor, a violent man who was shown mercy because I acted in ignorance and unbelief. [14]Our Lord's grace poured all over me along with the faith and love that are in Christ Jesus. [15]This teaching is a core belief worthy of unqualified acceptance: "Christ Jesus came into the world to save sinners" — among whom I am first! [16]But I was shown mercy for this reason, that Christ Jesus might thoroughly demon-

---

19. In this regard, see the recent discussion on "homosexuality" in Samuel Wells and Ben Quash, *Introducing Christian Ethics* (Chichester: Wiley-Blackwell, 2010), 296-310.

strate patience first in me as the role model for those who come to believe in him for eternal life. ¹⁷Now to the King of the ages, to the immortal, invisible, and only God, be honor and glory forever and ever. Amen.

Expression of thanksgiving for another is a standard although not uniform ingredient of Pauline letters. In most cases, epistolary thanksgivings function much like pastoral prayers, when thanksgiving is given and petitions offered to God for the well-being of the audience. In this case, however, Paul thanks Jesus for saving him from ignorance and unbelief (1:13) for a ministry of the gospel entrusted to him (vv. 11-12). This combination of conversion and commission is imagined as a pouring out of divine grace (v. 14) to demonstrate to others not only that "Christ Jesus came into the world to save sinners" (vv. 15-16) but also that such a salvation does not follow a conventional pattern of human existence but is the merciful effect of the one and only God (v. 17).

The epistolary thanksgiving, well known from extant letters of antiquity, is sometimes referred to as a *captatio benevolentiae* — a rhetorical device used when introducing a public speech to cultivate the goodwill of one's audience and also to establish the purpose or main themes of the speech (or letter) that follows. What is found in this Pauline letter, however, is a thanksgiving that only indirectly is given for the letter's recipient but rather is biographical (χάριν ἔχω . . . με, *charin echō . . . me*, literally "I thank . . . me"). In fact, this is an account of the origins of the Pauline apostolate and so not only explains the theological grammar of the gospel entrusted to Paul (1:10-11) but also describes the religious experience that shapes it as a sinner's conversion from ignorance and unbelief. Moreover, when this biography of conversion is contextualized by a prior reading of the Acts narrative, the reader more easily notes that Paul's dramatic conversion (Acts 9:1-9) is decisively linked to his missionary calling (Acts 9:15-16; 26:15-18). The critical role this thanksgiving performs within 1 Timothy is made even more clear by this intertext: Paul's conversion envisages the realistic demonstration of God's transforming grace that not only shapes his gospel but also underwrites Christ's appointment to his apostolic ministry (cf. Gal 1:11-17). As with Acts, Paul's conversion staged his commission as the most decisive moment of his life. Set within a pastoral exhortation, then, his testimony of conversion underwrites the instruction of those, like Timothy, who are called to safeguard his apostolate in his absence but who may be unprepared or even reluctant to do so (cf. 1 Tim 1:18-20; 4:14-16; 6:20-21; 2 Tim 1:6-7, 13-14).

Commentators often note that the use of biographical genre in letters follows from the strategic use of illustrative portraits in ancient rhetoric (Aristotle, *Rhetoric* 1366a34-b11, 1398a33-b20); Paul frequently uses biography to

1 Timothy 1:12-17

illustrate his theological instruction. What concerns most modern exegetes is whether the biographical snapshots included in the Pastoral Epistles portray the "real" Paul or an idealized, legendary Paul drawn from material found in his authentic letters but then air-brushed by a pseudepigrapher to suit a post-Pauline social setting.[20] The problem with this standard criticism is not so much methodological, even though its purchase for exegesis is rather thin; the problem is rather rooted in the failure to recognize the role performed by the Pastoral Epistles within the Pauline canon, where the biography genre portrays a canonical Paul, introduced and complemented by his story in Acts, who is the implied author of the Pauline canon. The irony presented by the biography of a canonical Paul is that it is not ultimately about Paul but about his tradents, whose experience of a responsible grace is cued by their apostolic leader and frames their reading of his epistolary deposit. The biography of his conversion both here and in Acts not only stipulates a core belief of Pauline orthodoxy (1:15), which regulates the theological interpretation of his canonical letters, but personifies the normative pattern of the transforming effect of grace in all matters of life (1:17).

The biography frames the problem of a sinner's ignorance of (rather than willfully ignoring) God's redemptive purpose, and so agrees with how sin was routinely understood in Hellenistic Judaism (cf. Josephus, *Antiquities* 3.231-32). The theme of human ignorance of God's ways is also an important narrative theme of Acts (Acts 3:17; 17:3), whose prior reading in canonical context alerts the reader to the deep logic of God's mercy toward someone who has acted in ignorance rather than in malice toward the risen Christ — in Paul's case, turning him against Christ without his knowing any better. Reading this passage under the light of Paul's story in Acts secures more firmly this theological point: God gives second chances to those whose prior rejection of God's Messiah is a matter of their ignorance of Scripture's messianic way of salvation rather than a matter of bad character. In this case, the attentive hearing of God's glorious gospel (or a wakeful response to a christophanic experience!) dispels one's ignorance and opens up one's heart to the truth of God. This principle is not very different from that received by Rabbi Yishmael (135 c.e.), who taught that "it is better that an Israelite sin unknowingly than to sin with intent" (SB 2:264), presumably because God's mercy is more readily available for the ignorant than for those who know the truth but reject it (1:13; cf. Lev 16:21; 22:14; Num 15:29-30; Heb 10:26).

Also in a text attached to an injunction to correct misguided "Torah

---

20. See, e.g., Arland J. Hultgren, "The Pastoral Epistles," in *The Cambridge Companion to St. Paul* (ed. James D. G. Dunn; Cambridge: Cambridge University Press, 2003), 151-53.

teachers," this rehearsal of Paul's conversion experience reassures Timothy that theological ignorance, which can prevent one from embracing the gospel, can be overturned by the operation of God's grace mediated through the proclamation of the gospel. Even for these opponents of Paul, Timothy has reason to hope for a change of direction — an optimism of grace that even enemies of God can be restored to Christian fellowship by the ministry of the "glorious gospel." No teacher of the church should be engaged in ministry without a robust confidence in a patient God who "wants everybody to come to a knowledge of the truth" (2:4) and in the transforming effect of God's mercy mediated through Christ Jesus for all who embrace it.

Even though "Christ Jesus" is the name used for Jesus in the Pastoral Epistles, here Paul adds "our Lord." The public profession that the risen Jesus is the church's Lord is the principal identity marker of Pauline congregations (cf. Rom 10:9). By this profession of faith, sinners admit their agreement with the central claims of Paul's gospel about Christ's atoning death, bodily resurrection, heavenly exaltation, and triumphant return (see 3:16). That is, believers share with the apostle the same core belief about Christ and experience that Jesus "came into the world to save sinners" and that those who profess him as "our Lord" do so "for eternal life." In Pauline dress, "eternal life" is an eschatological rather than existential term and refers to residence in the coming age that will "appear" with "Christ Jesus our hope" (1:1; cf. Tit 2:13; 3:7).

The catchphrase I have translated "this teaching is a core belief" (πιστὸς ὁ λόγος, *pistos ho logos*, 1:15) appears five times in the Pastoral Epistles (1 Tim 1:15; 3:1; 4:9; 2 Tim 2:11; Tit 3:8; cf. Tit 1:9) and nowhere else in the NT. In each case, it either introduces or concludes a Pauline formulation of God's way of salvation. "Christ Jesus came into the world to save sinners" summarizes what is found in the "glorious gospel" entrusted to Paul (1:10-11) and is what one scholar has called a Pauline "creedal cameo."[21] How these summaries originated is difficult to determine; they were likely created, however, as missionary "sound bites" — memorable yet dense phrases that helped converts conceptualize their experience of being initiated into Christian faith.

The key exegetical question for us concerns how these "sound bites" function within the church for current readers of the Pauline letters. Sharply put, these sayings articulate the core theological agreements of a Pauline grammar of faith and set normative guideposts for the formation of a healthy congregation. They add nothing new to Scripture's Pauline witness; their purpose is rather hermeneutical for catechesis or worship, supplying a theological constraint that regulates the contemporary appropriation of a Pauline letter as

---

21. Collins, *1 and 2 Timothy and Titus*, 43.

God's word. This initial (and in many ways programmatic) core belief that "Christ Jesus came into the world to save sinners" suggests that readers should aim Pauline texts at a soteriological result, perhaps to overturn ignorance about Christ but more critically to proclaim the effect of taking what is learned about him to heart, which results in the sinner's experience of God's transforming grace. The presumption, of course, is that when a community is formed by a common experience of this truth, it will be compelled by the Spirit to continue Paul's ministry of the glorious gospel in his absence.[22]

Hardly anywhere in the Pauline canon does the reader find a clearer expression of Pauline epistemology than in this biography of conversion. Clearly, the principal source of Paul's claims about Christ Jesus is his personal (and some would say private) experience of being saved from the consequences of ignorance and unbelief for a ministry of the gospel. As such, his apostolic witness and the truth claims of his gospel are rooted in a different epistemic soil than those of the believers who were with Jesus from the beginning and whose witness is based on what they saw and heard of him (cf. 1 John 1:1-5; 2 Pet 1:16–2:1; Acts 1:21-22). While Acts seeks to demonstrate the essential continuity between Paul's proclamation of grace, which is shaped by his personal experience of grace, and the Jerusalem apostolate, who were with Jesus from the beginning and were beneficiaries of his careful instruction (cf., e.g., Peter's summary of Gentile repentance in Pauline idiom in Acts 15:6-11), the careful reader recognizes the difficulty that an epistemology of personal experience may have for those requiring a more expansive, firsthand knowledge of God's way of salvation gained from "accompanying Jesus from the beginning" (Acts 1:21-22; cf. 2:29, 32).[23]

The concluding doxology (1:17) is characteristically Pauline, especially since it reflects on the apostle's own strategic role within the global economy of God's salvation (Rom 11:36; Gal 1:5; Eph 3:20-21). The terms of his praise size up the character of the God who has the capacity to make good on the stunning promise to save sinners for eternal life through Christ Jesus. This

---

22. Towner says this saying invites today's church "to view the Pauline 'pattern' and to replicate it." Philip H. Towner, *1-2 Timothy and Titus* (Downers Grove: InterVarsity, 1994), 154.

23. See now Mary Healy, "Knowledge of the Mystery: A Study in Pauline Epistemology," in *The Bible and Epistemology: Biblical Soundings on the Knowledge of God* (Milton Keynes: Paternoster, 2007), 134-58. Richard Bauckham's magisterial study *Jesus and the Eyewitnesses: The Gospel as Eyewitness Testimony* (Grand Rapids: Eerdmans, 2006) explores the epistemic importance of a testimony that can be trusted precisely because it claims to be firsthand. He makes passing mention of the oral traditions of Jesus received by Paul from eyewitnesses but makes no comment on the relative lack of influence these traditions had in shaping Pauline Christology (cf. Gal 1:16-17).

general depiction of deity to underwrite Paul's more particularly Christian claim about Jesus has a familiar ring in both Hellenistic and Jewish worlds, and this is precisely its purpose in this context, where Paul encourages the formation of a Christian congregation, a microcosm of the *oikonomia theou* in the pagan world: to invite a conversation between these two worlds on God's manner of saving sinners through Christ, whether one is shaped by religious or pagan beliefs. The religious person, for example, might pick up on the idiom of the biblical Psalter or prophets, which speak of Israel's God as the only God (cf. Deut 6:4; Isaiah 44) and King over all creation (e.g., LXX Pss 5:2; 23:7-10; 43:5; 46:3; 94:3). On the other hand, the additional pair of divine attributes, "immortal and invisible," resonate with claims made by Greco-Roman philosophers — even though God's transcendent and eternal majesty is also a central claim of Israel's Scripture (see Exod 33:20–34:8; cf. John 1:18). In *Lives of Eminent Philosophers,* for example, Diogenes Laertius (300 B.C.E.) writes, "First believe that God is a living being immortal and blessed, according to the notion of a god indicated by the common sense of humankind; and so believing, you shall not affirm of God aught that is foreign to his immortality or that does not agree with blessedness, but shall believe about God whatever may uphold both his blessedness and immortality" (*Epicurus* 10.123).

This doxology complements the one in 6:15 to form doxological bookends. It was widely commented on by the Church Fathers. Gregory of Nyssa aptly comments that by it "we know that of all these names by which Deity is indicated some are expressive of the Divine majesty, employed and understood absolutely, and some are assigned with reference to the operations over us and all creation."

1:18-20 Paul Repeats His Charge to Timothy

¹⁸Timothy my son, I entrust this instruction to you according to the prophecies once made about you so that you may fight the good fight with those ¹⁹who have faith and good conscience. Some have subverted and have shipwrecked their faith. ²⁰Among them are Hymenaeus and Alexander, whom I have handed over to Satan so that they may learn not to blaspheme.

Paul resumes his request that "Timothy my son" (cf. v. 2) stay in Ephesus to instruct the gospel's opponents (v. 3), but here adds the additional reason that to do so agrees with "the prophecies once made about you." While the source of these "prophecies" is not specified, Paul probably is referring to a charism

1 Timothy 1:18-20

of "prophecy" given by the Spirit and used in Christian worship to disclose the guiding word of the Lord to the people of God. In the NT prophetic utterance is typically directed to individuals about specific tasks at particular locations, as here, rather than about ecclesial offices (cf. Acts 13:1-3).[24] Paul's subsequent reference to this same gift in 1 Tim 4:14 implies that prophetic utterance is not extemporaneous or ad hoc but an element of a more formal liturgy by which the Spirit confers religious authority on a person for and within a particular congregation. The gesture of "laying on hands" probably takes its cue from biblical tradition (cf. Exod 29:10; Lev 4:15), when the congregation's leaders, whether elders (so 1 Tim 4:14) or apostle (so 2 Tim 1:6-7), mediate publicly God's decision to ordain someone for a special task. God's call is not therefore privately made or a matter of personal conjecture, but is confirmed before a congregation of witnesses that allows Timothy no wiggle room to maneuver out of the obligations of his ordination (cf. 4:13-16)!

Paul's evocative exhortation that Timothy "fight the good fight" draws on images of warfare, which are frequently employed by Paul (cf. 2 Tim 4:7; 2 Cor 10:2-6; Eph 6:10-20) and were widely used by the philosophers and literati of antiquity. For example, Epictetus asks rhetorically, "Do you not know that the business of life is a military campaign?" (*Dissertationes* 3.23.31). The so-called "War Scroll" found at Qumran (1QM 1.1-5) predicts the coming salvation of God in apocalyptic symbols of a cosmic battle between the forces of good and evil: "The first attack by the sons of light will be launched against the lot of the sons of darkness, against the army of Belial. . . . And after the war . . . (there) will follow a time of salvation for the people of God and a period of rule for all the men of his lot, and of everlasting destruction for all the lot of Belial." The battle Timothy is to engage in is against cosmic powers and principalities and is all the more urgent because its victory insures his participation in the future of God's salvation (so 4:16).

Identifying individual opponents, in this case "Hymenaeus and Alexander" (see 2 Tim 2:17; 4:14), is unusual in Pauline paraenesis. The apostolic practice of "delivering them over to Satan" (cf. 1 Cor 5:5; LXX Job 2:6) probably refers to their excommunication from the covenant community rather than to their spiritual testing. In either case, this text recalls the apostle's authority to maintain solidarity within the community, which he does not therefore delegate to his successor. Hymenaeus and Alexander have "subverted and shipwrecked their faith," whatever it is they have done, which is a verdict the apostle alone renders: "I have handed (them) over to Satan" (1:20a). The use of the image of a "shipwrecked faith," which has attracted considerable attention during

---

24. I. Howard Marshall, *The Pastoral Epistles* (ICC; Edinburgh: Clark, 1999), 409-10.

the history of the letter's interpretation,[25] recalls the dramatic story of Paul's shipwreck, in which the forces of evil are pitted against the forces of good, with everyone who stands with Paul saved from the sea (Acts 27:27-44).[26] That is, the subtext added by this intertext is that those who refuse to stand with Paul's gospel and whose faith is shipwrecked as a result are lost to God.

Not much is known about these two shadowy figures, although letter writers of antiquity frequently dropped names into their letters without comment to pepper their points. *Acts of Paul and Thecla* tells the story of someone named "Alexander" — perhaps alluding to this Alexander — who plots to win the affections of Thecla, a protégée of Paul's much like Timothy. According to this apocryphal story Alexander uses bribes to entice Thecla and when failing tries to take her by force but is repelled by miracle and political intrigue (3.26-36). Later stories like this one that embellish the careers of those mentioned in biblical texts function as a kind of Christian haggadah *midrash* — that is, a collection of narrative commentaries that help the Bible's readers more fully understand its application for them.

The well-known and oft-studied parallelisms between 1 Timothy and 1 Corinthians are nowhere more evident than in Paul's reference to the practice of "handing over" wayward believers to Satan for a spanking. This apostolic practice of church discipline is mentioned in 1 Cor 5:5, there with the prospect of excommunicating an errant member for unrepentant, persistent sin (cf. 1 Cor 5:9-13). Most scholars think this practice has its background in the story of Job, since 1 Cor 5:5 is remarkably close to the language of LXX Job 2:6, where God hands Job over to the Satan for spiritual testing. In a Pauline setting the devil's role remains the same, and again there is no threat to life. If the author of 1 Timothy has the Corinthians text in mind, the wayward believer's repentance and restoration to the covenant community is clarified as the principal motive of church discipline. Although exclusion from Christian fellowship is not mentioned in this case, the implied loss of participation in the community's covenant blessing of eternal life (so 1:16; cf. Jas 5:19-20) underwrites the seriousness of the case and the prospect of complete spiritual failure.[27] For this reason and with sublime irony, Paul claims that God sometimes uses even the Evil One as an agent of the believer's spiritual restoration.

Paul repeats his earlier charge, here with passing reference to Hyme-

---

25. See Jay Twomey, *The Pastoral Epistles through the Centuries* (Chichester: Wiley-Blackwell, 2009), 28-29.

26. Wall, "Acts," 344-54.

27. David Raymond Smith, *Hand This Man Over to Satan: Curse, Exclusion, and Salvation in 1 Corinthians 5* (LNTS 386; London: Clark, 2008), 146-48, who considers the act of "handing over" more like a liturgical act of cursing.

naeus and Alexander, not to delegate this same manner of church discipline to Timothy for use with his opponents in Ephesus. Again, the severity of this practice, which carries life-death consequences, appears to be available only to the apostle. This exhortation is of a piece with the Pastoral Epistles' persistent reference to Paul's associates who deserted him during a controversial and costly mission (cf. 2 Tim 4:9-15), which underscores the importance of maintaining the Pauline apostolate in the face of difficulty. If this letter's instruction is understood as the textual substitute for the now absent apostle, Timothy's ordination is to succeed him in Ephesus by doing what Paul would do were he there; failure to do so would be tantamount to excusing oneself from the battle and abandoning the faith. With this in mind, Paul begins to instruct Timothy and his congregation as though he were there in person.

2:1-7 Instructions regarding Congregational Worship

¹First, I request that petitions, prayers, intercessions, thanksgivings be therefore offered for everybody — ²even for kings and all those in positions of authority — so that we may lead a quiet and peaceful life in full godliness and holiness. ³This is good and acceptable in the eyes of God our Savior, ⁴who wants everybody to be saved and to come to the knowledge of the truth: ⁵There is one God and one mediator between God and humankind, a man, Christ Jesus, ⁶who gave himself a ransom for everybody, the witness at the right time. ⁷I have been appointed its preacher and apostle — I speak the truth and do not lie — and teacher of the true faith to the nations.

The letter's second chapter is currently among the most contested and scrutinized passages of the Pastoral Epistles. But the reasons for this are typically different from the evident concerns of the text, which are to bring clarity to the theological motive and public manner of Christian worship. The chapter's opening instruction about prayer scores this point: not only is prayer the quintessential worship practice, but the community's prayers are for everyone (vv. 1-2) to instantiate God's redemptive purpose for everyone (vv. 3-6) as defined and implemented by the Pauline apostolate (v. 7).

Two different and often competing human families are mentioned, the one comprising a secular household led by "kings and all those in positions of authority" (v. 2; cf. Tit 3:1-2) as head, and the other a sacred household led by God. Paul's instructions give partial recognition of the tension often provoked by competing loyalties between rival households in which believers hold joint membership. In this case, the stability embodied by a congregation's social relationships — between one another and with outsiders — serves a missiological rather than sociological end: if God wants to save everyone from death (v. 4) for eternal life (so 1:16), and Christ Jesus enters the world to mediate God's redemptive end (so 1:15; cf. 2:5-6), then the worship practices of the sacred household should purpose what God desires: namely, the salvation of everyone from ignorance of the truth about God.

This passage forms a compact unit whose instructions are founded on this theological premise. Paul's instruction regarding prayer is noteworthy, not only because it is placed "first" (v. 1), but because of its sheer length: it is the longest discussion of prayer in the NT. If the subtext of this instruction is the correction of the false teachers mentioned in the initial charge (1:3), those whose presence threatens to disrupt the organization of a Pauline congregation, then the purpose of this instruction would be to restore order — in this case to the congregation's worship practices. A particular manner of public prayers, for example, envisages God's reordering the sacred household against those "teachers of Torah" who seem more interested in divisive sophistry than in "full godliness and holiness" (2:2b). The "therefore" that begins these instructions (v. 1) may well assume the contrast between the false teachers (1:3-11, 19-20) and the apostle, whose own conversion from falsehood is mimetic of prophetic ministry (1:12-17; cf. 2:7). And there may be other divisions within the congregation as well, whether precipitated by the presence of false teachers or by the congregation's cultural surroundings. But the plain sense of this passage indicates no such threat, and Paul's emphasis on the practice of a congregation's prayers for everyone is a means of peacekeeping with everyone (2:2), which coheres with divine providence.

In this regard, two brief observations about the importance of congregational prayers should frame any interpretation of this passage. First, God's household must be ordered to serve God's redemptive purposes. The prayers of the household are an essential worship practice by which its members grow in their spiritual understanding of God's purpose for them in all of life. In making this more general point, the interpreter should not make too fine a distinction between the four general terms used to describe the congregation's prayers — "petitions, prayers, intercessions, and thanksgivings" (2:1). Paul's intent is rather to emphasize that the congregation's communication with God should seek what God seeks.

The catholic scope of the church's evangelistic concern is reflected by the next phrase, which repeats the preposition "for" (ὑπέρ, *hyper*) to include the very persons the congregation might otherwise be inclined to omit in their prayers: "kings and all those in positions of authority." While the historical record is severely gapped with respect to the persecution of earliest believers, most scholars agree that in certain regions believers had come under the attack of those who distinguished Christianity from the imperial cult and Christians from Jews (who enjoyed some protection under Roman law). Christians believe in the sovereignty of one God and the lordship of one Lord, Christ Jesus, which challenged the central ideological tenet of the empire's socio-political solidarity: the sovereignty of its emperor. The social friction between a powerless church and a powerful state is found everywhere in the NT (e.g., Acts 22–28; 1 Pet 3:13-17; Revelation 13) and may be a political subtext of Pauline paraenesis (e.g., Rom 13:1-7).

Yet, even though counterintuitive of a Christian congregation, whose instantiation of the *oikonomia theou* forms a counterculture of loving relationships within the world (cf. 1:4-5), the religious sentiment toward supporting those who led the secular household was widely shared in antiquity. Aelius Aristides (150 C.E.) writes, "It remains for each of us to go to our respective duties after a prayer to Poseidon, Amphitrite, Leucothea, Palaemon, the Nereids, and to all the gods and goddesses of the sea, to grant safety and preservation on land and sea to the great emperor, to his whole family, and to the Greek race, and to us to thrive in oratory and in other respects as well" (*Discourses* 46, *The Isthmian Oration regarding Poseidon* 42). In Paul's Diaspora Judaism, the practice of praying for one's pagan rulers was probably adapted from Darius's decree concerning the Jerusalem temple according to Ezra 6, specifically that his instructions for the rebuilding of the temple were motivated in part so that Israel would offer acceptable sacrifices to God for "the life of the king and his sons" (6:10; cf. Bar 1:11-12). It is later reported that Rabbi Hanina instructed Jews to "pray for the peace of the ruling power, since but for fear of it men would have swallowed up each other alive" (*m. 'Abot* 3.2). While Jews were sometimes accused of praying only for Israel, another rabbi taught that Israel's prayers should not fall short of the Lord's own interests (SB 2:643). If it is the Lord's design that all people, including the emperor, are saved, then the community's prayers should not fall short of God's purpose (cf. 1 Sam 12:23). The biblical Daniel exemplifies such political wisdom to ensure peaceful relations with hostile pagan powers. In other writings Paul extends this wisdom to a theological principle, so that civil authority is ordained by God to maintain a public morality that accords with God's desire for good works (cf. Rom 13:1-4; 12:2). Johnson points out that Jews and Christians of the first century felt a deep solidarity with their socio-political world as a faithful response to the Creator's provident care for all things.[28] Paul's instruction to Timothy is of a piece with the practices and core beliefs of his Jewish legacy.

---

28. Luke T. Johnson, *Letters to Paul's Delegates* (NTC; Valley Forge: Trinity, 1996), 129-31.

1 Timothy 2:1-7

A second observation in this regard extends to the theological motive of Paul's instructions for worship. If the ultimate purpose of a congregation's worship is to testify to its membership in God's household, then the subject matter of its prayers and petitions must support the vocation of a people who belong to God rather than to the Roman emperor. Worship gives public expression to a congregation's deepest commitments, and "worship" is a verbal noun precisely because its practices demonstrate covenant loyalty to God. Prayers are radical and countercultural and demonstrate what makes a holy God wholly other. In Pauline cast, worship practices are a principal means by which the people of God are public witnesses to and agents of God's merciful way of reordering life.

For this reason, then, Paul extends the scope of the congregation's prayers to include "everybody" (v. 1b). The motive for doing so is not political, as though the idea of church in this letter is complicit in a program of social domestication to cultivate a peaceful working environment in which believers are not denied social status and can flourish in Roman society as good citizens. Paul's principal motive is, rather, clearly theological: to pray for everybody is to pray after God's own desiring: "God our Savior wants *everybody* to be saved and to come to the knowledge of the truth" (v. 4). Prayers for the emperor's personal safety and political wisdom were ultimately offered to God in prospect of his salvation.

But Paul's intent here is to move the worship practices of a Christian congregation in a somewhat different direction: yes, the congregation should pray for the conversion of their pagan leaders, rather than their cooperation, so that an experience of divine grace will occasion their transformation and ultimately prompt social reform. The purpose clause describes the result sought by congregational prayers as a "quiet, peaceful, godly, and respectful life" — all terms that describe Christianity's social manner in the public square. But the congregation's public prayers reflect not a program of political domestication but a Christian mission that boldly evangelizes the surrounding pagan culture from top to bottom.

The repetition of "good" in the Pastoral Epistles generally carries the connotation of compliance with the will of God and thus embodies the community's missionary vocation and facilitates God's plan to save the world. Nonetheless, in canonical context where the Pauline canon is glossed by a prior reading of Acts, the biblical reader has been made aware of the conflict over Jesus that is provoked in the public square whenever the gospel about him is proclaimed to all the people (e.g., Acts 5:27-32; 17:5-15; 19:23-30). In this social setting, prayer is a resurrection practice of radical discipleship; its motive and subject matter are unsettling because it makes clear a people's priorities and loyalties. Prayer is a political act, not because it asks God to support the state but because it asks God to save the ruling elites.

At this point Paul clarifies the theological (and more subversive) motive for the congregation's public prayers. Worship is not a religious duty performed by good citizens to favor the emperor; Christianity is not a civil religion. Congregational prayers are offered to God according to God's criterion (v. 3) to mark out a household as belonging to God rather than to the emperor. In this reading, the subtext of Paul's instruction to pray to one God for the salvation of everyone (cf. 2:5), including the emperor, is clearly political, since such prayers refuse to admit that the emperor is sovereign or a deity or that as such he has ultimate control over humanity's destiny. While Paul's use of "acceptable" (ἀπόδεκτος, *apodektos*) may allude to the OT liturgy of offering acceptable sacrifices in worship of God (Lev 1:3-4; 17:4; etc.), the issue at stake is not so much that prayer has replaced the priesthood as the normative medium of Christian devotion; again, what pleases "God our Savior" is petitions that agree with the desire of God to seek the salvation of all people. God's endgame is mercy, not sacrifice.

The opening "for" (γάρ, *gar*) of v. 5 introduces a footnote to the final phrase of v. 4, "the knowledge of the truth," and serves to define in formal theological terms the catholic scope of God's plan of salvation. In fact, Paul's awkward phrase, "the witness at the right time" (v. 6b), probably links Christ's atoning ransom (v. 6a) with the assertion of his apostolic appointment (v. 7) to underwrite this summary of "the truth" as the plumb line for a ministry of the gospel. Within the bounds of the Pauline canon, then, the formulation in vv. 5-6a clarifies the theological subtext of every Pauline text.

1. "There is one God." This apt summary of Jewish monotheism not only serves to locate "kings and all those in positions of authority" in their proper place within the *oikonomia theou* but also to challenge any notion that supposes God has multiple plans of salvation, one for Jews and another for Gentiles: God, the only God, has but one plan. The singularity of God is an affirmation of the *Shemaʿ* (Deut 6:4) and is of special importance in Paul's Diaspora setting, where the God of Israel had competition from many deities, local and national. Chrysostom reminds us that the motive of Paul's confession, "there is one God," is to "distinguish the one God from idols, not from the Son" (*Homilies on 1 Timothy* 7).

2. "There is one mediator between God and humankind." Although laden with Christological freight, especially with inferences of the crucified Christ's mediation of God's new covenant (see especially Hebrews 8–10), Paul's primary meaning here is more diplomatic: God's offer of universal salvation is tendered by a single ambassador; any other source is bogus. Paul's

reference to himself as preacher and apostle (v. 7), who is appointed by the command of God (1:1), suggests an ambassadorial motif: Paul is Christ's "undersecretary" in God's kingdom, given the task of communicating God's gospel in Christ's absence. There may well be an even deeper inference that, in Paul's absence, it is now Timothy who is given this crucial task to perform.

Given the influence and importance of the emperor cult in the Roman world, Paul's insistence that there is but one mediator would probably have communicated a political message that rejected the divinization of the emperor and his role as the sole mediator of the gods. One God, one Messiah, one salvation all inform a particular, exclusive conception of the truth. In Paul's understanding, then, conversion to Christianity requires one to "come to the knowledge of [this] truth." It should also be noted that within a Jewish world Paul stresses the character of the Lord's mediatorial role as messianic rather than priestly; that is, Jesus' role is to offer a ransom for all people (v. 6) whereas the congregation's role is to pray for all people (v. 1).

3. "A man, Christ Jesus." The reference to Jesus' humanity seems awkward at first. Some suggest that it goes best with the next phrase, which speaks of Jesus' death. Certainly Paul's Adam-Christology requires this connection to the Lord's humanity and his self-sacrificial death (so Phil 2:6-8). Yet I doubt this connection is intended here. Rather, Paul extends his reference to Jesus' messianic role as the broker of God's promised salvation for all the families of earth. The plain sense of this phrase, then, is more epistemological: God discloses in one of us — "a man, Christ Jesus" — the truth about God's desire to save every one of us.

4. "[Christ Jesus], who gave himself a ransom for everybody." In Paul's social world, payment of a "ransom" freed a slave from indenture, and perhaps the most important biblical typology of God's way of salvation is God's liberation of enslaved Israel from its captivity to a pagan power to live in its own land and freely worship its own God. The politics of worship, which supplies an important subtext to the present instructions, is shaped not by Rome but by the exodus story.

Yet the reader may well have expected a more traditional Pauline dogmatics: "who gave himself a ransom *for sin*" (cf. Tit 2:14). Instead Paul repeats "for all" (ὑπὲρ πάντον, *hyper pantōn*; cf. 2:1) because under the present circumstances he is pressing for the catholic scope of God's salvation as the principal theological reason the congregation should pray even for pagan rulers. Sharply put, Christians pray for everybody because Christ died for everybody in agreement with God's chief desire.

Paul's mention of the Lord's payment of a "ransom" — one crucified Messiah in trade for all sinful humanity (cf. 1:15) — would have had special currency in a Roman world with a huge slave population, where it would have evoked images of a ransom price paid to set a slave free. Further, the prefix of the distinctive word Paul uses for ransom (ἀντίλυτρον, *antilytron*), ἀντί- (*anti-*, "instead"), adds the nuance of a substitution to the root word for "ransom" (λύτρον, *lytron*) to make it clear that Jesus exchanged his life as a man on behalf of everyone else. The very idea of a person substituting his life for a community or nation is the definition of the noblest covenant loyalty in Jewish literature of Paul's day (see *4 Maccabees* 6:29; 17:21-22; 2 Macc 7:37-38; cf. Deut 32:36; Mark 10:45).

5. Paul was "appointed its preacher and apostle . . . and teacher of the true faith to the nations." The formula's final line is hardly incidental to a Pauline conception of the *missio Dei*. Apostleship is a core theme of the Pastoral Epistles, no longer in defense of Paul's vocation but rather to define and underwrite the apostolicity of Scripture's thirteen-letter Pauline canon (see Introduction). Nowhere else in that canon is the purpose of his apostolic appointment more clearly stated than here: Paul is called to teach truth to the nations — an appointment that is framed for Scripture's readers by Paul's prior story in Acts, which plots his prophetic commission to carry the Lord's name "before the nations and kings and the children of Israel" (Acts 9:15). The purpose of Paul's mission to the nations is clearly glossed by this formula: so that everyone may "come to the knowledge of the truth" and be saved from death for eternal life (v. 4).

But this formula defines the missional nature not only of Paul's apostleship but also of the community that confesses itself to be apostolic. As J. Webster put it, "apostolicity is the church's standing beneath (Christ's) imperious directive, 'Go.'"[29] Most Protestants understand the church's apostolic mark within the bounds of the magisterial Reformation: that is, in terms of Scripture, whose instruction is paraded and practiced because it faithfully coheres to the apostolic witness of the Incarnate Word. But in doing so, Scripture is used by Christ's Spirit in service of the church's apostolic existence. The apostolic word forms a people that engages in the same missionary calling and movement that engaged the apostle, apart from which the church simply cannot claim to be apostolic.[30] And v. 7 formulates the church's apostolic calling and movement in Pauline terms.[31]

---

29. John Webster, *Holy Scripture: A Dogmatic Sketch* (Cambridge: Cambridge University Press, 2003), 51.

30. Cf. John G. Flett, *The Witness of God: The Trinity, Missio Dei, Karl Barth, and the Nature of Christian Community* (Grand Rapids: Eerdmans, 2010), 240-85.

31. That is, the Spirit who baptizes the church into this apostolate also empowers the church to continue to herald and teach faith and truth in the nations. The church has no choice

But surely there is an irony here. The occasion of Paul's concluding emphasis may well allude to the controversy provoked by his evangelistic mission among Jewish traditionalists, perhaps including the divisive Torah teachers mentioned earlier (1:7), who argue that converts from paganism must first meet the standards of Jewish proselytism before being initiated into a covenant-keeping community. The subtext of the letter's repeated appeal to a Pauline apostleship, especially if a Jewish opposition is in the background, is the prior biography (cf. 1:15-16) in which Paul self-identifies with those very Jewish opponents but by divine grace has become the role model for the nations of true faith. While Paul's apostolic calling underwrites his teaching ministry in a special way, his encounter with the risen One and transforming experience of God's grace are normative for everyone, especially for his Jewish detractors "among whom I am first" (1:15).

2:8–3:1a Worship Practices of Christian Men and Women[32]

⁸Therefore, I want men to pray publicly with their holy hands lifted up without anger or argument. ⁹Likewise, women should adorn themselves modestly and prudently with sensible attire, without braided hair, gold, pearls, or costly clothes, ¹⁰but rather with good works suitable for pious women. ¹¹Let a woman learn quietly in complete submission: ¹²I do not allow a woman to teach or to have authority over a man but to be a quiet (student). ¹³For Adam was formed first, then Eve, ¹⁴and Adam was not deceived, rather the woman was deceived, became a sinner, ¹⁵and yet will be saved through childbearing — if they continue in faith and love and holiness with prudence. 3¹ªThis teaching is a core belief.

Paul's instruction and warrant for congregational prayers turns to more particular injunctions for Christian men (v. 8) and women (vv. 9-15). The patterns of worship evince well-known caricatures of ideal males as self-controlled and able to curb their natural bent toward aggression, and of ideal females as prudent and engaged in good works rather than trivial pursuits. In urban congregations, female converts sometimes came from affluent Roman

---

but to follow the canonical Paul's example of apostolicity and so be led by the Spirit into the public square to make disciples of the nations (cf. Matt 28:19-20). Of course, it was the risen Jesus who warned Paul that he would suffer (Acts 9:16). The apostolic assembly should also expect to suffer (cf. 2 Tim 1:8-14; 2:1-7; 3:10-13), since there is hardly a battleground more fiercely waged in the public square than over competing notions of faith and truth (cf. 2 Tim 3:1-9).

32. For the full critical notation and expanded exegesis of this text, see Robert W. Wall, "1 Timothy 2:9-15 Reconsidered (Again!)," *BBR* 14 (2004): 81-103.

middle-class households, and so their exemplary behavior was demonstrated in reference to social practices apropos of the middle class: wardrobe (v. 9), philanthropy (v. 10), and schooling (vv. 11-12). In this Pauline setting (v. 7), however, the ideal woman's public life is prompted more by theological motive than by social propriety: God's desire to save every woman (vv. 3-6, 15a) from deception and sin (v. 14) is realized by the witness of influential Christian women who exemplify God's saving grace to outsiders by a public life of "faith and love and holiness with prudence" (v. 15b). By so doing, not so much by spoken word as by prudent deed, they provide an apt illustration of Paul's apostolic mission in the world (cf. v. 7).

My reading of this difficult passage is shaped to some extent by a deep awareness of the struggles it provokes among female students at Seattle Pacific University, especially those whose call to Christian ministry is sometimes demonized by the leaders of their conservative faith traditions.[33] Their vocational aspirations are dismissed by appeal to this single "text of terror," as if it presented a biblical norm that trumps all others. Prior to the nineteenth century, when it was picked up to quell the social pressures to free women from social pigeonholing exerted by a democratic America, these instructions were interpreted as referring to natural differences between genders in a manner generally agreed on by all and close to the plain sense of the text. This reading, however, can hardly be sustained today given what science now teaches us about gender and what women have taught us about the hostility toward them this reading has engendered.

Indeed, without doubt this passage presents an interpretive problem for practitioners of the canonical approach precisely because of the history of its effects within the church as a text of terror: How can such a text function canonically? Especially today, criticism's instinct is to find a way to silence the text because of its history in silencing women and even in legitimizing their abuse. In turn, then, criticism has sought to silence Paul's instructions by relocating them from their canonical setting in the text of 1 Timothy to the ancient world, where their history-of-religions meaning and authorial intent are understood as unsuitable for our culture. The effect of this interpretive move is to de-canonize the text and render it irrelevant for today's Christian women.

While proposing an exegesis that seeks to make plain the sense of this passage in its compositional setting, a canonical approach to any particular text, and even more acutely a text of terror, will resist treating it in isolation

---

33. The film *Agora* (2009) shows how this same text has also been used against gifted women in scientific and other vocations to challenge their ability and contribution to the pursuit of truth.

from other canonical texts — an interpretive reductionism that lies at the root of the current problem. That is, this letter's instruction is aimed at Christian women in a way that does not trump all other antecedent texts about women in the Pauline corpus (e.g., 1 Corinthians 7, 11, and 14; Gal 3:28, etc.), but rather it trades on and illumines them.[34]

Paul's instructions recalibrate well-known caricatures of competitive men and modest women found in the literature of the Greco-Roman world to transform them into ideal worshipers. He does not refer by name to specific individuals in response to problems they are provoking in the congregation; Pauline paraenesis does not intend to correct misbehavior, whether or not prompted by false teaching; rather, it intends to provide general patterns of worship that serve a redemptive end according to the theological formula in vv. 3-7. While these instructions speak to a particular class of influential women — those from the urban upper middle class with the financial means to dress well and leisure time to engage in philanthropic work and learning — they regulate a basic theological stance in the public square that is true for all Christians who influence the choices others make.

The attentiveness of the congregation's influential women is cued by "likewise," intimating that they share equally with men in the congregation's worship (cf. 1 Cor 11:4-5), and on this basis prompts a fuller set of instructions similar to those just given in telescoped form to Christian men. Paul's purpose is simply this: the congregation's worship practices, down to the individual believer, should personify the redemptive purpose of God our Savior set out by the preceding theological formulation. Furthermore, the opening exhortation, "I want men to pray" (v. 8a), introduces an elaboration of his prior instructions regarding a congregation's prayers (vv. 1-2) in a way that differentiates its members by gender and social class rather than by practice or "divergent doctrine."[35]

---

34. See Towner's expansive discussion and bibliography on this passage's history of interpretation and especially its social world: Philip H. Towner, *The Letters to Timothy and Titus* (NICNT; Grand Rapids: Eerdmans, 2006), 190-239. Korinna Zamfir and Joseph Verheyden's study, "Text-Critical and Intertextual Remarks on 1 Tim 2:8-10," *NovT* 50 (2008): 376-406, considers the problem created by the elliptical 2:9 in its transmission, concluding that it introduces a picture of worship that constricts the freedoms granted by 1 Corinthians 11, especially to women. As I do, the authors assume a reading of 1 Timothy in the context of a wider Pauline corpus; as such they find a still deeper contrast between Christian men and the apostle who alone can prophesy (2:7 in contrast to 1 Corinthians 11). This contrast may have in mind a canonical Paul and his ultimate purchase for the future of the church.

35. This passage does not depart from instructions about worship practices in 1 Corinthians. Here, too, every believer is allowed to pray publicly to God even though regulated by social conventions related to gender (cf. 1 Cor 11:1-16) and social class (cf. 1 Cor 11:17-34).

1 Timothy 2:8–3:1a

In this setting, worship affords a public expression of the earnest communicant's piety and civility (v. 2b). Christian men are exhorted to pray "with their holy hands lifted up" (v. 8). Their gesture is apropos of the devout Jewish man in prayer. Rabbi Joshua ben Levi said that "a priest should not raise his hands in holiness to God (so Ps 134:2) unless to give a blessing" (*b. Sotah* 39a). Perhaps for this reason, Paul adds that the purity of the worshiper's hands (which may also expect ritual bathing prior to worship according to Jewish tradition) extends to the heart: a man should enter into worship only if he can do so "without anger or argument."

Rabbi Hiya ben Ashi taught that "he should not pray whose dispositions are not calm" (*b. Erubin* 65a). The public gesture of raising "holy hands" represents not only the worshiper's inward purity but also his peaceful solidarity with other members of the community. More critically, the raising of hands in worship is hardly cultic but responds naturally to an experience of saving grace that has cleansed the heart and conscience (1 Tim 1:5b; cf. 1 Cor 6:11; 2 Cor 7:1). This gesture of worship, then, not only testifies to the theological belief set out in 2:4-6, it signifies to other congregants affirmation of solidarity with God's will. Christian men are to pray "without anger or argument" since competitive affections are not only antithetical to "loving relations" (1:5) but result from misplaced focus on human relationships rather than worshiping God.

The images of the ideal Christian woman are developed in a rhetorical unit bracketed by the repetition of "prudence" (σωφροσύνη, *sōphrosynē*, vv. 9, 15), which was the most universally admired female virtue of the period. It is noteworthy, however, that although prudence, especially when qualified by "modesty" (αἰδώς, *aidōs*) as here, carries a peculiar impress for Christian women, the same word is subsequently used in 3:2 more generally to characterize any Christian leader (see also Tit 1:8; 2:2, 5; cf. Acts 26:25). In this sense, the modesty of the ideal Christian woman is not exclusive to a particular gender but embodies the redemptive purpose of God for everyone, since it "abstains from whatever tends to sin."[36] Female modesty adorns religious existence and is the principal affection of a thoughtful, prudent outlook on all of life.

The contrast between secular and religious women is well known from antiquity. Secular women live a banal existence, lacking in moral scruples and religious devotion and typified by the trivial pursuit of fastidious personal appearance, while "pious women" are concerned with the well-being of their neighbors and exemplify "a life of productive virtue."[37] In modern parlance

---

36. Tertullian, *On the Apparel of Women* 2.2.
37. For examples, see Johnson, *First and Second Letters to Timothy*, 200, 204-8.

prudence, like civility, seems like a pale platitude. But in classical culture, *sōphrosynē* did not connote shyness or coyness but practical wisdom and savvy. If a woman's prudent practices exhibit the self-possession and competent dignity of the influential woman who knows how her world works and how to act wisely in the world, then this word may lose some of its current distastefulness. Put differently, Paul may be drawing on his wisdom tradition and its conception of *ḥokmah* — skill for living well — in describing a competent woman.

The subject, "pious women," combines the participle ἐπαγγελλομέναις *(epangellomenais)*, "promise-making," with the unusual noun θεοσέβεια *(theosebeia)*, "devotion to God," to form the image of one who makes good on her public profession of faith by acting in a manner consistent with her theological claims. This image is consonant with Hellenistic (especially Stoic) morality, which placed a premium on a piety that translates religious talk into ethical walk. Paul's definition anticipates his concluding exhortation regarding the seductive power of wealth (6:8-10) and the obligation of wealthy members to care for those on the margins (6:17-19). Again, however, his motive does not appear to be provoked by worry of conflict within the congregation or even with the self-absorption of the influential, but is illustrative of Christian women who have been saved from a banal existence to contribute to the congregation's welfare.

In this sense, the woman's public identity — that which is observed by others and by which an opinion of her is formed — is her dress. In fact, her relationships with others are in this sense also formed by what she wears. The first members of my Free Methodist Church refused to wear jewelry or expensive clothes for fear that they would offend the poor and prevent them from seeking God in worship. In this sense, they "dressed down" in order to form an unnatural solidarity with outsiders.

While doing "good works" is a social marker of the middle class in 1 Timothy (cf. 5:10, 25; 6:18-20), here it provides evidence of Christianity's positive effect on society — a persuasive societal standard for a newly introduced religion (cf. Acts 17:18-31) reconceived in 1 Timothy as another concrete witness to the transforming power of divine mercy (cf. 1 Tim 1:12-16). At the same time, these are worship practices of God's household observed by outsiders but not directed to them but to "those who are of the household of faith" (Gal 6:10).

A final contrast (2:11-12) applies female prudence to a theme of primary importance in this letter: what members of a Christian congregation are taught and by whom. While the issue of authority is clearly gender-based — teachable women learn from men in positions of authority to teach others — the construction of this social hierarchy is hardly a matter of mere gender. In fact, the relationship between women and men is introduced in v. 11 with studied neutrality — by asyndeton, in the third person, and without reference to a male. Simply put, a woman's prudence is shown in deference to her teachers as exhibited by careful listening.[38] Moreover, the term used, ἡσυχία (*hēsychia*, "quietly"), repeats the disposition of the entire worshiping congregation described earlier in v. 2b. This repetition creates an intertext that implies that a "quiet and submissive" woman during instruction personifies the quiet disposition of the entire congregation in its civic relations.[39]

But such studied neutrality begs for greater precision: From whom does the prudent woman learn, and about what? While inferences drawn from v. 11 may fairly respond to this practical question, Paul clarifies his intent by a subsequent injunction (v. 12) and appeal to Scripture (vv. 13-15a).[40] In fact, the shift from third to first person in v. 12 and from general exhortation to personal injunction (οὐκ ἐπιτρέπω, *ouk epitrepō*, "I do not allow") sharpens the instruction. Many suppose that this abrupt shift in tone signals a more direct response to a real problem. But again, without clear evidence in the text of a female problem, such speculation seems unwarranted. In fact, readers may just as well understand Paul's motive in rhetorical terms: he sharpens his tone to clarify his instruction that the influential Christian woman knows she should quietly learn (v. 11a) rather than teach (v. 12a) and should do so in a way (v. 11b) that does not usurp her teacher's authority (v. 12b).[41] The use of the imperative suggests that prudence is measured by the choices a woman makes in her education, especially with respect to her teachers. Paul himself defines the criterion that regulates this choice by the interplay of two infinitives, διδασκεῖν (*didaskein*) and αὐθεντεῖν (*authentein*, v. 12: "to teach . . . to

---

38. F. Young contends, however, that the instruction for women to listen envisages a worship setting rather than catechesis and follows the practice of the synagogue, in which men and women were separated and women listened to men pray. Frances M. Young, *The Theology of the Pastoral Letters* (NTT; Cambridge: Cambridge University Press, 1994), 35.

39. Had Paul wanted to silence women from speaking, there is reason to believe he would have used ἐπιστομίζω (*epistomizō*) instead of ἡσυχία (*hēsychia*) as he does in Tit 1:11 when instructing Titus to silence members from the so-called "circumcision" whose oral arguments were evidently disrupting the congregation.

40. Paul's midrash in 2:13-15 may illustrate a proper use of Torah in contrast to those misguided "teachers of Torah" who assert Torah's support for their false ideas "without understanding" (1:6-7).

41. Antiquity's sense of a woman's quiet disposition when instructed by a competent man (typically her husband or father) is nicely reflected in Aristotle, *Politics* 1.13. E.g., "the courage of a man is shown in commanding, of a woman in obeying. . . . Silence is a woman's glory."

have authority"), both of which exclude women in this setting. The exegetical concern is to explain why they are excluded.[42]

Both the syntax and lexicography of this text are subjects of vigorous debate in recent years, prompted in large measure by a feminist reading of this text. Most interpreters assume that the meaning and role of the first infinitive, "teach," turns on the meaning and role of the second, *authentein,* a *hapax legomenon* whose unstated referent is sometimes imagined in cultural and gender-specific terms. The reader should not assume that the plain sense of this text is simply its mirror opposite — that is, that the exceptional use of *authentein* rather than *exousia* or some other more common word for "authority" suggests an exceptional problem of rebelliousness, since no such problem is mentioned in this passage. Nonetheless, on this single basis several modern commentators assume that certain leading Christian women were behaving immodestly by seeking to usurp the traditional roles of male teachers, for which they were unprepared. Paul's instruction, the argument goes, seeks to tame these women into the "submission" mentioned in v. 11. In this reconstructed setting of intramural conflict, the use of *authentein* carries with it the sense of a bullying or presumptive authority; that is, only rebellious and not modest women are in view. The implication for some interpreters, of course, is that under different circumstances and in different times a woman would be allowed to teach if she did so prudently.

But I doubt this reading. In antiquity, *authentein* had no such technical meaning and was used in various ways to denote one's role or social status.[43] The principal use of *authentein* was hardly negative and seems rather more

---

42. P. B. Payne argues that the οὐκ . . . οὐδέ *(ouk . . . oude)* construction is always used to make a single prohibition, here of a woman who teaches while assuming authority over a man, whom we take to refer to a male tutor. Philip Burton Payne, "1 Tim 2.12 and the Use of οὐδέ to Combine Two Elements to Express a Single Idea," *NTS* 54 (2008): 235-53.

43. See Marshall's judicious discussion of recent interpretations of this word in *Pastoral Epistles,* 456-60. George W. Knight, *The Pastoral Epistles: A Commentary on the Greek Text* (NIGTC; Grand Rapids: Eerdmans, 1992), 141-42, demonstrates that the word had no negative connotation and in 1 Timothy refers to the proper exercise of an ecclesial "office" — in this case to teach the Pauline gospel to believers. Knight's conclusions have been challenged by Linda Belleville in "Teaching and Usurping Authority: 1 Timothy 2:11-15," in *Discovering Biblical Equality* (ed. Ronald W. Pierce and Rebecca Merrill Groothuis; Downers Grove: InterVarsity, 2004), 205-23, but her assumption that use of the word here is determined by some unspecified false teaching (cf. 1:3-11) and her overall study of this verse's syntax or lexicography are unpersuasive. See now Andreas J. Köstenberger, "A Complex Sentence: The Syntax of 1 Timothy 2:12," in *Women in the Church: An Analysis and Application of 1 Timothy 2:9-15* (ed. Andreas J. Köstenberger and Thomas R. Schreiner; 2nd ed.; Grand Rapids: Baker, 2005), 53-84. The relevant issue in adapting this text to today's church is hermeneutical and not only exegetical.

simply to define the exercise of one's authority as predicated by rank or competence, while its secondary use recognizes authority as one's birthright.

Both connotations are sounded in Paul's use here: first, *authentein* principally refers to virtuous teachers who are "apt to teach" (cf. 3:2). Second, the apostle recognizes a special familial relationship with his delegated successors, whose spiritual birthright as his "children" (see above on 1:2; also Tit 1:4) gives them special authority to teach others. Following the logic of this succession trope, the prudent Christian woman recognizes that Timothy (and perhaps other faithful leaders assigned the responsibility to teach others; so 2 Tim 2:2) has been granted authority to instruct her both by charism (2 Tim 1:6-7) and as a kind of birthright as Paul's "dear child" (e.g., 1 Tim 1:3-5; 2 Tim 1:13-14; 2:2). More plain in this regard, Timothy's approval by a "council of elders" (1 Tim 4:14; cf. 2 Tim 1:6) agrees with Paul's verdict based on "prophecies" made about his ministry (so 1 Tim 1:18). While these references are vague, they suggest a formal act of authorizing certain individuals to teach and care for the congregation's spiritual well-being (cf. Acts 13:1-3; 14:23). The overriding feature of Timothy's authorization — and I cannot state this point emphatically enough — is his intimate connection to Paul and his apostolate: he teaches Paul's pattern of healthy doctrine (cf. 2 Tim 1:13-14) and imitates what Paul does in ministry (cf. 2 Tim 3:10-14) for the sake of his congregation's spiritual health.

Paul's striking use of the indefinite ἀνήρ (*anēr*, "a man," 2:12) with *authentein* reflects the particular social world that comes with these instructions. The specifics of Pauline paraenesis included in any correspondence are shaped by the public square that comes with it — in the case of 1 Timothy, by the culture of Roman Ephesus, where teaching was an exclusively male occupation, and by the culture of Diaspora Judaism, which was reluctant to advance women to positions of authority over men and never under ordinary circumstances.[44] Within its canonical context, the reader should also note that Paul's instructions in this regard do not define the authority of a teacher in gender-specific terms but rather in terms of charisma or in a manner consistent with the content and redemptive consequence of his gospel. This is clear from this letter's repeated use of the διδάσκειν (*didaskein*, "teach") family of words (1:10; 4:6, 11, 13, 16; 5:17; 6:1, 2; cf. 1:3; 6:3), which not only indicates the right practices of Pauline catechesis but distinguishes between the faithful tradent who is authorized to teach others from those who engage in ἑτερο-

---

44. See M. Eugene Boring, *Hellenistic Commentary to the New Testament* (Nashville: Abingdon, 1995), on Philo's midrash on Exodus 15 in *Life of Moses* 1.32.180, which divides a joyful Israel into two choirs, one male and the other female, to celebrate God's victory over Egypt.

διδασκαλεῖν (*heterodidaskalein,* "divergent teaching") who themselves must be taught (1:3-4, 20).⁴⁵ The criterion that measures religious authority in the congregation, then, includes more than a personal relationship with the apostle but also personal virtue and spiritual maturity (4:12; also 3:6-7), theological orthodoxy (1:10-11; 6:2-3), a pedagogy that aims learners at Christian growth (1:4-7; 4:13), and sometimes, as with Timothy, the spiritual charism to do so rightly (1:18; 4:14; 2 Tim 1:6-7, 13-14). These requirements do not appear to include a preference for gender or age (cf. 4:12). Even so, it should be clear that this passage's definition of the ideal Christian woman is that she influences others by her prudent choices rather than by her instruction. Given the letter's portrait of a canonical Paul, it is also the case that pedagogical authority is a credential that Paul (or the spirit of the departed Paul) distributes (as in 2:12: οὐκ ἐπιτρέπω, *ouk epitrepō:* "I do not allow").⁴⁶

Sharply put, a continuing theological norm rather than social conventions current when the letter was composed supplies the ground floor on which these instructions for Christian women are read and applied today as Scripture. Even if this particular prescription is aimed at the dressing rooms or classrooms of ancient Ephesus and is not applicable to any other social world, its canonical function is to instantiate the practices of a particular Christian congregation to make all readers, male and female, aware that their social manners bear witness to the core beliefs of Paul's gospel in order to teach the nations (2:7). The prudent choices believers, whether male or female, make in what they wear, what they do, and what they learn and from whom, when observed by others, construct implicit contrasts with the choices others make and thereby help them determine decisions of an ultimate kind about which gospel to believe.

The illative γάρ (*gar,* "for") introduces Paul's reading of Eve's story in Gen 2:13-15a, which supplies a biblical warrant for his instructions and thereby helps clarify his motive. This midrash is not easily problematized as idiosyncratic since it rehearses the plain sense of the biblical story and agrees with contemporary Jewish interpretations of Eve's complicity in humanity's first transgression. This is a familiar Eve who personifies every woman's spiritual failure and her need for "God our Savior."

This summary sounds a note of disagreement with the recent history of interpreting this text, which either features a more negative appraisal of Eve

---

45. Marshall rightly argues that Paul would have surely used ἑτεροδιδασκαλεῖν (*heterodidaskalein*), as he did in 1:3, had he wanted to convey a negative impression of the kind of teaching he has in mind. Marshall, *Pastoral Epistles,* 458.

46. E.g., Johnson, *First and Second Letters to Timothy,* 205-8, which then shapes Paul's misreading of Eve's story in Genesis.

or blames Paul for misreading the biblical narrative and God's indictment of the man (cf. Gen 3:17). According to Paul's reading, Eve has come to illustrate an inferior woman who needs to be subject to her leading man. Contrary to the more compliant Adam, who was not initially deceived by the serpent's mischief, Eve chooses an independent course away from God, is deceived, and therefore sins (2:14; cf. 2 Cor 11:3). The order of humanity's creation, woman from man, hints at male priority (2:13; cf. 1 Cor 11:8-9) and might be read as offering a straightforward justification for each woman's submission to a male mentor (2:12). In fact, on the basis of this single text many congregations have silenced their female members on implicitly ontological grounds: they are by nature out-of-control and need the males' strong hand to keep them from straying!

To stipulate that *Christian* women act prudently on the basis of Eve's deception and fall into sin is hardly likely in a Pauline letter! According to Romans, *every* believer has been made alive "in Christ" and has been liberated from deception and transgression as the powerful and evident result of divine grace (Rom 5:12–6:23). Glossed by this theological grammar, the reader should not assume the unstated function of Eve's story in these instructions is to check the regenerate woman's natural propensity toward deception and sin; rather, we should assume that she can realistically aspire to live "with prudence" (2:15b) in the public square and influence other women there toward God's love as a result. Rom 5:12 pins the blame on Adam for the very indiscretion that 1 Tim 2:14 blames on Eve, and Rom 7:11 sounds an echo of the same "deception" as in 1 Tim 2:14 to preface Paul's theological essay on the moral and spiritual frustration of the "awakened" sinner in Rom 7:13–8:2, in which the rhetorical "I" quite probably stands for the universal recapitulation of Adam's sin. If viewed from this more positive angle, Paul's interest in the pair of pedagogical contrasts drawn in 2:11-12 — learning but not teaching, submitting but not leading — shifts the reader toward a more evangelical purpose that pertains to the community's regard of the female outsider and her prospective salvation.

1 Tim 2:15a remains "one of the strangest verses in the NT,"[47] and the use of Eve's story here turns on this question: Does Paul conclude its plotline with v. 14 or v. 15a? In part, the answer depends on a prior decision. If the purpose of the injunction is to domesticate Christian women and allow men to take the lead, then this Eve is likely an exemplar for the subordinate, fallen, and inferior woman who needs a man's firm grip. If, however, this instruction is approached as a worship practice motivated by the *missio Dei*, then the

---

47. William D. Mounce, *Pastoral Epistles* (WBC; Nashville: Nelson, 2000).

reader is more likely to regard this Eve as typological of God's way of salvation. In canonical setting, it seems entirely plausible that Paul would conclude his version of Eve's story with an image of her restoration rather than condemnation.

Marshall offers an unequivocal verdict that the subject of σωθήσεται (*sōthēsetai*, "will be saved," 2:15) "is clearly no longer Eve" but "woman" from v. 12 — that is, women in general.[48] But this is hardly a clear reading, especially if one follows the grammatical prompts in the text itself. The most natural antecedent of the singular verb is the Eve of vv. 13-14: she is "the woman" who is deceived and sins and will then be saved in childbearing. The shift from a singular verb *(sōthēsetai)* to a plural verb ("*they* remain ... with prudence") in v. 15 lends support to this reading as well, since Paul thus departs from his comment on a particular woman, Eve, to conclude his general exhortation to Christian women, which began in v. 9. The repetition of *sōphrosynē* has the rhetorical effect of forming an *inclusio* on female prudence to wrap around this paraenetic unit.

If the grammar of the text suggests that v. 15a continues the thought of vv. 13-14, then to what scene of Eve's biblical story might the reference to "childbearing" allude? The reader is naturally drawn to LXX Gen 4:1-2, which picks up Eve's post-Eden existence as a woman in the act of childbearing. 1 Tim 2:15a picks up Gen 4:1-2 to complete Eve's biblical story with its third and most crucial narrative step: her redemption. The first two steps are her creation, cued here by "For Adam was formed (πλάσσω, *plassō*) first" (v. 13), which echoes the central verb in the Genesis account of God "forming" man (LXX Gen 2:7-8). The sparse "then Eve" recalls that she was created from Adam (Gen 2:18-25, especially v. 22). The pivotal moment of Eve's story is cued by the verb ἀπατάω/ἐξαπατάω (*apataō/exapataō*, "deceive," 2:14), which repeats the central verbal idea from Scripture's story and the leading role performed by Eve (LXX Gen 3:13).

Both grammar and a theological sensibility shaped by a Pauline way of salvation suggest that Eve's story needs an ending, and it is cued by Paul's puzzling phrase σωθήσεται δὲ διὰ τῆς τεκνογονίας *(sōthēsetai de dia tēs teknogonias)*, "and yet she will be saved through childbearing" (2:15a). In our reading, this phrase recalls the moment the fallen Eve, now dismissed from the garden, apprehends that her relationship with God has remained intact after all: when giving birth to her first child (συλλαβοῦσα ἔτεκεν, *syllabousa eteken*, LXX Gen 4:1) she exclaims that God (and not Adam!) is her partner in

---

48. Marshall, *Pastoral Epistles*, 467; also, among others, Collins, *1 and 2 Timothy and Titus*, 76-77.

giving life to another (see below). This stunning development takes "Eve" from God's indictment to celebration with God and is picked up by the particle δέ (*de*, "yet") in 1 Tim 2:15a to complete the typology of everywoman's experience of salvation from sin.[49]

The articular phrase *dia tēs teknogonias*, which I have translated "through childbearing," can be understood as generic of the woman's physical act of giving birth or as a reference to a particular woman giving birth to a particular child — in my reading, Eve (rather than Mary) giving birth to her firstborn Cain (rather than the Messiah), in allusion to the Genesis narrative (rather than the Gospel narrative). In any case, the woman's recognition of participating in a new life with God is thereby attached to the quintessential female experience of bearing new life. But how is this act of childbearing redemptive for the sinful woman, especially when earlier in 1 Timothy the mediation of God's salvation is assessed Christologically (1:15; 2:5-6), not biologically? When responding to this question, the interpreter should consider the full meaning of σῴζω (*sōzō*)-words in 1 Timothy. While surely the sinner's pardon from sin through Christ is central to a Pauline definition, the earlier formula qualifies the realization of God's redemptive purpose in this important way: God wills that everybody be saved (πάντας ἀνθρώπους ... σωθῆναι, *pantas anthrōpoi ... sōthēnai*), evidently including "the woman" who "was deceived and became a transgressor" (v. 14b).

The reference to childbearing is not an echo of Gen 3:16 and Eve's judgment,[50] but of Eve's exclamation that ἐκτησάμην ἄνθρωπον διὰ τοῦ θεοῦ (*ektēsamēn anthrōpon dia tou theou*, "I have made a person with God," LXX Gen 4:1b) — a note that sounds her post-Eden reconciliation with God. In evident absence of the earlier prediction of increased pain, the woman realizes that God has chosen her to fulfill the creational promise of Gen 1:28.[51] In this reading of the phrase, "childbearing" — the quintessentially female act

---

49. Against the idea that the promise here is merely that a virtuous woman will be saved from a difficult pregnancy or even from death when giving birth, Bruce W. Winter suggests the opposite: wealthy women, preoccupied with other matters, did not want to have children; *Roman Wives, Roman Widows: The Appearance of New Women and the Pauline Communities* (Grand Rapids: Eerdmans, 2003), 109-12. But Marshall is correct is arguing that the spiritual sense of salvation — salvation from sin — is uniformly in view in the Pastoral Epistles; Marshall, *Pastoral Epistles*, 467. After all, it is Paul's conversion from sin and ignorance that defines the theological grammar of his apostolate (see above on 1:12-17).

50. Τεκνογονία (*teknogonia*) not only picks up the reference to τέξῃ τέκνα (*texēi tekna*) in LXX Gen 3:16 but more critically the repetition of τίκτω (*tiktō*) in LXX Gen 4:1. Not only does life continue beyond "the fall," Eve recognizes that it does so in full partnership with God.

51. So Terence E. Fretheim, "Genesis," in *The New Interpreter's Bible* (Nashville: Abingdon, 1994), 1:319-674.

— occasions an experience not unlike Paul's own (1:12-16) of God's mercy, in this case granted specifically to a woman at childbirth. Paul's use of Eve's story, then, is typological of every woman who when giving birth to a new life — a uniquely female experience — is awakened to a realization of her partnership with God, who has not abandoned her because of Christ Jesus. Eve's exclamation that she had created a child in partnership with God (cf. Gen 1:27-28) comes precisely at the climactic moment she discovers the truth about God's mercy: God promises her a new life as well. This conception of female salvation subverts later Gnostic Christian female myths (e.g., *Gospel of Thomas*) that claimed redeemed women will finally be repristinated as Adam/male.[52]

The triad of virtues, "faith and love and holiness" (2:15b), recalls the biography in 1:12-17, where Paul rehearsed his conversion experience as an encounter with "the faith and love that are in Christ Jesus" (1:14). Christian existence is an experience of belonging to Jesus, of becoming like him as the confirmation of the gospel's claim that "Christ Jesus came into the world to save sinners" (1:15). Moreover, in the immediate context where Paul teaches on the manner of Christian worship, this triad nicely summarizes the character of the worshiper whose approach to God is made with "faith and love and holiness."

Paul concludes his instruction of Christian women as he began it: with an appeal to prudence as the hallmark of the faithful woman (2:9, 15b). When competent self-control — or any other virtue relevant of a particular social location — comes to characterize the public manners of Christian women it has the persuasive power to evoke within other women recognition of the gospel's truth. This is the effect of personal testimony in public life: manners lend integrity to the gospel's truth claims. By such testimony, women "likewise" come to know that God desires to save them from the self-destructive results of deception and sin and to transform them into persons known for their virtue — "faith and love and holiness." I take it that this would have been a radical idea in a male-centered world.

Once again, Paul commends this saying about female modesty as another "core belief" that concentrates Pauline theological grammar (3:1a; cf. 1:15). These sayings in the Pastoral Epistles clarify the soteriological grammar of the Pauline gospel (see above on 1:15). In this case, a woman's salvation results in a transformed life characterized by prudent social practices. The axi-

---

52. See Pheme Perkins, "Gospel of Thomas," in *Searching the Scriptures: A Feminist Commentary* (ed. Elisabeth Schüssler Fiorenza, Shelly Matthews, and Ann G. Brock; New York: Crossroad, 1994), 2:558-60.

omatic value of the concluding conditional is made more clear by the change from singular "the woman" to plural "if they (i.e., women) continue." The force of the Eve typology is now made clear: every woman's partnership with God, awakened by her experience of childbearing, is prospective of a new way of living with God's powerful presence in her life. This conditional clause hardly indicates that the assurance of her salvation is tentative or conditioned on her human achievement (e.g., childbearing or domestic chores) rather than on Christ's work (cf. 2:5-6); the clause more plainly indicates that her moral character is the real effect of God's saving mercy and will develop over time as her partnership with God deepens.

3:1b-7 Profiles in Leadership: Household Administrator

¹ᵇSomeone who aspires to become an administrator desires a good work. ²Therefore the administrator must be blameless: the husband of one wife, clear-headed, modest, respectable, hospitable, a skilled teacher, ³not a drunk or a bully but gentle, peaceable, generous. ⁴He must manage his own household well, holding children in submission with complete respect — ⁵for if someone does not know how to manage his own household, how can he care for God's church? ⁶He must not be newly converted so as not to be arrogant and slip into the devil's condemnation. ⁷He must have good references from outsiders so as not to slip into disgrace, the devil's trap.

The next set of instructions profile the ideal administrator of God's household. Appropriately, such a person must be able to manage his own household well (3:4-5), blameless in his public conduct (vv. 2-3), and mature in his faith (v. 6), and must have good rapport with outsiders (v. 7). Each contribution to this résumé of virtue envisages a competency of the leader's role in safeguarding the Pauline apostolate and its gospel for a new generation of believers.

Later in 1 Timothy, Paul mentions a "council of elders" that confirms Timothy's prophetic calling (4:14) and uses "elders" again of a group of household "elders," whose worth within the congregation is measured by their active ministry of preaching and teaching others (5:17-20). Although undeveloped in 1 Timothy, Paul's repeated comments about the ministry of a congregation's "elders" suggest that they are important custodians of the Pauline tradition and thereby of the spiritual health of believers who meet together for worship, instruction, good works, and Christian fellowship. This rather straightforward political structure accords with Acts, where the house churches founded by Paul's mission on the analogy of Diaspora synagogues are yet another element of the church's firm embrace of its Jewish legacy (see Acts 18:5-6; 14:23; 16:4; 20:17).[53]

If cued by reading Acts in its canonical setting, the reader may well puzzle over the conception of Christian leadership drawn by this passage, which seems in stark contrast to the more charismatic body of Christ also found in the Pauline canon (e.g., Romans, 1 Corinthians). For this reason, biblical scholars put this text forward as evidence of a post-Pauline development of a more complex ecclesiastical structure to accommodate Roman society and safeguard the social institutions of the Christian religion.[54] L. T. Johnson rightly objects to this construction if it supposes that the church of the Pastoral Epistles describes the more complex institutional episcopacy that developed in the early catholic church.[55] Regardless of the date of composition, no such structure is found in the Pastoral Epistles, and their household organization is rather simple by comparison with the church's episcopacy, which did not fully develop until the third century. The ideal congregation of the Pastoral Epistles is elder-ruled (Tit 1:5-9), following the simple pattern of governance typical of Diaspora Judaism and other voluntary organizations of antiquity.

In any case, it bears repeating that "household" is the central metaphor for the church of the Pastoral Epistles and that Christian teachers catechize believers according to the social patterns of the *oikonomia theou* (1:4). The "living God" is *paterfamilias* of the sacred household (cf. 3:15). The political shape of this theological conception draws naturally on the experience of middle-class households in urban centers of the Mediterranean world (see 1:4-5; 5:1–6:2; 2 Tim 2:20-21; Tit 1:5; 2:1-10).[56] Those in charge of caring for the family household, from its administrator to its servant staff, had particular responsibilities and observed particular social conventions. The stability of the city-state, if not of the empire, was routinely considered by its politicians and philosophers to be dependent on maintaining its various households. While the vocation of God's sacred household is religious, its daily operations require effective administrators and a competent servant staff, like any other

---

53. Howard C. Kee, *To Every Nation under Heaven: The Acts of the Apostles* (NTC; Harrisburg: Trinity, 1997), 204-7. In Diaspora Judaism, πρεσβύτεροι (*presbyteroi*) formed councils that guided the religious business in Jewish neighborhoods of Roman cities, following the biblical pattern of Israel's tribal confederacy (e.g., Josh 24:1).

54. For a clearheaded summary of this perspective, see Joseph A. Fitzmyer, "The Structured Ministry of the Church in the Pastoral Epistles," *CBQ* 66 (2004): 582-96.

55. Johnson, *First and Second Letters to Timothy*, 74-76, 217-25.

56. The literature that locates the "household" in the Greco-Roman and Jewish social worlds is enormous. For an apt summary of both this background and its application to Pauline ecclesiology, see Philip H. Towner, "Households and Household Codes," *DPL* 417-19.

Roman household. Paul's instructions regarding the political organization of congregations is roughly analogous to its social and political practices — another example of missionary Paul's willingness to accommodate the outworking of Christian faith to those places where people actually live (cf. 1 Cor 9:19-23).

Given the centrality of the household motif in the Pastoral Epistles, I would suggest that the terms used in this chapter — "administrator" (bishop) and "servants" (deacons) — do not refer to established church offices of a highly organized episcopacy but are better understood as collective metaphors for a community's elders, whose practices and roles are informed by the administrator and servant staff of a Roman "household." That is, Paul's use of household as an ecclesial metaphor extends to spiritual leadership, which gives his instructions additional currency for those with experience in family households or who met for worship and fellowship in a family home (cf. Acts 16:40; 20:7-12).[57]

Moreover, Paul's use of household metaphors for congregational leadership should not imply that the elder's roles as household "administrator" or "servant" are mere tropes of the community's πρεσβύτεροι (*presbyteroi*, "elders"); in fact, the preface to his instructions (3:1b) indicates that he has certain individuals in mind. And subsequently he writes about real elders (5:1) and servants (6:1-2) of family households to create a purposeful ambivalence between sacred/transcendent and secular/historical households.[58] This interplay of hearth and holy place may also be inferred by the juxtaposition of *presbyteroi* in reference to both the household's older males (5:1, where *presbys* means "elderly") and the congregation's governing elders (5:17).[59] But the

---

57. Towner reflects the conclusion of most historians that "there seems to be no such thing as a straight-line development from a so-called informal Pauline church organization to the sort of setup indicated in Ignatius's (c. 110 c.e.) writings" (Towner, *Letters to Timothy and Titus*, 242). I suspect that the differences one finds within the Pauline canon between, e.g., the charismatic community of the Corinthians correspondence and the "household" of the Timothy correspondence is less a material difference that developed over time but rather the result of adapting a particular conception of a covenant-keeping community — the "Israel of God" (Gal 6:16) — to different kinds of theological crises. Paul's principal concern in the Timothy correspondence is organizing a congregation of tradents able to maintain and transmit his apostolic tradition in his absence and after his death.

58. Young, *Pastoral Letters*, 98-99.

59. It is for good reason that 1 Timothy makes an implicit connection between a congregation's "political" elders and its chronological elders, given the veneration of age in the ancient world. Note that the Qumran community's *Mevaqqer* was required to be between 30 and 60 years old (CD 14.7), somewhat younger than the age requirement of "real widows" in Pauline congregations (cf. 1 Tim 5:9).

larger exegetical point to make is that Paul's definition of spiritual leadership is rooted in a commonsense understanding of his social world, where appointment of virtuous persons to care and lead its institutions — rather than political conventions aimed at holding an office — was thought crucial to the well-being of the public square. For this reason, the résumé of virtues outlined in this chapter sounds a different note than what today's congregations may typically require of their applicants.

Like the household, the congregation needs only one administrator — the articular ὁ ἐπίσκοπος (*ho episkopos,* "the administrator") in 3:2 suggests this. If read as a synecdoche for the entire presbytery, however, the singular noun would be understood as referring to the council of elders who function collectively as an *episkopos* of the whole when supervising the daily affairs of God's household. Although a single administrator may indicate a role of singular importance beyond even that accorded to Timothy,[60] the verb προΐστημι (*proistēmi,* "manage," v. 4) is repeated in the letter to connect the administrative (3:4) and service (3:12) responsibilities of a common group of elders (cf. 5:17). Significantly in this regard, not only is the *episkopos* in Titus called "God's steward" (οἰκονόμος, *oikonomos*), thereby locating him within God's household, his qualifications (Tit 1:7-9) are shared and therefore logically related to those of the "elders" (vv. 5-6) by a connective γάρ (*gar,* "for," v. 7). So the instructions regarding leadership in 1 Timothy 3 and elsewhere in the Pastoral Epistles define the practical responsibilities of the congregation's elders and provide a set of moral markers that help define the kind of leader required to steward (3:2-7) and serve (vv. 8-13) the interests of the faith community as a microcosm of the *oikonomia theou* in and for the world.[61]

The word I have translated "to become an administrator" (3:1b, ἐπισκοπή, *episkopē*) refers to an "over-seer" (ἐπίσκοπος, *episkopos*) and is sparingly used in the NT (Luke 19:44; Acts 1:20; 1 Pet 2:12). Acts 1:20 quotes LXX Ps 109:8 and uses *episkopē* of Judas's vacated position within the Twelve, which is then filled by Matthias at God's bidding. Although vague, this may provide a context for reading the aspiration of a qualified administrator as an inward desire prompted by God's calling rather than by self-promotion.

---

60. Towner's discussion of a congregation's spiritual leadership makes the valuable observation that the order of appearance, first "overseer" then "deacon," reflects the congregation's need rather than a hierarchy of office. Towner, *Letters to Timothy and Titus,* 239.

61. Our contention that this passage describes in "household" idiom the duties of the council of elders follows the sense of Clement, who uses ἐπίσκοπος (*episkopos*) and πρεσβύτερος (*presbyteros*) interchangeably in his letter to the Corinthians (*1 Clement* 40–44), which was probably written toward the end of the first century and, we would allow, with a working knowledge of the Pastoral Epistles.

Episkopos (1 Tim 3:2) appears elsewhere with "elder(s)" (Acts 20:28; Phil 1:1; 1 Tim 4:14; Tit 1:7) and implies a responsibility shared with a group or perhaps even a political mechanism of accountability.

I have purposefully used "administrator" rather than the more familiar "bishop" to resist the anachronism of insinuating on the text what the "office of bishop" later became. This translation also indicates my preference to understand it as a collective metaphor for a council of elders who manages the mundane nuts-and-bolts of daily routines to insure the congregation's well-being. The virtue catalog of vv. 2-7 corresponds to this practical role, describing a manner of leadership that works behind the scenes for the common good of the household of God.[62]

Although the administrator has singular importance with respect to these organizational tasks, Timothy alone is charged with those responsibilities normally associated with a congregation's spiritual leader or "pastor" (see below on 3:14–4:7a). In distinction from the elders appointed to help manage the congregation's daily affairs, he alone is called "the pillar and foundation of the truth" (3:15) and is singled out by "prophetic utterance" (1:18) as vested with spiritual charism and so with religious authority that authorizes him to represent the apostle in guiding the congregation into its future (especially 4:7b-16). Neither the household's administrator nor its servant staff is accorded similar legitimacy.

If Acts is approached as Scripture's introduction to the Pauline canon, then Acts 6:1-7 tells a programmatic story of congregational leadership that contextualizes our reading of this text. There the settlement of the intramural conflict over widows between Hebrew and Hellenist members of the greater church of Jerusalem is prompted by an awareness of two related problems: not only were the material needs of widowed disciples from the Greek-speaking neighborhood neglected by the apostolic leaders, who lived across town in the Hebrew-speaking neighborhood (6:1), but the heavy burden of administering a community of common goods — since goods were laid at their feet for distribution (4:37; 5:2) — had subverted the apostles' principal vocation of preaching and prayer (6:2). In response to this crisis of leadership certain members of the Jerusalem community known for their virtuous character — "good reputation, full of the Spirit and wisdom" (6:3) — were selected and consecrated as the congregation's διάκονοι *(diakonoi)* to adminis-

---

62. See Johnson, *First and Second Letters to Timothy*, 218-19. Among the administrative functions performed by supervisors of other voluntary organizations in the Mediterranean world of antiquity, two appear most prominent: as liaison with other groups and in raising funds to support the community's programs and responsibilities. Typically the head of such an organization, and sometimes its primary patron, was also head of a family household.

ter the distribution of the community's goods. This organization, in which apostolic authority is shared with qualified "administrators," allows for the word of God to flourish and the number of converts to increase (6:7).

This division of labor is analogous to what we find in 1 Timothy, where Paul's apostolic authority is delegated to Timothy, an ideal tradent who is called a "good διάκονος *(diakonos)* of Jesus Christ" (4:6). While Timothy is charged to exemplify the Christian life (4:12), his principal role remains to engage in those same "apostolic" tasks of Paul: teaching healthy doctrine (1:10-11; 4:6, 13, 16; 5:17), interpreting the community's Scriptures (4:13), preaching the gospel of God (5:17), guarding the "mystery of godliness" as the church's "pillar and foundation" (3:15-16), and in all matters "standing guard over the (Pauline) tradition" (see 6:20). Significantly, these essentially repeat the tasks performed by the Paul of Acts. Moreover, not unlike the manner of Paul's calling (cf. Acts 9:15-16; 13:1-3), Timothy's ministry is made clear by "prophetic utterance" (1:18), confirmed by the laying on of hands, and empowered by spiritual charism (4:18), all of which underscore his spiritual authorization.

Three additional elements retrieved from Acts 6 illumine important subtexts of this letter's instructions for congregational leaders. First, a healthy congregation requires a competent administrative staff that supports and makes possible its ministry of the word. What is gained from Acts is a clearer sense of the practical reason for a simple division of labor between those called by God to serve "apostolic" roles such as Paul (2:7) and Timothy (4:6-16) and those elders who serve the congregation in "administrative" and "servant" roles.

Second, much as in Acts, the selection of the congregation's management staff is subject to a more pragmatic review of their personal virtue and spiritual maturity rather than by divine appointment as with those vested with apostolic authority. Those who are qualified to lead are identifiable by their public virtue, "witnessed" and approved by others (Acts 6:3), like the virtue that heads the list in 1 Timothy, ἀνεπίλημπτος (*anepilēmptos*, "blameless," 3:2). The more public virtue of the Seven, coupled with the Lukan catchwords of spiritual maturity "full of the Spirit and wisdom," envisages persons of moral and spiritual competence, which is the essential attribute for their community service.

Neither Acts nor 1 Timothy provides biblical readers with detailed job descriptions that narrow a pile of applicants according to their education, experience, calling, and success, which we might expect to find in today's résumés. We rather find the conventional profile of a virtuous person. What is clear, however, is that such a profile in virtue is appropriate for the administrative task in a household of believers. In fact, the aspiration of any believer who seeks to be a church administrator assumes prior experience managing the daily affairs of a family household (3:4-5). The experiences that prepare one for a supervisory role in the church are thus not those we seek in those who are to hold ecclesiastical "offices" but are more practically related to the routines and duties of running a household. Consistent with the rest of 1 Timothy, this profile is consistent with the use of "household" as the essential metaphor of church order, which extends to the next profile, that of household "servants" and their wives (3:9-13).

Finally, what is unclear in 1 Timothy is made clear by the Acts 6 intertext: the apostolate convenes the entire community not merely to advise them as their leaders but to participate with them in making a decision that accords with God's will. This is the subtext of Paul's opening conditional: for the prospective leaders to "desire a good work" (3:1) is to pursue work that agrees with God's will. The "therefore" that introduces v. 2 follows from "good work," which in the Pastoral Epistles is theologically rather than morally determined: the believer who does "good work" does God's will by God's grace.[63] While the interpreter should admit that the form of congregational leadership is not distinctively Christian and even formulaic in ancient Hellenistic moral writings, its theological subtext is not: the "good work" a manager may do is only by the grace of God and not to be understood as human achievement; and it is work that ultimately serves the redemptive interests of "God our Savior."

The moral philosophers of the day routinely condemned those who "aspire" to leadership positions, because ambition for public office is usually motivated by greed or a "desire" for sexual conquest. Paul here challenges this more negative reading of human desire, suggesting that divine grace can transform the motives behind a believer's actions. What Acts suggests, however, is that the congregation has the responsibility to determine whether this is true of every candidate who aspires to a position of leadership.

The run-on sentence in vv. 2-5 is structured to introduce "blameless" (*anepilēmptos*) as a virtue of principal importance. It introduces the entire catalog of sixteen characteristics that follow, nine positive and seven negative. Paul's choice of *anepilēmptos* as a hallmark virtue is somewhat surprising since it does not appear in Israel's Scriptures, which define political leadership more in terms of Torah observance or practical wisdom than of personal virtue. The "blameless" person, however, is well known in Hellenistic moral philosophy, and the holistic formula of virtue envisaged by this profile, especially with its pronounced concern for cultivating the respect of outsiders, is congruent with this ideal.

---

63. Marshall, *Pastoral Epistles*, 227-29.

Scholars continue to debate whether this catalog of virtues is generic or each virtue carries particular significance for the reader. On the one hand, similar lists are found in the writings of Philo and the Stoics, who were concerned with public morality. Epictetus, for example, defines the ideal citizen by conduct related to "marriage, raising children, reverence to God, care for parents" (*Discourses* 3.26). In similar vein, Onasander describes the competent military officer as "temperate, self-restraining, vigilant, frugal, hard working, alert, not too young or too old, a father if possible, a good orator, with a good reputation" (*General* 1.1). Isocrates writes, "Whenever you purpose to consult with any one about your affairs, first observe how he has managed his own. For he who has shown poor judgment in conducting his own business will never give wise counsel about the business of others" (*To Demonicus* 35). Cicero adds that the character of those responsible for the community's welfare must "in the first place be honestly acquired by the use of no dishonest or fraudulent means; let it, in the second place, increase by wisdom, industry, and thrift; and, finally, let it be made available for the use of as many as possible (if only they are worthy) and be at the service of generosity and beneficence rather than of sensuality and excess. By observing these rules, one may live in magnificence, dignity, and independence, and yet in honor, truth and charity toward all" (*De Officiis* 1.26). That is, Paul's list of a competent administrator's qualities agrees with the moral criteria by which any household manager would have been assessed. They are the stock qualities of someone capable of sensible decision-making and a prudent lifestyle who does not abuse his authority. A few of these characteristics are found elsewhere in the Pastoral Epistles as indicative of every earnest believer. The effect of such repetition is to relativize the leader's persona as exemplary of the covenant community in which every believer shares equally and is equally obliged to attain these marks of discipleship. In any case, the rhetorical role of this list is to evoke general impressions of the sort of person who can effectively manage the household of God.

On the other hand, a cursory comparison of the particular virtues cataloged here with comparable lists elsewhere in the Pauline corpus such as the profile of an *episkopos* in Tit 1:6-9 reflects differences that are probably related to different places and occasions. These lists, then, are not arbitrary and generic but reflect the particular concerns framed by the composition itself. For this reason, "the concept of 'good management of a household' provides the best access to the particular virtues of the supervisor."[64] This particular catalog really holds no surprises for the reader; it includes qualities one might ex-

---

64. Johnson, *First and Second Letters to Timothy*, 223.

pect of a competent manager: an ability to manage others well, to handle finances fairly, to make clearheaded decisions, to represent the community's membership at the highest level. Marks of personal maturity ("not a drunk or a bully but gentle, peaceable, generous") are coupled with those of a spiritually mature person (a "skilled teacher" who is not "newly converted") as appropriate for one who supervises a sacred household, especially one that is only recently founded and in a tough place — Roman Ephesus (see above on 1:3; cf. Acts 19).

Yet this particular list is noteworthy for its interest in a congregation's public life and with what outsiders think. For this reason, Paul's review of moral character concludes by asking for an outsider's letter of commendation in support of a candidate's moral character. Collins points out that the repetition of δεῖ (*dei*, "must," 3:2, 7) forms an *inclusio* that underwrites the necessity of a manager's good reputation among both the congregation's membership and outsiders. "Were an overseer not to have a good public reputation, he would likely fall into derision [and] along with him the community itself could possibly be derided."[65] Within 1 Timothy this pervasive interest in an outsider's opinion of the believer's social manners is theologically rather than politically motivated (cf. 2:8-15): the congregation's life together and its public practices embody for all to see God's will to save everybody (cf. 2:3-6). The motive of Paul's instructions is not a social program of domestication according to which the administrator is put forward as an exemplary citizen; rather, the administrator is an exemplary believer whose "good work" personifies the redemptive will of God for all to see.

Consistent with 1 Timothy's use of household as its primary metaphor of the church, marital fidelity and well-behaved children are listed as the marks of the excellent administrator. However, in the context of the Pauline canon where a solitary life committed only to God is celebrated (see 5:9-10; 1 Corinthians 7), the phrase "husband of one wife" might be understood more specifically as husband of *only* one wife. As a signature of his commitment, the administrator of a Pauline congregation may need to pledge to remain a widower in single-minded service of God's church should his wife die.

The objection is raised, especially by feminist readers, that this phrase assumes male leadership and as such excludes women from congregational leadership. They point out that Paul later stipulates that the "truly needy" widow is "the woman of one man" (5:9) who qualifies for congregational support for the leading role she performs within the household. In this case, gender is not the relevant criterion of acceptance but rather implies fidelity to the

---

65. Collins, *Timothy and Titus*, 86.

woman's congregational service. By simple inference, the same is true here: that is, the virtue of having "one spouse" represents not gender exclusivity but adherence to the social norm of faithfulness to the household.[66]

Significantly, hospitality is a hallmark of the covenant community. A host's good treatment of guests, a well-known characteristic of early Christian communities, was expected of any household headed by a virtuous person in the ancient world (cf. Acts 16:15, 34). To care for others, especially for one's own (cf. Gal 6:1-10; 3 John 5-8) as well as strangers (cf. Luke 6:31-36), reciprocates God's kind regard for everyone (cf. 1 Tim 2:4). The administrator's own hospitality, then, inculcates this practice within the household of believers where their obedience to God aims at love toward others (cf. 1:5).

3:8-13 Profiles in Leadership: Household Servants

⁸Likewise, servants must be respectful, not duplicitous, not indulging in too much wine, not seeking dishonest gain. ⁹They should hold fast to the mystery of the faith with a clear conscience; ¹⁰let those who serve first be tested and found blameless. ¹¹Likewise, women must be proper, not slanderous, prudent, faithful in all things. ¹²Let the servants be husbands of one wife who manage children and their own household well, ¹³for those who serve well acquire for themselves a good position and much confidence within the faith that is in Christ Jesus.

In this second pericope on a congregation's leaders, Paul turns to the household's servant staff. The catalog of virtues list characteristics of the ideal servant (vv. 8, 12-13) whose faith is tested and found blameless (vv. 9-10). Their spouses must be similarly qualified to serve others as well (v. 11), since caring for members of the household is their principal responsibility.

Unlike the metaphor "administrator," the term translated "servants" (διάκονοι, *diakonoi*) belongs to a word family (διακονία/διακονέω, *diakonia/diakoneō*) that has wide currency in the Pauline corpus and generally conveys the terms of a faithful servant's vocation.[67] Paul considers all believers "διάκονοι *(diakonoi)* of the new covenant" (2 Cor 3:6), whose competence in their common life and witness is a measure of divine grace mediated by God's

---

66. Bassler admits, however, that the transference to married men of an honor given to widows in antiquity who remain single out of respect for their deceased husbands should be considered "unusual." Jouette M. Bassler, *1 Timothy, 2 Timothy, Titus* (ANTC; Nashville: Abingdon, 1996), 66. Although vague, the exclusivity of this phrase pertains to marriage and could also be read as excluding polygamy or sexual promiscuity; cf. Knight, *Pastoral Epistles*, 157-59.

67. See Marshall, *Pastoral Epistles*, 486-88.

Spirit (v. 3). Even though Paul sometimes attaches this word to specific tasks — such as carrying the Macedonian offering to the Jerusalem congregations (Rom 15:25; cf. 2 Cor 8:19-20) — he principally uses "servant" as a metaphor for a community that serves the interests of God in the "ministry *(diakonia)* of reconciliation" (2 Cor 5:18), whose members are called "servants *(diakonoi)* of Christ" (11:23). Pauline use follows the Gospel's witness to Jesus' definition of the disciple as a "servant *(diakonos)* of all" (Mark 9:35; 10:43).

The use of "servant" here, however, is as another trope of a particular kind of spiritual leadership within the sacred household. Paul's interest again is not to draft a job description for those who hold the church office of "deacon" but to profile the characteristics of the council of elders, who collectively are faithful servants to God's household for Christ's sake. Perhaps for this reason, he says that the servant-staff of the sacred household must "hold to the mystery of the faith with a clear conscience" (v. 9) — a religious practice in clear distinction from the duties of a household administrator.[68] The servants of this household must exemplify the "mystery of godliness" defined by creedal formula in v. 16 (cf. Eph 1:9; 3:4), which functions in context as a criterion of Pauline orthodoxy that elders must surely observe as caretakers of the apostolate. According to Hellenistic religious mores, beliefs linked to a "mystery" implied the use of magical formulas or esoteric teachings or an initiation ritual known only to the membership. But in Pauline teaching, the "mystery of faith" is a public statement of what is believed, which marks out the confessing community as a people belonging to Christ. In this sense, then, the servant's responsibility within the household is to represent what is confessed to be true about Christ.

The structure of the catalog, which lists four virtues before adding the "mystery" phrase, suggests that a virtuous life is a mode of conduct that is the effective yield of one who "holds to the mystery of the faith with a clear conscience." To be sure, the virtues Paul lists — "respectful, not duplicitous, not indulging in too much wine, not seeking dishonest gain" (v. 8) — are apropos of a servant's "domestic" work in the household. But the critical point should not be lost on the reader: the servant's character is forged by Christian faith for the work of securing the congregation's faith and life together.

Nothing stated would suggest that this role is subordinate to that of the administrator; rather, if both administrator and servants are roles assumed by

68. The image of "holding" (ἔχω; *echō*) onto something as ethereal as a "mystery" is striking. If the articular πίστις (*pistis*, "the faith") refers to the material content of what is confessed as true (see Marshall, *Pastoral Epistles*, 214) and its genitive relationship to τὸ μυστήριον (*to mystērion*, "the mystery") is appositional, then what is embraced by the elders qua servant are the truth claims published by Paul's gospel, then rehearsed in 3:16.

the council of elders, the elders' household chores are simply different from those performed as administrator. The servant is less interested in the community's external affairs and more attentive to the spiritual formation of believers. (Perhaps for this reason Timothy himself is called a "good *diakonos* of Christ Jesus" in 4:6.) Unlike the ideal administrator whose public persona is best summarized as "blameless" (see above), the ideal servant's profile begins with "respectful" (σεμνός, *semnos*). The related noun was used earlier to characterize the administrator's relations with his own children (v. 4), which suggests that a servant's chores are in relation to the "children" who belong to the household of faith and pertain to cultivating the faith of God's extended family.

Perhaps for this reason Paul adds that the predicate of such service is spiritual testing (v. 10), and the present tense of the imperative "let those who serve" suggests that such testing is ongoing with this service: the one funds and equips the other. Collins relates this spiritual testing to the embrace of faith's mystery "with a clear conscience."[69] If a "clear conscience" refers to one's internal moral apparatus and the source of loving relations (cf. 1:5), then moral integrity must be seen as the complement of orthodox commitment, "holding fast to the mystery of faith." This formula of Christian existence, which views faith commitment and commitment to faithfulness as an integral whole, is central to the Pauline rule of faith.

How the servant's "blameless" character is tested and assessed by the congregation is unmentioned, except that a servant's character is tested as the necessary predicate of service. The adjective I have translated "blameless" (v. 10: ἀνέγκλητος, *anenklētos*) differs from the earlier word *anepilēmptos*, which concentrates on the "blameless" character of the competent administrator (v. 2). The word used here is a legal term for innocence (cf. Acts 23:29; 25:16), which when used elsewhere in the Pauline collection carries important theological freight: the believer who continues in the faith (Col 1:22-23) is pardoned of spiritual crimes and so participates with Christ in God's coming triumph (1 Cor 1:8). The believer's faithful response to spiritual testing is the barometer of spiritual vitality.

The central problem facing the exegete of this passage is how to understand γυναῖκας ὡσαύτως σεμνάς (*gynaikas hōsautōs semnas*), which I have translated quite literally, "Likewise, women must be proper . . ." (v. 11). Because the phrase is sandwiched between two halves of a virtue list that characterizes a household's servant-staff, the reader reasonably assumes that some connection exists between these women and the men who constitute the

---

69. Collins, *1-2 Timothy*, 88.

diaconate of elders. What remains unclear is the nature of their relationship, whether vocational (they were a discrete class of female servants) or marital (they were wives of the servant-elders). Grammar alone does not decide,[70] but the decision turns on understanding the title *diakonoi* as a metaphor for the elders, all of whom would have been male in this particular social setting.[71] These women, then, most likely comprise the "one wife" of the elder-servants. Of course, in an ecclesial setting that allows both female and male elders, this instruction properly targets "spouses."

The list that defines the wives' persona is noteworthy by what virtues are mentioned, which correspond to those of their husbands. In particular the concluding phrase "faithful in all things" parallels "mystery of the faith" in the earlier list (see above; cf. 5:16). While again no description of tasks is added to this list, Paul's evident point is that faith is most effectively formed within households led by a faithful couple — perhaps the motive that lies behind v. 12, which otherwise seems out-of-place.

3:14–4:7a Profiles in Leadership: The Household of God

[14]While I hope to come soon to you, I write these instructions to you [15]so that if I am delayed you will know how you must behave as the pillar and foundation of the truth within the household of God, which is the church of the living God. [16]Indeed, great is the mystery of holy living we confess: He was

> revealed in flesh
>   and confirmed by Spirit,
> seen by angels
>   and proclaimed among the nations
> believed worldwide
>   and exalted in glory.

4[1]But in fact the Spirit says that in the latter times some will abandon the faith, adhering to deceptive spirits and doctrines of demons [2]because of the hypocrisy of deceptive liars and cauterized consciences. [3]For example, they forbid marriage and eating foods that God has created to be received with thanksgiving

---

70. For an analysis of the grammar of this phrase, see Marshall, *Pastoral Epistles*, 492-94, who takes it with most scholars as referring to female deacons.

71. Bassler follows others in providing a history-of-religions explanation for the lack of theological or religious justification for the appointment of church leaders. A pattern of virtuous life rather than theological orthodoxy is more important in a Greco-Roman world deeply suspicious of new religions; Bassler, *1 Timothy, 2 Timothy, Titus*, 71.

by those who believe and know the truth. ⁴For everything God created is good and nothing received with thanksgiving is rejected ⁵since these things are sanctified by God's word and prayer. ⁶If you teach these things to believers you will be a good servant of Christ Jesus, apprenticed according to the teachings of the faith, the good doctrine, you have followed. ⁷ᵃHave nothing to do with profane and silly myths.

This is arguably the passage of gravitas in this letter, if not of the Pastoral Epistles as a collection. Here the letter's occasion is more clearly articulated: Paul has left instructions for Timothy so that he will know what to do in his absence (3:14-15a; see above on 1:3). Moreover, Timothy's pivotal role in forming Christian congregations as Paul's substitute is set out — again in household metaphors: Timothy is "the pillar and foundation of the truth within the household of God" (see the comment on 3:15b below). The formulation of this truth is expressed in an elegant Christological creed (v. 16), which is the lynchpin between the descriptions of Timothy as the household's truth-provider and of those apostates whose "doctrines of demons" pose a threat to believers (4:1-5), whom Timothy targets for instruction according to the "good doctrine" of Pauline faith (vv. 6-7a). In this way, "the church of the living God" (3:15c) is secured by the truth of the gospel.

Perhaps the abruptness of Paul's move to more personal instructions and mention of an apostolic house-call suggest its importance to the letter's recipient. In any case, at last Paul makes clear his central metaphor for "the church of the living God": believers are "the household of God" (οἶκος θεοῦ, *oikos theou*) in the world. The instructions given in this letter, then, forge the formation of a sacred household in a way that circumscribes its social relationships and religious practices as appropriate for those who think of themselves as members of God's family. The church is a sanctified place, and so even its mundane routines are consecrated by "God's word and prayer" (4:5). God rather than any one person is the household's actual *paterfamilias*. This passage does not break the flow of the chapter's definition of leadership as some suppose but rather clarifies the character of congregational leadership within the bounds of the sacred household and in functional terms appropriate to a household rather than by gender or social class. In particular Timothy's role is now reimagined as the house's "pillar and foundation" (3:15); his role is to uphold "the truth" of the living God in a manner that dispels the teaching of those who "adhere to deceptive spirits and doctrines of demons" (4:1).

This move to a more religious basis for leadership is especially important since the prior discussion of the household's administrator and servant-staff — the so-called "bishop" and "deacons" — is circumscribed by appeal to personal virtue rather than to any special religious role or sacred vocation. This omission has led modern critics to imagine the presence of the same kind of hostility that faced the Paul of Acts in Athens, where he was taken into custody because of the controversy provoked by his claims for a "new" religion (Acts 17:16-34). That is, in response to the suspicions among outsiders that Christianity would not be good for society, Paul presents Timothy with catalogs of virtue to use as criteria for appointing church leaders, in part to persuade the suspicious of the good intentions of this new religion that might actually improve the social order. It should be said that Luke fashions a Socratic Paul whose apologia presents not himself as a man of virtue but rather a Christian gospel that is adaptable to Athenian religious sentiment. The subtext of Paul's shift of emphasis from social virtue to religious practices at this point in his instructions to Timothy may make a similar point.

Because Paul purposes to instruct his young protégé in the manner of his religious practices and public life befitting the spiritual director of God's sacred family (cf. 1:18), the importance of his passing mention of a personal visit lies well beyond the routines of polite discourse. In Pauline letters, references to scheduled visits are vested with rhetorical importance: they promise "apostolic" house-calls laden with official importance.[72] Whether the promise is fictive or real, the very idea of an imminent visit implies the exercise of apostolic authority to fortify spiritual resolve (Rom 1:10-11; 15:20-22; 2 Cor 13:1-2) or to check on spiritual progress (1 Cor 16:3-7; 1 Thess 2:17–3:5; Phlm 22). Such apostolic visitations are anticipated following a protracted delay (3:15a), when letters become suitable substitutes for Paul's personal presence — an interim measure that seeks to address problems until the apostle can come to handle them in person. Read as a literary convention of Pauline letters, this reference to a personal visit suggests an approach to 1 Timothy as a textual substitute for the authoritative apostle that gives important instructions to carry out during his absence.[73] I would argue that this conception guides a canonical approach to this material as well (see the Introduction).

The reader knows that Paul has delegated to Timothy the responsibility

---

72. The classic study of this motif is Funk, "Apostolic Parousia."

73. Paul may well understand the difficulty of directing a congregation's theological formation at a distance and so devotes considerable space to defining the leadership of a congregation no longer under his immediate care. For example, he may have even imagined the prospect of awkward relations between young Timothy and certain women because of their social status (2:9-15) or age (5:1-16) and for this reason provides him more direction in the absence of his personal mentoring.

of organizing the congregation in Ephesus according to his instructions. But the relationship between delegate and congregation must be more adequately defined. Rather than using a metaphor of leadership related to particular household chores as he has for the elders, Paul defines Timothy in architectural metaphors: Timothy is responsible for the very structure of the *oikos* as its "pillar (στῦλος, *stylos*) and foundation (ἑδραίωμα, *hedraiōma*) of the truth" (3:15a).[74]

This phrase reminds the reader of the similar way Paul refers to "James, Cephas, and John" as "the reputed pillars (στῦλοι, *styloi*)" of the Jewish church (Gal 2:9). In the context of Galatians, the "pillars" metaphor conveys a sense of importance granted to these three leaders for deciding the future of the church's mission to the circumcised (Gal. 2:7; cf. Eph 2:19-22). In the context here, some have argued that the architecture images of 3:15 — house, pillar, and foundation — reflect the pagan temples of the various Ephesian deities, against which Paul posits the church as the actual dwelling place of the one God. Possibly so, especially if the repetition of *styloi* recalls Paul's mission to the uncircumcised. More likely, however, "pillar and foundation of the truth" refers specifically to Timothy, not to the church (as per Origen) or its magisterium (as per Calvin), and implies his role in the congregation as representative and guardian of the Pauline apostolate and the truth claims of Paul's gospel. In this regard, the text may well allude to the OT idea of Israel as God's "household" and to Timothy's performance of a role analogous to Moses' within Israel (Num 12:6-8; Deut 23:2-4; 31:30): that of cultivating the people's understanding of God and of God's law to insure their covenant-keeping and so their divine blessing (e.g., Deuteronomy 4–6).

If Timothy's Moses-like role is that of the authorized agent of the church's theological formation, then the puzzling placement of the Christological confession here (3:16) now makes perfect sense: it summarizes the truth found at the epicenter of the Pauline gospel. In using this verse against the Arian heretic Eunomius, Gregory of Nyssa wrote that this confession contains "all the declarations which the heralds of the faith are prone to

---

74. Johnson argues that the referent of the phrase "pillar and foundation of the truth" is "how one ought to behave" rather than the more natural "the church of the living God" — a delayed appositional phrase, then, similar to what the reader encounters in 1:7; Johnson, *First and Second Letters to Timothy*, 231-32. While we agree with Johnson that people more than place make better sense of the "pillar and foundation of the truth" metaphor in that people and not places transmit and uphold the truth, we do not agree that the referent of this metaphor is the entire congregation. The text addresses Timothy and not the congregation, and in this broader setting concerning leadership the delayed apposition seems more likely to be Timothy as the congregation's "pillar" whose instruction of the truth safeguards the congregation's faith and public conduct.

make. By these is increased the marvelous character of him who manifested the super-abundance of his power by means external to his own nature" (*Against Eunomius* 5.3).

The formula "great is the mystery of holy living (εὐσέβεια, *eusebeia*)" introduces an agreed-on confession of the pious.[75] While it is plausible to think that the core Pauline beliefs about Christ comprise the revelation of a "great mystery" (so Eph 3:3-4), in what way are they constitutive of a holy life? And what does this phrase suggest of Timothy's identification as the congregation's pillar and foundation? Even to hear the echo of *4 Maccabees* (6:31; 7:16; 16:1) in the combination of *eusebeia* with ὁμολογουμένως (*homologoumenōs*, "agreed") as Hanson does, perhaps to defend a "rational piety" against the asceticism mentioned in the next pericope, does not get one very far.[76] M. D'Angelo has recently and more helpfully demonstrated that moral philosophers since Plato considered *eusebeia* the Roman virtue that best combined religious observance with "family values." That is, the secular ideal of "holy living" presumed a profound devotion to one's family heritage, which was often expressed publicly by one's religious devotion to the deities and was therefore a principal motive of one's religious practices. The pious person was religious for the sake of the family household's reputation.[77]

This ideal may lie in the background of Paul's use here in locating Timothy's ministry within the household of God, where two properties of Christian existence, a vital piety and sound doctrine, are mutually inclusive. Timothy's religious practices, including his public profession of faith, indicate his piety, which not only upholds the sacred household as its "foundation of truth" but also personifies a commitment to the Pauline legacy.

Paul often adorns his letters with confessions of faith, although rarely one as theologically robust as this one (e.g., Rom 1:3-4; 16:25-27; 1 Cor 15:3-7; Phil 2:6-11; Col 1:15-20). In most cases, the lyrical line reminds the reader of what is already known and believed. If so, we may assume that the literary form and Christological content of this confession allude to a well-known verse in a Pauline catechism or book of worship. Most scholars now suspect that Paul's use of preformed creeds and hymns was intended to remind readers of their beliefs in order to prop up a letter's response to some crisis. It follows that this confession's opening formula cues the reader to what all believ-

---

75. Cf. Collins, *Timothy and Titus*, 106-7.

76. Cf. Anthony T. Hanson, *The Pastoral Epistles: Based on the Revised Standard Version* (NCB; Grand Rapids: Eerdmans, 1982), 83-84.

77. Mary R. D'Angelo, "*Eusebeia*: Roman Imperial Family Values and the Sexual Politics of 4 Maccabees and the PE," *BibInt* 11 (2003): 139-65.

1 Timothy 3:14–4:7a

ers agree by common confession is "the good doctrine" Timothy is charged to teach them (4:6) as the church's "pillar and foundation."

I doubt that the hymn's Christological subject matter envisages the distinction made by modern criticism between an existential act of trust in Jesus and a later institutionalized set of core beliefs about Jesus — the former more true of the real Paul and the latter more true of his later followers. No constructive distinction need exist between these two kinds of "faith." To profess faith in Christ is to affirm the church's core beliefs about his messianic death and his status as creation's risen Lord. To come to knowledge of the truth about Christ (2:4-6) is synonymous with the act of converting to Christ.

The modern history of this confession's reception within the academy often attends to its literary cues: the discrete lines of identical length, the similar structure of each line, the introduction by a pronoun without a clear antecedent, and an eschatological vocabulary different from that of the rest of the letter, all of which suggest that the text had an earlier life of its own. In this case, the text's confessional form is more formally cued by the introductory *homologoumenōs* and an economy of expression typical of an oft-cited passage used in worship or catechism. Each of six parallel lines begins with a passive aorist verb followed by a dative noun. Also typical is the transition from worshipful invocative to confessed creed, when the implied antecedent of a relative pronoun is the one who is confessed. In this case, the subject matter implies that the antecedent is Christ Jesus, and the creedal expression is doxological and reflects the attitude and tenor of a worshiper.

The confession's design, along with its placement at the letter's pivot point, envisages its import for the letter's recipient. The six lines in three pairs make three succinct claims about the risen Jesus cast in spatial rather than temporal images. Each pair envisages a dynamic interplay between heaven and earth, between what angels witness — that which remains an invisible "mystery" — and what the church witnesses — that which defines "the faith" (cf. v. 9). That is, the subject matter of the congregation's professed beliefs about the risen Christ is confirmed by a second congregation of heavenly witnesses, whose speech resounds throughout all creation, on earth and in heaven, in praise that the Creator's redemptive purpose is brought to realization by the Christ event. And this is the central truth claim that Timothy is charged to uphold (v. 14).

"Revealed in flesh and confirmed by Spirit." The first couplet introduces the church's most critical belief about Jesus, the affirmation of his divine self-presentation in human existence. It is not fully expounded according to the interests of modern historians who attempt to reconstruct the life of Jesus; rather, this is an expression of faith that his public life is nothing other than the presentation of God's redemptive purpose in history (cf. 2:5-6). The motive is not primarily to advance an incarnational Christology with its full array of epistemic claims as the ancient Fathers insisted but is messianic and so consonant with the soteriological claims of this letter (see 1:15). The heavenly complement of this belief is that his messianic mission is confirmed by the Spirit at his resurrection (cf. Rom 1:4; Acts 2:36). In fact, Collins contends that the revelation of Jesus to which this initial parallelism refers is the post-Easter manifestation of the risen Jesus.[78] The odd use here of δικαιοῦν *(dikaioun)*, which I have translated "confirmed," is similar to Paul's use of this same verb in 1 Cor 6:11 in reference to the authenticating witness of "the Spirit of our God." Accordingly, I take it that the first line refers to the whole of Jesus' public mission and not just his post-Easter visitations, which is then validated as messianic by the Spirit who mediated God's power in raising him back to life according to Pauline teaching.

"Seen by angels and proclaimed among the nations." The second couplet reverses the spatial interplay by beginning with a belief about the witness of angels. My translation of ἄγγελοι *(angeloi)* as heavenly "angels" (rather than as human "messengers") preserves the heaven-earth interplay of the creed. But why an interest in angels? In the Pauline canon a happy note is sounded: an angelic host welcomes the risen Son of God Messiah back into its heavenly embrace (Phil 2:9-11; cf. Rev 12:5-12); and I suspect that the creed links the first two parallelisms by maintaining the resurrection subtext of the previous line. That is, "seen by angels" affirms the gospel's witness to the angelic pronouncement of the Lord's resurrection (Matt 28:5-7) and is the assumed predicate of the apostolic proclamation of the risen Jesus among the nations (Matt 28:16-20).

"Believed worldwide and exalted in glory." This final couplet commends what Paul has already professed, that God wills all people saved (2:4-6) — a redemptive plan that is embraced on earth by those who believe in Christ, even as it is demonstrably realized in the heavenly exaltation of their risen Lord (Phil 2:5-11). While linking the second line of the preceding couplet, "proclaimed among the nations," with the first line of this one, "believed worldwide," makes perfect sense, the logical connection of earth and heaven in this couplet interplay is not immediately clear. I doubt the idea that the doxology's final line is predicated on a prior reading of Luke, as some scholars

---

78. Collins, *Timothy and Titus*, 108-9. Collins takes the parallel line as an allusion to Isa 53:11 so that the Spirit's "vindication" (δικαίουν, *dikaioun*) of Christ confirms that he is the "Righteous One" (δίκαιον, *dikaion*) of Isaiah's Servant oracle, which is an important "proof-from-prophecy" in the church's apologia for Jesus' messianic identity.

suggest, reading this as a nod to the Lord's ascension as the ultimate proof of his resurrection (so Luke 24:51-54; Acts 1:3-10). The accent is Pauline and expresses Jesus' heavenly exaltation as creation's Lord and thus the utter logic of the church's trust in him and proclamation of him in the world.[79]

Most commentators suggest that 4:1 marks a discrete break in the letter's design. But the connecting δέ *(de)* is best understood as introducing a contrast between Timothy's role in caretaking the "mystery of holy living" as the congregation's "pillar and foundation of the truth" and those who seek to subvert this truth with "doctrines of demons." The interplay of earthly and heavenly witnesses to Christ (3:16) forms an embodied manner of Christian discipleship that inclines believers to receive material goods, such as food or marriage, with thanksgiving to their heavenly God (cf. Acts 17:24-25).

There have been vague references to the manner and motive of teachers of "divergent doctrine" who compromise the Christian formation of Timothy's congregation (1:3-7, 19-20). Paul now condemns what they teach as characteristic of the "latter times" (see below on 2 Tim 3:1-9). His invective echoes Jesus' apocalypse (Matthew 24, Mark 13, and Luke 21), which also predicts the advent of false prophets who seek to subvert Israel's preparation for its Messiah (2 Tim 3:1-9), even as their arrival ironically heralds the imminent triumph of God, which will disprove their teaching and vindicate the gospel. Qumran's *Rule of the Community* predicts that "due to the Angel of Darkness all the children of righteousness will stray, and all their sin, their iniquities, their failings and their deceitful works will be under his rule in compliance with the mysteries of God" (1QS 3:21b-23a). Other Jewish literature of the day, framed by the images of an imminent apocalypse, speak of "deceitful spirits" set loose on God's people to turn their minds away from God (*Testament of Reuben* 2.1-2; *Testament of Judah* 14.8; 20). In particular, Matthew's Gospel characterizes those who lead the Jewish opposition against Jesus as "hypocritical" (Matt 6:2, 16; 7:5; 22:18; 23:13-29; 24:51). Paul's polemic against the false teachers reflects the connection of personal character with one's capacity to receive and transmit truth, which was fundamental in the moral literature of the day.

The powerful trope "doctrines of demons" recasts the earlier expression, "divergent doctrine" (1:3), in terms of a creation-denying asceticism that evidently sets aside marriage and certain foods. Paul's correction of this falsehood appears to follow naturally from the letter's use of "household" as metaphorical of the Christian congregation. In this regard, the quality of a faithful marriage as a credential of spiritual leadership or childbearing as the distinc-

---

79. See Marshall, *Pastoral Epistles*, 528-29.

tive mark of God's keen interest in a woman's salvation is of a piece with this household metaphor. Any opposition to marriage (and so to childbearing) or to certain foods, especially if received with thankful responses to the Creator's common grace, may signal teaching that subverts not only the sacred household's covenant with God but also its mission in the world.

Even more central to this letter's theological vision is the belief that faithful familial relationships instantiate a Pauline understanding of the *oikonomia theou*. Interactions among men and women, whether in public or at home, are regulated by patterns of loving relationships that reflect God's providential care of the created order. The claim that the church is a sacred household, organized by divine agency for God's glory, springs from the believer's "good conscience" cultivated by faith in the glorious gospel (1:5, 10-11) and subverted by those who reject a "good conscience" (1:19-20). Recalling these earlier passages glosses the characterization of the opponents as those who think with "cauterized consciences" (4:2) and so with beliefs that oppose the Pauline gospel (1:10-11) and the holy mystery confessed by God's church (3:15-16).

Given the vague cast of Paul's invective, however, scholars have found it difficult to place these opponents or their "doctrines of demons" anywhere on the religious map of earliest Christianity. Those who date the composition quite late identify these ascetic practices with mid-second-century Gnostic movements of the kind Irenaeus refutes in *Against Heresies*. Irenaeus writes, for example, that Gnostics "assert that marriage . . . is from Satan" (1.24.2) and that "some among them have introduced abstinence from animal food, thus proving they are ungrateful to God who created all things" (1.28.1).

Even if 1 Timothy is dated to the second century on other grounds, such a date is unnecessary in order to make sense of the text's plain meaning. Not only does Jesus commend a concern for social purity, reading 1 Timothy in its canonical setting and in relationship with Acts elaborates this sense. The James of Acts, for example, corrects Peter's myopic commentary on Cornelius's conversion by arguing that the purity practices (Acts 15:20) that complement a "purity of the heart by faith" (15:9) are the *sine qua non* of Christian fellowship. According to Acts, the leaders of the church gathered in Jerusalem to discuss issues of table fellowship. James in particular was concerned that the initiation of repentant Gentiles into the Diaspora church, most of whom were not Jewish proselytes and converted from paganism to Jesus, might threaten the Jewish legacy of the faith. Appealing to Israel's Scripture, his solution, repeated three times in Acts for rhetorical effect (15:20, 29; 21:25), concerns food and sex. Indeed, religious practices related to these things often defined the sometimes difficult social relations between repentant Jews and Gentiles. Perhaps Paul's harsh words about the "hypocrisy of liars" and his appeal to God's good creation (4:4) and to the alternate religious practices of "the word of God and prayer" (v. 5) have a similar setting in mind, one in which a world-denying asceticism is mandated by false teachers for converts who have recently left their pagan religions for membership in God's household (see above). James follows the pattern of Jesus, who allows for (but does not require) a celibate lifestyle as a property of a disciple's kingdom vocation (Matt 19:12) and considers all foods kosher (Mark 7:19).

Even Paul's constant rumination on food and human sexuality in his letters (e.g., Romans 14; 1 Corinthians 5–7, 8–11; 1 Thess 4:3-6) suggests a keen interest in these topics of his Gentile mission, even if it is in response to questions of his faithfulness to Scripture raised by his Jewish opponents. Although it is not clear from 1 Timothy and is perhaps assumed by it, Pauline teaching supports marriage (e.g., 1 Corinthians 7) and a normal diet (e.g., Romans 14) as indeterminate of the believer's purity before God in Christ. More critically, Paul recognized that disagreements over marital and dietary practices are inherently divisive and for this reason should be of principal concern for leaders of a congregation (1 Corinthians 5–12; cf. Acts 21:25 in narrative context).

The thankful reception of material creations such as good food or of healthy social conventions such as a covenant-keeping marriage is sanctified for holy outcomes by the church through "God's word and prayer [of thanksgiving]" (4:4-5). In this setting the consecrating agent is not the Holy Spirit but the holy household. Even these mundane activities carry religious importance for believers, especially when contrasted with non-Christian "households" whose use of food (or not) during religious rituals framed a different natural theology. In continuity with Jewish tradition table fellowship is consecrated for Christians by prayers of thanksgiving that recall the biblical story of creation in which "God's word" brings forth a creation (Gen 1:31) in which food (Gen 1:29-30) and marriage (Gen 1:28) are given strategic roles that serve the Creator's way of stewarding the world.

The subsequent conditional in 4:6-7a continues, I think, from Paul's correction of a creation-denying Christianity rather than serving as an introduction to a personal charge that follows in 4:7b-16. Ταῦτα (*tauta*, "these things") is frequently used in this letter (3:14; 4:6, 11, 15; 5:7, 21; 6:2, 11), but without clear indication of its referent. Here a case could be made that "these things" anticipate what comes next and in particular the canonical saying in 4:10. I think it more plainly concludes the implied contrast between those teachers who seek to influence a sacred household with "doctrines of demons" and Timothy, whose instruction follows the "healthy doctrine" of the Pauline legacy appropriate to his vocation as the household's "pillar and foundation of the truth" (3:15).

The adjective γραώδης *(graōdēs)*, which I translate "silly," literally refers to "old women," which some ancient philosophers employed as a trope for any person who promulgates useless tales and household remedies instead of profitable teaching. While sexist and derogatory at face value, this word is typically used in antiquity as a non-literal rhetorical ploy to denigrate "profane and silly myths" no matter the gender of one's intellectual rivals. Lucian, for example, used the expression against other schools of philosophy, calling their arguments "stories consisting of old wives' *(graōdēs)* fables" (*Philopseudes* 9).

Here Paul probably has in mind those mentioned in the preceding verses and any who oppose Pauline rule of faith and whose teaching leads to a lifestyle contrary to God's redemptive purposes. Later he criticizes those "old women" who spend their days "saying things they shouldn't" (5:13) rather than nurturing the congregation "with teachings of the faith" (4:6). In any case, Paul does not mention these *graōdēs* as serious intellectual rivals to "good doctrine," and his exhortation to "have nothing to do with" them is probably more practical than theological: Timothy should spend his time teaching the gospel rather than defending its truth against "profane and silly myths."

4:7b-16 Paul Charges Timothy to Serve Only Christ

⁷ᵇTrain yourself for holy living. ⁸While physical training has some value, holy living has value for everything, holding promise for both this life and the life to come. ⁹This teaching is a core belief and worthy of unqualified acceptance ¹⁰(for it is the aim of our work and struggle): "Our hope is set on the living God, who is the Savior of all people, especially those who believe." ¹¹Command compliance to these instructions and teach. ¹²Let no one despise your youth, but until I arrive set a pattern for believers in speech, in public conduct, in love, in faith, in purity. ¹³Pay attention to public reading, preaching, and teaching. ¹⁴Do not neglect the spiritual gift in you, which was given to you through prophecy with the laying on of hands by the council of elders. ¹⁵Practice these things; live by them so that your progress may be observed by all. ¹⁶Tend to yourself and to your teaching; for by doing this you will save both yourself and your auditors.

After an interlude that sounds an apocalyptic warning about apostate interlopers, Paul returns to practical instructions to guide the professional formation of his successor. Having already encouraged Timothy to ground his ministry in "good doctrine" (4:6-7a), Paul turns now to portray the sort of person who can effectively pastor those under his care. The overarching exhortation regarding the ultimate value of a holy life (vv. 7b-8) is underwritten by a canonical saying that clarifies its eschatological benefit (vv. 9-10, cf. vv. 15-16). The pattern of holiness commended by Paul includes both personal virtues (v. 12) and vocational practices (vv. 13-14). Timothy is to live in a holy manner that is observed by all (v. 15) so that the community may learn by his example of faithfulness what is necessary for salvation (v. 16).

The pericope opens with an exhortation to follow the habits of a well-trained athlete: "train yourself for holy living" (v. 7b; cf. 2 Tim 2:5). The word for training is γυμνάζω *(gymnazō)*, from which "gymnasium" derives, and envisages the practices and habits that form physical self-control. Paul, of course, is interested that Timothy develop spiritual self-control (cf. 2 Tim 1:7), which is decisive in securing his and his congregation's future with God (4:16).

"Holy living" translates the most distinctive catchword for Christian existence in the Pastoral Epistles, εὐσέβεια *(eusebeia)*, and is used to characterize both the ideal congregation (2:2) and those who provide for its spiritual leadership (6:3, 5-6, 11) by adhering to a standard set out preeminently by Christ Jesus (so 3:16; cf. 3:9) and his apostle (cf. 2:7; 1:16). Admittedly, the semantic field of *eusebeia* is quite fluid and depends on its compositional context. Its history of interpretation picks up on this multivalence, and the various translations reflect both its more academic sense of "religious instruction"[80] and, from Calvin and others, the act of "spiritual worship" that produces "purity of conscience."[81] As mentioned earlier (see 3:16), *eusebeia* is not used elsewhere in the Pauline canon,[82] even though it was widely used in the synagogues of the Diaspora, where Paul received his earliest religious training. He likely is trading on a well-known belief in his world that religious manners are important within the general population — much like his earlier reference to a woman's "modesty" (cf. 2:9-15) or a manager's "blamelessness" (cf. 3:2). Epictetus, for instance, would agree with Paul's sentiment: "In piety *(eusebeia)* toward the gods I would have you know the chief element is this: to have right opinions about them — that they exist and administer the universe well and fairly — and to have set yourself to obey them and to submit to ev-

---

80. For example, Basil writes of a "school of righteousness" that leads believers gradually into the truth beginning with "elementary lessons suited for our limited intelligence." *OHS* 56.

81. Calvin, *Epistles to Timothy*, 61.

82. See Collins's excursus on *eusebeia*, especially for its use as a religious virtue in the Greco-Roman world. It is a catchword for civil religion, in which one's personal piety includes practices that are of benefit for one's household and society as a whole (*1 and Timothy and Titus*, 122-26). Also Towner, *Letters to Timothy and Titus*, 171-75, who relates the word to Jewish thought.

erything that happens, and to follow it freely in the belief that it is being fulfilled by the highest powers" (*Enchiridion* 31). While knowing the public regard of the pious person in his world, Paul surely understands that the source of personal rectitude is the inward effect of God's righteous-producing grace (cf. 1:12-16).

The combination of personal discipline and holy living targets the coming age. Not only does holy living benefit "everything" (i.e., internal and external things), its effect transcends time and extends into the coming age (v. 9). Although what "promise" is in mind is undefined here, in the context of the Pauline corpus it is likely the blessing promised to Abraham, that of a people and a place (Gen 12:1-3; cf. Rom 4:13-20; Gal 3:14-29), which is now realized for the community of believers baptized into Christ for the coming age (Rom 4:17).

Paul supports his exhortation for holy living by an appeal to a canonical saying (vv. 9-10) that summarizes his theological legacy for his successors (see also 1:15; 3:1a). Most commentators agree that these five sayings scattered across the Pastoral Epistles formulate a Pauline way of salvation. The phrase "this teaching is a core belief" is therefore read as an introduction to what follows rather than concluding the preceding proverb about the value of "holy living." In fact, the plain sense of the saying makes better sense of Paul's concluding concern that Timothy "will save both yourself and your auditors" (v. 16b). Perhaps no other text in the Pastorals more clearly connects the expectation of future salvation with the present performance of one's sacred calling. Sharply put, should Timothy neglect "the spiritual gift in you" (v. 14), which includes the practices of a holy life (vv. 12, 15) and the Bible practices delegated to him (vv. 13, 16a), he would also neglect a "hope set on the living God," and the personal cost of doing so would be eternal.

This pointed and personal definition of salvation's future may explain Paul's parenthetical elaboration of the introductory formula, which anticipates that "struggle" accompanies the hard "work" of spiritual discipline (v. 10a; cf. v. 7b). This same pairing of "work and struggle" is frequently used in the Pauline corpus to characterize an apostle's missionary labor (cf. Rom 16:6, 12; 1 Cor 16:16; 1 Thess 5:12; Col 1:29), and that is the sense here: the truth of the canonical saying is confirmed by the sacrifice motivated by it. Similarly, Epictetus compares the human struggle in becoming morally excellent with an athletic contest — with a long race or hard-fought wrestling match (*Discourses* 3.25.3) in which it is necessary for the athlete to fix his attention on its victorious completion. The "work and struggle" of ministry, analogous to the hard work required of physical discipline, is endured by its promissory note: the victory of salvation in this life and for the life to come.

Such a definition, of course, is predicated on one's belief in a particular kind of God: "the living God, who is the Savior of all people" (v. 10b; cf. 2:3-4). The combination of "living God" and "Savior" underwrites a core Pauline belief that God enlivens "especially those who believe" as the promissory note for the life to come. Even though the universal reach of God's benefaction to "all people" continues an important theme of this letter (see 2:3-4; cf. 4:4), the use of the superlative, "especially" (μάλιστα, *malista*), restricts the *present* experience of God's promised salvation to those who have believed "the teachings of the faith" (4:6). Towner rightly concludes "there is no division here based on limited and unlimited atonement, and no need to posit two shades of meaning for the term 'Savior.'"[83] The plain sense of this core belief is that God has offered salvation to everyone, but not everyone has embraced it, since divine grace does not coerce an unwilling acceptance of the gospel.

The portrait of youthful Timothy is introduced by Paul's cautionary exhortation: "let no one look down on your youth" (v. 12a; cf. 1 Cor 16:10-11). In this light, the prior instruction to "command compliance to these instructions and teach" suggests that Timothy's curriculum offers more than catechesis into Pauline doctrine and includes a demythologizing of cultural biases that may have engendered age discrimination. To be sure, Timothy's precise age cannot be determined, but perhaps his youthfulness refers to a lack of work experience, especially when compared to the absent Paul or even to the elders of the congregation. The Roman world considered apprenticeship and field experience requirements of mature instruction; rather than a reference to chronological age, Paul's exhortation may reflect concern for an incomplete or inadequate résumé for a congregational leader. The earlier catalogs of virtues were focused on what sort of person leads a sacred household rather than on expertise gained from experience, but even they assumed a level of real-world experience, since virtue is not formed in a vacuum. In any case, the clipped allusion to a future apostolic visit (v. 12a) doubtless assumes that Paul's spiritual authority extends to the congregation even when he is absent, and on this basis Paul will examine the congregation's response to Timothy and his instruction when he is present (see above on 3:14-15a).

To insure a good visit, then, Paul sets out a series of five terms for well-regarded credentials that transcend age and job experience (v. 12): in his (1) public speaking and (2) social manners, Timothy should demonstrate a virtuous life consisting of the triad of (3) faith, (4) love, and (5) purity, the last probably sexual (cf. 5:11-15). As with most catalogs of virtues in the Pauline

---

83. Towner, *Letters to Timothy and Titus*, 312.

corpus, this one was no doubt created with the letter's recipient in mind, not necessarily because Timothy had a problem with any of these moral practices but because, taken together, they supply the *conditio sine qua non* of effective ministry.

A second triad — reading, preaching, and teaching (v. 13) — catalogs standard worship practices that are instrumental in cultivating a Jewish way of life (cf. 2 Tim 1:5; Acts 16:1-5). Rather than finding opponents hidden behind these instructions, we should see that these two triads together provide a thick definition of the congregation's spiritual leader: the worship practices (v. 13) of the virtuous leader (v. 12) will have a maximal effect in shaping the saving faith of the worshiping community (v. 16).

Not only the congregation's but Timothy's recognition of his spiritual authority is predicated on personal and public experiences of χαρισμάτα (*charismata*), which according to Pauline teaching are supernaturally apportioned by the Spirit according to the congregation's need and for the common good (1 Corinthians 12). Timothy knows that he has such a gift because prophecy (or revelatory speech) confirmed the particular charism that is "in you" (ἐν σοί, *en soi*, 4:14a; cf. 2 Tim 1:6-7). Nowhere is the nature of Timothy's gift defined, but the reader should assume a logical connection, perhaps even causal, between the different parts of this paraenetic unit. In this sense, the spiritual gift enables the performance of the prior worship practices.[84]

The congregation's acceptance of Timothy's divine authorization, however, is made public by a liturgical gesture, the imposition of hands. This gesture by the congregation's elders is not the effective means of Timothy's ordination (cf. 2 Tim 1:6: "*through* the laying on of *my* hands"). Rather, in this particular case, "*with* the laying on of hands" (μετὰ ἐπιθέσεως τῶν χειρῶν, *meta epitheseōs tōn cheirōn*) indicates that the elders provide public testimony to the prophecy's expected fulfillment (v. 14b; cf. Acts 9:17-18; 13:1-3). Especially in an apostolate shaped by Jewish tradition (cf. 2 Tim 1:3), the responsibility of the most revered (and typically most senior) group of leading men would include public recognition of those charged with administering the congregation's affairs — reminiscent of Moses laying his hands on Joshua as symbolic of the transfer of authority to his successor (Num 27:18-23; Deut 34:9; Acts 6:6; 13:3). The "presbytery" (*presbyteroi*, "council of elders") corre-

---

84. If Acts introduces and 1 Corinthians 12 glosses this text within its canonical setting, readers should assume that the spiritual gift was given to Timothy by the Holy Spirit (see 2 Tim 1:6-7). The connection between the spiritual gift (v. 14) and worship practices (v. 13) is similar to the effect of the Spirit's reception especially in Acts where Spirit-filling enables the community's leaders to interpret Scripture, preach, and teach others with greater skill and more positive effect; now see John R. Levison, *Filled with the Spirit* (Grand Rapids: Eerdmans, 2009), 347-65.

sponds to the *gerousia* of the synagogue, which made appointments within the congregation.[85]

The final piece of Timothy's spiritual résumé gathers evidence of his moral progress (v. 15). Paul's exhortation to "practice these things" (ταῦτα μελέτα, *tauta meleta*) reflects his prior instruction that Timothy "not neglect" (μὴ ἀμέλει, *mē amelei*) his spiritual charism. Consistent with the shape of Pauline paraenesis, the formulation of Christian character includes doing certain things and not doing others. Relevant evidence of progress concerns what is observable by others, including outsiders as well as insiders (cf. 3:7). Moral practice (rather than inward virtue) is a hallmark of Stoic philosophy, following Aristotle, for whom inward virtue is more like a habit developed in a person only over time by a routine of moral practices. In his famous essay, "On Progress in Virtue" (*Moralia* 75b-86a) Plutarch extols the virtue of the person who stands up under his own scrutiny rather than being disdainful of himself as an incompetent "witness" (81a), which may help one appreciate Paul's concluding charge for Timothy to "tend to yourself and to your teaching" (v. 16a).

The concluding reminder is variously understood. Its plain sense clarifies the eschatological significance of Paul's prior exhortation: Timothy's future salvation from God's future judgment depends on careful exercise of his charismatic leadership within the congregation (cf. Jas 3:1). To this point in the letter, Paul repeatedly confesses God as "our Savior" and salvation as realized according to God's desire and because of Christ's death (1:15; 2:4). In what sense, then, is Timothy responsible for his and his congregation's (or, even more inclusively, all his auditors') salvation? To posit a human agent of salvation resonates with Paul, who mentions in other letters the believer's responsibility for self-examination (e.g., 2 Cor 13:5; 1 Cor 11:27-32) and the dire consequence of failing to pass the test, which extends even to the apostle himself (1 Cor 9:27). Moreover, the covenant-keeping shape of a community's salvation forces a distinction between the divine source of humanity's salvation and its future realization, which is based on works (cf. Rom 2:6-11; 2 Cor 5:10). Paul's exhortation to Timothy assumes that it is also human performance that complements divine grace that brings the living God's redemptive plan and so "our hope" to realization (4:10; cf. 1 Cor 9:22; 10:32-33).

What is distinctive and perhaps confusing about this text when read within the Pauline canon is not its general conception of salvation, especially the importance of human agency, since Paul teaches elsewhere that the believer is responsible to "work out" her salvation in God's company and the

---

85. Johnson, *First and Second Letters to Timothy*, 253.

fellowship of believers (Phil 2:12-13; 2 Tim 4:1-7). Rather, the distinguishing feature of this text is that the believer's cooperation with God's saving grace aligns with the practices of Timothy's ordination (4:14). This more vocational (rather than moral or religious) formulation of human agency is an important elaboration of Pauline soteriology and sets the stage for 2 Timothy, where this idea is given rich texture, especially by the worship practices and holy persona of the faithful tradent, whose responsibility is to safeguard and transmit the memory and message of the Pauline apostolate. Given the connection between Timothy's Scripture (2 Tim 3:15-17) and his memory of Paul (2 Tim 3:10-14; cf. 2 Pet 3:15-16), by the time the Pastoral Epistles are added to complete the Pauline canon late in the second century, the public reading, preaching, and teaching of Scripture by faithful successors would surely have included this sacred deposit of Pauline letters.[86]

5:1-16 Caring for Widows

¹Do not rebuke an older man harshly. Encourage him as though he were your father, younger men as though brothers, ²older women as though mothers, and younger women as though sisters, with complete purity.

³Care for widows who are truly needy. ⁴But if a particular widow has children or a relative, they should first learn to practice their piety by taking care of their own household and so repay their parents, for this pleases God. ⁵If truly needy and completely on her own, the widow puts her hope in God and pleads and prays continually night and day. ⁶But the one who lives extravagantly dies even though alive. ⁷Instruct these things so that they will be blameless. ⁸Especially if someone does not care for a member of their household, he repudiates the faith and is worse than an unbeliever.

⁹Enroll a widow older than sixty, wife of one husband, ¹⁰with a reputation for good works — if she has raised children, if she has practiced hospitality, if she has washed the feet of believers, if she has helped those in difficult times, if she is accompanied by all kinds of good works. ¹¹But decline (to enroll) younger widows, for when they are distracted from Christ and choose to marry, ¹²judgment results because they invalidate the prior confession of faith. ¹³Moreover, by going from house to house they learn laziness, and not only laziness but how to gossip and meddle, saying things they shouldn't. ¹⁴Therefore, I prefer that younger widows marry, raise children, keep house, to give the opponent no opportunity to slander us. ¹⁵For some have already turned away to follow Satan. ¹⁶If any female believer

---

86. Cf. Childs, *Reading Paul*, 73-75.

has widows in her employ, she should care for them and not burden the church in order that it can help other widows who are truly needy.

The next several pericopes of instructions codify rules of engagement that order various relationships within God's household "with complete purity" (5:1-2). In agreement with biblical tradition, keen attention is paid to the welfare of widows who are old and "truly needy" and require financial support from one of three sources (vv. 3-10, 16) as well as those who are young and vulnerable to spiritual disaffection and require a husband and household to concentrate their talent and energy (vv. 11-15).

The instructions given Timothy in this passage are of a piece with other household rules in this letter that order relationships within the church according to the *oikonomia theou* (see 1:4b). Significantly, central to the political ideology of antiquity, the well-run family household is a necessary condition of civil society; likewise, an orderly congregation of believers is a necessary condition for maintaining a covenant-keeping relationship with God. Such cooperation with God envisages a keen sense of responsibility toward other members, not unlike that mapped in the preceding passage, in which Timothy's faithfulness has been made a measure of his future salvation (4:16). Relatives who fail to care for needy widows are as bad as unbelievers (5:8), and younger widows whose devotion to Christ is displaced by self-interest lose their religion and presumably their salvation (vv. 11-12).

Moreover, the manner of responsible care for the household's membership has a salutary effect on outsiders who find the virtuous widow "blameless" (v. 7; see 3:2, 7), while the younger widow who remarries rather than rejecting Christ squelches the opponent's slander (v. 14). This mixture of responsible care for insiders and conscientious regard for the opinion of outsiders (v. 10) is characteristic of Paul's household code, which reflects extraordinary sensitivity to people of all ages under the banner of God's desire to save everyone (so 2:4).

The repetition of purity (vv. 2, 22b; cf. 4:12) in reference to the young indicates a core emphasis of these instructions. Most commentators think the call to purity reflects a particular threat to the congregation's reputation, probably sexual,[87] whose likely source is the young. "With complete purity," then, is code for chastity. One might well understand this to be the subtext of Paul's instructions regarding younger widows who pursue new husbands rather than Christ (vv. 11-15), but one hardly thinks that the exhortation for Timothy to "keep yourself pure" (v. 22b) is similarly motivated. The particu-

---

87. So Josephus, *Against Apion* 2.198.

lar application in that case is purity of discernment in administrative matters. Purity, then, is what safeguards responsible decisions about both marriage and management of a congregation's jurisprudence.[88]

Paul prefaces his instruction regarding widows with a general principle of social manners within God's household (cf. Tit 2:1-6). The principle is a departure from the more intimate *Haustafeln* of Ephesians and Colossians, which order spousal and parental duties. In this paraenesis, instruction is given various age groups of both genders in the household (rather than of a "body," the principal metaphor of a Christian congregation elsewhere in the Pauline canon). The word for "older man" (πρεσβύτερος, *presbyteros*) is translated with respect to age and gender, even though the political sense of a congregation's ruling "elders" is in play in 4:14. The repetition here of *presbyteros* does imply an interpenetration of household and ecclesial social structures and roles, which substantially thickens its metaphorical use. In both cases, order is maintained by mutual respect rather than by abusive force. In this regard, the force of contrasting injunctions — sharp rebuke (ἐπιπλήσσεω, *epiplēsseō*), a *hapax legomenon*, and exhortation (παρακαλέω, *parakaleō*), a quintessentially Pauline formula of pastoral care — shapes every working relationship within the household.

Philo divided his Jewish congregation into six groups according to their ages: "old men, young men, boys, old women, grown women, maidens" (*Gaius* 227). Paul's initial prohibition against sharply rebuking older men (v. 1) reflects a sensibility of his Jewish upbringing that privileged elderly men. Ben Sira taught that "kindness to one's father will not be forgotten (by God)" (Sir 3:14), and treatment of elders was widely viewed in the ancient world as a litmus test of a community's moral maturity.

The members of primary concern for an orderly congregation are its widows (5:3-16). In part, this concern reflects Paul's scrupulous attention to the Torah, which demands the faithful community take special care of its widows and orphans — those most vulnerable to the vicissitudes of life (Exod 22:22; Deut 14:29; Zech 7:9-10). The letter of James reflects this same concern and considers care for widows in their distress a hallmark of the religion approved by God (Jas 1:27; cf. Acts 6:1-7).

---

88. Bruce W. Winter argues that these instructions are intended to insure that justice is done toward Christian widows in a setting where custodians of their dowries were breaking Roman law. In a public square where outsiders would have accused the congregation of unjust and unkind treatment of its widows, thereby undermining the integrity of the gospel, Paul is also concerned with a legal "purity" that avoids such an accusation of hypocrisy from non-believers. Winter, *Seek the Welfare of the City: Christians as Benefactors and Citizens* (Grand Rapids: Eerdmans, 1993), 61-78.

1 Timothy's concern for the treatment of widows adds another layer to the household motif. Roman law required that, if a dowry had been paid at marriage, the widow be provided for by the new head of her deceased husband's household — usually her son. If there was no son or the household was dissolved, then the proceeds of its sale would repay the dowry, and the widow would be returned to her parents. Of course, if there was no dowry paid, nor a family to which a widow could return — as evidently is the case for the "widows indeed," then a subsistent *providentia* was provided to the widow by the city-state (in this case, Ephesus). Essentially, Paul's code is an attempt to structure the congregation's welfare system according to Jewish practice (and the Torah) rather than Roman law (cf. Acts 6:1-6; 9:39; Jas 1:26-27; also Luke 7:11-17).

The congregation's widows are divided into three groups: those who are "truly needy," whose age precludes remarriage, who lack the financial support of an extended family, and whose piety is exemplary (5:3, 5-7, 9-10); those who should expect the financial support of their children (vv. 4, 8, 16); and those who are still young and should expect to remarry (vv. 11-15). I have translated the initial hortatory "care," which frames this entire passage. But this verbal idea, τιμάω *(timaō)*, is typically translated "honor" and envisages the kind of responsible support that is based on a person's honor rather than simply on financial need. It is welfare with good reason. In this first case, while the widows supported by the congregation are financially needy, their care is a sign of a congregation's honor because of the widows' "good works" (v. 10) and religious devotion (v. 5). In fact, her "hope is in God," to whom she continually prays and so, rather than exploiting the congregation's welfare system, her support is in answer to prayer; indeed, God is "our Savior" (2:3) and the welfare of the congregation, God's household, is God's concern (cf. 3:15).

The practice of putting names "on a list" (5:9) is well known from Hellenistic literature: mercenary soldiers signed on to wage Rome's wars by adding their names to a general's list (Herodotus, *Persian War* 1.59; 7.1), and new initiates were added to the rolls of a religious group (Oxyrhynchus Papyrus 416) or newly elected members to the Senate's roster (Plutarch, *Pompey* 13.7). This registry of widows in need of the congregation's material support has less to do with keeping a public record of who are really "widows indeed" than as an encouragement to follow the protocol of discernment that Paul stipulates.

In this regard, among a widow's qualifications are her age and faithfulness: she is "not less than sixty years old" and "the wife of one man" (5:9; cf. 3:2). Paul is appealing to current actuarial tables for defining an age beyond which women cannot remarry or be expected to do hard work. Moreover, the ideal of one marriage for a woman was honored in Roman society (Livy, *Roman History* 10.23.9) and in Judaism, according to which not remarrying provides evidence of marital fidelity to a woman's now deceased husband and of her devotion to the Lord (Jdt 8:4; 16:22; Luke 2:36-38). Paul is concerned that the congregation, whose vocation is to engage the wider culture with the gospel, is not at odds with social convention. At the same time, his concern that widows supported by the congregation be known for their *Christian* character is indicated by her piety (5:4) and "good works" (v. 10). Indeed, as Ambrose wrote, "the virtues of the widow have become the duties of old age" (*Concerning Widows* 2.9). The catalog of virtues in v. 10 is bracketed by "good works," which is thematic of the Christian life in the Pastoral Epistles and characteristic of the public operations of divine grace.[89] The presence of the exemplary widow in the congregation not only occasions its hallmark activity but is also a personal reminder of God's "great grace" residing in its midst (cf. Acts 4:32-35).

Even though the social convention of Paul's day — very nearly into the modern period — was that "younger widows" did not seek to remarry, the verbal mood of v. 14 is active: "I prefer that younger widows marry." That is, his exhortation is for a widow of marriageable age to seek a Christian husband as a necessary good. By doing so she will more likely avoid the unseemly behaviors described in vv. 11-13, thus giving "the opponent no opportunity to slander us" (v. 14). The "opponent" in this case is probably Satan, God's principal antagonist borrowed from Paul's Jewish apocalyptic background. Rather than a reflection of his world's misogyny, Paul's instruction is set against idlers (v. 13; cf. Tit 1:11-2), who are easily perceived by outsiders as morally lax (cf. Aristotle, *Nicomachean Ethics* 1097b). With respect to idle younger widows, this almost certainly would have carried a sexual innuendo (v. 11; cf. Dio Cassius, *Roman History* 47.15.4; 53.2.4) and so subverted the integrity of the gospel.

The chief threat to the spiritual vitality of younger widows is expressed in a compound verb, καταστρηνιάσωσιν *(katastrēniasōsin)*, whose meaning is difficult to determine (v. 11). The *kata-* prefix points to practices that are "against" Christ, which leads to setting aside an earlier "confession of faith" (πίστις, *pistis*, v. 12). The verbal root, στρηνιάω *(strēniaō)*, denotes a strong compulsion or inclination toward some desire, in this case to get married. I have translated the verb as "distracted" to convey a relational sense: pursuit of a marital relationship is at the expense of a relationship with Christ. If this is the case, then "Christ" in this passage is existentially adduced and refers to the living Christ rather than to "Christology" or to a body of beliefs about Christ that are jeopardized by a different preoccupation. What is imperiled is a prior confession of faith in Christ, which must have included a vow of single-minded devotion similar to that embodied in the older widows (v. 10). This

---

89. Marshall, *Pastoral Epistles*, 227-31.

concern is not unlike that expressed by Paul in 1 Corinthians 7, both in its preference that people remain unmarried to better serve the interests of Christ but also in allowing some to marry rather than be distracted by sexual desire (1 Cor 7:8-9). Against the backdrop of this antecedent Pauline text, 1 Timothy's subsequent and apparently contradictory instruction to marry (5:14) must be understood as the pastoral solution for the believer whose pronounced desire to find a husband now imperils her life with Christ (vv. 11-12).

Finally, the vague reference to the believer who "has widows" (ἔχει χήρας, *echei chēras*, v. 16) caused copyists to add to the text to make its intent more plain, and it continues to be variously interpreted. The feminine form of "believer" is used (πιστή, *pistē*), which indicates that the instruction is directed to Christian women. Most interpreters identify the widows as the woman's relatives, extending the earlier injunction that families should take care of their own. In this sense, to "have widows" in the family implies a responsibility toward them. While this reading is certainly plausible and continues the letter's interest in the financial responsibility of middle-class Christian women (cf. 2:10; 6:17-19), it does not explain why this instruction is necessary since it repeats a point made earlier (v. 8), nor why it focuses exclusively on female disciples.

Perhaps it is better to take the most common sense of "have" as to possess or own something. That is, this instruction is directed to wealthy female Christians (cf. 2:9) whose personal servants are widows, members of their extended household for whom they are thus directly responsible. The scope of the earlier rule is here expanded to include non-familial relationships within the household. This is consistent with Pauline paraenesis, in which the traditional hierarchy of household relationships in the Jewish and Roman world are reset to embody the mutuality that exists in Christ (so Gal 3:28; Col 3:11), thus showing a real world microcosm of the *oikonomia theou*, the aim of which is love (cf. 1:4-5), especially in social relationships where abuse is likely. It would also seem to bring balance in the subsequent instruction directed to household slaves in 6:1-2.

5:17-25 Care of Elderly Men

[17]Request a double honorarium for elderly men who lead well, especially those who labor in public speaking and teaching. [18]For the Scripture says, "Do not muzzle the ox that is threshing" and "The worker is worthy of his wages." [19]Do not respond to an accusation leveled against an elder if it is not confirmed "by two or three witnesses." [20]Discipline those who sin before the entire congregation in or-

der to provoke fear in those present. ²¹Bring testimony before God, Christ Jesus, and the elect angels so that you will discharge these instructions without prejudice and without making a biased claim. ²²ᵃDo not ordain anyone hastily.

²²ᵇDo not share in the sins of others. Keep yourself pure. ²³Stop drinking just water but use a little wine for your upset stomach and frequent illnesses! ²⁴The sins of some folks are blatant, leading to judgment, while others follow close behind; ²⁵on the other hand, the good works of still others are obvious and cannot remain hidden from view.

This pericope of household instructions initially deals with the household's elderly men (πρεσβύτεροι, *presbyteroi*) and elaborates the principle introduced in v. 1 that they are not to be rebuked harshly but treated as father figures. Those engaged in ministry should be fairly compensated (vv. 17-18), and those accused of malpractice should be fairly judged (vv. 19-22a). Negotiating the congregation's court is tricky business, especially for someone viewed as inexperienced. Spiritual and physical health is good preparation (vv. 22b-23), even though sometimes the wisest course of action is to patiently wait on the consequences of another's action before reaching a verdict on it (vv. 24-25).

Even as the earlier instructions concentrate on widows, presumably because of the community's special responsibility toward them, so also here a particular group of older men are in view: those who lead the congregation and especially those who have assumed important and sometimes difficult public roles (v. 17). Leadership in middle-class households of antiquity was typically determined by gender (male) and age (elderly), and this social norm here extends to God's household — even if Paul is probably less concerned about chronological age than spiritual maturity (see 3:6; 4:12). So Philo writes of Moses that he "applied the name of 'elder' not to one who is bowed with old age but to one who is worthy of honor" (*Sobriety* 16).

While "double honor" translates the literal sense of the Greek noun phrase, διπλῆς τιμή (*diplēs timē*), I have translated it "double honorarium" in a context concerned with the financial support of the congregation's older members. The formula "For the Scripture says" introduces the canonical use of LXX Deut 25:4, "Do not muzzle the ox that is threshing," followed by Paul's illustrative midrash "The worker is worthy of his wages." This is rather conventional wisdom but probably recalls instructions regulating the fair compensation of priests according to LXX Num 18:31.[90] Here and in the earlier use

---

90. For Paul's use of such introductory formulas, see Christopher D. Stanley, *Paul and the Language of Scripture* (SNTSMS 69; Cambridge: Cambridge University Press, 1992), especially 252-64.

of Deut 25:4 in 1 Cor 9:9 Paul uses *qal-wa-homer* reasoning to make the critical point. That is, he first appeals to Scripture's lesser claim — in this case about farm animals — to prove Scripture's ultimate claim — in this case about the wages of a laborer for the gospel: if we generally treat beasts of burden fairly, then how much more should we treat fairly those among us who labor on God's behalf.[91] Significantly, Luke's Jesus uses this same proverbial wisdom when instructing his disciples for mission (Luke 10:7), which gives Christ's affirmation to Scripture's instruction to compensate fairly those who work on behalf of a Christian congregation.

In 1 Corinthians 9, the issue was an accusation that Paul was not behaving as an apostle because he refused financial support. By his appeal to Deut 25:4 he agrees with those who say he is entitled to support, but because his "apostleship (is) in the Lord" (1 Cor 9:2), he declines his right to a fair wage (so 1 Cor 9:15a). But clearly the situation has changed in 1 Timothy, which is occasioned by the apostle's departure from the congregation. In this new setting, the prerogatives of Paul's apostleship, including the renunciation of financial support, have departed with him and are not passed on to others.[92] In his absence, then, successors who "lead well" and work hard to teach his gospel to others should be well compensated for doing so.

The support of the congregation's teaching elders is conceptually similar to the support of the widows of similar age, who were added to the welfare roll in part because of their "good works" (see 5:10). Here, the congregation compensates elders who "lead well" (καλῶς προεστῶτες, *kalōs prosetōtes*), especially in their "public speaking and teaching" (v. 17). I have translated ἐν λόγῳ *(en logō)*, "in public speaking," to pick up a fuller resonance of its pairing with διδασκαλία *(didaskalia)*. Not only was competence in public rhetoric considered a sine qua non for effective leadership in antiquity, the distinction between the two activities, *logos* and *didaskalia*, regards their different audiences and intentions, the first directed toward outsiders and the second to the church. And this is hard work! The word used for "labor" is not *ergon* as we might expect but κοπιάω *(kopiaō)*, which envisages the kind of sweaty exertion that exacts a physical toll on a daily laborer.

While nothing is said about a list of elders approved for financial support (cf. v. 9), a similar scrupulosity of attention is required of Timothy, including avoiding hasty ordination of an unfit elder (v. 22a). As before with the widows, Paul's instruction concerns not only the quality of work performed

---

91. Collins, *Timothy and Titus*, 144.
92. This change would be especially crucial in a second-century setting in which the ascetic Paul of the apocryphal *Acts of Paul* is being promoted as canonical for his followers.

but also the elder's character: those guilty of sin are unfit to lead a congregation (v. 20).

A protocol of jurisprudence (vv. 19-22) sets out guidelines for determining the congregation's financial support of its leading elders (vv. 17-18). Again, following Scripture's injunction regarding the gathering of credible evidence (v. 19; cf. Deut 19:15), Timothy is instructed not to "receive an accusation against an elder" in the absence of multiple witnesses. If the evidence proves the elder guilty, which by implication disqualifies him from leadership and financial support, he is to be publicly disciplined before the congregation. The purpose is not the spiritual repair of the guilty party (as in Jesus' example of jurisprudence according to Matt 18:15-17) but a spiritual doctrine of deterrence in which the public shame of the disgraced elder provokes the congregation's fear of a similar fate.

The appropriation of a familiar OT trope in which the prophet cross-examines Israel before a heavenly court that includes God, who then renders the verdict and executes the punishment, functions here as a cautionary note to Timothy not to preside over a kangaroo court. A trial before an impartial God, who fairly considers all relevant evidence (cf. LXX Sir 35:12; Rom 2:11; 1 Pet 1:17), requires an impartial handling of the evidence. The presence of "the elect angels" in this heavenly court is curious in this setting but perhaps trades on the connection in apocalyptic literature between the angelic guardians of God's elect people and the latter's perseverance into the coming age. In this case, the implication is that Timothy's attentiveness to this sacred jurisprudence helps to insure the congregation's end-time salvation (see 4:16). To blithely ordain (literally "lay hands upon") an elder (5:22a) or to exonerate him in a careless fashion is subversive of a congregation's perseverance.

As the apostle's delegate, Timothy is most immediately responsible to monitor the application of the *oikonomia theou* to the congregation's loving relationships (see above on 1:4-5a). Since this vocation requires character as well as competence (cf. 1:5), a public protocol that insures the selection of effective leaders melds naturally into more personal instruction headed by the exhortation "keep yourself pure" (5:22b; cf. 4:12; 5:2). The two are juxtaposed in this letter for good reason. Doubtless Timothy's youth may have been regarded as problematic by some in the congregation, in a social world that valued experience that comes only with age. Perhaps even Paul, who has said that Timothy's age is a problem for some (4:12), views Timothy's lack of maturity as a liability in gaining the congregation's confidence during the sometimes tricky negotiations of a disciplinary proceeding when the sin of an accused elder is not evident (5:24-25) and there exists the natural awkwardness of a young man's relationship with older men (v. 1). If the issue is Timothy's nerve (cf. 2 Tim 1:6-7), the "use of a little wine" would have been viewed as medicinal. Greco-Roman physicians prescribed wine for a "nervous stomach," and the Talmud stipulates wine as the "first among medicines" (*b. Baba Batra* 58b; cf. *b. Berakot* 35b), even though the Mishnah encouraged abstinence from wine to maintain one's *spiritual* health (*m. 'Abot* 6.4). Chrysostom makes the same distinction later when he writes on this verse: "Paul does not allow Timothy to indulge freely in wine, but as much as was for health and not for luxury" (*Homilies on 1 Timothy* 16).

Timothy's reluctance to drink wine, even for medicinal reasons, has been widely adduced as cultural in motive: drinking "too much wine" marks out those who lack the virtue to lead (3:8) whereas to abstain from drinking wine or even "a little wine" is not cause for concern. But the reasons could also be religious. Indeed, the asceticism that Paul has already demonized (4:1-4) may be a subtext here. That is, perhaps the problem is not Timothy but the congregation or the misguided teachers, eavesdropping on Paul's letter, who are once again reminded that wine, like food and marriage, is the good gift of a benevolent Creator.

But there is yet another possibility in the canonical context. If the canonical Paul — the Paul whose memory and message fund the tradition Timothy is to safeguard for the next generation (see 2 Tim 6:20) — is the Paul of Acts, then in this narrative world Paul enjoins the practices of the Nazirites, which include strict abstinence from wine, to demonstrate his faithfulness to his Jewish heritage (so Acts 18:18; 21:26; cf. Num 6:1-21). And perhaps Timothy is inclined as his faithful tradent to follow his example. Paul's exhortation, then, intends to grant Timothy a dispensation from his Nazirite vow of abstinence for reasons of ill health.

But even with a glass of wine in hand to settle an upset stomach, the best test of Timothy's fitness is discernment between the sinner who needs rebuke and repair and the saint who needs support and encouragement. Assessing people is the truck-and-trade of Timothy's job description. Appropriately, then, the final instruction (vv. 24-25) is given in the third person as though it were axiomatic. The contrast between obvious and hidden, whether regarding sin or good works, would seem to suggest that Timothy must wait on the consequences of behavior before assessing it. What is blatantly sinful or conspicuously good is not difficult for people to measure; however, the full effect of what is hidden from public scrutiny is more difficult to discern. Rather enigmatically, Paul reminds Timothy that the consequence of what one does "cannot remain hidden from view," perhaps also from Timothy but certainly not from the heavenly tribunal of "God, Christ Jesus, and the elect angels" (v. 21; cf. Heb 4:12-13).

6:1-2a The Conduct of Christian Slaves

¹Those who carry the yoke of slavery must respect their own masters as deserving every honor so that the name of God and the Teaching may not be reviled. ²Those who have believers as masters must not despise them because they are brothers; rather, they must serve them more faithfully since the recipients of good work are beloved believers.

Since most middle-class urban households of the Roman world included household slaves, paraenetic codes typically included instructions regarding slaves' responsibilities and conduct. Paul does not include additional instructions about the congregation's or Timothy's responsibilities toward slaves, and some think this is because the membership of urban congregations consisted mostly of slaves. I doubt that, especially since the letter also includes instructions for middle-class members (e.g., 6:17-19). What is remarkable about this version of the traditional household code is the motive of good conduct: slaves are to serve their masters well so that "the Teaching" may not be reviled (v. 1) and so that Christian masters are served even "more faithfully" (v. 2).

For some Christians, this passage and its vivid image of "the yoke of slavery" has made it a "text of terror"; few others in the Pauline canon occasion the inward, even visceral conflict this one does. I approach it as a text sanctified by the Spirit for sacred purposes and refuse to decanonize it, but I do so with full recognition that it has been used throughout history to support slave practices that dehumanize neighbors and prevent loving communion with them, in disobedience to Christ's command. No reciprocal virtue is asked of slave masters, and they are in fact viewed as roughly analogous to God in this instruction. That may lead readers to use this text to endorse a social hierarchy that sanctions oppression for God's sake, which I consider blasphemous. At the very least, before offering a theological explanation that elaborates certain aspects of the apostolic Rule, we must seek first the plain sense of this particular prescription.

Because most middle-class households in the Greco-Roman world included slaves, traditional conduct codes included rules that reflected their duties. The congregation addressed by the instructions of 1 Timothy evidently included household slaves, which the reader should expect since slavery was integral to the economy of Roman urban society. Many slaves were well educated and exercised enormous influence in shaping the daily routines of the household. At the very least, Paul seems alert to the effect the gospel might have on working relations between household slaves and their masters, which might in turn undermine the congregation's influence on the wider culture.

In fact, the reader may allow that this instruction in particular reflects, perhaps uncritically so, the missional concern for the outsider that is found throughout the letter.

Paul addresses two different slave-master relationships. In the first case (v. 1a), some slaves belong to a non-believing δεσπότης *(despotēs)*. Once again Paul begins with an exhortation for the congregation to give honor (τιμή, *timē*) to a social group (cf. 5:3, 17). In this case, however, some of those honored do not belong to the congregation but own slaves who do: they are the pagan "masters." Nor does the honor due them take the form of monetary compensation; they are outsiders and have no evident need of financial support. The extravagant approach to the master is striking and suggestive of an ironic subtext. The master is called a *despotēs*, a word used elsewhere in Scripture of the exercise of God's sovereignty over the world's affairs (Luke 2:29; Acts 4:24), whether in providential care of creation (a wisdom motif) or in the severe consequences of disobedience (Isa 1:24; 10:33). Additionally, the layer of adjectives, πᾶς *(pas)* and ἄξιος *(axios)*, heaped on a deserved *timē*, literally "every worthy honor," suggests a master with absolute power whose status alone deserves the respect of those under his authority. The true motive of the Christian servant's regard, however, is loyalty to the world's real *despotēs*, who is God (cf. 1:17).

This is implied by the articular ἡ διδασκαλία *(hē didaskalia)*, "the Teaching," which in combination with "the name of God" alludes to Pauline teaching about God — "healthy doctrine," the community's norm. This doctrine is succinctly set out in 2:3-6: the Christian's Master is the one God who is "our Savior." To discredit this teaching by careless or unprofessional conduct is to subvert the gospel, which is the means by which the world is put to rights.

A more surprising concern is reflected by a second kind of slave-master relationship, set out in v. 2, one that stands outside a traditional household code. The problem is hardly sociological, one in which "familiarity breeds contempt" between a Christian slave and Christian master. Rather, the problem is theological, roughly similar to what is worked out in Paul's letter to Philemon: What is the manner of a slave-master relationship within the household of God? To what extent is the institution of slavery undermined because of Christian faith? Surely the radical egalitarian impress of the Pauline gospel, memorably articulated by Gal 3:28, would unsettle things when applied to a hierarchical arrangement. Slaves may naturally come to despise their Christian masters who refuse manumission as a Christian practice in preference for being treated with honor like the pagan *despotēs* of v. 1.

But the use of the intimate "brothers" reverses the move in Philemon, where the master is pressured to resist the social norm and to treat his runaway slave as a "dear brother" (v. 16). The instruction here in 1 Timothy is so shocking to the modern reader precisely because the slave is asked to regard his master as a "beloved brother" (ἀδελφός ἀγαπητός, adelphos agapētos) in order to maintain a cultural norm that seems antithetical to "the Teaching" and to transform one's faithful servitude into a Christian practice. It is not the honorable master who is responsible for righting a broken relationship, even though he would be in a position of power to do so legally; rather, it is the powerless slave who takes responsibility for a ministry of reconciliation.

Perhaps a way forward is guided by the chiastic shape of this passage, which places the cautionary note about reviling Christian teaching about God (v. 1b) between the two instructions regarding a Christian slave's relationships with two different kinds of masters, pagan and Christian. That is, the congregation's witness to "the name of God and the Teaching" is located especially in the believer's most difficult social relations, and there especially between Christians. This upside-down conception of servanthood is completely consistent with Pauline paraenesis.

The insertion of a reference to "the Teaching" is hermeneutically crucial for this household paraenesis. "The name of God," which is a trope for God's reputation in the world, is linked to ἡ διδασκαλία (hē didaskalia), "the Teaching," of the community. I take its articular form as a technical reference to "healthy doctrine" that sets out the theological grammar of the Pauline gospel (cf. 1:10-11). That is, what is most worrisome about disruptive relations within the household of believers is not only that God's reputation is slandered by such behavior but that it is corrosive of a Pauline apostolate that is custodian of right teaching about God. And it is this worry that grounds the catholicity of this sacred text rather than a particular prescription shaped by the social institution of a Roman world far removed from its current readers.

A final cautionary note must be sounded, more hermeneutical than exegetical in timbre. Hardly another biblical passage is found that better illustrates the danger of applying biblical prescriptions to every social location. The slave catechism in antebellum America, composed by Christian masters to support a profitable social institution, included this text within its biblical justification.[93] Surely the use of an interpreted text must be avoided when its effect subverts Scripture's performance in cultivating loving communion with God and all others. For this reason, the catholicity of this sacred text is better placed not on its address to those under "the yoke of slavery," which too easily misses the irony of Paul's injunction and is transformed into a political reason

---

93. Twomey, *Pastoral Epistles*, 93-94.

1 Timothy 6:2b-10

for one to control another, but on the subsequent purpose clause, "that the name of God and the Teaching may not be reviled." Herein lies the real purpose of this letter for every reader and every working relationship.

6:2b-10 False Teachers

²ᵇTeach and encourage these things. ³If someone teaches differently and does not come to agree with the healthy teachings about our Lord Jesus Christ — teaching that accords with godliness — ⁴he is arrogant and understands nothing, but has an unhealthy interest in contesting the meaning of words that provoke envy, dissension, slander, evil suspicion, ⁵and persistent argument among those who are corrupt and deprived of the truth, who think that piety is profitable. ⁶Indeed, there is great profit when piety is combined with self-sufficiency! ⁷For we brought nothing into the world and so are able to take nothing out: ⁸we shall be satisfied with food and shelter. ⁹Those who are determined to be wealthy, however, are tripped up into temptation and a trap — many foolish and harmful desires — that plunge them headlong into ruin and destruction. ¹⁰For the love of money is the root of all kinds of evil. Some who have aspired for wealth have wandered from the faith and have impaled themselves with many pains.

This instruction is directed to Timothy, whose charge to "teach these things" is directed at those whose instruction does not square with Paul's teaching about Christ (vv. 2b-3), a religious disaffection that yields an impious character evinced in contentious debate (vv. 4-6) and rooted in a love for money (vv. 7-10).

Repetition of the letter's familiar exhortation for Timothy to instruct the congregation "about these things" (v. 2b; see 4:11; 1:3; 2:1; 5:1; cf. 3:14-15) cues a familiar problem: the presence of false teachers, in this case prospective, who require Timothy's correction. What is less clear is whether the placement of these instructions in the final form of the letter concludes its prior codification of the congregation's internal relations (5:1–6:2a) or introduces its benedictory (6:3-21). If the latter, these instructions to Timothy bring to focus the letter's abiding interest in the character and conduct of the congregation's spiritual leaders. The sharp contrast between true and false teachers forms an *inclusio* with 1:3-20, a passage that also set out the letter's theological crisis, namely the departure of the apostle and his succession in Ephesus by Timothy.[94] What 1 Timothy makes

---

94. Marshall identifies the former role of this transitional text as a scholarly consensus. But see Towner, *Letters to Timothy and Titus*, 390-92, who follows J. Thurén and others since and

1 Timothy 6:2b-10

more clear by repetition is that spiritual leadership not only concerns the substance of what is taught but also the sort of person one is when measured by the testimony of Jesus (cf. 1:15-16; 6:13). Thus, the content of teaching and character of piety form an integral criterion for effective ministry.

The present passage once again mentions those who "teach differently" (ἑτεροδιδασκαλέω, *heterodidaskaleō*; cf. 1:3). Here the criterion of orthodoxy is not the gospel entrusted to Paul (1:10-11[12-16]; 2:4-7) but "the healthy teachings about our Lord Jesus Christ" (6:3b). The translation "teachings about" takes "our Lord Jesus Christ" as an objective genitive, which agrees with the plain sense of 3:16 that adherence to Pauline Christology is a qualification for congregational leadership (cf. 2 Tim 2:8-13). Moreover, the use of "healthy" repeats the medical idiom used in 1:10 to introduce this same link between what a teacher believes and how he behaves. Put positively, then, the salutary effect of orthodoxy (διδασκαλία, *didaskalia*) is spiritual vitality (εὐσέβεια, *eusebeia*). While this letter makes the point in personal terms of the congregation's leaders, the connection repeatedly made between right doctrine and virtuous character is a routine focus of Pauline paraenesis, which typically extends to the entire congregation. In fact, the present passage elaborates the decisive exhortation of 3:14-15, according to which Timothy is the "pillar and foundation of the truth" in God's household — a role predicated on a firm commitment to the tradition's core beliefs about Christ (so 3:16).[95]

The caricature of "someone who teaches differently" is illustrative and need not have specific opponents in mind. As before, no one is named, nor is a particular heresy identified. The catalog of evil characteristics and unprofitable practices, carefully fitted into this setting, is axiomatic, emphasizing the unhealthy effect bad teaching will always have on the sacred household. Ironically, Paul's conception of congregational leadership does not focus first of all on the manner of one's life; rather, the beginning point is whether the content of the teacher's instruction conforms to what is confessed about

---

relates 1:3-20 and 6:2b-21 as follows: (1) Command (1:3; 6:2b), (2) Occasion (1:4-7a; 6:3-6), (3) Misunderstanding (1:7b-10; 6:5-6), (4) Contrasting role models (1:11-16; 6:11-15), (5) Doxology (1:17; 6:16), and (6) Commission (1:18-20; 6:20-21). The advantage of this structure is that by repeating this pattern to conclude the letter, Paul is able to highlight the dangers of wealth (6:7-10, 17-19), lacking in the initial panel, as the signal threat to Timothy's faithful leadership (cf. 6:11-16).

95. Johnson, *First and Second Letters to Timothy,* 297-98, argues for the possibility of understanding "our Lord Jesus Christ" as a subjective genitive, in which case *logoi* would likely refer to a body of sayings uttered by Jesus and transmitted in the gospel tradition (cf. Luke 1:1-2). What may be inferred by this reference to the Lord's "healthy words," then, is a kind of oral catechism the teacher draws on to initiate the congregation into the core beliefs and practices of Christian discipleship.

Christ, as proclaimed by Paul. If the teacher gets this right, then the manner of his conduct within a congregation will surely follow.

This singular point is scored in a single if elaborate sentence, consisting of stock polemical expressions and vice catalogs from familiar philosophical writings of the day (6:3-5).[96] The apodosis (v. 3a) introduces the contrary example of the teacher who does not follow the "teachings (λόγοι, logoi) about the Lord Jesus Christ."[97] Sharply put, it is practically impossible for such a person to embody a pattern of "godliness." The hallmark virtues of spiritual health are replaced by a malformed intellect and "an unhealthy interest in contesting the meaning of words"[98] (v. 4; cf. 1:6-7). Stupid does as stupid is! And the terrible consequence for a congregation under the influence of such a teacher is a house divided by "envy, dissension, slander, evil suspicion" (v. 4), the cumulative effect of a people "deprived of the truth" (v. 5). The ancient world did not judge the soundness of speech on the basis of merely what was said but also its salutary effect on the manner in which a people lives (Homer, *Iliad* 8.524).

The haunting refrain that such a teacher fakes godliness as a money-making scheme may have in mind the Lord's contrarian teachings about wealth, which is one of the most important *topoi* of his definition of discipleship. Money attitudes (v. 10) and practices (vv. 17-19) are among the most evident ways in which a Christian way of life challenges and perhaps even destabilizes the cultural norm. But the danger of acquiring wealth was commonly noted in conventional wisdom of the day. For example, "The love of money is the mother city of all evils" (Bion the Sophist according to Stobaeus,

---

96. See Robert J. Karris, "The Background and Significance of the Polemic of the Pastoral Epistles," *JBL* 92 (1973): 549-64. The familiarity of language actually helps the reader concentrate less on the words used and more on Paul's central point: the criterion of effective teaching is whether the substance and result of what is taught comport with the apostolic memory of Jesus.

97. The grammar of this phrase is ambiguous and debated among commentators. Plural λόγοι *(logoi)* is most likely not synonymous with "gospel," which is referred to by the singular noun in the Pastoral Epistles (2 Tim 2:9; 4:2; Tit 1:9). If one takes the genitive τοῦ κυρίου ἡμῶν Ἰησοῦ Χριστοῦ *(tou kyriou hēmōn Iēsou Christou)* as indicating the source of the *logoi*, then it probably refers to the "sayings/words of" Jesus; whether the author has in mind an oral or written collection of Jesus sayings is indeterminate. If one takes the genitive as attributive of the *logoi*, then "teachings about" Jesus is the preferred sense. In a setting that alludes to the gospel story of Jesus' Roman trial as canonical for the confession the "man of God" must now make, we prefer the attributive genitive and so an implicit reference to a proto-gospel about the life of Jesus.

98. Johnson places this sentence against the backdrop of ancient moral discourse whose rhetorical conventions include similar medical images as found here and whose disputations between rival schools of thought often equate "unhealthy" teaching with a teacher's ignorance and vice. Johnson, *First and Second Letters to Timothy*, 291-93.

Anthologium 3.417, c. 250 B.C.E.). Aristotle taught that "the life of money-making is limiting, and wealth is surely not the good we seek after, for it is at best only the means to something else" (*Nicomachean Ethics* 1.5.8). And Rabbi Jose b. Quisma (c. 110 C.E.) is reported to have said, "My son, even if you give me all the silver and gold of this world, I want to live in light of Torah nonetheless; because in the hour when one is separated from human life and he has no more silver nor gold nor jewels nor beads, only Torah and good works will accompany him" (*m. 'Abot* 6.9).

The repetition of "profit" (πορισμός, *porismos*) in superlative dress — "great profit" — cues the reader's move back to a right understanding of "godliness" grounded in "teachings about our Lord Jesus Christ" (v. 3b; so also 3:9, 16). However, rather than an appeal to a Christological formula as we might expect, the form of godliness that yields "great profit" is marked by the philosopher's ideal of "self-sufficiency" (αὐτάρκεια, *autarkeia*), which "cancels the material meaning of gain" and leaves only its spiritual sense.[99] Significantly, in 2 Cor 9:8 Paul posits that *autarkeia* comes from the overflow of divine grace, which enables the congregation to give generous gifts to the poor. This definition of the source of self-sufficiency, in which Paul combines grace and generous giving is vaguely similar to Stoicism, which honored Socrates because he refused to sacrifice his moral and religious ideals at the altar of wealth. In this regard, Plato famously proffers this dialogue on friendship in *Lysis:* "Will not the good man be measured by his self-sufficiency? Yes. Because the sufficient man has no need of anything other than the virtue of his sufficiency" (215a). Likewise, Diogenes the Cynic characterized the guiding norm of good teaching by describing the simplicity of his followers' clothing and diet. While Paul measures good teaching by its theological orthodoxy, the spiritual leader computes "what's in it for me" by a form of *autarkeia* characterized by freedom from the distractions of wealth. Paul's concern for a practical divinity, glossed by his missionary vocation, routinely compels him to reinterpret secular ideals — in this case the simple life — as the saint's proper response to the sufficiency of divine grace that empties the "self" from self-sufficiency, and with it the natural inclination toward self-centered "envy" and its effects on social relationships. In this sense, of course, while we take nothing of material value out of this world (so v. 7), which follows biblical wisdom (e.g., Ecclesiastes), the believer can certainly bring valuables of a spiritual kind from this world into the next (see v. 19). The eternal cast of divine grace means that its powers and gifts do not stop at heaven's door.

---

99. Johnson, *First and Second Letters to Timothy,* 294.

The locus of spiritual struggle is over the inward desires of the individual. Paul emphasizes this point by poetic resonance, using a series of π- words to create an interplay between a person's desire for riches (πλουτέω, *plouteō*) and "tripped up (ἐμπίπτω, *empiptō*) into temptation (πειρασμός, *peirasmos*) and a trap (παγίς, *pagis*)." Johnson translates ἐπιθυμία *(epithymia)* as "cravings" instead of "desires" to capture the central deception, which is that financial security defines sufficiency (cf. Jas 1:13-16).

Although what kind of "ruin and destruction" awaits those who are trapped is not specified, the canonical context suggests that it is God's final judgment (e.g., 2 Peter 2–3; Matt 7:13; Phil 3:19-20; 1 Thess 5:3; 2 Thess 2:3; Rev 17:8-11). Contemporary Jewish usage does as well and may be reflected in the Qumran *Rule of the Community*, in which the day of God's judgment is described as a "glut of punishments . . . for the scorching wrath of the God of revenge, for permanent error and shame without end with the humiliation of destruction by the fire of the dark regions" (1QS 4.11-13).

Paul can agree with the consensus of ancient philosophers and Jewish moral teaching that materialism is the source of every kind of mischief (see Jas 4:1-2). In fact, the placement of "root" at the head of the proverb, which I have translated "the love of money is the root of all kinds of evil," only intensifies the truth that greed is the source of every destructive power. But Paul's sense of this remains eschatological rather than existential. The "many pains" that are experienced by those who foolishly pursue wealth at the expense of genuine piety are for those who are destined for "ruin and destruction" at the final judgment of God.

The middle voice of the present participle of ὀρέγω *(oregō)*, used earlier of the mature leader who seeks to manage ably the congregation's spiritual affairs (3:1), here pictures by contrast a kind of malevolent ambition that inevitably brings a "leader" interested in his own fame and fortune to eschatological ruin (cf. 1:19-20). The reader cannot help but recall Paul's stunning conclusion to an earlier exhortation in which he bids Timothy to obey his sacred calling to save both himself and his congregation (see 4:16), presumably from this unhappy end.

6:11-16 Charge to Remain Faithful to Christ Jesus

¹¹But you, O man of God, flee from all this! Instead, pursue moral rectitude, piety, faith, love, endurance, gentleness. ¹²Fight the good fight of faith. Lay hold of eternal life for which you were called and have confessed the good confession before many witnesses. ¹³(I exhort you before God, who dispenses life to all things, and

before Christ Jesus, who made the good confession when testifying before Pontius Pilate.) ¹⁴Obey this command without fault or failure until the appearing of our Lord Jesus Christ, ¹⁵the timing of which God alone determines — God, the blessed and only Ruler, the King of kings and Lord of lords, ¹⁶who alone has immortality, dwells in unapproachable light, whom no human has seen or is able to see, to whom is honor and everlasting sovereignty, amen.

The contrast between the previous profile of the false teacher and the profile of the virtuous "man of God" is signaled by the characteristic address "But you." What follows is a series of hortatory exclamations that indicate the kind of piety required by God and demonstrated by Christ (vv. 11-12). Paul thus plots the movement toward a very different kind of destiny than awaits the false teacher, whose avarice tempts and traps him into a manner of life that leads to eschatological "ruin and destruction" (v. 9). The "man of God" will appear before a tribunal headed by God, who alone "dispenses life" (vv. 13-16), and Christ Jesus, who exemplifies "the good confession," with faultless testimony that assures his eschatological reward (v. 13).

The solemn idiom of this passage is less liturgical than juridical. The emphatic "man of God" recalls an important OT title for prophets (especially Elijah in 1-2 Kings), who are thus identified as God's witnesses to Israel and the bearers of God's word (cf. 2 Tim 3:17). The "man" here is, of course, Timothy, the ideal Pauline tradent. But the full importance of the title awaits Paul's salutation of Titus, where he says that God's word has now been disclosed to Paul "in due time *(kairos)*" to encourage the faith of God's elect (see below on Tit 1:1-3). In other words, Timothy's prophetic ministry is as a bearer of God's word given to Paul to bring the nations to an understanding of the truth (so 1 Tim 2:4-7).

The "flee/pursue" pair, typical of paraenesis, outlines what Timothy is to do in providing a witness to God for his congregation. The catalog of six virtues, headed by "moral rectitude" (δικαιοσύνη, *dikaiosynē*) and "piety" (εὐσέβεια, *eusebeia*), outlines the character of such a witness. Collins contends that these two virtues form an inseparable pair in designating a manner of life that exhibits a right relationship with God and God's people. Taken together they form a generic whole, a correct attitude (piety) and correct behavior (moral rectitude), which is then the root of all other virtues.[100] The familiar pairing of faith and love, already mentioned as the by-product of saving grace (1:14), together with the final pair of social virtues, patience and gentleness, thus flows out of a right relationship with God and neighbor. The

---

100. Collins, *Timothy and Titus*, 123-24.

purpose of this exhortation, however, is to remind Timothy of the manner of life required of the carrier of God's word.

A metaphor from athletic contests is used to underscore the seriousness of Timothy's pursuit of this manner of life. Already Paul has warned that Timothy's future with God depends on faithful attention to his vocation (4:16), and now again the reward of "eternal life" is predicated on "fighting the good fight of faith" (v. 12: *agōnizou ton kalon agōna*). The exhortation to "lay hold" suggests the effort of an athlete who trains hard for victory. Eternal life is not the entitlement of those whom God elects but God's gift to those who obey.

The pairing of the aorist verbs "call" (passive, i.e., called by God) and "confess" (active, i.e., Timothy confesses) recalls Timothy's prior ordination when the elders commissioned him to charismatic ministry in response to prophecy (4:14; cf. Acts 13:1-3). Here is emphasized a past event when Timothy responded to public confirmations — in prophecy and liturgy — of his sacred call to ministry: he "confessed the good confession" (v. 12, ὡμολόγησας τὴν καλὴν ὁμολογίαν, *hōmologēsas tēn kalēn homologian*) before a panel of witnesses that included God, who called him, and Christ Jesus, who exemplifies the faithful response to God's bidding (v. 13). The repetition of "good" in phrases that combine verbs with their cognate nouns frames a résumé of faithful witness that results in a verdict of eternal life. Moreover, the exhortation to "lay hold of eternal life" (αἰώνιος ζωῆς, *aiōnios zōēs*), sandwiched between these two phrases in v. 12, points to the eternal God who alone can give such life (v. 13). That is, the point scored by this logic is that the hard evidence demanded by God at the eschatological trial, which will confirm that a "good fight of faith" has been fought, consists of work that embodies "the good confession" of faith.

What Timothy confessed at his ordination has become the criterion of his present ministry and future status with God (see 4:14-16) and coheres to the confession the Messiah made before Pilate (v. 13). "Confession" literally means "same-saying" *(homo-logia)* and so invites the reader to recall the gospel tradition of Christ's Roman trial before Pilate as roughly analogous to the situation and demand now facing Timothy in Roman Ephesus. Initially, one realizes that this tradition is part of the body of "teachings about our Lord Jesus Christ" (v. 3), which forms the continuing criterion that measures the content and character of a teacher's faithfulness to the sacred tradition. For Timothy to "confess the good confession," then, is to give public expression to the same kind of response Jesus made when interrogated by Pilate.

In this regard, perhaps Paul has in mind the expanded gospel tradition of the church's memory of the Lord's responses to Pilate received in John's

Gospel (18:28-38).[101] The addition of the Lord's "testifying (μαρτυρέω, *martyreō*) before Pontius Pilate" uses an important catchword of John's Gospel, particularly in Jesus' Roman trial before Pilate, to whom he says that "to testify to the truth" of his kingdom, which is not of this world, is the very purpose of his messianic vocation (18:36-37).

The gospel's "teaching about the Lord Jesus Christ" (v. 3) is cued to trigger Timothy's memory of the pledge he made at his ordination (4:14). His personal struggle over its obligations, a central theme of 2 Timothy also hinted at throughout this letter, may well suggest the same kind of conflict that led Jesus to the cross. Timothy's opposition to false teachers, whose confession is "deprived of the truth" (v. 5), reflects such a conflict. Pilate's deeply ironic question put to the Lord, "What is truth?" is the implied question now put to Timothy, especially since a "knowledge of the truth" is God's chief desire (so 2:4) and therefore the central motive of Christian ministry and worship. To pledge one's allegiance to a sacred calling is to commit oneself to a costly ministry of the truth that encounters the same enemy and perhaps the same destiny as Jesus encountered. Paul strikingly calls Timothy's ordination "the command" (v. 14), and Timothy's absolute obedience to it — "without fault or failure" — intensifies the importance of compliance, since his salvation and that of others depend on it (so 4:16).

The image of giving testimony "before many witnesses" evokes a courtroom scene. The identity of these "witnesses" is unclear, but probably they are the elders who presided over his ordination (4:14; 2 Tim 1:6) and now assume the role as the jury that reviews evidence of his obedience. More important to this juridical trope is the mention of "the appearing of our Lord Jesus Christ" to complete his messianic mission. In the Pastoral Epistles (2 Tim 2:10; 4:1, 8; Tit 2:11, 13; 3:4; cf. 1 Thess 3:13; 5:23; 2 Thess 2:8), the idiom of Jesus' appearance regards his future work: if he came into the world initially to bring sinners salvation from their sin (1:15), then his future "appearance" will bring an impartial judgment of works (cf. Rom 2:5-11) that will include a judgment of whether Timothy is obedient to his sacred call.

The related verbs used in the Pastoral Epistles for Jesus' return are ἐπιφανερόω and ἐπιφαίνω *(epiphaneroō, epiphainō)* — the dramatic appearance of a ruler — which adds a material impression to Paul's belief in the Lord's eschatological presence and its spiritual effects for believers. In antiq-

---

101. The difficulty of dating either John's Gospel or 1 Timothy makes it equally difficult to determine whether John's Gospel was available to the author of 1 Timothy. Without doubt, however, the fourfold gospel canon was already in wide circulation during the formation of the NT canon, and so this intertext would have been in play when the Pastoral Epistles collection was first received as Scripture and added to the Pauline canon toward the end of the second century.

uity, this idiom gave religious expression to the belief that gods would show up at their shrines in response to vigorous worship. Such a belief extended to the deified emperor of the state cult, which justified the elaborate celebration that often accompanied his arrival, similar to our own political leaders, to convey a sense of their power and importance to the public. In 2 Maccabees, a Jewish text probably known to Paul's Diaspora community, this verbal idea is repeatedly used with dramatic irony to narrate God's "appearances" in defending Israel during its revolt against Antiochus *Epiphanes*. While Paul's Christological claim linking God's coming triumph with Jesus' return may well be echoed in the doxological refrain "King of kings, Lord of lords" (Rev 19:16), the point of this exhortation regards Timothy, not the cosmos, namely, whether Timothy will measure up to the Lord's standard when the Lord returns to assess Timothy's faithfulness. The certainty and effect of this eschatological tribunal may already be in view in the startling mention of the Roman judge who presided over the execution of Jesus: on that future day, the judged will become the judge. The jarring subtext illumined by the assumed tension between Rome (and its emperor cult) and Timothy's public confession of allegiance to the one and only King of kings and Lord of lords underscores the cost that must be paid for Christ's favorable verdict.[102]

The grammar of the concluding doxology (vv. 15-16) is awkward and its referent is unclear, whether it refers to the majesty that accompanies Jesus' arrival as "Lord of lords, King of kings" or to the sovereignty of the God who alone knows its date (cf. Acts 1:6-7). Most commentators agree that its subject is God and that it parallels 1:17 in summarizing the core beliefs about Israel's God. While one might allow that the Lord's appearance will witness to the truth of these claims, even as it is this God to whom the Lord testifies before Pilate, the primary focus of this passage is the contrast between Timothy and false teachers — their character and respective destinies. The impress of Paul's laudation is to underwrite the eventual triumph of those whose values and activities side with God's redemptive purpose. The unhappy future of

---

102. Towner notes that the imperial cult was an important medium by which Rome promoted the empire's political values. Paul's use of the "epiphany" motif "would have called to mind first and foremost the victories of Augustus (= Savior) that brought an end of the civil wars and introduced the *pax Romana* with its benefits to the Imperial provinces." Towner, *Letters to Timothy and Titus*, 418. Not only does Paul conceive his mission bracketed by the two epiphanies of Christ, but he thereby makes the subversive point that Christ's past and future epiphanies mark out the real appearance of divine power on earth and the realization of God's promise of a new creation. Not Rome's Caesar, but the church's God. It is easy to understand the offense Rome felt in Christ's "good confession," imitated now by Timothy!

those teachers who spread falsehoods rather than the gospel and who seek money rather than piety is made certain by the sort of God who awaits them: the transcendent authority of the one and only God guarantees a just verdict of what people have done with their lives that accords with who God is.

The catalog of divine attributes in v. 16 reverses what is essential to human nature — God is not mortal (ἀ-θανασία, *a-thanasia*), not approachable (ἀ-πρόσιτος, *a-prositos*), not visible (ὃς εἶδεν οὐδείς, *hos eiden oudeis*; cf. 1:17) — and explains why God's judgments, unlike those of human culture, are certain and final. In a world that deified its rulers — Caesar was routinely confessed as "Lord of lords" — and whose gods were paraded in public as "the most powerful, the mightiest of the gods, the far-seeing master who fulfills everything" — as Homer would say of Zeus (*Ode to Zeus* 1-2) — Paul's implied claim is that sovereignty belongs only to the Creator and lordship only to Jesus Christ. This doxology registers a community's unwavering confidence in the ultimate triumph of God's way of ordering reality precisely because of the nature of God who does the ordering.

Finally, the juxtaposition of the Lord's confession before Pilate, symbolic of Rome's unholy hegemony in Palestine, and the doxology of the incomparable "Lord of lords, King of kings" is politically pregnant. Similar to Paul's earlier instruction for the community to pray for civil rulers (2:2) while believing in the singularity of God's redemption through Christ Jesus (2:3-6) and instruction through the apostle Paul (2:7), the community's theocentric faith allows no wiggle room for Rome's claims. The idiom of faithful suffering in 2 Timothy, which is seen there as the consequence of following the pattern of Pauline teaching in a public square policed by Rome, makes it impossible for us to accept the modern critical verdict of the church's wholesale domestication in the Pastorals. At the end of the day, the church's confrontation of the empire is never seditious: the church is a household of good citizens. Yet, no matter how compliant the church is with Roman rule or how virtuous its leadership is, its core belief in one God who alone is King over all other kings, including Caesar, must be assessed as (and was) a challenge to Roman sovereignty.

6:17-19 Final Instructions for the Congregation's Wealthy Communicants

[17]To the rich of the present age: tell them not to be arrogant and not to count on the uncertainty of riches but on God, who richly offers us all things for our enjoyment; [18]to do good — to be rich in good deeds — and to be generous communi-

cants, ¹⁹storing up for themselves a good foundation for the future in order to lay hold of what is truly life.

Most recent commentators have recognized the close connection between this passage and the letter's opening, even suggesting they form an *inclusio* within which the entire letter is read. Both passages sound an alert against false teachers and both underwrite Pauline instruction as normative for Christian faith. Within the immediate context, however, this passage resumes Paul's instruction regarding wealth (vv. 3-10), in this case targeting rich Christians: those who place their hope in God rather than in their riches (v. 17) are most able "to be rich in good deeds" (v. 18), thereby preparing for themselves a future reward (v. 19). In fact, Marshall contends this passage forms an *inclusio* with vv. 3-10 that sandwiches the doxological refrain between to supply a final theological gloss on the special problem that having money occasions within the community of faith.[103] In particular, Timothy's "good confession" (v. 12) is exemplary of his congregation's "self-sufficient" piety, according to which greed is exchanged for generosity.

Jas 4:1–5:6 addresses the problem of poverty among believers, but this letter addresses the opposite problem, wealthy believers whose Christian confession must include use of their resources "to do good" (v. 18). This instruction continues from the prior affirmation of a sovereign and transcendent God whose eschatological judgment at the appearance of the church's returning Lord either "gives life to all things" (v. 13) or assigns those who substitute senseless desires for love of God to "ruin and destruction" (v. 9). This haunting sense of a future judgment is reflected by the location of the rich "in the present age," the idiom of Jewish apocalypticism, in which the symbols of present and coming "ages" are contrasted. Moreover, the storage of good works awaits a future whose prospect is "what is truly life" (v. 19). While the Pauline belief in the consummation of God's salvation is not cast here with customary urgency or in the idiom of its imminent arrival, the future reward of faithfulness remains an important motive for a community's obedience to God.

---

103. Marshall, *Pastoral Epistles*, 669. A. J. Malherbe shows how 6:17-19 fits within a longer discussion about the congregation's right uses of wealth that began in 5:1. Moreover, he contends that the passage immediately prior to this one, 6:11-16, typically thought intrusive, is of a piece with the thinking of 6:17-19 and 6:3-10: Timothy's "good confession" includes a moral mandate that includes a kind of contentment that rejects greed. Timothy (rather than Paul) becomes in turn the exemplar-on-the-ground for the wealthy of his congregation to imitate. Malherbe, "Godliness, Self-Sufficiency, Greed, and the Enjoyment of Wealth: 1 Timothy 6:3-19," *NovT* 52 (2010): 376-405.

The uncertainty of wealth is a theological and not an economic judgment. Christianity does not demonize money or possessions, but only a preoccupation with and privatization of them. Within apocalypticism, however, money (and doubtless the class system money sponsors in human culture) belongs to "the present age" indicted by God, which is passing away and will be replaced by a new creation in the coming age. In this letter, perhaps in response to the asceticism of false teachers (see 4:1-4), the generosity of the rich embodies the material generosity of God who "richly offers us all things for our enjoyment" (v. 17). The rapid repetition of πλοῦτος *(ploutos)*-words does not demand the forfeiture of wealth, which other biblical witnesses may imply (e.g., Revelation; Luke 6:20-26), but rather a reciprocal action according to which the congregation's wealthy follow the example of God, who richly gives good things for people to enjoy (vv. 17-18).

Unlike the previous instruction aimed at middle-class women whose wealth was to be put to use in public ways to demonstrate their virtue for evangelical ends (see 2:10), the purpose for the redistribution of personal wealth here is to "store up for themselves a good foundation (θεμέλιος, *themelios*)" for eschatological ends. While the repeated use of καλός *(kalos)* in this concluding exhortation (vv. 12, 13, 18, 19) may connect a "good confession" with "good deeds" in securing a favorable verdict from God, the use of *themelios* when a more appropriate metaphor would do may be an intentional allusion to the word's strategic use in the gospel tradition that tells of the "good person" whose fruitful production of good works is compliant with the teaching of Jesus (cf. v. 3), which is then illustrated by the parable of the builder whose house is constructed on a solid foundation that enables him to escape the coming storm (Luke 6:45-49; cf. Matt 7:24-27).

Paul defined an ideal woman's philanthropy as a public practice of worship that is especially directed toward outsiders (2:10). But wealth is to be used to benefit the congregation: it is the practice of a community of goods, which is the social hallmark of the church in Acts. I have tried to sound this echo by my translation of κοινωνικός *(koinōnikos)* as "communicant." The sense of shared partnership in this word-family suggests a generosity expressed within the bounds of the congregation.

The phrase I have translated "what is truly life" (τῆς ὄντως ζωῆς, *tēs ontōs zōēs*) concludes this letter's adumbration of the Christian conception of real living. The early doxology filled out the persona of "the living God" (3:15), who gives life to all things (6:13) but "eternal life" (1:16; 4:8; 6:12) in particular to those who obey God. The ultimate proof of what is "truly life" is a life with God that endures forever.

This exhortation is a window into the diversity of social classes in the urban congregations founded by the Pauline mission. While clearly there are poor people in the congregation (e.g., those who are "widows indeed" or household servants), there are also wealthy members with both time and money to engage in philanthropic works (see 2:9-10; 6:18). The measure of their religious commitment is how they use their time and money, whether on themselves or to improve society (cf. 2:9-10). For this reason, Augustine wrote in *City of God* that "Those who have given liberally of their riches have had great gains to compensate them for light losses. Their joy at what they assured for themselves more securely by readiness to give outweighed their sadness at the surrender of possessions they more easily lost because they clung to them fearfully" (1.10.2).

6:20-21 Concluding Benediction

²⁰O Timothy, stand guard over the tradition. Avoid worldly chitchat and fictions of the so-called "knowledge." ²¹By claiming it, some have missed the target concerning the faith. Grace be with you all.

In concluding his letter, Paul admonishes Timothy to defend his apostolic inheritance (v. 20a) by avoiding what the Christian faith does not target (vv. 20b-21a). Paul's benedictory prayer is extended to the entire congregation (v. 21b)

Paul's final words to Timothy are consistent with the role performed by the closings of most letters: exhortations repeat characteristic themes threaded through the entire letter and are followed by a fond farewell. In particular, the idea of an apostolic "tradition" (παραθήκη, *parathēkē*) is introduced, which 2 Timothy goes on to say is received from the apostle (1:12; 2:2a) and protected in the company of the indwelling Holy Spirit (1:14) to pass on to still other believers (2:2b). Marshall allows that "the elements of trustworthiness and faithfulness . . . were important associations of the term."[104] As a legal term, *parathēkē* actually envisages the cooperation of two parties who must share equally in this trust as it moves between them — the owner of whatever is deposited and its recipient, who safeguards it for an unknown future. Earlier Paul has written that the congregation's doctrinal standard, which takes its cues from "the glorious gospel of the blessed God," has been "entrusted" (ἐπιστεύθην, *episteuthēn*) to him (1 Tim 1:10b-11; cf. 6:3). And it is this apostolic legacy, instantiated in this letter's instructions as a kind of ecclesial template or "target," which is now entrusted to Timothy's care.

---

104. Marshall, *Pastoral Epistles*, 675.

1 Timothy 6:20-21

It is difficult to underestimate the importance of this benedictory exhortation for understanding the role this letter performs within the Pauline canon. The stunning mention of *parathēkē*, a new idiom for the Pauline gospel shaped by the anticipated succession of his apostolate, not only concludes 1 Timothy but then opens 2 Timothy (see 2 Tim 1:12-14), thus forming the vital lynchpin of this correspondence and suggesting the prospective role of the Pastoral Epistles collection within the entire Pauline canon. No matter how the issue of authorship is settled or how we understand the author's intentions, the late reception of the Pastoral Epistles, which completed the Pauline corpus, insinuates on its every part a "canonical" conception of a fixed apostolic *parathēkē*: even as Paul entrusts his memory and message to Timothy for safekeeping, so also the church entrusts the Pauline canon to faithful readers who approach it as an indispensable auxiliary of the indwelling Spirit to form a vital Christian congregation.[105]

The exhortation to "stand guard" is an aorist imperative from φυλάσσω *(phylassō)*, which carries the added sense of personal vigilance to whatever one protects. Timothy is custodian and apologist for a Pauline conception of God's way of stewarding life. And he assumes this work in the face of an opposition that chatters on about "so-called 'knowledge'" (v. 20b; cf. 1:3-4, 6-7, 9). I have translated κενοφωνία *(kenophōnia)*, which vividly pictures someone who "shouts out" (-φωνία, *-phōnia*) "empty things" (κενός, *kenos*), as "worldly chitchat" to underscore the trivial pursuit of speech within the community that does not target the formation of faith. In this sense, the instructions Paul has given to Timothy by which to organize a Christian congregation is intended to protect believers from "missing the target concerning the faith" (6:21; see 1:18-20). The articular πίστις *(pistis)*, here as elsewhere in the Pastoral Epistles, refers to the Christian faith, which is the content of Timothy's instruction.

Some scholars a generation ago speculated that ἀντιθέσεις τῆς ψευδωνύμου γνώσεως *(antitheseis tēs pseudōnymou gnōseōs)*, which I translate "fictions of the so-called 'knowledge,'" refer to second-century rivals of Pauline Christianity (e.g., Marcionism, Gnosticism) that the Pastoral Epistles were written to counteract. This is doubtful, and few scholars today take the benediction's plain sense in this way. "Gnosis" and "antitheses" were catchwords of philosophical discourse in antiquity, and Paul has in mind any kind of teaching that departs from his "healthy" tradition, which coheres to teachings about Jesus (6:3) as taught by Paul (1:10-11) and now passed on to Timothy for safekeeping.

---

105. Childs, *Reading Paul*, 69-75.

Even though the majority of mss. have the benediction in the singular, Ἡ χάρις μετὰ σοῦ *(hē charis meta sou,* "Grace be with you"), the critical text rightly retains the plural μετὰ ὑμῖν *(meta hymin),* "with you." Copyists expected the farewell to repeat the letter's individual address when it does not. But this begs the exegetical question: Why does Paul conclude a private letter with a public farewell? This concluding address extends the letter's future readers beyond its intended recipient. The personal and direct farewell to Timothy to protect Paul's apostolic legacy also has in mind future congregations of tradents who will benefit from Timothy's diligence. The canonical process, of course, confirms this communicative intent when a personal letter is reimagined and received into the Pauline canon as part of the church's sacred Scripture for generations of future readers. From a canonical perspective, then, the plural form of the letter's benediction underwrites the letter's continuing role as a means of God's saving grace.

A Rule of Faith Reading of 1 Timothy[1]

The Creator God: *"There is only one God, and he is none other than the Creator of the world, who produced all things out of nothing through his own Word, first of all sent forth."*

The theological grammar of the Pauline canon is theocentric. The doxologies of this letter (1:17; 6:15-16), especially when imagined as read aloud in a pagan setting like Roman Ephesus, properly refer to God as the One who "gives life to all things" (6:13) and who is fully alert to the presence of death all around. The subtext of every Pauline letter, then, is a messianic pattern of the Creator God's redemption of creation, broken apart and battered by humanity's sin, and the confirmation of God's provident love in bringing about this redemption in gracious response to the faithfulness of Christ Jesus, the incarnate Word sent forth to save the world from death. The Pauline adumbration of the apostolic Rule in effect outlines the Creator God's *via salutis*. According to this pattern of salvation, God, who alone is God, purposes to save everything from evil and death through the mediation of Christ Jesus, who alone is Messiah (1 Tim 2:3-7; cf. Romans 8; Acts 14:15-17; 17:22-29).

1 Timothy 1 Paul's initial claims about "the blessed God" in the epistolary greeting set out the subject matter of the "glorious gospel" entrusted to him and supply the theological foundations of his variegated instructions to Timothy: God is the one and only God (1:17), the world's "Savior" (v. 1), and "the Father" from whom are received the chief goods of human existence — "grace, mercy and peace" (v. 2). In fact, the Creator's way of sustaining the world, which is affirmed as the overarching theme of Christian instruction

---

1. See pp. 40-43 above.

(v. 4b), seeks the community's loving communion, which is entered into only when hearts, consciences, and faith are all transformed by the word of truth (v. 5).

Because ignorance and sin threaten humanity's loving communion with the Creator, "Christ Jesus came into the world to save sinners" (v. 15). The letter's initial canonical saying is an apt synthesis of a Pauline *via salutis* and stands as the initial article of "healthy doctrine" (v. 10) and the central claim of the "glorious gospel of our blessed God" (v. 11). Even now God's mercy transforms sinners into servants of this "glorious gospel," following the pattern of Paul's own experience of divine grace and missionary calling (vv. 12-17).

In this same regard, we should allow that Paul's personal experience of conversion shapes an intimate knowledge of "our blessed God" as the benefactor of a transformative power. Paul's missionary conception of how God saves people, although related to Israel's biblical story, is informed by an *experienced* communion with the Creator. As a Jew, Paul was thoroughly familiar with the biblical concept of divine grace: Scripture's story of Israel is a story of divine grace. God's election of and covenanting with a particular people, Israel, out of nowhere and for no prior reason, is here retold in deeply personal ways. After all, Paul is the worst of sinners (v. 15) — a blasphemer, persecutor, and arrogant man (v. 13) — who has been met by Christ as though faithful (v. 12) and treated by God with kindness and without good reason. In this sense, Pauline biography (vv. 12-17) secures the theme of salvation and vocation that shapes his instruction of Timothy and the apostolic tradition he is given to pass on to others (cf. 6:20).

Significantly, too, this passage locates the Pauline apostolate within the scope of divine providence. Paul's trope for God's way of putting the world to rights is οἰκονομία θεοῦ (*oikonomia theou*, 1:4), which not only supplies the subject of the community's confession of faith but is also a cipher for Paul's experience of God's saving grace, which liberated him from sin and ignorance (vv. 12-16). God the Savior acts in Christ not only to save Paul from sin (v. 15) but to appoint him to this ministry (v. 12; cf. Acts 9:15-16) so that he might be the role model of God's redemptive intentions for everyone who believes (v. 16; cf. 2:4-6). One cannot detach Paul's sense of his apostolic calling — its practices and its message — from his core belief in God's providential reordering of the world.

Salvation concerns this world where we make our home, which perhaps lies behind Paul's choice of "household," the most essential if also mundane social entity of his world. That is, salvation penetrates the ordinary, this-worldly practices of being human. It should not surprise the reader that this letter contains household codes that present patterns of social arrangements for its members as well as cautionary notes about foolish speech, food, marriage, and money. All of it aims readers at a species of human existence characterized by loving communion (1:5) for which God "who gives life to all things" (6:13) has created us.

Tertullian's profession of faith in "only one God" carries with it a political stance toward all other rulers whose arrogant claims to authority over the world are an affront to the world's Creator. The letter as a whole creates a tension within the congregation that on the one hand is encouraged to pray for "kings" (2:1-2) and generally cultivate the virtues of good citizenship while at the same time directing its praise to "the King of the ages . . . the only God" (1:17). Although Dibelius and Conzelmann are right that the doxology in 1:17 is probably not a "direct polemic against the cult of the emperor,"[2] the juxtaposition of Paul's conversion story with this concluding note of worship leaves no doubt that it is God and not the emperor who alone can save people and thus is worthy of their honor and glory. The politics of such faith leaves no doubt where the community of converts' allegiance is ultimately placed.

1 Timothy 2 A succinct formulation of Paul's theological conception is set out in 2:3-7. The predicates of divine providence are concentrated by the stunning claim that "God our Savior wants everybody to be saved." The repetition of πάντων ἀνθρώπων (*pantōn anthrōpōn,* vv. 1, 4, and 6), especially when coupled with the statement that Paul's gospel is proclaimed to the "nations" (v. 7), underscores the universal scope of God's salvation. Although some have understood this emergent emphasis as a response to Jewish exclusivism or to the elitism of proto-Gnostic sectarianism, these are highly speculative constructions. When read in its canonical setting, glossed by the narrative of Paul's mission to the nations in Acts, the universalism of God's redemptive plan is prophesied by Israel's Scriptures. For this reason, the Paul of Acts is called by the living Jesus to bear witness to him first of all to Jews and then to non-Jews (Acts 9:15-16). God's gospel is preached to all because God's salvation has been made available to all. Nonetheless, this is a radical vision in any world ordered by human sin, which divides "everyone" according to social class, race, gender, nationality, education, or religious affiliation.

The long-standing question may properly be asked whether the universal scope of God's salvation is fully realized in due time because it is a property of God's "will," or whether one's life with God is the shared responsibility

---

2. Martin Dibelius and Hans Conzelmann, *Die Pastoralbriefe* (4th ed.; HNT 13; Tübingen: Mohr, 1955), 31.

of the believer who must freely choose to embrace and enter into it. The strong sense of God's active "will" (θέλω, *thelō*, 2:4), which is typically softened by modern translations into something that God merely "desires" (NRSV) or "wants" (NIV), misses the dynamic tension in Pauline thought between divine sovereignty and human freedom. Although many have sought to resolve this tension one way (God wills to save only those individuals whose salvation God foreknows and preordains) or another (God desires everybody to befriend God in faith, but only some choose to do so and are saved), the Pauline canon nowhere supplies a dogmatic solution — perhaps purposefully so.

This very tension is, however, central to Paul's reasoning in Romans 9–11, where he defends God's faithfulness to promises made to Israel according to the Scriptures. Those chapters are difficult to follow and deeply contested. My sense of what they claim is twofold. First, God's promise of blessing to Abraham (= Israel) does not fail simply because most Jews have rejected Jesus as God's Messiah. Israel's story makes clear that only a "remnant" of humanity experiences the blessings that God promised to all Israel and to "all the families of earth." Second, there is nothing inherently unfair about God willing to save only some, because salvation is God's alone to dispense. Yet the appeal to Pharaoh's story to illustrate God's mercy is ironic: God "hardens the heart" of Pharaoh because Pharaoh's heart was already hardened against God. God's distribution of mercy, while according to God's will alone, is ever responsive to decisions that people make about God.

Against this antecedent text, the confession that the Savior is "one God" (and then also Jesus is the "one mediator," 2:5) clarifies that there is a single way of saving the world. The jarring juxtaposition of an inclusive belief in the global salvation of everybody coupled with an exclusive claim that it is according to the will of "one God" that anyone is saved is perfectly explicable when read within the bounds of Paul's Judaism. God's particular promise to Abraham of a special people, Israel, mediates God's general promise to bless "all the families of earth." It is this more inclusive idea of salvation that frames Israel's vocation as "light to the nations." While Israel's role as mediator of God's blessing to the nations is realized by "the man Christ Jesus," its vocation continues in the life and ministry of the church.

This sense of God's will to save everybody, then, is embodied in the worship practices and public witness of the church. Therefore, the theological formula of vv. 4-6 is central in this paraenetic letter: the true referent of Paul's instructions to his apostolic successor is not a particular "social world," which is only obliquely mentioned in 1 Timothy; rather, it is a God, the only God, who wills the salvation of everybody and who has therefore called the Messiah's people to the sacred business of bearing witness to this truth in the public square by both word (v. 7) and deed (vv. 8-12). The Pauline midrash of Eve's creation story (vv. 13-15a) is, then, a poignant reminder that the Creator's faithfulness to save sinners is the central theme of Scripture's theological narrative. God's salvation of a fallen woman, who experiences God's faithfulness in the act of giving new life, is exemplary of humanity's realization of God's redemptive purpose.

1 Timothy 3:1–4:7a This theological conception is made more robust by the claim in the next passage that the Creator who has willed in Christ Jesus to save a broken and fallen world is not some detached deity but a "living God" who enters into a covenant relationship with those saved from sin to form "God's household," where the truth is found (3:15; cf. 4:10; 5:6). This same "living God" is also "our Savior," who desires that all come into a knowledge of the truth of the gospel (so 2:3-4), which has the power and effect of saving sinners for eternal life (1:15-16). The mysteries of God's truth are apprehended more keenly by those members of "God's household" who not only have experienced the truth about God's mercy in deliverance from their sins but are served by congregational leaders who exemplify the "mystery of the faith" (3:9, 16).

At the very least, Paul's affirmation of a living God reflects the central Jewish conviction that Israel's God is personal and not at all like the ineffective lifeless deities of pagan religion (cf. 1 Thess 1:9; Rom 9:25-26; Acts 17:22-31). Neither is God "housed" in a pagan shrine; rather, God is present in the formation of a people belonging to God. In fact, the expression "God's household" nicely captures the twin impulses of Pauline theology: it is God who saves, and God's saving activity is directed at forming a sacred household, a family, a church, in which a living God is present. For this reason, the church's "living God" (3:15) is object of a more robust hope precisely because God is Savior of all creation — a salvation that is heralded already by those who have already believed (4:10).

God's ordering of human existence aims the covenant-keeping community at loving relations (1:5), which is invariably experienced as a "good thing" (cf. 4:4). For this reason, the community is instructed to give thanks to God for marriage as a "good thing" rather than to disparage it. Καλός (*kalos*, "good") is an important catchword in 1 Timothy (1:8, 18; 2:3; 3:1, 7, 13; 4:4, 6; 5:4, 10, 25; 6:12, 13, 18, 19) and almost certainly echoes Scripture's creation narrative and the Creator's positive assessment of what is made (Gen 1:31). Food and marriage are inherently good things, not because the sacred household's incantations of thanksgiving magically make them so but because these are "very good" creatures made by God for human flourishing. For this reason, the community's prayers of "thanksgiving" (εὐχαριστία, *eucharistia*) are prompted by the actual experience of God's good intentions for these material creatures. Perhaps this image of thanksgiving for food explains the use of the unusual word μετάλημψις (*metalēmpsis,* "receiving"), used as a purpose clause in 4:3 — a word that stresses the relational or shared nature of our thankful reception of God's good gifts. Food and marriage are means by which we cultivate a sense of partnership with God (cf. Gen 1:26) and one another. "Good" is attributed to whatever the Creator has made, whether in the natural order (food) or the social order (marriage) or as an expression of divine grace (salvation, moral virtue). Timothy's assessment of the "good" consists of every result of God's word, whether uttered in creation or proclaimed for salvation.

I write these words not long removed from Katrina's devastation of much of our nation's Gulf Coast, and only a few months removed from the Indian Ocean tsunami that brought untold tragedy to millions. There is much that happens in our world that does not square with our confession of a good creation and its benevolent Creator. Our prayers of thanksgiving and lamentation reflect a theistic perspective that assumes that God is a living presence in all of life, even in a world that sometimes groans under its bondage to decay (Rom 8:21-22). The "good" experience of divine grace in its variegated forms heralds the Creator's coming triumph even over those natural calamities that cause death and suffering, heartbreak and hardship.

This robust conviction of divine providence funds a healthy perspective on our mundane routines — eating food and getting married. Even they are consecrated as the sacred media of God's presence. Remarkably, in this passage the act of transforming the ordinary into sacred objects is not affected by the Spirit's intercession, as elsewhere in Paul, but by the thankful community's worship of God — by recalling stories of "God's word" and by calling on God in "prayer."

4:1b supplies interesting images that help to secure the theological importance of Pauline cosmology according to which "demonic spirits" are the disorderly occupants of the Creator's cosmic household (cf. 1:20; 3:6-7; 5:15). The fascinating interplay in this letter between multiple "households" that occupy the world superintended by divine providence (1:4) — civic (2:2), familial (5:1-2), cosmic (4:1-2), and creational (4:3-4) — frame a believer's response to the routines of daily life. On the one hand, what is not of God is delineated by "deceptive liars" whose false teaching leads to "cauterized consciences." On the other hand, what is of God and issues in holy living is confirmed by "God's word and prayer." Both by rejecting the "doctrines of demons" — that which does not cohere to a Pauline rule of faith and life — and by consecrating even daily routines, the believer actively participates in God's way of orderly reality.

1 Timothy 4:7b-16 The connection is made in this passage between a particular set of religious practices, embodied in the congregation's exemplary leader (4:7b-9), and the letter's repetition of the community's core belief that the "living God is the Savior of all people" (v. 10; cf. 2:4). In particular, the motive of the community leader's εὐσέβεια *(eusebeia)*, which I translate "holy living" (v. 7b), is its value for human "life" (ζωή, *zōē*). The repetition of "living" in this passage seeks to align a life of holiness with the Creator's intentions and so extends into the coming age: holy living has value for what is to come precisely because coexistence with a living God, the Holy One of Israel, is presumed. Moreover, this repetition presumes that the "living God" (θεὸς ζῶν, *theos zōn*) is interested in human flourishing, not only in the future but also in the present.

God "is the Savior of everyone, especially those who believe." The force of the qualification "especially those who believe" is variously understood, but at first seems at odds with the universalism of the letter's prior formulations of God's redemptive will. While the scope of God's salvation is impartial and universal, the scope of those who respond favorably to this good news is more narrowly limited to those who come to a knowledge of the truth and respond in faith to its claims. If this remnant within the whole is marked out by faith — by believing the "glorious gospel of our blessed God" entrusted to Paul (1:11) — the importance of getting the content of this gospel right is made clear.

For this reason, Timothy's salvation and that of members of his congregation (v. 16) depend on his Bible practices (v. 13), presuming that *what* he teaches agrees with the "good doctrine" of the apostolic tradition. Moreover, the refrain that God's salvation (i.e., "those who believe") depends on a species of perseverance defined by the performance of a leader's ministerial duties is a haunting reminder that God's salvation is not a universal entitlement but is worked out in partnership with those called and gifted to teach others (vv. 14, 16; cf. Jas 3:1-2). A sovereign God has recruited Timothy to serve God's redemptive interests by spiritual gift and ordination (v. 14). Not to progress in his ordination is tantamount to spiritual failure to serve Christ Jesus, a rejection of his apprenticeship to the apostle and of the "good doctrine" into which he has been initiated (v. 6). The result is the fearful prospect of not being saved by the very διδασκαλία *(didaskalia)* he has learned and is now called to teach others (cf. 1 Cor 9:27). The succession of leadership from Paul to

Timothy facilitates the succession of the glorious gospel on which basis "God our Savior" is made known and people are saved by faithful response (cf. 2:3-4).

1 Timothy 5:1–6:2 The Pauline household code is especially important in a letter in which the church is presented as God's household. Earlier it was claimed that God's people belong to a sacred household, a microcosm of the *oikonomia theou*, over which God is *despotēs* (1:17). Yet God's rule is benevolent because its aim is love (1:4-5). Relationships in the household are reordered in analogy to this overarching aim. When it posits an ancient (and patriarchal) social world rather than God as this household code's referent, modern criticism will generally fail to interpret the code's instructions regarding widows, elderly men, and slaves and the concern expressed for Timothy's reputation and health as instantiations of the *oikonomia theou*, which aims at loving relations within the household of believers rather than a sociology of domestication.

The danger of using imperial terms such as *despotēs* to depict God's relationship with the ecclesial household is that it can excuse an excessively hierarchical body politic. In such a political structure, those on the bottom will likely be oppressed — women, youths, and slaves. But the theological subtext of the household code is more radical: God is our Savior, God desires that everyone be saved, and the aim of God's economy is a love that issues from a transformed people who are competent at being virtuous and doing good works. This subtext fundamentally qualifies the patriarchy of the household code and prevents the abuse of power. A community shaped by "the glorious gospel of our blessed God" will seek to save people from their ignorance and sin, and the sociology of the community, however it is ordered, should serve that end.

The creational subtext of this household paraenesis, already introduced by the prior confession that everything God created is good (4:4), is envisaged by the tacit appeal to gender differences (5:1-2) and by placing young women in the home (5:11-16) and slaves in submission to their masters (6:1-2). That is, the congregation has a certain order or social structure, which is patterned after creation and "sanctified by God's word and prayer" (4:5). Even the exhortation for Timothy to drink wine to settle his nerves is an ancient naturopathic cure for stress (cf. 4:4-5). While reflecting the practices and norms of an ancient world, the self-worth of people (which includes their personal and physical well-being) is a condition of covenant-keeping.

The remarkable image of a fair-minded God who joins a panel of heavenly jurists to render a verdict on the disciplined elder (5:19-21) presumes that God's supervision of the household includes the rule of law. God hears testimony, weighs it, and renders judgments based on what is observed. For this reason, Timothy is instructed to proceed with careful attention to evidence (5:19) and without hasty decision (v. 22a). The use of the Scriptures and the Jesus tradition (v. 18) and the allusion to the biblical Torah (vv. 3, 8, 19) suggest a legal protocol that is predicated on discernment of God's will. That is, church discipline presumes a conception of *stare decisis* based upon divine precedent. Timothy does not act with partiality, because God is impartial. Even so, God the fair-minded Judge is finally "God, who is Savior of all people, especially those who believe" (4:10).

1 Timothy 6:3-21   1 Timothy was written to supply instructions for organizing a Christian congregation in absence of the apostle. While there are surely external threats to this project, such as false teaching mentioned or alluded to throughout the letter, the principal concern is whether the inexperienced Pauline believer, to whom the work has been delegated, is up to the challenge. The benediction is crucial in rounding out the letter's witness to the Creator by clarifying the theological motive that underwrites the manner of a congregational leader's response to God's way of ordering the world. As personified by Timothy, the selfless performance of those duties obliged by a sacred calling is to engage God's redemptive purpose for "all things"; and not to do so is to lose one's life without gaining it.

The gravitas of the Rule's beginning point is the oneness of the Creator God, who alone "dispenses life" (ζῳογονοῦντος, *zōogonountos*, literally "life-maker") to all things (πάντα, *panta*, 6:13). God alone is in a position to "richly offer us all things *(panta)* for our enjoyment" (v. 17; cf. 4:4-5). The sheer scope of God's life-giving generosity, which extends to all God's creatures, compels Timothy's obligation to live out his sacred calling (6:11-12) as well as the community's obligation to share its goods with other believers. To privatize one's wealth is incongruous of the earnest believer who makes confession of a Creator who gives away everything for the enjoyment of all others. And this image of a hospitable God makes Timothy's own pursuit of virtue as a "man of God" a reasonable obligation (so 6:11; cf. 2 Tim 3:17).

The theocentric cast of this letter's elaboration of the Rule is nowhere better illustrated than in the doxological formulation of 6:15-16. The nature of creation's salvation, which the one and only God orders and implements (2:3-7), is of a piece with the nature of God (see also 1:17). Images of God's transcendent majesty, who "dwells in unapproachable light" and whose sovereign power is as the "only (μόνος, *monos*) δυνάστης *(dynastēs)*" (6:15) "who alone *(monos)* has immortality" (v. 16), sets out God's impressive credentials. God's résumé not only underwrites the ultimate triumph of the *oikonomia theou* —

the pattern by which the leader of the congregation orders its collective life — but also affirms that God's salvation is life-affirming rather than world-denying. The congregation is set within history as a testimony of God's prevenient grace for all to see.

This doxology evokes confidence in a life-giving Creator and contextualizes the discussion of wealth that concludes this letter. When properly used, wealth funds a future secured by this God (v. 19). Nowhere is wealth itself demonized; rather, the reader assumes material riches is another of God's creatures, much like marriage or food, whose inherent nature is good and which are enjoyed when thankfully received as gifts from God (4:3-5). For example, wealth is a good thing when used to acquire food and shelter (6:8) or to fund good works that benefit others (vv. 17-18). Such expenditures are characteristic of those believers whose piety has combined with self-sufficiency in "the present age" to lay hold of eternal life (vv. 17-19). Those who are foolishly greedy and are determined to become wealthy (v. 9) at the expense of their faith in God (v. 10) do not count on God for their future (v. 17) and are plunged into a future of "ruin and destruction" (v. 9) rather than eternal life or "what is truly life" (v. 19). The choices the believer makes about money are theologically adduced, whether or not they are prompted by a robust confidence in the coming victory of the "only *dynastēs*" over the evils of the present age, which will pass away (cf. vv. 10, 17).

Christ Jesus the Lord: "*This Word is called his Son, and, under the name of God, was seen 'in diverse manners' by the patriarchs, heard at all times in the prophets, at last brought down by the Spirit and power of the Father into the Virgin Mary, was made flesh in her womb, and, being born of her, went forth as Jesus Christ; thenceforth he preached the new law and the new promise of the kingdom of heaven, worked miracles, and having been crucified, rose again the third day. Having ascended into the heavens, he sat at the right hand of the Father.*"

Although articulated in an incarnational idiom, Tertullian's confession of Jesus is of a piece with this letter's important confession of "the mystery of holy living" in 3:16. Paul's interest in what Jesus did in and for the world is central to his gospel. In fact, the first in a series of canonical sayings spread across the Pastoral Epistles claims just that: Jesus came into the world to save everyone from their sins (1:15). Subsequently, Paul adds that Jesus did so as a human mediator of God's redemptive will (2:4-6). To claim as Paul does that there is only one Messiah, Christ Jesus, is to claim that the messianic mission to save everyone from sin concerns the particular actions of a single person and no one or nothing else. In particular, Jesus died a Messiah's death, which may be interpreted as a gift since "he gave himself," as a "ransom" since the effect of his death is to free sinners from slavery to sin (cf. Rom 3:24; 6:3-11), and as a "witness at the right time" since he discloses God's redemptive purpose and grace by his actions in the world (cf. 2 Tim 1:9-10). Each of these human acts of mediation has a corresponding heavenly effect (3:16). The working partnership between God our Savior and Christ (who in 2 Tim 1:10 is called "our savior" and in Tit 3:4 "God") is inextricably linked in the outworking of creation's salvation from sin and death.

But in this letter, Jesus is also engaged in the appointment of Paul to a ministry of the gospel (1:12; cf. 2:7). In some sense, Paul's apostolate is the consequence of Christ's decision, even if "by the command of God" (1:1). Thus, a Pauline rule of faith is predicated and funded by "the healthy teachings about our Lord Jesus Christ" (6:3), by which false teaching is corrected and the community's standards maintained until Christ's return (v. 14). Paul's understanding of his gospel was based on what he knew about the risen Jesus. While decisively forged by the experience of his christophany on the Damascus Road (since he did not know the historical Jesus), this letter indicates that he was also informed by gospel traditions about Jesus, including Jesus' Roman trial (6:13). In any case, what seems clear is that the Pauline tradition that Timothy is to protect (and then pass on to others, according to 2 Timothy) is not somehow detached from the Jesus tradition.

1 Timothy 1 While more robust formulations of Pauline Christology await the reader, the letter's opening introduces Jesus as our only hope (1:1) and risen Lord (v. 2), who appointed Paul to his gospel ministry (v. 12) after coming into the world to save sinners like him (v. 15) for eternal life (v. 16). Paul claims that he was "foremost among sinners" and was mercifully saved by the Lord's messianic intervention before Jesus called him into gospel ministry. To believe this is to affirm the tradition's core belief about Christ Jesus.

Significantly, this pattern of a Pauline way of salvation is personalized in a biographical statement about a religious conversion and forms an existential impress of the "glorious gospel" better caught than taught in a concrete, historical, transformative, and personal encounter with the living Christ. It is crucial to note that this biography of Paul's conversion to Jesus grounds his apostolate in different epistemic and dogmatic soil from that of the Jerusalem Pillars, whose apostolic witness was based on their eyewitness testimony to Jesus in the flesh. Pauline commentary on Jesus is not predicated on these same historical memories of the incarnate "word of life" but rather on a deeply personal experience of conversion. While we must be careful not to reduce the Pauline conception of salvation to an internal and individual experience largely detached from the biblical narrative of Jesus' life articulated by the Rule, the initial canonical saying of the Pastoral Epistles collection concentrates on the apostle's conversion to Jesus in a way that is evidently hermeneutical of God's "glorious gospel."

At the very least, Paul's assessment of his past in Pharisaism — as "blasphemer, persecutor . . . (who) acted in ignorance and unbelief" (cf. Gal 6:12-16; Phil 3:4-11) — testifies to an abrupt departure from his old way of thinking about salvation, quite "apart from Torah" and covenant-keeping (Rom 3:21). Personal conversion concentrates God's promise of salvation on an individual's struggle with sin and ignorance, and its debilitating effect in separating the individual from God's redemption plan for all things. Certainly Paul was no unbeliever; to characterize his past, then, as "unbelief" (ἀπιστία, *apistia*, 1:13) is to claim something about his past in Judaism and the disjunction between its way of salvation and this new way he found in Christ (cf. Phil 2:3-9). His apostolate, instantiated and ongoing in the Pauline canon, bears witness to this new way.

Moreover, the converted Paul is enabled and appointed by a "patient" Christ (1:12) who has waited out Paul's prior life of unbelief and insolence to save him from sin for another work: to serve Christ as "an example to those who were to believe in him for eternal life" (1:16). Commission is the endgame of conversion. 1 Timothy includes this dynamic interplay between getting saved and getting called (cf. Acts 9) that adds a distinctively vocational gloss to a Pauline pattern of salvation. Rather provocatively, eternal life is predicated not only on believing in Christ (e.g., 1:16) but also on obeying what one is called by Christ to do (so 4:16; 6:12).

The core beliefs of "the glorious gospel" are introduced in the Pastoral Epistles by the formula πιστὸς ὁ λόγος *(pistos ho logos)*. This convention is pivotal for understanding the role performed by the Pastorals within the Pauline canon. These sayings hardly distort what Paul says elsewhere; rather, these are the tradition's canonical sayings and assert the core theological agreements of a Pauline grammar of faith. Each is a memorable statement, linked to memorable events (often narrated by Acts), which enable Pauline tradents in every age to recall and proclaim "the glorious gospel" in their own idiom to others in persuasive ways.

Critically, this initial core belief is programmatic of the redemptive purpose of the Christ event (1:15): Jesus came to save sinners. When added as a formal element of Pauline biography this saying functions to establish the canonical Paul as the ideal exemplar of the Christian convert whose encounter with the living Jesus transforms his ignorance and unbelief, frees him from sin, and empowers him for missionary service. At the same time, the reformulation of Paul's conversion from ignorance and sin as the basis of his missionary calling and message, which has already been framed by a prior reading of the conversion of the Paul of Acts, has the canonical effect of universalizing it as a normative pattern of salvation. In particular, Timothy is put on notice that the gospel does not sponsor the narcissism of private religion. Even if its principal sources are inward and spiritual (cf. 1:5), a ministry of this gospel engages in the hard work of the convert who is then called to serve Christ on behalf of a world in need of God's salvation-creating grace.

1 Timothy 2 Tertullian puts it that the Son "was made flesh and went forth as Jesus Christ." Paul elaborates this event by claiming this Jesus Christ is "the man" who mediates God's salvation for every other human (2:5). This emphasis on Jesus' human mediation is remarkable. Only Hebrews claims Jesus as a mediator, but there as the divine Son of a new covenant whose priestly intercession on behalf of the church is perfect and eternally effective. Here, however, it is precisely the *humanity* of Jesus that is central, not as a key element of a Christian polemic against pagan cults who divinized their saviors (too speculative) nor as a rejection of a Gnostic mythology of a heavenly mediator (too late), but as a core belief of the Pauline gospel, according to which a particular person, Jesus, represents all people whom God desires to come to a knowledge of the truth. The deep logic of the Pauline gospel is that not only does one God work in solidarity with one mediator to achieve God's intended result, but this mediator is in kind the very nature of those whom God wishes to save. Significantly, this formula contrasts with Gal 3:19-20, whose meaning is extraordinarily difficult to follow but appears to argue against the efficacy of Torah because its revelation is mediated indirectly by many angels rather than directly by one God. Glossed by this earlier Pauline claim, the repetition of "one God, one mediator" may well underscore the effective collaboration of God and Christ in the work of humanity's salvation.

Christ's identification with every person is expressed by the metaphor of a "ransom." Although the word ἀντίλυτρον *(antilytron)* is used only here in the NT, Pauline strategic use of ἀπολύτρωσις *(apolytrōsis)* in Rom 3:24 (cf. 8:23) carries a similar meaning. The root meaning is release from slavery at the expense of another — exodus imagery appropriated by Paul to emphasize that salvation from slavery to sin unto a life characterized by "faith, love, and holiness with modesty" results from a change in one's relationship with God. Christ Jesus effects that change by expending his life (cf. Mark 10:45). Further, the verbal idea that Jesus "gave himself" is Pauline (Gal 1:4) and indicates that the work of salvation is a gift and not a reward: salvation is *for* people, not an entitlement because of their election or a reward because of their achievement.

1 Timothy 3:1–4:7a Among the Apologists' deepest concerns when defending the prospect of a biblical canon in the face of "heresy" late in the second century was to have public and particular analogues of the apostolic Rule of Faith that would regulate how the sacred tradition was used by insiders and outsiders alike. Scripture, creeds, the episcopacy, and authorized biographies of early Christian leaders all helped to clarify what the church should believe and how it should live. No matter the date of its composition or the identity of its author, 1 Timothy is a pastoral letter that contains creedal sayings that function in canonical ways: to define the limits of Christian belief. While such theological definitions are found elsewhere in the Pauline canon, the Pastoral Epistles are especially valuable in this regard, and we may claim that their late addition to Pauline canon reflects the *Zeitgeist* of the canonical process.

In fact, 3:16 is a rich illustration of Pauline Christology, and the overall shape of its six lines follows the plotline of Tertullian's Rule. But the letter's confession illumines the Rule by envisaging the interplay between two spatial loci of Christ's cosmic triumph: heaven, where he is vindicated by God in the Spirit and by angelic mediation, and earth, where he once appeared in a body and is now preached among the nations/Gentiles and believed on in the world through the church's ministry. The essential importance of a local congregation's leadership is now clarified for the reader: leaders personify in their public practices, mundane and sacred, the risen Christ's heavenly triumph on earth. Even the outsider's assessment that leaders are "above reproach" is confirmation that they embody "the mystery of the faith" (3:9). The odd use of a moral formula, "mysteries of godly living" (v. 16), to introduce a Christological confession now makes more sense, especially as it relates to Timothy's prophetic role: the truth that he guards, articulated by this Christological creed, is not merely professed as though its incantation magically produces a spiritual effect, but is embodied in a holy life.

After reading the earlier Pauline letters, the reader of Pauline canon should be caught short by these moves. These beliefs, charted along a salvation-cosmic grid, are hardly those of a participatory Christology in which believers are made one "in Christ" and "with him" are being transformed into God's image. Rather, ordinary believers share in the Christ event with their congregational leaders, in whom they find truth personified.

1 Timothy 4:7b-16 The content of the exhortation to "train" oneself for "holy living" (εὐσέβεια, *eusebeia*) takes its cue from the prior catchphrase, "the mystery of holy living *(eusebeia)*" (3:16), who is Jesus Christ. The implication, then, is that the habits of holiness cultivated by instructions from the "good servant of Christ Jesus" (4:6; cf. 3:9) are characteristic of Christ. Read within the bounds of the Pauline canon, the prospect of a holy life is not self-willed but is the result of union with Christ. Perhaps this point is implicitly made in this text in which catalogs of public virtues, including the triad of "love, faith, and purity" (4:12), are linked to worship practices (vv. 13-14) and spiritual gifting (v. 14), which are conduits of divine grace.

1 Timothy 5:1–6:2a The purpose clause that provides the context for the difficult instruction regarding younger widows is καταστρηνιάσωσιν τοῦ Χριστοῦ *(katastrēniasōsin tou Christou)*, which I have translated "they are distracted from Christ" (5:11). Besides the difficult lexical problem of determining the meaning of the compound verb *katastrēniasōsin* there is the theological problem of the reference to Christ: What form does this "Christ" take in the congregation when a believer is "distracted" by other, more mundane preoccupations? And what is the presumed consequence of such a distraction when it threatens to "invalidate" (ἀθετέω, *atheteō*) a prior confession of faith in Christ (v. 12)? The plain sense of this passage makes it difficult to suppose that what is set aside is a lifestyle consistent with faith in Christ or that the real threat is the prospect of marrying a non-believer. Such is not mentioned.

Rather, the danger in view is a functional kind of apostasy when the believer is so overwhelmed by her desire for another that the obligations that have bound her by pledge of loyalty to Christ have been replaced by another. The plain sense of this instruction underwrites a pattern of salvation that is covenantal. The believer must live according to God's economy and is responsible to maintain her devotion to Christ to maintain the covenant and stay saved. In this sense, a self-inflicted judgment befalls the apostate, whose own disobedience brings with it the loss of promised blessing, including eternal life. Salvation from sin is a gift from a gracious Benefactor realized through Christ (1:12-16), but it also is something attained by responsible and faithful discipleship to Christ.

1 Timothy 6:3-21 This passage has importance because it reverberates with echoes of the "healthy teachings about our Lord Jesus Christ" (6:3a), which roots what is believed about the exalted Lord Jesus (3:16) in the soil of history and so closer to the Rule's conception of a messianic *life*. Not only did Jesus "come into the world to save sinners" (1:15) by giving himself as "a ransom for everyone" (2:6), but his teaching about godly living — specifically as it concerns personal wealth — and the content and motive of an event when he made "the good confession" during his Roman trial (cf. 6:13) are new elements added to the gospel of the Pauline tradition. Clearly, the sacred παραθήκη *(paratheke)* over which Timothy is charged to "stand guard" (6:20) includes more than the doctrinal claims of the gospel entrusted to and proclaimed by Paul (cf. 1:10-11); here it includes gospel traditions about the historical Jesus, who is the community's Lord. The word I translate "teachings" (λόγοι, *logoi*) about Jesus can also be rendered "words" or oral "sayings" from Jesus himself, which would imply a Christological source of Pauline tradition. That is, any teaching that disagrees with Paul is unhealthy for Christ's disciples, who cannot possibly live godly lives (εὐσέβεια, *eusebeia*) unless they are rooted in a knowledge of what the Lord Jesus did and said (cf. Matt 28:19-20).

The canonical effect of this move is twofold. The shape of the dogmatic standard of Christian teaching combines gospel stories and sayings of Jesus with Pauline instruction to function as a "Gospel–Letter" canon, especially in a setting where heresy threatens the congregation. Accepting this sacred deposit, then, the vocation of spiritual leadership is to "stand guard" (6:20) over it, to oppose those who depart from its doctrinal standard (v. 3) and to "teach and encourage these things" among other believers (v. 2b).

The clipped allusion to the gospel story of Jesus' Roman trial presumes the reader knows it in detail, and one's memory of its details is cued here to establish the typical circumstances of the "good confession" made by a spiritual leader before others. Critical in this regard is the interplay between the good confession of "Christ Jesus" and his return as the exalted "Lord Jesus Christ" (v. 14), which is probably rooted in Pauline teaching of Christ's faithfulness to God. The prerequisite of the reappearance of the exalted Lord to complete God's redemptive plan is his prior obedience to God, even to death on the cross (so Phil 2:5-11; cf. Rom 3:21-26). The reference to Pontius Pilate, found only here among the NT letters, resists the abstraction of Jesus' obedience into a glib profession of his messianic death or that he is risen Lord. To confess one's allegiance to God in the manner of Jesus requires the clearheaded recognition of the costs of Jesus' obedience to God's command: an excruciatingly painful Roman execution suffered in isolation and public scorn.[3]

Timothy's obedience to his calling, if patterned after Jesus' obedience to his messianic calling and in a similar pagan setting, requires extraordinary courage and singular commitment.

The Community of the Spirit: *"Christ sent instead of himself the power of the Holy Spirit to lead such as believe."*

---

3. See Robert W. Jenson, *Canon and Creed* (Louisville: Westminster John Knox, 2010), 54-58, which sharply distinguishes the history of the fourfold Gospel's depiction of Jesus' life and ministry from modern reconstructions of historians.

Tertullian's sparse theological prescription locates the Spirit and its power to lead God's people exclusively among those who believe. More than any other biblical witness, the grand theological innovation of the Pauline canon is to locate the Spirit of God within particular congregations of Christ's disciples as the instrument of their spiritual transformation in public witness to Christ during his bodily absence. The Spirit's presence on "such as believe" marks out those who by faith participate with the risen Christ in a transformative newness of life that heralds the victory of God over sin and death. In this sense, the Spirit is God's gift to and agent within the company of saints who draws them ever closer in loving communion with God and each other, but then also forges a profound anticipation of what is yet to come, when they hope to experience the full measure of God's promised restoration of all things in a new creation. In the meantime, it is this Spirit that reorders the community according to "God's way of stewarding reality," which makes it difficult to live at ease in Babylon.

The addition of the Pastoral Epistles to complete the Pauline canon adds a depth to its ecclesiology for its subsequent readers.[4] The conception of the church as a charismatic (and sectarian) "body of Christ" whose membership is wholly gifted and that is formed and led by the baptizing Spirit, is now supplemented by a more mundane conception, the "household of God," organized and led by Spirit-filled individuals such as Timothy who take on the household chores themselves as the "pillar and foundation of the truth" (see 3:15). This addition has resulted in a more robust and pragmatic conception of the church: by locating the Spirit in a congregation's ordained leaders, the future of the church and, indeed, of the Pauline apostolate, of which it is the custodian, is placed in the hands of virtuous leaders, whose political role is in part to legitimize the Christian faith to outsiders in the public square.

The addition of this dimension to Pauline ecclesiology does not add order to chaos, as though the charismatic congregation of Corinth lacked the orderliness and concern for public decorum exhibited by the household. Paul is ever alert to this danger in setting out rules in 1 Corinthians 12–14 to regulate the practice of charisms distributed by the Spirit. After all, "God is not a God of disorder but of peace" (1 Cor 14:33). In fact, Paul's extended essay on worship practices in 1 Corinthians 11–14 envisages a primary concern for social order, even if it is primarily internal to the congregation (but see 14:22-23). Even though his address in this case is directly to the congregation with-

---

4. Robert W. Wall, "The Function of the Pastoral Letters within the Pauline Canon of the New Testament: A Canonical Approach," in *The Pauline Canon* (ed. Stanley E. Porter; Leiden: Brill, 2004), 1:27-44.

out expectation that his apostolic office is mediated by delegated or appointed leaders, the reader should assume (from personal experience and church history) that some level of congregational oversight existed similar to what we find in 1 Timothy. Otherwise, how were Paul's instructions enforced? There is no indication that Paul expected the Spirit to police the congregation's worship practices. Käsemann's understanding of a conflict between Paul's apostolic charisma, which led his missionary church, and a system of ecclesial offices, found in the Pastorals, which has institutionalized and domesticated the church ("early catholicism"), is artificial.[5] It is difficult to imagine a vital congregation lacking either, and so the different conceptions within the Pauline canon as a whole are much closer to the truth than one bit or another. 1 Timothy's conception of a "household" church supplies a practical overlay, then, which, when placed on 1 Corinthian's conception of a "body" church, insinuates a clearer understanding of how Paul's apostolic instructions are enforced in a congregation.

1 Timothy 1 The instructions and complement of exhortations that form this letter's main body typically regard the nature and practices of effective leadership — but a leadership that will effectively translate and transmit the Pauline legacy — the apostle's rule of "healthy doctrine" and the proclamation of "the glorious gospel" entrusted to him — for a pagan audience. While love is the moral aim of the *oikonomia theou* and is spiritually adduced (1:5), it is threatened not by misbehavior but by bad theology. Paul makes this clear by opening the letter with the charge that Timothy correct the divergent doctrine of those teachers who fail to uphold the "healthy doctrine" of his apostolic tradition lest they "make a shipwreck of their faith" (1:19).

The practical connection made between doctrinal orthodoxy and moral orthopraxy is inescapable; no teaching should subvert the centrality of Christ to God's redemptive plan for all the families of the earth. Thus, the purpose of Torah is to reveal God's moral compass and so expose a sinner's need for God our Savior (1:8-10). It may be intimated in this passage that Torah teaching helps form the congregation's inner life, from which springs love (1:5). But the plain sense of Paul's argument, reflected in Romans (5:12-21; 7:1-12) and also by the Paul of Acts (13:38-39), is that Torah no longer mediates God's paternal relations with "God's household" as Savior and Father (1:1); nor is it the means by which God's way of stewarding life is observed by faith. This is all now replaced by Christ, whom Rom 10:4 refers to as the *telos* of faith. The two

---

5. Ernst Käsemann, *New Testament Questions of Today* (Philadelphia: Fortress, 1969), 129-47.

uses of *telos* in the Pauline canon, Christological and ethical, are not at odds, since the "in faith" formula by which the *oikonomia theou* is apprehended according to 1 Tim 1:4b is invariably christologically adduced, whether in confession (3:16) or trust (1:4).

Moreover, teaching must serve useful purposes. Teachers who encourage a congregation to attend to idle speculations about God (1:4), who wander into "vain (= foolish) discussion" (v. 6) or who instruct others about important matters of the Torah without sufficient "intelligence" (v. 7) thus subvert the theological formation of any congregation that aims at cultivating loving relationships. If the canonical role of the Pastoral Epistles is "ecclesiastical discipline" — that is, to provide a normative set of instructions for adapting Pauline tradition to future Christian congregations — then the reader is alerted in this opening exhortation to the ongoing problem of those teachers whose "divergent doctrine" and disruptive pedagogy provoke ecclesiastical chaos. Order is maintained to the extent that compliance to the tradition is observed by a congregation's teachers.

What emerges from the letter's opening is a clear understanding that a community of loving relationships is the primary setting that constrains the spread of sin that so easily distorts the gospel and prompts a manner of teaching that is divisive and self-serving. Timothy's correction of teachers is the practice of the leader of such a community, who understands that the orderly instruction of healthy doctrine requires more than truth and has a more interpersonal aim of reconciliation and restoration of "shipwrecked faith." There is no sense in this text that the opponents mentioned are outsiders or forever cut off from the church. Rather, they are disciplined by Paul or corrected by Timothy as the means of forgiveness for their sin and healing of the community.

The mention of "prophecies once made about" Timothy (1:18) invite reflection on the role of the Spirit in and on the individual believer. In this case, the indwelling Spirit of prophecy has publicly indicated Timothy's call and has given to him the necessary charism to fulfill it (cf. 4:14), similar to what we find with Paul in Acts (Acts 9:15-16; 13:1-4). Much has been made of the focus of the Spirit's activity on an individual in 1-2 Timothy rather than in and on a whole congregation elsewhere in the Pauline canon. Of course, this can be explained by different addressees: to a congregation or to a congregation's leader. More importantly, one might allow that the Timothy correspondence allows the reader insight into a Pauline pneumatology focused on the individual. The inborn Spirit is linked with the formation of an individual's virtue over a lifetime — perhaps alluded to in 2 Tim 1:6-7, for example — which surely has its roots in Jewish Wisdom. But the Spirit's presence and the liturgical/apostolic gestures associated with it indicate the Spirit's special gifting of an individual believer who is sanctified and commissioned for a particular ministry by the "laying on of hands."[6]

Paul mentions a second congregational practice of disciplining contrary teachers (who ignorantly engage in the same activities that Timothy has now assumed in the apostle's absence): they are turned over to Satan, who curiously becomes their instructor of last resort! This image is a trope for excommunication (cf. 1 Corinthians 5), but its use here implies that something bad has happened or surely will happen to the excommunicated one that may prompt his recanting and subsequent restoration. "Satan" symbolizes all kinds of nasty stuff — evil, sinning, destruction, death — but Satan's relationship to a Christian congregation or to its disaffected membership as somehow important to their "learning" process is more difficult to assess. Moreover, Satan clearly is subject to Paul's religious authority, which is like God "delivering" sinners over to death in Romans 1.

Finally, a comment is in order regarding Paul's apostolic office (1:1). The canonical approach is not easily distracted by the historian's legitimate concerns about who actually wrote this letter, when, to whom, and for what reasons. The letter's continuity with Paul's earlier or "genuine" letters and its fit within the Pauline canon are established on theological rather than historical grounds, by *what* is written rather than by who wrote it. And on this ground, there is essential continuity between Paul's self-understanding as expressed in the letter's salutation and subsequent biography-thanksgiving with other Pauline letters. The characteristics of Paul's apostolic vocation locate this letter within the Pauline canon as an elaboration and confirmation of his apostolic witness to God's word. As exemplified by Paul and described more fully in the instructions that follow, the congregation's vocation is missional. God's mercy finds and forgives sinners in spite of their past history and theological ignorance (1:13; cf. v. 7), but God's love and grace "overflow" not only to bear witness to God's mercy (v. 16) but to enable believers to serve God (vv. 11-12).

Significantly, then, the terms used in the letter's salutation not only recall the risen Jesus' commissioning of the Paul of Acts (cf. Acts 9) but also the manner by which Paul describes himself and his apostleship in other Pauline letters. The conventionality of this text is precisely its point! Elsewhere in the Pauline canon the sender introduces himself, as here, as an "apostle" (Rom 1:1; 1 Cor 1:1; 2 Cor 1:1; Gal 1:1; Eph 1:1; Col 1:1) who by the "command of God" (Gal 1:1; also 1 Cor 1:1; 2 Cor 1:1) serves the interests of the risen Christ and those the Spirit has gathered "in him" (1:12; cf. Rom 15:31; 2 Cor 5:18). The familiar terms of the letter's Pauline biography used to define the exemplary

---

6. See John R. Levison, *Filled with the Spirit* (Grand Rapids: Eerdmans, 2009), 240-41.

nature of his apostolic vocation recall other letters as well to construct a coherent profile of his spiritual authority and his enduring importance for the future readers. Moreover, his experience as a Christian convert is considered normative of the "glorious gospel" because it secures the validity of the gospel's core meta-saying proclaimed to the nations: Christ Jesus came into the world to save sinners. In fact, the church's identity as a redeemed and missionary people is underwritten by this biography of its apostle.

In this regard, the reader should note that 1 Timothy follows the concern of other NT witnesses (2 Peter and 1 John) that a Christian congregation's theological understanding and its moral life are ordered by the apostolic witness of the "word of life" (cf. 1 John 1:1-5; 3:11). Indeed, the church confesses itself to be an apostolic people. But Paul's deeply affecting experience of the risen Jesus is quite different from that of the other apostles, who "have heard . . . seen with our eyes . . . touched with our hands the word of life" (1 John 1:1). As a result, the Pauline tradition is necessarily shaped by a converting encounter of the sinner with Jesus and by an experience of forgiveness and transformed existence rather than by a historical memory of what Jesus said and did. This sensibility forged by the apostle's conversion is perhaps apropos of a missionary community whose leaders, represented by Timothy, are called to continue Paul's gospel ministry.

1 Timothy 2 There is hardly a more important demonstration of the church's political theology than the jarring juxtaposition of Paul's instruction for the congregation to pray for its civic rulers (2:1-2) while confessing at the same time there is but one Savior and God, whose work in the world is brokered by a single Messiah, Jesus (vv. 3-6), and the instruction of his apostle (v. 7). And it is difficult to imagine a community of better citizens than the virtuous women engaged in philanthropic acts to help their neighbors (vv. 9-10). This is not a people bent on sedition! But the story of the founding of the Ephesian church in Acts 19 suggests that Paul's Christian mission there was unsettling precisely because its affirmations and practices did not tolerate alternate gods, pagan lifestyles, or different ways of salvation. Yes, the community prays for its rulers and performs good deeds on behalf of its neighbors, but its allegiance and so its motives for doing all that are regulated by a firmly circumscribed "knowledge of the truth" in a single deity, to whom its prayers are offered and for whose redemptive purpose all worship and moral practices are performed.[7] Moreover, as I argued above, the keen accent on Paul's

---

7. Cf. Christopher K. Rowe, *World Upside Down: Reading Acts in the Graeco-Roman Age* (Oxford: Oxford University Press, 2009).

missio Dei in the opening of this letter, which shapes the congregation's vocation in turn, understands these practices as aimed at Christian conversion: to pray for the emperor is to pray for his conversion to Christ — hardly an act of political acquiescence!

The initial instruction makes the keen impress that the church is a household distinguished from other households by its worship practices. It does not gather together individuals who each engage in private worship of personal deities. The congregation's social manners consider the well-being of all its neighbors by praying "first of all" for outsiders (2:1-2a) and by engaging in selfless philanthropic acts (vv. 9-10) in order to live at peace with its neighbors (v. 2b). While much has been made of the hierarchical (and domestic) cast of the church's practices in this regard, a socio-political motive is surely not the emphasis of these instructions, which are more theological and missional in aim. As God's household, the congregation is not principally concerned for the spiritual and social welfare of its own membership, as could be argued from the Corinthian correspondence, but invites all people because its public manners are motivated by the theological belief that God the Father is also "our Savior" whose will is to save everybody.

In this light, Paul's instructions to guide the community's worship practices help forge a public identity. There is ever an eye cast to the household of outsiders and its salvation — since God wants "everyone" saved. Thus, for example, believers are to pray for the salvation of the *paterfamilias* of the competing civic household (v. 2a). Yet, as a feature of its political identity, these same prayers envisage a separation from the body politic and its ruling elite: Christians are finally a household belonging to God, not to Caesar. For this reason, the "peace and quietness" that worship aims for is not a matter of good citizenship but an expression of a holy life set apart to serve God's will (v. 2b). For this same reason, the congregation's men raise their "holy hands" during public worship to emphasize their solidarity with God's purpose for every human life.

The reader should recognize the ambivalence formed within the Christian household who practices these things in the presence of outsiders. The confession that there is but one transcendent God, who alone is the world's Savior and who has worked out the salvation of everyone through a single mediator as taught by a particular apostle, whose tradents have formed the congregation in Ephesus, would have left them open to the charge of *misanthrōpia*. The congregation's worship practices, which include prayer for outsiders and philanthropic works, are hardly the effect of cultural domestication but of obedience to God.

This is an important distinction, especially for American Protestant churches, which have sought to maintain a delicate balance between civil servant and criticizing prophet. Too often the church's voice in the public square has taken on the timbre of extremism, either uncritically patriotic or critically anti-American. To a large extent the collapse of the more missional or evangelical conception of good citizenship envisaged by this letter's instruction is the result of a social orthodoxy mostly concerned with good works, however defined, rather than with sound doctrine. Protestantism has become a way of life, perhaps even for some a political ideology, a way of thinking about the other, rather than a theological system organized by the five grand *solas* of the Magisterial Reformation: *sola gratia, sola fide, sola scriptura, solus Christus,* and most especially *soli Deo gloria.* Indeed, this letter is concerned with the shape of the church's social identity (2:1-2), but this identity is deeply rooted in the church's theological confession (vv. 3-6) and missional motive (v. 7). The inherent and fragile liberalism of Protestant religion, so profoundly concerned with the well-being of the other, can only be maintained when regulated by the apostolic Rule of Faith.

Elsewhere in the Pauline canon, prayer gives expression to the Spirit's witness of a believer's familial relationship to God (Rom 8:16-17) and to the inward sense of hope for creation's future restoration that such an experience evokes in the believer's heart (Rom 8:23-24). Moreover, the Spirit makes the community's prayer even more effective by interceding "on behalf of the holy ones" according to God's will (Rom 8:27). While certainly compatible with this more charismatic understanding of worship, 1 Timothy's instructions to pray according to God's redemptive will extends the Pauline idea of worship beyond the cultivation of the congregation's spiritual relationship with God to include the public square. This identification with outsiders does not subvert a Pauline congregation whose covenant markers are its profession of faith that Jesus is Lord and its internal experience of the Spirit. Rather, it confirms that a Pauline congregation's worship practices must embody an activist sense of vocation as light to the nations (2:7; Acts 13:47). While the Christian household leads a quiet life, it certainly is not a passive life!

If the whole of this chapter's instructions map a pattern of worship, then it deals with more than those spiritual practices of a gathered household. Especially in his description of the "modest" woman, Paul includes social practices — philanthropic works toward the community's poor and the manner by which one learns from another — that proffer a more robust understanding of worship that extends to everyday relationships.

Finally, the church's self-presentation as a catholic and apostolic community is elaborated in Paul's understanding of his apostleship in 2:7. His missional vocation as herald of Christ and teacher of the nations marks out what it means to be apostolic. Protestantism has especially defined its apostolic mark in terms of Scripture and its practice. While that is true enough, J. Webster rightly adds that "apostolicity is the church's standing beneath [Christ's] imperious directive, 'Go.'"[8] The church must engage in the same missionary calling and movement that engaged the apostle Paul, apart from which the church is simply not apostolic.[9] And 2:7 formulates that calling and movement.

1 Timothy 3:1–4:7a The principal metaphor of the church in 1 Timothy is the "household of God" (3:15). Similar to Paul's use of "body" or "temple" in 1 Corinthians, the use of "household" images in 1 Timothy is not incidental to the letter's subject matter: the letter is occasioned by the organization of a Christian congregation in a pagan place that is rife with various threats to "church order." Paul imagines the congregation's members and the necessary tasks that build up a faithful congregation as roughly analogous to those of the extended family household of the Roman world. He can even ask this rhetorical question of the household's prospective administrator: "If someone does not know how to manage his own household, how can he care for God's church?" (v. 5). Indeed! Management style (vv. 2-13), maintaining proper boundaries between different members of the household (5:1–6:2), fostering good relations with other households (2:1-2; 3:6-7) within the wider culture (2:8-15), proper use of money (6:3-10, 18-20), inculcating a memory and a sense of legacy in the next generation (1:10-19a), and a proper succession of family leadership (3:14-16; 4:6-16; cf. 2 Tim 2:2) are all keen interests in maintaining a stable household, whether ecclesial, political, or familial.

While the use of the "household" metaphor in 1 Timothy surely draws from the author's social world and its familiar conduct codes, caricatures, and schemata, it is also an important biblical image for God's covenant people. Israel's traditional household does not distinguish between its religious life and its public life or between its domestic and national life. In fact, Torah demands that the inculcation of a people's covenant obligations take place in the everyday routines of family life (Deuteronomy 6). For this reason the first congregations of believers maintained an intimate connection with their Jewish legacy, and in this light the "household" became the place where believers would regularly gather for instruction, for *koinōnia,* to share meals, and to

---

8. John Webster, *Holy Scripture: A Dogmatic Sketch* (Cambridge: Cambridge University Press, 2003), 51.

9. Cf. John G. Flett, *The Witness of God: The Trinity, Missio Dei, Karl Barth, and the Nature of Christian Community* (Grand Rapids: Eerdmans, 2010), 240-85.

worship (Acts 2:42-47; 5:42; 16:15, 34, 40; 18:8; 20:7-12). In fact, the Israel for whom God's promises are fulfilled is cast in Acts by the idiom of Amos's prophecy of the church as the net result of God's "rebuilding" of David's house (Acts 15:16-18), including households of repentant Gentiles (Acts 11:13-14; 16:34).

It should not surprise the reader of this letter, then, especially if she has already read the biblical story of Israel and the narrative of the church's beginnings, to find that this letter opens with the catchphrase *oikonomia theou*, "God's way of stewarding the world," which depicts God as the world's "house *(oiko-)* steward." While Paul distinguishes between the household and the church as different social realities with different missions (cf. 5:3-16), there is no doubt that he observes structural similarities between the two (cf. 3:4-5). In this sense, God our Father is the heavenly *paterfamilias* of the earthly "household of God."

From the Muratorian document, which remains our earliest canon list (c. 200 C.E.), I deduce that the reception of the Pastoral Epistles into the canon of sacred writings was due to the church's recognition of their utility for "the regulation of ecclesiastical discipline" (62-64). Whatever the occasion of their writing, which remains contested, the occasion of their canonization was almost surely practical: to organize Christian congregations in a manner that safeguards and transmits the gospel's truth according to Paul. From this canonical perspective, then, the various instructions of 1 Timothy presume the authority of a Pauline rule of faith and life, which regulates the worship and religious practices of a Christian congregation. The author's irreducible theological principle is embodied concretely in his use of the household metaphor, which serves as the letter's principal *typos* for ordering a competent community's life.[10] The interplay between οἶκος θεοῦ (*oikos theou*, "God's household," 3:15) and οἰκονομία θεοῦ (*oikonomia theou*, "God's way of stewarding the world," 1:4) forms the theological gravitas for the entire letter, since the various elements of a congregation's public life must embody the Creator's pattern for social relationships.

Of course this made perfect sense for the letter's first urban readers, whose meeting place was typically a member's home where believers gathered for worship and Christian fellowship (e.g., Acts 16:40; 18:7; 20:7-12). Whether the family household remains the most essential unit of human culture today is debated among sociologists. Yet even when the currency of other metaphors that organize Christian congregations into cohesive and competent

---

10. See Raymond F. Collins's excellent excursus on this point in *1 and 2 Timothy and Titus: A Commentary* (NTL; Louisville: Westminster John Knox, 2002), 102-6.

communities displaces the household as more relevant, the patterns and codes of the family household found in this letter continue to instruct its faithful readers.

For example, this particular chapter catalogs the qualities of those who can competently lead a Christian congregation — not by the spiritual charisms of church office but according to the virtues of competent workers. These qualities and their presumed roles within the church are illumined by analogy to the typical Roman household. That is, the household administrator takes care of the congregation's day-to-day business, especially with outsiders, while its servant staff attends to the household's internal affairs. The collective task of the congregation's leadership team, whether as a household administrator or servant, is to help Timothy organize believers into a working congregation that will cultivate the faith and witness of its membership. For this reason, the congregation's "administrator" is also able to teach believers (3:2), and the servant staff personifies the "mystery of the faith" for the religious benefaction of other believers.

If one assumes that the elder-administrator manages the sacred household by God's gospel, one should expect the catalog of virtues that mark such a person out among other elders to embody the core ideals of God's sense of propriety about human relationships. The "theological basis" for the leader's spiritual authority is the array of virtues he displays. But a virtuous life alone does not qualify a person for ecclesial leadership. Other qualifications are necessary: business acumen, rhetorical skill, and counseling experience, for example. People are appointed to supervise the church's affairs not simply because they are virtuous people; their appointment is based on a congregation's apprehension of their ability to lead in the ways of God in a particular location (cf. Jas 3:13; Deut 1:13).

Today's American churches, which are often preoccupied with legal rights and denominational slights, too easily dismiss this chapter's catalog of human virtues as yet another biblical reflection of social hierarchy. Not only is the household symbolism of this passage thereby missed; the canonical argot is also missed. For what remains normative in Paul's discussion of church leadership is no longer the specific attributes of a biblical catalog — or its ancillary metaphor — as though a congregation selects a leader by a checklist. Rather, what is normative from congregation to congregation is the underlying theological principle that shapes these instructions: religious leaders are qualified by character rather than charisma.

In fact, the elevation of personal character as the criterion of leadership is different from teaching elsewhere in the Pauline canon that defines Christian ministry (if not congregational leadership) by the Spirit's charismata distributed according to the Spirit's will and set within an egalitarian worshiping community (1 Corinthians 12–14, Romans 12, Ephesians 4). In a charismatic community, where the Spirit is Lord and alone determines church order by giving spiritual gifts (1 Cor 12:11), the very idea that male supervisors are selected on the basis of their virtue and approved even by outsiders strikes the reader as strange. Some clarity is gained by merely recognizing the use of different metaphors of "being church" such as the human body (1 Corinthians) and the household (1 Timothy): each metaphor proffers a distinctive way of imagining the social roles and relationships within a congregation's membership and the congregation's corporate identity and sacred calling as a missionary people belonging to Christ. But Paul's use of the "body" metaphor regards the internal dynamic between believers, which is sometimes conflictive even though they share God's benefaction equally in Christ.

In 1 Timothy, for reasons that have occasioned a great deal of scholarly speculation, much more attention is granted a different kind of dynamic between believers and outsiders. Paul's use of the household metaphor is not easily reduced to a mundane matter of naming God's church after its customary meeting place. The church is reimagined as a sacred household precisely because that enables readers to understand why and for what ends a congregation and its leadership are organized in the manner envisaged by these instructions. In fact, even if the household metaphor and its top-down management style responds to instability triggered by false teaching, which I doubt, the initial reception of the Pastoral Epistles as Scripture toward the end of the second century was doubtless prompted by the early catholic church's battles with internal "heresy." The organization of the church after the model of the Roman household provided a political structure, and a firm definition of a Pauline Rule of Faith helped settle conflicts that threatened the church's future at the very moment the Pastoral Epistles were received as Scripture.

While helpful in this practical way, the use of the household metaphor was theologically motivated: God's desire to save the outsider (2:4) requires an idiom that pays close attention to the conventions and manners of outsiders and so increases the prospect of their conversion to Christianity.[11] While Paul consistently adapted his sense of the church's missionary vocation to various epistolary settings, his metaphor of the church as a Spirit-ruled "body" concentrated on its internal dynamics: each believer performs a Spirit-assigned and -enabled role within and for the benefit of the whole church. Moreover, the very expression that a congregation is a "bodily" whole

---

11. Jouette M. Bassler, *1 Timothy, 2 Timothy, Titus* (ANTC; Nashville: Abingdon, 1996), 106-7.

is apropos of an apocalyptic community whose very existence under the Spirit and in Christ is situated over-and-against the surrounding world order.

While this idea is not totally absent in 1 Timothy, the Pastoral Epistles show a much keener interest in what outsiders think and how they might respond to the gospel on the basis of what they observe of believers in the public square. Outsiders' opinions count in a way that is simply not found in the rest of the Pauline canon. Indeed, there are three kinds of outsiders according to 1 Tim 3:6-7. The first is the ordinary citizen who gives public testimony whether a prospective congregational administrator is "above reproach" (3:7, *apo tōn exōthen*). Such outsiders are also subjects of God's redemptive purpose, "sinners for whom Christ came into the world to save" (1:15), whom God desires to save (2:3-4), and therefore to whom the church should present itself as a compelling testimony of God's mercy. But evidently there are outsiders, once of "the faith," who now pose a moral and spiritual threat to believers (4:1-2). Even these Timothy is told to point in a different doctrinal direction (1:3). There are also demonic outsiders (3:6-7; 4:1; cf. 2 Tim 2:26) who may influence believers negatively and are to be avoided.

While 1 Timothy's household code surely envisages a Pauline sense of the *oikonomia theou* — divine providence — the fact that this code trades on Roman models of the middle-class household further suggests an accommodation with Rome's way of ordering society, but in a subversive way and to convert it to God. In this regard, the administrator's role is not truly analogous to the *paterfamilias* of the Roman household, since the church is God's household and God alone is its head. For this reason, leadership is to be according to character rather than inherited. The result is an ethos not unlike the charismatic community, even though one's fitness to lead is predicated on human virtue rather than spiritual charism. Moreover, the administrator's various duties in the household are those one would expect of one who manages a Roman household: instruction and role modeling, administrative oversight, and public representation, all of which are supported by the qualities cataloged.

Another intriguing element of this notion of community is reference to a female order of servant leadership. On the one hand, the servant staff of a middle-class Roman household would typically include men and women. The qualities required of the women match those of the male "helpers." This is qualified, of course, by 2:11-12: 1 Timothy would not include women engaged in public teaching. It should be pointed out, however, that there are examples of female heads of households in antiquity, which on occasion extends to the structure of the congregation (cf. Acts 16:14-15).

L. T. Johnson's contested interpretation that the crucial phrase of 3:15b, "the pillar and foundation of the truth," refers to Timothy rather than to the church deserves attention. In agreeing with his exegesis, I note two of its most important implications for this letter's definition of "ecclesiastical discipline." The first concerns the political structure of a Christian congregation. Neither the congregation as a whole nor its elder-administrator in particular is vested with primary epistemic authority. This role belongs to another individual, Timothy, who is appointed by the Spirit and confirmed by apostolic authority to insure the succession of truth to the "next congregation." His religious authority as "the foundation of truth" is charismatic and not subject to a human assessment of his competence. Second, as custodian of the apostle's Rule of Faith, Timothy's leadership is not practical but theological. He leads by teaching, interpreting, adapting "the truth" about Christ (3:16) as the congregation's internal standard of compliance to God's saving word.

This leads us to a final theological reflection on this chapter's elaboration of the Rule's core belief in the church as a community of the Spirit. In *Against Heresies* Irenaeus notes the importance of a succession of spiritual leaders — "bishops" he calls them — in caring for the apostolic deposit to make certain it arrives on a congregation's doorstep with the interpretive apparatus necessary to form a people belonging to God. Even if one links this deposit with the canonical writings — the Pauline tradition with his canonical letters, for example — it seems imprudent to think of this tradition as self-interpreting, as if the Pauline canon provided a self-evident answer to every contemporary question or crisis that any rank-and-file believer can readily discern. A congregation requires holy elders who in the company of the Holy Spirit can draw on the various auxiliaries the Spirit has assembled, including Scripture, to meet the spiritual needs of God's people in their own day. For this reason, Paul is deeply concerned about the character of the congregation's magisterium and the apostolic Rule that monitors its teaching ministry.

1 Timothy 4:7b-16 1 Tim 4:16 is an extraordinary text, not only because it conditions an individual's salvation on personal virtue and performance of the ministerial practices but because of what it suggests about the importance of spiritual leadership in cultivating a church's life with God. Before Paul's haunting exhortation of Timothy, instructions are set out that catalog the personal practices of the "good servant of Christ Jesus" (v. 6). This conception of church is different from that of the Corinthian correspondence, where Paul's emphasis responds to possible abuses in congregational worship practices and so presses for a dynamic and loving interdependence within the diverse membership of a charismatic body of Christ. While the evident contingencies that shaped the concerns there are different from those of 1 Timothy, our concern is the role the latter's pastoral conception performs in the entire Pauline canon. Put vaguely, this passage, elaborated in 2 Timothy, underwrites the importance of individual spiritual leaders to the well-being of a Christian congregation.

From this angle, charisma is given to a Spirit-filled leader to enable performance of ministerial duties (vv. 14-16) rather than in different forms to each within an entire congregation to empower a loving and effective ministry of the whole (e.g., 1 Corinthians 12–14). The congregation's salvation, while purposed by "the living God who is the Savior . . . especially of those who believe" (v. 10), is nonetheless conditioned on the growing faithfulness of its spiritual leader and his dedicated practices of a sacred (and personal) calling (vv. 15-16). Central to these ministerial practices are those that facilitate the congregation's catechesis: "the public reading of Scripture, preaching and teaching" (v. 13) as exemplified by the canonical Paul (cf. 2 Tim 3:14-17). This triad of Bible practices, which carry over from the Diaspora synagogue, not only include the "public reading" of Scripture but also midrash — that is, the act of "preaching and teaching" the read text as sacred commentary on the congregation's life. These Bible practices are made more urgent by Paul's prior contrast between the "good minister of Christ Jesus" and the false teachers (4:1-6). That is, theological catechesis into the "healthy doctrine" of Pauline tradition shapes a congregation's identity as a people belonging to the living God.

Perhaps more central to Timothy's professional résumé is the formation of his personal character. On the one hand, the sort of leader one is determines what sort of public activities one engages in. Even if the formation of a congregation after the manner of God is the public task of its spiritual leader, this work is conditioned on the formation of the leader after the manner of God. Obedience is still the result of a robust internal spiritual apparatus. God's way of stewarding the real world includes a reordering of social relations, but also an ordering of one's spiritual life. Finally, there is something of a tension that lies close to the surface of Paul's instruction of effective leadership. The spiritual discipline required for holy living exemplifies the gospel to a congregation that holds promise "for this life and the life to come" (4:8). In this life, then, the minister typically must deal with this-world things — ridicule of one's youth, purity of public conduct, and canonical practices — but also with inward affections that set one's "hope" on the transcendent God and future salvation. Paul makes clear in this passage that the one has everything to do with the other.

1 Timothy 5:1–6:2   Much has been made of the social world that comes with these texts. Frances Young observes that "the Pastoral epistles are part of a concept of society in which everyone is subordinate to someone else."[12] Such a place, she goes on to argue, cultivates a keen sense of obligation and duty toward others in which the law of reciprocity provides the primary constraint of group behavior. Widows who receive the church's assistance are those without viable means of self-support but with "a reputation for good works" (v. 10). By contrast, widows who disobey this law of reciprocity and engage in practices contrary to the household's welfare (cf. v. 13) and open it up to public scorn (so v. 14) receive reprimand rather than charitable help. Submission to authority is therefore an ecclesial practice; the honor and respect due to any congregational member is predicated on whether she does what is expected of her. More importantly than internal relations, one's future with Christ depends on working within stipulated boundaries of the household to prevent "turning away to follow Satan" (v. 15).

The central theological problem the contemporary interpreter confronts in the plain sense of these instructions is the hierarchical social structures they engender. Household servants are asked to maintain their servile relationship to their masters, young single women are consigned to a domestic life, and *de facto* widows must conform to certain social and religious standards to be supported by the congregation's welfare system. Timothy's relationship with the older men of the congregation is a deliberate and cautious one. In fact, relationships within the congregation are generally drawn in a manner that agrees with the household codes of antiquity, which intended to form social solidarity at the expense of individual freedom.

Paul's own politics were more conservative (cf. Rom 1:28-31; 13:1-7), whether shaped within the Diaspora where Judaism's relationship with pagan religion/philosophy and Roman authority was tentative or by the accommodation principle of his missionary vocation (1 Cor 9:18-23). Without doubt, this "don't rock the boat" mind-set is deeply rooted in his primary religious conviction that the boat needs saving. His ambition matches God's since God's salvation is for everyone (1 Tim 2:4), and his pragmatism is such that the conversion of outsiders requires the congregation to live in a manner that wins high approval ratings in the public square.

In this sense, then, the politics of the sacred household is of a piece with the overarching sense of the *Missio Dei* in the Pauline corpus. The practical issue is how to witness to the gospel truth according to Paul within a pagan culture without causing undo distraction from its radical message (see 1 Tim 2:1-7). As a hermeneutical collection, the Pastoral Epistles provide instructions for

---

12. Frances M. Young, *The Theology of the Pastoral Letters* (NTT; Cambridge: Cambridge University Press, 1994), 92.

using the Pauline tradition with a primary concern for the outsider's salvation, but not at the expense of cooperative relations. The way forward in this regard is not to replace Pauline religion with civil religion, or to accommodate the beliefs and practices of pagan culture/religion — to become more "hip" or "relevant" in order to convert the pagan to a religion that is no longer genuinely Pauline. There is a fascinating if somewhat subtle balance or dialectic maintained in these letters between the radical Pauline gospel set out in the ten-letter corpus and practices of good citizenship that resist confrontation, sedition, revolution, disrespect of the emperor, or even separation from the imperial culture. The Pax Romana goes unchallenged in public practice, but the gospel and the way of life it shapes remain a subversive force that seeks to reshape and reform the culture from inside out. Even Paul's sexual ethic, which surfaces in muted tones in this chapter, is driven by a missional pragmatism: celibacy is encouraged, not as a gift of God but as that which facilitates a believer's single-minded attentiveness to the congregation's missionary vocation (so 1 Corinthians 7). Getting entangled in a sexual/marital relationship is a distraction, sometimes necessary and unavoidable, but still unfortunate.

The canonical approach to this problem, while recognizing the practical value of these instructions, seeks to recognize the continuing theological effect of adding the Pastoral Epistles (and this passage) to the final form of the Pauline canon when appropriated by its subsequent readers. As I have already argued, the relevant interpretive issue does not concern the canonicity of this letter's instructions regarding social relationships or whether they carry the same force in different social environs as those that shaped congregational life in Paul's world or even in the second-century community who first received the Pastoral Epistles as Scripture. The effect of this passage when read as Scripture does not concern the nature of a community's social relations but rather a community of tradents whose principal obligation as Christians is to submit to the church's apostolic tradition.

Thus, for example, while slaves are admonished to respect their masters and submit to the social norm — play nice and don't rock the boat — they are to do so to maintain their religious rather than social identity: they are God's slaves, whose real identity is secured by following "the Teaching" (6:1) — by an apostolic Rule of Faith that reorders the household of believers into the *oikonomia theou*. No alternative source can substitute for this apostolic rule, which is the criterion of the community's life together. The community's primary obligation, then, is religiously and not politically adduced and concerns the preservation and continuation of the apostolic legacy founded by Paul and now contained for future generations in the corpus of his canonical letters.

1 Timothy 6:3-21 When reading this passage in canonical context, the Christian practice of sharing goods (6:17-19) is cued by its thematic development in Acts, where it not only cultivates public favor toward the community (Acts 2:42-47) but functions as a clear barometer of its spiritual health (Acts 4:32–5:11; cf. 1 Tim 1:18-19) and acceptance of apostolic instruction (Acts 8:18-24; cf. Acts 6:1-7). While certainly alert to the corrupting potential of wealth, whether in making one too proud (1 Tim 6:9-10) or too complacent (v. 17), the emphasis of this passage is similar to that of Acts: wealth is a commodity to share for the benefit of other believers to serve religious rather than purely social ends: sharing goods embodies for all to see the inauguration of God's victory in the resurrected Christ.

In this regard, the most important contribution this passage makes in elaborating the Rule's core conviction about the church regards its middle-class membership and the link between the responsible use of shared wealth and a future with God. While neither acquiring nor having money is demonized (or blessed), wealth does obligate one to follow God's example as Benefactor and to share with the poor. Wealth, then, is not privatized to secure one's financial future, which is uncertain, as any bear market attests (6:17); rather, wealth affords the opportunity for some believers to secure their spiritual future with God by the practice of good deeds (vv. 18-19; cf. 2:9-15). The theological contribution this passage makes is not the connection of good deeds with end-time salvation, which is a consistent teaching of the Pauline tradition. It makes that point in regard to a particular social group within the congregation whose special status shapes a particular command much the same way that Timothy's calling shapes a different command, whose performance secures his future salvation. Perhaps the household metaphor helps display this kind of participatory ecclesiology, in which one's responsibility in the congregation depends on one's social class or religious office.

Christian Existence and Discipleship: *"In putting on our flesh, Christ made it his own; and in making it his own, he made it sinless . . . because in that same human flesh he lived without sin" (On the Flesh of Christ 16).*[13]

---

13. Tertullian does not supply a core belief about the Christian life in his articulation of the apostolic Rule of Faith; and so we have imported a grammar statement from his seminal essay on the incarnation, *De Carne Christi*, to complete his articulation of the Rule. In our mind, this statement captures the essence of his conception of Christian existence as a new creation, but one conceived of as a bodily or material, even a mundane creation rather than of a form cast in docetic and largely inward ways. In his incarnation, the Son assumes a human body like our human bodies — finite, frail, an "earthen vessel" capable of sinning. That Jesus lived a sinless life is not due to having a special body unlike our own; but it is due to his selfless devotion to the

1 Timothy 1 The canonical effect of noting Paul's departure for Macedonia (1:3) cues the "post-Pauline" setting for the letter's readers, who receive instruction from the departed apostle, ever mindful that his message and memory are normative in the formation of Christian faith and life. Paul's importance for the future of the church is unmistakable from Acts, so to "teach divergent doctrine" subverts a congregation's fellowship with God.

From a canonical perspective, the presentation of Paul's relationship with Timothy exemplifies his relationship with every faithful reader: the church constitutes his "children in the faith," schooled by his apostolic tradition, guided by his example, and formed in a community of disciples whose faith adheres to the "healthy doctrine" shaped by the gospel entrusted to him. If these resources are not drawn on, the individual's faith can be "shipwrecked" by a flawed inward spiritual apparatus — a repudiated "conscience." The repetition of conscience in this opening passage and later in defining the qualified servant (3:9), also in a context of doctrinal purity, suggests an institutional role that serves leaders, such as Timothy, in protecting the Pauline apostolate. To cultivate a "good conscience" not only enables one to maintain solidarity with the apostolic tradition but also to detect and so correct teaching divergent from it.[14]

The biography of the canonical Paul (1:12-16), while also illustrating the gospel's theological center, underwrites a particular kind of conversion experience as the norm for all who believe in Christ Jesus for eternal life (v. 16c). While salvation from sin by God's grace brokered through Christ Jesus is arguably the doctrinal locus of the Pauline canon, what is lacking otherwise and supplied by this letter is a canonical testimony of Paul's experience of being saved from sin for eternal life with God. The hermeneutical importance of this biography of conversion for the Pauline canon, especially with the three accounts in Acts, cannot be overestimated. It provides the résumé of the former sinner (v. 13) and tells of how he was subsequently treated by the risen Christ (vv. 14-16a) and of the transformative experience that resulted from his encounter "in the world" with Christ (v. 16b). In this sense, then, the meaning of justification set out by Scripture's Pauline witness regards more than a conception of getting saved from sin: it also engages a vital experience of transformation.[15]

Father, maintained by the power of the Spirit. Likewise, the prospect of the believer's doing the good works of God's will is not so much the effect of Christ's death and resurrection, as Paul puts it in Romans 6; it is by his sinless example that sin itself is abolished, which his disciples may now imitate even if ultimately in martyrdom — the "baptism by blood."

14. See Robert W. Wall, "Conscience," *ABD* 1:1129-30.
15. See N. T. Wright's doctrinal sketch of Pauline justification in *Justification: God's Plan and Paul's Vision* (Downers Grove: InterVarsity, 2009), especially 79-108.

The firm connection of God's glorious gospel entrusted to Paul (vv. 10-11) with his conversion experience, however, suggests that a Christianity that sponsors an experience-only religion, which I have seen in increasing numbers of students who come from mega-churches, is just as wrongheaded as it is to avoid or dismiss the testimony of a genuine experience of God's presence. The revelation of God is mediated by both the articulate and accurate instruction of the gospel and a profound experience of God's saving grace that confirms its truth.

1 Timothy 2 The character of Christian discipleship is embodied by the faithful woman of influence whose steady modesty bears witness to the transforming effect of the triumph of divine grace over sin in her life. Yet the modesty instantiated in her quiet submission to her male tutor often offends the sensibilities of today's reader. However this offense is finally handled by the interpreter, the canonical status of this passage within the Pauline witness resists every effort to de-canonize it. Not only does the dogmatic soil into which this and every sacred text is rooted compel our serious attention to its spiritual instruction, the historical particularity of the instructions given to middle-class Christian women reflects the responsibility and struggle of being a Christian with the means of influencing others in the public square. And it is this particular struggle, not the struggle of being a Christian woman, that is presented as normative, although I would admit the one often bleeds into the other.

The Pauline conception of the *oikonomia theou* allows for a variety of social hierarchies between "strong" and "weak" believers in various guises or a political hierarchy of spiritual leaders and communicants who are all baptized into a mutual whole by their common commitment to the one Lord and a single pattern of salvation. Yet the evident particularity of 1 Tim 2:9-15 rubs raw the assumption that its literal sense has continuing authority for women of every age, especially in our day when men learn in quiet submission to women teachers who are authorized to teach by their talent and training. That a text's "original" social world is not the same as the social world inhabited by current readers compels fresh adaptations of its plain sense for a contemporary world. This move is made even more clear by the various images of women disciples found in the NT, including some who teach men (cf. Acts 18:26), part of the whole witness that makes it impossible to use the sense of any one text to establish a biblical norm.

If the congregation's social identity embodies its theological commitments, the instructions given to its female and male members, if dissonant to modern ears, provide apt illustrations of the manner and scope of God's redemptive purpose for Scripture's faithful readers. That these instructions are not intended to function as a social code for domesticating unruly Christian women but rather frame a missional exhortation to save non-Christian women underscores a theological motive of normative and ongoing value in every age.

This distinction between theological and sociological motives is consistent with Paul's reading of Eve's biblical story, which appeals to a canonical text (Genesis 1–3) to clarify its theological claim on new readers. Indeed, new meanings are often retrieved from Scripture not by hard-nosed critical analysis but whenever social pressures exerted by new historical exigencies bring to light layers of meaning hitherto hidden from the interpreter's view. In the case of 1 Timothy, Paul's instructions to Christian women adapt both biblical texts and philosophical traditions to an urban, pagan setting in which the worship practices of a Christian congregation are pivotal to its public witness in the Greco-Roman pagan world. Following this author's own interpretive practices, then, today's readers may adapt this biblical text and contemporary social philosophy to update this text's meaning for today's church.

While the text's particular definition of prudent behavior may no longer define the ideal woman, neither can the church fail to read this troubling text as Scripture. No interpreter has the authority to undo the usefulness of a text the church has recognized as divinely inspired and sanctified for holy ends: the interpretive task is to listen carefully for God's word apropos in forming the wisdom of today's readers.

In concluding her seminal work *In a Different Voice*, Carol Gilligan envisions the character of the "mature" (or ideal) woman in terms of developmental psychology.[16] Using first-person narratives of women's experiences, Gilligan proposes to complement extant constructions of adult development built largely with the raw materials of male experiences and dispositions. She finds that women approach moral dilemmas differently than do men. For example, they seek to maintain the sometimes uneasy alliance between personal integrity (being true to oneself) and an ethic of care (sacrificing self for the good of others). The female sense of self, even of self-enhancement, is organized around the maintenance of intimate friendships and interested affiliations. In fact, a woman's sense of social relations, typically more complex and engaged than that of a man, is constructed by experiences of separation from friends or of attachment to them. This growing, developing, maturing sense of knowing oneself and being true to oneself is inseparable from a maternal

---

16. Carol Gilligan, *In a Different Voice: Psychological Theory and Women's Development* (Cambridge: Harvard University Press, 1982), especially 151-74.

ethic of caring for others; that is, "the underlying epistemology correspondingly shifts from the Greek ideal of knowledge as a correspondence between mind and form to the Biblical conception of knowing as a process of human relationship."[17] Learning about oneself as a function of living in and for caring relations with others forges a generous respect for life's ambiguities and an awareness of a differentiated social reality. The result is a much more complex articulation of the sometimes messy interplay between personal responsibilities and individual rights, which are settled by the courageous cession of one's individual rights for the good of significant others.

This "ideal of self-sacrifice" is central to a morality of caring for and empowering others, but never at the expense of a woman's self-worth or contentment. For this reason, the principle of equity, which integrates justice and love, is preferred over mere equality, which is primarily concerned with fairness and equal rights, or matriarchy, which replaces one form of social privilege with another. That is, a woman's independence, which pursues equal power with men, and her dependence, which expends her talent on behalf of the important men in her life, are equally bankrupt vocations.

Finally, what is most satisfying is a woman's interdependence in an ever-widening circle of friends, male and female, for whose destinies she assumes responsibility even as they respond to her in equally responsible ways. As Gilligan puts it, "In a different voice of women lies the truth of an ethic of care, the tie between relationship and responsibility, and the origins of aggression in the failure of connection."[18] Although careful to note that family life differs across ethnic, national, and socioeconomic lines, Gilligan makes the important observation that typically a woman's awakening sense of the profound depth of this truth is in her experience of "childbearing."

From this powerful contemporary perspective, then, 1 Tim 2:15a, "yet the woman will be saved through childbearing," is translated into the climactic moment of a woman's moral formation when she is saved from anti-social "aggression in the failure of connection" and begins to assume the responsibility of caring for herself and then for another.[19] While the Pauline commentary on Eve's biblical story is shaped by a particular understanding of apostolic faith, Gilligan's sociological insight informs a contemporary reading of this text. In the woman's experience of mothering new life a grand truth about God's saving grace is learned: salvation is finally covenantal, cooperative, relational, and rooted in a profoundly hopeful sense of a renewed life —

---

17. Gilligan, *Different Voice*, 173.
18. Gilligan, *Different Voice*, 173.
19. Gilligan, *Different Voice*, 76.

a life that is transformed from deception and transgression into one characterized by Christian virtue.

Timothy 3:1–4:7a The concern for the virtue of individual believers is nowhere more evident than in this passage. While taking care not to displace Scripture's interest in the corporate good, this passage recognizes the importance of individual exemplars who take the lead in guiding the people of God. In this regard, the competence of the leader is principally measured in terms of the personal virtue required to get the job done. While this emphasis surely borrows from the moral traditions of antiquity, it is theologically grounded in God's way of salvation. The kind of corporate ethos cultivated by virtuous individuals provides the context in which disciples of Christ come to a knowledge of the truth and are rightly formed into persons who obey God and live according to God's pattern of life.

An awareness of threats that arise in "the latter days" (4:1-5), here cued by the Spirit (v. 1) rather than from the apostle, echoes the dangerous practices that threaten the congregation addressed by 1 Corinthians 7–10. The response to the "doctrines of demons" that subvert mundane activities such as eating and marrying recalls Paul's prior discourse on creation in Romans 1. These pastoral instructions regarding the most ordinary practices of human existence, especially when recalling their wider Pauline canon, point readers back to what Paul has written, which shapes a vision of discipleship that covers all of life.

Among the more important themes of 1 Timothy is the attention it sustains toward middle-class disciples and the distinctive features of their social existence. Against the apologia for an ascetic lifestyle that we find elsewhere in the NT (e.g., James, Revelation), 1 Timothy argues against despising worldly things and against a self-interested "love of money" that privatizes rather than shares wealth with others. This theme is indicative of the need, especially in the second century, to accommodate Pauline witness to increasingly middle-class congregations.

1 Timothy 4:7b-16 The repetition of εὐσέβεια (*eusebeia*, 4:7-8) cues the reader's attention that Paul's instructions underscore "piety" as a hallmark of Christian existence. But its meaning is hardly technical; the variegated history of this word in antiquity and its use in the Pastoral Epistles suggest a broad expanse of meaning that includes inward affections and public practices. But its use here makes clear that the holy life is not something that God imputes, as though the believer's godly character is the irrepressible effect of God's grace alone. The imperative that opens and frames this passage, "train yourself for *eusebeia*" (v. 7b), bids Timothy's active participation in a disciplined process of becoming godly through his performance of a variety of personal (v. 12) and professional (v. 13) practices (v. 15).

This passage also underscores the importance of canonical practices in forming a congregation that perseveres in grace and hopes for salvation. Those communicants who are saved with Timothy and Paul are those who mind apostolic teaching (v. 16) and who are recipients of the teacher's "public reading, preaching and teaching" (v. 13). Paul's cultivation of a successor to stand in his place during his absence, as Timothy is told to do (1:3), is to supply the church with a mechanism of instruction that defines the terms of covenant-keeping for the next generation (cf. Acts 20:17-34). Understood canonically, the role of ordained leadership within a Christian congregation is catechesis: it is to initiate believers into their future with God by grounding them in the apostolic tradition. The leader does this not only by establishing her practical authority in obeying her sacred calling as confirmed by the church but also by engaging in canonical practices of reading, preaching, and teaching Scripture.

1 Timothy 5:1–6:2 The democratization of the church in the West has forged a deep antipathy for this passage. The hierarchical structures that order household relations, especially instantiated in the domestication of young widows and the servile responses of slaves to their masters, are routinely dismissed as without merit (and worse) for today's church. Modernity's forces that shaped the Magisterial Reformation also shaped liberal democracy's interest in the individual's right to pursue life, liberty, and happiness on his or her own terms. The result is often an individualistic idea of salvation, a detachment of religious observance from Christianity's sacred traditions and practices, and an attenuation of a robust theology of the church as the context in which the Spirit forms disciples in the company of the saints. The central question this passage occasions, then, is: What kind of disciple is formed within a hierarchical Christian community such as envisaged by this text?

Sociologist and gadfly Malcolm Gladwell is well known for his thesis that particular cultures help shape particular kinds of personalities that make those who embody them either highly successful or deficient in the performance of particular roles or tasks.[20] In this sense, a person's success is predictable by the advantages and inheritances she has enjoyed growing up, whether deserved or not, and by the cast of her social world that shapes who she is and how she thinks. He famously argues that a hierarchical culture inculcates a keen sense

---

20. Malcolm Gladwell, *Outliers: The Story of Success* (New York: Little, Brown, 2008).

of deference to those in authority, which tends to reproduce excellent servants but people ineffective at performing tasks that require inventiveness or self-assurance. For example, the cockpit of an airplane requires cooperation between two competent individuals. Hierarchical cultures produce ineffective co-pilots precisely because they show deference to the pilot when making dangerous decisions or when they need to correct the pilot. On the other hand, a co-pilot whose persona is shaped by the forces of a liberal democracy tends toward a bold self-assurance that enables her to correct the pilot's mistakes.

While critics have accused Gladwell of facile generalizations, his study evokes an interesting question rarely if ever asked of this passage: What task is best enabled within a *hierarchical* religious culture? That task is preserving and transmitting an inherited tradition to the next generation of tradents, which is the occasion of these letters and their principal role within the Pauline canon. Perhaps no other unit of this letter's paraenesis better illustrates the canonical effect of adding the Pastoral Epistles collection to the final redaction of the Pauline canon: the ethos of a congregation able to be cultivated to produce successful readers of "the Teaching" (ἡ διδασκαλία, *hē didaskalia*, 6:1; cf. παραθήκη, *parathēkē*, 6:20), instantiated in the Pauline canon. In this sense, the repeated exhortations for an individual believer to remain pure in relation to others (5:22; cf. 4:12; 5:2) and to practice "good works" toward others (5:10, 25; cf. 2:10) are not rooted in conventional notions of social virtue but rather in a definition of Christian existence whose very substance and consequence are set out by an apostolic tradition consisting of the personal example of Paul and his gospel ministry.

The formation of the Pauline canon is not only a function of a community's awareness of the canonical Paul; it is the textual creation of and for a community of believers that come to recognize the indispensability of "the Teaching" for its very survival as the household of God. To put the matter this way underscores the importance of a pattern of discipleship that forms an ecclesial mind-set that willingly submits to apostolic instruction, especially in those settings where it is threatened by rival teachings, personal immaturity, impure desires, impertinent practices, and unruly protocols, all of which are in play in 1 Timothy. But resistance to such behaviors is not motivated by a sense of civic responsibility; rather, the real disciple is called to preserve, defend, and transmit the faith of the apostles to others with integrity and without essential change or distortion.

On the other hand, the theme of personal competence that attends the description of honored members of the community resonates with contemporary culture. Those worthy of support or double compensation (5:17) are those who do good work or who spend their days in useful (v. 10) rather than trivial (v. 13) pursuits. This portrait of the community member corrects the tendency of any volunteer organization to reward loyalty, sometimes uncritically and often in trade for genuine productivity.

Moreover, an emphasis on civility characterizes the honorable member: how speech is used, a concern for public appearances, responsibility for the well-being of needy family members, the hearing of evidence instead of hearsay when rendering legal decisions, and concern for personal hygiene, hospitality, and good works are all sound practices of a just and civil society. Of course, rather than reflecting a later domestication of primitive Christianity, this portrait underwrites the missionary motive that is central to the long-term maintenance of the Pauline apostolate.

1 Timothy 6:3-21 The catchphrase "man of God" is a formal address of the congregation's spiritual leader (cf. 2 Tim 3:17). While Timothy's principal role is to safeguard and transmit the canonical heritage (1 Tim 6:20), which includes the Pauline biography (so 1:12-16) and gospel (so 1:10-11; 2:6) as well as gospel traditions about Jesus (so 6:3), this passage profiles the character of a leader who flees from greed and pursues "moral rectitude, piety, faith, love, endurance, gentleness" (v. 11). Certainly, this text as much as any other in the Pastoral Epistles shapes how we should understand the canonical function of the letter's recipient, Timothy: whatever historical circumstances may have occasioned the concerns of this particular exhortation, its continuing application is aimed at every congregation's spiritual leaders who, following Timothy, find themselves in this text characterized as exemplary tradents of Paul's "glorious gospel," which sets the norm for what they teach to other believers and how they practice their piety before them.

But as the history of interpretation and many modern translations commend, this passage extends its charge beyond the formal offices of the church leadership to every generation and member of God's household. Every disciple is a custodian of the church's παραθήκη *(paratheke)*, and every custodian is obliged to embody a manner of piety that resists self-centered greed (6:9-10) and to pursue rectitude directed toward "good works" toward others (vv. 17-18), which lends integrity to the gospel truth the church protects and transmits to the next generation. Nowhere in this letter should one suppose that the manner of Timothy's discipleship is somehow substantively different from that of the rank-and-file. He is their leader, the delegate of Paul's apostolic office, and as such the congregation's bulwark. But to divorce the manner of his life from ordinary Christian existence as if it were peculiar to his calling is to miss the overarching purpose of the letter's instruction: what goes for the "man of God" goes also for every member of the "household of God."

The concern for the disciple's interior life is perhaps nowhere better expressed in this letter than in its benediction's interest in a species of godliness content with the mundane materials of human life, money, food, and shelter. This interest elaborates the Rule's summary of the Lord's teaching about an incarnational discipleship. The problem with money is not only the time and energy required to make it, which distracts one from the time and energy required to cultivate one's life with God: it also corrupts how one thinks about the future. Rather than trusting in God's benevolence, one trusts instead in riches. And when this shift takes root from within, one becomes more interested in privatizing wealth than sharing it with others. Paul links generosity with eternal life precisely to subvert the greed that drives self-interest and leads away from love of others, without which the household will fracture and fail.

Consummation in a New Creation: *"Christ will come with glory to take the saints to the enjoyment of everlasting life and of the heavenly promises, and to condemn the wicked to everlasting fire, after the resurrection of both these classes shall have happened, together with the restoration of their flesh."*

The old objection that Pastoral Epistles depart from other Pauline letters by lacking eschatology no longer enjoys the support of scholars. This letter, for example, plainly indicates its confidence in the coming victory of God (4:16; 6:14-15, 18-19). What should be said, however, is that Paul's core beliefs about God's coming victory are adapted to the particular concerns of his letters. Because the Pastoral Epistles address the pastoral crisis of a departed apostle and give directions to guide the hard work of preserving and adapting normative traditions linked to his apostolate in his absence, these core beliefs, including those regarding the future of God's salvation, are sometimes articulated in settled, formulaic terms. But this genre, apropos in instructions that seek to transmit an apostolic tradition in the absence of the apostle, does not indicate the demise of Pauline eschatology or the replacement of his apocalyptic religion for a more domesticated or institutional one. Although the outworking of the Pastoral Epistles' epiphany eschatology awaits 2 Timothy and especially Titus, its core conception of an eternal life shared with a gracious, glorious God preceded by an end-time judgment of works is a crucial subtext of this letter.

Christ's return to initiate the restoration of all creation is always linked to the present moment, whether as motive for some immediate response or in expectation of a reward for faithfulness presently rendered. This connection of future hope and present response is a critical dynamic of Pauline paraenesis and is found at work throughout the Pastoral Epistles.

1 Timothy 1 Christ Jesus is our only hope. It is he who came into the world to save sinners for eternal life (1:16). "Eternal life" in Pauline thought is life whose only source is the eternal God. "Eternal life" affirms a manner of life experienced in relationship with the living and merciful God. While in Pauline thought eternal life typically refers to existence in the coming dispensation of a new creation, 1 Timothy's instructions are centered on present experiences, and thus "eternal life" could be an idiom of transformed existence and not merely the promise of life after death.

1 Timothy 2 According to 2 Peter 3:11-13, the holiness that becomes a congregation's public life during the present age at the same time heralds the coming of the new creation in which right living is the anticipated norm. This testimony confirms and defends, then, the apostolic preaching about God's future against opponents who ridicule it as a fraud (2 Pet 3:2-7). Likewise, the Pauline canon routinely links ethical exhortation with eschatological expectation. The purpose of this moral calculus is not primarily prescriptive — to provide a code of conduct for living "between the times" as the guarantee of one's admission into the coming age. Rather, the holiness of those who belong to Christ bears confident witness to the coming cosmic triumph of God's grace at his return. According to Pauline teaching, God's promise of a new creation, which has not yet arrived, is already being realized in the transformation of deceived sinners into virtuous saints. For this reason, Paul concludes the story of the woman's salvation in the future tense: her salvation, embodied by her modest conduct in public, is proleptic of God's future triumph over evil and to the establishment of virtue as the rule of life in God's new creation.

1 Timothy 3:1–4:7a Nowhere in the Pastoral Epistles is the persistent criticism of a diminished Pauline eschatology exposed as mistaken more clearly than in this passage. The contrast between the beliefs of those who confess the "mystery" of Christ (3:16) and those who depart from the faith (4:1) is in events of "the latter times." The Spirit's prophetic word assumes that Christ has inaugurated the final dispensation in the history of God's salvation. Indeed, the catalog of events set out in the preceding confession, especially when linked to other Pauline letters for elaboration, reflects the church's confidence that a new age has begun with the death and vindication of Christ.

Against modern criticism, which seeks to date and locate "the latter times" in antiquity, the history of interpretation of this phrase indicates its timelessness. Chrysostom, in recognizing his opponents in these words of Paul, boldly announced that "it is now the last time." While Calvin admits that Paul's "warning was advantageous in the age of the Apostle," he opines that "to us in the present day it is not less useful."

Thus, Paul's sharpest polemic against those apostates who teach "different (i.e., non-Pauline) doctrine" (1:3, 10-11) is given as a Spirit-inspired prophecy of the church's "latter times" (4:1), when trouble from false prophets is expected (cf. Matt 24:9-14). The future is here (cf. Acts 20:28-30), so Paul rebuts creation-denying asceticism (4:3-4) as contrary to "the faith" (v. 1) and a lie (v. 2) precisely because the new age that Christ has inaugurated heralds a restored creation rather than creation's demise.

The mention of the Spirit is more important than pointing out the church's opposition to falsehood or Paul's prophecy regarding the church's eschatological battle with the devil and those spirits and doctrines it controls (cf. Rev 12:10-12). In this context, focused on Timothy's role in the congregation, this is the very Spirit of prophecy whose utterance called him to his ministry of safeguarding the truth about Christ. Timothy's future is right now as well.

Paul's regard for creation such that "everything God created is good, and nothing received with thanksgiving is rejected" (4:4) trades once again on the biblical narrative of creation (see 2:13-15a) — in this case noting that God created marriage and food to eat for good ends (cf. Gen 1:26-31). Such pastoral encouragement is apropos in a letter whose instructions intend to supply Timothy with a map of the *oikonomia theou,* which the faithful congregation then must instantiate. Yet in a passage about the church's "latter times," Paul's celebration of a good creation heralds the coming renewed creation in which the original intentions of "everything God created" are restored. In this sense, the church's ordinary time, in which good food is thankfully eaten and marriage thankfully enjoyed, heralds the Creator's coming triumph over the "deceptive spirits and doctrines of demons."

This response to an opponent's creation-denying asceticism completes a Pauline conception of the future. Among the core values the early Apologists retrieved from the Pastoral Epistles that may have led to the expansion of the Pauline canon to include them is the recognition that other Pauline texts supported Marcion's negative appraisal of the natural order (cf. Tertullian, *De Praescriptione Haereticorum* 33). Evidently Christian teachers in Corinth had already taken Paul's predictions of Christ's imminent return as implying indifference to material things, including marriage (cf. 1 Corinthians 7) and perhaps even food (cf. 1 Corinthians 8–10), which soon will pass away (1 Cor 7:31). While the date of 1 Timothy's composition may well preclude an anti-Marcionite *Sitz im Leben,* almost surely the letter's reception as Scripture does not. The Apologists may well have recognized in this text a useful corrective to teaching found in Marcion's Pauline canon: the church's positive response to its material life heralds the in-breaking of a renewed creation at the end of the age.[21]

1 Timothy 4:7b-16 This passage is aimed at the coming victory of God and the prospect of participating fully in God's promised salvation. In this sense, the hope that is "set on the living God who is the Savior of all people" sustains the prospect of Timothy's salvation and that of those given into his charge (4:16). Timothy's personal hope will be realized by the present performance of his sacred calling (cf. 2 Tim 1:12), which offers an interesting gloss on Pauline eschatology. The radically transcendent, otherworldly nature of Paul's apocalyptic conception of salvation typically rules out a future that depends on institutional forms or human practices. God's salvation goes forward in history in an irrepressible manner that depends on nothing and no one for its ultimate realization. While the eschatology disclosed in the Pauline canon surely attaches the faithful outworking of God's promised salvation to the righteousness and sovereignty of God in the Christ event (cf. 3:16), this passage provides this promise with an ecclesial mechanism that makes a congregation's ordained leaders, their virtuous character and ministerial practices, critical to the ongoing realization of this promise.

This is especially the case "in these latter times" (4:1) when the perseverance of the congregation is threatened by "profane and silly myths" (v. 7a) of those who have "abandoned the faith" for the "doctrines of demons" (v. 1). One role performed by the Pastoral Epistles within the Pauline canon is to clarify the church's missionary vocation, worked out in other Pauline letters, for a post-Pauline setting. The successors of Paul's message and mission must establish a protocol and working principles, much like those found in a "household," that will effectively transmit Paul's theological and personal legacy to the next generation of his spiritual progeny (2 Tim 2:2). While this is critical if the church is to extend the Pauline witness to the ends of the earth during the present evil age, it is also critical if it is to enter into the coming age.

1 Timothy 5:1–6:2 Ch. 4 made clear that the sacred household lives during the "latter times" (v. 1), which makes even more urgent the exhortation to Timothy to pay close attention to those ecclesial practices and manner of life that "will save both yourself and your auditors" (v. 16) on the day of judgment

---

21. This is precisely the sort of move we find in Tertullian's comments in *On the Apparel of Women* 9, where he uses 1 Tim 4:3-4 as a corrective to asceticism shaped by 1 Corinthians 7.

(5:24). The motive to order household relations according to Paul's instruction is that "they will be blameless (ἀνεπίλημπτος, *anepilēmptos*)" (5:7), which gives an eye to the Lord's reappearance to complete his messianic mission (see the use of *anepilēmptos* in 6:14).

This inference expands the reason that Paul is disinclined to support the community's younger widows and advise them to remarry in order to prevent their "distraction from Christ" (5:11). The warning directed at kinsfolk who refuse to care for family members — "he repudiates the faith and is worse than an unbeliever" (v. 8) — surely has the future horizon of God's final review in mind. Likewise, the repetition of the moral standard of "good works" in this unit (5:10, 25; 6:2) is brought to focus in 5:24-25 by the prospect of a future when the community's present faithfulness will be judged. What is made clear by this text's elaboration of God's eschatological judgment is that a criterion of good works will be employed, and this recognition now motivates compliance to the instruction given. While "the teaching" of the Pauline apostolate is surely missional in cast and emphasizes salvation from sins by faith in Christ (so 1:15), it also presents an understanding of divine providence that is worked out by repayment of "the sins of some folks" (5:24) and a reward for the "good works" performed by others, suggesting that the prospect of eternal life entered by faith can also be forfeited by moral or theological apostasy.

1 Timothy 6:3-21   The logical connection Paul makes between Christ's reappearance (6:14; cf. 3:16) and his doxological confession of God's sovereign lordship over all creation (6:15-16) suggests that the one is inextricably related to the other. Christ Jesus comes into the world to vindicate the "glorious gospel of the blessed God" (cf. 1:15). In the first case, Christ comes into the world to save sinners like Paul from their ignorance and sin. But in this second case, Christ's reappearance corresponds to a time (καιρός, *kairos*) that only God knows (δείκνυμι, *deiknymi*, 6:15) to vindicate the truth about God (vv. 15-16).

The Second Advent does not meet here the need for a theodicy in view of the Gentile mission (as in Romans 9–11) but does safeguard the future of the Pauline tradition. For this reason, this pronouncement of the Lord's return is placed at the letter's conclusion to supply the theological motive of its entire paraenesis: Timothy organizes the congregation according to the patterns of the *oikonomia theou*, shuns evil, embraces virtue, heeds his calling, and safeguards the Pauline *parathēkē* in order to participate in the coming triumph of God's gospel.

In particular the problem of personal wealth is glossed by this eschatological vision. Since no one can take anything material with them from "the present age" (6:7) into the coming age (so v. 17), the wise are content to spend their lives in pursuit of profit that endures: personal virtue instead of money, and money used to fund "good deeds." This kind of religious accounting, which displaces the love of money for the love of others, avoids a future of "ruin and destruction" (v. 9) and builds a foundation for eternal life with God (vv. 17-19).

Paul's striking use of θεμέλιος (*themelios*, 6:19) for a "foundation for the future" that consists of good works (v. 18; cf. 1 Cor 3:11-12; Eph 2:20) provoked Calvin's attention for fear that its textual meaning would incline one toward a belief that "we obtain eternal life by the merit of good works," which he considered an "excessively frivolous" doctrine.[22] But attention to the purchasing value of good works safeguards the believer, instead, from the eternal embarrassment of entering into God's presence empty-handed. Nonetheless, the Rule's emphasis on the believer's material (fleshly) restoration in the coming new creation squares with Paul's exhortation on the right use of wealth since it imagines an eschatological dividend that contributes in some tangible way to the quality of eternal life.

The letter's elaboration of the Rule's belief in the parousia is not easily assessed since Paul's conception of the future of God is consistently concentrated by "the appearance of Christ Jesus" to vindicate God's gospel. The contribution the Pastoral Epistles collection might add to this general belief regards what the tradents must do to persevere to this end when this gospel is vindicated (6:14; cf. 2 Tim 4:1-2, 8; Tit 2:13). In this sense, the legacy of Paul and the church's future with God are linked together.

---

22. John Calvin, *The Second Epistle of Paul the Apostle to the Corinthians and the Epistles to Timothy, Titus and Philemon* (Grand Rapids: Eerdmans, 1964), 100.

Case Study: John Wesley and the Early Methodist Societies

The aim of instruction is loving relationships that come from a pure heart, good conscience, and earnest faith. (1 Tim 1:5)

Early British Methodism instantiated some of the key themes that Paul develops in the Pastoral Epistles. John Wesley, the founder of Methodism, followed Pauline precedent in holding right doctrine ("orthodoxy"), right conduct ("orthopraxy"), and right character ("orthopathy") in dynamic tension.[1] This case study offers first an overview of the ecclesial structures that Wesley developed to form, inform, and transform his followers. It then delineates five specific ways in which early Methodist doctrine, practice, and experience embodied ideas embedded in 1 Timothy 1:1-20: (1) in the recognition that "healthy teaching" (1:10; cf. Tit 2:8) is crucial for the spiritual and moral welfare of the Christian community and that "divergent doctrine" is correspondingly destructive; (2) in the insistence that the aim of healthy teaching is to foster "loving relationships that come from a pure heart, good conscience, and earnest faith" (1:5); (3) in the affirmation that the law, that is, the moral teaching of Scripture, as interpreted and codified by the historic church, has a crucial role to play in the Christian life (v. 8); (4) in the belief that Christians who are growing spiritually and morally need "role models" to imitate (v. 16); and (5) in the conviction that Christ's saving work is offered to all persons without exception (v. 15) and therefore that the internal dealings and external mission of the church, God's "house-

---

1. For an explication of the meanings of "orthodoxy," "orthopraxy," and "orthopathy" in recent Wesleyan theology see Theodore Runyon, *The New Creation: John Wesley's Theology Today* (Nashville: Abingdon, 1998), 146-67, and Richard B. Steele, Introduction, in *"Heart Religion" in the Methodist Tradition and Related Movements*, ed. Richard B. Steele (PWS 12; Lanham: Scarecrow, 2001), xxx-xxxv.

Case Study

hold" (οἶκος θεοῦ, *oikos theou*, 3:15), must bear consistent witness to "God's way of ordering the real world" (οἰκονομία θεοῦ, *oikonomia theou*, 1:4), such that "everyone [might] be saved and come to the knowledge of the truth" (2:4).

I do not claim that Wesley specifically used the Pastoral Epistles as a blueprint or formal constitution for the array of large-group and small-group structures he developed for the spiritual nurture of his followers. Wesley certainly believed that the theological principles he espoused and the spiritual and moral character and conduct he sought to foster in his disciples[2] reflected scriptural norms, and, because the Pastorals represent the most thoroughgoing statement of church order in the NT canon, it is no surprise that many of the teachings and practices characteristic of early Methodism are consonant with Paul's instructions to Timothy and Titus. But that does not mean that Wesley's ecclesiastical experiments were driven primarily by his reading of the Pastorals. His understanding of "primitive Christianity" was funded from many sources, both biblical and sub-apostolic, and many of his most successful experiments in organizing the movement began as rough-and-ready responses to immediate problems or opportunities and were legitimized (at least in his eyes) by their worthwhile outcomes.

The overview of the structures of early Methodism given here is very brief and heavily dependent on more detailed accounts readily available in the scholarly literature.[3] My aim here is simply to show how these structures functioned together to enable the early Methodists to live as the "household of God" (3:15).

I

Historians of the eighteenth-century Methodist Revival often note that neither of the categories used by Max Weber and Ernst Troeltsch to analyze ecclesiastical polities, namely "church" and "sect," applies very well to the early

---

2. See Wesley, *The Character of a Methodist* (1742) and *The Principles of a Methodist* (1742), in *The Methodist Societies: History, Nature, and Design*, WJW 9:30-46 and 47-66.

3. Thomas R. Albin, "'Inwardly Persuaded': Religion of the Heart in Early British Methodism," in *"Heart Religion,"* 33-66; Frank Baker, *John Wesley and the Church of England* (London: Epworth, 1970), 74-87; idem, "The People Called Methodists — 3. Polity," in *A History of the Methodist Church in Great Britain* (ed. Rupert Davies and Gordon Rupp; 2nd ed.; London: Epworth, 1965), 1:211-56; Henry D. Rack, *Reasonable Enthusiast: John Wesley and the Rise of Methodism* (Philadelphia: Trinity, 1989), 237-50; John S. Simon, *John Wesley and the Methodist Societies* (2nd ed.; London: Epworth, 1937), 97-113.

Methodist societies.[4] Wesley was fiercely committed to the principle that Methodism was a renewal movement within the Established Church. He recruited few ordained clergy as "assistants," and those were nearly all, like himself and Charles Wesley, Anglican priests (not dissenting ministers). He insisted that worship services in Methodist facilities never be scheduled to conflict with those of nearby Anglican churches and expected those who attended the one to attend the other as well. He was careful not to register Methodist properties as dissenting meetinghouses under the Act of Toleration of 1689, an action which would, in effect, have *made* Methodism a dissenting church. He was frequently called on to defend Methodism against detractors, and did so forcefully, but always with courtesy and candor, the better to defuse public fears that his movement was a new manifestation of the sectarian radicalism that had ravaged Britain in the previous century. In short, Wesley meant for his "connexion" to reinvigorate Anglicanism from within and extend its ministry to those segments of the British population that the Anglican parish system, having not adapted to the massive demographic shifts caused by the Enclosure Laws and the Industrial Revolution, was failing to reach. That the ultimate *effect* of Wesley's innovations was the establishment of the Methodist Episcopal Church in America during his lifetime and of the Methodist Church in Great Britain shortly afterward is apparent. But "separation" was not his *intention,* and for the first several decades of the Revival it was by no means obvious that separation was inevitable. Wesley's aim was to create a network of societies that would restore to the national church a sense that it was truly the "household of God" — a place for spiritual nurture and fellowship — not a department of the state — an agency for social control.

The basic administrative unit of early Methodist polity was the "society." Broadly speaking, a Methodist society included on its rolls all those in a given town or in a given district in a large city who had formally placed their spiritual welfare in the hands of John Wesley (or, more immediately, in the hands of those appointed by Wesley as preachers or society administrators). Wesley traced the origin of the societies to "the latter end of 1738," when "eight or ten persons came to me in London who appeared to be deeply convinced of sin, and earnestly groaning for redemption."[5] Crucially, the only qualification Wesley set for *joining* a society was soteriological, namely an earnest desire "to

---

4. See, e.g., Baker, *John Wesley;* John Rawson, "The People Called Methodists — 2. 'Our Discipline,'" in *A History of the Methodist Church in Great Britain,* 1:181-209; Rack, *Reasonable Enthusiast,* 249; and Bernard Semmel, *The Methodist Revolution* (New York: Basic, 1973), 20.

5. Wesley, *The Nature, Design, and General Rules of the United Societies,* WJW 9:69.

flee from the wrath to come." But to *remain* a member in good standing, one had to demonstrate the spiritual and moral seriousness of that desire by making demonstrable progress in one's faith. A Methodist society, then, was "a company of men 'having the form, and seeking the power of godliness,' united in order to pray together, to receive the word of exhortation, and to watch over one another in love, that they may help each other to work out their salvation."[6] Note that the scriptural citation built into this statement of purpose is from the Pastoral Epistles (2 Tim 3:5) and underscores a point that is central both to Wesley's reading of Paul and to his conception of religious revival, namely that saving faith requires close congruence between a Christian's inward motives and convictions (the "power" of godliness) and her outward conduct and comportment (the "form" of godliness). Wesley set down three general tests that society members had to pass "to evidence their desire for salvation": (1) avoiding all conduct demonstrably harmful to oneself or others, (2) doing good to the bodies and souls of others, "especially to them that are of the household of faith" (Gal 6:10; cf. "household of God," 1 Tim 3:15), and (3) "attending upon all the ordinances of God."[7]

A Methodist society usually met only when Wesley or one of his itinerant preachers was in town: rarely more often than once a month and usually about once a quarter. Society meetings were festive occasions, often marked by the celebration of the Lord's Supper, a watch night, a covenant renewal ceremony, or a love feast.[8] But the presence of the appointed authority figure also meant that society business was transacted, spiritual progress or decline assessed, and discipline of erring members meted out. Yet as important as these monthly or quarterly large-group meetings were, they were too infrequent to provide the kind of intimate fellowship and close pastoral oversight that were important keys to early Methodism's rapid growth. This was achieved through the weekly meetings of smaller groups within the society, the classes and bands.

The class meeting was first introduced into Methodist polity in February 1742[9] and was swiftly adopted throughout the connection. A class was a neighborhood group, ideally numbering about a dozen persons, but sometimes growing to three times that number, depending on the size of the society and the availability of qualified leaders. Persons of both sexes and all ages

---

6. Wesley, *General Rules*, *WJW* 9:69.
7. Wesley, *General Rules*, *WJW* 9:70-73.
8. Albin, "Inwardly Persuaded," 52-58.
9. See Wesley's journal entry for Monday, February 15, 1742, in *WJW* 19:251, his *Plain Account of the People Called Methodists* (1749), *WJW* 9:260, and his *Thoughts upon Methodism* (1786), *WJW* 9:528.

could attend. Meetings were held weekly, usually in members' homes, but sometimes in other convenient venues. Originally, classes were organized to facilitate fund-raising, but Wesley quickly realized that, because the leaders whom he appointed were in close touch with the members, they could also provide reliable, up-to-date information about the spiritual and temporal welfare of the members and their families. Accordingly, class leaders were soon used not only to collect funds but also to disperse funds to indigent members, to visit the sick, and to inform the preacher "of any that walk disorderly and will not be reproved."[10]

The band meeting was imported into early Methodism from Moravian precedents in 1738, and two sets of rules — one regulating the conduct of band meetings and one regulating the daily lives of band members — were soon drawn up.[11] These rules proved to be adaptable to a wide variety of needs and situations, and within a few years there were special bands for married men, married women, single men, and single women. Candidates for membership in a Methodist society were first registered in a "trial band" for two months, to determine their seriousness and staying power. Veteran Methodists who had fallen into sin were sometimes temporarily enrolled in a "penitent band," where their moral and spiritual rehabilitation was carefully supervised. Conversely, Methodists who had made significant progress in their spiritual lives might join a "select band," where they could "press after perfection" and provide Wesley himself with a trustworthy circle to whom he could "unbosom" himself.[12] It is tempting to suppose that just as a society was divided into classes, so its classes were simply further subdivided into bands. But that oversimplifies matters. The classes were organized geographically (i.e., by neighborhoods, as noted above), whereas the bands were organized according to the life situation or spiritual condition of the members. Thus, the members of a single band might come from several classes. But the bands were kept very small, usually between four and eight members, so it might happen that all the members of a band belonged to the same class.

Classes and bands had somewhat different objectives. As Thomas Albin has shown, the classes tended to offer "doctrinal instruction . . . supplemented by practical guidance in Christian living, that is, by the enforcement of the *General Rules* and by the leader's deliverance of earnest exhortations and reproofs to the members."[13] For example, a letter from an early Method-

---

10. Wesley, *General Rules*, WJW 9:70.
11. Wesley, *Rules of the Band Societies* (1738), WJW 9:77-78, and *Directions Given to the Band Societies* (1744), WJW 9:79.
12. Wesley, *Plain Account*, WJW 9:269-70.
13. Albin, "Inwardly Persuaded," 45.

ist class leader, Abraham Jones, to John Wesley, gives, in quick succession, a summary of the spiritual condition of his class, an account of his expostulations with a female member who had begun to doubt "the being of a God," and a review of his thoughts on the relative merits of extemporaneous and formal prayer.[14] In contrast, the bands could sustain very high levels of trust and confidentiality, and accordingly could engage in very searching examination of conscience and promote deep transformation of character and conduct. Each week, band members were asked what "known sins" they had committed since the last meeting, what temptations they had encountered, how they had been "delivered," and whether they were keeping anything secret from their companions.[15] Put differently, classes emphasized doctrinal and moral "instruction" (cf. 1 Tim 1:5), or what we would call "orthodoxy" and "orthopraxy," whereas bands sought to capitalize on that instruction and move their members toward "loving relationships that come from a pure heart, good conscience, and earnest faith," that is, "orthopraxy" and "orthopathy."

II

Having summarized the polity, discipline, and pastoral practice of early Methodism, we shall now explore five ways in which that movement embodies Paul's teaching in 1 Tim 1:1-20. The first of these is Wesley's agreement with Paul's contention that "healthy teaching" is central to the life of a healthy Christian community (1 Tim 1:10). For Wesley, the criterion of "healthy teaching" was the general doctrinal content of the Bible, which he called, following Paul, "the analogy of faith."[16] Wesley defines this as "the grand scheme of doctrine which is delivered [in Scripture], touching original sin, justification by faith, and present inward salvation." He goes on to assert: "There is a wonderful analogy between all these; and a close and intimate connexion between the chief heads of that faith 'which was once delivered to the saints.' Every article therefore concerning which there is any question should be determined by this rule; every doubtful scripture interpreted according to the grand truths which run through the whole."[17] The analogy of faith thus corresponds closely to the ancient church's Rule of Faith, which was later codi-

---

14. Dated December 12, 1742, in Wesley, *Letters II: 1740-1755*, WJW 26:95.
15. Wesley, *Rules of the Band Societies*, WJW 9:78.
16. Wesley, *Justification by Faith* (1746), WJW 1:183.
17. John Wesley, *Explanatory Notes upon the New Testament* (1754; reprint, Grand Rapids: Baker, 1981), vol. 1, note on Rom 12:6.

fied in the ecumenical creeds and given its definitive Anglican form in the Thirty-Nine Articles and the Homilies. Wesley faithfully subscribes to these statements of the "core beliefs" of historic Christianity.

Nevertheless, he was widely criticized in his time as an "enthusiast," one who taught "divergent doctrines" based on the intense religious experiences of his followers. Wesley stoutly repudiated this charge, insisting that his aim was not to teach anything more or less or other than the doctrines of Scripture and the ancient church but to help believers experience the truth of those doctrines for themselves, in ways that would cleanse their hearts and lives of sin.[18] When believers have an authentic experience of the Holy Spirit, nothing new is added to the doctrinal content of what they believe; rather, they receive a powerful and personal "inward impression" of the historic faith onto their souls. For Wesley, the Bible is the source and norm of Christian truth, but this truth may and must be "confirmed" by the experience and practice of all true believers — always presuming that their experience and practice are shaped, tried, tested, and corrected by the faith community.

A second way in which early Methodism displays themes developed in 1 Timothy 1 was in regarding the "aim" of healthy teaching as the cultivation of "loving relationships that come from a pure heart, good conscience, and earnest faith" (1:5). Wesley firmly insisted that embracing the core beliefs of the historic faith is fundamental to the Christian life, but he cautioned against the kind of religiosity that is reflected either in the proliferation of confessional statements and dogmatic treatises or in wild flights of speculative fancy.[19] Such religiosity is driven not by the love of divine truth but by an unholy infatuation with doctrinal controversy or by an arrogant desire for Gnostic superknowledge. It is sheer egotism masquerading as theological sophistication that drives people to want to draw the boundaries of faith too precisely or to differentiate between "insiders" and "outsiders" too sharply. In his note on 1 Tim 1:6, Wesley observes: "An affectation of high and extensive knowledge sets a man at the greatest distance from faith, and all sense of divine things."[20]

In his sermon *Catholic Spirit* (1750),[21] Wesley extends "the right hand of

---

18. Wesley, *The Witness of the Spirit, Discourse I* (1746), *WJW* 1:267-84, *The Witness of the Spirit, Discourse II* (1767), *WJW* 1:285-98, and *The Witness of Our Own Spirit* (1746), *WJW* 1:299-313.

19. See especially his four "appeals" (1743-45) in *The Appeals to Men of Reason and Religion and Certain Related Open Letters, WJW* 11 passim, and W. Stephen Gunter, *The Limits of "Love Divine": John Wesley's Response to Antinomianism and Enthusiasm* (Nashville: Kingswood, 1989).

20. Wesley, *Explanatory Notes*, vol. 2, on 1 Tim 1:6.

21. Wesley, *Sermons II: 34-70, WJW* 2:79-95.

fellowship" to other Christians, irrespective of their "opinions" on theologically peripheral matters, providing their "heart is right with God and neighbor" and their faith is expressed in works of love. It is crucial not to confuse Wesley's catholic-spirited Christianity with "speculative latitudinarianism" (i.e., "indifference to all opinions" and "unsettledness of thought" with respect to the "main branches of Christian doctrine"), "practical latitudinarianism" (i.e., a complete unwillingness to subject Christian worship — one's own or that of others — to pertinent theological tests), or "indifference to all congregations" (i.e., the sort of religious solipsism which eschews Christian fellowship and refuses to submit oneself to guidance and discipline of others). Wesley's objection both to persnickety dogmatism and "enthusiastic" speculation is not driven by disregard for the core convictions of the faith. These matters were nonnegotiable. But he insisted that as long as the doctrinal center was holding, disputes about peripheral matters that might create animosity between the disputants had to be put aside, lest Christians commit grave sin in their very attempt to define religious truth. For the knowledge of religious truth is ordered to the experience and practice of genuine love to God and neighbor.

> But while he is steadily fixed in his religious principles, in what he believes to be the truth as it is in Jesus; while he firmly adheres to that worship of God which he judges to be most acceptable in his sight; and while he is united by the tenderest and closest ties to one particular congregation; his heart is enlarged toward all mankind, those he knows and those he does not; he embraces with strong and cordial affection neighbors and strangers, friends and enemies. This is catholic or universal love. And he that has this is of a catholic spirit. For love alone gives the title to this character: catholic love is a catholic spirit.[22]

In his late sermon *On Zeal* (1781) Wesley forcefully delineates the function of orthopraxy and orthopathy in the Christian life. He says little here about Christian doctrine per se: his immediate concern is the shameful history of religious warfare and persecution, in which zealots have imposed their orthodoxy on others by force. *True* Christian faith, *true* Christian zeal, is *more* than doctrinal correctness: it is heartfelt love of God and neighbor, self-disinterested obedience to God's law, and deep commitment to the Christian community. Wesley visualizes saving faith as a kind of bull's-eye, with a center point and three concentric rings around it:

---

22. Wesley, *Sermons II: 34-70, WJW* 2:94.

> In a Christian believer love sits upon the throne, which is erected in the inmost soul; namely, love of God and man, which fills the whole heart, and reigns without a rival. In a circle near the throne are all holy tempers: long-suffering, gentleness, meekness, goodness, fidelity, temperance — and if any other is comprised in "the mind which was in Christ Jesus." In an exterior circle are all the works of mercy, whether to the souls or bodies of men. By these we exercise all holy tempers; by these we continually improve them, so that all these are real means of grace, although this is not commonly adverted to. Next to these are those that are usually termed works of piety: reading and hearing the Word, public, family, private prayer, receiving the Lord's Supper, fasting or abstinence. Lastly, that his followers may the more effectually provoke one another to love, holy tempers, and good works, our blessed Lord has united them together in one — the church, dispersed over all the earth, a little emblem of which, of the church universal, we have in every particular Christian congregation.[23]

Although this image does not correspond exactly to Paul's formula, "loving relationships that come from a pure heart, good conscience, and earnest faith," the basic point is the same: divine grace transforms the Christian's beliefs, dispositions, conduct, and dealings with others.

A third parallel between Paul's teaching in 1 Tim 1:1-20 and the faith and practice of early Methodism is the very high — but carefully qualified — estimate of the law in the Christian life. Paul insists that "the law is good if used lawfully" (1:8), but then adds, somewhat perplexingly, that it is not for the just or innocent person but for all sorts of people who "act contrary to healthy teaching" (v. 10). We have here a new formulation of the familiar Pauline paradox (cf. Rom 7:7-12; Gal 3:19-29), according to which people can live wisely and well neither with nor without the law. The law always has the effect of making the temperamentally disobedient feel lasciviously "free" and the habitually obedient self-righteously secure. It provides legitimacy for the efforts by the state and/or the church to restrain vice and crime, but it also provides occasion for those not disposed toward vice or crime to imagine that their law-abidingness constitutes righteousness before God, and therefore to obviate their need for faith in Christ's pardoning and empowering grace.

Wesley wrestled mightily with these issues, first in his series of sermons, *Upon our Lord's Sermon on the Mount* (1748-50),[24] and then in his three sermons on the law, which we will examine here. In the first of these, *The Origi-*

---

23. *WJW* 3:313-14.
24. *WJW* 1:466-698.

nal, Nature, Properties and Use of the Law (1750),[25] Wesley argues that "the original of the moral law" is not "of so late an institution as the time of Moses," but is "enrolled in the annals of eternity," and, "with regard to man, it was coeval with his nature."[26] God is good and just, and God's law, which is the expression of God's nature, is likewise good and just. Human beings, who are made in God's image, are therefore just and good to the extent that their character and comportment correspond with the law inscribed on their hearts. Yet in the exercise of their moral freedom — which *also* reflects the divine image in which they are made — they are capable of breaking the law and thereby becoming not only evil and unjust but also deeply untrue to themselves. In humanity's "fallen" condition, therefore, the law, applied to our hearts by the Holy Spirit, has three salutary effects: (1) it convinces us of our fallenness, (2) it alerts us to our need for conversion to Christ, and (3) it "prepares [us] for larger communications of the life of God."[27] Wesley draws these three uses of the law from continental Protestantism, but he gives the third use, which had been so hotly debated by Lutherans and Calvinists, a distinctive twist. It is not merely to regulate outward Christian conduct (as Calvinists and Philippist Lutherans had allowed), but also to propagate deeper Christian faith, to "keep us with [Christ]," who is himself "the end of the law." As we contemplate the "height and depth and length and breadth" of the law, which is perfectly embodied in the person and work of Christ and beyond our attainment on our own, we are impelled to put aside all futile efforts at self-justification and to rely on his pardon *for* sin and his empowerment *over* sin. Thus, "to use the law lawfully" is to regard it not simply as a moral ideal that we cannot attain but as a moral reality that Jesus Christ *has* attained and that he invites and enables us to share through communion with himself.

This communion is affected, of course, by faith: that point is elaborated in the second and third sermons, titled *The Law Established through Faith, Discourses I and II* (1750). In *Discourse I*, Wesley inventories three ways of "making void the law through faith," namely (1) failing to preach the law at all (out of a misguided preference for "the gospel," which, in Wesley's view, cannot be rightly understood apart from the divine law), (2) "teaching that faith supersedes the necessity of holiness" (when, in fact, faith is the indispensable means to holiness), and (3) "living as if faith was designed to excuse us from holiness."[28] This corrective against antinomianism is balanced, in *Discourse*

---

25. *WJW* 2:1-19.
26. *WJW* 2:6-7.
27. *WJW* 2:15-16.
28. *WJW* 2:20-32.

II, by a discussion of three corresponding ways of "establishing the law," which are: (1) preaching the demands of the law, as Jesus did, which apply "not only with regard to the outward actions which it either forbids or enjoins, but also with respect to the inward principle, as to the thoughts, desires, and intents of the heart," (2) preaching faith in Christ "to produce all manner of holiness, negative and positive," and (3) putting the law into concrete practice in our own hearts and lives.[29] The law is "for the lawless and rebellious, godless and sinners" (1 Tim 1:9) only in the sense that it exposes and condemns their evil, but their evil consists precisely in their failure to allow the law to be *for* them in the deeper and proper sense of articulating the pattern of, and furnishing the incentive and means to, friendship with God.

Wesley's sermons on the law provide a useful hermeneutic for the seemingly draconian rules of his accountability groups. These rules, customized as they were to the conditions of eighteenth-century English life, were nevertheless intended to help the Methodists fulfill the majestic divine laws inscribed on the human heart — laws without which human life cannot flourish and by means of which fallen human beings are restored to wholeness. Wesley understood the dangers inherent in the rigorous pursuit of holiness: legalism, sanctimoniousness, hypocrisy, self-deception, spiritual tyranny, etc. But he feared that apart from the quest for holiness Christian faith falls prey to moral laxity — as Moravian quietism and Calvinistic antinomianism had shown. And he believed he could prevent those pursuing holiness from succumbing to Pharisaism by requiring them to face those conscience-searing questions described above. These questions alerted members to the discrepancy between their high ideals and their actual attainments, not in order to demythologize their ideals or inure them to failure but to limn "the Christian's pattern"[30] and remind them that the spiritual power needed to live accordingly was available through faith and through the practice of the means of grace.

This brings us to the fourth element in 1 Timothy 1 that was central to the way early Methodists were formed in the Christian faith, namely the appeal to "role models." Paul calls himself both "the chief of sinners" and "the *hypotyposis* (example or paradigm) for those who come to believe in [Christ Jesus] for eternal life" (1:16). He takes his own story to provide both a negative

29. *WJW* 2:33-43.
30. This was the title Wesley gave to his "extract" of *The Imitation of Christ* by Thomas à Kempis. This extract was first published in April 1735 and repeatedly thereafter. In his *Plain Account of Christian Perfection* (1777), Wesley tells us that he first read *The Imitation of Christ* in 1726 and that it had revealed to him "the nature and extent of inward religion, the religion of the heart" (*WJW-Jackson* 1:366-67).

and a positive example, from which Timothy can learn. Although Wesley never directly pointed to himself as a "role model" for imitation, or at least never claimed to have attained the state of "Christian perfection" that he urged his followers to pursue, his published *Journal* gives us a (carefully "stage-managed") portrait of his own spiritual struggles and experiments. Moreover, Wesley published a number of character sketches of saints, both ancient and modern, which illustrated moral and spiritual qualities worthy of imitation. These included extracts of martyrologies and biographies of Catholic, Anglican, and Puritan saints,[31] a memorial sermon for his rival George Whitefield,[32] a collection of spiritual autobiographies by his own preachers, and two works (a funeral sermon and a biography) on his associate John Fletcher. This proliferation of journals, eulogies, testimonies, hagiographies, and martyrologies should not surprise us. Whenever Christians organize themselves for the pursuit of holiness, such writings become important forms of devotional literature. The unanswerable argument for the claim that, in principle, Christian holiness is attainable by everyone is that, in fact, it has been attained by some. And those who have attained it are distinguished from the rest, not by any superhuman traits of their own, but by the spiritual power that comes from determined faith in Christ.

The fifth parallel between early Methodism and 1 Timothy 1 is that both promoted the belief that God's saving love is universal in scope. This idea is adumbrated in Paul's salutation to Timothy, where the words "grace, mercy and peace" (1:2) envision the joining of the pagan and Jewish worlds. It is further elaborated, albeit indirectly, in the creedal statement "Christ Jesus came into the world to save sinners" (v. 15), which I take, following Wesley, to refer to "*all* sinners, without exception."[33] And it is later explicitly affirmed in two places: "God our Savior . . . wants to save everybody and wants them to come to a knowledge of the truth" (2:3b-4), and again, "Our hope is set on the living God, who is the Savior of all people, especially those who believe" (4:10).

None of the controversies in which John Wesley was embroiled was more bitter or protracted than his dispute with English Calvinists over the question of predestination. Wesley, following Arminius, held the following view: (1) that Christ died to save all persons from sin and death; that God does not violate the moral freedom of any person by unchangeably decreeing

---

31. The first edition of the *Christian Library* was published between 1749 and 1755 and ran to fifty duodecimo volumes. The second edition was published between 1819 and 1827 in thirty octavo volumes. I have consulted the latter. The martyrologies and saints' lives are found in Vols. 1-4, 15-17, and 27-29.

32. Wesley, *On the Death of George Whitefield*, WJW 2:324-47.

33. Wesley, *Explanatory Notes*, vol. 2, on 1 Tim 1:15.

whether she will accept full pardon for her sins through the atoning death of Jesus Christ; (2) that each person must, by the exercise of that same moral freedom, cooperate with the Holy Spirit in repenting of her sins and amending her life in accordance with the divine law and the example of Christ; and (3) that there is no fixed limit beyond which the Holy Spirit's transforming power is incapable of healing and sanctifying a person and therefore no theoretical reason why she could not attain "Christian perfection" in this life. Wesley did not assert that all persons *will* be saved, for that is a speculative claim of the sort that Wesley avoided, much less that all persons *must* be saved, for that is a necessitarian claim, which nullifies human freedom every bit as much as Calvinist predestinarianism. Accordingly, we should not regard Wesley as a "universalist." He affirmed that God *desires* the salvation of everyone and freely *offers* everyone all the conditions "external" to themselves by which that salvation is brought into effect, namely, pardon *for* sin through Christ and power *over* sin through the Holy Spirit. But Wesley rejected the notion that God *imposes* on people the "internal" conditions of their salvation, namely faith in Christ and yieldedness to the Spirit, for he regarded these internal conditions as functions of free moral agency, the infringement of which would violate the very thing that makes a personal relationship with God possible and that makes a human being able and worthy to enter communion with God. Wesley elaborates this position in many writings,[34] but there is perhaps no more succinct or precise a statement of it than in his notes on 1 Tim 4:8-10. The KJV reads: "For bodily exercise profiteth a little: but godliness is profitable unto all things, having promise of the life that now is, and of that which is to come. This is a faithful saying and worthy of all acceptation. For therefore we both labour and suffer reproach, because we trust in the living God, who is the Saviour of all men, especially of those that believe." Here is part of Wesley's gloss on this passage:

> *Therefore* — Animated by this promise. *We both labour and suffer reproach* — We regard neither pleasure, ease, nor honour. *Because we trust* — For this very thing the world will hate us. *In the living God* — Who will give us the life he has promised. *Who is the Saviour of all men* — Preserving them in this life, and willing to save them eternally. *But especially* — In a more eminent manner. *Of them that believe* — And so are saved everlastingly.[35]

---

34. E.g., Wesley, *Free Grace* (1739), *WJW* 3:542-63; *Predestination Calmly Considered* (1773), *WJW-Jackson*, 10:204-59; and *Thoughts upon Necessity* (1774), *WJW-Jackson*, 10:457-74.
35. Wesley, *Explanatory Notes*, vol. 2, on 1 Tim 4:10.

Wesley's Arminianism is neatly revealed in these clipped comments. The Calvinists of Wesley's day were committed, above all, to the concept of the sovereignty of God, and were willing to attenuate the reach of divine *love* rather than minimize the efficacy of divine *power:* whatever God wills, God infallibly accomplishes; whatever God does not accomplish, he must not will; therefore whomever God does not actually save, God must never have willed to save in the first place. In contrast, the starting point of Wesley's theology is the *love* of God displayed on the cross of Christ. Accordingly, Wesley taught that God desires the salvation of all people and freely offers to everyone all that is needful for their salvation but, out of respect for their moral freedom, does not force anyone to accept his offer. Wesley believed that the very love that impels God to seek our salvation prevents God from overruling our capacity to accept that offer freely. If it did not, the "offer" would become an act of coercion and God's "love" for us would be indistinguishable from capricious and arbitrary favoritism.

Whatever position one takes on the dogmatic and exegetical issues at stake here, it is important to understand that Wesley's Arminianism is funded by pastoral and missional considerations. It is precisely *because* he regards our capacity for free moral choice so highly — even to the point of making our eternal destiny hinge, finally, on our own decision to accept or reject God's love — that he organized his accountability groups as he did. As we have seen, the only entrance requirement for these groups was an expressed desire "to flee from the wrath to come," but the condition of remaining a member in good standing was behavior that demonstrated the sincerity of that desire. The discipline exercised over these groups was as searching and severe as it was because the presumed consequences of spiritual and moral failure were so dreadful. But this discipline was not a matter of spiritual tyranny or coercive control. It was regarded, by leaders and followers alike, as the means by which they experienced and practiced the divine economy for themselves. God orders the world by vanquishing sin — by canceling the conscience-searing guilt of it through the blood of Jesus Christ and conquering the life-diminishing addictiveness of it through the power of the Holy Spirit. Wesley's societies understood themselves to be microcosmic exemplifications of God's redemptive love for humanity as a whole. Accordingly, they displayed in their own context a way of life very similar to what Paul exhorted Timothy to establish in the house church at Ephesus.

2 Timothy

2 Timothy is more direct and personal than 1 Timothy and appears to recognize what the first letter only obliquely suggests: the charisma and indwelling spirit of the faithful tradent are indispensable for transmitting the apostolic tradition to the next generation (see 1 Tim 6:20). The letter's oblique mention of Paul's death (4:7-8), perhaps imminent, makes his personal absence from Timothy even more ominous because of its permanence. If this letter is read within canonical context as the second letter of a Timothy correspondence, the benediction of the first letter becomes transitional, shifting attention away from an interest in forming a competent congregation to a second letter that calls faithful individuals to preserve and transmit the Pauline tradition to the next generation of believers. While statements of a self-aware Paul continue to function much like his final speeches in Acts, where he reminds audiences of his unique importance for the church's future (e.g., Acts 20:17-35), the real problem is no longer Paul. Paul's legacy as presented in this letter no longer needs defending: it needs preserving. The threat that occasions 2 Timothy — and, in fact, the entire Pauline corpus — is disintegration of a community's memory of Paul, without which the next generation is left without an apostolic compass.

Two related but discrete claims follow from these observations and help today's readers understand this letter's crucial role among the Pastoral Epistles and within the Pauline corpus. First is the importance of Paul and his legacy for the future of the church. His life and message are remembered not merely as exemplary of Christian faith but as integral to the church's apostolic tradition. To put the matter sharply, the church that confesses to be apostolic cannot exist without remembering the apostle Paul, and the church cannot remember him without careful and self-critical appropriation of his canonical letters and his portrait in Acts. It is this canonical deposit that delimits —

in a way that only a canon of texts can — what in particular the church must remember to make good on its confession of apostolicity.

But, second, Paul's death occasions a succession that is not dependent on an apostle who is uniquely and irreplaceably important. A succession of Paul's apostolate depends rather on those who continue to do what is remembered of his life and to proclaim what is remembered of his gospel. It is an imitation of his missionary vocation rather than his apostolic persona. Significantly, the public manner of this succession is not an institutional or ecclesial project but a profoundly interpersonal one: the Pauline tradition is perpetuated by Spirit-filled individuals — loyal tradents — whose calling is to "hold to a pattern of healthy teaching you have heard from me . . . and protect the good tradition" (1:13-14) for every generation (cf. 2:2) until "that day" (1:12).

2 Timothy is a letter of succession. It is picked up and read by those who have come to recognize the importance of Paul — his memory and message — for the future of the church. It thus shapes a particular approach to the entire Pauline corpus, since there Pauline instruction has been "textualized to become the written vehicle by which the church, guided by the work of the Holy Spirit, is continually instructed by his letters."[1] Again, however, the personal nature of this letter's address may well suggest that the tradent's ongoing work is not a congregational project but belongs to a magisterium of faithful teachers, each of whom is gifted, called, and schooled for this work. The added phrase, "competent to teach still others" (2:2), is thickened by the repetition of teaching words in the Pastoral Epistles, finally and distinctively of Paul himself (1:11), which underwrites the importance of this activity as the transmission of a sacred deposit to others. The teacher's curriculum is Scripture's Pauline corpus, performed in the church and in conversation with the Spirit and the rest of Scripture.

1:1-2 Paul Greets Timothy

¹From Paul, an apostle of Christ Jesus by God's will for the purpose of the promise of life realized in Christ Jesus, ²to Timothy, dear child: Grace, mercy, and peace from God the Father and Christ Jesus our Lord.

The letter opens with a single sentence that supplies the reader with necessary information to frame what follows. The address is similar to those of other Pauline letters: Paul introduces himself as "an apostle of Christ Jesus" (1:1; cf.

---

1. Brevard S. Childs, *The Church's Guide for Reading Paul: The Canonical Shaping of the Pauline Corpus* (Grand Rapids: Eerdmans, 2008), 97.

1 Tim 1:1) who acknowledges his close relationship to the letter's recipient before greeting him with familiar salutation (1:2; cf. 1 Tim 1:2). Paul's apostleship, and the religious authority it presumes, is linked to Christ Jesus, who has commissioned him (cf. Acts 9:15-16) in full accordance with God's will (1:1; see the comments on 1 Tim 1:1 and Tit 1:1-3). The effect of this familiar greeting, besides the rhetorical role it performs within the letter, is to locate and secure this correspondence within Scripture's Pauline canon as important for the spiritual formation of its readers.

On closer inspection, however, important differences in this greeting from others in the Pauline corpus not only define more carefully the letter's intended readers but the particular role the letter continues to perform as Scripture. For example, the purpose of Paul's apostolate is indicated by a κατά (*kata*) phrase that concerns the "promise of life." According to 1 Tim 4:8, this is the divine promise marked out by piety that heralds the blessings of the coming age. While several reasons have been suggested for its addition here, it doubtless orients the recipient to the overarching pattern of Paul's apostolate, which Timothy is appointed to grasp (cf. 1:13-14; 1 Tim 6:20) and transmit to other believers (2:2). The prospect of an apostolic succession, occasioned by Paul's current absence and imminent death (cf. 4:6-8), is the central image of this letter and shapes the nature of Timothy's sacred calling and charisma (cf. 1:10-11; 2:8-11), which the letter seeks to clarify.

But God's biblical promise of life to Israel is also thematic of Paul's reading of the OT narrative. According to Rom 4:13-25, God's promise of life "to Abraham and his descendants" is brought to realization through faith in Jesus Christ. The mention of Paul's ancestral religion (1:3) alludes to that biblical promise, not only to sound a note of thanksgiving for Timothy but also to mark out the purpose of an apostolic succession in which he now is called to participate.

The sense of the phrase, "realized in Christ Jesus" (τῆς ἐν Χριστῷ Ἰησοῦ, *tēs en Christō Iēsou*), is plain: the future of Paul's apostleship, linked now to God's promise of life, has been secured in advance by the messianic work of Jesus. This added point about a realized promise is not incidental in a letter whose intended reader is reminded that God is faithful to a promise made even when God's people are often not (cf. 2:13).

Timothy is greeted as a "dear child" (see above on 1 Tim 1:2), which I take as a trope for a special kind of mentoring relationship that is at once intimate but also shaped by the obligations of the family business passed on by father to son. This conception of a working relationship has particular resonance in a letter of succession whose instructions guide the faithful protégé to assume the goods and responsibilities of Paul's apostolate after his departure.

Paul's traditional salutation combines the Hellenistic "grace" with the Jewish "peace" and is complemented here by the familiar biblical motif "mercy" (see 1 Tim 1:2) to ground the close working relationship between Paul and Timothy in confidence in God's merciful presence. Even as God's grace and peace extend to all people, so are all relationships within the community of believers imbued with this quality of divine mercy.

1:3-7 Paul Thanks God for Timothy

³I give thanks to God, whom I serve, as did my ancestors, with a clear conscience. I remember you in my prayers day and night. ⁴I long to see you, remembering your tears, so that I may be filled with joy. ⁵I take hold of your earnest faith as a reminder — the kind that first found a home in your grandmother Lois and mother Eunice and I am certain is in you.

⁶For this reason, I remind you to reignite God's gift that is in you through the laying on of my hands. ⁷For God did not give us a cowardly spirit but a Spirit of power, love, and discernment.

Paul's thanksgiving, expressed in the manner of his Jewish heritage (1:3), rehearses a set of powerful memories that define Timothy's call to ministry. His religious education, supervised by his mother and grandmother, has cultivated an "earnest faith" (v. 4), which has been personally confirmed by the apostle at his ordination (v. 6). Timothy is also reminded that with a call comes the Spirit of power and a spiritual gift that animates his ministry (vv. 6-7).

Typical of the canonical letters of Paul, personal greetings are followed by a note of thanksgiving, typically sounded with mention of the apostle's intercessory prayer for his letter's recipients. While offered to God in the idiom of worship, the content of Paul's petition often signals, as here, the letter's occasion and thus anticipates the exhortation and instruction in the letter's main body. But the word choice of this particular thanksgiving is striking. Instead of the characteristic and more formal εὐχαριστέω *(eucharisteō)*, Paul expresses his thanksgiving for Timothy emphatically: χάριν ἔχω τῷ θεῷ *(charin echō tō theō)*, "I give thanks to God." Moreover, *charin* is an expression of personal gratitude to God more than of worship and perhaps reflects the apostle's deeply personal relationship with his protégé and successor.[2] Signifi-

---

2. Cf. Jouette M. Bassler, *1 Timothy, 2 Timothy, Titus* (ANTC; Nashville: Abingdon, 1996), 128.

cantly, the phrase χάριν ἔχω *(charin echō)* is found only here and in 1 Tim 1:12, where Paul gives thanks to Christ Jesus for his conversion and calling as a minister of the gospel. This intertext within the Timothy correspondence forges a keen impression that Paul's gratitude to God extends in two integral directions: he is grateful for his own ministry as an apostle and grateful that a well-groomed successor is ready to take the apostolate over from him as death approaches.

Paul allows that his practice of expressing gratitude to God is offered with the "clear conscience" of his ancestral religion. What is surprising to the reader is not that Paul has the "clear conscience" of one whose theology and practices are shaped within the embrace of Israel's sacred heritage; the exegetical question is why he should mention this at all, especially in light of 1 Tim 1:13, where he speaks of his former life as a Jewish blasphemer of Christ. Perhaps Paul is reacting to an accusation leveled against his apostolate, much like the accusation leveled against Jesus (cf. Matt 5:17-18), according to which his theology and practices are contrary to his ancestral religion. The theodicy question that confronts readers of the Pauline canon is not that of his innocent suffering, although this dimension of the problem is very much in play in this letter (cf. 2 Tim 2:8-10); rather, the challenge against which Paul contends is whether God is faithful to promises made to Israel according to Scripture. This expression of continuity with his ancestors, then, lays claim to something more important than what appears at first reading: Paul's Gentile mission is in continuity with the biblical promises God made to Israel (so Romans 9–11).

This passing mention of his Jewish faith may also cue the canonical Paul of Acts, whose mission engages pagan culture in a way that retains the church's Jewish legacy. Strikingly, the impress of Timothy's circumcision in Acts (16:1-5) assures "the Jews who were in those places" that Paul's mission will bring the Jewish past forward into the Christian present. This implicit anti-supersessionism is a central feature of the Pauline apostolate, which not only corrects the exclusive use of those passages within the Pauline canon that might justify the church's "gentilization" of the Pauline gospel (e.g., Gal 2:15-21) but for which the Pauline tradent is appointed to continue into the future.

Thanksgiving always occasions a remembrance of the past; we express our gratitude to God for gifts already received. Much has been made of Paul's repeated invocation of what he remembers in this letter, especially since his death seems imminent. Collins is among the letter's recent interpreters who has recognized its extensive personal reminiscences as conventions of the testamentary genre, concluding (with many others) that 2 Timothy is an epistolary example of a farewell discourse — Paul's "last will and testament" written for his spiritual heir.³ But Johnson correctly points out that in antiquity memory was the mode by which personal models of imitation were invoked.⁴ That is, Paul's personal reminiscence, whether of himself or others, is the literary convention of a particular kind of paraenesis, characteristic of this letter, which prepares a trusted apprentice, Timothy, for his succession to leadership by imitation of the now departed (although not yet deceased) apostle. The admonition is not to be Paul, whose calling and charisma have been uniquely bestowed on him (so Tit 1:3; cf. 1 Tim 1:10-11; 2:7), but to be like him in personal virtue and the practices of ministry.

But this observation begs the question: What exactly does Paul remember and why is it strategic to this letter's model of apostolic succession? With evident poignancy, Paul remembers Timothy's "tears." I doubt there is much exegetical value in speculation on what prompted Timothy's tears. What is more important is that in recalling these tears Paul desires to see Timothy and "be filled with joy." This phrase recalls Phil 2:1-2, where "filled with joy" is used as a topos of friendship sustained in difficult moments by common fellowship in Christ. Implicit in that evocation of joy are warnings of threats, made clear by the letter, that may eventually subvert Paul's fellowship with the community if they are not averted.⁵ Likewise, the very mention of Timothy's "tears" alongside the prospect of Paul's joy may sound a warning of spiritual testing that will not only threaten their working relationship but subvert Timothy's apostolic succession as well.

Paul also recalls the origins of Timothy's faith in his own familial household. The point is not incidental when this text is read alongside the opening of 1 Timothy. In a context where false teaching had some influence, Paul provides Timothy with a taxonomy of Christian instruction for a household of faith managed by God (οἰκονομία θεοῦ, *oikonomia theou*): the aim of religious instruction is loving relations cultivated within the community characterized by an "earnest faith" (πίστεως ἀνυποκρίτου, *pisteōs anypokritou*, 1 Tim 1:5). Significantly, Paul personalizes this claim by not only thanking God for Timothy's earnest faith (literally "the earnest faith in you," 2 Tim 1:5) but also placing its formation within a particular household led by Timothy's mother and grandmother.

If the reader has read Acts in preparation for the study of the Pauline canon, she will have already observed that Timothy's mother is Jewish (so

---

3. Raymond F. Collins, *1 and 2 Timothy and Titus: A Commentary* (NTL; Louisville: Westminster John Knox, 2002), 181-85.
4. Luke T. Johnson, *The First and Second Letters to Timothy* (New York: Doubleday, 2001), 340-41.
5. So Stephen E. Fowl, *Philippians* (THNTC; Grand Rapids: Eerdmans, 2005), 81-82.

Acts 16:1), which fills in a missing detail of this text: that is, Timothy's "earnest faith" is of Jewish origin, in agreement with Paul's (1:3), which makes his apostolic succession more viable. I have translated the key verb of this expression of trust, ἐνοικέω *(enoikeō),* as "find a home," in order to highlight its οἶκος *(oikos,* "house") root-family and so its participation in the pivotal metaphor for church in the Pastoral Epistles. In addition to the repetition of παραθήκη *(parathēkē,* "tradition," 1 Tim 6:20; 2 Tim 1:14), then, the repetition of *oikos*-words fashions a crucial Pauline intertext between the two Timothy letters. In particular, ἐνοικέω *(enoikeō)* alludes to Timothy's role as the "pillar and foundation of truth" of "God's house" (1 Tim 3:15), the microcosm of the *oikonomia theou* in the world (see 1 Tim 1:4b). If Timothy's earnest faith has been cultivated at a Jewish address, the confidence Paul expresses in the earliest stages of its formation extends not only to Timothy's succession to apostolic ministry but also to the ministry in the household of God for which he has been ordained.

Moreover, a carefully crafted passage sometimes is inserted between the epistolary thanksgiving and main body of Pauline letters to introduce the orienting theme of the letter's instruction (e.g., Rom 1:16-18). I would argue that 2 Tim 1:6-7 is such a passage. Simply put, this passage, personal and direct, is about Timothy's succession to the Pauline apostolate, and the rest of the letter will clarify the character and practices required for such an ordination.

The opening phrase, "for this reason" (1:6), reclaims not only the confidence Paul has just expressed in the origins of Timothy's "earnest faith" but also, I suspect, its allusion to Paul's earlier charge that Timothy conduct himself as the sacred household's "pillar and foundation of truth" (1 Tim 3:15). None of this comes as a surprise, since the reminder/remember idiom recalls a shared experience: Paul exhorts Timothy to act on what they both know is true. The verbal idea translated "reignite" (ἀναζωπυρέω, *anazōpyreō),* plays off the verb used to cue the memory of this shared experience (ἀναμιμνῄσκω, *anamimnęskō),* the one *ana-* word triggering the other. The ongoing operation of "God's gift (χάρισμα τοῦ θεοῦ, *charisma tou theou)* that is in (Timothy)" is confirmed by recollection of his "earnest faith."

The exegetical task is to define more carefully the nature of Timothy's charisma and why Paul should say it needs reigniting. When this work is executed within the bounds of the Pauline canon, a reading will necessarily be informed by two antecedent texts, Romans 12 and especially 1 Corinthians 12–14. Paul used *pneumatika* when addressing the Corinthians about "spiritual things" (1 Cor 2:13; 9:11; 12:1-3) and shifted to *charismata* when speaking of God's allocation of particular supernatural "gifts" to different individual believers (12:4-11). Hays argues that this difference is crucial to Paul's rhetoric of reconciliation. The unity of Christian fellowship depends on the community's distinction of the work of God's Spirit in its midst from general "spiritual things" flooding the cultural marketplace. The Spirit allocates the *charismata* to equip the church for the ministry of reconciliation — crucial for the public witness of a community conflicted over rival claims (1 Cor 1:10-12).[6]

Significantly, two of the Spirit's attributes mentioned here, power and love, are used in Paul's Corinthian exposition of God's charisma. That is, the Spirit is the source of the power (δύναμις, *dynamis*) of God, which makes the proclamation of God's gospel effective (1 Cor 2:4-5; 4:19-20). The aim of the Spirit's activity — and so of the ministry of the *charismata* it has apportioned — is the cultivation of a loving congregation (so 1 Corinthians 13). This same point is made for a different kind of conflict — between Timothy and Paul's opponents — in the opening of 1 Timothy: Timothy has been told that the aim of his instruction is love, which suggests that all the instruction that follows has the same moral aim (see above on 1 Tim 1:4-5; cf. 1 John 3:11). Remarkably, Paul contrasts genuine love of the sort produced by the indwelling Spirit with meaningless public demonstrations of religious piety (1 Cor 13:1-2), much as he does in 1 Tim 1:4-7, where he indirectly castigates immature Torah teachers for engaging in a pedagogy interested in trivial matters. The discerning exercise of God's charisma empowers real love that confirms the reception of God's word (cf. 1 Cor 4:19-20).

Thus read within the context of the Pauline canon, the exhortation to "reignite" the divine charisma confirms the tradent's prior personal gifting of the Spirit, which was intended to bring the many and not just the one to spiritual maturity. Timothy's charism is accompanied by God's Spirit, whose "power" (rather than Timothy's personal talent or eloquence of speech) animates the gift and makes it effective for the public ministry to which he has been called (see 1 Tim 1:3; 3:15-16; 4:14-16; 6:20-21). The aim of his charismatic ministry is not finally the conversion of pagans but the cultivation of loving relationships among believers, which is the hallmark of the *oikonomina theou* (1 Tim 1:4-5).

The decision to understand "Spirit" (πνεῦμα, *pneuma*, 1:7) as divine rather than human is based not only on this Pauline abstract but also on the purposeful textual interplay with the "indwelling Holy Spirit" of v. 14. The "cowardly spirit" should not be psychologized as a deficient human spirit but

---

6. R. B. Hays, *First Corinthians* (Louisville: Westminster John Knox, 1997), 207-9; also Margaret M. Mitchell, *Paul and the Rhetoric of Reconciliation: An Exegetical Investigation of the Language and Composition of 1 Corinthians* (Louisville: Westminster John Knox, 1993), especially 266-83.

rather refers to some hypothetical divine spirit whose effect is contrary to the Holy Spirit of genuine Christianity (cf. 1 Cor 12:1-3). While some interpreters take this as a negative trait of Timothy's flagging spirit — his charism needs reigniting because self-doubt has quenched it — this is hardly Paul's point here and does not suit the tenor of his general exhortation.

J. R. Levison has recently argued that the distinction between human spirit and divine Spirit may, in any case, be unnecessary here, if the divine Spirit and the human spirit are of a piece. While the act of giving the Spirit, signaled by the apostle's laying on of hands, may indeed refer to the special gifting and empowering of the believer for the work of ministry, Paul's attachment of a catalog of virtues to the spirit may indicate that he is exhorting Timothy to draw on a "holy spirit" given by the Creator to every person at birth. Consonant with Jewish tradition, then, Paul reminds Timothy that God has already given him the resources required — "power, love, discernment" — to make Timothy's work as custodian of his apostolate possible (cf. 1:13-14).[7] But Paul speaks of both kinds of spirit-filling and probably has both in mind here: the given Holy Spirit aiding and enhancing the created holy spirit for the hard work ahead.

Two elements of this pivotal passage remain unexplained by its intertextuality with 1 Corinthians 12–14. The first is more incidental and concerns the third element of the Pauline triad that characterizes the indwelling Spirit's performance: σωφρονισμός *(sōphronismos)*, translated "discernment." Its more precise definition is contested, but most agree that it represents intellectual competence in moral thinking that enables one to weigh competing goods and decide rightly between them. Love and power are readily understood from its 1 Corinthians co-text as necessary controls in the effective performance of a spiritual gift, but discernment is not, especially if it is perceived as a secular virtue. While this word is used only here in the NT, it belongs to the *sōphron-* word family, which is used often in the Pastoral Epistles. Most uses are in virtue lists used to characterize competent persons capable of good works apropos of their position or task. For example, the woman who is saved according to 1 Tim 2:15 maintains both *sōphrosynē* ("prudence") and love *(agapē)* as the public marks of the faithful life (see above on 1 Tim 2:9-15). *Sōphroneō* frames a discussion of *charismata* in Rom 12:3, where Paul admonishes each believer to "discern" the particular portion of divine grace he or she has received to use it more effectively in the body of Christ, in whom each "belongs to one another" (v. 5). Read within this canonical context, then, this third virtue in 2 Tim 1:7 recalls a much broader valence of spiritual gifting

---

7. See John R. Levison, *Filled with the Spirit* (Grand Rapids: Eerdmans, 2009), 240-41.

that thickens a belief that not only is the indwelling Spirit the agent of the community's spiritual formation but its presence gives gifted individuals the capacity to discern how best to use a particular charism in ministry toward others within the household of God.

The other addition to this example concerns the liturgy of "the laying on of my hands" (cf. 1 Tim 4:14), about which much has been written.[8] Most locate it in the Diaspora synagogue where "laying on of hands" was a liturgical gesture in the ordination of rabbis — not merely the transference of spiritual authority to those who qualified but a public recognition of that authority for a congregation to observe.[9] Certainly, the Spirit's gift is confirmed by (διά, *dia*) apostolic authority, and the imposition of hands is personal ("my hands") rather than congregational (see above on 1 Tim 4:14). This personification of a congregational practice suggests that Timothy has been chosen by the apostle as his successor and that Paul's apostolic authority has in some sense been transferred to Timothy. In this sense, it is a gesture of succession rather than merely of apostolic authority as, for example, in Acts 8:17. That succession and not just ordination is in mind is secured by the allusion to the OT pattern of succession (Moses to Joshua: Deut 34:9; cf. Num 8:10), which may well elaborate Paul's prior affirmation of continuity with the practices of his ancestral religion (1:3). The connection in Acts between the Spirit's baptism and the laying on of apostolic hands, suggests that Timothy's succession comes with the Spirit's power and gift for ministry in Paul's absence.

Perhaps, too, the combination of indwelling Spirit and apostolic hands recalls the famous story of the succession of prophets, Elijah and Elisha, told in 2 Kings 2. The witness of the Spirit's coming upon Elisha by the guild of prophets (2 Kgs 2:15; cf. 1 Tim 4:14) is the pivotal symbol of a transference of authority. Interestingly, the other symbol of succession is Elijah's instruction for Elisha to remain behind as he departs for another place (2 Kgs 2:2, 4, 6; cf. 1 Tim 1:3). The poor results prompted by shame (2 Kgs 2:16-18), plotted as Elisha's initial act on his own, may also resonate with Paul's subsequent exhortation for Timothy not to be ashamed. And so the reader can only imagine the significance of the cloak that Paul asks Timothy to bring him while staying in Troas (2 Tim 4:13), if this sounds a final echo of Elisha's sheepskin as the medium of the Spirit of power transferred from one prophet to the next!

---

8. See now the comprehensive examination of this gesture by J. F. Tipei, *The Laying On of Hands in the New Testament: Its Significance, Techniques, and Effects* (Lanham: University Press of America, 2009).

9. For a succinct summary, see Benjamin Fiore and Daniel J. Harrington, *The Pastoral Epistles: First Timothy, Second Timothy, Titus* (rev. ed.; Collegeville: Liturgical, 2007), 136-37.

If this allusion is also in play, Paul's reminder underscores two integral points: Timothy is gifted for ministry by the Spirit and is authorized to use this spiritual gift by apostolic authority as Paul's chosen successor. For this reason, the laying on of his hands is personal and direct. There is no formal contradiction between this text and 1 Tim 4:14, where a council of elders officiates over a liturgy of ordination. Rather here a different significance is made to illumine the nature of an apostolic succession: Timothy's spiritual charism empowers his imitation and so continuation of Paul's mission. Such a succession, directed by Christ's Spirit and confirmed by Christ's apostle, is not a matter of maintaining an apostolic *office* but an apostolic ministry. Timothy's vocation is not to *Christ's* apostolate, which requires an extraordinary charism given to only a few (Rom 1:5, 11; cf. Acts 8:18-20). Rather, his gift and call pertain to the responsibility to "pass on the things you heard from me to faithful people" (2 Tim 2:2). What Timothy and "many other witnesses" heard from Paul is analogous to the Pauline corpus, which every Christian of every generation is to pass on to faithful people.

1:8-14 Unashamed of a Sacred Calling

⁸Therefore, do not be ashamed of the Lord's testimony or of mine, his prisoner's. Rather, share the suffering for the gospel by the power of God: ⁹God saved and called us with a holy calling, not according to our works but according to God's own purpose and grace. God gave grace to us in Christ Jesus before time began, and ¹⁰now it has been revealed through the appearing of our Savior Christ Jesus, who abolished death and illumined life and immortality. For this gospel ¹¹I was appointed herald, apostle, and teacher;[10] ¹²for this reason I suffer as I do. But I am not ashamed, for I know the one in whom I have placed my trust and am convinced that God is strong enough to protect my tradition until that day.

¹³Hold to a pattern of healthy teaching you have heard from me with the fidelity and loyalty that are in Christ Jesus. ¹⁴Protect the good tradition through the Holy Spirit who indwells you.

The letter's initial exhortation challenges Timothy to accept the costs of his "holy calling" (1:8-9a) and to succeed Paul in a ministry of the gospel revealed by Christ Jesus (vv. 9b-10), which he was appointed to publish and because of which he now suffers (v. 11). In commending this apostolic legacy to Timothy

---

10. Most mss. add ἔθνων (*ethnōn*, "to the nations") to διδάσκαλος (*didaskalos*, "teacher"; cf. 1 Tim 2:7), which does not explain its omission in mss. A, a, and 1175.

for safekeeping, Paul instructs him to uphold faithfully the "pattern of healthy teaching" of the "good tradition" learned from the apostle (vv. 13-14).

L. T. Johnson is among those commentators who find reflected in the expressions of this letter's opening thanksgiving (1:3-5) and transitional statement (vv. 6-7) a mirror image of Timothy's self-doubt.[11] J. Bassler is another who takes Paul's exhortation of a "reignited" charism without irony as the pastor's exhortation to someone lacking inward fortitude to get on with the business at hand.[12] Hilary did as well, wondering why otherwise Paul would need to remind Timothy of his ordination, an event he surely would have remembered (*De Trinitate* 11.23). Although I do not think the real issue at stake is self-doubt, at the very least the history of interpretation would seem to suggest that this is a letter occasioned by a colleague's vocational crisis, no doubt exacerbated by the apostle's absence.

One of the most important elements of Hellenistic moral teaching is the use of personal example, which then the student is to emulate as a moral norm. As often found in the Pauline letters, biographical vignettes illustrate a manner of life worthy of imitation, modeled by Paul according to "the testimony of our Lord" (1:8).[13] The present passage is an exhortation of imitation, marked out by repetition of two key terms. First is the exhortation not to be ashamed of the gospel: "do not be ashamed" (v. 8), "for I am not ashamed" (v. 12). This literary *inclusio* reflects the Greco-Roman culture of Paul's world, even as it reflects the socio-psychology of that society, which shapes a criterion of value in terms of what prompts a person's honor or embarrassment. For Paul, of course, this criterion is shaped by a personal call by the risen Christ to preach God's gospel: what is deemed foolish by the world's standards — namely, the cross of Christ — is wisdom in God's mind (cf. 1 Cor 1:18-25).

The cultural background of this exhortation has been clarified by modern criticism.[14] Ancient codes of conduct were typically fashioned to stipulate what behaviors or situations to avoid because they would bring shame to individuals and disrepute to their households and public associations. Most people understand intuitively what to avoid in order to escape public ridicule; the

---

11. Johnson, *First and Second Letters to Timothy*, 358-59.

12. Bassler, *1 Timothy, 2 Timothy, Titus*, 129.

13. See George W. Knight, *The Pastoral Epistles: A Commentary on the Greek Text* (NIGTC; Grand Rapids: Eerdmans, 1992), 372, who rightly takes τοῦ κυρίου (*tou kyriou*) as an objective genitive — a testimony "about the Lord."

14. See, e.g., David A. DeSilva, *Despising Shame: Honor Discourse and Community Maintenance in the Epistle to the Hebrews* (Atlanta: Scholars, 1995), for a sustained and helpful exegesis of a biblical book (Hebrews) with this cultural ethos in mind.

social shaping of intuition, especially during one's early education (so v. 5), remains to this day an effective means of maintaining social order. The virtuous person — the one who is "above reproach" — is capable of detecting and avoiding shameful behaviors in order to maintain good relations with those who count. Chrysostom's homily on this text observes that heresies — he notes those of Marcion, Manes, and Valentinus — arise because their teachers are "ashamed of the divine economy." He adds that when the cross of Christ is "viewed aright, it will appear full of dignity and a matter for boasting. For it was that death on the cross that saved the world when it was perishing."

Typically, only those who influence us or are important to us can say or do that which evokes in us feelings of shame. In this case, Paul's mention of himself and the Lord as potential objects of Timothy's shame is ironical. While imitation of Paul's scandalous testimony of Christ (cf. 1 Cor 11:1) may provoke the ridicule of outsiders, it is precisely being like Paul that counts; it is offending Paul, not so much outsiders, that Timothy must avoid.

The repetition of παραθήκη (*parathēkē*, "tradition," 1:12, 14) clarifies the letter's core thematic, which turns on the ultimate importance of Paul's "pattern of healthy teaching" (v. 13) for the future of the church (cf. Acts 20:29-35). Paul's appointment as "herald, apostle, and teacher" (v. 11; see also 1 Tim 2:7) carries with it a sacred trust that he has protected with God's help (v. 12b)[15] but is now passing on to Timothy to guard, with the Spirit's help (v. 14). Rather than reading 2 Timothy as Paul's "last will and testament," this is a letter of succession that sets out a Pauline pattern of instruction with the firm exhortation for Timothy to recall what he "has heard" from Paul (v. 13) so as to pass it on to others (cf. 2:2).

If the occasion of this letter is the unbroken succession of the Pauline apostolate, the gospel about God's power to save sinners (1:8-11) now logically extends to God's power to "protect my tradition" (vv. 9-12). Especially if the successor's firm grasp of the tradition is predicated on the "fidelity and loyalty that are in Christ Jesus," then his task is not conditioned on raw talent but on God's capacity to deliver the goods — in Pauline idiom, "not according to our works but according to God's own purpose and grace" (v. 9; cf. Eph 2:8-9). Not only have this purpose and grace been publicly disclosed in the Christ

---

15. The translation and meaning of 1:12b is contested among interpreters. *Tēn parathēkēn mou* could be taken (NRSV, NIV) as an allusive reference to what Paul has entrusted to God, including his apostleship, gospel ministry, suffering, and imprisonment, or to what God has entrusted to Paul (NASB, RSV). Both make good sense, but we prefer the latter because we take the purpose of this exhortation as providing warrants for a smooth succession. In this setting, the interplay between what God has entrusted to Paul and what Paul has then entrusted to Timothy (cf. 1 Tim 6:20) makes most sense.

event for all to see (v. 10), but the medium of divine power, the "indwelling Holy Spirit," comes with the "good tradition" received by Timothy to secure what has now been entrusted to him (v. 14; cf. v. 6). This proto-Trinitarian formulation of an empowering God, our Savior Christ Jesus, and the indwelling Spirit supplies the theological soil in which the forward movement of the apostolic tradition is rooted.

The reader should note the echoes of Rom 1:16 sounded by this passage, which fashions an important intertext within the Pauline canon. In setting out the main point of his magisterial letter to the Romans, Paul famously asserted that he was not ashamed of the gospel he was preaching throughout the empire. The same constellation of catchwords that introduced readers to the Pauline canon in Romans 1 — shame, gospel, power, salvation, belief — are repeated in 2 Timothy 1, but in a new setting with new meaning apropos of a succession of the Pauline *parathēkē* to faithful tradents represented by Timothy. Paul remains unashamed of his appointment as the gospel's herald (so v. 12), no doubt because he continues to believe what he defended in Romans, namely that the gospel agrees with Scripture's promise. The shame that he might but does not experience would not be, then, due to his imprisonment and the assumption of personal failure or futility some may have associated with it. If Timothy is embarrassed by the controversy provoked by the gospel, Paul has reason to worry that Timothy's sense of shame may then subvert his missionary work. If a tradition bearer imitates the tradition's founder, then it seems reasonable that Paul would encourage Timothy by the same reality that persuaded him to continue preaching the gospel in the face of public ridicule: the compelling kerygma, testified to in Scripture, that God has the power to save sinners from death and does so through our Savior Christ Jesus, according to God's own purpose and grace "before time began" (vv. 9-10).[16] If this confession of faith is embraced as true, then feeling shame about the testimony of our Lord or the ministry of his gospel is a real impossibility.

Paul's passing reference to his imprisonment evokes a sense of the costs involved. If shame avoidance would prompt the wise of this world to remove themselves from those activities or situations that will land them in prison for

---

16. The phrase I have translated "before time began" (πρὸ χρόνων αἰωνίων, *pro chronōn aiōniōn*, 1:9) has long puzzled commentators. If it is part of a creedal formula in vv. 9-10 that characterizes God's way of salvation (see Marshall, *Pastoral Epistles*, 704-8), then it helps to express the belief that the nature of salvation — its "purpose and grace" — must instantiate the nature of God. What God does reflects who God is. If the eternal God existed "before time began," so too must redemption's plan, including "the appearing of our Savior, Christ Jesus" and its gracious effect. This is not quite yet a robust commitment to incarnational Christology, but it surely marks a development on the way there.

Christ's sake, then a rethinking of the source of shame is called for as a crisis of discipleship (cf. 1 Cor. 1:18–2:5). The jarring juxtaposition of shame and gospel in Romans and now here does just this.

Even though Timothy's imitation of Paul is the focus of this entire correspondence, the addition of "the Lord's testimony" is a reminder that Paul himself is the imitator of a Lord whose faithfulness proved costly. The gospel traditions of Jesus establish the normative pattern of the teacher's piety (1 Tim 6:3) and more directly of Timothy's compliance to his sacred calling (6:13). Even though "the Lord's testimony" in Pauline idiom would include an account of Christ's costly faithfulness to God (Rom 3:21-26; Phil 2:5-8), the summary here in 2 Timothy 1 regards only "the appearing of our Savior Christ Jesus, who abolished death and illumined life and immortality" (v. 10). While perhaps alluding to Christ's share of suffering, the focus of this formula is Christ's triumph as "our Savior." That is, the transformation of the concept of shame that follows the lead of the faithful Messiah and his apostle requires a shift of focus from suffering to its redemptive effect. And it is God's "own purpose and grace" that plot "the appearing" of the crucified and risen One as the climax of the gospel narrative, which is instantiated in the costs of Paul's mission and the content of his message. Therefore, this same plotline should continue to shape the narrative of apostolic succession.

The kerygmatic claim that Christ Jesus is "our Savior" who "appeared" to defeat death is exceptional apart from the Pastoral Epistles and deserves comment. There were many saviors in antiquity, both political and religious, and Paul uses "Savior" of Jesus in Phil 3:20 with evident political meaning. Greeks loved and told tales of the grand appearances of legendary heroes (e.g., Alexander). We populate our symbolic worlds with valorized political leaders, whether Caesars or American presidents, and present them as "our savior[s]." Their public "appearances" occasion considerable pomp and circumstance. A Christian citizen's confusion over which allegiance to pledge is bound to occur. In Philippians, implicit in the politics of this confession of faith, Paul claims that Christians must not negotiate a dual "citizenship" that splits loyalties between this age and the coming age (3:18-19).

The summary of the gospel Paul heralds is spread across a long and complex sentence that consists mostly of participial phrases in aorist tense to secure its truth as definitive (1:9-10). The gospel is the means by which this truth "comes to light" (φωτίζω, *phōtizō*). The repetition of "gospel" brings two ideas together. If suffering and shame result from a ministry of the gospel, then suffering is justified by the gospel's critical role: its proclamation discloses the truth about God's salvation without which people would die without "life and immortality." Because proclaiming the gospel effects the redemptive purpose and transforming grace of God, Paul repeats (for Timothy's benefit) that he is not ashamed to proclaim it. Of course, the opposite would be equally true: if the gospel did not have salutary effect, the glad acceptance of public shame or personal suffering would be non-rational.

The experience of suffering and the prospect of shame signal an important subtext of this letter: the preaching of the gospel provokes a political disturbance. This is so not because Paul's mission is directly opposed to Roman rule: Acts makes this clear. Rather, it is because the embrace of the gospel forges a vision of life and daily practices that threaten the empire's way of doing business. The juxtaposition of the "power of God" and the believer's "suffering for the gospel" is a political declaration (1:8), which implies that a life molded by a Pauline "pattern of healthy teaching" under the aegis of the indwelling Spirit constitutes a real problem for those who hold secular power. Of course Paul makes clear that his gospel does not summon the congregation to political revolution; it rather announces the epiphany of a Savior, who is Jesus (v. 10) and not one of Rome's pretenders to his messianic throne.

The idiom of time in this exhortation is important to note. Because it concerns a succession, the past interplays with the present and the present interplays with the tradition's forward movement into the future to form a continuum of the sacred. Thus, Paul speaks not only of his past appointment to proclaim the good news of what has "now been revealed" in the coming of Christ Jesus (1:10), he also speaks of God's pattern of grace as something planned "before time began" (v. 9; cf. Rom 8:28-30; 1 Cor 2:7; Eph 1:4) — a "promise of life" that God has already brought to realization for those who are "in Christ Jesus" (cf. 1:1).

The memory of his apostolic appointment and the gospel Paul has proclaimed and for which he is now imprisoned fashions a sacred tradition that he passes on to Timothy for a future "until that day" (1:12). This apocalyptic catchphrase, which Paul uses often and often strategically (see 1:18; 4:8; cf. Rom 2:16; 13:12; 1 Cor 1:8; 1 Thess 5:4; 2 Thess 1:10), refers to a future, finite, and final date of reckoning, when God the Judge will demand a rigorous accounting of one's faithfulness. The repetition of "until that day" in the positive example of Onesiphorus's household (1:18) suggests that its sense here is to underwrite Timothy's faithful succession, for which he will be rewarded by God on "that day."

The phrase I translate "pattern of healthy teaching" has added importance in a concluding exhortation about apostolic succession. While Timothy's reception of what he has heard from Paul is inherently important because what he has heard speaks of God's redemptive purpose and because its faithful reception has a powerful effect on the believer, the pair of imperatives to "hold" and "protect" this apostolic word invites a more practical question: What is the tradent to do now that he is in possession of what has been handed on? Commentators are mostly interested to identify the body of Pauline teachings in succession here and are right to see "healthy teaching" and "good tradition" as synonymous. The tradent's competence is characterized by his earnest faith in God (1:5) and loving relationships with others (cf. 1 Tim 1:5), which are formed "in Christ," where believers dwell with the Lord's Spirit (1:14). Especially in light of the later allusion to death (4:6), the present exhortation for a faithful and loving Timothy to pass on this teaching to others (2:2) has real purchase.

Less often considered, however, is the performance of this good tradition implicit in the anarthrous noun ὑποτύπωσις *(hypotypōsis)*, "a pattern" (1:13). Although exceptional in the NT, the word had broad currency in the Greco-Roman world when referring to an "outline" or "sketch" of someone's teaching. Rather than understanding this as referring to a personal role model, I take this word in its curricular sense, much like the role performed by the Torah when appropriated by the Deuteronomic Moses to prepare Israel for entering the Promised Land. D. Trobisch has argued, not without problems, that Paul himself collected, edited, and put into circulation a canonical edition of his principal letters (Romans, 1-2 Corinthians, and Galatians) for the training of tradents.[17] Certainly such an activity of canon-building agrees with the portrait of Paul found in the Pastoral Epistles and with the Pastorals' imperative to preserve and transmit the memory and message of Paul to others.[18] In any case, I suspect this mention of a *hypotypōsis* set within this exhortation of succession alludes to just such a proto-canonical collection of "healthy teachings" that Timothy can entrust to still other tradents to insure the preservation of the Pauline tradition (see 2:2).

1:15-18 The Example of Onesiphorus

15You know this: all those in Asia, including Phygelus and Hermogenes, have turned their backs on me. 16May the Lord give mercy to Onesiphorus's household, since he often refreshed me. He was unashamed of my chain, 17but upon arriving in Rome he diligently sought and found me. 18May the Lord give him opportunity

---

17. David Trobisch, *Paul's Letter Collection* (Minneapolis: Fortress, 1994). Although I am favorable toward Trobisch's argument, see S. Porter's measured criticisms in "When and How Was the Pauline Canon Compiled? An Assessment of Theories," in *The Pauline Canon* (ed. Stanley E. Porter; Leiden: Brill, 2004), 1:113-24.

18. Childs, *Church's Guide,* 69-75.

to find mercy from the Lord on that day. (And you know how well he served us in Ephesus!)

This is the first of four biographical footnotes in this letter (with 3:11 and 4:6-8, 16-18). Timothy is said to know about Paul's betrayal by Phygelus and Hermogenes in Asia (1:15) and the service of Onesiphorus's household to Paul in Rome (vv. 16-17) and, while Timothy was present, in Ephesus (v. 18b). On this basis, Paul hopes that Onesiphorus will receive the Lord's benefaction (vv. 16a, 18a).

While contributing little to the letter's substantive instruction, the biographical material constructs a portrait of a frail Paul. More than mere reminiscences about the failures of missionary colleagues and personal trials, these snapshots frame the imminence of an apostolic succession when a sacred trust between people is a necessary but unstable commodity. The power of a sovereign God will surely sustain the tradition (1:12; 2:11-13), but Paul recognizes, as few biblical witnesses do, that God entrusts what is holy to a sanctified people who are, as Nietzsche ironically observes, "free spirits" who are prone to behave "all too human." An apostolic succession is not a done deal by any means: while Paul is confident about the future of the gospel entrusted to his care, he has reason to be a tad anxious about who is next in line.

With other teachers of antiquity, he recognizes that the continuation of his memory and message boils down to imitation of the right people and avoiding the influence of others. The present passage expands the preceding exhortation of succession by recalling the theme of Paul's imprisonment from 1:8, now with added characters to clarify its main concern. While the text's chiastic shape (a-b-a') centers the reader on his imprisonment as a potential source of public shame (vv. 16b-17), Paul sandwiches it between contrasting responses within the church: the disaffection of those in Asia who abandoned him (v. 15) contrasts sharply with the hospitality of Onesiphorus, who served him (vv. 16a, 18).[19] Of course, the subtext of this rhetorical footnote is plain: Timothy, join in Onesiphorus's diaconate and you too will receive the Lord's mercy "on that day" (see v. 12).

Nothing else is known from the canonical tradition of Phygelus, Hermogenes, and Onesiphorus, but they are mentioned in the second-century apocryphal *Acts of Paul and Thecla*. There Phygelus and Hermogenes (along with Demas from 4:10) are portrayed as heretical adversaries of Paul, prompted by jealousy of his success (*Paul and Thecla* 4). They disagree in

---

19. Cf. Collins, *1 and 2 Timothy and Titus*, 214.

particular with Pauline teaching about the resurrection of believers (*Paul and Thecla* 14; cf. 2 Tim 2:14-9), which they claim has already been realized spiritually and inwardly rather than bodily at the future return of Christ (*Paul and Thecla* 11-14; cf. 1 Corinthians 15). If read as a second-century haggadah midrash of 2 Timothy's Pauline biography, these apocryphal fictions may have been composed to help readers understand Paul's cryptic reference to the disaffection of "all those in Asia" (1:15). Accordingly, Phygelus and Hermogenes refuse to participate in the succession of the Pauline apostolate because of moral failure (= jealousy) and heresy (= denial of a bodily resurrection). The faithful tradent must rather "hold to a pattern of healthy teaching . . . with the fidelity and loyalty that are in Christ Jesus" (v. 13), presumably like Onesiphorus.

This note opens and concludes in the confidence that Timothy knows the details of the incidents mentioned. The introductory formula, οἶδας τοῦτο (*oidas touto*, "You know this"), recalls the earlier use of *oida* in v. 12, where it was linked with a certain knowledge that rejects a potential shame. The same is true here. Timothy's recollection of these men supplies information that puts away shame for faithful imitation.

What is not made plain by this text, however, is what the Asians actually have rejected: what is the referent of the "me" against whom their backs are turned? Is this a trope for their rejection of Paul's gospel, a spiritual disaffection? Or rather, especially in light of the positive example of Onesiphorus, does this refer to a financial or personal abandonment of Paul in his time of need? The *Paul and Thecla* midrash, shaped in response to heresy, clearly interprets it as a spiritual disaffection. Even so, Paul does not distinguish between different kinds of personal support (cf. Philippians 4): refusing to give financial support is tantamount to rejecting the gospel. The "me" of this passage, then, is an apostolic "me," which includes the apostle but also implies the One who appointed and empowered him as the gospel's "herald, apostle, and teacher" (cf. 4:4). There is no better commentary on this point than Acts 27, where the safe passage of sailors through a stormy sea depends on their personal attachment to Paul and compliance with his instructions received from the Lord (vv. 33-35).

Paul's invocation of divine blessing for Onesiphorus's "household" (οἶκος, *oikos*, 1:16; cf. 4:19) seems awkward here when accompanied by verbs singular in number. Why does Paul mention this particular "household"? Collins raises this question, suggesting that the Christian midrashist who wrote *Paul and Thecla* fills in this gap by portraying Onesiphorus's entire family as hospitable and heroic (*Paul and Thecla* 3). He also suggests that the hospitable household was a representation of social stability in ancient literature and for this reason is an important theme in Acts (e.g., ch. 16) and the Pauline canon (e.g., 1 Cor 1:16)[20] — and, I would add, the Catholic Epistles collection (e.g., 2 John).

In its canonical setting, however, this use of *oikos* so near the beginning of the letter recalls the word's typological use in 1 Timothy, where the church is the "household of God" (3:15) and the microcosm of the loving *oikonomia theou* (1:4b-5a). This suggests, then, that the hospitable practices of Onesiphorus represent a household belonging to God that thus personifies the aim of the Pauline apostolate.

The reference to Rome (1:17; cf. 4:16) in combination with "chain," an evident metaphor of imprisonment, recalls the ending of Acts, where Paul awaited his trial before Caesar while under house arrest and doing what he always does in Acts: presenting the gospel to all comers (Acts 28:30-31). The elaborate rehearsal of Onesiphorus's mission in Rome, however, according to which he arrives, diligently searches, finds Paul, and serves him, sounds an important note, especially in light of the parenthetical comment about Ephesus (1:18b). This is the kind of successor Paul wants Timothy to be in Ephesus: a tenaciously faithful servant of the Pauline tradition. The full measure of this desire is not made complete until the very end of this note in a grammatically convoluted but strategic parenthesis, where Paul adds another "you know," namely that Onesiphorus "served" (διακονέω, *diakoneō*) Paul very well. What Timothy should recall is not the variety of ways Paul was served but that this service to the apostle's needs is the hallmark of the very diaconate to which Timothy himself belongs (see 1 Tim 4:6).

The redundancy and incompleteness of Paul's double reference to the Lord's mercy are difficult to untangle. The verbal mood is optative and expresses a prayer-wish, literally "May the Lord give (Onesiphorus) to find mercy from the Lord." Whether both references are to the same Lord Jesus (1:2) or to different "Lords" within the Trinity, the plain sense of the petition is that Onesiphorus "find mercy" even as he "found" Paul in Rome.[21] But one would like to know what Paul does not mention: What should God "give" Onesiphorus that would enable him "to find mercy . . . on that day" (see v. 12)? If one agrees with those who take Paul's prayer-wish as an early example of a Christian prayer for the dead, then its missing element is God's response to Onesiphorus's résumé of good works, especially to Paul in both

---

20. Collins, *1 and 2 Timothy and Titus*, 216.
21. Bassler confidently asserts that if to different Lords, the first must be Jesus while the second to God (*1 Timothy, 2 Timothy, Titus*, 137), but Fiore and Harrington just as confidently assert the opposite (*Pastoral Epistles*, 144)! The resolution of this ambiguity is, again, exegetically insignificant.

Rome and Ephesus, finding it sufficient to render a merciful verdict. If Onesiphorus is still alive, the unstated desire of Paul's prayer is likely God's persevering grace to enable his friend to remain a faithful disciple a bit longer, until "that day" finally arrives.

2:1-3a A Faithful Succession

¹You then, my child, be empowered by the grace that is in Christ Jesus. ²And pass on the things you and many other witnesses heard from me to faithful people, competent to teach still others. ³ᵃShare the suffering. . . .

This pivotal exhortation reprises and extends the letter's central theme: Timothy's succession of Paul involves the catechesis of others. The grace that saves also empowers Timothy (2:1) to carry the legacy of the Pauline apostolate to "faithful people" who will be enabled to teach still others (v. 2).

The emphatic σὺ οὖν (*sy oun*, "You then") indicates that the following triad of related imperatives — be strong, pass on, share the suffering — aims the preceding example of Onesiphorus at Timothy: even as Onesiphorus served the imprisoned Paul (1:15-18) and so shared in his suffering, so too should Timothy — in his case to pass on the goods of the Pauline apostolate to others. Moreover, by recalling the letter's opening address, "my child" (see 1:2; cf. 1 Tim 1:18), Paul reminds Timothy that the predicate of his responsibility in protecting and passing on Paul's legacy is their close personal relationship. This is family business.²²

The first exhortation (2:1), which I translate "be empowered" (*endynamaō*), can be read in the middle voice, which would suggest that Timothy himself must own the power made available to him "in Christ Jesus" through the indwelling Spirit (cf. 1:14). Earlier, Paul reminded Timothy that the Spirit of "power" dwelled in him, not only to supply him with the "charisma of God" (1:6-7) but to cooperate with him in protecting the apostolic tradition (1:14) and so a Pauline pattern of faith (1:13). The exhortation here elaborates this idea in different words. For this reason, I prefer to translate the prepositional phrase ἐν τῇ χάριτι (*en tę chariti*) instrumentally, "by the grace,"

---

22. Commentators are generally unclear how the following exhortations relate to the prior material — as the diversity of their proposals indicate! Clearly, however, Paul expects Timothy to imitate Onesiphorus's faithfulness to Paul. The formula "my child" often introduces traditional materials, especially in Jewish proverbial literature (e.g., Sir 2:1; 3:1; 4:1), as here. What is important about this text is not the commonplace metaphors and exhortations employed but the role assigned to Timothy that they support.

rather than as naming the location or source of Timothy's strength. Thus "grace" is less a theological concept and more an experience of charisma that enables Timothy to perform those tasks necessary for the apostle's successor. The source of this charisma is "in Christ Jesus" and therefore will not quit on Timothy but is there through the Spirit to appropriate whenever necessary.[23]

The second exhortation (2:2) puts the matter plainly: Timothy's central obligation to Paul is to "pass on" to others what he and other "witnesses" have heard the apostle say. For the Church Fathers, this exhortation, along with 1 Tim 6:20 and 2 Tim 1:13-14, forms the biblical imperative for an ecclesial episcopacy whose responsibility it is to maintain and manage an unbroken and indissoluble connection with the Lord's apostles and their witness to the incarnate "word of life" (cf. 1 John 1:1-3). This doctrine of apostolic succession provided a principal theological warrant for the church's Rule of Faith and its use as the *norma normans* — a "rule that rules" — by which to measure publicly any claim to theological orthodoxy. The Rule proved invaluable not only in developing a range of materials for use in Christian catechesis and proclamation but also in controlling the influence of non-apostolic Christianities, especially during the second and third centuries.

But the form of apostolic succession envisaged by this letter is different in important respects. The preservation of the Pauline *parathēkē* within the church is secured not by its unbroken episcopate but by faithful successors who teach others to teach still others what they have heard from the apostle (2:2). This more democratic kind of expansion may be reflected by Paul's use of the generic ἄνθρωποι (*anthrōpoi*, "people") for those spiritually competent recipients of Timothy's ministry.[24] Paul does not yet think of them as comprising an episcopate but as a community of believers whose teachers remain faithful to his "pattern of healthy teachings" (1:13-14; cf. 1 Tim 3:1-7). Nor, finally, does he view the principal threat to their succession as heretical teaching but as a failure of nerve in the face of shared suffering (2:3a; cf. 1:8-12a).

If the words of a Greek sentence are ordered by their importance in meaning-making, the witness to what Paul himself taught is the most valuable qualification for participating in a succession of his apostolate. The

---

23. Bassler, *1 Timothy, 2 Timothy, Titus*, 138-39. For a Pauline conception of grace as "an event" along with its OT background, see James D. G. Dunn, *The Theology of Paul the Apostle* (Grand Rapids: Eerdmans, 1998), 319-23. Grace is not a "thing" but an actual experience of divine power or empowerment based on the believer's reception of the Spirit; so Dunn, *Theology*, 419-34.

24. Contra Knight, who claims that only males are intended since Paul's exhortation concerns the instruction of a congregation's magisterium and only males could teach in the social world that comes with this text (*Pastoral Epistles*, 391).

aorist form of the verb ἀκούω (*akouō*, "hear"), which opens this critical statement about succession, picks up and elaborates 1:13, where what is "heard" from Paul is "a pattern of healthy teaching." This is the content, then, of what a tradent must "pass on" to other believers. Collins argues that the implicit sense of this verbal idea "pass on" is to explain the tradition as one passes it along.[25]

The phrase διὰ πολλῶν μαρτύρων (*dia pollōn martyrōn*) could be understood instrumentally so that Timothy's religious formation as a Pauline tradent is said to be facilitated by "many witnesses." However, this makes little sense of the images of Timothy's relationship with Paul scattered across this letter and based on their intimate and immediate access to each other. The question remains, then: What role do these other ear-witnesses perform in a narrative of apostolic succession? Perhaps they are the elders who witnessed Timothy's ordination (1 Tim 4:14), but this also seems unlikely in a letter that depicts Timothy as commissioned by Paul himself (2 Tim 1:6).

More likely this crowd of "many witnesses" are yet another memory of those who could still recall what Paul taught and so are able to police Timothy's imitation of the apostle for accuracy. This would be especially important for a community whose accurate "hearing" of Paul's gospel is a condition of its future salvation.[26] The shape of succession is catechetical and forward-moving.[27] The exhortation to teach others is, of course, central to the Pastoral Epistles' vision of organizing a Christian congregation. Who has the authority to teach and what they teach are truck-and-trade concerns of church ministry.

The reader would be surprised to learn that the letter's conception of Pauline succession was something other than a succession of instruction (Pauline doctrine) and instructors (Pauline tradents). The contribution of 2:1-3 to this overall scheme regards the recipients of διδασκαλία (*didaskalia*). Two adjectives are used to define the community of reception: "faithful" and "competent." The quality of πιστός (*pistos*, "faithful") in the Pastoral Epistles is measured by Paul's example (1 Tim 1:12) and his canonical (or "faithful") teaching (1 Tim 1:15) — that is, by the Pauline tradition. The faithful community of reception is a community of faithful *tradents* (1 Tim 4:10, 12; 5:16). The second adjective, ἱκανός (*hikanos*, "competent"), is a more practical quality

---

25. Collins, *1 and 2 Timothy and Titus*, 220.
26. Cf. Marshall, *Pastoral Epistles*, 725-26, who argues that Paul's intent is not the identity of these nameless witnesses but their authority to validate what Paul said.
27. Future tense "will be able" (2:2c) envisages a future realization in what is presently taught. A faithful succession of a tradition always looks ahead to the next generation of believers.

and speaks of effectiveness in learning what is taught and then also in teaching others, which is thematic in the Pastoral Epistles.

The final exhortation, sharply issued in a single imperative, the Pauline catchword συγκακοπάθησον *(synkakopathēson)*, "share the suffering," repeats Paul's earlier charge for Timothy to "share the suffering for the gospel" in imitation of his own mission and of "our Lord" (1:8; cf. 1 Tim 2:5-7). This exhortation and the following three illustrations make clear the personal expense of an apostolic succession. It is the gospel's claims that are provocative, not Paul's persona nor surely that of Timothy, who evidently needs reminding that he already possesses both the charisma and indwelling Spirit to conjure the power necessary to suffer (1:8) and to cooperate with the Spirit of power to safeguard the tradition (1:14). If this succession guarantees the trajectory of the Pauline tradition into the future, then suffering is the expected expense paid by its tradents. Conflict is the inevitable consequence of imitating the testimony of our Lord and his apostle. The question remains, however: What manner of suffering does Paul envisage — martyrdom, shame, or something other?

2:3b-7 Three Examples of Suffering

³ᵇ... like a good soldier of Christ Jesus. ⁴None who soldiers gets entangled in daily affairs so that he might please the enlisting officer. ⁵Likewise, if anyone competes and does not follow the rules, he will not be crowned. ⁶The hardworking farmer must receive the first share of the crop. ⁷Think about what I say, for the Lord will give you clarity in everything.

The exhortation to "share the suffering" sounds a cautionary note, which is elaborated by these three well-known examples of noble sufferers: the "good soldier" (2:3b-4), the disciplined athlete (v. 5), and the "hardworking farmer" (v. 6). The concluding note to "think about what I say" (v. 7) is appropriate for Paul's "child" (v. 1).

The diverse and abrupt character of paraenetic literature sometimes makes it difficult for the reader to follow. There is no plotline and no clear rhetorical design that enables the reader to track easily the argument made. But an overarching flow is followed, the bits of exhortation are linked together by repeated words that help readers cobble together a vision for life and work, and familiar materials are used. Here Paul uses familiar topoi, as when he lists cardinal virtues to habituate or vices to avoid. Stories of the good soldier, disciplined athlete, or hardworking farmer are used even today to illustrate moral instruction. Their use in canonical texts is routine, since their ambiguity allows for flexibility when applying the gospel truth to faithful practice. This same literary characteristic, however, sometimes makes it difficult for the reader to understand the particular motive and plain sense of what is written. Here the topoi of hard workers shape an impression of why the faithful tradent must share in the suffering of the Lord's apostle. The importance of hard work is characteristic of faithfulness and a familiar feature of Pauline exhortation (cf. Col 4:13).

Timothy surely understands in general terms the task at hand: he is a custodian of memories, of a Pauline pattern of instruction, of an apostolic tradition, which he has been commissioned to pass on to others in Paul's absence. The idiom of suffering cues the personal and political expense of this work, which, even though conducted in the company of the indwelling Spirit, is vulnerable to the tradent's unfaithfulness and the treachery of others. Opponents are mentioned in this letter, those who, unlike Onesiphorus, have abandoned Paul or have rejected his instruction, and implied by allusions to imprisonment and abuse are the political elites for whom the preaching of the Christian gospel and the alternative way of life it sponsors constitute a threat to Rome's prerogatives.

What initially surprises the reader is that these examples, the soldier, athlete, and farmer, do not follow from the nature of Paul's suffering, namely imprisonment (1:18) and physical abuse suffered during his mission to the nations (cf. 3:11). Nor do they suggest suffering resulting from difficult circumstances, whether social rejection or financial hardship. These examples are of competent professionals whose personal sacrifice and hard work pay dividends of excellence, so that they represent a kind of "no pain, no gain" philosophy.

The first example, the disciplined soldier (2:3-4), does not baptize professional soldiering as a Christian profession. Rather, this vignette of the "good" soldier typifies the species of suffering the faithful tradent should anticipate.[28] The analogy is plain: "Christ Jesus" is likened to the soldier's enlisting officer, and single-minded attentiveness to the task of soldiering that pleases the officer is likened to the Lord's pleasure in Timothy's single-minded attentiveness to the tasks of succession. The adjective καλός *(kalos)*, "good," to describe this single-minded soldier repeats the earlier use in reference to the "good" *parathēkē* (1:14), which Paul has entrusted to Timothy to

---

28. The history of interpretation into the modern period (see Jay Twomey, *The Pastoral Epistles through the Centuries* [Chichester: Wiley-Blackwell, 2009], 132-38) reflects effort not so much to settle the plain sense of the text but rather more clearly to adapt Christian faith to its political setting.

pass on to others. That is, the good soldier is likened to the good tradent: they are both professional protectors.

In Hellenistic moral discourse, soldiering represented dedicated service and a willingness to suffer for a noble cause.[29] It speaks of rigorous training that puts aside personal pleasure to become battle-ready and of sacrifice of personal prerogatives, whatever they might be, in obeying a chain of command. The "good soldier of Christ Jesus" is single-minded in his obedience to a sacred calling (cf. 1:6-7).

The second example, the competitor, functions similarly. In antiquity as today the successful athlete is put forward as an example of one whose hard work pays off in competitive excellence (cf. Phil 3:12-14; 1 Cor 9:24-25). Paul's use of this topos here, however, features the athlete's attention to the rules of the game, or perhaps a precise regimen of training as decisive for victory (cf. 2:10-13; 4:8). The relevant issue for the purpose at hand is one's personal struggle and sacrifice not in becoming successful but in obeying the rules: Paul wants Timothy to be a loyal son.

The exegetical question remains, what kind of suffering does the compliant athlete embody that is analogous of the faithful tradent? Perhaps the key is hidden in νομίμως *(nomimōs)*, which I translate "follow the rules." Towner points out that these rules may be either the rules of the game, which the athlete must follow to avoid being disqualified, or the standard protocol of preparation that an athlete submits to in preparation for a contest.[30] I suspect the latter is in play here, so that Paul's implied exhortation to Timothy is to continue or make use of the rigorous preparation that has prepared him for the work at hand. Interestingly, Paul uses this same word in 1 Tim 1:8 when speaking of a "lawful" use of the rule of law to criticize Torah teachers who make claims without understanding. Without pressing this intertext beyond its breaking point, perhaps the antecedent text glosses this one to suggest that the suffering experienced in the tradent's training results from the hard work in preparing to teach the word of truth rightly (see 2:15).

The third topos is also used frequently of someone worthy of imitation (cf. 1 Cor 9:7, 10; Jas 5:7): the hard-working farmer (2:6). The word order of this text privileges the farmer's toil (κοπιῶντα, *kopiōnta*) over his reward, even though the two are integrally linked: hard work begets a crop. Again, the exhortation to "share the suffering" is linked to hard work. In this case, however, there is a future benefit or reward stipulated as its motive. Bassler suggests reading all three examples as parables whose primary point is made here

---

29. Johnson, *First and Second Letters to Timothy,* 365.
30. Towner, *Letters to Timothy and Titus,* 494.

in the third: Timothy's suffering, resulting from doing the work he is being told to do, is the condition of his future reward (cf. 4:8; 1 Tim 4:13-16).³¹

The sentence that concludes this triad of examples (2:7) is puzzling. Kelly calls it a "parenthesis" without a clear role to perform.³² Perhaps it is best understood as a tagline similar to a liturgical formula placed in a poetic or proverbial passage to signal a transition or pause. This sense seems to be picked up by the Majority Text, which prefers δώῃ (*dōē*, optative: "may he give") to the critical text's δώσει (*dōsei*, future indicative: "he will give") — a prayer-like refrain that seeks the Lord's support for a difficult task ahead. Towner, however, finds here a possible allusion to LXX Prov 2:6 and the way of wisdom: that is, wisdom clarifies the path one should travel into the future. If this allusion holds, it links suffering with the way of wisdom so that the cost of discipleship is the purchase price of spiritual understanding.³³

2:8-13 Suffering as a Resurrection Practice

⁸Remember Jesus Christ: raised from the dead, from the family of David. This is my good news ⁹for which I suffer bad news, bound like a common criminal. But the word of God cannot be bound. ¹⁰Because of this I endure all this for the elect, so that they may also experience salvation in Christ Jesus with eternal glory. ¹¹This teaching is a core belief:

> For if we shared in death, we will share also in life;
> ¹²if we persevere, we will also share in rule;
> if we deny, he will also deny us;
> ¹³if we are faithless, he remains faithful (for he cannot be other than what
> he is).

This passage begins with a reminder of a core belief of Paul's gospel: "Jesus Christ (is) raised from the dead" (2:8). On this basis, Paul endures suffering so that those who believe its truth may experience salvation (vv. 9-10). A canonical saying elaborates this claim by describing how Christian existence is formed from beginning to end by participation with the risen Christ (vv. 11-13).

Christian ministry serves the redemptive interests of the risen Lord, for whom one should expect to suffer. This passage continues to unpack this

---

31. Bassler, *1 Timothy, 2 Timothy, Titus*, 141.
32. J. N. D. Kelly, *A Commentary on the Pastoral Epistles* (BNTC; London: Black, 1963), 176.
33. Towner, *Letters to Timothy and Titus*, 496-98.

theme, which was introduced earlier in Paul's exhortation for Timothy to share in his suffering (1:8-12; 2:3-6). Paul now "remembers" the testimony of the resurrected Jesus (2:8a; cf. 1:3, 9-10), who supplies the theological core of his gospel ministry (2:8b; cf. 1:8, 11) and legitimizes his own suffering and imprisonment (2:9; cf. 1:11-12): his suffering is a resurrection practice. He claims that the purpose of his gospel ministry is the eternal salvation of those who are in Christ Jesus (2:10; cf. 1:9-10), and enlists yet another canonical saying (= "teaching of a core belief") for support (2:11-13; cf. 1 Tim 1:15; 3:1; 4:9).

Chrysostom rightly wonders why Paul would encourage Timothy to "remember Jesus Christ" (2:8a), but then answers his own question that "it is directed chiefly against the heretics, at the same time to encourage Timothy by underscoring the divine blessings accompanying sufferings, since Christ, our Master, himself overcame death by suffering" (*Homilies on 2 Timothy* 4). In this letter, the exhortation to "remember" rarely introduces apologetics but rather important elements of the Pauline gospel tradition, including Jesus' "resurrection from the dead" and his messianic credential as a "descendant of David" (cf. Rom 1:3-4). Chrysostom may be right, however, that Paul may be anticipating his later correction of Christian teachers (see 2:18), even if his immediate concern is Timothy's reluctance to share in his and the risen Lord's suffering. In this light, then, remembering Christ's resurrection recalls the deep logic of Paul's gospel by which Jesus triumphs over sin and death by "becoming obedient to the point of death, even death on a cross" (Phil 2:8). It is further logical that this same obedience-suffering-triumph pattern is reflected in his own missionary experience (2:10), which he trusts Timothy will share.

The formulation of Paul's exhortation strikes one as odd. The reordering of the name, "Jesus Christ," is unique in this letter and may suggest that it is borrowed from an early Christian creed or hymn already known by Timothy. More critically, the reader expects to remember the Christological formula in "proper order" by putting the historical Jesus' Davidic descent first, followed by his resurrection (and exaltation) as God's Son, as in Rom 1:3-4. The strange sequence here prioritizes the Lord's resurrection perhaps because Hymenaeus and Philetus are arguing against Paul's interpretation of it (2:18), or more simply to underwrite suffering as a resurrection practice — motivated by the victory of the risen Jesus and expected as a consequence of faithfulness.[34]

---

34. The verb "raise" (ἐγείρω, *egeirō*) is represented here in a perfect passive participle, which indicates that resurrection is a past activity of God's whose consequence continues into the present. This is true of the risen Jesus, who is alive, but also of those believers who participate by faith in his resurrection. That is, the Christological pattern of suffering-death-resurrection applies to believers whose obedient suffering for Christ's sake has the ongoing consequence of resurrection from the dead, not only in transformed existence but in the coming age.

But one must still explain why Paul would include a reference to Jesus' Davidic lineage since the Pastoral Epistles show no explicit interest in it, and he could have easily edited it out for consistency's sake. After all, his subsequent adumbration on this confessional note speaks of the long-term effects of Christian baptism into Jesus' resurrection (2:10-13) and of false teaching about the resurrection (vv. 14-19). Paul's inclusion of Jesus' descent from David, while part of a preformed creed, may not be messianic at all but merely explanatory of his human suffering: that is, David represents the Lord's family tree (cf. Matt 1:1-17) and explains why Jesus could be expected to suffer and why Paul (and Timothy) should therefore expect to suffer.[35]

But could this reference rather allude to the church's claim of Jesus' royalty, central to the passion narrative as the explanation of his rejection by both Israel and Rome? To remember Jesus Christ's Davidic descent is to remember the church's claim regarding his kingship, especially developed in the church's fourfold Gospel at the time of the Pastoral Epistles' canonization, which would have been especially provocative to imperial Rome and would therefore help explain why Paul suffers "like a common criminal" (2:9).

But this conclusion begs a different kind of question with deep roots in the modern period. Paul's exhortation to remember his proclamation of Jesus Christ disguises the central (and perhaps continuing) problem of his apostolate. Unlike the Jerusalem pillar apostles, he did not hear, see, or touch "the word of life." In fact, other apostolic traditions make their eyewitness the central evidence of their ecclesial authority and principal justification of the Christian gospel (1 John 1:1-3, 5; 3:11; Acts 1:20). The Jesus remembered by Paul is not Jesus before crucifixion and resurrection but the Jesus he encountered in a vision on the Damascus Road — an encounter that he interpreted through the grid of his messianic Judaism, according to which the Messiah is a "descendant of David" (Acts 13:22-23). Within its canonical setting, then, this act of remembering the risen Christ of Davidic descent is read in a substantively different sense than the appeals to this same Christ in a text like 1 John or 2 Peter, which assumes a personal encounter with the historical Jesus. The authority of the Pauline apostolate, clearly worked out in the narrative world of Acts, is predicated on a different sort of witness — one that regards the exemplary virtue and costly obedience of Paul as central (Acts 20:17-25; 24:21; 26:19-23).[36]

In any case, the interplay of three powerful contrasts conveys the extent

---

35. See below on 4:16-18, in which a Davidic psalm of lament (LXX Psalm 21) is echoed to add a missiological layer of meaning to Paul's own lament of abandonment and the Lord's "rescue" of him.

36. Contra Childs, *Church's Guide*, 74-75.

of Paul's suffering for Christ's sake, which is then glossed by his confidence in the resurrection of Jesus and its effect on human existence (2:8b-9). First is the contrast between Paul's proclamation of "good news" (εὐαγγέλιον, *euangelion*) and his personal experience of "bad news" (κακοπαθέω, *kakopatheō*, literally "suffer bad"). Second, this experience of "bad news" is elaborated as his treatment like a "common criminal," a second *kakos* ("bad") word, κακοῦργος (*kakourgos*, literally "bad-doer"). These two contrasts frame a third, the dramatic irony between a "bound" Paul and the unbound word of God. Paul recognizes that he (and, by implication, Timothy) is a mortal agent who serves an eternal purpose. Such an honest appraisal of his missionary vocation, similar to what we find in Acts, is the subtext of the succession theme in this letter: because of their shared mortality, Paul charges Timothy to continue his mission and message after his death (cf. 4:6), which Timothy is also to pass on to others who will teach still others as their successors (2:2). Paul's capacity to respond faithfully to his suffering does not derive from stoic self-will but from his confidence that God will call out still others to advance the gospel without him. Perhaps Paul here is also challenging a reason for Timothy's timidity (cf. 1:7), who may not be worried only that he will end up imprisoned like Paul: his reluctance to embrace his gift and vocation for gospel ministry may also have to do with the real effectiveness of a gospel that claims God's salvation from suffering and death while those who proclaim it are suffering and dying, seemingly without God's protection. If so, then, Timothy's confidence in the trustworthiness of God's unbound word, which proclaims the prospect of "eternal glory" (2:10), including his own participation in the coming age, is encouraged by remembering that "Jesus Christ (is) risen from the dead."

The relationship between Paul's suffering and his saving gospel is made even clearer in 2:10. He believes that those ushered into God's salvation during his evangelistic crusades are the fruit of his suffering. That is, God's salvation mediated by his gospel is effective not in spite of but because of his suffering and imprisonment. In my opinion the subtext of this causal connection between Paul's suffering and the salvation of "the elect" is not supplied by Jewish mysticism (as in Col 1:24); nor does Paul suppose that Timothy or other tradents must suffer as the badge of their faithfulness as his successors. Paul is no masochist! His comment is simply a deeply felt personal reflection on his present situation and the hard work required to obey his sacred commission to carry the word of God and so share in Christ's suffering (cf. Acts 9:15-16) — the very sort of comment we would expect to find in a literary "last will and testament." The larger principle expressed is this: a believer's life is empowered by God's grace, even to endure great suffering, in order to bear witness to the truth of the gospel.

But what are we to make of the evocative reference to "the elect" (cf. Tit 1:1)? In a letter that grounds the succession of the Pauline apostolate in Jewish tradition (see 1:3-5) it is not surprising that Paul would appropriate an important OT trope for the covenant community to stipulate the church's position in the presence of God. The modern discussion of the Protestant conception of election is hopelessly muddled in the offense of its particularity: if only certain people are the "elect" of God, then most are not, through no fault of their own. But Scripture's theology of election, especially witnessed in the ancestral narratives of Genesis, is not interested in this problem of theodicy but with how people respond to God's own choosing. The problem is not God, to whom salvation belongs; we are the problem. This is mostly so because election comes with a vocation: biblical Israel is chosen by God to be a light to the world, and most often Israel trades on its status as God's elect people without then also obeying God's call to be a holy nation, a priestly kingdom.

The real choice God has made is not of a particular apostle, Paul, or of a particular people, Israel. God has chosen a particular Christ, Jesus, and sent him into the world to save all humanity from sin (1 Tim 2:5-6). It is the resurrection of Christ Jesus that makes this choice perfectly clear, and it is "in Christ Jesus" that those who identify with him by faith "may also experience salvation" with "eternal glory" (2 Tim 2:10).

In this sense, then, the mention of an "elect" community is a Pauline way of speaking of the risen Christ as God's chosen Messiah, through whom God dispensed grace πρὸ χρόνων αἰωνίων (*pro chronōn aiōniōn*, "before time began," 1:9). He is not referring to individuals who are predestined by God for salvation but of those who by faith participate in the salvation that God's Chosen One has brought to earth (cf. Tit 3:4-8). The importance of this point extends to the succession theme mentioned above: Paul exhorts Timothy to succeed him in ministry, not only for the sake of the non-believers who will be initiated into the elect community in Christ as a result, but also to encourage those already saved to endure to the end in order that "they may also experience salvation" (2:10).

Especially in the writings of Hellenistic Judaism (Philo, Josephus), the language of "glory" develops a connotation of human reputation (cf. Josephus, *Antiquities* 15.376) that differs from OT (LXX) use of "glory," where it typically refers to the "weightiness" or ultimate importance of God's ongoing presence among God's people. In his doxologies Paul often recalls this biblical idea to celebrate God's "eternal glory" (see 1 Tim 1:11; 3:16; 6:15-16; Tit 2:13). Here he splits the difference and speaks of faithful believers — those whose reputation is to endure suffering with their faith intact — as those who will ultimately participate in the eternal glory of God.

2 Timothy 2:8-13

The canonical saying added in 2:11-13 is as complex as it is compressed, consisting of four conditional statements without subjects or objects. To fill in these gaps, the reader must "remember Jesus Christ" in the manner mentioned at the opening of this passage: he "is raised from the dead, from the family of David" (v. 8a). In fact, the very purpose of the surprising *gar* ("for") that introduces this saying is to point back to that confession as the saying's antecedent.[37] That is, it expounds a Christian confession of faith in the living Christ's resurrection from the dead.

The four lines of the saying are each expressed as a conditional: "if . . . then." Paul adds a footnote to the final line, presumably because of the theological difficulty it raises. The first, "for if we shared in death, we share also in life" (2:11b), is programmatic. Again, assuming that this canonical saying is an expansion of what is remembered of Paul's preaching about the risen Christ (v. 8a), allusions to his participatory Christology (e.g., Rom 6:1-14) are noted: both verbs are *syn-* constructions, and the aorist protasis and present apodosis, both indicatives, express the present effect that has logically followed from the believer's prior baptism into the dying and rising of Christ. The importance of the confession that "Jesus Christ is raised from the dead" is more fully expressed in Rom 6:8 by "for if we shared in the death of the risen Christ, we now share life with him" (cf. 2 Cor 7:3; 1 Thess 4:17). There the prior initiation of the believer into the death of Christ redefines Christian existence in terms of moral rectitude and freedom from sin. Here in 2 Timothy, this same core belief underwrites the faithful tradent's imitation of Christ's faithfulness in suffering for the gospel (cf. 1:8).

The second and third lines expand on this meaning by forming a parallelism based upon verbal tenses: in both lines, the present experience of Christian fidelity (protasis) yields a realistic hope for future blessing (apodosis). Again both lines are glossed by the opening remembrance of the risen Christ. The plain sense of the second line thus reads "if we persevere (present indicative) with Christ, we also will share in his rule (future indicative)," to express a thoroughly Pauline thought.

The three *syn-* verbs in the first two lines demonstrate the movement of

---

37. Most commentators neglect the opening γάρ *(gar)* when interpreting 2:11-13. Those who do not argue that it is a rhetorical device used to introduce a discrete saying, that it comes from the source of the saying, or, better (with Bassler, *1 Timothy, 2 Timothy, Titus*, 143), that 2:8a is too far removed from v. 11 to be the referent of *gar*, which is, rather, the promise of salvation in v. 10. While we agree that the canonical sayings of the Pastoral Epistles summarize Pauline soteriology, the elliptical nature of the saying suggests that Paul intends to reach back to the Christ formula that introduces and is therefore implicit in this entire passage. If so, the reader's appropriation of it to gloss and fill out this canonical saying is reasonable.

Paul's participatory Christology: to die (past), to live (present), and to rule (future). This idea lies at the center of his "epistolary and theological vocabulary" of Christian existence expressed in his "baptismal catechesis."[38] Moreover, perseverance is a hallmark of the justified, whose inward dispositions are transformed by divine grace (Rom 5:3; 8:24; 12:12; 1 Cor 13:7).

The third line, "if we deny (Christ), he will also deny us" (2:12b), retains this same dynamic between present existence and future blessing but restates its truth in negative terms, perhaps as a warning against disaffection.[39] If it is a warning and not merely a dogmatic assertion, Paul has in mind those who have rejected his interpretation of the risen Christ, such as Hymenaeus and Philetus (2:16-18). Paul thus considers them apostate, outside the "elect," and their "eternal glory" thereby imperiled (cf. 2:10, 19). If, however, apostolic succession is the implied referent of this saying, then denial of the Pauline apostolate and in particular his teaching about Jesus Christ (cf. 2:8b) is the problem, so that this becomes a warning for Timothy to continue in his work as an interpreter of the word of truth (cf. 2:15).

The idea that Timothy's salvation is conditioned on the performance of the practices of his sacred calling is already found in 1 Tim 4:14-16 and may be implicit here. The Lord's faithfulness to a promise made is undeniable, and for this reason the warning implicit in this line should be read in a qualified way: God's preference is always for the remediation and repentance of the faithless, and so the eschatological denial of their "eternal glory" must be seen as a last resort when every effort of correction, whether mediated by Timothy or Satan (see 1 Tim 1:19-20), is rebuffed.

Paul breaks from this negative pattern in the apodosis of the fourth line, "if we are faithless, he remains faithful" (2:13a), to conclude on a positive but theocentric note: the resurrection vindicates the faithfulness of God to promises made to the elect community of a Davidic Messiah. The rhetorical effect of ending the canonical saying in this way underscores the certainty of divine promise, which, while dependent on human agency for its fulfillment, is nonetheless independent of human influence. Sharply put, whether Timothy finally agrees to succeed Paul in the gospel ministry, which remains an open question at this point, his decision will not affect God's decision to grant eternal life to those who trust in Christ Jesus. The assumption, of course, is that if Timothy fails Christ, God will raise up another gifted tradent to succeed Paul.

38. Collins, *1 and 2 Timothy and Titus*, 226-27.
39. The ms. evidence is mixed. The critical text renders the protasis as a future middle, ἀρνήσασθαι *(arnēsasthai)*, even though most translate it with present force. The Majority and Western traditions have a present indicative, ἀρνούμεθα *(arnoumetha)*, which seems a more natural but easier (and therefore later) rendering.

Our faithlessness grieves the Lord, but does not subvert God's plan for the covenant-keeping community and the prospect of future blessings for those who remain faithful to him.

The explanatory footnote Paul adds at the end of the saying is introduced by *gar* ("for") and functions here to tease out an original and stunning implication of the Lord's resurrection: Christ's faithfulness to God's redemptive purpose and grace (cf. 1:9) coheres with who he is and so makes faithlessness to God on his part a real impossibility. While Paul routinely declares that God raised Jesus from the dead in confirmation of his messianic triumph, Jesus' faithfulness is not predetermined by his nature but rather is the exercise of a free and public choice that his disciples must now imitate (e.g., Phil 2:5-11). But Paul seems here to suggest something that actually subverts imitation: what believers are capable of doing — denying the truth of Paul's proclamation of Christ — is something that Christ is unable to do. What, then, are we to make of this parenthetical comment, especially in light of the participatory Christology that underwrites this canonical saying?

If one takes this footnote as proffering a fuller explanation only of the preceding apodosis, especially if understood by the letter's theme of apostolic succession, it would suggest that the risen Christ will not deny the Pauline apostolate but rather will secure its future since he has a personal stake in Paul — a clear theme of the portrait of Paul in Acts. That is, not only did Christ convert and commission Paul (cf. 1 Tim 1:12-16; 2:7; 2 Tim 1:10-11; Acts 9:1-21), Paul's gospel brings to light the full meaning of the "appearing of our Savior Christ Jesus" (so 1:9b-10) and so God's redemptive purpose and saving grace (so 1:9a). It is on this Christological ground that the Pauline tradition must be carried forward in the apostle's absence by faithful tradents.

2:14-26 True and False Teachers

¹⁴Remind them of these things and warn them before the Lord[40] to avoid disputed teachings. There is no benefit, and it only destroys the auditors. ¹⁵Make every effort to prove yourself in the presence of God as a worker who is unashamed to interpret the word of truth. ¹⁶Avoid profane chatter, for it will lead many into god-

---

40. Most mss. have τοῦ κυρίου (*tou kyriou*, "the Lord"), but there is support from a variety of ms. families for τοῦ θεοῦ (*tou theou*, "God"), which is favored by the UBS because the committee judged it the more difficult reading and because it agrees with the sense of the parallel wording of 1 Tim 5:4, 21 (cf. 2 Tim 4:1). We prefer "Lord," however, not only because of stronger ms. support but also because it better relates the injunctions of this pericope to the preceding reminder about Jesus Christ in 2:8-13.

lessness, [17]and their word will have the effect of spreading gangrene. Among them are Hymenaeus and Philetus, [18]who have missed truth's target, claiming that the[41] resurrection has already occurred and subverting the faith of some.

[19]Even so, God's firm foundation stands, displaying this marker: "The Lord knows those belonging to him" and "Let all those calling upon the Lord's name turn away from unrighteousness." [20]That is, in an impressive house there are not only gold and silver utensils but also some made with wood and clay; some are for special uses, some for ordinary uses. [21]Therefore, if someone thoroughly cleanses himself of these (teachings), he will be sanctified as a "special utensil," useful to the master for every good work.

[22]Stay away from the passions of youth and instead pursue righteousness, faithfulness, love, peace with those who call on the Lord from a pure heart. [23]Avoid foolish and thoughtless discussions, since you know they produce conflicts. [24]The Lord's slave must not quarrel but should be kind toward all, able to teach, patient, [25]schooling opponents with gentleness. Perhaps God might permit them a change of mind, then knowledge of the truth, [26]and so they will come to their senses, escaping the devil's trap, which holds them captive to do his will.

The act of remembering what is confessed about the risen Christ (2:8) issues in an expansive exhortation to remind, warn, and avoid instruction contrary to it (v. 14), which is disruptive of the spiritual formation of Timothy's congregation (vv. 14-16). By avoiding "thoughtless discussions" and schooling false teachers with gentleness, Timothy enables God to bring them to their senses, not only so that they might escape the devil's trap (vv. 25-26) but also so that their teaching is exposed as contrary to the word of truth (v. 15). In contrast to the likes of Hymenaeus and Philetus, who have missed the target of faith (vv. 16-18), the faithful minister is set apart as a "special utensil" (vv. 20-21), one who works hard to interpret the word of truth rightly (v. 15) while pursuing righteousness "from a pure heart" (vv. 22-26; cf. 1:12). This contrast, which resonates with the OT contrast of true and false prophecies, provides the thematic focus of this entire portion of the letter's instruction and stands at the heart of Paul's exhortation of his young protégé, who is encouraged to work hard in aiming a true word about the Lord's resurrection at his congregation (cf. Romans 6).

Paul begins this passage by repeating the exhortation to remember.

---

41. The article is omitted by some early and important witnesses, but we include it because of its overwhelming ms. support. If the omission is correct, however, Paul may be reporting a misguided claim for a particular kind of resurrection that may be a substitute belief in "the" resurrection of Jesus.

Even though my translation of the opening injunction adds the implied object "them," the text itself lacks an object and is more sharply concentrated on actions Timothy is asked to undertake as Paul's delegate and the congregation's spiritual leader: "remind . . . warn . . . avoid" (2:14). This exhortation purposefully recalls the preceding passage, which opens with "remember Jesus Christ" (v. 8a): the act of reminding the community of "these things" is an act of remembering their participation with the risen One.

Barrett contends that there is no connection with the prior material: this new exhortation is much too abrupt, he claims, and signals a change of topic and literary style.[42] But Bassler rightly observes that what follows is "logically connected" to the letter's prior summons to share in the immediate costs and eternal benefits of suffering occasioned by opposition to Paul's gospel.[43] The most prominent difference noted between true and false teachers is a contrasting teaching style, which continues the letter's interest in the pedagogy of theological catechesis (cf. 1 Tim 1:4-7; 4:6-7; 6:4). Paul's opponents are provocateurs, drawn to "disputed teachings"[44] (2:14) and inclined toward "profane chatter" (v. 16). Because their teaching is not shaped by the pattern of Pauline instruction (and so in the company of the indwelling Spirit; cf. 1:13-14), neither is it aimed at loving relations (cf. 1 Tim 4:4-5). There is "no benefit" for the community, and this manner of instruction even subverts God's redemptive purpose.

Positively, Timothy is advised to be a hard "worker" (ἐργάτης, *ergatēs*), one who presents himself "proven" (δόκιμος, *dokimos*) in a review before God, presumably in the future when God will measure the worker by his lack of shame when teaching the "word of truth" (2:15). On this basis one might anticipate a positive result. But the plain emphasis here is on the character of the worker, forged in a costly struggle and personal suffering, and on the content of instruction, both of which must pass God's test for excellence.

Images of the hard worker, the soldier or farmer, are common in the NT (cf. 1 Tim 5:18; 2 Tim 2:3-7; Jas 5:4; Acts 19:25). The character of the worker here — he is unashamed when interpreting the word of truth — are glossed by the letter's overarching theme of succession: the worker who passes God's muster is one who is faithful to the Pauline apostolate and unashamed to suffer when passing it on to others (2:2-7; cf. 1:8). The use of ὀρθοτομέω

---

42. Barrett, *Pastoral Epistles*, 105-6.
43. Bassler, *1 Timothy, 2 Timothy, Titus*, 149.
44. "Disputed teachings" translates the infinitive, λογομαχεῖν (*logomachein*), literally "word-battles" (cf. 1 Tim 6:4). The root verb, *macheō*, is a military expression often used in the polemics of philosophers who charged their opponents with engaging in "word-battles" rather than in dialogue over substantive ideas.

(*orthotomeō*, "interpret," literally "make a right path") echoes its only other uses in the biblical canon, where it is used of a wisdom of obedience that wins divine approval: the wise pave a "right path" in God's direction (LXX Prov 3:6) that leads to deliverance (Prov 11:5). Perhaps the diction of this echo helps the reader sense the force of the following warning against "worldly chitchat" (2:16), which repeats 1 Tim 6:20 and recalls that letter's concluding exhortation that Timothy mind the apostolic *parathēkē* rather than impious practices that miss the target. A word on target safeguards the tradition and leads to salvation.

The repetition of λόγος *(logos)* in this passage is important to note. On the face of it, the "word" of the faithful tradent spreads the "truth" of the Lord's resurrection, whereas the "word" that subverts Pauline instruction about the resurrection spreads like gangrene (2:17). In this setting, the substance of the true word consists of historical memories of Paul's core claims about the risen Jesus (2:8; cf. 2 Cor 6:7; Eph 1:13; Col 1:5; see 1 Tim 3:15-16; 6:3-5) and its implication for Christian existence, namely that the believer participates with the risen Christ in both his suffering and eschatological glory (so 2:10-13).

But in what *form* is this "word of truth" articulated? Virtually all commentators understand "word of truth" as a trope for the Pauline gospel. But could it refer instead to a textual rather than verbal word — that is, to an early collection of Pauline texts that has been put into circulation for use by delegates like Timothy when they are pressed by disagreeable teachers, as here, to make corrections in Paul's absence? As mentioned above, Trobisch's thesis that Paul himself may have initiated the formation of the Pauline canon is considerably more plausible when glossed by this letter's theme of apostolic succession. The critical text in support of this speculation comes in 2 Tim 3:14-17, where the memory of Pauline instruction (v. 14) is paired with Israel's "sacred writings" (v. 15) to perform the divinely inspiring work of Scripture that brings Timothy to maturity for doing God's good work (vv. 16-17). In fact, the subsequent charge to "preach the word" (4:2) may imply the performance of traditional Bible practices (cf. 1 Tim 4:12-13), in which the interpretation (*orthotomeō* here) of a proto-canon of Pauline letters, edited and put into circulation by Paul, is used in his absence for the community's catechesis into his tradition (cf. 2 Tim 2:2).

Characteristically, Paul notes the contrasting content and pedagogy of a pair of false teachers. He rarely spells out what his opponents teach and rarely names them; he is generally more interested to use them as rhetorical foils to clarify what he teaches (so, e.g., 1 Tim 4:1-4). However, in 2 Tim 2:17b-18a, Hymenaeus (see 1 Tim 1:20) and Philetus are named as having departed from a Pauline interpretation of the Lord's resurrection (cf. 1 Cor. 15:12). The medical images used to make this point were commonplace in the philosophical discourse of antiquity. The implicit contrast between "healthy teaching" (1 Tim 1:10; 6:3; 2 Tim 1:13) and the spread of gangrene is a vivid reminder in familiar terms of the awful effects on the human spirit of any departure from Pauline orthodoxy: it putrefies spiritual health. And the mention of this pair of troublemakers, whose reputation is no doubt familiar to the reader, may well be a rhetorical ploy to indicate their potential for wreaking havoc that only intensifies the urgency of Paul's exhortation to Timothy to remind and warn members to avoid their influence (2:14) and instead listen keenly to the word of truth (v. 15).

A few mss. substitute the indefinite "a resurrection" (cf. 2:18), which indicates that an unspecified resurrection of some kind is being taught. By choosing to retain the articular form, "the resurrection," even though the support is mixed, I take it that the false teaching of Hymenaeus and Philetus has reinterpreted Paul's teaching about the resurrection of Christ and its theological implications for Christian existence, set out in the prior canonical saying and elaborated in Paul's standard letters (especially Romans and 1 Corinthians). Although the text does not discuss their teaching, most interpreters think they are promoting some version of an overly realized eschatology that promises an escape from present suffering (cf. 2:10) — perhaps a kind of "prosperity gospel."[45]

Significantly, F. Watson's reconstruction of a late second-century contest between Tertullian and "Valentinian Gnosticism" over a normative Pauline interpretation of Christ's resurrection, reflected in the Apologist's rejoinder to the so-called "Treatise on the Resurrection" (or "Letter of Rheginus"),[46] suggests what was happening when the Pastoral Epistles were added to complete the final redaction of the Pauline corpus. According to Watson, Tertullian's definition of the apostolic tradition argues for a more material doctrine of the resurrection — an actual resurrection of the physical body — against those who, like the author of the "Treatise" (and perhaps not unlike Hymenaeus and Philetus), proffer a spiritualized or "realized" reading of Pauline texts on Christ's resurrection (which avoids the Gospel's Easter narrative). In a highly suggestive comment, Watson allows that this Valentinian reading of Paul is "truly and radically Pauline" but is possible only "outside the canonical context," by which he

---

45. For a summary of the history of interpretation, see Marshall, *Pastoral Epistles*, 771-74.
46. See M. L. Peel's introduction and translation of this letter in James M. Robinson and Richard Smith, *The Nag Hammadi Library in English* (rev. ed.; CGLP; San Francisco: Harper and Row, 1990), 52-57.

means a biblical canon in which the fourfold canonical Gospel is "foundation" and whose narrative of Christ's bodily resurrection grounds Tertullian's material reading of the church's future resurrection and justifies his objection of an overly spiritualized and individualized reading of Paul.[47]

But if the addition of the Pastoral Epistles to the Pauline collection (at a time when, according to Peel, the "Treatise on the Resurrection" was being circulated by "heretical" Paulinists) had a hermeneutical purpose, namely to guide the church's continuing appropriation of the apostle's standard letters for Christian theological formation, then perhaps this entire pericope beginning with Paul's declaration of Easter faith in 2:8 performs a corrective or constraining task for the church's future use of the Pauline witness in forming the church's orthodox doctrine of the resurrection. While the existential impress of Christ's resurrection is retained (vv. 11-14), the form of the creedal remembrance in v. 8 not only recalls the fourfold Gospel narrative of Jesus Christ but also explains the importance of the otherwise curious addition about his Davidic or human ancestry. That is, Tertullian rightly understood the importance of predicating the spiritual effects of our participation with the risen Christ on an actual event (or, as Watson might say, on the canonical Gospel narrative of the earthly Jesus).

In this regard, Paul clearly anticipates suffering for those who follow in his footsteps (2:9), and participation in the coming victory of the risen Christ is conditioned on faithful perseverance through it (2:12a; cf. 4:7-8). His response here is clipped and uncertain but seems similar to the responses in Romans 6 and 1 Corinthians 15 to Christians who are struggling with similar crises of faith. While the believer's participation in Christ's resurrection comes with a new capacity for good works, it does not deny the body's "mortality" (Rom 6:12) or "the sufferings of the present moment" (Rom 8:18). There simply is no spirit-body duality and no "already" that absorbs salvation's "not yet" to allow for a soteriology that avoids present physical suffering (cf. 2 Tim 3:12). Paul's use of medical or "bodily" terminology counters a body-denying resurrection that seeks to avoid suffering, ironically similar to the creation-denying asceticism rejected in 1 Tim 4:3-4.[48]

---

47. Francis Watson, "Resurrection and the Limits of Paulinism," in *The Word Leaps the Gap: Essays on Scripture and Theology in Honor of Richard B. Hays* (ed. J. R. Wagner, Christopher K. Rowe, and A. K. Grieb; Grand Rapids: Eerdmans, 2008), 452-71.

48. Johnson notes that medical metaphors were often used in the Greek world to distinguish truth and falsehood. Truthful instruction produces moral and spiritual health, whereas falsehood produces spiritually sick people. To characterize false teaching as "gangrene" is to contrast its unhealthy result in Christian formation with that of the "word of truth" (*First and Second Letters to Timothy*, 393-94).

Christ's second appearance "to judge the living and the dead" (2 Tim 4:1), especially when glossed by Pauline teaching about a future resurrection of the body (1 Corinthians 15), resolves this problem of theodicy when believers suffer because they are faithful to the Lord. The haunting line in the canonical saying about the reciprocity of denying God (2:12b) only underscores the plotline of the salvation that will come to those who persevere (2:12a; cf. 4:1b).

I take it that the emphatic "even so" (μέντοι, *mentoi*, 2:19) draws a necessary conclusion from v. 13: God's faithfulness to the truth of Paul's gospel remains secure. In the face of the threat posed by the rival gospel of Hymenaeus and others, then, the rock-solid referent of "God's firm foundation" remains the apostolic tradition (cf. 1 Tim 6:19-20; 1 Cor 3:10-12; Eph 2:20; also Rom 15:20), on which the congregation's faith is made secure (see 1 Tim 3:15). The citation of LXX Num 16:5 cues the story of Korah's (= Hymenaeus's) rebellion against the sacred leadership of Moses (= Paul) and Aaron (= Timothy), forming an intertext that adds an important layer of meaning to the reader's understanding of what is at stake in this current conflict. Korah's rebellion was democratic: on the premise that the presence of God made every member of the community equally holy (Num 16:3), Korah and his Levitical colleagues demanded equal authority to exercise the priestly role granted exclusively to the Aaronic priesthood. But Israel is not a democracy: it is ruled by God alone and is sanctified by God's choice of leaders, namely Moses and Aaron (Num 16:8-11). Korah's rebellion is finally not against Moses and Aaron but against God. Paul draws on this intertext to make a similar point: God has appointed Paul as an apostle of Christ Jesus (2 Tim 1:1), has entrusted him with God's glorious gospel (1 Tim 1:11), and has sanctified his teaching as the means of salvation. In this same sense, Hymenaeus and Philetus are not progenitors of an apostolic tradition since they have no portfolio from God to define the word of truth that saves.

The second quotation in 2:19 is more difficult to pin down but is probably composed of bits and pieces from various OT texts (e.g., Sir 17:26; 35:3; Job 36:10; Isa 26:13) that create a biblical prohibition of duplicity: there should be consistency between a congregation's profession of the Lord's name and its holy conduct (cf. Jas 3:6, 9-12). In this case, rivals of Paul's apostolic tradition are engaged in twin evils: they do not interpret the "word of truth" rightly, and their false teaching "spreads like gangrene" through the congregation, provoking spiritual defection and contaminating its life with God. Marshall argues that the opponents' duplicity may even be "regarded as a form of blasphemy."[49] If so, then 1 Tim 6:1's concern that the blasphemy of unruly slaves

---

49. Marshall, *Pastoral Epistles*, 758.

might have a negative effect on the opinions of outsiders helps here: teaching contrary to Paul's gospel threatens not only a congregation's spiritual life but the salvation of non-believers as well.

The analogy of the "impressive house" (οἰκία, *oikia*) in 2:20-21 is added to illustrate the truth of these biblical markers. The expansive use of *oikia/oikos* in the Timothy correspondence alerts the reader that this "house" is a trope for the local congregation (cf. 1 Tim 3:15), perhaps one that meets in the large common room of a wealthy member's urban home. For this reason, the motive of the analogy is clear, if also imprecise: if one expects to find in an "impressive house" utensils made of precious materials for use on special occasions, so also in God's household one should expect to find members who serve "special uses." One also expects to find utensils made of ordinary materials, such as "clay and wood," which serve more mundane purposes. But the conclusion Paul draws from this analogy in v. 21 has no interest in that part of the analogy; his interest is to define those precious members who serve special uses rather than those who have more ordinary duties to perform — such as Timothy, whose name *Timotheos* in Greek creates a purposeful wordplay with τιμή (*timē*, "honor"): his calling and charism have given him a special role to perform (cf. 1:6-7).

In fact, the use of τις (*tis*, "someone") is purposefully vague and would seem to include any member of the household who "thoroughly cleanses himself of these (teachings)." In light of a congregation unsettled by a misinterpretation of Easter, I have added "teachings" in parenthesis to complete the thought of the phrase, ἀπὸ τούτων *(apo toutōn)*: each member *(tis)* must take the responsibility to purge false teaching from the congregation, particularly as filled out with the reflexive pronoun ἑαυτοῦ (*heautou*, "himself").

The effect of the community's decision to "cleanse" itself of false teaching is to be cleansed or "sanctified" by God; this divine cleansing produces the raw material of a "special utensil." Paul's practical sense of ἁγιάζω (*hagiazō*, "sanctify") is that the convert's participation in Christ's death and resurrection transforms him from "ordinary," as it were, to "special" (see the use of *hagiazō* in 1 Cor 6:11).

The hard evidence of sanctification by faith is the polar opposite of gangrene's self-destructive spread: the production of "every good work," characteristic within the Pastoral Epistles of the Christian life, coheres to and provides evidence of God's redemptive purpose (see 3:17; 1 Tim 2:10; 5:10; Tit 1:16; 3:1). The perfect passive participle of ἑτοιμάζω *(hetoimazō)*, which I translate "useful," underscores the collaborative activity of one whose choices allow another to prepare him for the good work of a "special utensil."

I have translated εἰς ἀτιμίαν *(eis atimian)* "for ordinary use," which seems apropos for utensils made of wood and clay. The common mistranslation of this phrase in moral terms — for "dishonor" (KJV, NASB) or "ignoble" (NIV) — tries to press the analogy too far as a moral contrast between Paul and his unrighteous opponents or even between God's and the devil's intentions (cf. 2:25b-26).[50] There is no indication here of the destiny of the opponents, even though most commentators think they are likely damned. The response of Moses to Korah is precisely the point Paul wants to make for Timothy: any contrast between the Pauline "word of truth" and the teaching of his rivals regarding the Lord's resurrection — extended to any member of God's household who stands with Paul — is rooted in a prior choice *God* has made regarding the Pauline apostolate. To cleanse oneself of teaching that disagrees with his gospel is not finally to agree with Paul but with God (cf. Rom 9:20-23).

The contrasting catalogs of purity and profanity that follow in 2:22-26 extend the conclusion Paul has drawn from his analogy of the "impressive house" by characterizing those who cleanse themselves of bad theology and are made useful by God's sanctifying grace to produce "every good work." The second-person singular imperatives seem to indicate that these exhortations are directed to Timothy. But the imperatives themselves are typical and do not seem personalized, as indicated by the exhortation to "stay away from the passions of youth" when Timothy is approaching forty years of age.[51] The antecedent of this paraenetic unit is more likely the *tis* of v. 21, namely tradents who have made themselves useful to God, which doubtless would include young converts who might need to control their passions. The conviction of a realized resurrection by which these new converts have already been initiated into a new existence, perhaps formalized at Christian baptism, may well have formed the impression that one need no longer worry about unrighteousness. Such a teaching would subvert the believer's sense of needing to repent and grow in Christ, preventing their escape from "the devil's trap" (v. 26).

The initial exhortation to "pursue righteousness," with its complement of virtues, repeats the same attributes of Christian existence found elsewhere in the Pastoral Epistles. Johnson notes, however, that "peace" is found otherwise only in opening salutations (1 Tim 1:2; 2 Tim 1:2), so its use here may

---

50. So Ben Witherington, *Letters and Homilies for Hellenized Christians: A Socio-Rhetorical Commentary on Titus, 1-2 Timothy and 1-3 John* (Downers Grove: InterVarsity, 2006), 1:341.

51. So C. F. D. Moule, "The Problem of the Pastoral Epistles: A Reappraisal," *BJRL* 47 (1965): 433-34. But Johnson, *First and Second Letters to Timothy*, 400, and Bassler, *1 Timothy, 2 Timothy, Titus*, 154, now followed by others, take νεωτερικός (*neōterikos*, "youthful"), as a reference to innovations in theology rather than to age.

highlight a particular kind of peacekeeping that avoids the "foolish and thoughtless discussions" that produce interpersonal conflict rather than knowledge of the truth (2:23-25). The word I have translated "thoughtless" (ἀπαίδευτος, *apaideutos*) is the antonym of "teaching," namely the kind of "schooling" that brings even enemies to repentance and a knowledge of the truth (1 Tim 2:4). Towner comments that the irony of Paul's criticism is that the effect of the opponents' pedagogy is precisely the opposite of what they intend: they seek to educate by debating the merits of Paul's gospel, but they only produce thoughtless Christians who are prone to spiritual defection.[52]

The address of the final exhortation to "the Lord's slave" recalls the ironic use of *doulos*, "slave," in Rom 6:16-20: the believer, baptized by faith into the resurrection of Christ for "newness of life" (v. 4), is now no longer a slave to sin but "a slave to righteousness, leading to sanctification" (v. 19; cf. v. 22). The hortatory cast of this material locates this powerful vision of spiritual conversion within a passage that corrects a misreading of Romans 6 that supposes that the virtuous life — indeed sinlessness — is the natural state of one baptized into Christ. Clearly, the imperatives befitting the Lord's slave commend a pattern of moral resolve characteristic of the "special utensil"'s self-cleansing and purposeful pursuit of righteousness (2:21).

Moreover, the description of the prospective repentance of the opponents indicates the conditional nature of the believer's covenant-keeping. The precise meaning is contested among scholars, but Paul's persistent optimism in the capacity of the truth to change the minds of his opponents is a theme of these letters (v. 25; 1 Tim 1:19-20; 2:4; 3:6-7; cf. Tit 1:1). The "slave's" pattern of life, especially his pastoral kindness "toward all" and the ability to teach the truth to others, suggests that the repentance of opponents is the principal motive of the tradent's moral rigor.

Although their repentance is plainly the goal of Timothy's gentle and deliberative approach to the group that includes Philetus and Hymenaeus, less clear is the meaning of God granting them permission to change. Why should God's permission be so equivocal, expressed with μήποτε *(mēpote)* with the subjunctive of δίδωμι *(didōmi):* "perhaps God might permit," especially if "The Lord knows those belonging to him" (v. 19)? Perhaps the issue at stake is less about divine foreknowledge and rather concerns the mechanics of "repentance from below" and the powerful role of the "word of truth" in prompting people to turn from error back to God.

The distinctive use of "knowledge of the truth" in these letters (1 Tim 2:4; 2 Tim 2:25; 3:7; Tit 1:1) gives formulaic expression to an element central to

---

52. Towner, *Letters to Timothy and Titus*, 545.

Pauline thought: "the criteria of knowledge" are employed whenever the Christian missionary combats misinformation and ignorance. Even though God's role in conversion is clear, the gospel's accessibility to all depends on its rational presentation. Paul's earlier exhortation regarding the right interpretation of the word of truth (v. 15) makes plain this final exhortation: God's permission of restoration is granted only to those who respond to the "word of truth," kindly but rationally presented, and "come to their senses."

This helps discern the nature of the relationship between the devil and God, which remains difficult to assess with any exegetical precision. The final phrase in 2 Tim 2:26, literally "for that one's will" (εἰς τὸ ἐκείνου θέλημα, *eis to ekeinou thelēma*) is ambiguous: is the pronoun's antecedent the devil, just-mentioned, or God, since God's intention to grant repentance is expressed in the principal verb of the sentence. My translation reflects my decision in this regard: it is the devil who holds Paul's opponents "captive to do his will" (cf. 1 Tim 4:1-2). So the devil is an agent of God's redemptive purpose, which is that all come to a "knowledge of the truth" and be saved (so 1 Tim 2:4). For that reason, Hymenaeus is consigned to Satan for church discipline in 1 Tim 1:18-20.

Paul demonizes false teaching elsewhere (1 Tim 4:1-2; 5:15), but in 1 Tim 3:6-7 "the devil's trap" (2:26) is a spiritual test used to distinguish immature leaders from mature leaders, particularly with regard to reputation among outsiders. So in 2 Tim 2:26 the "devil's trap" symbolizes the manner of the opponents' spiritual immaturity, which disqualifies them from leadership, and also the ineffectiveness of evangelism that results from their immaturity.

Although the profile of Paul's opponents in 2 Timothy is important historically,[53] the most important element of this passage is the profile of the ideal tradent. Again, drafting both the persona and tasks of a competent successor, into whose hands the community can entrust its future, is central to this kind of testamentary literature. The moral purpose of one's life — to "pursue righteousness" (2:22) — is a decisive ingredient of Timothy's success as Paul's successor and custodian of the Pauline apostolate.

According to the Dead Sea Scrolls (CD 1.11; 20.32; 1QHab 2.2), the individual who had the most important role in shaping the life of the community was called "the Teacher of Righteousness" (*moreh hatsedeq*), a sobriquet that reflects his spiritual authority to interpret Torah and to exemplify the manner of holy life that might "direct (Israel) in the path of God's heart" (CD 1.11) and so the terms of eternal life (cf. 1QpHab 7.1-5). Significantly, the Scrolls

---

53. Witherington summarizes and applies a methodology for identifying "the opponents in Ephesus and their teaching" in *Letters and Homilies*, 341-47.

also speak of the Teacher's opponent within Israel — a so-called "Wicked Priest" (1QpHab 11.4-8; 4Q171 4.8-10) who is sometimes called "the liar" because he teaches falsehoods (1QpHab 10.9) — one who might lead Israel into Belial's traps (so CD 4.15; cf. 2 Tim 2:26). While the idiom used in the Scrolls to describe their unfriendly competition over Israel's future with God reflects the ascetic values of the Qumran community, it does emphasize the importance of purity in a way that rings true to the polemic Paul uses in 2 Timothy 2 both to castigate his opposition (vv. 16-18) and to encourage Timothy to live a holy life (vv. 20-21).

I continue to like Heifetz's basic concept of leadership.[54] He asks, "Does leadership mean influencing people to follow the leader's vision? Or, does leadership mean influencing people [a congregation] to face and engage its own most significant challenges?" The latter, he says. This helpful shift of emphasis from the persona of the leader (often overemphasized) to her hard work before a people who seek to be faithful at a particular time and in a particular place defines the role of the leader both in naming the work and engaging people to participate in doing it. I also like Peter Drucker's laconic observation to those who thought leadership was mainly about personal charisma or other personal qualities: "What is leadership? It is work." Drucker also emphasizes as I do that leaders are people who pay particular attention to the mission or purpose of the group or institution they lead. They think about the mission, describe it, communicate it, keep it constantly before the group, and develop goals on the basis of it.

3:1-9 The Last Days

¹Know this: The last days will be dangerous times. ²For people will love themselves and money; they will be braggarts, arrogant, blasphemers, and disobedient to parents. People will be ungrateful, unholy, ³without empathy, unresponsive, and spiteful. They will lack self-control and gentleness, without love for what is good. ⁴They will be traitors and reckless, deluded lovers of pleasure rather than lovers of God. ⁵They will make a public appearance of godliness but will resist its power. Have nothing to do with them. ⁶Now some slither into households and take control of immature women weighed down by sins and driven by various desires. ⁷These women are forever learning but never able to come to knowledge of the truth. ⁸In the same way that Jannes and Jambres opposed Moses, so also these

---

54. Anthony B. Robinson, *Transforming Congregational Culture* (Grand Rapids: Eerdmans, 2003).

people oppose the truth. They ruin the mind and counterfeit the faith. ⁹But like those others, they won't get very far: their mindlessness will be obvious to all.

The "last days" of human history will be morally perilous (3:1). Misdeeds of every kind will abound (vv. 2-5a) and those who live during this apocalypse of evil are to have nothing to do with those who practice them (v. 5b). Paul goes on to describe false teachers who oppose the truth and subvert the faith of the congregation's immature members (vv. 6-8); ironically, this time of great peril for the faith is also when those who practice falsehood will be publicly exposed as religious frauds (v. 9).

Paul's description of the dangers of moral decay is characteristic of Jewish apocalypticism and its polemic of "the last days" (3:1). But in this setting, the pericope continues the prior exhortation that Timothy should aspire to be a "special utensil" for "every good work" in the household of God: it provides another "good work" to his job description that sounds an alert that dangerous teachers are present. Central to Paul's warning is a lengthy catalog of vices, which not only engages in cultural criticism of an apocalyptic kind but also provides a negative example of the sort of person Timothy must avoid becoming (vv. 2-5; see Tit 3:10).

Each vice is easily found in the polemical writings of Greco-Roman philosophers such as Aristotle and Thucydides, and most are found in other Pauline letters, though some are cataloged only here in the NT. The rhetorical purpose of such lists, even those crafted with a particular occasion in mind — in this case an apostolic succession — is to create an impression rather than to describe bad people precisely and literally. In fact, the combination of "last days" (3:1) and "people" (ἄνθρωποι, *anthrōpoi*, v. 2) would seem to indicate that Paul is engaging in cultural criticism of a biblical kind. "Last days" is a well-known prophetic catchphrase (LXX Joel 3:1-5; Isa 2:2; Hos 3:5), used only here in the Pauline canon (but see 1 Tim 4:1). It refers to a particular but indeterminate time of testing, ending in divine judgment (2 Pet 3:1-7; Rev 13:11-18). It is a "dangerous time," then, not in the way of violence but in a spiritual sense because it is a season that may prompt spiritual defection that will result in God's eschatological indictment. The future tense of ἐνίστημι (*enistēmi*, "will be") expresses a certainty: the mention of "the last days" is not the prediction of some future time but describes a present already upon the readers that tests their allegiance to God.

The opening exhortation, "Know this," is followed by a set of images that concern a community's intellectual understanding. The essential crisis of the "last days," which makes it a dangerous time, is that it is a fertile time for those who "ruin the mind and counterfeit the faith" (3:9). The confusion of those households into which they "slither" prompts a species of learning that "is never able to come to knowledge of the truth" (vv. 6-7) and so does not lead to salvation (cf. 1 Tim 2:4). Perhaps this reflects the epistemic crisis occasioned by Paul's departure when the teacher par excellence is no longer on site pointing out the bad guys and discriminating between their fraudulent teaching and his own "healthy teaching" (see 4:2-4). Significantly, then, this passage is juxtaposed with Paul's programmatic statement about Scripture's utility in making people wise for salvation and mature for every good work (3:15-17).

The catalog of vices, the most extensive in the Pauline canon, is introduced with an explanatory γάρ (*gar*, "for") to indicate that the characteristic vices of the present age are actually danger signals. "People" does not refer to particular individuals but is used as a trope of human culture disposed against God's way of ordering the world — the *oikonomia theou*, which aims at loving relationships (see 1 Tim 1:4-5). To make this point more expressive, the list of vices is carefully crafted into a vaguely chiastic shape, bracketed by pairs of *phil*-words that express love's mislocation: "lovers of self and money" (3:2a) who are "lovers of pleasure rather than God" (v. 4b). Sandwiched between is a series of eight alpha-privatives, "disobedient" through "without love for what is good" (vv. 2c-3) around the catchword διάβολοι (*diaboloi*, "spiteful," v. 3).[55] The rhetorical effect creates a memorable literary alliteration when read aloud, but it also conveys a dismal portrait of human existence lacking in a robust experience of divine love. For this reason, Paul can conclude that even though there remains an external form of εὐσέβεια (*eusebeia*, "godliness"), an important catchword in the Pastoral Epistles for the practice of true religion, without the presence of God there can be no means of "power." The repetition of δύναμις (*dynamis*, "power") is ironic, since it recalls the prior use in 1:7-8 in reference to God's power conveyed by the indwelling Holy Spirit (cf. 1:14) in the company of the Pauline gospel. The absence of "power" indicates an absence of the Spirit and of the gospel's truth, and this absence indicates a lack of salvation.

Paul concludes this catalog with an exhortation to "have nothing to do with them" (3:5b). Most take this to resume the letter's earlier warning about opponents of his gospel, whose spread of gangrenous influence has undermined the faith of some believers (so 2:17-18). I doubt this, since Paul has just written that Timothy should engage the opponents to correct them in prospect of their repentance and redemption (so 2:22-26). Rather, this warning

---

55. Knight makes the attractive observation that the central position of διάβολοι (*diaboloi*), "spitefulness," actually recalls the person who cannot escape the "devil's trap" (2:26), which has soured him on household relationships; *Pastoral Epistles*, 429-32.

concludes Paul's biting criticism of secular culture in general, whose denial of the truth about God results in a way of life devoid of grace. To separate from those who populate and define such a world is to promote the work of God.

The use of an explanatory γάρ (*gar*, "now," 3:6) signals a more particular reason for Timothy to be on the alert for the tactics of those who appear godly as a pretense to gain influence — a classic depiction of malevolence. I have translated ἐνδύνω *(endynō)* as "slither" to capture this sense, but the word literally means "power into" and clearly plays off the previous *dynamis:* without God's power at work, the power used is abusive of human love. In this case, their tactic is to influence "immature women," based on a common caricature of middle-class women in antiquity. (Working-class women, perhaps employed as household servants, would not have the luxury of time to sit down and listen to the teaching of these people, nor would it have been polite to do so in Paul's world, were it permitted.) Epictetus denounced middle-class women as "silly," because they often used their freedom and leisure on material passions rather than critical thought (*Discourses* 15).

The description of these women as "weighed down by sins and driven by various desires" is obviously not a blanket statement about all women, immature or otherwise, but continues an important theme of the Timothy correspondence concerning the salvation of Christian women (see 1 Tim 2:9-15; 5:13-15).[56] While certainly shaped by the patriarchy of Paul's world and perhaps even echoing its philosophers, who sometimes deprecated women to score rhetorical points, the core principle at stake in this text concerns the sacred space of the Christian household as the locale of spiritual nurture: a person's immaturity makes him susceptible to falsehood. Especially when approached as a canonical text whose audience is universal and ongoing, Paul's concern is updated and aimed at any uneducated or spiritually immature person with time on his hands. With this in mind, I have translated the noun γυναικάρια (*gynaikaria,* literally "small women") as "immature women" to clarify this working principle: these are female believers whose spiritual immaturity, not yet brought to maturity by the word of truth, are more easily seduced by false appearance.[57]

Paul's symbolic world is primarily Jewish and biblical. His unqualified description of moral and social chaos is a feature of apocalyptic writings such

---

56. The addition of ἡδοναῖς *(hēdonais)* in a few mss., which specifies that a woman's sexual desire makes her weak and vulnerable, reflects a more negative caricature of women than is intended here.

57. Johnson, *First and Second Letters to Timothy,* 411-14, reminds readers that this same theme continues in a more exaggerated form in the second-century *Acts of Paul and Thecla.*

as *2 Esdras* and Daniel, which had significant influence on Jesus' understanding of salvation's future (cf. Mark 13:5-27). And Paul's reference to Jannes and Jambres for comparison (3:8) roots his entire "last days" polemic in the story of the exodus. Although their names are not found in the OT, these two shadowy figures were reputed to be members of the Pharaoh's court in the Pseudo-Jonathan Targum on Exod 1:15 and Midrash *Tanḥuma* on Exod 32:1. CD 5.17-19 says, "For in ancient times God visited their deeds and His anger was kindled against their works; for it is a people of no discernment, it is a nation void of counsel inasmuch as there is not discernment in them. For in ancient times, Moses and Aaron arose by the hand of the Prince of Lights and Satan in his cunning raised up Jannes and his brother when Israel was first delivered." In fact, their story was evidently so familiar to Timothy that Paul did not need to recall anything but their names to make his point. The outcome of that story was known, and, just as God delivered Israel from the Pharaoh, despite the opposition of Jannes and Jambres, so also will God expose these current teachers as frauds and the evident folly of those who are bamboozled by them and reject the faith.

If conversion is depicted as a "coming to the knowledge of the truth" (1 Tim 2:7; cf. 2 Tim 2:25; 3:7b), then logically those who are indicted by God — the "Jannes and Jambres" of the community — are those who oppose this same truth. The "word of truth" — the Pauline gospel — is the criterion of divine judgment, and this seems a crucial point to make in a letter of succession in which the principal task is the preservation and transmission of the Pauline apostolate. Timothy's task participates in the apocalypse of divine judgment precisely because he is commissioned to handle the word of truth, on which God's end-time verdict will be based.

This is a haunting passage. Spiritual immaturity is described as a disciple's desire to learn but without "ever coming to a knowledge of the truth" (3:7b), consigned thereby to judgment. An enemy from within. But then the evident enemies of God are further described as those who not only "oppose the truth" and "ruin the mind" but are without the intellectual equipment — they are ἄνοια (*anoia*, literally "without a mind") — needed to come to a knowledge of the truth and repent. Unlike that of Hymenaeus and Philetus, their situation is truly hopeless.

3:10–4:5 Prepared for Every Good Work

¹⁰You, however, have closely observed me — my teaching, way of life, purpose, faith, loyalty, love, patience, ¹¹physical abuse, and my suffering in places like

2 Timothy 3:10–4:5

Antioch, Iconium, and Lystra. What abuse I put up with, and the Lord rescued me from it all! ¹²In fact, anyone who desires to live a godly life with Christ Jesus will be persecuted, ¹³while evil people — swindlers! — become ever worse, deceiving and being deceived.

¹⁴You, however, stay steady in what you have learned and found convincing, knowing from whom you learned: ¹⁵from infancy you have known the holy writings, which enable you to be wise for salvation through faith in Christ Jesus. ¹⁶Every Scripture is God-inspired and is useful for teaching, for showing mistakes, for correcting, for training in rectitude, ¹⁷so that the man of God is mature, made mature for every good work. 4:¹In the presence of God and Christ Jesus, who is coming to judge the living and the dead, by his appearing and by his kingdom, I firmly command: ²Proclaim the word! Stand ready at all times! Refute! Rebuke! Always encourage with patient instruction! ³For a time will come when people will not tolerate healthy teaching. Because they are self-centered, they will accumulate teachers who say what they want to hear. ⁴They will turn from hearing the truth toward conspiracies.

⁵You, however, remain sober-minded whenever suffering bad news. Do the work of a preacher of the good news. Carry out your service fully.

This passage begins (3:10), concludes (4:5), and is centered (3:14) by the rhetorical formula σὺ δέ (*sy de*, "you, however"), which marks off three discrete but integral sections that conclude this letter's climactic exhortation. Each describes an object worthy of careful observation. The first section (3:10-13) is a reminiscence of a missionary career full of persecution and faithfulness. Paul is observed as someone worthy of careful observation and imitation. In the pivotal central section (3:14–4:4), the community's Scripture is observed as "holy writings," a source of wisdom and therefore worthy of close observation and ready use. The concluding exhortation (4:5) calls Timothy to a sober-minded attentiveness to his service as Paul's worthy successor.

If personal example is an important rhetorical convention in a speech of succession (e.g., Acts 20:18b-21), we would expect to find its use in a letter of succession as well: imitation of the apostle's past practices and core beliefs is imperative for a future succession. Paul begins his final exhortation to Timothy by asking him to recall observations of "my teaching, way of life, . . . and my suffering." There is a sense in which the witless rejection of truth, characteristic of the present evil age and set out in the preceding polemic, has already prepared the reader for this apostolic profile, its polar opposite. Each of the nine virtues listed, which include appropriate behavior (moral), missionary tasks (vocational), teaching (theological), suffering (experiential), and anticipated destiny (eschatological), if characteristic of Paul, is characteristic of his apostolate as well. It is this memory that comprises a practical criterion of succession.[58]

Historians who dispute the authenticity of this profile face the conundrum of using the Pauline biography of Acts to do so, even though typically disputing its historical reliability![59] Against those who think it strange that Paul would ask Timothy to recall examples from his so-called "first missionary journey" (Acts 13–14) even though he did not join Paul until later in the narrative (Acts 16:1), Kelly suggests that a pseudepigrapher would more likely have drawn examples from Acts 16–20, where Paul and Timothy are together.[60] Moreover, the participle παρηκολούθησας (*parēkolouthēsas*, "closely observed"), made emphatic by its placement at the head of the sentence, does not necessarily denote eyewitness scrutiny but rather profound reflection on a role model that results in imitation. In any case, these virtues define the ideal mixture of personal characteristics, experiences, and practices exemplified by Paul and then characterizing his successor.[61]

Not surprisingly, the first virtue cataloged is διδασκαλία (*didaskalia*, "teaching"). The adumbration of this catchword in the Pastoral Epistles integrates a range of interests, including the orthodoxy of what is taught (1 Tim 1:10; 4:6; 6:3; 2 Tim 1:13; Tit 1:9; 2:1, 10), its religious purpose (1 Tim 1:5; 4:16; 2 Tim 4:3), and its social manner (2 Tim 3:16; 4:13; Tit 2:7). In sharp contrast to subversive teachers who take their cue from the likes of Jannes and Jambres (cf. 3:6-9), the succession of the Pauline apostolate depends on a faithful transmission of his instruction (2:8-13), its aim and manner (2:14-26), to still others (2:1-2).

Two other comprehensive terms are added to form this first triad of virtues: ἀγωγή (*agōgē*, "way of life") and προθέσει (*prothesei*, "purpose"). Although used only here in the NT, ἀγωγή (*agōgē*) as used in the LXX (Esth 2:20; 10:3; 2 Macc 4:16; 6:8; 11:24; *3 Maccabees* 4:10), followed in earliest Christianity (e.g., *1 Clement* 47:6; 48:1), implies not just a "way of life" but catechesis into a culture or world where such a life is shaped. I would argue this is the sense of Paul's use here: to "observe" Paul is a form of catechesis or initiation into a manner of life, an idea that stands behind the concept of mimesis in

---

58. Fiore and Harrington argue that ancient use of παρακολουθέω (*parakoloutheō*), "observe closely," comprehends both life and instruction; *Pastoral Epistles*, 168: Timothy is to imitate Paul in everything in order to insure the forward movement of his apostolate.

59. E.g., Dibelius and Conzelmann, *Pastoral Epistles*, 119.

60. Kelly, *Pastoral Epistles*, 199.

61. Bassler notes that Stoics used this word when assigning competence to those capable of knowing and following the truth; *1 Timothy, 2 Timothy, Titus*, 164.

antiquity.[62] The final overarching virtue, προθέσει *(prothesei)*, recalls the word's earlier use in 1:9 of God's purpose that shapes how Paul understands his apostolate. The impression of this triad, then, is of a comprehensive purview of the person whose tradition Timothy is charged to safeguard and transmit. It is extended by a second triad that gathers together qualities of Christ (cf. 1 Tim 1:14-16; 6:11-15; 2 Tim 1:13) to characterize self-sacrificial service to others.

The final triad (3:11) reprises themes mentioned earlier and to be mentioned again (4:6-7): Paul's imprisonment and anticipated death. Acts 13–14 provides stories that help elucidate this "physical abuse and my sufferings . . . in places like Antioch, Iconium, and Lystra." In many ways, the rule of life found here in 2 Timothy is anticipated by a prior reading of Paul's speech at Miletus (Acts 20:18-35) in both purpose and content. In both, Paul distills his experiences into a general mark of Christian discipleship: "anyone who desires to live a godly life with Christ Jesus will be persecuted" (3:12; cf. Acts 14:22; 20:23-24, 29-30).

But such a sentiment is really quite extraordinary, since the nature of a godly life is drawn by the conventional virtues of exemplary citizenship. Why then should Christians be subjected to such abuse? Why should Paul's "teaching, way of life, purpose, faith, loyalty, love, patience, physical abuse, and suffering" (3:10-11) pose such a threat to those who hear the gospel? The pessimistic assertion that "evil people . . . become ever worse" (v. 13) comes from apocalypticism's playbook and reminds the reader that a faithful but hard succession of Paul will take place during "the last days" (v. 1) when evil will proliferate because of the insidious progress of bad theology (cf. vv. 2-9).

The abruptly inserted γόητες *(goētes)*, which I translate "swindlers," was a familiar pejorative of ancient rhetoric when dismissing an opponent, but in wider Hellenistic use it referred to the snake-charmer or magician skilled at deception. This usage not only explains why Paul would add the comment, "deceiving and being deceived," but in this compositional setting it may also recall those swindlers just mentioned, Jannes and Jambres, who are the nameless "enchanters" of the exodus story (*epaoidoi*, LXX Exod 8:18-19, a synonym of *goētes*). This potential intertext supplies an important subtext to this catalog of evil: even as those "enchanters" deceived the Pharaoh, whose hardened heart prevented him from turning to God, so also the newer religious "swindlers" deceive the public, whose hearts are thereby hardened against the gos-

---

62. Cf. S. Critchley, "The Catechism of the Citizen: Politics, Law and Religion in, after, with and against Rousseau," *CPR* 42 (2009): 5-34.

pel. This description of religious culture in "the last days" underwrites the difficulty of the task before Timothy.

The second "You, however" cues a related but different theme of mimesis, already introduced by the letter's opening thanksgiving: the apostle must be remembered as a Jew (see 1:3; so also the canonical Paul of Acts). And as a religious Jew, he is a reader of Israel's Scripture and reads it alongside other readers, including Jesus. As with Jesus, whose messianic interpretations of Scripture led him into conflict with other biblical interpreters (e.g., Matt 5:17-20), Paul's testimony of personal suffering is in large part due to his interpretation of Scripture. In fact, the preceding résumé of persecution (3:10-11), when contextualized by the Acts narrative of the canonical Paul, points readers to his controversial role as a teacher of Israel and to episodes of intramural disagreements with other Diaspora Jews provoked in part by his messianic interpretation of Scripture (Acts 13:14-52; 17:1-5; 28:23-28). The issue is not over divergent Bible practices or a battle for the Bible's authority in the synagogue, since on these issues Paul's use of Scripture is traditional (see especially Acts 17:2-3a). Paul seems alert to the interpretive conflict his reading of Scripture provokes and of course what prompts it: his good news of Christ Jesus' death and resurrection (see 2 Tim 2:8, 17-18; cf. Acts 17:3-5) for which he "suffers bad news" (2:9a). It is this account of the Messiah that has poured the "firm foundation" of God's household and that supplies the hermeneutical lens for reading Scripture. But it is also the cause of Paul's suffering.

If the opponents alluded to or mentioned by name in this letter are Jewish, their disagreement is not so much a "parting of the ways," which is a history of religion assessment, but Christological (cf. 1 Tim 1:12-17). They divide from Paul over biblical interpretation, not over a doctrine of Scripture. The Pauline tradition is a scriptural tradition, and so Timothy's succession of the Pauline apostolate comes with Israel's Scripture, and with a particular interpretation of Scripture that reads its promise of salvation by the memory of Christ Jesus, who was "raised from the dead, from the family of David" (2:8). Timothy imitates, then, not only Paul's godly character but his Bible practices and a share of his conflict and suffering (1:8).

Imitation of Paul's Bible practices requires more than careful observation: it requires a catechesis in which the student is initiated into the core beliefs of his teacher. "Knowing from whom you learned" (3:14b) is pivotal but variously understood, in part because the textual witness to the pronoun τις (*tis*, "whom") has been corrupted in its transmission. Although the earliest mss. support the critical text's preference for the plural form and therefore a plurality of teachers, including those responsible for Timothy's childhood education (so v. 15a), the majority of later mss. use the singular, παρά τινος *(para tinos)*, plainly referring to Paul. I prefer this reading, even if it was produced by scribal redaction, since it fits better the intentions of this canonical letter, in which only the instruction of the apostle is counted as normative.[63] Again, the more relevant issue of Timothy's catechesis is not that it is biblical or even Jewish but that it initiates him into a Pauline understanding of God's gospel, which is the substance of the "in what" (ἐν οἷς, *en hois*, v. 14a) he has learned from Paul.[64]

The use of "you learned" (ἔμαθες, *emathes*) in both clauses of v. 14 makes clear the ultimate aim of Timothy's catechesis, which is for him to "stay steady" (literally "remain") in the things learned from Paul. The motive to do so derives from confidence in Paul and his interpretation of the gospel. While I would agree with those commentators who understand that Timothy's confidence in what he learns from Paul is based on Paul's virtue (cf. 3:10-12) — a Hellenism according to which the reliability of what is taught is predicated on the virtue of the one who teaches it — the use of πιστόω (*pistoō*, "find convincing") in the LXX rather justifies the reliability of what is promised on the hard evidence of its fulfillment (cf. 2 Sam 7:25; 1 Kgs 1:36; 8:26; 2 Macc 7:24; 12:25; Ps 92:5; Sir 27:27; 29:3).

If this is the sense of Timothy's confidence in Paul's instruction, one would expect a more functional idea of catechesis, and, indeed, that is what we find: Paul's reading of Israel's Scripture, however idiosyncratic, imparts wisdom about Christ Jesus that saves.[65] The catchphrase "the holy writings" (τὰ ἱερὰ γράμματα, *ta hiera grammata*) has occasioned considerable discussion of its precise meaning here and its later implications as typological of Christian Scripture. Most now agree that the phrase is a technical term for Israel's Scripture in Greek translation, that is, the Septuagint.[66] But the substantive *grammata*, literally "letters," probably also carries a more colloquial connotation of a child's elementary education, more like learning the letters of an alphabet. In this case, the addition of the adjective *hiera* — "holy letters" — would imply a course of religious education for which Scripture would be the student's principal text.[67]

---

63. Contra Towner, *Letters to Timothy and Titus*, 581.

64. Cf. Marshall, *Pastoral Epistles*, 787, who understands the antecedent of this phrase more formally as the *parathēkē*.

65. For an expansive and creative interaction with this idea, see Francis Watson, *Paul and the Hermeneutics of Faith* (London: Clark, 2004).

66. For this linguistic background, see G. Schrenk in *TDNT* 1:763-65; 3:221-30. Philo (e.g., in *De Vita Mosis* 3.39) and Josephus (e.g., in *Antiquities* Preface 3; 10.10.4) use this same phrase in reference to the LXX.

67. Cf. J. A. Sanders, "Canon, Hebrew Bible," *ABD* 1:838. Keck rightly notes that Paul

The technical use of the phrase implies that these "holy writings" did not yet include a collection of Pauline letters, and there is no indication in this letter that Paul considers his letters "Scripture" in the same way the author of 2 Peter does (2 Pet 3:15-16). Rather, 2 Timothy considers normative what has been *heard* from the apostle — as the author puts it, "the pattern of healthy teaching you have heard from me" (1:13; cf. 2:2; 3:10-11). Nonetheless, the depiction of Paul's relationship with Timothy in this letter of succession makes logical a subsequent formation of a Pauline canon of his letters.[68] When 2 Timothy was received as Scripture in the second century and added to the Pauline canon, 2 Peter's verdict on Paul's letters would already have been in play and used by Christian readers to gloss this passage. That is, not only would the LXX be picked up as *graphē* but Paul's letters as well, one part of an emergent canon of "gospels of the apostles" (to use Irenaeus's apt phrase) that would ultimately extend the church's canon of holy writings to include a second testament. This kind of expansion is characteristic of canonization when texts are received and rendered in more expansive ways to aim meanings at a catholic, ongoing audience of Christian readers. While the communicative intent of 2 Tim 3:15-16 does not include a NT, its canonical intent does.

Having learned the Bible "enables (Timothy) to be wise for salvation through faith in Christ Jesus" (3:15b). Collins contends that this phrase stands at the vertex of a chiasm that pairs elements of Timothy's religious formation (vv. 14 and 17) with Scripture's role in his formation (vv. 15a and 16).[69] That is, Timothy's experience of salvation based on a Pauline reading of Scripture supplies convincing evidence of the efficaciousness of that reading. The verbal idea for wisdom rarely occurs (cf. 2 Pet 1:16) but is consistent with the premise of the LXX Wisdom tradition that God's word is the source of wisdom about life — what Paul earlier called *agōgē*, "way of life" (3:10) and the *oikonomia theou* (1 Tim 1:4). That is, Scripture's role is not to provide knowledge that makes one become a believer but to form the believer's skill set — that is, to enable the believer to become wise in the ways of God — that guides spiritual formation.

---

rarely uses Scripture for prooftexts but draws the structure of his arguments from Scripture: he reasons from the text. In Keck's phrase, "Paul not only reads his Bible in light of Christ but also reads the Christ event in light of his Bible . . . to show their coherence because God is consistent"; Leander E. Keck, *Romans* (ANTC; Nashville: Abingdon, 2005), 38.

68. Cf. Trobisch, *Paul's Letter Collection;* Robert W. Wall, "Acts," in *The New Interpreter's Bible* (Nashville: Abingdon, 2001), 10:215; Childs, *Church's Guide*, 69-75.

69. Collins, *1 and 2 Timothy and Titus*, 262, although he incorrectly posits this claim as part of a polemic against the opponents rather than as an apologia for the Pauline tradition.

The present participle, δυνάμενα (*dynamena,* "enabling"), implies that this new power to order his thinking after God's word, which directs Timothy to his salvation (εἰς σωτηρίαν, *eis sōtērion*), is coterminous with learning from Paul. The phrase "through faith in Christ Jesus" is quintessentially Pauline (1 Tim 1:14; Gal 2:16; 3:26; Rom 3:22). Salvation from sin and death is impossible apart from the risen Christ, a core belief summarized by the various canonical sayings spread across the Pastoral Epistles (e.g., 1 Tim 1:15; 2 Tim 2:11-13). While διὰ πίστεως (*dia pisteōs*) denotes Timothy's affirmation of Paul's core beliefs about Christ Jesus, the orthodoxy of his affirmation is never detached from an experience of transformed existence (cf. 2:10). One begets the other. The authority of Scripture, then, is its capacity to cultivate faith and with it the experience of salvation.[70]

What the reader may sense, however, is a tension between a biblical way of learning Jesus and Paul's way of learning Jesus on the road to Damascus. The epistemology of conversion is different from the epistemology of catechesis. At the very least, one should recognize that the canonical sayings that summarize the core beliefs of the Pauline gospel are distillations of an experienced salvation, not a salvation just adduced from the plain sense of Scripture. Scripture is not a converting ordinance. One must encounter Jesus and trust him for salvation before one can recognize him as Torah's *telos.*

The term for Scripture changes to πᾶσα γραφή (*pasa graphē,* "every Scripture") in 3:16, following its typical NT use. No reason is given for this change, and the meaning of the term itself is ambiguous and so remains contested.[71] Although *grammata* and *graphē* do not appear to be interchangeable, I find no compelling reason to think Paul has different texts in mind with the two terms: both refer to his Bible (the Septuagint). Nonetheless, the change from a plural term to a singular term seems syntactically significant. If the adjective *pasa* with an anarthrous singular noun *(graphē)* is generally understood as referring to a specific thing ("every") rather than to a collective whole ("all"), then v. 16 may be read as extending the general claim made in 3:15 about Israel's Scripture to its every part. If learning *ta hiera grammata* cultivates a wisdom that saves, then the ecclesial performances of its every part *(pasa graphē)* are inspired by God to produce salvation — a classic form of deductive logic. In fact, Paul may have in mind those biblical texts cited (e.g., 2:19) or echoed (e.g., 3:8-9, 13; cf. 4:13) in this letter.

---

70. Robert W. Jenson makes this point in "The Religious Power of Scripture," *SJT* 52 (1999): 89-105, and then extends it by arguing that "spiritual" exegetical strategies (e.g., figural readings) are more productive of this end than modern criticisms.

71. For a fine summary of the four exegetical options possible and current state of research, see Towner, *Letters to Timothy and Titus,* 585-88.

This syntax coheres to rabbinical thinking that every part of Scripture held a word from God. In fact, Rabbi Akiva regulated readings of Scripture by his "*ribbui* (inclusion)–*mi'ut* (exclusion) rule," which stipulated that even the most familiar and least significant grammatical particles (such as "and," "or," "the," and "a") could hold important meanings since by them God discloses those included or excluded from covenant blessings. Moreover, the substantive "Scripture" implies simultaneity, so that, even though expressed in a different genre or a different theological idiom, "every Scripture" bears common witness to the truth about God.

Excursus: The Septuagint as the Christian Old Testament?

Before pressing on to consider the meaning of *pasa graphē* in 3:16-17, there remains a question that is more hermeneutical than exegetical: Which version of Israel's Scripture should the church receive as canonical, the Hebrew text of the Masoretes or the old Greek text that comes with the apostolic tradition? Since in my view the final redaction of Scripture's two-testament witness has hermeneutical value, the scope and arrangement of the canonical OT in particular is decisive for a range of exegetical practices (e.g., textual criticism and intertextuality). The following observations are more conceptual than technical, and their purpose is to occasion a conversation about a question rarely raised anymore among scholars and clergy.[72]

Admittedly, the textual and social histories of the church's "old" LXX are exceedingly complex and deserve our close attention to help contextualize this conversation. At the very least, such an interest should result in the critical recognition that there existed no single LXX text in earliest Christianity, and in any case the translation of the sacred text into Greek was based on a Hebrew *Vorlage*. For this reason, considerable modesty should attend any claim we make for the tension that surely exists between "the" old LXX and the MT. Yet it remains axiomatic among scholars that no translation envisages a purely pragmatic or philological interest; the translator's choices typically communicate his theological or ideological preferences. I hesitate to

---

72. One who is raising this question is Ross Wagner, who follows the lead of B. S. Childs in "The Septuagint and the 'Search for the Christian Bible,'" in *Scripture's Doctrine and Theology's Bible* (ed. Markus N. A. Bockmuehl and Alan J. Torrance; Grand Rapids: Baker, 2008), 17-28. I acknowledge my gratitude to Professor Wagner for staking out a set of important issues that deserve a hearing and that should stimulate vigorous debate among those who read the OT as the church's Scripture.

claim that the apostolic appeal to the LXX in earliest Christianity was predicated on a different theology than would have been shaped by the Hebrew *Vorlage* or that the cultural sensibility of a Greek translation reflected a more liberal, less parochial faith than that of the rabbis and their Hebrew text. But one may assume that the LXX was exchanged for more literal translations of the Hebrew Bible into Greek during the second century C.E. for deeply held theological and sociological reasons, which likely register formative Judaism's claims for a particular canonical text (Hebrew, not Greek) and legal address for Israel's Scripture (the synagogue, not the church). This move became necessary precisely because Judaism's LXX had become, perhaps already by the end of the first century, a Christian text and because its use in apostolic preaching and writing came to warrant a decisively *Christian* gospel. Quite apart from the gospel's distinctive claims for a risen Jesus as Son of God and Messiah according to the Scripture, the church had become a community of mostly converts from paganism who brought with them all kinds of cultural values and religious practices that were antithetical to Judaism.

Moreover, the LXX was preserved by the church's scribes and, unlike Jewish texts, in codices rather than scrolls for a Christian community that had long since moved beyond Palestine and had become mostly Gentile and Greek-speaking. At the same time, the formation of the Hebrew Tanakh had become a pivotal symbol of formative Judaism following the destruction of the Second Temple. Indeed, the Book of Acts, written during the first quarter of the second century when all this was happening, includes a snapshot or two of intramural conflicts provoked when Hebrew is replaced by Greek in language and cultural sensibilities (e.g., Acts 6:1-7).

Josephus and the enduring legacy of *Pseudo-Aristeas* aside, there is even some evidence that the rabbis of different Judaisms disparaged the LXX not only as a poor (i.e., non-literal) translation of the original Hebrew but as a translation born out of a wrong culture in an inferior language and now identified with a rival religion. My sense is that the old LXX of the apostles had come to symbolize a parting of the ways and, worse, a Christian supersessionism. And so the translation of the Hebrew Bible into a standardized, more literal Greek text in the second century envisages a deeply canonical motive within Judaism: the preservation of a single — that is, normative — sacred text for Greek-speaking Jews of the Diaspora. Perhaps countervailing currents underwrite a similar motive within the church for its own Greek version of Israel's Scripture (LXX).

While the textual tensions between the LXX and MT should not be exaggerated, tensions remain nonetheless. Even though some conflicts may be explained by textual criticism — that the LXX translates the Hebrew text at an earlier stage of its canonical shaping — the Septuagintal shape and scope of the community's Scripture were nonetheless canonical for the apostles and quoted as such in the canonical texts we now receive under their names. If our primary concern is the textual witness embedded in the NT canon, then a range of questions is important for the church to consider. Should the scope of the first testament be expanded to include all those books quoted and, importantly, alluded to in the second testament because they are in the received LXX of the apostles even though not in the final form of the MT? And if the MT is received as the church's normative biblical witness, why should the shape of the Christian OT follow the LXX rather than the MT witness? Is it not because the LXX makes better sense of the apostolic proclamation of Jesus, witnessed by a two-testament canon centered by the juxtaposition of prophecy's promise and gospel's fulfillment?

Does the NT canon demonstrate a preference for the LXX over the Hebrew text when they disagree, especially in service of kerygmatic ends? On balance, probably not. According to Wagner, at least at the level of explicit quotations in the NT, the MT and LXX share "an undeniable core that decisively shapes the contours of mainstream Christian practice and belief."[73] However, the use of the LXX in Acts is an apt illustration of the strategic preference of the Greek text over the Hebrew in the narrator's extended quotations of biblical prophecy in support of distinctively Christian claims. Moreover, quite apart from the different shape and scope of the LXX, the translation of Hebrew words into the Greek language creates a range of new and different connotations. For instance, the resonances of *nomos* ("law"), which translates Hebrew *torah* ("instruction"), broaden its meaning to include the more abstract meaning in Hellenistic philosophy of the cosmic rule instituted by the Creator by which all creation is patterned (cf. 1 Tim 1:3-11). Paul's use of *nomos* is necessarily multiform because it reflects the variegated uses of this word forged by Hellenistic culture and understood as such by his Greek-speaking audiences. In any case, this is a dimension of a text's texture or intertextuality that requires recognition of how the overtones of a language and a culture's transmission of ideas communicate the mind of Christ.

St. Augustine defended the authority of the LXX on the basis of its catholicity along with its apostolicity. Some have expressed the view, without evidence, that the LXX presented a global alternative to the more parochial interests of Judaism and its MT. Even if that is not the case, we should pay attention to Augustine's words:

---

73. Wagner, "Christian Bible," 23.

> [E]ven if anything is found in the original Hebrew in a different form from that in which these men [the LXX translators] have expressed it, I think we must give way to the dispensation of Providence which used these men to bring it about, that books which the Jewish race were unwilling, either from religious scruple or from jealousy, to make known to other nations, were, with the assistance of the power of King Ptolemy, made known so long beforehand to the nations which in the future were to believe in the Lord. And thus it is possible that they translated in such a way as the Holy Spirit, who worked in them and had given them all one voice, thought most suitable for the Gentiles. (*On Christian Doctrine* 2.15)

In this light, Wagner's use of Childs's rubric, "the search for the Christian Bible," is apropos of the Christian interpreter's quest for the particular form and text of the biblical witness the church believes to be appointed by the Holy Spirit and received as canonical on this basis. According to 2 Tim 3:14-17, the future of Paul's apostolate depended on Timothy's recognition that God inspires a *particular* holy text, the LXX, for teaching and training, for showing mistakes, and for correcting those in the household of God. Whatever we may finally decide about the range of critical and practical problems that attend Scripture's claim for a divinely inspired LXX and whatever we want to make of its purchase for his tradents, Protestants especially (ironically) are compelled to include the LXX in the quest.

The adjectives θεόπνευστος (*theopneustos*, "God-inspired") and ὠφέλιμος (*ōphelimos*, "useful") are existential marks that evince the performances of every Scripture as divinely inspired — that is, as indispensable for wisdom-making. But the syntax is problematic because of the absence of a verb that could relate these two adjectives to their common subject, *pasa graphē*. The form and placement of the first could be either attributive or predicate. Although it is difficult to sense any real difference between the two alternatives other than in translation, some think that — at least rhetorically — an attributive *theopneustos* makes a more decisive claim for Scripture's ontology: "every God-inspired Scripture" by its very nature *must* be "useful" for wisdom-making. Yet if the second adjective is self-evidently predicate — that is, "every Scripture is useful" rather than "every useful Scripture" — I think the first must also be rendered as a predicate adjective in order to preserve their parallelism as well as the function of the conjunction καί (*kai*, "and") that links them.

The sometimes contentious history within Protestantism of interpreting the first adjective, *theopneustos*, will not be rehearsed here.⁷⁴ Yet its meaning is not self-evident. Hellenic religious literature sometimes described the speeches of religious men as "inspired," usually in reference to "mantic" experiences or the "inspired" reception of their rousing speeches by others. For example, *4 Ezra* (written about the same time as 2 Timothy) narrates the inspiration of the prophet Ezra this way (14:38-41): "And on the next day a voice called me, saying, 'Ezra, open your mouth and drink what I give you to drink.' So I opened my mouth, and a full cup was offered to me; it was full of something like water, but its color was like fire. I took it and drank; and when I had drunk it, my heart poured forth understanding and my wisdom increased, for my spirit retained its memory and my mouth was opened and no longer closed."

Theopneustos is likely Paul's coinage, bringing together *theos*, "God," and the aorist stem of *pneuō*, "breathe." The new word sounds an echo of two biblical stories famous for God-breathing in order to convey a sense of Scripture's power to animate a congregation's spiritual formation. The first is a passage of enduring importance for the Jewish conception of human life: according to LXX Gen 2:7, God breathed "the breath of life" into the man and thus he "became alive." The second is Ezekiel's stunning vision of exiled Israel's "dry bones" rattling around in the desert without life (Ezek 37:1-14), which is read aloud at Passover to remind Israel of God's promise of restoration. The prophet recognizes that there is no *pneuma* ("breath") in Israel's corpse (37:8b), which sets the stage for God's commissioning of *to pneuma*, "*the* spirit," that is, God's Spirit, to command "the fourfold spirit to breathe into these corpses and they will live" (37:9b).

I suspect Paul has both in mind, thus connecting Scripture with the divine impartation of life-in-relationship-with-God. When God breathes into something "dead" a new and distinctive kind of life begins: eternal life in covenant with God. The implied voice of *theopneustos* is passive: God breathes life into a people through a scriptural medium. It may even be another facet of Paul's resurrection theme (cf. 2:8), in which God brings to "newness of life" the community that engages its inspired Scripture — in a manner apropos of a sacred performance — to animate its life-with-God.

In this case, it is Scripture's agency rather than the "ground" of God's creation or the "fourfold spirit" of Ezekiel's vision that conveys the life-giving breath of God. Yet when these two OT intertexts are taken together to fund another layer of meaning to a Pauline idea of Scripture, the community's

---

74. A still useful summary of the recent history of this battle is Kern R. Trembath, *Theories of Biblical Inspiration: A Review and Proposal* (Oxford: Oxford University Press, 1987).

graphē is recognized as a material creature (so Gen 2:7) that becomes the auxiliary of God's Spirit (so Ezek 37:9) to enliven God's people for God's work.[75]

J. R. Levison considers the importance of these same two OT texts in forging a Pauline theology of the new creation. He argues that Paul's reading of Gen 2:7 and Ezekiel 36–37 is transformed by his belief in the resurrection. Rather than locating the "spirit of life" in the first Adam as other Jewish interpreters (including Philo) do, Paul now locates the divine Spirit in the risen Christ, the second Adam, in whom the Holy Spirit vivifies a new life in all who believe. In Levison's reading, Christ's resurrection and the individual believer's baptism into Christ's spiritual body personalizes Ezekiel's prophecy "that bones and sinews and flesh can rekindle, and that the spirit can come from the four corners of the earth to fill the moribund nation, to re-create Israel into a new people who will till the land until it becomes a garden of Eden."[76] The mortality of the first Adam, in whom the divine breath is stilled by sin, provides, then, the prophetic foil for the second Adam's life-giving Spirit, who reorders the relationship between mortality and immortality.

Paul's conception of Scripture is reworked within this same matrix of meaning. Not only his coinage of *theopneustos*, when probably *enthousia* is expected, even the use of a fully formed (or mature) "man of God" as the endgame of using Scripture recalls the transforming effect the risen Adam's life-giving Spirit has on the faithful mortal into whom it breathes new life; and, indeed, it is Scripture that this life-giving Spirit uses to lead this new creature "through a valley of very many, very dry bones back up the garden path to Eden."[77] Perhaps Paul's conception of individual (and not just national) restoration targets Timothy in whom the spiritual gift may need rekindling (see 1:6-7).

The catalog of Scripture's uses, which includes both priestly ("teaching . . . training rectitude") and prophetic ("showing mistakes, for correcting") roles, is patterned on rabbinic uses of Torah. Not only is Torah the "curriculum" used by rabbis-like-Moses when teaching the congregation truths about God (so Deuteronomy), Torah is also used by prophets-like-Moses when calling the congregation to repentance as in Jeremiah and Isaiah. Paul's point in exhorting Timothy, then, is to underwrite both roles with Scripture in hand: Timothy is to reprove and correct false teachers as a prophet, while teaching

---

75. See John Webster's superb development of this idea in *Holy Scripture: A Dogmatic Sketch* (Cambridge: Cambridge University Press, 2003), 42-67.
76. Levison, *Filled with the Spirit*, 315.
77. Levison, *Filled with the Spirit*, 316.

and training the congregation to live holy lives before God and each other. Such are the aspirations and "good work" of "the man of God" (3:17a) who is brought to maturity by Scripture.

The repetition of ἄρτιος . . . ἐξαρτίζω *(artios . . . exartizō),* translated "mature . . . make mature," draws on rarely used words from a glossary of spiritual formation that envisages a process during which things are added to make a person or group complete. In other words, Scripture's different uses supply goods that add to whatever else has been received from the tradition — in this case, from observing Paul's life and listening to him teach (3:10-13). William Abraham reminds us that Scripture is a piece of and of a piece with a broader, more expansive canonical heritage that includes creeds, sacramental practices, liturgical conduct, icons, ecclesiastical disciplines, exemplars, and teachers.[78] Whether one agrees with all the historical or philosophical detail of Abraham's sophisticated analysis, one must surely agree with his rejection of a *sola scriptura* principle if it results in the detachment of the biblical canon from the other analogues of the church's apostolic tradition, especially the ecumenical creeds. This passage confirms this idea by juxtaposing Paul's sainted biography with Scripture's performance as indispensable bits that form the faithful tradent to full maturity.

The scope of the final clause, which indicates the purpose (ἵνα, *hina,* "so that") of Scripture's use, is debated, whether it refers only to the maturity of a single "man of God" or to the entire congregation. The catchphrase "man of God" (see 1 Tim 6:11) generally identifies one who belongs to God, no matter their gender. However, in this letter of succession it refers to the ideal tradent who safeguards and transmits the Pauline apostolate for future believers. That is, the purpose of the community's "holy writings" is to bring to maturity those who truly are of and for the apostolic tradition.

Even though the plain sense of this text does not include Paul's letters among the community's "holy writings," which refers only to the LXX, by the time the Pastoral Epistles were added to the corpus of Pauline letters some time during the second century, Paul's letters had become not only textual media of Paul's apostolic legacy but recognized as Christian "Scripture" within the church (so 2 Pet 3:15-16). When read as Scripture today, then, this passage tells how all Christians should use Scripture, and perhaps the Pauline canon in particular, and for what ends: as a divinely inspired source for a heavenly wisdom that saves and to bring those tradents to maturity to produce "every good work" (3:17b).

---

78. William J. Abraham, *Canon and Criterion in Christian Theology* (Oxford: Clarendon, 1998), 27-56.

The phrase "every good (ἀγαθός, *agathos*) work" is repeatedly used in the Pastoral Epistles (in 1 Tim 2:10; 2 Tim 2:21; 3:17; Tit 1:16; 3:1; *kalon ergon* in 1 Tim 3:1; 5:10, 25; 6:18; Tit 2:7, 14; 3:8), and according to Marshall is a theologically rather than morally determined conception of Christian existence. Yes and no. That is, it is the manner of a public life produced by God's saving grace and characterized in the Pastoral Epistles by the primary practical virtues of the day.[79] That is, grace transforms the believer to live in harmony with the *oikonomia theou* — God's way of ordering human existence that aims at loving relations (see 1 Tim 1:4-5). This moral payoff is the target of the redeemed community's use of its every Scripture.

Paul uses the formula "in the presence of God" (4:1) in these letters to introduce the practical implication of a prior instruction (1 Tim 2:3; 5:4, 21; 6:13; 2 Tim 2:14). Its juridical sense — similar to "as God is our witness" (see 1 Tim 5:21) — puts Timothy on notice that the previous claims about Scripture should inspire him to action.[80] This use of the formula is expanded by creedal emendation to make the call to action more pointed (as in 1 Tim 2:3 [4-6]): the divine witness is joined by "Christ Jesus, who is coming to judge the living and the dead" (cf. 1 Tim 4:1). The expectation of end-time judgment, which surely includes Timothy's own (see 1 Tim 4:16), is here aimed at prospective readers by the merism "the living and the dead." While the universal scope of divine judgment mirrors the universal scope of God's desired salvation of everyone (cf. 1 Tim 2:3-4), its use here makes more urgent the prior claim that the "man of God" is brought to maturity by Scripture (3:17) to safeguard the congregation from false teachers (cf. 3:1-9; 4:3-4) and for its future salvation (cf. 1 Tim 4:16; 2 Tim 4:6-8).

The source and meaning of the messianic formula "coming to judge the living and the dead, by his appearing and by his kingdom" (4:1b) are both contested, and the syntax is awkward. The plain sense of the exhortation itself, however, is clear: present choices are motivated by expectation of a future judgment. The formula itself probably reaches back to 2:8 to draw implications for the future appearing of the risen Lord, who is alive not dead. The

---

79. Marshall, *Pastoral Epistles*, 227-29.

80. Scholars have long recognized the difficulty of determining whether 4:1-5 follows from the prior claims about Scripture (3:14-17) or from the earlier warning about false teachers (3:13), interrupted by the author's excursus on Scripture, or begins a concluding exhortation to the entire letter. Our sense of the more limited role of 4:1-5 within the letter follows from an assessment of how the formula, "in the presence of God," is used elsewhere in 1-2 Timothy and also the repetition of the σὺ δέ *(sy de)* conjunction that holds together 3:10–4:5. In our view, then, the command issued by Paul in 4:2 is predicated on Timothy's appropriation of the holy writings in a manner that targets the community's salvation.

purpose of the living Jesus' return to complete his messianic mission is to make judgments about the past and present performances of everyone, including those members of the community who have denied the faith (2:12-13). The criterion of the Lord's verdict is nowhere stated. But in a letter of succession, it seems to be tied to the perseverance of the apostolate "for that day" (1:12), which is the criterion of whether a people have remained faithful to "the pattern of healthy teaching" that God entrusted to Paul (1:12-13), Paul to Timothy (1:14), and Timothy to still others (2:1-2). The apocalyptic idiom of the re-"appearing" of the risen Jesus is important to the Pastoral Epistles, where it is linked with the final victory of God's reign over death and evil — the core Pauline belief about the future of God's salvation. But Paul's use of ἐπιφάνεια *(epiphaneia)* in 1:10 of Jesus' messianic work in abolishing death and inaugurating life suggests that the Lord's parousia is the endgame of a process already underway. In this way, reference to the Messiah's judgment of Timothy's fidelity to the present tasks of succession given him is made more urgent.

In particular, the principal command given Timothy to "proclaim the word (λόγος, *logos*)" (4:2a) reiterates Paul's previous instruction (1:13; 2:15; 1 Tim 4:14-16), and the additional four commands — "stand ready ... refute ... rebuke ... encourage" (4:2b) — are ancillary to this main one. The immediate purpose of Timothy's ministerial duty to "proclaim the word" is to refute falsehood (so 4:3-4) and clarify the gospel (so 4:8; see above on 2:15), the latter agreeing with the normal sense of the verb used here, κηρύσσω (*kēryssō*, "proclaim"). Moreover, in this hortatory setting, both "refuting and rebuking" a congregation's bad theology and teaching it good theology (catechesis) are roles performed by Scripture (so 3:16b). This is not to make the mistake of thinking the divine *logos* is a biblical one; rather, it is to affirm a Pauline conception of Scripture whose sanctified utility is to clarify the truth about God.

The resumption of Paul's apocalyptic polemic against false teachers in 4:3-4 (see 3:1-9) adds little except to concentrate the reader's attention on the problem of a congregation's tendency to substitute unreliable conspiracy theories for healthy teaching of the Pauline tradition. I have translated μῦθοι (*mythoi*) "conspiracies" (4:4) to help create a more particular impression of the worry expressed by this text. That is, the situation described is not one created by the teachers themselves but by members of the congregation who do "not tolerate healthy (= Pauline) teaching ... and accumulate teachers who say what they want to hear" (v. 3).

B. Childs, following G. Lohfink, contends that the persistent repetition of Paul's warning that his opponents are intolerant of "healthy teaching" (4:3;

cf. 1 Tim 1:10; 4:6; 6:3; Tit 1:9; 2:1) is "the most important normative concept in the Pastoral Epistles."[81] The ready word that Timothy must proclaim in the face of opposition imitates Paul, the exemplary teacher to whom God's "glorious gospel" has been entrusted (1 Tim 1:11; cf. Tit 1:3). This imitation extends beyond the doctrinal content of the gospel but, clearly, to pedagogy as well: a "patient instruction" that includes the rhetoric of refutation and rebuke as necessary (4:2). The reader should assume that this becomes necessary because of the ease by which Christian congregations "turn from hearing the truth toward conspiracies" (v. 4).

The picture drawn is of a Christian community that has heard the word proclaimed (4:2) but some of whose members have rejected its truth claims (v. 4), presumably because they do not wish to pay out its social expense. Paul repeatedly notes in personal reminiscences of imprisonment (1:8; 2:9), suffering (1:8, 12; 2:9; 3:11; 4:14), and rejection (1:15; 4:10, 16) that "anyone who desires to live a godly life with Christ Jesus will be persecuted" (3:12). I doubt the persuasive power of opponents in initiating this spiritual disaffection has to do with the content of what they said — or, better, I doubt Paul would ever admit as much of an intellectual rival, given the divine source of his own gospel. He uses *mythoi* to underscore the kind of unreliable evidence that finds a home in self-centered people who are not really interested in considering the gospel truth. My translation, "conspiracies," attempts to cast this situation in terms of alternative theories of existence, for which there is no evidence and which foster an unhealthy outlook and leave people utterly unprepared for the future appearing and judgment of Christ Jesus.

Paul's contemporaries were well aware of the contrasting merits of mythology and truth-telling. Most philosophers considered the politician's penchant for conspiracy-making as opposing the truth and common sense. Philo, for example, contrasted *mythoi* and lasting truth (*Abel and Cain* 13), and Epictetus even questioned the great Homer's enduring importance as an author of "his myths" (*Discourses* 3.24.18). Similarly, Gregory of Nazianzus commented on this text for his own day that

> there are certain persons who have not only their ears and their tongues but even, as I now perceive, their hands too, itching for words. They delight in profane babblings and the oppositions of science, falsely so-called, and strive over words which tend to no profit. Paul is the preacher and establisher of the "word cut short"... who calls into question all that is excessive or superfluous in discourse. (*Orations* 27.1)

---

81. Childs, *Church's Guide*, 163.

The final σὺ δέ (*sy de*, "you, however," 4:5) introduces yet another contrasting image of Timothy as the ideal tradent and successor of the Pauline apostolate. The more general exhortation to "remain sober-minded" probably has the preceding "teachers" (v. 3) in view. The virtue of sober-mindedness characterizes the one who does not rock the boat — in this case, in order to maintain Paul's example. If the criterion of succession is whether Paul is imitated, then even as Paul "suffered bad news" (so 2:9; cf. 3:10-12), so must Timothy; and even as Paul preaches good news (cf. Acts 21:8; 2 Tim 1:8, 11-12), the same is also Timothy's "service."

4:6-8 Paul's Death Is at Hand

⁶As for me, I've already had my fill, and the time of my death is at hand. ⁷I have fought the fight, finished the race, kept the faith. ⁸At long last there remains for me the champion's wreath for rectitude that the Lord will give me on that day. He is the just judge, not only of me but of all those who have loved his appearance.

This final exhortation forms the poignant conclusion of Paul's instructions to Timothy, which supply the guidelines of a faithful transmission of the apostolic tradition to the next generation of believers. Paul predicts his imminent death (4:6), which makes this succession necessary, while confidently rehearsing a life of faithfulness (v. 7) that assures a "champion's wreath" when the Lord returns to justly "judge the living and the dead" (v. 8; cf. v. 1).

The preceding triad of exhortations, each introduced by σὺ δέ (*sy de*, 3:10, 14; 4:5), finds an effective rejoinder in this statement that begins with an emphatic ἐγὼ γάρ (*egō gar*, "as for me"). Indeed, this passage stipulates what every succession must: the leader's impending "death" (ἀνάλυσις, *analysis*, literally "departure," 4:6). If the apostolic tradition is to have a future, there must be a succession from the apostle to the next generation of leaders who imitate his character and mission (vv. 7-8; cf. 1 Tim 2:7).

Much has been made of the use of σπένδω (*spendō*), translated "had my fill." The verb comes from a priestly glossary and literally refers to a libation poured over a sacrifice to God (Exod 30:9; Num 28:7; Hos 9:4; 4 Maccabees 3:16). An imprisoned Paul's dramatic use of *spendō* in Phil 2:17 to speak of his death in sacrificial terms has led some to find a martyr's death in its use here.[82] But this is hardly the plain sense of the text; a better reading is that Paul simply recognizes that the end of his life has now ar-

---

82. So Knight, *Pastoral Epistles*, 458.

rived even though he is still busy making plans for the immediate future (see 4:9-13).

Perhaps significantly, Paul predicts that his death is a καιρός (*kairos*, "time"), an undetermined moment, the word sometimes functioning as an eschatological catchword for the "God-only-knows" timing of important events of the history of salvation (see below on Tit 1:3; cf. 1 Thess 5:1; Acts 1:7). In any case, the last day of Paul corresponds to the very last of the "last days" of this present evil age, when Christ Jesus will appear "to judge the living and the dead" (4:1). Some interpreters have held that the reward may be granted in this life,[83] but surely Collins is correct in observing that the reference to "on that day" has the Lord's second coming in mind and echoes LXX Zeph 1:14's vision of "that great day of the Lord." That day will unfold in a series of fearsome final events that bring judgment against the enemies of God's people. This intertext identifies the enemies with subversives mentioned here and earlier (3:1-9) along with those mentioned in the letter's benediction (4:10, 14-16) who have harmed Paul. Timothy must not be included among them but rather must stand with Paul and his apostolate during this fragile time of transition.

Paul does not anticipate a negative verdict for himself but a "champion's wreath for rectitude that the Lord will give me on that day" (4:8a). The reason for his optimism is supplied by three memorable metaphors, each given action by consummative perfects: "I have fought the fight, finished the race, kept the faith" (v. 7). This combination of a soldier's completed fight, an athlete's finished race, and a believer's confirmed faith recalls the similar triad of exemplary sufferers in 2:3b-7. These now are exemplars of laborers whose work has been brought to purposeful completion. The reader, whether ancient or current, would naturally assume that the labor envisaged has followed a battle plan, a race course, or a confession of faith that guides the action to its particular end.[84]

Paul's labor is not necessarily motivated by the prospect of a "champion's wreath," but that is the reasonable expectation based on his Christology: Christ's faithfulness to God's redemptive will is the predicate of his resurrection and exaltation as Lord (cf. Phil 2:5-11). In "the wreath for rectitude," "rectitude" (δικαιοσύνη, *dikaiosynē*) is not epexegetical of the wreath's composition but explanatory of what champions are: they are righteous. Paul tri-

---

83. Cf. Twomey, *Pastoral Epistles*, 182-84.

84. The parallel between 4:7 and Acts 20:24 is significant, not only because it challenges an axiom of Acts criticism that the narrator does not know the Pauline letters but more importantly for us because it links the speech of succession in Acts 20 with the climax of this letter of succession when Paul predicts his imminent death.

umphs at day's end because he has lived a faithful life, enduring his hardship with sobriety and responding to his many critics with patient instruction. The implication is certain: Timothy must now do likewise as Paul's exemplary successor.

The choice of *dikaiosynē* as the signature of eschatological reward is significant in a Pauline text, not only because it occupies the center of this particular description of the apostle's future — and by implication the destiny of his apostolate that includes "all those who have loved his appearance" (4:8c) — but also because of its purchase for the deep logic of the Pauline canon. For example, interpreters may hear an echo of Paul's keynote statement in Rom 1:17, especially if the final member of the preceding triad, "kept the faith," is understood as the principal condition for his eschatological reception of a "wreath of rectitude." As elsewhere in the Pastoral Epistles (see 1 Tim 1:12-16), Paul thus personalizes his gospel's core conviction to supply evidence of its veracity; indeed, his faithfulness to the Lord — he has "kept the faith" — will be rewarded by the Lord's faithfulness to him on that day when he appears to judge the living and the dead.

The meaning of the final phrase of this passage, which I have translated quite literally "all those who have loved his appearance" (4:8c), remains difficult for Protestants whose sola fideism inclines them — against Paul! — to detach their future "wreath of rectitude" from their present performance of rectitude. The verbal aspect of the perfect participle of ἀγαπάω *(agapaō)* is actively intensive, indicating that one's love (or longing) for the Lord's reappearing is cumulative and is confirmed concretely by acts of love for him (cf. Phil 3:20).

4:9-22 Final Instructions, Greetings, and Benediction

⁹Do your best to come to me quickly; ¹⁰Demas, who is in love with the present world, has deserted me and has gone to Thessalonica. Crescens has gone to Galatia, Titus to Dalmatia. ¹¹Only Luke is with me. After you pick up Mark, bring him with you; he has been very useful in serving me. ¹²I sent Tychicus to Ephesus. ¹³When you come, bring the coat I left with Carpus in Troas, also the books and especially the parchments. ¹⁴Alexander the coppersmith has done me great harm: the Lord will repay his deeds. ¹⁵Watch out for him, for he opposes our teaching.

¹⁶No one took my side at my first defense; everyone deserted me. May it not be charged against them! ¹⁷The Lord took my side and enabled me so that the message might be brought to fulfillment through me that all nations might hear it. I was also rescued from the lion's mouth; ¹⁸the Lord will rescue me from every

evil act and save me for his heavenly kingdom. To him be the glory forever and ever, amen.

¹⁹Greet Prisca, Aquila, and the household of Onesiphorus. ²⁰Erastus stayed in Corinth, and I left a sick Trophimus in Miletus. ²¹Do your best to come before winter. Eubulus, Pudens, Linus, Claudia, and all the brothers send greetings.

²²The Lord be with your spirit. Grace be with you all.

The conclusions to most Pauline letters follow the literary conventions of the Hellenistic world, which are noteworthy for their miscellany: they often include epistolary summaries, travel itineraries, greetings, and good-byes to friends and colleagues, with general exhortations interspersed, finally concluding with a benedictory prayer. A colleague friend of mine once called the epistolary benedictory "a garbage dump" for this reason. Whatever its rhetorical role might be within the Pauline letter, which is typically to sum up the letter itself, this closing presents the standard fare: a newsy recap of the behaviors of others (4:9-15) intending to guide the reader, followed by personal comments about Paul's hard situation (vv. 16-18), concluding with greetings to colleagues and a final blessing (vv. 19-22).

The confused manner of modern criticism when reading this letter's benediction envisages different reactions to its highly personal nature: some take it as the intentional deception of a pseudepigrapher who adds this concluding brief to give it the appearance of a genuine letter, while still others have taken these same personal particulars at face value as evidence of the letter's authenticity. Neither would deny the plain sense of the passage, which depicts a vulnerable apostle at life's end, isolated and abandoned by others. The central exegetical question, then, is: What does the passage hold for the intended reader, the ideal tradent, in concluding this letter about the succession of Paul and his apostolate?

At the most obvious level, the number of people and places mentioned reminds readers of the catholicity of Paul's apostolate. But at a practical level, hidden in what is said are exhortations regarding what is to be avoided or embraced. In this sense it is a clever summary of what has already been written. For example, Timothy must not imitate Demas, who is "in love with the present world" (4:10a). This phrase continues the apocalyptic idiom of judgment just drawn in vv. 1-8: "the present world" (literally "the now age") is what human sin has made it, and the practices and outlook of this world are contrary to Christ's kingdom and so avoided by his disciples in order to avoid his judgment (cf. Rom 12:1-2; 2 Cor 4:4; Gal 1:4; Eph 1:21; 2:2). Not only is Demas's departure from Paul's mission surprising, given his passing but seemingly positive mention in Col 4:14, but the pair of departures in this concluding passage reminds the reader of the letter's idiom of suffering and the costs of continuing Paul's legacy. Nor should Timothy imitate Alexander the coppersmith (cf. 1 Tim 1:20; also Acts 19:33-34), who "has done me great harm . . . (and) opposes our teaching" (4:14-15). Like Demas, Alexander will be "repaid" by the Lord (v. 14b), which again trades on a Pauline conception of retributive justice: good work is compensated by reward whereas apostasy is compensated by judgment.

Alexander and Demas form a third pair of apostates in 2 Timothy — along with Phygelus and Hermogenes (1:15) and Hymenaeus and Philetus (2:17) — who are examples of a failed Pauline succession. To "desert" Paul as Demas did or to "oppose" Paul's gospel as Alexander did is to be unfaithful not only to the Lord but also to the apostle's legacy and example in fighting the fight, finishing the race, and keeping the faith (4:7). The implication of such spiritual failure is that the likes of Demas and Alexander will not share in Paul's eschatological reward (v. 8).

A positive pair of examples is personified by Luke and Mark, but again in a severely abbreviated manner: Luke is "with me" and Mark "has been very useful in serving me" (4:11). Luke is thus the opposite of Demas, and Mark of Alexander. They also carry with them canonical profiles from Acts, which create highly suggestive intertexts that permit us to elaborate the importance of their pairing. In Acts, the person of the narrator appears in stories that prepare readers for dramatic transitions in Paul's career: to Europe (16:10-16), from Europe (20:5-16), to Jerusalem and imprisonment (21:1-18), and to Rome, the city of his appointed destiny (27:1–28:16). The narrator's presence thus marks out episodes that depict Paul's departure and is therefore of strategic value in defining the importance of Luke, the presumptive narrator, to post-Pauline Christianity.[85] If Paul's passing reference "only Luke is with me," is read in canonical context, the reader will be prompted to read the speeches placed with the "we"-passages in Acts (Acts 16:31; 20:17-35; 22:1-21; 28:17-22). The effect is to remind the reader of the importance of carrying on Paul's legacy to the next generation, the central theme of this letter.

Although nothing is said about how Mark made himself useful to Paul (4:11), assuming this is the Mark of Acts (it was a common name), the remark is the opposite of Paul's dismissal of Mark as unreliable in Acts (15:36-41; cf. 12:12; 13:13).[86] The silence of the Acts narrative about Barnabas from that mo-

---

85. This observation trades on the argument of Thomas E. Phillips, "Paul as Role Model in Acts: The 'We' Passages in Acts 16 and Beyond," in *Acts and Ethics* (ed. T. E. Phillips; Sheffield: Phoenix, 2005), 49-63.

86. The verb ἀναλαμβάνω (*analambanō*, "bring with") in 4:11 is a synonym of συμπαραλαμβάνω (*symparalambanō*, "bring along with"), which Luke uses to tell Mark's story

ment on implies that the Paul of Acts was right in his assessment of Mark. The positive verdict on Mark in 2 Timothy constructs, at the very least, a useful intertext that sounds a redemptive note and may hide an exhortation for those tradents who have survived spiritual failure and whose calling, along with Timothy's, has been reignited by the indwelling Spirit of power (cf. 1:6-7).

In the midst of this posting of "troop movement" as Towner calls it,[87] Paul mentions his need of coat, books, and parchments (4:13). This request seems not only abrupt but perhaps even awkward following the dramatic announcement of Paul's imminent death (vv. 6-8). At the very least, this image of an engaged apostle should gloss statements earlier in this letter (1:8-12; 2:8b-10; 3:10-11) and elsewhere in the Pauline canon (e.g., 2 Cor 4:7-18; Phil 1:12-30) that articulate his faithful response to the threat of death. Much like the closing of Acts, which portrays Paul awaiting his fate by doing what he has always done (Acts 28:30-31), here he faces death by staying in the moment, keeping warm and studying, presumably in preparation for ministry (perhaps in Spain? see Rom 15:24) and not for death. While the plea to "come before winter" (4:21) may only reinforce the request for warmer clothing, it may also be a weather report about winter navigation in the Mediterranean world, which, if glossed by the Acts story of Paul the missionary traveler, would almost certainly indicate his plans are for sea travel and further ministry.

The next pericope of this concluding passage (4:16-18) is among the most fascinating of the letter. At its center is the claim, which Paul repeats, that he was "rescued" (ῥύομαι, *rhyomai*) by the Lord from evil for salvation (see 3:11). Paul's idiom of "rescue" cues the exodus typology (cf. LXX Exod 6:6; 12:27; 14:30). Once again Paul personifies the saving grace of God, as in the biography of his conversion in 1 Tim 1:12-16. In this case the Lord "rescues" Paul from danger for safety in his heavenly kingdom — recalling Israel's Promised Land.

The note of praise that he was "rescued from the lion's mouth" echoes LXX Ps 21:21-22 and locates Paul's poignant review of personal hardship and heartbreak in a lament psalm that pleads to God for well-timed help and ultimately finds it. The psalmist's finding of God's rescuing grace has two effects, both of which are strategic in concluding this letter. First is the "missiological" result of Paul's suffering: "all the ends of the earth/families of the nations shall remember and turn to the Lord" (Ps 21:28) is read as an intertext not only of the suffering of the Davidic Messiah (cf. 2 Tim 2:8) but also of

---

(Acts 12:25; 15:37-38) and may be read as another linguistic link that brings these two texts into conversation.

87. Towner, *Letters to Timothy and Titus*, 626.

Paul's own courageous suffering, which is an indispensable apologia of his ministry to the nations.[88] Second is the effect of remembering the psalmist's suffering for the future of Israel. Suffering provides testimony that "my soul lives for the Lord" (Ps 21:30c), which has the effect that "my offspring will serve him . . . they shall announce his righteousness to a people yet to be born" (vv. 31-32). Again, if the Psalm is reread as a personification of Paul and its concluding lyrics as analogous to the "succession" of his apostolate, the implication is that his suffering bears testimony of his loyalty to the Lord, with the effect that his tradents — his "offspring" — would carry his story with them into the coming generation of believers "because the Lord has acted" (Ps 21:32b; cf. 2 Tim 4:18b).

This canonical setting may be expanded by the story of Paul's suffering in Acts, especially as a Roman prisoner. For this reason, some interpreters have offered elaborate reconstructions to fit these vague references to opposition and a "first defense" in this letter within the plotline of Acts 22–26. But the timing and location of Paul's "first defense" (4:16) are indeterminate and of little exegetical value in any case.[89] Certainly the Acts narrative of Paul's arrest and imprisonment in Jerusalem and then Caesarea is noteworthy for the lack of support from James and the other leaders of the Judean church. The Paul of Acts must depend on his own scruples, Roman politics, family members, and ultimately the Lord for his personal safety. In fact, this intertext may allow the reader of 2 Timothy to conclude that the "no one" on "Paul's side" also included earnest believers and not just religious renegades such as those listed in the letter, presumably because they did not think Paul's mission to the Gentiles was on God's side (cf. Acts 21:18-26). Perhaps this then explains why Paul would add the refrain "may it not be charged against them" (4:16b), which is otherwise a curious note to sound in a concluding passage that includes the hope that God would punish others who opposed him (v. 14b).

Final greetings of the kind found in 4:19-21 are a typical convention of Hellenistic letters. But in a letter of succession this kind of name-dropping, especially when set within the context of the Pauline canon, may serve a special role. On the one hand, the greetings come with a particular agenda set out in 2:2, where Timothy is instructed to pass the "things heard from me to faithful people." Those greeted by name are these "faithful people" who be-

---

88. This is the thrust of Towner's fine intertextual study of this passage in *Letters to Timothy and Titus*, 642-49.

89. But see William D. Mounce, *Pastoral Epistles* (WBC; Nashville: Nelson, 2000), 594-98, who understands that "the primary question of the passage is the historical setting of the defense" (594), agreeing with the current consensus that this passage refers to an initial public hearing of the evidence rather than to the first of two imprisonments.

long to the magisterium instructed to "teach still others." The simple catalog of their names, along with all the others found in these concluding words, commend to readers a "cloud of witnesses" favorably linked to Paul that underwrite the succession of his *parathēkē* and the faithfulness of the Lord to its future.[90]

On the other hand, some of these names cue other biblical stories that elaborate the essential characteristic of these believers as Pauline tradents: the faithfulness of Prisca and Aquila recounted in Acts 18 (cf. Rom 16:3; 1 Cor 16:19) and of Onesiphorus (2 Tim 1:15-18) to Paul and his mission. The repetition of Onesiphorus's "household" (οἶκος, *oikos*; cf. 1:16) seems important, not because it deflects attention from Onesiphorus, who has since died, but in light of the strategic role *oiko-* words perform in the Pastoral Epistles, in which the church is the "household of God" (1 Tim 3:15) and a this-worldly microcosm of the cosmic *oikonomia theou* (cf. 1 Tim 1:4). Within this context the repeated mention of this household, which would have been known to the letter's first readers, cues the memory of virtues (e.g., hospitality, loyalty, and courage) that are characteristic of the ideal tradent.

Finally, the benedictory prayer (4:22) is in two parts, concluding this letter in the manner of 1 Timothy (see above on 1 Tim 6:21). The second part is a conventional blessing written in second-person plural — "you all" — and addressed to the entire congregation. While similar to other Pauline letters, this letter is addressed to an individual rather than a congregation, and so the first part of the benediction is singular in address. We might imagine the entire congregation eavesdropping on the correspondence between apostle and apprentice when it was read aloud. From a canonical perspective, the plural form in the second part may cue the reading of a canonical letter by an ever-changing audience of faithful readers for whom it is a textual means of God's saving grace.

The mention of Timothy's human "spirit" in these final words recalls the mention of the divine "Spirit" in the letter's opening words (1:6-7) and provides the letter with a literary *inclusio* that frames its instruction by the interplay of God's indwelling Spirit and Timothy's spirit. This interplay supports the letter's theme that the ideal tradent "protects the good tradition through the Holy Spirit who indwells you" (1:14). Evidently, the effect of this individual's ministry extends to and is measured by the forward obedience of the entire congregation.

---

90. Bassler, *1 Timothy, 2 Timothy, Titus*, 179.

A Rule of Faith Reading of 2 Timothy[1]

The Creator God: *"There is only one God, and he is none other than the Creator of the world, who produced all things out of nothing through his own Word, first of all sent forth."*

Images of God intent on saving all things, so central to Pauline theology, opened the first letter (1 Tim 1:12-17) and remain a subtext of 2 Timothy. But in a letter of succession such as this one, God is powerfully engaged in preserving the Pauline apostolate as strategic to God's redemptive plan to save all creation. Not only do Paul's appointment as "herald, apostle, and teacher" of the gospel and his subsequent suffering serve "God's own purpose and grace" (1:9; cf. vv. 1, 11); the very exercise of divine power protects his apostolic legacy "until that day" (v. 12).

What also seems clear from this letter is that God's rescue of Paul from his various personal enemies (3:11), typically mentioned in pairs as though they are ganging up on the apostle (1:15; 2:17; 4:9-18), is not to preserve an ecclesial "office" but a particular person whom God has appointed for a special task (cf. 4:17; see below on Tit 1:1-3) — a salient dimension of Paul's portrait in Acts as well as the Pastoral Epistles. What is remembered about the person and proclamation of Paul forms a "pattern of healthy teaching" (1:13), funds the "good tradition" (v. 14), and is passed on to the next generation because God's desire to save everyone is subject to the continuing ministry of a particular apostolate.

2 Timothy 1 Timothy's sense of vocation is recast in the terms of his being Paul's successor, whose individual charism is animated by God's indwelling,

---

1. See pp. 40-43 above.

empowering Spirit (1:6-7, 14). His capacity to hold onto and protect the pattern of instruction received from Paul is enabled by "the Holy Spirit who dwells in you" (v. 14). The repetition of "that day" (vv. 12, 18; cf. 4:8), which links God's protection of what is remembered of Paul (1:12; cf. 2:2) with Paul's personal well-being (1:18), suggests that God's final judgment depends in some sense on a community's treatment of Paul and his apostolic legacy.

What makes this peculiar conception of divine power more remarkable is its close connection with the distinctive emphasis of the Pastoral Epistles on the saving activity of God, who along with Christ Jesus (1:10) is "our Savior" (cf. 1 Tim 2:3). It is God who has "saved us . . . not according to our works but according to God's own purpose and grace" (1:9). While the initial reference to God's δύναμις (*dynamis*, "power") pairs the Holy Spirit with a ministry of the gospel that calls people into the realm of God's grace by the knowledge of one who can be trusted "until that day" (v. 12), the subsequent mention of God being "able" (δυνατός, *dynatos*, v. 12) marks a continuation of salvation's history that is conditioned on God's powerful protection of the apostolic tradition. Presumably those who come under the umbrella of Pauline instruction are in a better position to come to knowledge of the gospel truth (so 1 Tim 2:4).

This eschatological pairing of a particular apostolic tradition with God's redemptive purpose explains why Paul's succession is a crucial moment in the history of salvation. Paul's exhortation that Timothy maintain the Pauline prototype assumes that the indwelling Spirit will enable him to protect and transmit the apostolic παραθήκη (*parathēkē*) as a distinctive practice of his ministry. In fact, loyalty to Paul and the preservation of his memory for the next generation of believers are critical features of divine providence. Quite apart from what consequences the actions of those who "turned their back on Paul" (v. 15) and of Onesiphorus, who "sought and found Paul" (v. 17), might have "on that day" (v. 18), the point scored by this etiology is that the criterion of God's eschatological verdict is personal connection with Paul. To remain loyal to and unashamed of Paul is to assure one's participation in God's coming victory.

The drumbeat of references to time (1:3, 9, 10, 12, 18) and place (vv. 5, 15, 17) ground this conception of God's saving action in the real world. A Pauline theological conception is concentrated by the claim that God's restoration of a broken creation is brought to realization by the faithfulness of Jesus, and this secondary claim that God will protect the Pauline tradition is of a piece with this same redemptive plan.

2 Timothy 2 Among the most arresting images of Scripture's God is the scrupulous attention God pays to what is happening on the ground. God not only observes the human endeavor but also makes decisions about individuals, including their eternal destiny, based on what has been observed and heard. And this mostly concerns manner of life: that is, "the Lord knows those belonging to him" (2:19) by what they do.

Timothy is addressed as a "worker," then, who publicly trades in interpretation of the "word of truth" and whose tangible effort in doing so "proves" his mettle before "the presence of God" (2:15; cf. 4:1). The expectation of God's eschatological review of good or bad workers is thematic in these letters. Timothy's salvation depends on the faithful performance of his sacred calling (see 1 Tim 4:16). This idea of divine approval might offend the sensibility of those who dismiss the idea that human achievement has any place in God's way of thinking and who suppose that God is interested only in the orthodoxy of our faith or in the act of trusting God with our future. We may suppose that God's actions typically involve forgiving people without placing demands on them. This passage, along with others in Pastoral Epistles, suggests otherwise: the worker must "prove" herself by God's standard and under God's scrutiny.

The close attention God pays to interpreters of the word of truth, like Paul and Timothy, reflects the importance of that word in communicating God's interests to others. God works in collaboration with others, and the quality of their work reflects on the quality of God's interests for the world. To get the truth content of God's word right and to aim the teaching of that word so as to produce a redemptive result — two abiding concerns of the missionary Paul in this letter — reflect God's interest in what is said about God and how it is said. Again, God's scrupulous attention to these things reflects God's serious interest in them.

Balancing God's careful attentiveness in evaluating the hard work that brings salvation to everyone is God's faithfulness to follow through with what has been promised: the promise to save creation from sin and death is a done deal because of God (2:19). Much has been written about the stance of these letters toward false teaching and teachers. Paul's absence has created an epistemic crisis, in response to which those who disagree with his missionary practices and core beliefs now seek to subvert the succession of his apostolate. Clearly God's faithfulness toward the promise to save everyone is instantiated in God's protection of the Pauline tradition "until that day" (1:12). What is sometimes overlooked, however, is the sheer scope of God's redemptive will, even to "permit a change of mind" that enables false teachers to "escape the devil's trap" and come back to a "knowledge of the truth" (= conversion: 2:25b-26). The virtuous performance of Timothy's pastoral workload, which includes "schooling opponents with gentleness" (v. 25a), cooperates with God in making good on God's promise to save everyone.

2 Timothy 3 The "last days" mark out a dangerous time for God's creation (3:1). People love what God despises and their rebelliousness unsettles God's way of ordering the world (vv. 2-9). The relevant question is how the Creator responds to an unhealthy world that has rejected the very word that formed it.

This letter's response to this question is set out by a series of exhortations organized and introduced by three instances of *sy de*, "you, however" (3:10, 13; 4:5). Each of these three hortatory units is best understood in the context of a letter of succession. In this sense, then, God's principal auxiliary in putting creation to rights is Paul, and by implication his apostolate — "my teaching, way of life, purpose, faith, loyalty, love, patience, suffering" (3:10-11) — whose example is "closely observed" (v. 10) by the faithful tradent as the right pattern in dealing with evil people.

Insofar as evil people do not tolerate "healthy (i.e., Pauline) teaching" (4:3), Paul's successor must "stay steady in what you have learned... knowing from whom you learned." In particular, learning about God's "salvation through faith in Jesus Christ" is the role of the community's "holy writings" whose practices God inspires to bring the tradent to "maturity for every good work" (3:16-17; cf. 1 Tim 4:13-16). While no indication is given that Timothy's Scripture includes a collection of Paul's "holy writings," the juxtaposition of 3:10-13 and 3:14–4:4 would imply that Timothy's learning curve is drawn by Paul and that what he has observed of Paul's teaching is at the very least hermeneutical of his holy writings. Within the bounds of the canonical process, of course, this inspired and inspiring body of Scriptures would come to include the Pauline canon, and it is this corpus of letters that has fixed and authorized the memory of what is "closely observed" of Paul for every generation of believers "until that day."

It should be said at this point that the church's recognition of a fixed collection of Pauline letters as Scripture would have resulted from the church's various uses of them for "teaching, showing mistakes, correcting, training in rectitude" (3:16b) by which a Pauline "pattern of healthy teaching" (1:13) would have been recognized. In this way a "textualized" Paul, even though secondary and inferior to Paul himself, is nonetheless appropriated by future generations of his tradents in the manner of Timothy, that is, by continuing to "stay steady in what you have learned and found convincing, knowing from whom you learned" (3:14). Learning God's word from Paul during the present time characterized by his absence is defined and governed by the Pauline canon used in the company of the inspiring Spirit.

2 Timothy 4 The final unit of exhortations (4:5) repeats the letter's thematic of "suffering bad news" as a hard worker (cf. 2:15) whose ministry of the word (4:2) is carried out in service to God (cf. 1:8-14). The "bad news" is that this ministry is conducted in the "last days" of a broken and futile creation, held now in the devil's trap. But it also is ministry conducted in full view of God and Christ Jesus, whose victorious reappearance will be to judge evil rather than to redeem it. In sounding this apocalyptic note, consistent with Pauline instruction, a second conception of God as "righteous judge" (4:8; cf. v. 1) is added. On "that day" (v. 8; cf. 1:12, 18) God will determine reward (4:8, 14; cf. 1:18; 2:17-19) or punishment (4:14) on the basis of works done.

The principal theodicy of the Pauline canon regards the faithfulness of God to biblical promises made to Israel, which remains the central controversy of his mission to the Gentiles and the initiation of repentant Gentiles into the covenant community (Romans 9–11). Paul resolves this problem by appeals to his missionary experience among Gentiles but also by his peculiar reading of Scripture, which he believes has scripted the very *ordo salutis* his mission brings to realization.

The opening testimony of this letter, however, introduced a more traditional theodicy regarding suffering of the innocent: Paul and all those who imitate him suffer because of their obedience to God. This apostolic theodicy is resolved by Paul's appeal to a sacred calling. Moreover, his development of the theme of suffering in ch. 2 clarifies that suffering results more from the hard work of ministry than from unjust persecution — a commonsense "no pain, no gain" kind of suffering.

Christ Jesus the Lord: *"This Word is called his Son, and, under the name of God, was seen 'in diverse manners' by the patriarchs, heard at all times in the prophets, at last brought down by the Spirit and power of the Father into the Virgin Mary, was made flesh in her womb, and, being born of her, went forth as Jesus Christ; thenceforth he preached the new law and the new promise of the kingdom of heaven, worked miracles, and having been crucified, rose again the third day. Having ascended into the heavens, he sat at the right hand of the Father. Christ will come with glory. . . ."*

Paul's epiphany Christology compresses the Rule's narrative formulation of the Christ event into two decisive moments in the history of salvation. In "the appearing of our Savior Christ Jesus" (1:10), God's own purpose and grace is revealed (vv. 9-10). This opening formula elaborates the Rule's core belief about Christ in terms of salvation. The incarnate Word, "brought down by the power of God . . . made flesh . . . as Jesus Christ," is now heralded by Paul's gospel (v. 11), which is proclaimed and protected by this same divine power (vv. 8, 12).

The centerpiece of the gospel's proclamation, which concerns the world's salvation, is this confession: "Jesus Christ, raised from the dead, from the family of David" (2:8). The addition of the Lord's Davidic descent to his resurrection underscores precisely what the Rule does: God's Son lived a human life, having been born into Israel's royal family as expected of the Messiah and "heard at all times in the prophets." In his programmatic speech at the synagogue in Pisidian Antioch, which supplies Scripture's own setting for hearing the Pauline kerygma for the nations, the Paul of Acts develops the relationship between the Psalter's prediction of a Davidic Messiah and Jesus' resurrection as its proof (Acts 13:16-41).[2] In this sense, the resurrection of the Davidic Messiah vindicates Scripture's testimony of God's faithfulness to a promise to cleanse the world of sin for a new life with God.

The second epiphany is set in the indeterminate future when the risen "Christ will come with glory." The very idea of a second coming is predicated on the belief that God raised Jesus from the dead. The prosecution of Christ's messianic business is in two stages. If salvation is the order of the Messiah's business in the first stage and its success is confirmed by his resurrection, then judgment is the Messiah's business in the second stage and will complete his work. Putting the matter this way raises a question: In what sense does the Messiah's reappearance "to judge the living and the dead" (4:1) and to reward the faithful (vv. 6-8) complete his mission to save the world? On the one hand, the idea of a final judgment is of a piece with Paul's apocalyptic theology, inherited from his Judaism. No one is excused, not even the apostle (v. 8): there is coming a day when an impartial God will judge even "the secrets of all" (Rom 2:16). The expressed hope is that because God's Christ is a "just judge" (4:8), rewards will be dispensed to those whose faithful performances are deserving. What is remarkable about the adumbration of this point, apropos in a letter of succession, is that these performances are ascertained in terms of a particular vocation. The mention of Christ's second epiphany is placed amid a series of crucial exhortations, beginning with 3:10, which set out the importance of Timothy's imitation of Paul, which will prepare him for the apostle's final departure (4:6-8).

On the other hand, the mere mention that Christ will bring his kingdom with him when he appears again (4:1) resonates powerfully with the inheritance promised by God to the covenant community, which includes the full measure of a transformed existence currently experienced in part by those baptized by the Spirit into Christ. What seems clear from the portfolio

---

2. See Robert W. Wall, "Acts," in *The New Interpreter's Bible* (Nashville: Abingdon, 2001), 10:191-94.

of references to the kingdom of Christ in the Pauline canon is that its future appearance with Christ is heralded by a particular manner of purified life that follows from being "washed and sanctified, when you were justified in the name of the Lord Jesus Christ and in the Spirit of our God" (1 Cor 6:9-11; cf. Gal 5:21; 1 Thess 2:12; Eph 5:5). In 2 Timothy, the deep logic of this claim is applied to Pauline tradents, whose present fidelity to Paul and his legacy prepares them for the coming victory of God and God's Son.

2 Timothy 1 The pivot point of the letter's Christology is introduced in its opening chapter. Christ Jesus has publicly "appeared" as "our Savior" to abolish death and illumine life (1:10) according to God's redemptive purpose and grace (v. 9). Indeed, in the letter's opening and most decisive claim, God's "promise of life" has been brought to realization "in Christ Jesus" (v. 1). In this sense, he is the agent of God's plan, not only to realize it but also to reveal its terms. The catchword used of his advent in the Pastoral Epistles, ἐπιφάνεια *(epiphaneia)*, interprets his saving role as revealer of God's transcendent will to save everyone (1 Tim 2:4-6). In fact, the use of "our Savior" in reference to Christ (2 Tim 1:10) rather than to God as in 1 Timothy (1:1; 2:3; 4:10) may very well imply that his revelation of God's redemption instantiates God.

The passing reference to "the Lord's testimony" (1:8), if then related to this initial epiphany, implies what about his earthly life might have been embarrassing for a follower but revelatory of God's salvation, namely, following a Messiah (and his apostle) who was rejected by Jewish leaders and executed as a Roman criminal because his claim as Israel's king rivaled that of Caesar. "It is a disgrace to be on the wrong side of the law,"[3] and Paul later remarks with irony that while he is bound as a common criminal, the word of God is not (2:9). Of course, it is precisely in this shameful act of Christ's faithfulness that God's promise of life is realized.

Young argues that the epiphanic idiom of 2 Timothy combines the Lord's two epiphanies, in the past to save and in the future to judge, in a way that may have been thought subversive of the lord Caesar, who made similar claims to be savior and judge of the world.[4] If this is the case, the exhortation for Timothy to be unashamed and to "share the suffering for the gospel" is underwritten by this core Christological sentiment, and the second epiphany will vindicate the first.

In addition to the Lord's public agency of God's redemptive plan in past

---

3. Frances M. Young, *The Theology of the Pastoral Letters* (Cambridge: Cambridge University Press, 1994), 66.
4. Young, *Theology of the Pastoral Letters,* 65.

and future epiphanies, this chapter also alludes to his present status between these two advents in its repeated use of the "in Christ" formula (1:1, 9, 13) as the location where Christ is spiritually present to believers, who experience God's grace (v. 9). The final use of the "in Christ" formula is extraordinary, not because it posits faith and loyalty (ἀγάπη, *agapē*) but because these characteristics are now applied to the tradent's succession of Paul's apostolate so that his existence "in Christ" enables him to hold onto and protect the Pauline tradition for those others with whom Christ's suffering is shared (cf. 2:1).

2 Timothy 2 The prior exhortation to be unashamed of the Lord's suffering is elaborated in this chapter. Once again, Timothy is encouraged as a faithful tradent to "share the suffering like a good soldier of Christ Jesus" (2:3; cf. 1:8). In this case, however, the matter is put differently than before, when suffering was joined with shame to explain why Timothy might be unwilling to make good on his charism and calling. The examples of suffering exemplify hard work and self-sacrifice (2:4-6) rather than the effect of a ministry aligned with a pair of purported Roman criminals (Jesus and Paul), which some might take as shameful (or imprudent) behavior. The memory of the risen Christ (v. 8) is put forward as a sufficient motive that prompts soldier-like work as an interpreter of "the word of truth" who passes muster in the presence of God (v. 15).

Paul's remembrance of Christ's resurrection is the theological setting for reflection on the prospect of suffering and as such is extended here in two directions. First, a canonical saying is added (2:11-13) to explain the elect community's participation with Christ in a shared experience of salvation. The combination of familiar Pauline tropes for the community's baptism into the body of Christ — sharing in his death, life, and rule (vv. 11b-12a) — not only sets out salvation as a partnership with Christ but provides a reason for suffering the costs of a hard gospel ministry: the ministry not only shares in the cruciformity of the past Christ event but thus secures one's participation in his future reign.[5]

If Paul's exposition of Christian baptism into the dying and rising of Christ in Romans 6 is an apt co-text with the first two lines of the saying in 2 Tim 2:11-13, then the reader more easily recognizes that his concern to uphold an Easter faith is practical, not apologetic. Paul does not concern himself with whether "Jesus rose again the third day," but in believing that he did teases out the implications for human existence. He seems well aware that in-

---

5. Michael J. Gorman, *Inhabiting the Cruciform God: Kenosis, Justification, and Theosis in Paul's Narrative Soteriology* (Grand Rapids: Eerdmans, 2009).

terpretations of truth claims have real effects in how people live their lives. Incorrect interpretation of the word of truth about the resurrection will have a negative effect on the congregation's life. Paul wants Timothy to get the teaching about Christ's resurrection right in order to enable the congregation to live its life in a manner that pleases God.

The second direction Paul takes his confession that "Jesus Christ is raised from the dead" is to correct those who claim that it "has already occurred" (2:18). The canonical role of Pauline orthodoxy is to delineate falsehood from the word of truth. It is a mistake to think of this in terms of control; rather, the matter is more practical and concerns the ongoing relationship between the risen One and those who exist "in him." According to Romans 6, Christ's resurrection initiates "newness of life" in those who believe. Believers are baptized into the body of the risen Jesus, in and with whom they sin no more and live as sanctified instruments of God's righteousness toward God and neighbor. When Paul mentions that "the faith of some" is threatened by the instruction of his opponents (2:18), clearly he has in mind a particular set of core beliefs about Jesus that include his resurrection as Davidic Messiah. Faith in this word of truth carries with it the expectation that those who get the resurrection of Jesus right will experience salvation (v. 10; cf. Rom 10:9). The problem with a realized eschatology of the sort taught by Paul's opponents, then, is that, by getting the resurrection of Jesus wrong, they undermine the prospect of an experienced salvation. In fact, claiming that Christians who participate in Christ's resurrection will avoid suffering actually will prevent them from owning a realistic hope that could interpret their faithful endurance of transitory suffering as the criterion of their future eternal reward (cf. 4:7-8).

This comment perhaps begs another more provisional one about a role performed by the Pastoral Epistles within the Pauline canon. The mention of teachers who move Pauline teaching in wrong directions — in this case, Hymenaeus and Philetus — may suggest a continuing problem within Pauline Christianity. The definition of Pauline orthodoxy set out in biographical statements and theological formulas in these letters may well establish a rule of faith that enables tradents to distinguish right from wrong readings of Paul. In this rather limited sense, these letters may well function more like the Catholic Epistles, which help sort out apparent or even real conflicts within the Pauline canon while also correcting misuses of Paul that might move the church away from its apostolic faith. In particular, the canonical saying in 2:11-13, along with others in the Pastoral Epistles, elaborates a soteriology that does not presume the elect's future with God has already been secured by Christ regardless of the choices they continue to make about him.

2 Timothy 3 Paul's commentary on suffering with Christ concludes with a discourse on the last days (3:1-9) followed by a profoundly personal exhortation in which he charges Timothy to "remain sober-minded whenever suffering bad news" (4:5) by conducting his ministry of the gospel according to what he has learned from a persecuted Paul (3:10-13) and from Scripture (3:14–4:4). Two Christological formulas of Christian existence are used to secure this charge.

First, for the first time Paul speaks of his suffering as "persecution" (3:12); since suffering is shared (1:8), he transforms a personal experience into a Christian rule that "anyone who desires to live a godly life with Christ Jesus" will also be persecuted. One finds Paul almost glibly exhorting others to adopt a particular attitude — in this case toward suffering — "with Christ" or "in Christ." While this formulaic appeal to Christ seems rhetorical, used to add weight to an exhortation or command, it is nonetheless true that Paul considers the whole of Christian existence and ministry a partnership with the living Christ.

The second formula is attached to performances of Scripture, which enable one to be "wise for salvation through faith in Christ Jesus" (3:15). In this case, salvation is substituted for the more familiar "justification" to make a typically Pauline point about the value of Scripture in confirming and explaining the gospel message about Jesus. Christ is made known by Scripture and by the pattern of salvation that his death and resurrection secure. Clearly this salvation has a history since this formula does not speak of conversion but of a wisdom that directs Timothy forward in partnership with Christ.

Moreover, Scripture is used to make people "mature for every good work" (3:17), which makes possible an acceptable résumé of good works for "that day" of Christ's coming judgment (4:1, 7-8). What seems clear from this text is that Scripture both supplies a deeper knowledge of Christ and cultivates those inward dispositions of Christ-likeness that enable the "man of God" to act on what is known.

2 Timothy 4 Christ's mediation of God's salvation gathers around his two earthly appearances, past and future. If the purpose of the first is to reveal God's redemptive plan and grace (cf. 1:9-10), the purpose of the second is to "judge the living and the dead" (4:1). His future appearing "on that day" consummates God's plans for a restored creation. In this letter, Christ's future and salvation's future are fully integrated as a day of personal vindication when those who have "fought the fight, finished the race, kept the faith" are justly rewarded. Only they will "love his appearance" (v. 8; cf. v. 18).

Several things are assumed by this Christian affirmation. Not only is the risen Christ presently alive "at the right hand of the Father," but "in the presence of God" he observes and makes judgments about work taking place on the ground, whether it is acceptable in God's sight. This implies that a believer's baptism into Christ is not merely "mystical" but critical: Christ is coming to make judgments about the quality of one's performance, whether the fight has been waged, the race finished, and the faith kept. Everything is seen and fairly evaluated by this messianic judge.

In this letter of succession a premium is placed on the tradent's loyalty to the apostolic tradition and his willingness to pass it on to the next generation. While the tradent's spiritual résumé must certainly list his contributions as a hardworking interpreter of Pauline orthodoxy (2:15), which also is observed by the Lord (2:14), a premium is placed on his response to the prospect of suffering, which imitates Jesus and occasions a test of fidelity to his ordination and to the apostolate. Christ appears as the judge of loyalty as well, which is why spiritual disaffection is considered such a grievous sin in this letter.

The Community of the Spirit: *"Christ sent instead of himself the power of the Holy Spirit to lead such as believe."*

The idea of an apostolic succession framed by this letter concerns particular individuals — Paul and Timothy. Nonetheless, the plural address of the concluding benediction indicates that this otherwise personal letter is knowingly overheard by the entire congregation, finally acknowledged by Paul and blessed (4:22b). The letter's instructions and exhortations for a particular individual are thus heard as relevant for every member. The universalizing tendency of the canonical process — so that this personal letter now belongs to the whole church — makes the very point implied by its benediction: the congregation itself shares the responsibility of insuring that the Pauline apostolate moves forward from this generation to the next.

Corporate metaphors for the church, however, such as "household of God" (1 Tim 3:15), are mostly absent from this letter. The word "church" is not used, though it is common for commentators to vest references to the households of individual believers, such as Onesiphorus (1:16) or even those households infiltrated by false teachers during the "last days" (3:6), with ecclesial import. For this reason, perhaps no other core belief of the Rule's theological grammar suffers more than this one when the Pastoral Epistles are not distinguished from each other and grouped together as though one size fits all. The mutually glossing character of these letters may allow for an expanded understanding of family households in 2 Timothy that includes an ecclesial subtext, especially the "impressive house" of many utensils (2:20-21). But what is thus implied about congregational life and faith is indirect. The congregation is understood as a sanctified household whose "pillar and support" is provided by Timothy's good work (see 1 Tim 3:15).

2 Timothy 1 This letter's two most important texts in elaborating the Spirit's role in the faith community are in its opening passage. In fact, of the seven uses of πνεῦμα (pneuma) in the Pastoral Epistles, most refer to the human spirit and here we have the only two that add a significant conceptual layer to a fully Pauline pneumatology. They also provide a theological explanation of the canonical role of the Pastoral Epistles, which is to uphold the importance of Paul and his apostolate into the community's future. Timothy's experience of the indwelling Spirit enables him to protect and pass on the apostolic tradition (= the Pauline canon) to others. One might even say that the succession of the apostolate is conditioned on the Spirit's presence and work.

The Spirit's indwelling presence both to gift the tradent and to protect the tradition is initiated by the liturgical gesture of laying on of hands (1:6). This is different from the Spirit's baptism of believers into the body of Christ, which is initiated by faith rather than by the apostle's choice. The Spirit gives gifts to individuals to enable a variety of worship practices that bring the entire congregation to maturity in Christ (1 Corinthians 12–14). Moreover, the Spirit's presence in the community witnesses to the community's present union with Christ as God's children and future heirs of a new creation (Romans 8). But the gifting of the ordained individual through apostolic mediation in a congregational setting suggests that the tradition itself is formative of a congregation's life and faith (1:9-10).

The emphasis of this letter is vocational: the crisis that occasioned its reception is the tradent's responsibility to preserve and transmit the Pauline legacy (gospel, memories, vocation) to the next generation. References to opposing teachers are vague and give no real indication of how they subverted congregational life. All that is mentioned, other than the usual hardball rhetoric typical of the period, is their asceticism. Comparison of 2 Tim 1:6 and 1 Tim 4:14 is critical in discerning both the differences and the complementarities of the two letters. In 2 Timothy, Timothy's authority is symbolized by Paul's laying "my hands" on Timothy (rather than the hands of the council of elders). The gloss of the "Timothy crisis/occasion" in 2 Timothy is more personal and has to do more with the relationship between Paul and Timothy and with whether Timothy has the spiritual chops to preserve and continue the Pauline legacy (2:2).

The Spirit's role in enabling Timothy's ministry is not carried out in a vacuum. A considerable prehistory has prepared Timothy for the Spirit's influence. Thus what is mentioned in 1:3-5 is not incidental to what is mentioned in vv. 6-7 and elaborated in vv. 13-14. Timothy's spiritual apprenticeship under his mother and grandmother and then Paul is the long preparation necessary for the right performance of the indwelling Spirit. This pattern is like what one finds in the opening chapter of Acts: the community did not await Pentecost passively but actively. Not only were the forty days between Easter and the Ascension full of instruction (Acts 1:3-8), but the ten days the community waited for God to fulfill the Lord's prophecy of the Spirit's arrival were spent in worship (1:12-14), instruction (1:15-22), and an experience of God fulfilling prophecy (1:23-25). The notion that the Spirit arrives upon a community or its covenant mediators as a sudden, unexpected apocalypse of power is challenged by this alternate pattern of a community waiting actively in preparation for the Spirit's baptism. In Timothy's case, the presence of the Spirit and the charism it conveys to enable his ministry come as a piece with his memories of childhood — as Paul's child (1:2) but also as Eunice's child and Lois's grandchild (v. 5).

2 Timothy 2 Paul suffers bad news to insure the realization of good news, the full experience of the salvation promised by God (2:10; cf. Tit 1:1-2). Here the community of the Spirit is called "the elect," which recalls an OT trope for Israel's privileged or secured status as God's covenant people. While election language elsewhere in the Pauline canon may also include resonances of divine providence (e.g., Rom 8:29-33), the addition of the canonical saying in 2 Tim 2:11-13 makes it clear that the individual's eternal status within the elect community is not predetermined but conditioned on faithfulness: after all, God denies those who deny God while remaining faithful to the promises made to all (vv. 12b-13a). Such fidelity toward God is mediated or monitored by the apostolic tradition. While salvation comes from God through Christ Jesus, the word of truth that publishes this good news is articulated by bearers of the tradition (v. 15). In this sense, the elect community's future experience of eternal glory is predicated on its ongoing connection to Paul and his gospel.

The second and more familiar church metaphor, "household," is employed to underscore this point. The "special utensils" that one finds in an "impressive house" implies that there are gifted and delegated members in a congregation, who are set among its rank-and-file as carriers of this saving word of truth. The various threats to the entire congregation are targeted at them: passions trump personal virtue, and thoughtless debate overwhelms the kind of hospitality that schools opponents in knowledge of the truth. There is hardly another biblical writing that underwrites more clearly the importance of the character and practices of a congregational leader for "escaping the devil's trap" while marking out those who belong to God.

In fact, the Timothy correspondence makes clear the potential threat of bad theology on the community of faith. Disputed teaching "destroys" the community, has "subverted the faith of some," and could lead believers into "godlessness." But the warnings raise a theological question: Why does the Spirit not safeguard the church's faith and prevent these outcomes? Should we not expect Christian faith to be secured by the Spirit's presence within the community? Paul's exhortation for Timothy to combat the influence of bad theology by teaching good theology underscores an important theme of biblical instruction: while the Spirit initiates the believer into the community on the basis of trusting what the Creator has done for every creature in Christ, the believer must then respond to God in covenant-keeping ways in order to maintain membership. Timothy's ministry of the word is recognized as critical to this end, since the Spirit utilizes the truth of that word to secure and bring to maturity those who trust in it.

The Nicene church confessed itself to be an "apostolic" community, a community whose practices are cued by the apostles' witness to Christ and mission in the world on his behalf. Timothy's warning of teachers whose work is reviewed "before the Lord" (2:12), who recognizes those belonging to him (v. 19), assumes the verity of this apostolic definition.

2 Timothy 3 Precisely because the church does not remove itself from the world but rather engages it with redemptive practices issues in the warning that "the last days will be dangerous times" (3:1). The community's relationship with outsiders is thematic in the Pastoral Epistles, not only in a missional way, to save outsiders from sin, but also prophetically, calling on them to end their sinning. The catalog of vices in 3:2-5 profiles the counter-community that is the target of God's just wrath (cf. Rom 1:19–2:5). The chaos caused by false teachers who enter households to draw people away from the truth (3:6) forms an apt contrast with the "special utensils" of the "impressive house" to make a larger point coherent with Pauline teaching and captured by this household metaphor: those who are set apart as carriers of God's word present a "pattern of healthy teaching" that orders and empowers a people's life together in a manner that aims at loving relations (cf. 1 Tim 1:4-5). The repetition of *phil-* words to characterize those affected by false teaching as "lovers of self and money" (3:2) who "love pleasure rather than God" (v. 4) clearly sets in contrast a community that is not ordered by the *oikonomia theou*.

Paul's creative use of θεόπνευστος *(theopneustos)* as a predicate of the community's Scripture commends its role as an auxiliary of the Spirit "to lead such as believe." Readers of C. S. Lewis's Narnia mythology will recall the breath of Aslan that brings to life creatures who have been hardened into stone by the wicked witch. Lewis thus captures this creational sense of breath as life-generating that follows the lead of Paul's conception of Scripture as a medium of divine breathing, which enlivens readers/auditors to newness of life (cf. Rom 6:4). Much of this interpretation of the divine inspiration of Scripture has been elaborated in my exegesis of 3:16 and below under the rubric of "Christian existence," and need not be repeated here. Two additional observations can be made, however, regarding the Spirit's use of a written *graphē* in forming its community and what this might say about that community. While much has been made about the importance of the magisterial office in the Pastoral Epistles and the practices of educating a congregation's membership, Young points out that this may reflect a Hellenistic cultural interest (mostly among its elites) in book-learning, reinforced by a Jewish reverence for the written text (cf. 4:13). Moreover, learning from books occurred in the household, where the hierarchical structure facilitated practical learning more than did schools, which typically gathered a very small number of people around esoteric topics.[6] Naturally, such an interest was already picked up by the church during the formation of its canon, which included a textualized deposit of Pauline teaching the Spirit could now appropriate in the apostle's absence to instruct its audiences for salvation through faith in Christ Jesus and to bring them to maturity for a life of good works. Centuries later this same text was picked up by the Reformers in an early modern cultural setting, in which book-learning was made popular and more democratic with the aid of the printing press. In this new setting, Paul's exhortation for Spirit-led uses of Scripture was heard again as formative of a priesthood of all believers.

Even though this text was rather quickly appropriated during the canonizing process to authorize the formation of Christian Scripture, including a canon of Pauline texts, and still much later to authorize Protestantism's Scripture principle, it seems prudent to note that the manner and purpose of the Spirit's use of Scripture expressed in this text are entirely Jewish and that "every Scripture" originally referred to Israel's Scripture in Greek translation. This profound interest in learning from the sacred book, which guides the theological and moral formation of a Christian congregation and its spiritual leader, is one indicator among others of an essential continuity in the practices and core beliefs of the synagogue and the church.

2 Timothy 4 The repetition of "healthy teaching" (4:3), especially in combination with a pedagogy of "patient instruction" (v. 2), establishes a Pauline rule of faith that regulates the formation of a Christian faith in the presence

---

6. Young, *Theology of the Pastoral Letters*, 81-84.

of God that is prepared for Christ's end-time judgment (v. 1). The importance of Christian catechesis is stated in negative terms, in the observation that people seem intolerant of truth and are easily persuaded by conspiracy theories. Hardly a better historical example of this exists than an American popular culture so easily attracted to Dan Brown's various novels, such as *The Da Vinci Code*, which persist in depicting the church as engaged in censorship, violence, and intellectual fraud as a matter of institutional self-preservation. Typically, the Pastoral Epistles are not interested in giving historical examples, and Paul does not do so here. His point is theologically adduced: the memory and manner of his apostolate — what he proclaims and how he does so — provide a normative model that his tradents follow to produce theologically healthy congregations. There is hardly a more important congregational practice than a rigorous pattern of catechesis that patiently and carefully initiates members into the word of God so that they will resist the turn toward conspiracies, which will continue to occupy popular culture of the last days.

The benediction of this letter provides a fascinating profile of the canonical Paul. The network of relationships of friends and foes that surrounds him should not be read as the final words of a weakened and slightly paranoid Paul, now awaiting his death (4:6-8) in winter's cold, alone and without creature comforts. The theological implication of this profile regards his indispensability from the Lord's perspective, who "will rescue me from every evil act and save me for his heavenly kingdom" (v. 18; cf. v. 1). His persistence in making the gospel accessible so that "all nations might hear it" (v. 17) and his confident trust in God's ultimate approval secure the ground for the succession of his apostolate within the church. The keen personalizing of his relationship with the Lord — "the Lord took my side . . . the Lord will rescue me" (vv. 17-18) — may well underscore Paul's peculiar and distinctive role in God's redemptive plan, but in this letter of succession the underlying purpose of these ruminations is to legitimize the church's decision to safeguard the Pauline canon for the next generation of tradents.

Christian Existence and Discipleship: *"In putting on our flesh, Christ made it his own; and in making it his own, he made it sinless . . . because in that same human flesh he lived without sin" (On the Flesh of Christ 16).*

While the exercise of spiritual leadership in a congregation is a matter of the Spirit's charism and apostolic ordination (1:6-7), it is also a matter of moral competence. In fact, the youth (or inexperience) of Timothy, which is alluded to in the letter's address to a "dear child" (cf. 2:1; 1 Tim 1:2) and mentioned more directly elsewhere as a potential problem (2:22; cf. 1 Tim 4:12), implies that Timothy's credentials to lead are not based on extended practical experience in leading a congregation but on his virtue and his gift to lead. The interpreter of these letters should allow that the virtue that marks out a group leader is not esoteric or heroic but practical: what enables the leader to do the job well. It is also noteworthy that some are not distinctively "Christian" but secular, indicating again the concern of the Pastoral Epistles that outsiders think well of the community and perhaps also of the gospel it heralds.

It also seems clear that the paraenetic cast of the Timothy correspondence is hardly detached from theological conviction but rather flows from it. A Pauline moral freight, whatever the literary genre that carries it, loads theology and ethics together as two parts of a dynamic whole. Hardly any interpreter of the Pastoral Epistles denies the coherence of their theological content, even if it is hardly innovative. But this should not be unexpected in a letter of succession that sets out traditional or canonical beliefs as a congregation's "pattern of healthy teaching" (1:13). Yet the clear subtext of Pauline paraenesis and its various conventions — catalogs of virtue and vice, household codes and topoi, biographies of what to imitate or avoid — is a theological orthodoxy that must be embraced if a healthy or loving manner of life is to be lived.

Tertullian's discourse on the incarnation, where we find the Rule's core belief about Christian existence, makes this point remarkably well. If the manner of Christian existence is that of the disciple/student who follows after/learns from Christ, then the believer must seek to imitate Christ's manner and message. Especially in this letter, the dual-epiphany theme allows Paul to define Christian virtue in terms of Christ's suffering and resurrection (e.g., 2:3-26) but then also provides added incentive to imitate Christ by appeal to his reappearance "to judge the living and the dead" (4:1-8). But grounding this manner of life, which is itself hardly a Pauline innovation but mostly derived from his Jewish education if not also from secular philosophy, is the effect of the Christ event, which "abolished death and illumined life and immortality" (1:10b). In Tertullian's idiom, Christ put on human flesh and in doing so "made it sinless" or virtuous.

2 Timothy 1 Paul exhorts Timothy to revitalize God's gift in him, which enables him to perform the various tasks of his holy calling. The implied question, which is not incidental to this letter or to the church's reading of it, is: How does one go about reinvigorating a spiritual charism? The surprising lack of doxology in Paul's initial exhortation suggests that spiritual renewal, at least in Timothy's case, is not the result of giving praise to God; rather, the testimonial idiom that pervades the hortatory materials of 2 Timothy suggests that Timothy — along with all Paul's faithful tradents — is directed and renewed by his memory of the apostle, of what he does with and says about the gospel entrusted to him (1:8-9, 13; 2:2; 3:10-14).

Spiritual renewal also turns on one's appropriation of the indwelling Spirit: Timothy's gift comes with God's Spirit, who produces "power, love, and discernment" rather than timidity. These are virtues cultivated within the human spirit that enable the gifted one to "protect the good tradition" passed on to him (1:14). Paul's gesture of laying on of hands is similar to the badge the Wizard of Oz gives the lion to wear as a reminder of the power already inside him. The resident power is Paul's to recognize but not to grant; it is the indwelling Spirit's power that provides the gift and competency according to God's will that enables Timothy to guard the tradition from its various threats.

The contrast between a "cowardly Spirit" and one that generates these virtues suggests a remarkable level of cooperation between the divine and human. Σωφρονισμός *(sōphronismos),* "discernment," in particular is a decisively humanistic competence, the inward performance of which checks and balances the kind of power that derives exclusively from the Spirit's presence. In this sense, Timothy's spiritual charism as well as his salvation and "holy calling" cannot originate with him "according to (his) works" but from God's grace alone (1:9). This exercise of weighing competing goods and choosing rightly among them is more human in nature — a competence acquired by experience and training. The new powers given by the Spirit to those who live in Christ are necessarily constrained and directed toward loving ends by this "calm desire of edifying" others, as Calvin puts it.[7] Without this internal apparatus of moral discernment, the minister of the gospel might misuse these powers in the manner of the false teachers of the "last days" described later in the letter (3:1-9). It is not what one knows, who one knows, or one's spiritual gift that qualifies one for leadership; rather, it is the indispensability of a discerning witness to the gospel that prevails.

A culture of shame acts as a preventative if also distasteful medicine against those who are inclined toward spiritual or vocational disaffection. The prospect of being publicly shamed into faithfulness can work properly only when the Lord is taken seriously! Ironically, shame becomes an unnecessary deterrent when the Lord is well known and his victory is entirely trusted as trustworthy (1:12). The practical connection in this passage, then, between Timothy's gift and God's power, which is managed by the motive of shame, should not go unnoticed; however, the assumption is that disgrace as

---

7. John Calvin, *The Second Epistle of Paul the Apostle to the Corinthians and the Epistles to Timothy, Titus, and Philemon* (Grand Rapids: Eerdmans, 1964), 110.

a motive for obeying God becomes less effective as the believer becomes more mature.

Although this letter's ethic is more personal and concerns the moral competence of spiritual leadership, the example of shameless Onesiphorus and his well-timed hospitality toward Paul is a helpful reminder of the importance given to the moral practices of a Christian household. Elsewhere the community's practice of extending hospitality to strangers and outsiders instantiates divine mercy (Luke 6:27-36), but here it is mentioned in contrast to the actions of Phygelus and Hermogenes, who have rejected Paul and his tradition. This discriminating use of hospitality as an act of loyalty toward insiders (rather than an all-inclusive love extended even to enemies) is similar to what is in 2 John, where the criterion of Christian fellowship is doctrinally based (2 John 8-11; cf. 1 John 1:3). The congregation's moral practices, then, are not only cultivated by a Pauline "pattern of healthy teaching" (cf. 1:13) but are to some extent regulated by it as well.

2 Timothy 2 More than in any other Pauline letter, discipleship is marked out as genuine in 2 Timothy by perseverance in suffering. Living without sin in Christ is not an escape from daily struggle. Ch. 2 makes clear, however, that a disciple's suffering for Christ's sake is not necessarily the physical or emotional result of persecution or ridicule at the hands of God's enemies. Perhaps because it is addressed to a successor of the Pauline apostolate, who is gifted by the Spirit and ordained by the apostle to teach others (2:2), Timothy's share of suffering results from a demanding workload that requires self-sacrifice and hard work (vv. 3-6). That is, the work assigned to Timothy, if modeled after Paul's and acceptable in God's sight, requires him to "interpret the word of truth" (v. 15) in a manner that avoids idle and thoughtless chitchat (vv. 16, 23), avoids vice in pursuit of personal virtue (v. 22), and seeks to persuade opponents to knowledge of the truth (v. 25). This is the workload of the "special utensil" of an "impressive house" which God sets apart to wage a hard-fought battle with the devil.

The plotline of Paul's story of the believer's baptism into the risen Christ, especially found in Romans 6, can be traced in the canonical saying quoted in 2 Tim 2:11-13: believers share in the death, life, and coming reign of the living One (vv. 11b-12a), and this makes a difference in how they live and what they experience. Even so, an ambivalence characterizes this story of God's victory (cf. Rom 6:12): God's firm foundation stands (2:19), and God remains faithful to a redemptive plan even when the covenant community fails God (v. 13). But this has a condition: "if we persevere." The prospect of spiritual failure hangs on every imperative. To illustrate, another pair of opponents, Hymenaeus and Philetus, once believers, are now at work "subverting the faith of some" (v. 18).

Despair is a constant threat for the Christian facing persistent opposition and hardship in the world, even within the congregation. The conflicts with Paul's opponents provide, however, a setting in which the faithfulness of God to the community is disclosed (2:13, 19). Even the exercise of God's grace, which "permits a change of mind" and allows the opponent to return to a "knowledge of the truth" (v. 25), reveals divine providence and is a constant source of courage and confidence in the midst of suffering and opposition. In fact, this dependence on the faithfulness of God that extends even to opponents is the source of Timothy's protection. Paul's bold and repeated claim that God has kept him from harm's way (1:12; 3:11; 4:17; cf. Acts 27), rather than an appeal to the rule of law or ecclesial office, testifies to the real power behind the apostolate.

2 Timothy 3 The apocalyptic scenario that begins this chapter imagines a cache of vices that describe those who oppose the word of truth (3:8). Again, Paul's implied claim is that the word of truth, which sets out a pattern of healthy teaching, orders human life in a manner that loves God rather than self-centered pleasure (v. 4). When this truth is rejected, the results are morally catastrophic. "Knowing this" is central to Christian catechesis instruction (v. 1), and so the very mark of spiritual immaturity is to "forever learn but never come to knowledge of the truth" (v. 7) even as the essential characteristic of the enemies of God is that they "ruin the mind and counterfeit the faith" (v. 8). Knowing the apostolic rule of faith is baseline for Christian existence, not only because it empowers good works but enables one to know who and what religious impiety and ethical impurity to avoid. But the stated purpose of this Pauline apocalypse is to sound a cautionary note ever present to its readers "until that day": the cultural situation of the present age is "dangerous" precisely because it makes the prospect of sharing in Christ's sinlessness a very hard possibility. While moral purity and genuine piety (cf. 1 Tim 6:3-10) herald the coming victory of God over sin and death, intermingling with "deluded lovers of pleasure rather than God" is a threat to Christian existence that must be avoided (3:4-5).

Imitation of moral exemplars is a topos of paraenetic literature to this day. And there is no better example of its use in the NT than this Timothy correspondence. The prospect of Timothy's succession to the Pauline apostolate adds urgency to the normal import of role models. Paul's repeated depiction as Timothy's role model, closely observed (1:13; 2:2; 3:10, 14; 4:6-8), must be read in the context of a letter of succession with its clear expectation that Timothy's imitation of the departed Paul is indispensable in the succession to his apostolate into the next "post-Pauline" generation (cf. Acts 20:17-35). It is, of course, this approach that the reader now takes toward the Pauline canon: it is the indispensable resource for learning the Pauline tradition in the absence of the apostle who founded it.

The piety Paul exemplifies is set out in a catalog of virtues headed by his teaching and pattern of life (v. 10). Once again, the prospect of suffering — in this case the result of persecution rather than of hard work — is mentioned, including place-names that correspond to the narrative of Paul's suffering in Acts. The interpreter who appropriately prepares for this letter by reading Acts will recall that the Lord's commission of Paul indicated that he would "suffer much for the sake of my name" (Acts 9:16). It is less clear from the story itself — or from this letter — why suffering is anticipated as a dimension of loyalty to the tradition, other than that imitation of the apostle includes sharing in his suffering. The juxtaposition of 3:1-9 and vv. 10-13, however, explains the suffering of the righteous in apocalyptic terms as the historical precipitate of spiritual warfare between the forces of good and evil. The suffering theme in this letter makes it difficult to defend the premise that the Pastoral Epistles, taken as a whole, indicate a move toward a domesticated church that averts hardship by conforming to social convention.

Paul writes that the "man of God" (= Timothy) who uses Scripture is "made mature for every good work" (3:17). Much has been written about the Pastoral Epistles' interest in "good work(s),"[8] not only because the phrase is not found in the letters thought to be authentically from Paul but because it occurs so often in Pastoral Epistles: fourteen times and in a variety of settings. The addition of "every" to "good work" in 3:17 (cf. 2 Cor 9:8; Col 1:10; 2 Thess 2:17) suggests a habit of doing good things, following Aristotle's teaching. The theological shape of this idea is that Christian existence is marked out by good work of all kinds (cf. Tit 2:7), such as philanthropic work (1 Tim 2:10), domestic work (1 Tim 5:10), monetary policy (1 Tim 6:18), and vocational work (2 Tim 2:21). Most often, good works are described by Christ-like virtues and result from the believer's baptism into Christ by faith. That is, good works naturally result when someone is saved from sinning and remade by divine grace into an agent of moral rectitude.

This idea as it gets worked out in the Pastoral Epistles is no different from what is found elsewhere in the Pauline canon — that is, surely good

---

8. See I. H. Marshall's excellent excursus on "goodness and good works in the Pastoral Epistles" in *A Critical and Exegetical Commentary on the Pastoral Epistles* (ICC; Edinburgh: Clark, 1999), 227-29.

works has not displaced the importance of depending on divine grace for salvation (2 Tim 1:9 repeats the Pauline formula of salvation by grace alone). But its role as the measure of the Christian life is expanded. In particular, Paul elaborates on Scripture's role as the Spirit's auxiliary in bringing one to moral maturity. In this case, Scripture's role is not to provide direct answers to moral problems; rather, it is to cultivate a spiritual maturity that enables the "man of God" to discern those moral practices that, when executed "in the presence of God and Christ Jesus" (4:1), will secure their approval. Catalogs of virtues and vices and lists of practices found in the Pauline canon suggest what these moral practices look like on the ground.

Excursus: The Role of Scripture in the Formation of a Faithful Church

A proper theology of Holy Scripture attaches both its production and performance — that is, its material existence as a literary text — to God's providential care for creation and in particular to God's desire to repair all things broken according to God's redemptive purposes. The Bible's authority is not predicated on the identity and intentions of its divinely inspired authors,[9] on the divine nature of its inerrant propositions, or on the artfulness of the biblical text understood in its original historical settings. Rather, the Bible's authority as God's word for the church is predicated on God's persistent use of the Bible to bring to realization God's purposes for the world. In this sense, the Bible's authority is defended here by a long history of evident usefulness as an auxiliary of God's Spirit in the reordering of its faithful readers according to the Creator's good intentions for them — what Paul calls "wisdom for salvation" and "maturity for good works" in 2 Tim 3:15-17.[10]

---

9. The modern conception of the divine inspiration of biblical authors (rather than of particular texts) is of a piece with Protestantism's definition of apostolicity in terms of historical figures. That is, the primary justification of Scripture's authority is the divine inspiration of Christ's apostles, whose verbal inspiration enables them to write sacred texts that are infallible in content and plenary in scope. What follows defines the divine inspiration of Scripture differently and so shifts its basis for Scripture's authority accordingly.

10. It is one of the principal theses of W. J. Abraham's "canonical theism" that the church's epistemic criterion is divine revelation, especially in the Son, not Scripture. Scripture and all other auxiliaries of the Spirit function first and foremost soteriologically. These earthen vessels are transformed under the Spirit's direction into a "complex means of grace that restores the image of God in human beings and brings them into communion with God and with each other in the church." *Canonical Theism* (Grand Rapids: Eerdmans, 2008), 3. While Abraham needs to develop a more adequate description of the overlapping relationship between Scrip-

Scripture must also be attached to belief in the Son's incarnation of God's truth and mediation of God's redemptive purposes. The Son is the definitive medium of God's self-presentation, not Scripture. It is by him that we come to know the truth about God and experience God's redemptive purpose for all of life. It is critical to an incarnational Christology that this absolute claim for truth is *particular;* that is, truth resides in history in the body of a single creature, the man Christ Jesus (1 Tim 2:5), who is the Son of God bodily or "creaturely" (so Col 2:9). The Bible can lay no claim to absolute truth; its claim to truth is predicated on the trustworthiness of its witness to the truth incarnate in the Son.

This is not a judgment that the church makes about its Scripture but a judgment made on behalf of all believers by the Holy Spirit, whose activity sanctifies texts and gathers them into the biblical canon — a material "creature" which is "hallowed" — set apart — in order to facilitate God's redemptive purposes. The role of the Holy Spirit, in the absence of the incarnate One, is to find substitutes or material "auxiliaries" that are sanctified to continue to present the way, the truth, and the life to the community of disciples that it indwells. Scripture is sanctified by the Spirit for its use as a holy instrument of God's self-presentation by which the way of God is known and life with God is made possible.

Some scholars still press for the usefulness of an analogy of Scripture's nature to Christ in that both have "two natures," human and divine.[11] But J. Webster's cautionary note seems right: "The Word made flesh and the scriptural word are in no way equivalent realities." The most we should allow is that one can speak of both Christ and Scripture as "human" and "divine." But they are not equivalent humanities or divinities, nor do the Son and Scripture perform equivalent roles as agents of God's salvation or media of God's revelation. As Webster writes, use of this analogy "can scarcely avoid divinizing the Bible" and claiming an "ontological identity" between the God-like propositions of the Bible and Christ who is God.[12] At a theological level, this will lead to idolatry; at a practical level, it will lead to the use of Scripture as the "epistemic criterion" by which all truth in every domain is measured and confirmed. (Our concerns with the claim of the Bible's "inerrancy" reside here; such a claim seems misdirected to us.)

---

ture's role in revealing God's word and its role within the life of a congregation to cultivate a maturity that enables it to perform good works, I agree with his essential "thesis."

11. See now Peter Enns, *Inspiration and Incarnation: Evangelicals and the Problem of the Old Testament* (Grand Rapids: Baker, 2005), 13-21.

12. John Webster, *Holy Scripture: A Dogmatic Sketch* (Cambridge: Cambridge University Press, 2003), 23.

Given these difficulties with Scripture's analogy to Christ, even if used modestly for illustrative purposes, inclines us toward another analogy: Scripture's analogy to the church. This analogy avoids the ontological difficulty mentioned above. Further, it makes theological sense. That is, assuming that God's redemptive purposes are embodied in the covenant-keeping community and that the Spirit hallows the material or textual properties of Scripture — a "treasure in an earthen vessel" — in order to redeem and reorder the community according to the ways of God, then it follows that the nature of this reordered community is of a piece with the nature of the sanctified text.

If the church confesses that its creaturely existence is marked out as "one, holy, catholic, and apostolic" — these are the material properties of God's redemptive purposes when embodied in the mature church — then it follows logically that the material properties of Scripture properly used/read "to teach, correct, reprove, and train in justice" in bringing believers to maturity as the people of God (2 Tim 3:16-17), are of a piece with the church: that is, Scripture is similarly marked out by the same Spirit that calls the church into existence by its oneness, holiness, catholicity, and apostolicity. What is true of the church is also true of its Scripture.

We can define each of these markers as a material property of Scripture:

(1) The oneness of Scripture: If the oneness of the church is defined by its uniqueness and its unity — neither of which is easy to defend on the evidence — so too is the oneness of Scripture defined by its uniqueness and its unity — also difficult to defend against the assured conclusions of modern criticism.[13] A further question may be raised about the church's multiple canons: In what sense is the Bible "one" if it exists in multiple literary or canonical forms? In short, the Bible is unique in the same way the church is unique: in the distinctiveness of its purpose and practices.

(2) The holiness of Scripture: If the holiness of the church is characterized by the unfolding sanctification of its membership as the concrete effect of its purity practices (religious and moral, individual and corporate) with the effect that it is set apart for worship of and witness to a holy God, so too is the holiness of Scripture characterized by the effect its various practices have in purifying its readers and making them holy. This analogy is also hard to sustain in the face of a "scandal of appearances." The church is more hypocritical than holy, and the reading of the Bible is easily corrupted to serve self-centered ambition. For Scripture to have its holy effect on readers, its interpretation and practice must be orderly — that is, ordered by aiming our reading and use to God's redemptive purposes for all creation.

---

13. See, e.g., Daniel J. Treier, "Scripture, Unity of," *DTIB* 731-34.

(3) The catholicity of Scripture: If the character of the church's catholicity is its global reach and its inclusion of a network of redeemed yet diverse members (cf. Rev 5:9-10), so too is it in the very nature of Scripture to be read by all Christians of every shape and size as their common book. M. Gorman puts Scripture's catholicity this way: "all Scripture is written for all God's people in all ages and all places."[14] A catholic approach to Scripture, then, does not find what is there not to like but recognizes what is true in all that is written and so what to embrace as God's vision for all of life. The catholicity of Scripture also insists that no right interpretation is a private matter but is for the body of Christ shaped by the apostolic witness to him.

Not only does the catholicity of Scripture attend to the usefulness of its every part, but it also suggests that every part is useful for all the church. This marker became pivotal during the canonical process when the canonicity of certain sacred texts was disputed precisely because of the limited geographical scope of its usefulness. Again, the late arrival of the Pastoral Epistles to the Pauline corpus was not due to questionable authorship or content. The mistake often made by modern criticism is to equate the terms of a text's compositional history — who wrote it and when — with its canonical authority. While a text's apostolicity, however this is finally defined (see below), is also required for its reception as canonical, so also is the catholic scope of its reception and religious utility.

(4) The apostolicity of Scripture: The church is of and by the apostles; their witness to the incarnate Word of life is the plumb line of Christian proclamation and the criterion of the community's *koinonia* with God and God's Son (1 John 1:1-5). As Irenaeus put it, the fourfold Gospel of Jesus congregates "the gospels of the apostles." The apostles' teaching and exemplary life define Christian discipleship (2 Tim 1:12-14). As B. S. Childs put it, "apostolicity became a dynamic term to encompass historical, substantive, functional, and personal qualities of the most basic core of the faith."[15] In this sense, to confess itself as apostolic is to admit a community's canonization of Christ's apostolate as the principal carrier of his divine truth. By analogy and in the absence of the apostles, Scripture's apostolicity assumes that it is the medium of the present witness to the incarnation.

Our study of Scripture's nature — what kind of text it is — intends to guide our approach to its interpretation and instruction. If Scripture is all of

---

14. Michael J. Gorman, *Elements of Biblical Exegesis: A Basic Guide for Students and Ministers* (rev. ed.; Peabody: Hendrickson, 2001).

15. Brevard S. Childs, *The Church's Guide for Reading Paul: The Canonical Shaping of the Pauline Corpus* (Grand Rapids: Eerdmans, 2008), 21.

the above, then our interpretations and instruction of it must be of a piece with what it is. Consider Webster's central point again: if our proper understanding of a theology of Scripture is shaped in relationship with the triune God and our beliefs about a God who is at work in history in putting to rights a broken, fragmented world, then our readings and uses of Scripture must seek this same result. Sharply put, biblical interpretation and instruction must serve the interests of the Holy Trinity, whose chief purpose is to put the world to rights.

---

2 Timothy 4 The spiritual maturity facilitated by Bible study forges a way of thinking about the source of "healthy teaching" (= a Pauline rule of faith) that enables individual believers to distinguish gospel truth from conspiracy theories (4:3-4). What is crucial to understand about the practical role of this critical discipline, characteristic of the spiritual leader brought to maturity by the Spirit's use of Scripture (3:17), is that the succession of Paul's apostolate is not of his apostolic office but of his theo-logic, which shapes a way of thinking and teaching about God. We have argued that the succession of Paul is not of those special tasks only he is given by God to perform (see below on Tit 1:3); rather, the succession of Paul regards the church's magisterial office in which his apostolic tradition is passed on from teacher to other teachers so that they can prepare still others to teach (2 Tim 2:2) — not unlike the holy calling issued in Jesus' "Great Commission" by Matthew's Jesus (Matt 28:20). The images of the act of effective teaching and the role of the teacher of Pauline doctrine set within the sacred household help to form the special vocabulary of the Pastoral Epistles and its distinctive definition of Christian piety.

The most striking feature of the concluding benediction is how ordinary Paul's concerns seem for his personal well-being (e.g., 4:13, 21), especially when read after the announcement of his imminent death (v. 6). There is a sense in which this jarring contrast is similar to the ending of Acts (Acts 28:17-31). In that rhetorical seam linking Paul's story in Acts with the Pauline canon that follows, Paul awaits his audience with the Roman emperor by simply being Paul: preaching the gospel to all who visit him in his rented flat in downtown Rome (Acts 28:30-31; cf. Rom 1:13-15). Here also in 2 Timothy Paul awaits his death by living his life. He expresses concern about his colleagues and missionary network, those who are for and against his instruction; he wants his coat before winter comes, perhaps in preparation for a mission trip to Spain; he wants his library, presumably to continue his study. The Christian life mostly consists of those mundane tasks and concerns that have come to define who we are by sacred calling. Yes, the awareness of one's death occasions a time of retrospection (so 4:7), but the reality of death does not prompt one to abandon what one has been called to do as a servant of God.

Consummation in a New Creation: *"Christ will come with glory to take the saints to the enjoyment of everlasting life and of the heavenly promises, and to condemn the wicked to everlasting fire, after the resurrection of both these classes shall have happened, together with the restoration of their flesh."*

The old objection that the Pastoral Epistles depart from the other Pauline letters by their lack of eschatology is puzzling both methodologically and theologically, and few scholars who specialize in these texts would agree with it any longer. What should be said, however, is that Paul's core beliefs about God's coming victory over death are always adapted to the particular concerns of the particular letter. Because the Pastoral Epistles address the pastoral crisis of a departed apostle and the hard work of preserving and adapting the normative traditions linked to his apostolate to different settings in his absence, these core beliefs are sometimes articulated in settled, formulaic terms, which are the literary shape of a norm. But the use of this genre in the Pastoral Epistles does not indicate the end of eschatology beyond Paul or the replacement of his apocalyptic religion with a domesticated or institutionalized one.

In the context of this letter of succession, images of the future gather around the perseverance of an apostolic tradition "for that day" (1:12) or the Lord's coming judgment of individuals "on that day" (4:1, 6-8). That is, the criterion that orchestrates the end of time is imitation of Paul (1:18) and adherence to his teaching (2:15; 4:14); on this basis tradents will "experience salvation in Christ Jesus with eternal glory" (2:10), and to deny Paul's gospel is ultimately to deny the Lord (vv. 12-13). In fact, the Pastoral Epistles' routine use of the phrase "in the presence of God" (2:15; 4:1) suggests a divine review of work done (or not done). We have argued that loyalty to the person of Paul and his apostolate is a criterion of this review.

The framework for this adaptation of Pauline eschatology is the two epiphanies of Christ. The first "appearing of our Savior Christ Jesus" illumines the nature and target of God's grace (1:9-10), while his second appearance will be "to judge the living and the dead" (4:1). Confession of Christ's past exaltation as the risen and vindicated One (so 1 Tim 3:16) underwrites the church's hope for his future epiphany to judge the unfaithful and reward the faithful.

The present situation of the church is between these two appearances in the time called "the last days." During that time self-love trumps love for God and counterfeit religion is more popular than apostolic faith (3:1-9; cf. 4:9). How life and faith are worked out in such a situation — whether the fight is fought, the race finished, and the faith kept (4:6) — not only determines the succession of the Pauline apostolate into the future but whether one will participate in the coming reign of God (1:18; 4:7-8, 14-16, 18). In this sense, then, the future of God breaks in on the present of God's people as the motive of faithful endurance, since the believer's future depends on how faithfully life is currently lived in the presence of God and Christ Jesus (v. 1).

2 Timothy 1   The repetition of "that day" in the letter's opening chapter illustrates what is distinctive about the eschatology of a succession letter: the future of God's salvation is replaced by concern for the future of Paul's apostolate. God's eschatological power, the effective working of which insures the complete realization of what God has purposed to do, is now exercised to preserve Paul's legacy as "herald, apostle, and teacher" (1:11-12). This idea is not self-serving but is inextricably attached to the gospel that announces the "appearing of our Savior Christ Jesus." Nonetheless, there can be no doubting Paul's strategic importance in God's redemptive plan, which is reflected in the expression of hope that Onesiphorus's household will "find mercy from the Lord on that day" (of judgment; cf. 4:1).

2 Timothy 2   The Lord's second appearance "on that day" "to judge the living and the dead" (4:1) is based on his resurrection, which concluded his first appearance. In Pauline thought, Christ's resurrection has begun a new age, heralded by a new humanity united with the living Jesus, in whom "newness of life" is experienced and the "old" passes away. The implicit eschatology of the canonical saying in 2:11-13 trades on Paul's resurrection Christology, rooted in his Damascus road christophany and the changes in him that followed from it (cf. 1 Tim 1:12-16): believers die, live, and will reign with Christ "on that day."

Framed by the two-epiphany model, anticipation of the elect's participation with Christ in the coming victory of God over death is muted somewhat by the warning that God will deny those who deny God, who remains ever faithful to the plan. The conditional nature of promised covenant blessings is an incentive not to fear but to "wage the fight, finish the race, keep the faith," without which there does not remain a "champion's wreath" (4:7-8).

Images of ill-health and destruction are used to intimate God's future judgment of the consequences of false teaching. This ultimate consequence of bad theology is a principal theme of other NT letters (e.g., 2 Peter, Jude) and is of a piece with the essential Pauline understanding of God's coming victory over sin and death. That is, the new creation, inaugurated at the Lord's return, will be purified of all those various causes of ill-health, whether of body, soul, or intellect (ignorance). Ironically, it is the resurrection of Jesus that provides evidence of his return and the nature of its effect on the cosmos.

The apocalyptic connection between the devil and death is implicit in ch. 2's concluding purpose clause, which allows that Timothy's schooling of his opponents toward repentance will result in their escape from the "devil's trap." Coming to the truth and so "to their senses" is a trope for conversion to Christ, the destiny of which is eternal life (1:10).

2 Timothy 3 According to the periodic compartmentalization of history sponsored by apocalyptic Judaism, "the last days" is a season of spiritual testing over an indefinite period of time immediately prior to the Messiah's final actions to inaugurate the new creation promised by God (e.g., the rewriting of LXX Joel 3:1 in Acts 2:17). The present moment is "the last days," and they are "dangerous times" precisely because faith is imperiled — that is, these are dangerous days for an immature people because of an overabundance of clever pundits who "ruin the mind and counterfeit the faith" (3:8) to promote a "deluded love of pleasure rather than of God" (v. 4).

Against this apocalyptic scenario, Paul gives a triad of exhortations that prepares Timothy, in full view of God, for the coming of Christ Jesus to judge the living and the dead. In particular Paul presents himself as a role model for the end of time (3:10-13) and Scripture as an auxiliary of the divine breath to make "the man of God" "wise for salvation" and "mature for every good work" (vv. 14-17).

2 Timothy 4 In a letter that emphasizes suffering for Christ's sake as the mark of fidelity to the gospel, the resolution of the problem of theodicy — why would a good God allow people to suffer as result of covenant-keeping — is delayed to "that day" when those who have "finished the race and kept the faith" will be vindicated and rewarded. Not surprisingly, the eschatological Paul personifies this expectation, when his good works are to be duly rewarded (4:8).

This formula of divine justice cuts two ways. On the one hand, there is a day set aside for God's vindication of those who remain faithful, especially to their holy calling (cf. 1:9), "whenever suffering bad news" (4:5). On the other hand, God's vindication is conditioned on their meeting certain performance standards. God's sense of justice is not *sola fideistic* or somehow muted by Christ's work on behalf of the elect. God demands evidence — "every good work" — of one's faithful endurance (v. 7; cf. 2:13). In this sense, only those who follow Paul's example have reason to "love Christ's appearance" (4:8), when he will judge the living and the dead. Certainly not Demas or Alexander the coppersmith, who have abandoned Paul or done him great harm: their repayment from Jesus the judge will be something other than a champion's wreath!

Paul repeats his witness to the Lord's rescue from personal difficulty (4:17; cf. 3:11), which is a remarkable feature of this letter but hardly unique in the biblical witness. He interprets these events as typological of God's eschatological rescue of the faithful from death "for his heavenly kingdom" (4:18). Consistent with the Pastoral Epistles' depiction of a canonical Paul, his life personifies salvation's future.

This idea of a future judgment based on works, not faith, is consistent with Pauline instruction elsewhere. In Rom 2:5-6 — a hard text avoided by most Protestant interpreters — Paul writes that God's rectitude will be disclosed "on the day of wrath" by a judgment of every individual based on works, since "God shows no partiality" (Rom 2:11). Even when Paul later argues that these holy works that result in eternal life are the by-product of being set free from sin by God's grace through faith in the risen Christ (Rom 6:4-11, 22-23), the deep logic of his gospel is that lack of one surely evinces lack of the other.

Case Study: John William Fletcher, John Wesley's Designated Successor

> *Hold to a pattern of healthy teaching you have heard from me with the fidelity and loyalty that are in Christ Jesus. Protect the good tradition through the Holy Spirit who indwells you. (2 Tim 1:13-14)*

Wall has argued that 2 Timothy is a "succession letter," that is, an exhortation by the apostle to his young protégé to accept the mantle of church leadership after the apostle's death — a death presumed to be imminent — and a delineation of various personal qualities and ministerial practices vital to the faithful and productive execution of that role. Accordingly, it seems appropriate to select for this case study John Fletcher, who was designated as the successor of John Wesley, who was profiled in the case study for 1 Timothy, and to examine through the interpretive lens of 2 Timothy why Fletcher was so designated.

Wesley sought out Fletcher, unsuccessfully as it turned out, to govern Methodism after Wesley's death. This succession narrative can tell us much about how Christian leaders actively identify promising members of the rising generation on whom to confer the mantle of spiritual authority and about the complex reactions of the chosen successors, who must wrestle with whether they are truly called to and fully adequate for the daunting interpretive and practical tasks ahead.

I

John William Fletcher was born on September 11 (?), 1729, in Nyon, Switzerland. This town is located in Canton Vaud, in the predominantly French-speaking southwestern corner of the country, and French was not only Fletcher's mother tongue but the language in which he wrote many of his letters and some of his poetic and theological writings, even after he had become an English citizen and Anglican clergyman. His parents were well-to-do members of the minor nobility and were able to send him to school in nearby Geneva. Fletcher's most recent biographer notes the significance of this move for his later theological development. During the late seventeenth century, many Swiss Protestant cantons, including Vaud and Geneva, had adopted the Swiss Consensus Formula (1675) as a reassertion of traditional Calvinist doctrine against the so-called "reasonable orthodoxy" of Moïse Amyraut (1596-1644), a Huguenot theologian who taught at the Protestant Academy of Saumur. Amyraut had affirmed "universal grace," that is, the doctrine that redemption was available to all who had faith in Christ. Although Amyraut considered himself a follower of John Calvin rather than of Jacob Arminius, he stoutly rejected the anti-Arminian Canons of the Synod of Dort (1618-19) for much the same reason that Arminius had rejected the teachings of Theodore Beza and Franciscus Gomarus, namely, that they ascribed the damnation of the reprobate to the express will of God. When John Fletcher began his university studies, his home canton of Vaud continued to affirm the strongly predestinarian Consensus Formula against Amyraldism, whereas Geneva had begun to entertain the ideas of Amyraut. There is strong evidence that Fletcher's early theological views were influenced by Amyraldism, and that this predisposed him, when he later moved to England, to the Arminian theology of John and Charles Wesley.

During his student years, Fletcher appears to have felt the first inklings of a calling to the ministry. Yet he held back from applying for ordination, partly because of his theological objections to the Consensus Formula, which as a citizen of Vaud he would have been required to sign, but partly also because of a sense that, despite the rather perfervid piety he now displayed, he lacked the requisite spiritual maturity. Some years later, he described his spiritual condition during this period:

> At eighteen years of age I was a real enthusiast; for though I lived in the indulgence of many known sins, I considered myself a religious character, because I regularly attended public worship, made long prayers in private, and devoted as much time as I could spare from my studies to reading the prophetic writings and a few devotional books. My feelings were easily excited, but my heart was rarely affected; and, notwithstanding these deceitful externals, I was destitute of a sincere love to God, and consequently to my neighbor. All my hopes of salvation rested on my prayers, devotions, and a certain habit of saying, "Lord, I am a great sinner, pardon me for the sake of Jesus Christ." In the meantime I was ignorant of

the fall and ruin in which every man is involved, the necessity of a Redeemer, and the way by which we may be rescued from the fall by receiving Christ with a living faith.[1]

Feeling unqualified for the cloth, Fletcher briefly considered a career as a soldier, but several opportunities for service were foiled by circumstances beyond his control. And so in 1750, at the age of twenty-one, he traveled to England to seek his fortune. For a year he attended a boarding school to learn English, and then he became the private tutor of the sons of Thomas Hill, a member of the landed gentry in Shropshire, a position he held for nine years. Hill's duties in Parliament required him to shuttle frequently back and forth between his country estate and London, and he regularly took his family — and his sons' tutor — with him. On one such visit to London Fletcher encountered the Methodists, and their principles and practices resonated deeply with him. He promptly joined the London society and found great comfort in reading Wesley's *Journal.* This precipitated the kind of spiritual crisis that was typical of members of the Wesleyan revival. Though his outward life was irreproachable, he was plagued by intense scrupulosity and a deep fear that his "pretended piety" was self-serving and hypocritical.

On January 24, 1754, Fletcher experienced a profound sense of release from the guilt and power of sin, and, after the usual period of self-doubts and spiritual vicissitudes, he found an assurance of salvation that would endure for the remainder of his life. On August 24 he composed a Covenant with God, in which he promised to "give, restore, consecrate [and] dispose" his mind, body, property, and life to God's service and to "seek, ask, demand [and] importune" from God the forgiveness of all his past sins and any future ones, grace in time of temptation, and power to practice the means of grace — prayer, meditation, Scripture study, and the reception of the Eucharist — with fervor and diligence.[2]

By 1757, Fletcher's vocation to the Christian ministry had come into sharp focus for him. In March of that year he was ordained a deacon and then a priest and installed as curate at Madeley in Shropshire. But he did not immediately take up residence in the town, nor did he leave the Hills' service, al-

---

1. "The Conversion of Mr. Fletcher, Related by Himself, In a Letter to his Brother," *WJF* 4:48-49. This curious document actually consists of two separate letters. Neither the dates on which these letters were composed nor the name of the editor who rather awkwardly stitched them together for this brief essay is given.

2. The text of this covenant is reproduced in full and exhaustively analyzed in Patrick Philipp Streiff, *Reluctant Saint? A Theological Biography of Fletcher of Madeley* (trans. G. W. S. Knowles; Peterborough: Epworth, 2001), 34-40.

though his responsibilities as their sons' tutor waned as the boys grew older. Opportunities to preach in Anglican churches in the area came along, and the Wesley brothers were eager to recruit him for itinerancy in the Methodist societies. In 1758, John Wesley introduced Fletcher to Lady Selina Hastings, the Countess of Huntingdon, a prominent sponsor of Methodist activities, and thereafter she frequently invited him to preach and celebrate the Eucharist in her private chapel. Moreover, there was considerable opposition to Fletcher's desire to become the vicar of Madeley — both from his Methodist friends, who argued that such rustication was "the snare of the devil,"[3] and from the regional ecclesiastical authorities, who did not want an evangelical serving as a parish priest in their diocese. Nevertheless, by autumn 1760 the official obstacles to his appointment, though not Wesley's opposition, had vanished, and in a manner that Fletcher himself regarded as providential. On October 26 of that year Fletcher preached his inaugural sermon at Madeley. He would serve as the vicar of that parish for the remainder of his life.

Doing so did not end his affiliation with the Methodists. It did, of course, reduce his freedom to itinerate, but it also enabled him to perform several services to Methodism that full-time itinerancy might have prevented. First, he sponsored the establishment of Methodist bands and classes in and around Madeley and so enabled Methodist sentiments to penetrate church life more deeply there than could happen in most Anglican parishes, whose priests were hostile or indifferent to the revival. Second, in 1768 he was able to accept the presidency of the Countess of Huntingdon's new theological seminary in Trevecca, Wales. Regrettably, his service in that capacity ended only three years later, when an irreparable split occurred in Methodist ranks between the Arminian followers of the Wesleys and the Calvinist followers of Whitefield and the Countess. Yet it is worth noting that Fletcher was held in such esteem by both sides that, despite his outspoken affiliation with the Arminians, he was not dismissed from his office by the Countess but quietly resigned as an act of solidarity after the ouster of an Arminian faculty member. Finally, and most importantly, Fletcher emerged in the 1770s as the most profound and articulate theologian of the Arminian wing of the Methodist movement, but also as one committed to rapprochement with the Calvinists.

As we have seen, Wesley had tried to dissuade Fletcher from settling at Madeley, and in subsequent years he repeatedly urged him to resign his pas-

---

3. John Fletcher, Letter to John Wesley, October 27, 1760, in *"Unexampled Labours": Letters of the Revd. John Fletcher to Leaders in the Evangelical Revival* (ed. Peter S. Forsaith; Peterborough: Epworth, 2008), 116-17, quoting Wesley's own words from an earlier letter to himself, now lost. On the following day he wrote to the Countess of Huntingdon and mentioned Wesley's inflammatory words; see Streiff, *Reluctant Saint?* 64-65.

torate and take up full-time service as a Methodist traveling preacher. Most Methodist preachers of the time were laymen, and opportunities for rapid advancement in the Connexion were open to Anglican priests who were willing to forsake the comfort and security of parish life for the rigors of itinerancy. But very few were willing, and until the 1780s Wesley made little effort to recruit them and certainly had no thought of conferring holy orders on his most talented "assistants." Fletcher was a conspicuous exception, however, and Wesley tried not only to solicit his assistance but also to appoint him as his successor. Indeed, on one astonishing occasion Wesley apparently offered Fletcher immediate command of the Connexion in his stead, volunteering to remain as Fletcher's adjutant. We do not have Wesley's original letter, but we do have a quotation from it in a letter that Fletcher wrote to Wesley's brother Charles, dated August 19, 1761:

> Your brother [John] has done me the goodness to write to me very recently. The extract from his letter is: "You are not fit to be alone. You will do and receive much better among us. Come, and if you do not want to be my equal, I will be below you, etc." In my last I mentioned to him that I was prepared to quit my benefice without repugnance should providence give me the signal, far from feeling myself attached here by particular views: but I make a distinction between his obliging invitation and the ordering of providence: I don't care to leave my post before I have been relieved by the sentry: I came passively, I will go in the same way.[4]

As far as we know, John Wesley never again offered to subordinate himself to Fletcher, but he continued to seek Fletcher's services as a traveling preacher and to offer him control of the revival after his own death. Of particular interest is a letter from Wesley to Fletcher dated January 15(?), 1773, in which he acknowledged that the "wise men of the world" were right in expecting the revival to die with him unless someone were found who had the sanctity, learnedness, and spiritual authority to govern the increasingly obstreperous and disunited band of preachers. I will quote from and analyze this letter below. Here it suffices to note that in his reply Fletcher assured the aging patriarch that in the event of his death Fletcher would "help your brother" to "gather the wreck, and keep together those who are not absolutely bent to throw away the Methodist doctrines and disciplines." He made no

---

4. Forsaith, *"Unexampled Labours,"* 134. This letter, like so many of Fletcher's letters to Charles Wesley, was written in French; Forsaith gives the original text as well as a translation. I have slightly amended the punctuation and capitalization of the translation. See also Streiff, *Reluctant Saint?* 133 and 326, which give a slightly different translation of the same letter.

mention of resigning his living at Madeley, but he affirmed his readiness "to resume my office as your Deacon, not with any view of presiding over the Methodists after you, but to ease you a little in your old age, and to be in the way of recovering, perhaps doing, more good."[5]

But what exactly did being Wesley's "deacon" mean? It clearly did *not* mean agreeing to be Wesley's successor. Wesley was surely right in supposing that *if* Fletcher were ever to become the leader of the Methodists, he would have to begin itinerating when Wesley was still alive to itinerate with him, groom him for his role, and prepare the other preachers and the societies to acknowledge his authority. Fletcher apparently *was* willing to join Wesley occasionally on his preaching tours, although the first practical opportunity to do so would not arise for several more years. But he would never accept the designation of heir presumptive. How are we to explain his refusal? It appears that he had several reasons.

First, we must take at face value Fletcher's repeated assertion that he never felt that providence "gave him the signal" to resign his pastorate. Whether he ever *desired* to be the leader of the Methodists, he felt *called* to be the vicar of Madeley, and whatever veneration he may have had for John Wesley, it did not override his profound conviction that God intended him to remain at his post in Shropshire.

Second, Fletcher was a person of great modesty and self-diffidence, and these lifelong aspects of his character were deepened, not abated, by his conversion experience in 1754, when he first felt the assurance that divine grace was operating in his life. It would surely be incorrect to accuse him of harboring a "spirit of cowardice" (2 Tim 1:7), for he was never averse to giving bold Christian witness in private conversation, from the pulpit, or in print. Yet Fletcher exhibited humility almost to a fault and was naturally reluctant — even if he had felt divinely called — to take center stage.

Third, if it was gauche of Wesley to propose, in 1761, that Fletcher resign from Madeley after less than a year of service there, it was odd of Wesley to suggest, in 1773, that Fletcher undertake full-time itinerancy when he was embroiled, on Wesley's behalf, in a furious controversy with the Calvinist branch of the Methodist movement. Space does not permit us to go into this convoluted story. It is sufficient here to say that the minutes of the Methodist Annual Conference of 1770 appeared to the Calvinists to confirm their worst fears about Wesley, namely, that his long-standing repudiation of the doctrines of double predestination and limited atonement would finally lead him

---

5. Letter of John Fletcher to John Wesley, February 6, 1773, quoted in Wesley, *Short Account, WJW* 11:301-2.

to compromise on the doctrine of salvation by faith alone and thereby to capitulate on the very thing that supposedly qualified Methodism as "evangelical." Whatever other services Fletcher made to the Wesleyan branch of Methodism, his contributions to the Minutes Controversy were outstanding. He produced a stream of apologetic treatises, uncompromising in content but irenic in tone, between 1771 and 1775, which included six *Checks to Antinomianism,* two *Equal Checks to Pharisaism and Antinomianism,* and a number of ancillary works. In vindicating the Minutes from the charge of Pelagianism, Fletcher furnished Arminian Methodism with a thoroughgoing program for balancing free grace against free will, faith against good works, and human depravity against Christian perfection.

A fourth reason Fletcher had for refusing to undertake the full-time itinerancy that was the condition for his becoming the eventual leader of the Methodists was that he simply did not have the physical strength to do so. Always of a frail constitution, by the mid-1770s he was suffering from what would prove to be a fatal case of tuberculosis. This argument cut no ice with Wesley, who had boundless confidence in the therapeutic properties of horseback riding and who, when the Minutes Controversy had finally subsided, managed to convince Fletcher that, as he tells us, "nothing was so likely to restore his health as a long journey." In autumn 1776 Fletcher managed to log "eleven or twelve hundred miles" with Wesley, "partly in the chaise and partly on horseback," but finally collapsed and was bedridden for much of the following year.[6] In late 1777 he returned briefly to Madeley, burned his private papers in expectation of his death, and then journeyed to Switzerland, hoping against hope that the dryer mountain air would help his health. By this time it was clear, even to the indefatigable Wesley, that Fletcher would never recover and would never live to succeed him as leader of the Methodists.

Fletcher's symptoms did improve for a time. He spent three years in Nyon, writing, preaching, and ministering to the people, especially the children. In spring 1781 he returned to England. He soon renewed his acquaintance with Mary Bosanquet, a longtime friend and leading Methodist laywoman, and on November 12 they were married. Judging from their letters to each other and from her subsequent testimonies, their brief marriage was one of uninterrupted joy, or at least of constant mutual edification. But the prog-

---

6. Wesley, *Short Account, WJW* 11:304. Wesley concludes his account of the journey by chiding Fletcher's "kind but injudicious friends" who forbade him to continue merely because he was "spitting blood [and showing] other symptoms" and affirms that if Fletcher had continued "only a few months longer," he would have quite recovered his health.

ress of Fletcher's illness was relentless, and he died in the Madeley vicarage on August 14, 1785. His funeral was held there three days later with a neighboring Anglican clergyman presiding. Wesley conducted a memorial service for him in London on November 6 and preached a eulogy that was immediately published and later expanded into a short biography. Mary Bosanquet Fletcher, who was ten years her husband's junior, outlived him by thirty, and died on December 9, 1815, herself a revered figure in the Methodist movement.[7]

II

Let us now look at why Wesley regarded Fletcher as a worthy successor. We shall see that much of what Wesley admired in Fletcher closely parallels what Paul prized, or hoped to develop, in Timothy. Many specific qualities are listed, but these can be classified under two general headings: sanctity of character and aptitude in teaching and preaching.

Fletcher's sanctity was renowned in his own time, and it is remarkable that when Wesley undertook the sad task of composing the eulogy for his memorial service he chose Ps 37:37, "Mark the perfect man, and behold the upright."[8] After Wesley himself, Fletcher had emerged as the most thoughtful, balanced, and penetrating exponent of the hallmark Methodist doctrine of Christian perfection,[9] and the point of Wesley's eulogy was that Fletcher had not only skillfully defended the attainability of perfection but had himself attained it. Of course, we must allow for the possibility of some hagiographical exaggeration in this sermon, as well as in Wesley's later biography of his disciple. Although these works were as historically accurate as the documents to which Wesley had access, they also served as apologiae for the Methodist cause. This is less true, however, of Wesley's private correspondence, which, though certainly driven by his strategic objectives, is remarkably free of flattery and exaggeration. It is noteworthy, therefore, that in his letter to Fletcher of January 15(?), 1773, Wesley cites the vicar's exemplary spiritual, moral, and intellectual qualities, as well as his administrative and oratorical skills, as the reasons he should agree to be Wesley's successor:

> But who is . . . qualified to preside both over the preachers and people? He must be a man of faith and love and one that has a single eye to the ad-

---

7. See Henry Moore, *The Life of Mrs. Mary Fletcher: Consort and Relict of the Rev. John Fletcher, Vicar of Madeley, Salop* (New York: Waugh and Mason, 1832).
8. Wesley, *Death of Fletcher*, WJW 3:611.
9. See especially his *Last Check to Arminianism*, WJF 2:483-669.

vancement of the kingdom of God. He must have a clear understanding; a knowledge of men and things, particularly of the Methodist doctrine and discipline; a ready utterance; diligence and activity, with a tolerable share of health. There must be added to these, favor with the people, with the Methodists in general. For unless God turn their eyes and their hearts towards him, he will be quite incapable of the work. He must likewise have some degree of learning; because there are many adversaries, learned as well as unlearned, whose mouths must be stopped. But this cannot be done unless he be able to meet them on their own ground. But has God provided one so qualified? Who is he? *Thou art the man!* God has given you a measure of loving faith and a single eye to His glory. He has given you some knowledge of men and things, particularly of the whole plan of Methodism. You are blessed with some health, activity, and diligence, together with a degree of learning. And to all these he has lately added, by a way none could have foreseen, favor both with the preachers and the whole people. Come out in the name of God! Come to the help of the Lord against the mighty! Come while I am alive and capable of labor![10]

The parallels here with Paul's catalogs of the necessary personal qualifications for worthy church leaders (1 Tim 3:1-13) and especially his urgent charge to Timothy himself (2 Tim 4:10–5:5) are striking. Deep piety, public respectability, and wide experience in secular and ecclesiastical affairs are all prized by Wesley in Fletcher, and by Paul in Timothy.

Yet it is important to note that much of what Paul and Wesley prized in their respective chosen successors were qualities and qualifications they prized in *themselves,* or at least came to regard as fundamental to their witness. In the introduction to his exposition of 2 Timothy, Wall writes of Paul: "His life and message are remembered not merely as exemplary of Christian faith but as integral to the church's apostolic tradition." Something analogous might be said of Wesley. He believed that the unrelenting quest for "perfection in love" was central to the faithful Christian life and that the distinctive contribution of Methodism to the ecumenical church was its avowal that, by disciplined cooperation with the activity of the Holy Spirit in one's soul, every Christian might properly expect to be perfected in love in this life. Wesley was, of course, sensitive to the possibility that anyone who actually claimed to attain that lofty goal might be guilty of spiritual pride (thereby falsifying the claim) or at least publicly ridiculed for it, and he never claimed it of himself. But he was not averse to claiming it of his followers. And who better to lead

---

10. John Wesley, *The Letters of John Wesley* (8 vols.; ed. John Telford; London: Epworth, 1960), 6:10-12.

the Methodists after his death than someone who not only possessed the necessary practical qualifications but whose life was an unblemished illustration of the attainability of the spiritual goal toward which every faithful Methodist pressed? Such, Wesley believed, was John Fletcher.

But Wesley also recognized that it was not enough for his chosen successor to exemplify personal sanctity. He also had to be able to articulate Methodist convictions clearly and persuasively and to defend them against the distortions that would arise within the movement and the misrepresentations that would be made by its enemies. And there was no question that Fletcher stood alone among Wesley's ordained lieutenants in his skill as a theological expositor and controversialist. This is stressed not only in the letter quoted above but in a remark in Wesley's biography of Fletcher with reference to the latter's contributions to the Minutes Controversy:

> ... [O]ne knows not which to admire most, the purity of the language, (such as scarce any foreigner wrote before,) the strength and clearness of the argument, or the mildness and sweetness of the spirit that breathes throughout the whole; insomuch that I nothing wonder at a serious clergyman, who, being resolved to live and die in his own opinion, when he was pressed to read them, replied, "No; I will never read Mr. Fletcher's *Checks*; for if I did, I should be of his mind."[11]

Particular note must be made of Wesley's admiration for Fletcher's ability not only to defend the Methodist message against its detractors with great theological acuity and biblical erudition but to do so with unfailing respect and charity for his opponents. This resonates with Paul's emphasis on the tradent's need for "teaching competence" (1 Tim 3:2; 2 Tim 2:24; 4:2), for a thorough understanding of and a sincere commitment to the Pauline gospel (1 Tim 1:10; 4:6; 6:3; 2 Tim 1:13; 4:3; Tit 1:9; 2:1; cf. 2:13), and for purity and holiness of life, which exemplify the teaching (2 Tim 2:22-25; 4:1-5; cf. 1 Pet 3:15-16). Thus, rhetorical skill, orthodox belief, and personal sanctity are equally indispensable and mutually reinforcing. Wesley says the same of Fletcher and underscores — in full agreement with Paul, but perhaps even more explicitly — that Fletcher's gracious and respectful manner in refuting the Calvinists was as critical to the success of his apologetic as the strength of his theological arguments. And it was certainly Fletcher's intention to engage in debate for the sake of the truth, not for the pleasure of winning, and therefore to display patience and gentleness with his adversaries. The title pages of his *Second,*

---

11. Wesley, *Short Account, WJW* 11:300.

Third, and *Fourth Checks* carry this epigraph: "Reprove, rebuke, exhort, with all long-suffering and (Scriptural) doctrine; for the time will come when they will not endure sound doctrine (2 Tim 4:2). Wherefore rebuke them sharply, that they may be sound in the faith. But let brotherly love continue (Titus 1:13; Heb 13:1)." And on the title page of the *Fifth Check*, Part I, we read: "As deceivers and yet true. In meekness instructing them that oppose themselves (2 Cor 6:18; 2 Tim 2:25)."[12] By flagging these verses Fletcher testifies to his conviction that the "how" of doctrinal controversy among Christians is as important as the "what" — and indeed, that a fixation on the what without proper attention to the how is a profanation of the message and has destructive consequences for the faith community.

One final point: I noted above that despite Wesley's repeated blandishments, Fletcher did not allow himself to be designated as Wesley's successor. Here is another remarkable similarity between the Wesley-Fletcher relationship and the Paul-Timothy relationship — but also a significant difference. For it appears that Timothy, like Fletcher, was reluctant to play Elisha to his mentor's Elijah; yet their reluctance was driven by quite different reasons. Timothy seems fearful of leadership. Or at least Paul must exhort him to "reignite God's gift that is in you" (2 Tim 1:6) and to "be empowered by the grace that is in Christ Jesus" (2:1), chides him for being afraid or ashamed of the gospel (2 Tim 1:7, 8; cf. v. 16), and points to himself as an example of bold, unblushing witness for Christ. In contrast, Fletcher shows no more fear or shame in his public ministry than Wesley — a fact that Wesley deeply admired. And Fletcher's refusal to be named as the heir to Wesley's leadership was driven primarily by his clear sense of his pastoral calling, though modesty and ill health (*pace* Wesley's letter) may have played some role here as well. Moreover, 2 Timothy leaves us feeling that Timothy still has crucial decisions to make before he can live into the role to which Paul has appointed him, whereas the Wesley-Fletcher correspondence leaves no doubt that Fletcher had made up his mind and that his mentor would have to make other arrangements for the succession.

---

12. See Wesley, *WJF* 1:65, 133, 203, and 332 respectively.

Titus

A canonical approach to Titus recognizes its integral relationship to the Timothy correspondence at the point of its canonization: while written separately in response to different circumstances, the letters probably circulated together before being added to an extant ten-letter Pauline corpus to complete it as a canonical collection. Approaching the Pastoral Epistles as a discrete sub-collection within the Pauline canon seems self-evident by the sheer number of linguistic similarities among them, including a cache of common themes (e.g., Savior, healthy teaching, godliness), use of the same literary genres typical of paraenesis (e.g., letter form, canonical sayings, household codes, catalogs of vices and virtues), and shared use of the "household" metaphor for a Christian congregation. More importantly, the letter is addressed to a faithful tradent who, like Timothy, is also addressed as Paul's "true child" (1:4) and given similar responsibility in Paul's absence to instruct the congregation and cultivate its faith and moral practices.

While the crisis that occasions the reception of these letters is the apostle's departure and succession, there are various other real (and sometimes different) threats to the theological security of the congregation mentioned in each letter, including the presence of false teachers and the problems they create in the household of believers. In particular, Titus bears a striking family resemblance to 1 Timothy, since both letters are heavily laden with instruction and exhortation whose focus is to organize a Christian congregation of new believers in a pagan place under trying circumstances that include fierce opposition, immature faith, inexperienced leadership, and, most especially, the absence of the charismatic apostle. The similarity of the two letters and the shorter length of the letter to Titus raise the question why it should be received as Scripture for the church.

The most obvious cue to Titus's critical importance to the church is "three passages (1:1-3; 2:11-14; 3:4-8) that are among the richest theological concentrations in the entire New Testament . . . a real mini-summa of Christian theology."[1] These passages supply a soteriological glossary for the entire Pauline canon. Their use of "salvation" and of "Savior" for both God and Jesus Christ is mindful of the wider Pauline witness, which refuses to separate God's providential action from the death and resurrection of Christ. In addition, the second epiphany text (3:5-7) includes the most important formula of the Spirit's work in salvation within the Pauline canon, which thereby inclines the Pauline reader toward Nicaea and a Trinitarian understanding of salvation.

Especially when contextualized by the story of the canonical Paul in Acts, the letter's expansive greeting (1:1-4) is exceptionally important. There is hardly another passage that underscores the enduring importance of the Pauline apostolate more definitively than this one. God's word given to Paul is now preserved and received in the Pauline canon, entrusted to the church as Scripture, and the source of its "healthy teaching."

Moreover, the different social locations of the Pastoral Epistles — the urban and urbane Ephesus of Timothy and the uncivilized Crete of Titus (cf. 1:12) — create something of a cultural merism such that readers might accept the similar instruction of both letters as providing guidance for every congregation. The credentials for leaders, the household codes, and the pastoral instructions and exhortations in both letters, directed to disparate places, suggest that the claims of Paul's gospel and his instructions to congregations and their leaders do not change from place to place. God is Savior of both and all in equal measure. And even slight differences detected in the instructions of 1 Timothy and Titus may indicate the dynamic adaptability of the Pauline apostolate to different social settings.

The secondary crisis facing Titus concerns his theological opponents, whom Paul routinely castigates (1:10-16; 3:9-11). In part, the issue is political and related to their subversive effect on Titus's religious authority in the congregation; however, they also disrupt the spiritual formation of new believers (1:11). Vague references to their teaching would seem to indicate a Jewish influence: they are members of "the circumcision" (v. 10) who pay "attention to Jewish myths and commandments" (v. 14) as well as "disputes about the law" (3:9) and who "profess to know God" even though they are "worthless for any good deed" (1:16).

Paul appears less concerned about the content of their teaching, which he only hints at, than about its divisive result within the congregation. The

---

1. Raymond F. Collins, *1 and 2 Timothy and Titus: A Commentary* (NTL; Louisville: Westminster John Knox, 2002), 299.

passing mention of Titus in Gal 2:1-3 as a non-Jewish believer at the center of controversy initiated by Jewish believers may provide a useful co-text to illumine the identity of the opponents Titus encounters in Crete. If "those of the circumcision" also believe that converts to Christianity should be purified by Torah observance and circumcision before their initiation into the community of "elect ones," then Titus will come under special scrutiny and even hostility in Crete. He will have to argue as Paul does in Galatians that new life with Christ is initiated by trust and not by compliance with Judaism's proselyte protocol. The instruction in 1:14-15 that Titus not pay attention to the opponents' teaching adds a liturgical trope, "defile-clean," to secure his separation from them and suggests that the letter's readers do the same: do not pay attention to them! While this idiom does suggest a Jewish influence contrary to the Pauline gospel, the apostolic directive is less interested in the opponents' identity than he is in cultivating the religious and political chops of his protégé. Again, the primary crisis facing Titus is not the presence of the circumcision on Crete but the absence of his spiritual mentor and the church's apostle.

Titus is depicted in 2 Corinthians as a missionary colleague of Paul who travels with Paul throughout Asia (2:13-14) and Macedonia (7:5-7, 13-14), working with Paul as his "partner and coworker" (8:23). Paul has put him in charge of the collection of an offering from the Macedonian congregations to benefit the impoverished Jerusalem church (8:1-7; 12:18). Several impressions are made about Paul's relationship with Titus on the basis of these few passages. First is the intimacy of their relationship, indicated most poignantly by 2:13-14: despite a clear sense of the Lord's direction in leading Paul to Troas to preach the gospel, he could not continue his mission there because he could not find Titus — a conflict of divine and human spirits that was resolved in favor of finding Titus in Macedonia (7:5-7). Second is the shared nature of their work together, in which Titus furnishes Paul with missionary reports that shape Paul's responses to the congregation (7:7, 13-14).

This commission takes on greater importance when glossed by Paul's account of the Jerusalem Council in Gal 2:1-10, according to which his refusal to circumcise Titus comes to symbolize not only his Torah-free mission to the nations but also the agreements between the Jewish and Gentile missions of the church. Indeed, not only did the Jerusalem Pillars extend fellowship to Paul (Gal 2:7-9) and presumably to the non-proselyte converts of his mission (cf. Acts 15:4-21), they also encouraged the Pauline mission to "remember the poor" (Gal 2:10). Titus, who would be given the task of collecting money for the poor of Jerusalem, stands as a witness of this concord. At its core, especially when interpreted against the backdrop of the Jerusalem agreements, this collection and Titus as its agent symbolize a new and unified *koinōnia* between Jews and Gentiles. In fact, in some sense this Gentile offering to a Jewish congregation instantiates a Pauline understanding of God's redemptive plan, in which Gentiles are grafted into and become participants in God's promises to Israel (Rom 11:17-24).

Titus is addressed as a "true child according to a common faith" (1:4). He is more than Paul's missionary associate: he is a loyal tradent whose task is to adapt Paul's pattern of healthy teaching and congregational formation to a new setting in Paul's absence. In this sense, every faithful reader of Scripture's Pauline deposit assumes a similar vocation and so self-identifies with Titus (and Timothy) in receiving this biblical word. Frances Young has famously said that "theology is always earthed in a context."[2] The worlds that shape the ideas and idiom of Paul's instructions to Titus (and Timothy) are Greco-Roman — the morality of its philosophers and the social politics of its households — and Jewish — the theology of Judaism's Scriptures and the structure of its synagogues. But this sacred letter comes to us "earthed" in a canonical context that supplies the normative setting for its reading and application in the church. The problem that occasioned the writing of Titus also occasions its faithful reading wherever Christian congregations are organized in non-Christian places, so that "the faith of the elect ones" gathered together there for Christ's sake is enriched by God's word (cf. 1:1-3).

1:1-4 Paul Greets Titus

¹From Paul, a slave of God and an apostle of Jesus Christ for the faith of God's elect ones and a knowledge of truth that agrees with godliness, ²in hope of eternal life that God, who does not lie, promised before time began ³and revealed God's word in due time through the preaching entrusted to me by the command of God our Savior. ⁴To Titus, my true child according to a common faith: Grace and peace from God the Father and Christ Jesus our Savior.

Paul typically opens his letters after the fashion of other letter-writers in the Greco-Roman world: "writer to recipient, greetings." This literary formula is not incidental to the particular intentions of the letter, however, but often commends the proper posture of the recipient to what is written. Paul's expansive greeting to Titus, longer than in any canonical letter except Romans,

---

2. Frances M. Young, *The Theology of the Pastoral Letters* (Cambridge: Cambridge University Press, 1994), 1.

particularly helps confirm its utility as a context for reading the letter. In a complex but coherent sentence (1:1-3), then, Paul establishes his apostolic credentials for Titus's reception of the instructions that follow before greeting him (v. 4).

The memory and message of Paul are secured by his office as an "apostle of Jesus Christ" (v. 1) and by his vocation as the one entrusted to proclaim "God's word" and impart a "knowledge of truth" about "eternal life that God promised before time began" (vv. 2-3). Paul interprets his apostolic call as an act of divine revelation that occurred at καιρὸς ἴδιος *(kairos idios)*, at God's appointed time: Paul has been singled out within the bounds of God's redemptive plan for the world as a vessel of divine revelation (cf. 2 Cor 4:1-15).

But why does Paul take such care in establishing the terms of his apostolic office in a brief letter to a "true child" whose work is forged "according to a common faith"? Titus needed no reminder of Paul's importance. The real purpose of this greeting is rhetorical, not to prove the author's apostolic mettle to an unconvinced student but to frame the substance of an apostolate whose enduring importance every faithful follower must firmly embrace. When read as Scripture whose instruction is timeless and universal, Titus comes to represent every Pauline tradent called on to secure Paul's gospel in ever-changing social locations. Unlike the equally expansive greeting of Romans, which is mostly about Christ, who supplies the core of Paul's gospel, this letter's superscription is about Paul, who has been entrusted with God's word to preach to others. Moreover, this calling was given by command of "God our Savior" and is evidently fitted into the overall redemptive scheme of God, which was planned "before time began." The purpose of Paul's apostolate, then, has a timeless quality, so that "the knowledge of truth" provided by the gospel is always at work forming the faith of God's "elect ones."

As we argued in commenting on the apostleship motif in 1-2 Timothy, the portrait of Paul cultivated by the Pastoral Epistles underwrites his indispensable importance for the church's going forward. The present spiritual crisis facing the current readers of the Pauline deposit in Scripture is precisely the same as what Timothy and Titus faced: the departure of Paul and his apostolic charisms raises the serious question whether his mission and message, delegated to others in his absence, will have the same salutary effect on people as his successors carry the gospel into new places. This question has been answered by the formation of the Pauline canon, the textual form of the Pauline legacy carried forward by subsequent generations into ever changing places so that new and different readers may receive knowledge of truth and godliness that will cultivate their hope for eternal life.

The titles appended to Paul's name function much like an email signature block: they form impressions of another that help fashion a working relationship. In this case, the exceptional pairing of "slave" and "apostle" communicates an impression of Paul that forms the recipient's posture toward the letter's instruction. While an unusual title for Paul, "slave of God" is familiar to Jewish readers of David's story, where the king speaks of himself as God's "slave" (1 Sam 23:10-11; 2 Sam 7:27; cf. 1 Kgs 8:28; Ezra 5:11; Isa 42:19; 49:3). If Paul is alluding to David's self-designation, he may thus be indicating that complete loyalty to God, regardless of high office, is a necessary attribute of an agent of God's salvation (1:3). This powerful sense of personal loyalty is deepened when received in a world that includes members of urban congregations with a résumé of slavery (see 1 Tim 6:1-2).

The second marker, "apostle of Jesus Christ," is more typical of Paul and expresses his missionary vocation (cf. Acts 9:15-16) as herald and teacher of God's gospel (see 1 Tim 2:7). But Jerome also thought Paul mentioned the title to awe his readers with his authority. Maybe so, but apostleship is the shape of Paul's slavery to God. Calvin explains that Paul's slavery to God defines a general class to which all believers belong (1 Pet 2:16), while "apostle of Jesus Christ" explains Paul's "particular office" within this class.[3] In this sense, the purpose of the pairing would be to distinguish Paul from all other believers (including Titus) in the manner and obligations of his service to God: his apostolic authority and gospel ministry are a function of his slavery to God. Paul is not engaged in self-promotion to establish the importance and continuation of his apostolate.

The κατά *(kata)* phrase that follows explains the principal purpose of Paul's apostolate, which is to inform and so form the faith of "God's elect ones." His use of this familiar OT idiom of the covenant community for the church does not suggest God's predestination of its membership "before time began" but refers to those whose act of "faith" in Christ Jesus marks them out as a people belonging to God (see above on 2 Tim 2:10; cf. Rom 8:33; 16:13). Paul's preaching of the gospel intends to prompt this act of faith.

But the "faith of God's elect ones" is understood as not only a converting choice but also a theological content that agrees with "a knowledge of truth," which Paul has been appointed to teach the nations (see 1 Tim 2:3-7). In this setting, a religious conversion assumes that one has come to knowledge of the truth. The special claim of the Pastoral Epistles' definition of Paul's apostleship, found nowhere else in the Pauline canon, is that only he is the authorized teacher of God's gospel for the nations. In this claim Paul does

---

3. John Calvin, *The Second Epistle of Paul the Apostle to the Corinthians and the Epistles to Timothy, Titus and Philemon* (Grand Rapids: Eerdmans, 1964), 162.

not lie (1 Tim 2:7), which is repeated here of God, whose promise to grant eternal life to those who embrace the truth of what Paul teaches is similarly grounded in the epistemic claim that God "does not lie" about the promises (1:2). This declaration of truth-telling anticipates Paul's harsh characterization of both his religious opponents (v. 10) and Cretan culture (v. 12) as "liars." At Qumran "knowledge of the truth" identified the community as God's covenant people — perhaps in contrast with other Jewish groups with different beliefs (1QS 6:15; 9:17-18; 1QH 10:20-29). The same sense distinguishes the Pauline apostolate from its opponents.

The familiar pairing of "godliness" (εὐσέβεια, *eusebeia;* see above on 1 Tim 3:16; 6:3-6, 11; 2 Tim 3:5) with the gospel truth in the Pastoral Epistles concentrates the reader's attention on Paul's practical divinity: the firm embrace of the gospel's truth will always exert an influence on the manner of believers' devotion to God and relationships with one another. While "the faith of God's elect ones" requires a rigorous intellectual affirmation and understanding of what Paul teaches, faith is never just that. In the Greco-Roman world, "godliness" was a cardinal virtue. Epictetus, an important Stoic philosopher, understood it as the very foundation of a moral life. Hellenistic Jews, such as Paul, recognized that obedience to God generated love for one another: piety begets morality. Thus, in the Pastoral Epistles, a life of "godliness" is often described in terms of religious practices and beliefs (e.g., 1 Tim 6:3) that animate a particular lifestyle (e.g., 1 Tim 6:5-6; cf. 2 Tim 3:5).

The formula "in hope of eternal life," in combination with "promised before time began," ascribes a temporal perspective to what is known to be true. It will be repeated in 3:7 to bracket Paul's instructions to Titus. It suggests the theological motive or objective for Titus's compliance with all these instructions: the realization of promised eternal life for God's people.

The keenly providential cast of this greeting links God's promise of eternal life to the present disclosure of God's word through Paul's preaching ministry. The promise of "eternal (αἰώνιος, *aiōnios*) life," which God made "before time began (πρὸ χρόνων αἰωνίων, *pro chronōn aiōniōn*)," is the sort of promise only God can make. In Pauline discourse, eternity is not a characteristic of life but is life instead of death and encompasses all creation (Romans 8). This promise, which concerns the future of the covenant community and the renewal of creation, was first made to Abraham (Rom 4:20-21) and is only now secured because of the death and resurrection of Christ (Rom 4:23-25). The antecedent of the αὐτοῦ (*autou,* "his") whose "word" Paul preaches is God, and the content of that word therefore concerns God's faithful fulfillment of Abraham's promise through Christ (see 2 Tim 1:9-10; 2:15; 4:2).

"In due time" dates God's act of disclosing and entrusting the gospel to

Paul. It therefore marks the occasion of Paul's proclamation of God's saving word and glosses other temporal references found in this passage. Καιρὸς ἴδιος *(kairos idios)*, a divine appointment — "in due time" — is a trope of divine providence. This expression of Paul's commission is thick with theological importance, since it implies that he has been singled out by God within the bounds of God's redemptive plan as a vessel of divine revelation for the redemption of the world (cf. 2 Cor 4:1-15).

We suspect that this emphasis on Paul's role has to do with the nature of opposition Titus is facing in Crete from "the circumcision," whose principal appeal is to God's word in the Torah (i.e., Genesis 17) to support the purity practice of circumcision as conditional of membership in God's elect ones. Against this biblical appeal is the revelation of God's word to Paul (1:3), whose truth, especially when contextualized by a prior reading of Acts, is confirmed by his missionary experiences (see below on vv. 10-16).

God's promise of salvation is worked out within the covenant community's history for all to see. The public announcement of the promise of "eternal life," which God made "before time began," has now evidently entered a new dispensation, inaugurated "in due time" with God's command that Paul preach the gospel (see 2 Tim 1:9-10). It is the apostolate of this Pauline gospel that stipulates a pattern of healthy teaching that Timothy (2 Tim 1:13-14) and now Titus are to pass on to others.

Titus is called Paul's "true child" (1:4) who shares "a common faith" with Paul. The sense of profound solidarity with Paul based on Titus's proven (or "true") kinship and theological agreement affirms his readiness to function as a caretaker of the Pauline tradition in the apostle's absence.[4] The familial fiction used here of Titus is not a badge of close friendship with Paul but rather functions more like the guild idiom in which a child is apprenticed to his father to learn the family craft (see 1 Tim 1:2). In this sense, the adjective "true" (γνησίως, *gnēsiōs*) connotes someone whose apprenticeship is completed and whose right to assume the family's trade is proven.

The distinction of Paul's salutation to Titus is the addition of "our Savior" to "Christ Jesus" (1:4), which intentionally pairs Christ with the earlier "God our Savior" (v. 3) in the outworking of God's redemptive plan. What is made clear by this letter is that Christ's decisive role as "our Savior" has already been disclosed at his past "appearing" (3:6), which balances an exclusively apocalyptic Christology that locates the decisive moment of his messi-

---

4. In a similar way, the author of 1 John introduces his letter by stipulating that the apostolic tradition is the epistemic criterion by which *koinōnia* between the community and God is measured (1 John 1:3).

anic work at his future coming (2:13). Christ's participation with God in fulfilling the promised salvation is coextensive with salvation's entire history.

The centrality of the Savior idiom in this letter, especially here where it is attached to the distribution of grace and peace, may well have a political subtext. In Greco-Roman culture, "our savior" had wide currency in reference to generous benefactors. A city official who distributed needed benefits to the rank-and-file would be hailed as the people's "savior." Julius Caesar was celebrated as the "savior" of common folk and was even worshiped as god personified.[5] Deities such as Zeus were petitioned as savior by those in need of healing or rescue from harm's way. This use of "savior" agrees with its use in the OT: God delivers Israel from enemies and for a better life (Deut 32:15; Pss 24:5; 25:5; 27:9; 42:6; Isa 12:2; 60:16). The subtext of Paul's salutation, then, is that any claim for Caesar's kingdom without end, characterized by peace and grace, is a fiction. Such an eternal kingdom, occupied by the elect ones, who are marked out by their faith in God's word, is possible only as the outcome of God's active faithfulness.

1:5-9 A Qualified Elder

⁵The reason I left you in Crete was to put to rights what is lacking there and to appoint elders in every city. As I directed you, ⁶appoint only those who are without fault — the husband of one wife with faithful children who cannot be accused of self-indulgence or rebelliousness — ⁷for it is necessary that the administrator be without fault as God's household-manager, not stubborn, not irritable, not a drunkard or a bully, not acquisitive. ⁸Rather he should befriend strangers, befriend what is good, modest, upright, devout, under control ⁹with a firm hold on the teaching of the faithful word so that he may be able to exhort with healthy teaching while refuting those who speak against it.

Unlike most Pauline letters, in which expressions of thanksgiving and prayer follow the greeting, this letter moves directly to say why Paul wrote the letter, which was his decision to leave Titus in Crete "to put to rights what is lacking there" (1:5a). And what is lacking most is the appointment of elders who are "without fault" to manage the affairs of the household of God (vv. 5b-9). This initial charge presumably repeats Paul's verbal directive to Titus, which may raise the question of why he wrote it down. But the plural number of the con-

---

5. W. Dittenberger, ed., *Sylloge Inscriptionum Graecarum* (4 vols.; 3rd ed.; Leipzig, 1915-24), §§347, 760.6.

cluding benediction makes clear that Paul's audience includes other readers: these instructions to Paul's missionary associate publish a private conversation for a wider audience and thereby anticipate the letter's subsequent performances as Scripture.

According to Acts, Paul's missionary pattern included the routine of appointing elders to supervise the practical matters of congregational life as an initial step in bringing stability to the fledgling churches (Acts 14:23; see above on 1 Tim 3:1-7; 5:17-22). What is more curious, when compared to the sequence of instructions in 1 Timothy, is that this instruction to find elders comes first. Paul does not say why priority is given to this task, though the explanatory γάρ (*gar*, "you see," 1:10) linking this passage to the next may imply that the administration of church order was more critical there because Cretan culture lent itself to disorder.

Two words for leaders are used interchangeably, "elder" (1:5) and "administrator" (v. 7), suggesting that the work of the congregation's elders is to manage the household of believers. "Administrator" does not refer to a discrete ecclesial office but extends the household metaphor to include congregational leaders: a strategic role of the elders is to steward the congregation's internal affairs and its relations with outsiders (see above on 1 Tim 3:1-13).[6]

Catalogs in Pauline letters, such as this one listing qualities of competent leaders, are not generic codes but are carefully crafted units of paraenetic discourse for particular audiences and occasions. That is, these are qualities especially appropriate for the leaders of a Cretan Christian congregation. Such lists were as commonplace in Paul's world as they are in ours, with specific personal qualities stipulated for specific tasks and settings. Among these qualities, the importance of a public reputation for personal integrity is listed first and is primary: only "those who are without fault" in a variety of settings — social, religious, political, and financial — are to be appointed. Isocrates, *To Demonicus* 35 (250 B.C.E.), opines that "whenever you purpose to consult with anyone about your affairs, first observe how he has managed his own; for he who has shown poor judgment in conducting his own business will never give wise counsel about the business of others." Paul extends this quality of overall competence to both private (home) and public affairs: Christian leaders must be "without fault," and the criterion by which they are to be measured is their effectiveness at getting good results in regard to morality (see above on 1 Tim 3:1-13). This close connection between character and job performance is especially characteristic of Jewish professional ethics. Since

---

6. The two terms are "interchangeable and refer to the same leadership position" according to Jouette M. Bassler, *1 Timothy, 2 Timothy, Titus* (ANTC; Nashville: Abingdon, 1996), 186.

Crete had a large Jewish population, from which both converts and contention came (cf. 1:10-16), it is natural that Paul drafted a profile of leadership in continuity with the church's Jewish legacy.

In particular, the elder must be "husband of one wife with faithful children." This phrase does not appear outside the Pastoral Epistles, and its precise sense is difficult to pin down (cf. 1 Tim 3:2; 5:9, 14). Josephus mentions polygamy (along with levirate marriage) as a practice still current among some priestly families (*Antiquities* 17.1, 2, 14), who appealed to the multiple wives of the patriarchs and to the Torah's instruction where it assumes polygamy (Exod 21:8-11; Deut 21:15; 25:5-10). But polygamy was banned at Qumran (CD 4:20-21), and monogamy had become the norm throughout the Greco-Roman world. Paul may simply be lending his approval to what is generally accepted by society, but he may also be responding to religious ascetics who condemned marriage (cf. 1 Tim 4:3) or, opposite, to affluent and influential believers who indulged in the Roman practice of concubinage, especially if they were logical candidates for leadership positions in their Christian congregations. Perhaps aware of this background, Ambrose understood Paul's intent as encouraging "chastity in marriage to protect the grace of (a believer's) baptism" (*Letters* 63.62-63). Whatever the particular sense, Paul's larger point is that a stable, monogamous marriage is evidence of a successful household that may carry over to leadership of a Christian congregation.

A related metric is whether the elder's children are "faithful," which may indicate an ability to cultivate faithfulness among the "elect ones" (see 1:1). In Paul's world, fathers exercised final authority over their children's religious choices (cf. Acts 16:1-3). Faithful children embody the faithfulness of their parents; the implication is that spiritual children, like biological children, imitate their parents and in this sense supply evidence of the parents' faithfulness or rebelliousness. If children are "self-indulgent or rebellious" and not "true children," that casts a negative light on the legitimacy of their parents' faith. Of course, a catalog like this does not say how this evidence is to be measured, so the profligate life of a dependent is insufficient to disqualify the parent. The implied connection between the domestic household and the congregation is not absolute but a useful typology in making the general point that the body of good work produced in one household may indicate potential to produce a body of good work in another. This may be especially true of the parent who constrains the "rebelliousness" of his children in a cultural setting where "there are many who are rebellious" (1:10).

Rather than assigning one elder to the ecclesial office of "administrator," Paul uses ἐπίσκοπος *(episkopos)* as an elaboration of his household metaphor of the church's council of elders (cf. 1 Tim 4:14), whose shared role is as "household manager" (οἰκονόμος, *oikonomos;* see 1 Tim 1:4) of God's household (see above on 1 Tim 3:1-7, 8-13).[7] These are not terms for particular ecclesial offices but collective metaphors for the responsibilities of the appointed elders. The catalog of qualities, whether of abstaining from harmful actions (1:7) or engaging in virtuous actions (vv. 8-9a), is commensurate with good supervision (see above on 1 Tim 3:1-15). The overarching virtue is that a good elder-administrator is "without fault" or accusation (1:6, 7; see 1 Tim 3:2, 10): he has a clean record. The sense of ἀνέγκλητος *(anenklētos)* is not of moral perfection but of good politics. The manner of the elder's work and life does not leave room for a lack of credibility, even among outsiders (see 1 Tim 3:7).

Epictetus characterizes the good philosopher as the "manager of a well-ordered house" (*Discourses* 3.22.3-4). The good administrator places a firm hand on the household by "teaching the faithful word." The curious combination of *pistos* and *logos,* which we have translated "faithful word" (1:9), has been understood in several ways. It may more vaguely confirm the reliability of the gospel message,[8] an elaboration of the prior uses of *pistos/pistis* in the greeting (vv. 1, 4) and the present passage (v. 6), as a word that targets the formation of the covenant community's faith, or as a word that is carried forward by its faithful handlers like the prophets and apostles.[9] In this setting, this word is the one entrusted by God to Paul (v. 3), which the administrator faithfully handles in ordering the spiritual life of the household of believers.

The following purpose clause qualifies the use of this "faithful word" as an epistemic criterion to cultivate a pattern of faith in the household by encouraging its members and refuting its opponents. The word translated "healthy" is an ancient medical term used in the Pastoral Epistles of those practices that encourage a congregation's spiritual health (see above on 1 Tim 1:10; 6:3; 2 Tim 1:13). In light of the next pericope, the administrator's primary practice is adapting this Pauline word to refute opponents.

1:10–2:1 A Defiled Opposition

[10]You see, there are many who are rebellious, who are unreasonable and who mislead, especially those from the circumcision. [11]They must be silenced because

---

7. Young connects this word with the role of slaves in antiquity. The *oikonomos* was a skilled servant, often educated and competent in handling business affairs on behalf of his master. *Theology of the Pastoral Letters,* 102-3.

8. George W. Knight, *The Pastoral Epistles: A Commentary on the Greek Text* (NIGTC; Grand Rapids: Eerdmans, 1992), 293.

9. Philip H. Towner, *1-2 Timothy and Titus* (Downers Grove: InterVarsity, 1994), 691.

they are shaking up entire households, teaching what should not be taught for dishonest profit. ¹²One among them, a prophet of their own choosing, said, "Cretans are always liars, evil beasts, gluttons for laziness." ¹³This testimony is true. So refute them firmly that they may grow a healthy faith ¹⁴and not pay attention to Jewish legends or the demands of people who have turned from the truth. ¹⁵All is clean to those who are clean, but to those who are defiled and without faith, their mind and conscience are defiled. ¹⁶They profess to know God but their works deny God; they are detestable, disobedient, and disqualified for every good work. 2¹You, however, speak in a manner consistent with healthy teaching.

The opening conjunction "you see" (γάρ, *gar*, 1:10) introduces a passage that explains why the appointment of virtuous elders has become urgently necessary: to silence the threat posed by "the circumcision" (vv. 10-16) in order to "grow a healthy faith" (v. 13) secured by "healthy teaching" (2:1).

The elders are necessarily identified by their children, who are "not accused of rebelliousness" and so provide inside testimony that they are not among the "many who are rebellious" on the island. Moreover, the elders "keep a firm hold on the teaching of the faithful word" to refute "those from the circumcision" who teach "what should not be taught." Apparently, the opposition is strong, since "there are many who are rebellious," and they have targeted Christian families, "shaking up entire households." The letter's keen sense of social order (cf. 2:2-10), following 1 Timothy's expansive use of household codes, is less about the domestication of social relationships as it is a concern that some have rejected the prerogatives of the Pauline apostolate (cf. 1:1-3) for the beliefs and leadership of "the circumcision." In any case, the tone of this text is made more urgent by the scope and present tense of Paul's injunction to silence them: they "are shaking up" entire families and thereby subverting the *oikonomia theou* (see 1 Tim 1:4).

The historical identity of "the circumcision" is indeterminate for lack of information. But if understanding of it is cued by a prior reading of Acts 10–11 and Galatians 2, several things might be assumed by the reader. "The circumcision" is mentioned in the narrative of the Gentile Pentecost (Acts 10:45; 11:2) as a protest movement in the Jewish church that polices Peter's more liberal interpretation of the initiation of repentant but non-kosher (i.e., uncircumcised, non-proselyte) Gentiles into the covenant-keeping community. In Paul's account in Gal 2:1-10 of the Jerusalem meeting, Titus represents God's approval of Paul's "mission to the uncircumcised" and so of Jerusalem's decision to initiate faithful Gentiles into the covenant-keeping community on the basis of their faith in Christ alone.

Titus's faithfulness both to Paul as his "true child" and to the truth claims of Paul's gospel instantiates the new dispensation of God's salvation announced by Paul's mission to the Gentiles. Against this new day, which God had prepared "before time began" (1:2), are these Jewish Christians of conservative cast who protest on the basis of the Torah's plain teaching that repentant Gentiles such as Titus must maintain Judaism's purity practices, such as circumcision as covenant-keeping. Paul's delegation of his Torah-free mission to pagans in Crete to this uncircumcised Greek may have been especially offensive to "the circumcision." In any case, their concerns regard the form of purity, which is a condition of covenant-keeping with God for eternal life as disclosed in Scripture by a God "who does not lie" (1:2b).

Rather than teachers of integrity who are "without fault" (1:6), they are religious renegades who have denied the truth of God's word disclosed to Paul. The catalog of vices in vv. 10-12 includes several words found only here in the NT and is the reverse of the virtues listed in vv. 7-9a. These teachers usher in spiritual chaos rather than order, subvert the gospel truth rather than champion it, and bring mischief into Christian households rather than encouragement and edification. Rather than exemplifying the purity they demand, they teach "for dishonest profit," both spiritual and material (see 1 Tim 6:3-10). This may mean that their financial support comes from misled members of the congregation. In any case, the plain sense of this passage is clear: "the faith of God's elect ones," rooted and cultivated by God's word entrusted to Paul, is now imperiled by teachers from "the circumcision."

Epimenides the Cretan (c. 650 B.C.E.) is the unnamed author Paul quotes in v. 12 to castigate Cretans as liars and cheats, in agreement with the assessment voiced by their own public intellectuals. In the ancient world, the verb "Cretanize" was often used of duplicitous acts. It may seem curious to Cretan Jews (including his opponents) that Paul would refer to Epimenides as a "prophet" — a carrier of the word of the Lord. However, according to *Seder Olam Rabbah* 21, the non-Jewish world has its own "prophets" who speak accurately "of their own" and should be heeded by them. In this sense, Aristotle says of Epimenides that he is a prophet not because he forecasts the future but because he brings the hidden to light (*Rhetoric* 3.17.10). But in fact the low regard for Cretan integrity in religious matters was widely shared, in part because some actually claimed with straight face that they possessed the tomb of the immortal Zeus (Callimachus, *Hymn to Zeus* 8-9). While Cretan Jews certainly would not have shared this fiction with their pagan neighbors, Paul may be coloring them with the same cultural brush, if only for rhetorical effect, in making his larger point: only he possesses God's word for this moment (1:3), and these teachers have substituted "Jewish legends" for his "healthy teaching" (v. 9).

The plural "legends" (1:14) is generally used negatively in the ancient world, not only because they are fictions that some parade as true but because some would then appeal to these "truths" to justify unhealthy lifestyles (Plato, *Leges* 1.636; *Republic* 2.376E-383C). Josephus reports that some Jews of Crete were susceptible to superstition (*Antiquities* 17.327). More likely, "legends" is Paul's term for speculative midrash about OT characters used to authorize beliefs and practices that opposed and even subverted Paul's witness. Likewise, the addition of "demands of the people" probably refers to rules, based on these speculations, regarding what was "clean" or "defiled." If these rules were Jewish in cast, then probably certain foods and purity practices related to proper "table fellowship" between Jews and repentant pagans are implied.

The logic of the familiar but cryptic phrase that things are "clean to those clean but defiled to those defiled" (1:15) is similar to Paul's argument against the ascetics in 1 Tim 4:1-5. Not only is God the Creator of good things, so that material goods such as food or social institutions such as marriage may be gladly received, but God's kingdom is "not food and drink but righteousness and peace and joy in the Holy Spirit" (Rom 14:17). The interpreter must be careful not to generalize the meaning of "clean to those clean but defiled to those defiled" to cultural or intellectual matters, which can lead to world-denying censorship of the sort demonized in 1 Tim 4:1-5. While elsewhere in the Pauline canon certain kinds of religious practices are condemned (e.g., 1 Corinthians 8–10) or philosophical speculation chastened (e.g., Colossians 2), the reason is not for fear that they might contaminate Christian existence but that they do not edify it.

The ritual idiom of "clean" and "defiled" also recalls the topos of hygiene and disease widely used by moral philosophers to describe the human condition (see 1 Tim 6:4-5; 2 Tim 2:17). The opponents have diseased (or "defiled") minds and consciences (1:15b), so that Paul charges Titus to find elders who can restore these teachers to a "healthy faith" (v. 13) by instruction of "healthy teaching" (v. 9). And Titus himself, as a faithful tradent of the Pauline apostolate, must exemplify this by public speech "consistent with healthy teaching" (2:1).[10] The optimism that Paul places on public instruction is shaped by his Jewish tradition but is also rooted in a religious epistemology that holds that an apostolic account of truth will always win out since it is

---

10. We have put 2:1 as the concluding exhortation of 1:10-16 to help make Paul's larger point that the badge of effective leadership is teaching of good theology, which is the preferred and most effective response to false teachers. Knight rightly notes that the imperative λάλει *(lalei),* "speak," is a synonym for "teach." *Pastoral Epistles,* 305.

communicated in the company of God's Spirit (cf. 1 Corinthians 2–4). Paul repeats an earlier exhortation to avoid those teachers whose "public appearance is godly but who resist God's power" (2 Tim 3:5) in his contention here that "those of the circumcision" profess faith in God while the manner of their lives exposes that their faith is fraudulent (1:16).

While church order is maintained by challenging the personal integrity of those who subvert the Pauline apostolate and the erroneous substance of what they teach others — and nowhere in the Pastoral Epistles is the polemic sharper than here — there is a remarkable consistency in stipulating a redemptive endgame. Perhaps illustrative of the Lord's epiphany to "rescue us from lawlessness and cleanse a people for himself" (2:14), the refutation of "the circumcision" is not directed to the excommunication of its members but is a rescue operation that seeks to restore them to a "healthy faith" (1:13).

2:2-10 A Healthy Household

²Older men are to be prudent, mild-mannered, healthy in faith, loving, patient. ³Likewise, the manners of older women are to be reverent, not slandering or addicted to heavy drinking, but teachers of virtue ⁴so that they may mentor young women in loving their husbands and children ⁵in modesty, purity, as good homemakers, subject to their own husbands so that God's word may not be ridiculed. ⁶Likewise, encourage young men to be prudent ⁷in every way. Put yourself forward as a role model of good works, and in your teaching be sound and serious, ⁸a healthy word above criticism, so that the opponent may respect us, finding nothing bad to say. ⁹Slaves should be subject to their own masters in everything, doing what is asked without talking back, ¹⁰not skimming from the top but demonstrating a good faith in everything, so that in everything they may adorn the teaching about God our Savior.

The exhortation to "teach healthy things" (2:1) is not only a corrective to the false teaching of "the circumcision" but also formative of a healthy community, just as bad theology provokes unrest and chaos in the community (1:11). The logic of this sociology extends to the administration of household relations. The virtues of the older men (2:2) and women (v. 3) put them in sharp contrast with the leaders of "the circumcision," and their mentoring influence in the congregation is also sharply contrasted with the domestic practices of young women (vv. 4-5) and men (v. 6). Titus's own leadership role is as a "model of good works" (vv. 7-8). Finally, household slaves within the Christian household are distinguished not by age or gender but by their subordinate role, in which their competence "adorns the teaching about God our Savior" (vv. 9-11).

The instructions found in 1 Timothy (3:1-13 and 5:1–6:2) and now here in Titus assume the social world of Roman households, which in the Pastoral Epistles is typological of the Christian congregation, "God's household" (1 Tim 3:15). One's status and role in either household, domestic or sacred, depend on gender, age, social rank, and marital status. To a large degree public reputation was measured by the quality of one's conduct toward members of the extended family: Was the father/husband attentive to the financial needs of his family? Did children obey his caring and careful direction? Did their mother devote herself to the efficient management of the household? Were household servants helpful in making the various endeavors of family members successful? True to the spirit of his age, Paul draws these familial obligations in terms of personal virtue rather than job description. This letter makes clear the inextricable connection between personal moral conduct and "professional" competence, so that one implies the other. Chrysostom captures this ancient metric nicely: "when observers see a slave who has been taught the philosophy of Christ display more self-command than those taught by their own philosophers, they will in every way admire the power of the gospel" (*Homilies on Titus* 3).

Among the household virtues listed by Paul, several are shared with important Hellenistic moral philosophers such as Aristotle, Epictetus, Seneca, and the Jewish teacher Philo. In part, Paul's appropriation of generally accepted moral norms is of a piece with his missionary strategy, not wanting God's household to live on the margins of society, where they would have no influence on others. At the same time, we must be alert to the decisively Christian ground into which these common norms are rooted: "sound (or healthy) doctrine" (2:1) and belief in "God our Savior" (v. 10). For this reason, the interpreter must not detach this ethical teaching on relationships within the congregation from the densely theological passage that follows in vv. 11-14, which articulates Paul's account of "sound doctrine." Good theology shapes and explains good character.

The abrupt introduction of this material might be explained on literary grounds as a convention of paraenesis, but it makes better sense if one recognizes the implicit connection with the preceding alert to the threat posed to households by the false teachers (1:11). That is, the appointment of qualified elders targets the rebellious teachers "from the circumcision," even as the effect they are currently having on entire households provides good reason for the household code here. This is grounded in Paul's programmatic statement in 1 Tim 1:4-5, positively construed, that Pauline catechesis inculcates God's way of reordering spiritual and social relations in a manner that targets love for God and one another. In other words, this is precisely the claim Paul makes in greeting Titus (see above on 1:1-3).

The repetition of "sensible" (σώφρων, *sōphrōn*) and cognate words in 2:2, 4-6 marks out its importance within the household of faith, to such an extent that it is used again later as evidence of Christian conversion (v. 12). In Greek literature (there is no precise Hebrew equivalent) it is one of four "cardinal virtues" that personify those who are able to control their frivolous desires: mind over emotion. Because the desires of men and women differ, so did the public expression of their moderate, sensible lifestyle (e.g., Aristotle, *Politics* 1.5.8). A sensible lifestyle is frequently listed by moral philosophers as the most important quality of virtuous youth, as in v. 6. Paul also uses this word group to bracket 1 Timothy's profile of the modest practices of influential women (1 Tim 2:9, 15) and to name the effect the indwelling Spirit is to have on Timothy as Paul's faithful successor (see 2 Tim 1:7). Paul's point here, then, is that the mature believer's choices reflect or bear witness to conversion to Christ and represents the earnest believer's commitment to "sound doctrine" rather than to self-centered appetites. Virtue is for Paul the calling card of Christian faith.

"Older men" are those around fifty years old according to the medical formula used by Hippocrates in a world where life-expectancy for males was probably mid to late forties. Their moral profile is arranged in a pair of triads, a device that conveys the sense of a complete listing and that is frequently used in paraenesis. The first triad consists of social virtues headed by a "prudent" or sober manner (νηφάλιος, *nēphalios*; cf. 1 Tim 3:2, 11), while the second is introduced by the familiar Pauline catchword "healthy" to define the spiritual characteristics of the mature Christian man. This second triad recalls the famous "Pauline triad" in 1 Cor 13:13 (cf. 1 Thess 1:3) as the ideal of a Christian life. More critically, given Paul's missionary sensibilities, the virtues of "faith, love, and patience," had wide currency in the religious if not also secular world of his day. The subtext of this triad, of course, is that "healthy faith" is only formed by "healthy teaching" of the kind transmitted by the delegates of the Pauline apostolate.

"Older women" are also in their fifties. They are marked out by their "reverent" (ἱεροπρεπεῖς, *hieroprepeis*) manners (see 1 Tim 2:15; cf. 2 Tim 2:21), a catchword used by Hellenistic Jewish writers such as Philo to describe the religious practices of exemplary believers (*Abraham* 101; *Abel and Cain* 45; cf. *4 Maccabees* 9:25) and therefore in sharp contrast to those accused of practices that "defile" the household (1:15-16). Paul continues his emphasis on the practical importance of edifying speech: the women are not to "slander" (διαβόλους, *diabolous*) others but are "teachers of virtue," a contrast that evokes a more cosmic contention between the powers and principalities aligned with the devil, who slanders God, and those aligned with the agents of Christ, including the apostle.[11] "Addicted to heavy drinking" (δουλόω, *douloō*), sandwiched between, names a form of slavery that contrasts with the apostle's slavery (δοῦλος, *doulos*) to God (1:1). This principled concern with what is spoken reflects a social world in which speech and virtue were intimately linked. Control of one's speech is especially critical for teachers (James 3), so temperance in both drink and language was often sounded as a cautionary note for congregational leaders. Moreover, idle talk and drunkenness were elements of the caricatures of older (especially middle-class) women that Paul draws on but then demythologizes in presenting women as tradents with a religious portfolio equal to that of the household's older men.

The primary purpose of the public display of the older women's virtue is to cultivate female modesty in younger women — those "twenty-somethings" who were beginning their careers as homemakers and wives. Although women had other careers in the ancient world, typically made necessary by financial need or social class, the ideal role women performed in the polite society of Paul's world was domestic. The list here (2:4-5) is the standard job description of an ideal Roman wife, baptized into a Christian motive, "so that God's word may not be ridiculed." The repetition of "God's word" reminds the reader that this is the pattern of teaching entrusted to Paul (1:3), which is now delegated to faithful tradents in his absence (cf. 2 Tim 1:12-14).

The list of domestic practices in 2:5a is appropriate for "young women who love their husbands and children" (v. 4). No reason is given for the expansive and particular attention Paul gives to young wives but then not to young husbands; it is unwise to speculate about the circumstances of this concern and better to fill out what is addressed to husbands in other household codes in the Pauline canon.[12] On the face of it, the list presents the well-regarded practices of the competent woman whose management of her home was the sine qua non of an orderly society. Home management was the sphere of a woman's singular influence, where her virtue could have its most telling result. The exegete must not lose sight of the organizing conception of divine providence in these letters, which supposes that the Creator's way of ordering reality insinuates certain social patterns on human existence. The chaos of "the last days" is understood in part as the result of social

---

11. Cf. Bassler, *1 Timothy, 2 Timothy, Titus*, 194.
12. Cf. Knight, *Pastoral Epistles*, 308-9.

anarchy, when lovers of self will disobey even their parents (2 Tim 3:1-2; cf. Rom 1:28-31).

A passage about young wives, then, reflects a Pauline way of thinking about human life, in which what happens at home is a measure of agreement with God's plan to restore order through the gospel ministry of Paul and his delegates. In this sense wives who are "good (ἀγαθός, *agathos*) homemakers" provide examples of those who know God and whose "every good (ἀγαθός, *agathos*) work" compounds evidence of their obedience to God's word (cf. 1:16).

Contemporary protests against this portrait of an ideal woman are misplaced if their motive is to decanonize this passage as hopelessly irrelevant for today's Christian women. The text defines female competence in terms of the Greco-Roman household; other prospects for women are not demonized but perhaps thought irrelevant at that time. Moreover, this ideal need not be demonized as making a woman of today a victim of patriarchal society when in fact the opposite may be true: ambitions shaped by a preference to be like males have left women even more disaffected and unfulfilled.[13]

On the other hand, to reify this portrait of the ideal young wife of Roman society as a normative pattern for all Christian women, thereby trumping a single life or a call to ministry or to a career outside the home, is also subversive of its canonical role. This canonical text is present to all its faithful readers, but the conservative pattern it stipulates is not prescriptive for all, but sets out a principle of the importance of female relationships within a loving household, in which older "teachers of virtue" mentor younger women in manners that underwrite rather than discredit the claims of the gospel (see above on 1 Tim 2:8-15; 3:6-7; 5:9-16).

The sparse imperative for young men to be prudent in decision-making (2:6) focuses on a signal virtue, prudence or modesty, again with a *sōphron*-word (see above on v. 2). It recalls a richly textured range of conservative practices, male and female, that underwrite the claims of God's word, especially in earshot of outsiders who otherwise might be suspicious of the faith community. This purpose is indicated in two ἵνα *(hina)* clauses, which stipulate the religious purpose of a young wife's domestic practices and of Titus's ministerial practices is to prevent ridicule of God's word (2:5b) and to promote respect from opponents (2:8b). This regard for the outsider is prompted

---

13. Although published in 1972, the work of conservative intellectual Midge Decter remains a perceptive treatment of the tensions felt by many middle-class women today precisely because of the increased freedoms they have. See especially her *The New Chastity and Other Arguments against Women's Liberation* (New York: Coward, McCann, and Geoghegan, 1972).

by soteriology, not sociology, and represents the canonical shape of the Pauline mission to the nations: "God our Savior wills everybody to be saved and to come to knowledge of the truth" (1 Tim 2:3b-4).[14]

The coda directed to Titus in 2:7-8 reminds him that domestic and sacred households require similar tasks that share a commitment to social propriety. Paul links Titus with the young men but names a motive similar to the one given to young women: "put yourself forward as a role model of good works . . . so that the opponent may respect us, finding nothing bad to say." The list of "good works" is similar to 1 Tim 4:12-16, including practices that take seriously the content and manner of "teaching" (διδασκαλία, *didaskalia*), the quintessential task of the faithful tradent.

As many as half of those who lived in the Roman cities of Paul's world were slaves, and a sizeable percentage of the others were former slaves. Slaves were included as important members of middle-class households and were responsible for a wide variety of chores inside and outside the household. Standard household codes in the ancient world prescribed duties to domestic servants, encouraging them to work hard to insure their masters' success and good reputation while guarding against illegal practices (e.g., "skimming from the top"). Ironically, in the ancient world the formal "liturgy" for manumission often included an announcement that the freed slave was now in service of some local deity or the emperor. Perhaps this is the subtext of Paul's concluding phrase, if only in a metaphorical sense: Christian slaves are to live as though they are now slaves to the God who freed them from sin.

The verbal idea of the concluding purpose clause in 2:10, "adorn" (κοσμέω, *kosmeō*), comes from the "cosmos/cosmic" word family, and its most common use refers to the "cosmetic" that one applies to make one's public appearance more appealing to others. According to Paul, then, healthy relationships within the household provide an external beauty that presents the inward beliefs of the faith in a comely form that impresses the world: believers should appear in public as the very picture of spiritual health. Putting on and wearing what is taught about God our Savior is a public adornment that is especially important in a world where the honor or shame of a household is judged on what is seen and heard in public. Here, for example, the motive of both the young wife's (v. 5) or servant's (v. 9) "submission" to the husband or master is also for public consumption. In Paul's instructions, the honor that accrues to a Christian household comes from conduct that protects "the teaching about God our Savior" from public ridicule (see above on 1 Tim 6:1-2).

---

14. See Lewis R. Donelson, *Colossians, Ephesians, 1 and 2 Timothy, and Titus* (Louisville: Westminster John Knox, 1996), 176-77.

From the perspective of moral philosophers, people were made more sensible by cultivating a life of the mind and were thereby saved from making foolish choices. Hence the importance attached to good teaching (e.g., Dio Chrysostom, *Orations* 32.15-16). From Paul's perspective, however, the Christian motive for complying with this otherwise secular household code is to underwrite the truth of the gospel's central claim that God is our Savior.

2:11-14 Salvation's Appearance

¹¹For the grace of God has appeared, educating us about salvation for all people ¹²in order that by rejecting godliness and worldly desires we may live modest, upright, and godly lives right now, ¹³while we wait for the blessed hope and the appearing of the glory of the great God along with our Savior Jesus Christ, ¹⁴who gave himself for us to rescue us from total lawlessness and to cleanse a special people for himself, eager for good works.

The conjunction "for" (γάρ, *gar*) indicates that the important theological formula that follows explains the reason for Paul's directions to the Christian household that precedes it. The theological motive for those practical virtues is the "teaching about God our Savior" (2:10b), and this passage formulates the core beliefs of that teaching in a single sentence. Salvation is an epiphany of divine grace that trains all people to reject godlessness for godly lives (vv. 11-12) and to hope for the coming victory of God that will bring to realization the saving initiative of Christ (vv. 13-14). Because of the distinctive glossary of theological terms, most found only here in the Pauline canon, most scholars think this formula is lifted from a worship book or liturgy with only slight modification, known to the letter's recipient, and placed in the letter as a reminder of the tradent's core beliefs that fund "the teaching about God our Savior."

The catchphrase "God our Savior" (2:10; also in 3:4) is especially well chosen since it resonates with both Jewish and pagan readers. In the Hellenistic world, pagan deities were thought of as benefactors who granted favors (or "grace") to their subjects, especially when making holy "house calls." God's appearance when grace is dispensed serves an educative purpose: "educating us" to live in a socially acceptable manner. The assumption of the household code in 2:2-10 is that a Christian's public life embodies the truth claims of the Christian gospel for all to see — a sight that is hardly repulsive but rather highly attractive to those who look on (vv. 5, 8, 10).

This crucial claim is made even clearer by repetition of key words that link the purpose clause in 2:10b with the opening line of this theological summary: "in everything . . . for all people," and "the teaching about God our Savior . . . educating us about salvation for all people" (see above on 1 Tim 2:3-6). The word we have translated with "educating about salvation" is σωτήριος *(sōterios)*, an adjective form that appears only here in the NT. Its precise meaning is unclear, but its plain sense here is not and is surely Pauline. The essential idea is picked up from Jewish wisdom: teaching about God provides the knowledge necessary for salvation (see 2 Tim 3:15; cf. 1 Tim 2:4; 2 Tim 2:25; 3:7). Pauline theology is missionary theology: its endgame is not declension of nouns that define God's existence but conjugation of verbs that help people mark out God's saving activity in the world. People come to knowledge of the truth as the condition of their conversion to Christ. Sharply put, then, if the household code is the moral "cosmetic" the church brings into the public square for the world to see, then 2:11-14 states what thus gets taught about God's way of salvation.

This theological foundation of the Christian household is constructed as two core beliefs about God our Savior. The first is that "the grace of God has appeared (ἐπιφαίνω, *epiphainō*)" (2:11). The unusual personification of grace is a poetic way of recalling the person and work of Jesus (see 1 Tim 1:15-16); that is, the appearance of Jesus supplies a catechism of God's grace. We learn about grace, then, from the "the healthy teachings about our Lord Jesus Christ" (1 Tim 6:3), but, since "Christ Jesus came into the world to save sinners" (1 Tim 1:15), grace is also learned by a concrete experience of salvation from sin (so 1 Tim 1:14-16). Paul clearly wants Titus to reflect on the community's actual experience of God's grace — grace alone, its meaning and singular importance for advancing the gospel.

This passage mentions two elements of this experience of God's saving grace, both with implicit reference to the preceding instructions for the household of faith. (1) The sphere of God's grace extends to all people. Although Paul's reason for emphasizing the inclusiveness of salvation here is not clear, he probably has the household code (rather than his opponents) in mind. That is, the grace of God is for everyone in the community and excludes no one by gender, age, or social class. For this reason, every member and every relationship of the household of God must exemplify the results of God's grace in their life together. (2) The grace of our divine Benefactor saves us not only *from* sin and death but also *to live* in new ways that accord with God's high standards. The sharp contrast between vice ("godlessness and worldly desires") and virtue ("modest, upright, and godly lives") in 2:12 expresses Christian conversion in practical terms: their real experience of divine grace schools believers into a moral household of the kind described in vv. 2-

10. Grace, again personified, has its effect in Christian formation by the mediation of the Spirit through word and sacrament.

The second core belief about God our Savior named here concerns the "blessed hope" of a future appearance of "our great God along with our Savior Jesus Christ" (2:13). The confusing syntax of this passage is reflected in the differences among translations. Marshall lists three main interpretations: (1) it refers to two persons, God and Jesus Christ, both of whom are co-saviors of the world; (2) it refers only to Jesus Christ, whose "glorious appearing" discloses God; and (3) it refers only to Jesus Christ, who is in fact "our God and Savior."[15] All three readings agree that only one person makes an "appearance": Jesus Christ. The question is whether Jesus will appear as God incarnate or as the medium of divine glory or our salvation. I prefer the first of Marshall's three readings, translating the conjunction καί *(kai)* as "along with" for clarity. While the grammar and patristic evidence favor the third alternative, the canonical context does not. Nowhere else in the Pauline canon do we find θεός *(theos,* "God") used of Jesus, whereas in this letter's opening both God and Jesus are titled "our Savior" (1:3-4). Moreover, while the omission of an article before "Savior" may be explained as indicating its pairing with τοῦ μεγάλου θεοῦ *(tou megalou theou,* "of our great God"), it does not require it; in fact, it is more unlikely that *tou megalou theou* refers to both God and Christ without clear indication of an intent or precedent to do so. Finally, the attribution of "Savior" to Jesus Christ and of a future "epiphany," when interpreted by Paul's messianic Christology, does not require that Christ also is divine — only risen and exalted. This is not to deny those vague indications within the Pauline canon that nudge the reader toward Nicaea. But it is puzzling, if *theos* is taken as attributed to Christ, that there is no clear sense of his deity in 1 Tim 3:16, even though it was probably written after Titus and stands as the fullest Christological confession of the Pauline canon.

To what, then, does the "appearing of the glory of the great God" refer if not to Christ's parousia? The epiphany of God's glory, as with that of God's grace (v. 11), expresses an effect or experience of salvation. "Glory," δόξα *(doxa),* is typically found in doxological refrains in the Pastoral Epistles

---

15. I. Howard Marshall and Philip H. Towner, *A Critical and Exegetical Commentary on the Pastoral Epistles* (ICC; Edinburgh: Clark, 1999), 276-82, who prefer, with other conservative exegetes, the third alternative because it makes better sense of the absence of the article with "savior" and of the earliest history of interpretation, which clearly reads the phrase as a Pauline confession of the Second Person as both God and Savior. See also Murray J. Harris, "Titus 2:13 and the Deity of Christ," in *Pauline Studies: Essays Presented to Professor F. F. Bruce on His 70th Birthday* (ed. Donald A. Hagner and Murray J. Harris; Grand Rapids: Eerdmans, 1980), 262-77; Knight, *Pastoral Epistles,* 322-26.

(1 Tim 1:11, 17; 3:16; 2 Tim 4:18), which imagine God, even though invisible and heavenly, as a substantial and personal deity whose presence is manifestly experienced.[16] In this sense, the future appearance of God's glory anticipates a fully realized experience of God's salvation from sin that will arrive at the return of Jesus to complete his messianic work.

The community's hope for this future moment is "blessed." The blessing motif is rare in a Pauline vocabulary of salvation. The connection of blessing with the gospel of God's salvation from sin (1 Tim 1:11) is behind Paul's quotation of LXX Psalm 31 in Rom 4:7-8, where God promises covenant blessing on those who are forgiven from sin. If the first epiphany of grace has abolished death, then this second epiphany of grace as the object of the community's "blessed hope" must be a final justification, when the full effect of the Christ event is to be realized in a new creation freed from all sin and death. Only in such a setting will the glory of the great God, in whom no darkness exists whatsoever (1 John 1:5), be finally disclosed. E. Radner has argued that what the church "blesses" — in this case its hope — identifies publicly for all to see what it believes about who God is and what God does.[17] The community's public expression of its expectations for salvation's future thus indicates its core beliefs about the enduring results of God's grace. In this particular formula the plural participle προσδεχόμενοι *(prosdechomenoi)*, "awaiting," has a pair of integral objects: ἐλπίδα *(elpida)*, "hope," and ἐπιφάνειαν *(epiphaneian)*, "appearing." That is, the kind of hope blessed by the community is of an experience of divine glory that will ultimately vindicate for all to see the community's proclamation of God's salvation.

The "glory of God" is, of course, a prophetic idiom (especially in Isaiah and Ezekiel) and refers to the power and splendor of God's character that finally "will fill the whole earth." Certainly Paul's primary concern lies with the concrete demonstration of God's glory at the end of human history. As with God's grace, this consummation is also linked with the (re-)appearance of Christ on earth. God's grace has already made its appearance in the messianic mission of the Suffering Servant "for the salvation of all people." But this salvation and its transforming results (2:11-12) are harbingers of God's restored creation, in which the redeemed community will live forever (cf. Isa 66:18-23), and this hope is blessed precisely because believers have this end in sight.

The striking personification of God's grace (2:11-12) and coming glory (v. 13) to fulfill God's promise of a new creation is Christological to the bone

---

16. Collins, *Timothy and Titus*, 353.
17. Ephraim Radner, "Blessing: A Scriptural and Theological Reflection," *Pro Ecclesia* 19 (2010): 7-27.

and is elaborated as Christology in v. 14. The prior arrival of God's grace with Christ and the blessed hope of the future arrival of God's glory also with Christ are both predicated upon his atoning death. Christ volunteers himself, a sacrifice for sin, both to "redeem us from sin" — the sinner's "new exodus" out of his "Egyptian" captivity to sin and death — and "to purify a people for himself" — a liberated Israel's Passover in preparation for their long journey to their future Promised Land.

With the final phrase of 2:14, "zealous for good deeds," we come to the key to the interplay between moral teaching and theological confession, which forms the literary structure of the letter's paraenesis. Why must the congregation of believers live according to the standard Paul establishes in vv. 2-10? Because the grace of God has already appeared with the death of Jesus "for us," and grace is the power of God for a transformed life that purifies the covenant community from sin for a performance of "good works," which characterize the new life that heralds the coming triumph of God over sin and death.

This formulation of the Christian life sounds loud echoes of another epiphany of God's grace: the theophany at Sinai, which founded Israel as a Torah community. The Passover typology is already cued by the use of λυτρόω *(lytroō)*, "rescue," a verb used rarely in the NT but an important and repeated catchword in the Passover narrative, where God's deliverance of Israel from Egypt is called an act of "redemption" (e.g., Exod 6:6; 13:13-15; 15:13; Deut 7:8). Especially if Christ's rescue of the "elect ones" (1:1) from "total lawlessness" — a community without the rule of law — for a thorough "cleansing of a special people eager for good works" (see 3:5) prepares them for the "glorious appearing of the great God," then the Passover typology includes Sinai and Israel's purification (Exod 19:10-15) in preparation for a divine visitation (Exod 19:16-20). Paul recalls Moses to establish a pattern of covenant-keeping by which the church behaves as a "holy nation" by being "zealous for good works" according to God's law and in response to God's liberating grace (cf. Exod 19:3-6). In light of the exhortation to Titus to use this theological material when refuting Paul's opponents from the circumcision (2:15), its decisively biblical cast, reimagining the Christ event as typified by the exodus and his coming epiphany by Sinai, is especially apropos in doing battle with rebellious Jewish teachers (see 1:10-11).

As an apt summary of Pauline soteriology, 2:11-14 performs an important canonical role in arranging the apostle's argument logically. "The grace of God our Savior" breaks into human existence — it is an epiphany or apocalypse of sheer mercy — to train all people to think rightly. "Jesus Christ our Savior" gave his life to rescue all sinful people from their "total lawlessness," which would otherwise lead them away from God's grace to self-destruction.

Those who are saved from their sins and submit their lives to the training of divine grace will eagerly pursue a life of good works pleasing to God. This manner of transformed existence, perhaps along with even faith itself, is impossible prior to divine action. People are trapped in "total lawlessness" from which only an act of divine mercy can deliver them. The "good works" are the covenant-keeping works of a special people whose "blessed hope" is the appearance once again of God our Savior to grant them, as before, the promise of eternal life (see 1:1-3).

2:15–3:8c Salvation's Bath

¹⁵Talk about these things. Encourage and refute with complete authority; let no one disregard you. 3:¹Remind them to be subject to rulers and authorities, obedient, prepared for every good work. ²They should disrespect no one, but be peaceful, kind, showing complete civility toward everyone. ³For we too were once foolish, disobedient, deceived, enslaved to desires and various pleasures, living in evil and envy, hateful, and hating others. ⁴But "when the goodness and friendship of God our Savior appeared ⁵ — not because we had done works of moral rectitude but because of God's mercy — God saved us through a bath of rebirth and renewal of the Holy Spirit, ⁶whom God poured out on us abundantly by Jesus Christ our Savior, ⁷so that, having been made righteous by that grace, we may become heirs of the hope of eternal life." ⁸This saying is a core belief. I want you to insist on these things so that those who have come to believe in God may give careful attention to good works.

This passage includes the second grand theological formulation of the epiphany of God's salvation in Titus, which is very much like the first in 2:11-14. They are mutually glossing: in both, instruction and exhortation of both Titus and his congregation (2:1-10; 2:15–3:3) are followed by highly compressed statements on the epiphany of God's goodness (2:11-14; 3:4-8a) that serve as the doctrinal foundation for the present experience of God's salvation. As in the first instance, this text also concludes with an exhortation to "give careful attention to good works" (2:14b; 3:8bc). Salvation is confirmed by its concrete moral effect on those who experience the Spirit's outpouring.

The title I have given to this pericope derives from the translation of λουτρόν *(loutron)* as "bath" (3:5), used only here and in Eph 5:26 to portray the full effect of God's activity in Christian existence as a thorough washing that rids the covenant-keeping community of vice, cataloged here in 3:3. The passage opens with a series of exhortations for Titus to engage in the work of a faithful tradent, which centers on review and reminder. The first task continues from the exhortation of 2:1 to "talk" about "healthy teaching": Titus is to review the preceding instructions and theological formula (vv. 1-14) and "talk (λαλέω, *laleō*) about these things" (v. 15a) with others — not only because this is speech consistent with Pauline or "healthy" teaching but because Titus does so as a delegate of the Pauline apostolate and so as one "with complete authority." The reader should recall Titus's connection to the Pauline apostolate defined in the letter's greeting (1:1-3): Titus's "complete authority" is predicated on his relationship with Paul as his "true child" and as such as "heir" of the ministry entrusted to the apostle of Jesus Christ "by the command of God our Savior."

The repetition of ἐλέγχω (*elenchō*, 2:15b; see 1:9, 13) recalls the earlier polemic against "the circumcision," mindful of the chaos its teachers are provoking in Christian households. The management style envisaged by the preceding household code, then, is the criterion by which not only are these teachers refuted but order is "encouraged" and restored. The plain sense of the following exhortation, "let no one disregard you" (2:15c), is that Titus's authority will be challenged when he attempts to refute teachers who oppose Paul's apostleship in the Cretan congregations founded by his mission. There is no sense that the possible disrespect is due to his young age, as with Timothy (1 Tim 4:12-14), or from the congregation itself.[18] Rather, the challenge is likely to come from Paul's opponents, who will dismiss as bogus Titus's appeal to Paul's apostolic credentials. For this reason, the initial exhortation to "talk about these things," including the theological formulation of Christ's epiphany as typified by exodus in a manner consistent with Paul's "healthy teaching" (2:1), suggests that the more effective appeal is to the content of the material and its usefulness in producing a redemptive result (cf. 2 Tim 1:8-14).

The community's relations within wider society continue from 2:1-10 and fill out the last bit of the letter's household code. The reminder to be "subject to rulers and authorities" (3:1a) is not only Pauline moral instruction (Rom 13:1-7; 1 Tim 2:1-2; also 1 Pet 2:11-17) but also the political imperative of Rome's imperial culture, which not only shaped Judaism's Diaspora community but is an admonition frequently found in the moral handbooks of antiquity. By Paul's day, the Roman Empire was more than three centuries old, and its social and political structures informed and formed all of life. Perhaps this exhortation, then, reflects the sober realism of a Jew who recognizes the importance of cooperating with civil powers as a means of a peaceful and even constructive coexistence (see 1 Tim 2:2).

---

18. But see Marshall and Towner, *Pastoral Epistles*, 296.

The irony of such behavior for Christians, who confess that God alone, not Caesar, is the Benefactor of a lasting peace, was nicely captured years later by John of Damascus, who wrote, "If men honor emperors . . . how much more ought we to worship the King of kings" (*Apologia against Those Who Decry Holy Images* 3.41). In fact, the rhetorical design of this instruction for Christians to be subject to civil rule and exemplify the marks of good citizenship, which is sandwiched between the two great epiphany formulations, which appropriate the idiom of imperial culture to confess allegiance to God and the hope of eternal life that only God can grant, must finally be read as subversive of Rome and of its Caesar. It is the friendship of God and not of Rome's Caesar that makes an appearance to liberate a people from lawlessness and to reorder them to live just lives in the present age (cf. 2:12).

The connection of the community's "obedience" to God's will and the production of "good works" (3:1b) is thematic of the Pastoral Epistles. But coming on the heels of an admonition for the Christian community to be subject to civil authority, especially when read alongside Acts 4:19-20; 5:29-32, this reminder to obey God is clearly ironical. On the face of it, the instruction commands the congregation to be law-abiding citizens, contributing "every good work" to a civil society. Perhaps Paul is recalling by using similar language the conflict caused by the teachers from "the circumcision" who are "disobedient and disqualified for every good work" (1:16) and therefore up to no good. However, since the theological subtext of this instruction is the "cleansing of a special people who are eager for good works" (2:14), what may be initially read as an exhortation to good citizenship (3:2) is in reality a reminder to act in a manner worthy of a covenant people who belong to God, not to the Caesar. As such, the social virtues listed, which are crucial in cultivating a civil society — respectful, peaceful, kind, prudent — may also be read as religious dispositions that mark out a people in whom the "grace of God has appeared" (2:11). In this sense, good citizenship in the present age may actually herald the coming victory of God's kingdom on earth.[19]

The "once but when" contrast gives rhetorical definition to the letter's second epiphany passage (3:3-7) and reflects the Christian experience of conversion. Undergirding the Pauline canon are two epiphanies: the past epiphany of Jesus Christ on earth to redeem sinners and his future epiphany to reestablish the glory of "the great God" in a new creation. Between these narrative moments is the ongoing experience of "a bath of rebirth and renewal of the Holy Spirit" (v. 5). Paul's Jewish scruples share with those of Hellenistic

---

19. Cf. Philip H. Towner, *The Letters to Timothy and Titus* (NICNT; Grand Rapids: Eerdmans, 2006), 771-72.

moral philosophers of his day (especially the Stoics) a core conviction that a truly religious people must convert from a life of sensual or illicit passions to a holy life (cf. 1 Cor 6:9-11; Eph 2:1-10; Col 3:1-8). For this reason, the manner of life from which the sinner is converted is shown in the kind of self-destructive passions listed: "foolish, disobedient, deceived, enslaved to desires and various pleasures, living in evil and envy, hateful and hating others" — all of which bear a striking family resemblance to the vices already attributed to Paul's opponents (1 Tim 4:1-2; 2 Tim 3:1-13; 4:3-4; Tit 1:16; 2:12). In particular, the final pair of this list, "hateful and hating others," is the opposite of "God's way of stewarding the world," which cultivates the inward affections necessary for "loving relationships" (1 Tim 1:4-5).

Personal transformation is an operation of God's grace executed within the bounds of a community's history of salvation that began "before time" (see above on 1:1-3). This theological belief concentrates Paul's canonical witness. But the idea is not novel to Christian faith.[20] For example, the following inscription dedicated to the Roman god Mithras and found near Rome, though it is from the second century C.E., contains an idea that probably extends back to the ancient church: ". . . the one well-pleasing to god who is reborn and re-created through sweet things." This ancient parallel speaks of conversion as new creation, and "sweetness" may well refer to the purifying role that honey performed as an ancient salve.

The confession of faith articulates in a single sentence the final canonical saying (πιστὸς ὁ λόγος, *pistos ho logos*, 3:8a) of the Pastoral Epistles collection (see above on 1 Tim 1:15; 3:1; 4:9; 2 Tim 2:11). This saying, like the others, is a dense formulation of the Pauline apostolate's core beliefs. It not only provides yet another substantive summary of a Pauline way of salvation, but currently functions within the Pauline canon as a hermeneutical key that regulates the reader's quest of the word of God in any of its letters.

The temporal phrase "But when" not only introduces a soft contrast with the vice list of 3:3 but recognizes that a decisive change of direction has already taken place in salvation's history because God's grace has made its friendly appearance "by Jesus Christ our Savior" (v. 6) and in the Pentecost "of the Holy Spirit" (v. 5). As a result, sin ends for the immoral community represented by the rogue of v. 3, who in conversion to Christ has become the kind neighbor capable of "every good work" (vv. 1-2) because of the good work of God's grace (so 2:11).

The two virtues Paul mentions in 3:4, "goodness" (χρηστότης, *chrēstotēs*) and "friendship" (φιλανθρωπία, *philanthrōpia*), describe the God who wants

---

20. Collins, *Timothy and Titus*.

not only to save everyone (see 1 Tim 2:3-4) but then to act on that desire by appearing as "our Savior," saving us from vice to restore the community of elect ones for virtue, giving them a moral competence that is "prepared for every good work" (v. 1). This is the nature of salvation, and it is in the very nature of our God to do all this. Bassler comments that the combination *chrēstotēs kai philanthrōpia* was frequently used in antiquity, in both secular and Jewish writings of Paul's time, to describe the actions of exemplary humans.[21] "Mercy" is the chief attribute of the benevolent judge (Plato, *Apology* 34-35). Both are also qualities of the benevolent ruler to whom cities would gladly open their gates in surrender. For example, the Rosetta Stone speaks of Ptolemy V's "kindness" toward those he conquered, aimed to insure that his new subjects show him their love and gratitude in return (cf. Plutarch, *Cicero* 21.4). And no biblical passage scores this same point with greater theological power than 1 John 4:19: "We love because God first loved us." That is, the divine act of loving us in Christ not only discloses the nature of God as love (1 John 4:9) but thereby models the nature of a people in whom God abides (1 John 4:12, 19).

What follows this affirmation about God is a dense and syntactically uncertain confession that this "God our Savior appeared . . . God saved us" (3:4-5). This is a core belief of the Pauline apostolate, and it encloses yet another core belief that contrasts humanity's failed attempts to earn God's salvation by "works of moral rectitude" with the ultimate triumph of God's mercy (v. 5), the contrast made in Romans (e.g., Rom 3:21-31; 4:1-5; 9:30–10:13). Here, the conflict between human works and divine mercy is made even more emphatic in the Greek text by the location of the main verbal idea, "God saved us," after the contrast has been asserted rather than before, as it is in most translations. That is, the rhetorical design of this letter's reformulation of the centerpiece of the Pauline gospel has the appearance and act of God's salvation enclosing and glossing the contrast between works and mercy in terms of the divine nature. In this sense, then, humanity's "works of moral rectitude" do not work as the means of our salvation because they are at odds with who God is.

Curiously in a letter whose background noise includes rumblings from teachers of "the circumcision," "works of righteousness" is not attached to law-keeping or other purity routines required by a Jewish pattern of proselytism. Here the phrase appears to represent a much broader sweep of works so as to subvert *any* human effort, no matter how pleasing to God. Grace breaks into human existence to save sinners from total lawlessness because of the epiphany of a good and friendly Benefactor, not because of humanity's religious and moral performances.

---

21. Bassler, *1 Timothy, 2 Timothy, Titus*, 207; cf. Knight, *Pastoral Epistles*, 338.

This letter makes clear God's delight in good works (2:4, 14; 3:1, 8, 14),[22] thus sharpening the idea that God befriends us not because we get things right but because a merciful God rights things. Clearly, a Pauline pattern of salvation does not rule out good works from the believer's life; it simply rejects the idea that "good works" of any sort are the precondition, rather than the consequence, of the saving grace that has arrived with God's appearance and is now brokered through the Spirit of the risen Christ. People are in need of "rescue from total lawlessness" (see 2:14); God's epiphany is an apocalypse of truth so that everyone might "come to knowledge of truth" and be saved from their sin (see 1 Tim 2:3-4).[23]

What follows this main idea that "God saves" is an expansive prepositional phrase that summarizes the saving work that is mediated "through" (διά, *dia* of agency) the Holy Spirit (3:5b). "Nowhere else does Scripture speak as fully and explicitly about the content and activity of the means of salvation as it does here."[24] The phrase unravels a string of three nouns, all indefinite genitives and metaphors of salvation that together set out in bold relief the comprehensive work performed by the Spirit poured out at Pentecost "through Jesus Christ our Savior" to conduct and complete God's rescue of sinners. The key exegetical question regards the relationships among these three nouns and their relationship to "the Holy Spirit," which then shows up in the translation and interpretation of this text as the quintessential summary of Pauline pneumatology in the letters.[25]

Before treating this important triad of nouns, it seems important to identify the occasion of the Spirit's reception by the community. The verb ἐκχέω *(ekcheō)*, "poured out" (3:6), while also used figuratively in Rom 5:5 of the Spirit who "pours out" God's love into the heart of every believer, more

---

22. Marshall, *Pastoral Epistles*.

23. The current battle over a normative definition of Pauline justification, prompted by the New Perspective scholars such as N. T. Wright and J. D. G. Dunn, is deeply vested in this contrast and in the kind of "works" Paul rejects. Douglas A. Campbell, *The Deliverance of God: An Apocalyptic Rereading of Justification in Paul* (Grand Rapids: Eerdmans, 2009), views God's epiphany in apocalyptic terms so that God's mercy makes its appearance with stunning and surprising force. The very idea of God's universal judgment of works, which Paul speaks of in Rom 2:1-11, is the belief of "the teacher" — Paul's interlocutor and opponent. Paul's pattern of salvation is utterly theocentric from beginning to end. It is teachers from groups such as "the circumcision" who claim that covenant-keeping works are the criterion of God's final justification.

24. Knight, *Pastoral Epistles*, 342.

25. For a recent history-of-religion treatment of Scripture's pneumatology and an appraisal of Paul's distinctive contribution, see now J. R. Levison's superb study, *Filled with the Spirit* (Grand Rapids: Eerdmans, 2009). Also, Towner, *Letters to Timothy and Titus*, 779-86, who sees an intertextual link with Ezekiel 36 as the backdrop for hearing the echo of Joel 3:1-2.

likely recalls the main verb of Joel's prophecy of the day of the Lord, when the Spirit is "poured out" on Israel to cue a terrible day of judgment intended to prompt Israel's repentance and eventual survival (LXX Joel 3:1-4). While Paul is familiar with Joel's prophecy (Rom 10:13; 1 Cor 1:2), it seems to shape not his conception of the Spirit but his teaching that justification is by faith alone. Although the latter is clearly here too (3:5a), most interpreters think the saying is cued by the story of Pentecost in Acts and in particular by Peter's use of Joel to prove that the Spirit's baptism of believers inaugurates salvation's "last days" (Acts 2:17-18; cf. 10:45). The change of tense from future (Joel 3:1; Acts 2:17) to aorist here (3:6) indicates what Acts makes clear: God's promise of the eschatological Spirit has now been realized, the dispensation of salvation's "last days" has commenced, and everyone who calls on the risen Lord will be saved from their sins (Acts 2:21 as interpreted by Acts 2:22-41).[26]

Calvin (with others) hears an echo of Ezek 36:25 (cf. 1:15), where God promises to "sprinkle clean water upon you . . . to cleanse you from impurity." Calvin's syntactical decision to separate "bath of rebirth" from "renewing of the Holy Spirit" allows him to reconnect "bath of rebirth" with Christian baptism (= "sprinkle clean water") as "a visible symbol of (the Spirit's washing of regeneration) beheld in baptism."[27] This reading of the awkward syntax of the phrase is unwise because the single *dia* indicates that "rebirth and renewal" are the same and more fully elaborate the Spirit's role in the working out of God's saving mercy. But I do not fault Calvin's reading for finding in this phrase an argument for baptism, which we think entirely appropriate, even if unintended by the letter's author.

The subsequent *dia* phrase, "by Jesus Christ our Savior" (3:6), picks up the Pentecost claim (and the Christology of Acts 2:33) that the crucified and exalted Jesus is the one by whom God's prophecy of the Spirit's outpouring is fulfilled (Acts 1:4-5). The relationship between God our Savior and Jesus Christ our Savior is thereby cast in Acts as prophecy and fulfillment: Jesus fulfills what God has promised according to Israel's Scriptures. Read against this canonical backdrop, the double use of "savior" in this saying carries the same theological freight: the promise of eternal life made by God our Savior "before time began" (1:2) has now been fulfilled by Jesus Christ our Savior, who pours out the Spirit on the "elect ones" as the bath of salvation. To assume that a fully Nicene conception of a triune Deity stands behind this Pauline

---

26. See Robert W. Wall, "Acts," in *The New Interpreter's Bible* (Nashville: Abingdon, 2001), 10:60-70.

27. Calvin, *Epistles to Timothy*, 195.

confession would surely be anachronistic, but the shared responsibility of "God our Savior" who "pours out" the Holy Spirit "by Jesus Christ our Savior" coheres closely to a Trinitarian conception of salvation.

What must be allowed when constructing this intertext between Acts 2 and Titus 3 are the different conceptions of the Spirit at play in the two texts. According to Acts, the Lord pours out God's Spirit to empower a ministry that continues what he had begun to do and say according to the Gospel (so Acts 1:1-2). The Spirit's entry into the community is marked by signs and wonders, by extraordinary feats of biblical interpretation, and by persuasive preaching, all of which confirm the Gospel narrative about the risen Jesus. But in the narrative world of Acts the Spirit is not an agent of salvation poured out by God to transform the sinner into a saint. While Luke's conception of a vocation-minded Spirit is certainly present in a passage like 2 Tim 1:6-7, the Pauline formulation of the Spirit's work, here in Titus 3, is more focused on its agency in the personal transformation of the believer. While the clear allusions to the Pentecost tradition suggest that it is shared by storyteller and letter-writer alike, it is equally clear that Paul received and shaped this tradition with a different conception of the Spirit. Within the bounds of this epiphany saying, God poured out the Spirit through Jesus Christ in order to bathe believers in regeneration and renewal, not to empower their mission to the end of the earth.

We have translated λουτρόν *(loutron)* as "bath," aware of its use as a trope for Spirit baptism, which is borrowed from the Pentecost tradition: God pours the Spirit like water over the covenant community. The noun is used of a bath or washing with water, and some have argued that it is used of water baptism, though Spirit baptism is more likely. The effect of this bath is the spiritual cleansing of the Lord's "special people" for "good works" (2:14; cf. Eph 5:26; see also the use of *louō* in Heb 10:22). The eschatological importance for Paul of such a spiritual bath is unambiguous in Rom 2:1-16, which affirms the belief that God's final justification will appraise whether or not a person has performed holy works during her life (cf. Rom 6:22; 2 Cor 5:10). "Good works" are produced in the believer's life by the indwelling Spirit's operation and supply hard evidence that the sinner's "total lawlessness" has been washed away and that her life is being directed by the Spirit of life. In this sense (and with the opposition of "the circumcision" as a subtext), the indwelling Spirit is at work in this special people to produce what the Torah cannot and was never intended to produce: a new life of virtue (3:1-2) cleansed of vice (v. 3) as testimony that God's salvation has arrived.

The single preposition *dia* indicates a single Spirit baptism, but with a pair of effects: παλιγγενεσίας *(palingenesias),* "rebirth," and ἀνακαινώσεως *(anakainōseōs),* "renewal."²⁸ *Palingenesia* appears elsewhere in the NT only in Matt 19:28. Most commentators pin its meaning to its general use in antiquity for rebirth or restoration, but the Matthean use can be helpful for understanding Titus.²⁹

Matthew's Jesus responds ironically to Peter's question regarding the future reward of those who have given up material goods to follow Jesus: the reward will be the task of "judging the twelve tribes of Israel" in the *palingenesia* — an expansive exercise of authority that doubtless includes Israel's restoration. "In the *palingenesia*" in Matthew's redaction of this saying has been variously understood and translated, but probably refers to an extended period of time "until the end of the age" (Matt 28:20). That is, it makes little sense to place the apostolic practice of judging in the eschaton, when it will be too late to matter. Rather, the *palingenesia* is a hopeful figuration of the present age when apostolic authority will be exercised on God's behalf to bring about the promise of a restored Israel.³⁰ Such is what the Spirit's coming at Pentecost inaugurates according to Acts.

In Titus, the washing away of the community's total lawlessness and its performance of good works (2:14) testify not only to the presence of the indwelling Spirit but also to the fulfillment of God's promise of a restored Israel. *Palingenesia* may thus recall Paul's teaching that God's promise now extends to repentant Gentiles, represented here by Titus, who have been grafted into the restored Israel to receive the eschatological blessings promised by God (so Rom 11:11-24). Implicit in this new reality is the authority of the Pauline apostolate to bring the "word of faith" near so that those who call on the Lord's name will be saved (so Rom 10:9-13). The instruction of the Pastoral Epistles to mind the Pauline apostolate ultimately targets this redemptive plan (see above on 1 Tim 2:3-7).

The last of the three nouns is ἀνακαίνωσις *(anakainōsis):* God pours out the Spirit through Jesus Christ to bathe believers in rebirth and "renewal" (cf. Isa 44:3). The same word is used in Rom 12:2 of the transformed way a graced community thinks about God's will (cf. Col 3:10), but it also cues the root word *kainos*, which is used in the Pauline canon to denote the creation of something "new" in Christ Jesus (2 Cor 5:17; Gal 6:15; Eph 2:15; 4:28), and *kainotēs*, used in Rom 6:4 of the "new life" that results from participating in the death and resurrection of Christ and with "the Spirit" in Rom 7:6 in a for-

---

28. Cf. Towner, *Letters to Timothy and Titus,* 783.
29. For a survey, see Mounce, *Pastoral Epistles,* 449-50.
30. W. D. Davies and Dale C. Allison, *A Critical and Exegetical Commentary on the Gospel According to Saint Matthew* (ICC; Edinburgh: Clark, 1988), 3.

mulation that denotes the Spirit-led manner of the covenant community's slavery to God.³¹ The issue at stake in Titus is the congregation's moral and spiritual transformation from a life of vice to one of virtue initiated by God's epiphany (3:3-4; cf. Gal 5:16-26) and conducted under the direction of the Holy Spirit. In this regard, the combined meaning of "rebirth and renewal" seems to envisage transformed existence, however vaguely, as the end-product of a maturing process in God's direction (cf. 2:11-12) — some even think of two discrete stages ("rebirth," then "renewal") — by which every believer becomes a morally competent person.

The ultimate purpose (ἵνα, *hina*, "so that") of God's epiphany for the work of salvation is finally stated: "having been made righteous by that grace, we may become heirs of the hope for eternal life" (3:7). First, the application of God's saving grace makes sinners righteous. This affirmation evokes one of the most contested features in Pauline studies today: the meaning of "justify" in a Pauline pattern of salvation, which is put into play by the opening chapters of Romans (and so of the Pauline canon).³² My translation of the passive participle tips my hand in the debate. The expression is a judicial metaphor: a judge renders a verdict of acquittal based on evidence of innocence. Here God gives the verdict of "not guilty" on the sole basis of Christ's faithfulness (Rom 3:21-31). But if this verdict is then applied individualistically as an internal matter of the heart and thereby detached from any real change in the way one lives, then we would suggest that it is far wide of the mark. According to this "core belief," the pouring out and reception of the Spirit issue in the "rebirth and renewal" — that is, the transformation — of human existence. While a righteousness of works is not a precondition for God's rescue operation of sinners (so 3:5a), a righteousness of works is its certain outcome.

The setting into which this confession is placed makes this redemptive calculus clear. The preceding theological formula (see 2:11-14) concludes that grace redeems a lawless people to be law-abiding (so 2:14), and this result is illustrated by a conversion from vice to virtue (3:1-4). Even more clearly, the main body of this letter concludes with another *hina* clause: a people who believe what Paul teaches about God will "give careful attention to good works"

---

31. N. T. Wright, "Romans," in *The New Interpreter's Bible* (Nashville: Abingdon, 2001), 10:560-61.

32. Most recently Campbell has entered the fray with *Deliverance of God*, which is devoted to a study of justification in Romans 1–4. While Campbell seeks to remove the human element entirely from his radically apocalyptic rereading of Paul's argument, he also argues that Romans 5–8 and its depiction of a liberated and transformed humanity is crucial to a fully Pauline notion of justification. It is more than a verdict of innocence; it is God transforming a people after God's own righteousness.

(v. 8b). In fact, the letter's theme of "good works" (1:16; 2:7, 14; 3:1, 8, 14) leads the reader to an inescapable impression that the full purchase of God's saving mercy is more than forgiveness of sin or the imputation of undeserved righteousness: a salvation brokered by the Spirit produces good works, by which the covenant community's future with God is finally secured (cf. Rom 2:1-16; 6:22).

This observation leads us naturally to the second purpose of God's epiphany to save the world: so that "we may become heirs of the hope for eternal life" (3:7). The metaphor of a future inheritance, much used in the NT, has its background in the OT promise of land. An inheritance of a replenished and sanctified land — a "new creation" — is home to a restored Israel and therefore an essential blessing promised to God's covenant people.[33] In this case, "eternal life" is the covenant blessing promised by God to the "elect ones" (see 1:1-3) and the destiny of those on whom God has poured out the Spirit for *palingenesia* — an extended process of regeneration and renewal directed by the church's apostolate. The catchphrase "eternal life" is a theme of the Pastoral Epistles (1 Tim 1:16; 6:12) and, significantly, is used with "hope" in Tit 1:2. The literary effect of repeating this combination of a community's hope for eternal life at the beginning and end of the letter is to form an *inclusio* that focuses Paul's exhortation and instruction about the present situation and status of his apostolate on salvation history's outcome, "a future unending life with God."[34]

Excursus: The Canonical Effect of Titus 3:5b-6

The Titus 3 formula about the work of the Spirit of Christ as the apocalypse of God's salvation is hermeneutical of Pauline pneumatology in two different ways. First, the repetition of core beliefs about the Spirit's role in salvation confirms and secures Paul's traditional teaching about that role. Within its canonical setting, this formula reminds readers of key antecedent texts on the Spirit in the final form of the Pauline corpus, as a kind of refresher course. Clarification of this matter would have been practically important when the Pauline canon was being completed and finalized and when controversy over the role the Spirit among Christians was provoked by Montanus's "New Prophecy" movement. That movement, Tertullian's support of it for mostly

---

33. Walter Brueggemann, *The Land: Place as Gift, Promise, and Challenge in Biblical Faith* (Philadelphia: Fortress, 1977).

34. Knight, *Pastoral Epistles*, 347.

moralistic and epistemic reasons,[35] and the broader church's misunderstanding of Tertullian suggest that reflection on an apostolic doctrine of the Spirit was still confused and in a somewhat fluid state. Against this backdrop, then, this saying about a congregation's reception of God's Spirit through "Jesus Christ our Savior" is strategic for clarifying and securing the limits of a normative Pauline pneumatology.

That the Titus saying resists any separation of the Spirit from God's pattern of salvation serves to underwrite the traditional Pauline conception: the Spirit is received not by "works of moral rectitude but because of God's mercy" (3:5a). Neither should it strike one as odd that the Spirit's reception is logically linked to the community's "hope for eternal life" (Romans 8). And the experience of "renewal" echoes Paul's decisive introduction to the Christian life in Rom 12:2 (cf. 1 Cor 2:6-16; 6:9-11). Whether soteriological, eschatological, Christological, or transformative, the community's life in the Spirit is canonically underwritten by this formula to secure its place for those who "hold to a pattern of healthy teaching heard from (Paul)" (2 Tim 1:13).

The variation found in this formulation, however, suggests that an affirmation of Pauline teaching did not come at the expense of the adaptability of its theological principle to ever-changing circumstances and crises. This quality of the church's canonical heritage is suggested by the claim that the Spirit is "poured out on us by Jesus Christ." While this affirmation certainly sounds a Pauline tone, the experience of rebirth and renewal that results is "on us" — a corporate filling rather than one that is inward and individual (as in Rom 5:5). Rather than an experience of divine love poured out into the realm of Christ by the Spirit, the referent here is the experiences of rebirth and renewal poured out "on us" by Jesus Christ (cf. Luke 3:16; John 16:7). This elaboration of the activities of the risen Jesus to include the gift of the eschatological Spirit to prepare heirs for eternal life brings Easter and Pentecost together as integral to the gospel's power. This Christological reworking of the gift of the Spirit — it is "by Jesus Christ" that the Spirit is given to the covenant community (cf. Acts 2:33!), which then can experience rebirth and renewal because of its presence — makes more firm the Christological shape of that experience (cf. Rom 8:9-17). The community's reception of the Spirit not only helps it remember those crucial beliefs about Christ formulated for the Pastoral Epistles (1 Tim 3:16; 2 Tim 2:8) but also to produce a manner of life that bears the image of Christ. It is for Paul the Spirit of Christ who enlivens the community in accordance with the image of God in Christ. And this newly released

---

35. See now David E. Wilhite, *Tertullian the African: An Anthropological Reading of Tertullian's Context and Identities* (MS 14; Berlin: de Gruyter, 2007), 167-76.

transformational power is concurrent with the entire process of salvation, from new birth to eternal life.[36]

Second, this formula glosses the Pauline tradition in a way that creates a kind of canonical harmony linking the distinctive contribution of Pauline pneumatology to other salient traditions within the broader apostolic community that also found their way into the biblical canon.[37] If one of the marks of Scripture, analogous of the church, is its catholicity, then these vital connections underwrite a truly catholic spirit against one that is parochially Pauline. In this sense, the hermeneutics of the canonical process goes against the grain of modernity's familiar reductionisms: a Pauline canon within the canon, Pauline conceptions pitted against other biblical conceptions to defend an insoluble and adversarial diversity, or facile harmonization that seeks to rid Scripture of its diversity altogether. This robust formulation of the Spirit's work in salvation introduces non-Pauline features into a traditional Pauline rubric in such a way as to form a seamless, complementary whole. I would argue that this reflects the conception of apostolicity that guided the canonical process and is finally instantiated in the church's single biblical canon. There the reader finds the gospels of different apostolates bound together to form an illuminating whole that is greater than the sum of its parts.

To illustrate: I have mentioned the allusion to Luke's Pentecost tradition that reimages the pouring out of the Spirit by Christ for a Pauline setting (see above).[38] Another example of canonical harmonization is the pair of experiences that the Spirit's reception effects when poured out "on us." Once again the more traditional Pauline conception of "renewal" is combined with "re-

---

36. For the importance of this distinction and the collocation of key Pauline texts it envisages, see Levison, *Filled with the Spirit*, 267-69.

37. The stimulating discussion by Brevard S. Childs on a canonical approach to a "gospel harmony" in *The New Testament as Canon: An Introduction* (Philadelphia: Fortress, 1984), 157-209, provides a hermeneutical model for what I have in mind here. See in particular his discussion of the longer ending of Mark as a biblical example of harmonization (205-9) in which different bits and pieces of disparate gospel traditions are pulled together to form a new coherent whole "to function as a formal device to aid the reader in linking the parts" (207).

38. A few British scholars have argued that the linguistic similarity between Acts and the Pastoral Epistles is so striking that Luke must have either had a hand in the letters' composition or produced them entirely under Paul's name following his death. So C. F. D. Moule, "The Problem of the Pastoral Epistles: A Reappraisal," *BJRL* 47 (1965): 430-52, followed by Ralph P. Martin, *New Testament Foundations: A Guide for Christian Students* 2: *The Acts, the Letters, the Apocalypse* (rev. ed.; Grand Rapids: Eerdmans, 1986), 301-3, and S. G. Wilson, *Luke and the Pastoral Epistles* (London: SPCK, 1979). While I would disagree with this construction, it is important background music when making the connection between this formulation of the Spirit's outpouring and Acts 2.

birth," a conception of Christian existence not found in Paul. Rather this noun echoes the extraordinary use of *gennaō* in the Johannine tradition to speak of believers as God's children, reborn of God (John 3:3-8; 1 John 2:29; 3:9; 4:7; 5:1, 3-4, 18). At first glance, the evident creation sense of this new birth idiom shares much in common with the Pauline new creation motif, which is more eschatological and communal in scope.[39] In John, however, new birth initiates *individual* Christians into the presence of the Spirit to live with the purity of Jesus — real children do not practice sin! — in preparation for the imminent apocalypse of God's kingdom (John 3:3; 1 John 2:28–3:3). This passing nod in the direction of John also allows the reader to expand the meaning of "bath" within this Pauline setting to include water baptism, since both the fourth Gospel and 1 John combine the gift of the Spirit and water baptism as markers of this new birth (John 3:5; 1 John 5:6; cf. Acts 19:1-7). In this sense, then, Christian baptism confirms or perhaps symbolizes the filling of the Spirit in regeneration and for renewal.

Finally, then, the grammar of this saying focuses the apocalypse of God's salvation on the Holy Spirit's "bath of rebirth and renewal" rather than on the traditional Pauline formulation of justification — "not because we had done works of moral rectitude but because of God's mercy." Thus it may correct the Paulinist's (not Paul's) historic tendency to separate the two: God's pardon of sin and our purity from sin are of a piece in the Spirit's work in salvation. In fact, the Spirit's work envisages the concluding *hina* clause: "so that those who have come to believe in God (for pardon of sin) may give careful attention to good works (for purity from sin)" (Tit 3:8c; so 1 Cor 6:9-11).

3:8d-15 Final Instructions, Greetings, and Benediction

8dThese practices are good and useful for people: 9avoid foolish controversies, genealogies, disputes, and battles for the Torah; they are without profit and useless. 10After two warnings, have nothing more to do with a divisive person, 11knowing that someone like that is twisted: he sins and condemns himself.

12When I send Artemas or Tychicus to you, do your best to come to me in Nicopolis, for I have decided to winter there. 13Eagerly send Zenas the lawyer and Apollos on their way so that they may lack nothing. 14Let our people learn to devote themselves to good works to meet necessary needs so as not to be unproductive.

---

39. Although now see Levison's discussion of Paul's "new creation" motif (*Filled with the Spirit*, 307-16), especially in comparison with his discussion of the same motif in the Fourth Gospel (367-72).

¹⁵Everyone with me greets you; greet those who love us in faith. Grace be with all of you.

Benedictions of Hellenistic letters are typically a hodge-podge of vague exhortations, miscellaneous instructions, personal itineraries, and farewells. All these elements are present in this passage: a familiar exhortation to engage in those practices that protect the congregation from divisive people (3:9-11) is followed by travel plans (vv. 12-13), a concluding exhortation to engage in good works (v. 14), greeting (v. 15a), and a benedictory prayer (v. 15b).

The letter's conclusion begins with the formula, "These practices are good and useful for people." The pronoun ταῦτα *(tauta)*, which is generously translated "these practices," has no clear antecedent. My decision to begin the benediction at this point is based on the plain sense of the text rather than on clear linguistic markers. The most likely antecedent is the one nearest the pronoun, "good works" in the preceding clause (3:8b). But that clause is better understood as rounding out the general purpose of the theological agreement affirmed in the canonical saying as a whole. Another candidate is *(peri) toutōn*, "on these things," a clause earlier, which looks back to the theological goods of the prior canonical saying as well.

A third and preferable antecedent is the concluding catalog of ecclesial practices in 3:9-11, which, by focusing on what is good "for (all) people" (vv. 2, 8), is linked to the catalog of civil practices in vv. 1-2. The two lists together provide a thick (if somewhat vague) portfolio of Titus's pastoral concerns motivated by the theological sentiment of the canonical saying sandwiched between. It is precisely because a generous and good Benefactor has appeared that Paul's delegate is prompted to exercise the duties of his appointment.

Paul urges Titus to avoid "foolish controversies, genealogies, disputes, and battles for the Torah" (3:9).[40] This note about what kinds of conversations to avoid recalls the letter's earlier admonition about "the circumcision" and exhortation to nurture the "healthy" faith in a congregation that resists "Jewish legends" (1:13-14). Paul's concern is pastoral and pedagogical. Even though he belongs to a community of interpretation that is engaged in a battle for the Torah's theological meaning (see Romans!), his exhortation is for Titus not to get embroiled in debates that have no spiritual dividend — "they are without profit and are useless" (cf. 1 Cor 3:30). This language reflects a situation influenced by a particular brand of Jewish vitality excited by scrupulous attention to a code of conduct that legislates, or so it is claimed, a lifestyle

---

40. For distinctions among these four conversations, see Towner, *Letters to Timothy and Titus*, 795-96.

pleasing to God. Family myths and related genealogies of family trees were important literary conventions in ancient Jewish writings, especially commentaries on Genesis (*Jubilees*, Pseudo-Philo, 1QapGen, 4Q559, etc.), and even in the biblical Gospels (Matt 1:1-17; Luke 3:23-38). Locating one's family within Jewish history was a basis for an individual's religious authority. Paul's concern is that debating the meaning and motive of the Torah — but not the Torah itself — is finally "unprofitable and worthless" for Christian formation (cf. Rom 7:12-13).

The instruction that guides Titus in conducting a quasi-legal disposition of a "divisive person" (3:10) is reminiscent of the advice given in 1 Tim 5:19-21 regarding the discipline of a divisive elder. Here, cued by the earlier concerns about rebellious members of "the circumcision," the concern registered is the subversive effect of bad theology or anti-apostolic sentiment among the Christian families of Crete. But both here and in 1 Timothy Paul's preeminent concern is for order and stability, not only in securing a place where faith is more easily nurtured but also to present a good image to the general public. A contentious community in a culture that values social stability discredits the gospel. Toward this end, then, a pattern of congregational discipline that stipulates "two warnings" (cf. "two or three witnesses" in 1 Tim 5:19) prior to self-condemnation and excommunication (public or celestial rebuke in 1 Tim 5:20-21; also 1 Tim 1:20) is an appropriate ecclesial practice because it insures both internal and external well-being.

In this light, Paul's subsequent reference to "Zenas the lawyer" (3:13), who is otherwise unknown, may be especially pertinent. A lawyer in Paul's Jewish world was an expert in legal casuistry able to adapt the Torah's legal code to the ever-changing questions of faithful living. In the wider Hellenistic culture, the skills of a jurist depended on his detailed knowledge of the Roman constitution. Since "Zenas" is a Gentile name and probably reflects his work as a lawyer attached to the Roman courts, it may well be that Paul has recruited him to present a "secular" perspective to dismantle the debates over Jewish law now dividing the church of Crete. His traveling companion Apollos (v. 13) may well be the Alexandrian Jew introduced in Acts 18, who is subsequently mentioned in 1 Corinthians 1–4 as a church leader and Paul's missionary colleague. But it was a common Greek name, and the connection, while apropos to this context, should not be pressed — at least on historical grounds.

Paul plans to winter in Nicopolis (3:12), the name of which means "a city that overcomes." Nicopolis is a port city on the west coast of Crete just across the Bay of Actium from Italy. Paul asks Titus to join him there after he is relieved of his missionary duties by either "Artemas or Tychicus" — the latter mentioned in Acts 20:4. Some hypothesize that the historical referent of Luke's prior reference to Paul's three-month rest in Acts 20:3a is to his winter stay mentioned here in Titus. Perhaps it had become Paul's custom to take winters off to rest and plan for his next missionary campaign — perhaps in this case to Spain. Historical speculation aside, the plain sense of this personal detail expresses uncertainty about who will replace Titus on Crete, concern for his missionary colleagues, and authority over the details of the church's work, all of which open a window into the routines of Paul's mission that add color and texture to his biblical portrait (see 2 Tim 4:9-22). This concluding glimpse of Paul also interacts with the letter's opening, which introduced readers to the importance of his apostolate in the outworking of God's redemptive plan (1:1-3). By this self-assessment, Paul's attention to the details of his mission is an act of obedience to his calling.

The final repetition of the now familiar exhortation to engage in "good works" (3:14), in this case to aid the needy (cf. Gal 2:10), not only expresses Paul's concern for a solid public reputation, but a concern that the future of his apostolate cohere to its organizing motto: "a knowledge of truth that agrees with godliness" (1:1).

This letter's benediction is similar to those in 1-2 Timothy: greeting complemented by blessing (3:15; see above on 1 Tim 6:20-21; 2 Tim 4:22). The recipients of the greeting are identified only as "those who love us in faith," which prompts the question whether Paul has purposely singled out faithful tradents for blessing from those who oppose him and do not "love us" with the right kind of faith, such as the teachers from "the circumcision." This might make good sense if ἐν πίστει (*en pistei*, literally "in faith") is locative of those insiders of a Pauline brand of faith and is thus the final bit of a polemic that has been sustained throughout the letter. Although the meaning would be clearer if *pistis* were articular, this reading makes the best sense.

For those insiders who "love in faith," then, Paul dispenses a final blessing. As in 1 and 2 Timothy, grace is given to "all of you," which indicates the congregational scope of the exhortations and instructions addressed to the apostolic delegate. In some sense, the blessing works canonically as a warm embrace of all those faithful readers who are intent to move the Pauline apostolate forward into the next generation of believers.

A Rule of Faith Reading of Titus

The Creator God: *"There is only one God, and he is none other than the Creator of the world, who produced all things out of nothing through his own Word, first of all sent forth."*

In contrast to the lofty doxology of the sovereign, ineffable Creator that both introduces and concludes 1 Timothy (1:17; 6:13-17), Titus introduces God in more active terms, as "our Savior" (1:3), whose benefaction of grace (2:11; cf. 3:4) is of a piece with a divine nature that "does not lie" (1:2) and in sharp contrast to the Cretans, whose nature is to lie (v. 12). This same God made a promise "before time began" to grant eternal life to those who come to a knowledge of truth (v. 1; cf. 1 Tim 2:4). This very promise God has fulfilled through Jesus Christ, "who gave himself to rescue us" (2:14), and the Holy Spirit, "whom God poured out on us" in "a bath of rebirth and renewal" (3:5-6). God's Word, spoken before time began to "produce all things out of nothing," has been spoken again "in due time" through the ministry of the apostle Paul (1:3), whose preaching reveals God's way of salvation, which will restore order to all things.

Most especially, however, this is a God whose epiphany of grace and kindness has erupted into human history to radically change its direction toward a destiny of life rather than death. The Creator "gives life to all things" (1 Tim 6:15) because only the Creator can; but Paul's glorious claim — a claim whose only possible lyric is doxological — is that the Creator comes with Christ to put to rights whatever leads the world toward death. The subtext of this divine epiphany is a political claim: that in doing so, the triune God accomplishes for us through Christ and in the realm of the Spirit what no Caesar or empire could. Hardly a holy text that instructs the church to domesticate its faith and life to live at peace with its pagan surrounding, Titus's epiphany texts remind the reader that the church's singular faithfulness to the ways of God, often at odds with the norms and values of popular culture, actually presents the world with its only hope for life.

Titus 1 The theocentrism of this letter is nowhere more evident than in Paul's opening address (1:1-3) where God is introduced as "our Savior" whose "word" is revealed and entrusted to Paul at a *kairos idios* to disclose to the world that the time of its salvation has come. The word revealed to Paul — a word that secures the high purchase of his apostolate — concerns God's promise of eternal life, which the community of "elect ones" has heard and received by faith. Their faith is testimony to everyone, to the Cretans and especially to those of "the circumcision," that knowledge of the truth Paul proclaims "agrees with godliness."

What is extraordinary about the letter's address is that, unlike the equally expansive greeting of Romans, in which Paul sets out the Christological terms of his gospel to the nations (Rom 1:1-5), here is a clearheaded assessment of the *apostolic* terms of Paul's ministry of the word. In a sense, the *kairos* of divine providence has shifted from the Christ event to the Paul event, doubtless to frame the importance of a Pauline reading of the gospel for the next generation and beyond (see above on 1:1-3).

But the subsequent attribution of the congregation's administrator (*episkopos*) as "God's household-manager" (*theou oikonomos*, 1:7) is significant as well since it links the role of the congregation's leaders (= elders) with God's way of ordering reality, mentioned at the beginning of the Pastoral Epistles as the principal aim of apostolic instruction (*oikonomia theou*, 1 Tim 1:4). In this sense, leadership of God's household follows the redemptive pattern of the Creator's care for the world, the very task for which God created humankind (cf. Gen 1:27-28). Church orders are first of all understood as the ordering practices appropriate for God's household, which must transcend the ordinary duties of managing any human organization. The reputation and results of this particular household in the public square carry additional implications about God. Perhaps for this reason the administrator's outlook is not sectarian but inclusive of strangers and concerned to embody a blamelessness that enjoys the favor of outsiders.

The striking relationship between saving faith and good works in Titus is introduced by the haunting refrain of 1:16: "they who profess to know God, but their works deny God, ... are disqualified for every good work." God is a hard rationalist whose judgment between the clean ("growing a healthy faith") and the defiled ("without faith") is based on the evidence of works. Given the essential congruence between truth and life, one is considered unfit by God even if in possession of knowledge of the truth about God — perhaps by hearing Pauline preaching (1:2-3; cf. 1 Tim 2:4-7) — who then fails to live a manner of life consistent with what is professed as true (2:1).

Titus 2 Two notes are sounded by this letter's household code (2:2-10) that underwrite the importance of public conduct in supporting Christian teaching about God. It goes without saying that the practice of correct (i.e., Pauline) teaching about God and the godly character of the teacher are important themes in the Pastoral Epistles (so v. 7). Healthy instruction by virtuous teachers is the motor that drives the Pauline apostolate forward (cf. 2 Tim 2:2). In this case, however, the reception and application of instruction by young wives (Tit 2:5) and slaves (v. 10) in demanding relationships most subject to abuse are stipulated as a kind of test of whether God's word is upheld or ridiculed (v. 5) and whether "teaching about God our Savior" is considered a thing of beauty (v. 10). The truth about God is disclosed in a variety of forms, both in what is proclaimed and by whom, but also in how it is received and in what setting.

The first grand formulation of Paul's theological grammar found in this letter describes teaching about "God our Savior" that beautifies Christian existence. It is introduced in typical Pauline fashion with a personification of divine grace: God's grace has made its appearance in human history (2:11). The powerful operation of the Creator's grace sent forth to heal a broken and battered world is a core belief of Paul's theological grammar (Rom 5:15; 8:18-27; 1 Cor 15:10; 2 Cor 6:1; 8:1; Gal 2:21; Col 1:6, etc.), but here it is combined with the verb *epiphainō*, recalling its use in the LXX of the appearance of Israel's transcendent God, whose theophany reveals a word that sanctifies (LXX Exod 33:2-3) and who is present to render help in time of need (LXX Ps 117:27-28). Scripture's antecedent images of God's epiphany, then, explain this effect of God's grace: grace has appeared in the world to save and to teach everybody.

However, the subtext of Paul's recapitulation of this biblical idea is draped by a repetition of "good works" (2:7, 14; 3:1, 8, 14). The point is not only that the various means of divine grace cleanse and catechize believers to attend to good works eagerly (2:14; 3:8); it is that the epiphany of the Creator's grace transforms human existence from "total lawlessness" (2:14; cf. Gen 1:2) to something that is very good (cf. Gen 1:31). But this transformation, while it is expected by God and is even the criterion of God's final justification, is not itself required by God, since mercy is not prompted by "works of righteousness" (3:5). God's epiphany is an apocalypse of sheer mercy.

The remarkable use of the active participle of *paideuein*, "training," puts into play a more robust conception of grace that moves beyond a stock juridical notion — that God acquits repentant sinners of their guilt in a heavenly law court — to include a more formative idea of the powers unleashed by grace that retrain converts to reject "godlessness and worldly desires" and willingly embrace new patterns of thinking and living (cf. Rom 12:1-2). This is the theological conception into which Paul grounds his pedagogical concerns. That is, if the Creator's word is grace-filled, then its revelation retrains those who humbly receive it for performances that accord with the Creator's purposes for human existence. This idea continues in the second theological formation in Titus, 3:4-8 (see below). What is clear is that both escape from a sinful life, which leads to self-destruction, and the production of good works, which cultivates a life with God, depend on God's grace.

Much has been made of the title, "our Savior," which is used in Titus of both God and Jesus Christ (1:3-4; 3:4-6). Whether or not the co-saviorhood of God and Christ is adapted to the letter's Cretan setting in response to Crete's peculiar Zeus legend,[1] at the level of the canonical text the apocalypse of a transcendent God's grace is here linked to the advent of Christ "to give himself for us" (2:14; see above on 2 Tim 1:10). The antecedent of "for us" must be "for all people" (2:11): God's promise of salvation, even though it is worked out within the bounds of the covenant community, is an offer made to "all people," since God "wills everyone to be saved and come to knowledge of the truth" (so 1 Tim 2:4). This deep desire to save all people seems logical of a Creator whose Word "produced all things."

While there is no question that this connection elevates the Christ event as a rescue operation with heavenly origins, our interest here is how this same connection secures the "blessed hope" in the future coming of God and restoration of God's broken and battered creation. Not only has the Word that brought forth all things been roundly rejected, but the consequence is a collapse of the world into "total lawlessness" (2:14), a state of rebellion clearly detected on Crete (see 1:10-12). In this sense, then, the epiphany of God's grace "along with our Savior Jesus Christ" rescues a "special people" (= "the elect ones" of 1:1) from this spiritual chaos to herald the "glorious appearing" of the Creator to restore cosmic order once for all.

Titus 3 The second formulation of the letter's epiphany theology (3:4-7) is introduced by another personification, in this case not of God's grace rescuing the lost but of God's "goodness and friendship," which bathes with the

---

1. See Philip H. Towner, *The Letters to Timothy and Titus* (NICNT; Grand Rapids: Eerdmans, 2006), 694-712.

Holy Spirit those who have been found (v. 4). These too are characteristics of the Creator that are reproduced in the new creation rescued from sin and prefigured by the community born again and renewed by the Spirit.

What must be assumed about the church's experience of salvation is the presence of the triune God at work in the church. Soteriology moves from this ontology. The God who shows up to save people does so as "grace" that retrains people who are eager for good works or as "friendship" that saves these people by bathing them in the Holy Spirit. This understanding of the functional properties of the divine nature is not incidental to a theological reading of this text; rather, it supplies its deep logic since God's salvation is a move that God our Savior naturally makes, and salvation of the kind summarized by Paul occurs in those ecclesial places where God is present.

The timing (or circumstance) of the epiphany of God's goodness and friendship (3:4) is grammatically linked to God's act of saving people by pouring out the Spirit in a "bath of rebirth and renewal" (v. 5). *Palingenesia*, "rebirth," is a creational word that recalls the OT story of the "genesis" of creation, when "the Creator of the world produced all things by his own Word" in the company of the Spirit of God upon the water (LXX Gen 1:2), and the "genesis" of exiled Israel, to whom God promised restoration within a new creation. While its use here is exceptional in the Pauline canon, whose typical idiom is the law court rather than the maternity ward, the idea of a new creation is important (cf. Rom 8:18-25; 2 Cor 5:1-5, 16-17). Even though the regeneration of human nature is more typical of John's apostolic tradition and reminds the reader of its extraordinary catch-phrase *gennaō tou theou*, "born of God" (1 John 2:29; 3:9; cf. John 3:3), this idea is consistent with the letter's soteriology: even though the Creator does not save the world because of "works of righteousness" — salvation is an apocalypse of sheer grace and goodness, the offer of friendship — the purpose for saving people is to remake them "righteous by that grace" and so participants ("heirs") of the new creation.

Christ Jesus the Lord: *"This Word is called his Son, and, under the name of God, was seen 'in diverse manners' by the patriarchs, heard at all times in the prophets, at last brought down by the Spirit and power of the Father into the Virgin Mary, was made flesh in her womb, and, being born of her, went forth as Jesus Christ; thenceforth he preached the new law and the new promise of the kingdom of heaven, worked miracles, and having been crucified, rose again the third day. Having ascended into the heavens, he sat at the right hand of the Father."*

God's way of salvation is thematic in the Pastoral Epistles, and Paul's epiphany Christology compresses the Christ event into the two decisive moments in the history of salvation, which are clearly set out in the Timothy correspondence. Titus extends this theme, then, by coordinating an already robust expression of Christ's two epiphanies with two epiphanies of the Creator God, who appears as Benefactor to distribute the gift of salvation by pouring out the Spirit (3:5-6). These co-epiphanies of God and Jesus Christ as co-saviors envisage a joint operation of salvation in the past that forges a blessed hope for their future work of purification (cf. 2 Tim 4:1) that brings to completion the promise of a new creation (cf. Tit 2:13-14).

The apostolic Rule is ever alert to this partnership between the Father and Son — in Tertullian's articulation, in God's "own Word," by which all things are produced, and then "this word," instantiated in God's Son, who is carried to earth by the Spirit for the work of salvation. The downward mobility of the Son into history is given expression by Paul in the familiar idiom of sacrifice: he appeared to "give himself for us to rescue us" (2:14; cf. 1 Tim 2:6). The creative Word that produces a good and hospitable world (Gen 1:29-31) comes again as "goodness and friendship" to befriend us in the Son's self-sacrifice.[2]

Titus 2 While the title "Savior" is used of Christ in Titus, the title "Lord" is not. The rhetorical effect of this omission is to intensify the role Jesus performs with God in co-saving the world from sin: the singular purpose of both epiphanies of Jesus Christ, past and future, is to save the world for eternal life with God. The apostolic Rule defines the narrative of the Christ event; it is Scripture's role as its analogue to elaborate the implications and results of this redemptive event. Paul does so in this dense formulation of the nature and result of Christ's saving work. Three discrete claims, "almost hymnic in its structure,"[3] are made.

(1) He "gave himself for us." If the purpose of the epiphany of divine grace is educational, then the curriculum is Christ's act of self-giving. While

---

2. One assessment of the Christological goods of this letter turns on the exegesis of the difficult clause we have translated, "we wait for the blessed hope and glorious appearing of the great God along with our savior, Jesus Christ" (2:13). If one concludes that "the great God" refers to "our Savior, Jesus Christ," then the heightened dogmatic claim here is for the return of the divine Christ or perhaps the exalted Christ (see Rom 1:3). Towner, *Letters to Timothy and Titus*, for example, thinks this is crucial "to sharpen the gospel's penetration into Cretan culture" (65). True, in some sense God and Christ cooperated for the work of salvation, but this is grounded not on ontological commitments but in more functional terms consistent with the subsequent phrase and Pauline teaching elsewhere (e.g., 1 Tim 2:5-6).

3. Raymond F. Collins, *1 and 2 Timothy and Titus: A Commentary* (NTL; Louisville: Westminster John Knox, 2002), 353.

the verbal idea "give" is often used in reference to a gift, with the reflexive pronoun it also carries the implication of self-sacrifice, as in 1 Tim 2:6, where Jesus' death is interpreted as a "ransom for everybody" from slavery to sin (cf. Gal 1:4). Within the Pauline canon, this gift of martyrdom is an act of Christ's faithfulness to God's redemptive will (Phil 2:5-8; cf. Rom 3:22-26), but its saving effect is "for us" (cf. Luke 22:19-20; Rom 5:6).

(2) He did so "to rescue us from total lawlessness . . . for good works." The effect of Jesus' self-sacrifice is presented here not as a ransom paid to release someone from slavery but as a rescue operation "from total lawlessness." This is linked closely with God's liberation of Israel from Egypt (Exod 6:6). Read by the exodus story, the enemy no longer is an unrepentant Pharaoh but "total lawlessness," in which *anomia,* "lawlessness," is contrasted with "good works." In a sense this idiom is also taken from the exodus, the most elemental of biblical narratives, but in an ironic way since liberated but disobedient Israel quickly demonstrated its need for God's law. In this fuller sense, "good works" are the covenant-keeping responses God demands of a holy nation, a royal priesthood (cf. Exod 19:5-6); the effect of Jesus' self-sacrifice is to liberate a people from lawlessness in order to perform the "good works" of a people covenanted with God for salvation.

D. Campbell's recent book on Pauline justification, *The Deliverance of God,* argues against a traditional Protestant understanding of a Pauline *via salutis.*[4] Drawing largely on a close reading of Romans 5–8, he describes Paul's idea of salvation as apocalyptic and participatory. That is, if all people exist in "total lawlessness," they are incapable of responding rightly to God's epiphany of grace. They require an "apocalypse" of salvation that is not predicated on their faith, their knowledge of the truth, or their desire for God, which their state of lawlessness does not allow; rather, they require an abrupt act of divine deliverance to rescue and retrain them, in which God engages because of the faithfulness of the risen Christ. Only after this apocalypse of salvation happens are a liberated people's faith and good works even possible.

The "good faith" Paul calls for in Tit 2:10 is not the means for appropriating one's individual salvation from lawlessness that comes with Christ. Rather, faith is the entire community's public demonstration of the truth that God has already acted in Christ Jesus to save everyone from their total lawlessness — an act of supreme righteousness that brings to realization God's desire that everyone come to a knowledge of this truth (cf. 1 Tim 2:4).

---

4. Douglas A. Campbell, *The Deliverance of God: An Apocalyptic Rereading of Justification in Paul* (Grand Rapids: Eerdmans, 2009).

(3) Finally, Christ did this "to cleanse a special people for himself." Paul shifts typologies from exodus and Sinai to priestly purification to draft a second effect of the crucified Christ's faithfulness to God's redemptive will. Towner hears in this phrase an OT echo of Ezekiel 36–37, in which the prophet draws together concepts of purification from idolatry (= "lawlessness") and election.[5] In the act of election, an epiphany of unconditional grace, Israel becomes God's special people (Ezek 36:28; 37:23; cf. Exod 19:5), but by an act of purifying grace through Christ the status of a spiritual Israel as the elect ones of God is reclaimed and restored (see above on Tit 1:1-3; Ezek 36:25, 29, 33). Once again, the focus of this image is on God's unconditional mercy in rescuing people who otherwise cannot rescue themselves from their moral and spiritual poverty.

Titus 3 The repetition of "Jesus Christ our Savior" (3:6) cues the act of the exalted One by whom the Holy Spirit is sent to pour out a "bath of rebirth and renewal" (Acts 2:33; cf. John 16:7; 20:22). The logic of the Rule is implied here: having given himself for us, which "rescues us from total lawlessness," Jesus Christ "ascended into the heavens" from where he "sent instead of himself the power of the Holy Spirit." This formula elaborates the nature of this power that Christ delivers with the Spirit: unlike Acts, which tells of a Spirit baptism that empowers prophetic ministry, Titus recounts how this power saves those believers on whom the Spirit is poured as a "bath of rebirth and renewal." The present work of the exalted Christ is still vested in salvation, but at a distance and mediated by the Holy Spirit.

The Community of the Spirit: *"Christ sent instead of himself the power of the Holy Spirit to lead such as believe."*

The Spirit is mentioned five times in the Pastoral Epistles (1 Tim 3:16; 4:1; 2 Tim 1:7, 14; Tit 3:5). The occurrences in 1 and 2 Timothy are more individualistic and vocational and concern the Spirit's role in safeguarding the tradition, similar to the role the Spirit performs in Acts, filling certain believers to enable their charismatic exegesis of Scripture, persuasive speech, signs and wonders, and missionary movements, all to underwrite a ministry of the gospel according to God's plan. Only in Tit 3:5 is the Spirit linked to the cooperative work of God and Jesus Christ in saving those who believe. This expanded role given the Spirit in this formula of salvation reflects Paul's great innovation in his understanding of the indwelling Spirit's role as an agent of divine

---

5. Towner, *Letters to Timothy and Titus*, 761-66.

grace, not only in witnessing to those in Christ of their new status as God's children (cf. Romans 8) but also to empower new patterns of living together as the body of Christ (cf. 1 Corinthians 1–4 and 11–14). This stunning commentary on the Spirit's role in God's salvation of the redeemed community represents a final synthesis of Pauline pneumatology and operates as such within the Pauline corpus.

Although the full measure of God's goodness will be realized by justified "heirs" at a future epiphany (2:13), the Spirit is present while the exalted Christ is absent for an experience of "rebirth and renewal" (3:5) that undergirds "the hope" and heralds the inauguration "of eternal life." The juxtaposition of these two core beliefs that "Christ will come with glory" and "Christ sent instead ... the Holy Spirit" supplies a subtext of this saying, so that the reader understands that the experiences of regeneration and renewal, mediated by the Spirit, are signals that point to the coming age; and this real experience of transformation provides the hard evidence that secures hope for eternal life.

Titus 1   The regenerated and renewed community of the Spirit is none other than God's "elect ones" (1:1), whose faithful reception of God's word entrusted to and proclaimed by Paul (v. 3) has trained them in a "knowledge of truth that agrees with godliness" (v. 2; cf. 2:11). The members know on this basis that God has promised eternal life. Because this God "does not lie," they await its fulfillment.

As it does so, the community is organized into a household that belongs to God (2:14; see comment on 2 Tim 2:19). Its elders are appointed because of their moral competence, social virtues, and spiritual maturity and have experience apropos to the work of a household administrator.

This shift of ecclesial metaphors from a mutually edifying "body" of integral spiritual charisms to an orderly "household" led by competent human elders may well reflect a social location in which real threats to the community's survival exist and are increased by the absence of the authoritative apostle. Rather than empowering members of the body of Christ with spiritual gifts (so Romans 12; 1 Corinthians 12–14; cf. Ephesians 4), the Spirit "bathes" them (3:5) in forming a regenerate household that is by nature at odds with the surrounding pagan culture of "liars, evil beasts, and gluttons for laziness" (1:12). Grace mediated by the apostolate's "healthy teaching" trains a cleansed membership in knowledge of the truth that agrees with godliness and so, again, an intelligence — a coherent way of thinking — that is at odds with those who are defiled, without faith, and "disqualified for every good work" (v. 16).

Titus 2 The social manners of this household, cleansed in the Spirit's bath and trained by God's word carried by the apostle's instruction (cf. 2:1), reflect roles that take responsibility for the well-being of one another, but with an eye to outsiders so that God's reputation is protected from public scandal. Twice in setting out the purpose of the letter's household code (vv. 5b, 10b), household chores are related to teaching about God. The assumption carried over from 1 Timothy is that the healthy teaching of the apostolate initiates the community into God's way of ordering a very good world — the *oikonomia theou* (1 Tim 1:4, 10-11).

Older women therefore mentor young wives "so that God's word may not be ridiculed," and domestic slaves demonstrate a "good faith" in all they do "so that they may adorn the teaching about God our Savior" for the public to witness. The social practices of a community's life together are, again, not detached from its instruction in the faith. The virtuous manner of wives and slaves are indicators of the epiphany of divine grace that catechizes household members into the practices of God's salvation (2:11). As a result, believers are enabled to reject "godlessness and worldly desires" (v. 12) and to be "eager for good works" (v. 14), such as those cataloged in the code. A community of competence is known by its social and moral practices and by its resistance to a lawlessness that only results in social chaos. The decisive claim of this material, however, is that the source of this competence is the grace that has arrived "right now" with Christ our Savior.

Titus 3 The community's extension of "good works" from the household into the town square is nowhere more evident than in the instructions in 3:1-2 (cf. 1 Tim 2:1-2). Unlike 1 Timothy, where Paul instructs the community to pray for everyone, including "rulers and authorities," the repetition of "every good work" in Titus clarifies that a special people, who have been rescued and cleansed by Christ from lawlessness for good works of a religious kind (2:14), are also engaged in acts of good citizenship with and for their non-Christian neighbors (cf. Rom 13:1-10).

Although generic in form, the catalog of conduct includes "*every* good work," including speech acts that avoid slander. "Peaceable" is opposite to a verbal contentiousness that Paul warns teachers against (3:9; cf. 2 Tim 2:23). Applied to rules of public speaking, however, this virtue characterizes both the quality and outcome of the community's conversations with its neighbors.

Significantly, the stipulation of "every good work" (3:1) is sandwiched between important epiphany formulations of salvation, both of which conclude with a purpose clause that indicates that the community saved by grace is marked out not only by its profession of an orthodox faith but by its activism of "good works" (2:14; 3:8). That is, the presence of God's saving grace in the community is not just an inward property, and it does not force believers to the margins of society in radical nonconformity but rather toward the mainstream of society for "every good work" (cf. 1 Tim 2:10; 3:6-7). This expression of Hellenism's household code, unlike the fuller elaboration in 1 Timothy, includes concern for the well-being of the state — for the civic household — and for the rule of secular law. While we resist imagining too much what this may or may not imply about the intended readers of Titus, the theological principle is plain: God's rescue of a "special people" from "total lawlessness" carries with it the expectation of public works apropos of the good neighbor.

What is clear from the Pauline corpus is the apostle's dislike of conflict, which is ironic given his assessment of the gospel's provocative effect on people. In part, one might ascribe this dislike to a metaphysics of common sense: conflict is bad for business. But Paul's resolve to maintain order and work for solidarity in important matters, such as agreement about the core claims of the gospel, reflects a proper understanding of divine providence. If God our Savior is one God (so 1 Tim 2:3-4), then the social and spiritual manners of the community in which God's saving grace appears and is worked out will be of a piece with God's redemptive plan. In Paul's mind, this looks like "good works" when viewed on the ground, and these good works extend beyond households of believers (Tit 2:2-10) into the public square (3:1-2) for all to see.

The connection made between the community's salvation and Christ's pouring out of the Spirit for "rebirth and renewal" is central to the church's teaching of baptism. The Pauline understanding of baptism is mostly limited to spiritual renewal, but Augustine and Tertullian connected baptism to reception of the Spirit and to the believer's regeneration. The salvation-creating power that shows up with the epiphany of God's goodness and friendship is mediated through the Spirit's presence. Unlike the Fathers, however, Protestantism separates the transforming effect of a believer's new birth from the sacrament of baptism.

Christian Existence and Discipleship: *"In putting on our flesh, Christ made it his own; and in making it his own, he made it sinless . . . because in that same human flesh he lived without sin" (On the Flesh of Christ 16).*

The Rule's theological agreement on Christian discipleship stipulates that the faith community, which is freed from the guilt and power of sin because of Christ's faithfulness to God, should live out that freedom. In effect, the various catalogs of Pauline paraenesis, which contrast former vice and prospective virtue (e.g., 3:3-4; cf. 1:15), give expression to this theological point. According to Paul, a conversion from "total lawlessness" to moral rectitude is by grace (see 3:7) and is the anticipated dividend of the believer's participation in the death and resurrection of Christ (Romans 6).

In this sense, the steady drumbeat of "good works" in this brief letter (2:7, 14: 3:1, 8, 14; cf. 1:16), especially since each occurrence strategically concludes an exhortation or unit of instruction, has the rhetorical effect of cultivating a clear sense of the theological importance of the morally competent life. The ethical instruction of the Pastoral Epistles coheres to, as Young put it, "the fundamental theological presuppositions which undergird the discourse."[6] Her point is to dislodge the moral patterns we find here from recent sociological analysis that asserts that the content of this way of ordering human existence, viewed as excessively "patriarchal," "Hellenistic," or "secular," is detached from an essentially religious and theological mooring.[7]

That is, the plain sense of the moral life that emerges from this letter is that it is predicated not so much on a particular social location (without continuing relevance) but on a theological belief in the epiphany of God's grace (2:11; 3:4). God's word proclaimed by Paul and received in faithful response by the elect ones (1:1-3) concerns the spiritual resources available to the community to produce a transformation of human existence that reorders its members' relationships within the household (2:2-10) and with outsiders (3:1-2). To proclaim salvation from "total lawlessness" admits to a religious, not a philosophical need. While it might also admit to the deleterious effect of keeping company with those "who are rebellious, who are unreasonable and mislead" (1:10) and who engage in Cretan-like practices that produce ill-health (1:11-16; 3:3), moral transformation does not require an epistemology; it requires the means of grace. For this reason, the beginning point of Pauline ethics is not a conception of social propriety that targets what is good and thus defines human aspiration; it is rather the epiphany of a transcendent Benefactor who brings gifts of grace, goodness, and friendship into the world with Jesus Christ.

Of course, we easily recognize the codes of virtues and vices as rhetorical conventions of antiquity, Jewish and philosophical. If the collective life of society, a family household, or a voluntary organization like a Christian congrega-

---

6. Frances M. Young, *The Theology of the Pastoral Letters* (Cambridge: Cambridge University Press, 1994), 39. Of course, Young argues that no assessment of a moral good is neutral or benign but is shaped by a world when interpreted and targets a world in response.

7. Cf. Lewis R. Donelson, *Pseudepigraphy and Ethical Argument in the Pastoral Epistles* (HUT 22; Tübingen: Mohr, 1986).

tion is ordered by virtue, then its good health for the long haul is insured. This is also true for individuals such as the congregation's leader (1:5-9) or individual members of the Christian household who might occupy very different roles based on age, marital status, or task (2:2-10). One contribution the Pastoral Epistles collection makes to the Pauline canon as a whole is the close attention given to the "good works" of a competent life, whether in the world or the household. This theme is not lacking in the paraenetic materials found in other Pauline letters (e.g., Romans 12–13, Ephesians 4–6, Colossians 3–4, and 1 Thessalonians 3–4), but the force of the Pastoral Epistles is to add this emphasis as a strategy of the Pauline apostolate.

What the interplay between the letter's definition of "good works" and its two theological formulas also clarifies is that what is new in Pauline descriptions of Christian discipleship is not its constructions of moral rectitude: Paul is pedestrian in this regard. The Pauline innovation is in locating the real source of a transformed Christian existence in the epiphany of God's grace and friendship. While it is the product of "healthy teaching" (2:1), the Pauline assumption is that this training is a means of divine grace (vv. 11-12) — a "sacrament of the word" — whose reception is possible only by the Spirit's baptism of rebirth and renewal (3:5-6). In this sense, a Pauline conception of the good life is not so much a prescription of what Christians ought to do as a description of a way of life that is possible because of the apocalypse of God's saving grace through Christ and the pouring out by the Holy Spirit. The location of mentions of "good works" in Titus, then, provides an interpretive cue that guides our understanding of Pauline ethics, which is profoundly theocentric. In Paul's absence, this definition of discipleship is secured by the Pauline canon for future tradents as a trusted means of grace in training a people to be eager for good works.

The pairing of "rebirth and renewal" in a lean theological formula to describe the transforming effect of the Spirit's baptism (3:5b) invites theological reflection on the nature of salvation following the believer's justification "because of God's mercy" alone (v. 5a). Many interpreters take "rebirth" as synonymous with "renewal" and both as "express[ing] the concept of renewed life in connection with conversion."[8] Calvin, for example, argued that "God saved us" indicates that at least from God's perspective "our salvation is completed, while the full enjoyment of it is delayed till the end of our warfare."[9] In this sense, he separates the "bath of rebirth" from the Spirit's activity

---

8. Towner, *Letters to Timothy and Titus*, 782.

9. John Calvin, *The Second Epistle of Paul the Apostle to the Corinthians and the Epistles to Timothy, Titus and Philemon* (Grand Rapids: Eerdmans, 1964), 194.

in renewing life and interprets it as a sacrament of baptism that provides the outward symbol of God's inward justifying mercy obtained by Christ. In this sense, "rebirth" occurs when justification does.

Wesley thinks differently about this moment of the *via salutis:* no one event of divine grace is more strategic to him than new birth. The believer's regeneration is the linchpin holding justification and sanctification together in an innovative, powerful way. Probably in response to the Calvinism of his England, which collapsed regeneration and justification, Wesley more carefully distinguished between them as discrete operations of God's grace. While agreeing the two occur at the very moment the sinner trusts Christ for salvation, in his sermon "Great Privilege" Wesley distinguishes carefully between the two: justification occurs when the sinner is pardoned from the guilt of past sin, and regeneration occurs when the same person is released from sin's captive power to begin a new life under the direction of the Spirit.

New birth, then, regards a supernatural change in human nature. If God's justifying grace rights the sinner's personal relationship with God, God's regenerating grace transforms her senses in her inmost soul. She becomes a child of God, reborn with God's image with new capacities needed for a participatory partnership with God. In his sermon on "The New Birth" Wesley says, "As soon as he is born of God there is a total change in all his particulars — he sees the light of the world, he hears the voice of God, he feels the love of God shed abroad in his heart by God's Spirit. And now he may properly be said to live." New birth occasions a vast, inward change. All the resources necessary to live a holy life are given by God at this moment. Understood this way, regeneration marks a gateway into the hard work of sanctification and into still other operations of divine grace brokered by God's Spirit. Precisely because regeneration changes the will, the believer need not willfully sin. Because regeneration transforms the senses, it is now possible to resist evil tempers and thoughts. Because regeneration restores the image of a loving, truth-telling God within the believer, she is assured of God's love and confident of participating in God's coming victory. Because regeneration purifies the human spirit, God's Spirit can bear witness in our spirits, which in Wesley's understanding paves the path for a robust cooperation between God's people and God's Spirit, the broker of God's sanctifying graces.

Central to Wesley's conception of Christian perfection is a dynamic cooperation between the divine and human spirits that marks out the believer's new birth as God's child (cf. Romans 8). New birth initiates the believer into a long sanctification in the Holy One's direction; new birth is integral to rather than distinct from sanctification. Wesley described three integral movements marking out a full sanctification: the pure and irresistible gift of new birth, the process of growth in grace, and that unpredictable instant of Christian perfection, when the believer is entirely sanctified by the Holy Spirit at God's timing.[10]

While "rebirth" is a supernatural event that changes our nature, then, "renewal" envisages a working arrangement between God and the believer who is sanctified by grace in proportion to the amount and quality of grace received. The various practices of Christian discipleship — works of piety and mercy — when complemented by the ordinary means of grace ordained by the church occasion a profuse outpouring of God's salvation-creating grace that transforms the believer into a conspicuous saint.

Consummation in a New Creation: *"Christ will come with glory to take the saints to the enjoyment of everlasting life and of the heavenly promises, and to condemn the wicked to everlasting fire, after the resurrection of both these classes shall have happened, together with the restoration of their flesh."*

The old objection that the theological conception of the Pastoral Epistles collection departs from the Pauline original letters over its lack of eschatology is puzzling. What is lacking from the entire Pauline canon is a conception of the future that approximates Tertullian's robust statement of apostolic orthodoxy. Paul's eschatology bears down on the coming victory of God over sin and death, already realized in a proleptic sense on the cross and at the empty tomb, and the inauguration of eternal life with God in a new creation. Because the Pastoral Epistles address a pastoral crisis occasioned by the departure of the authoritative apostle, his message and memory are compressed into dense theological formulas and clipped biography for easy transmission. But the use of this highly portable genre, appropriate for the form and function of these letters, does not indicate the replacement of Paul's apocalyptic eschatology with a domesticated or institutional eschatology.

The expectation of a future with God is the motive for doing good works. The reader already has taken note that Christ's second epiphany occasions the final judgment of God (2 Tim 4:1) and that it is a judgment of works so that good works will be rewarded "on that (future) day" (2 Tim 1:12, 18; 4:8; cf. 1 Tim 4:16; 6:19) and works of betrayal condemned (2 Tim 4:14, 16). The effect of this conception when reading the letter to Titus is the insinuation of this eschatological vision on any commendation or condemnation of the household or its opponents. For example, the assumed destiny of those rebel-

---

10. For an expanded exposition of these ideas, see Robert W. Wall, "John's John: A Wesleyan Theological Reading of 1 John," *Wesleyan Theological Journal* 46 (2011): 105-41.

lious teachers from "the circumcision" who mislead entire households or of those who deny God (1:10-16) is a future without God (cf. 1 Tim 6:9; 2 Tim 3:1-9). Likewise, if Titus or any other puts himself forward as a "role model of good works," God will reward him (cf. 2 Tim 4:8; 1 Tim 4:16; 6:14).

This general assessment of the connection between eschatology and ethics is nowhere more clearly articulated than in the image of a community of virtue (2:12) awaiting the "blessed hope" of Christ's coming epiphany (2:13; cf. 3:7) in testimony of a people cleansed from lawlessness and now eager for good works (2:14). In this sense, the production of good works, which is the effect but not the condition of God's saving grace, has soteriological purchase. Paul's conception of salvation worked out in the history of those who belong to Christ includes a future review in which good works are the measure of whether or not a people will realize the promise of eternal life (see 1:1-3; cf. 2 Timothy 2)

Finally, then, this letter elaborates the belief in a future judgment in which the saints and "the wicked" are distinguished according to their works. The wicked are rebellious because they deny the intervention of divine grace, while the community that will realize the heavenly promises in a restored creation is marked out by its embrace of God's word entrusted to the Pauline apostolate.

Case Study: Phoebe Palmer and the Wesleyan Holiness Movement

> *But when the goodness and friendship of God our Savior appeared — not because we had done works of moral rectitude but because of God's mercy — God saved us through a bath of rebirth and renewal of the Holy Spirit, whom God poured out on us abundantly by Jesus Christ our Savior, so that, having been made righteous by that grace, we may become heirs of the hope of eternal life. (Tit 3:4-7)*

The letter to Titus summarizes and synthesizes the pneumatology of the entire Pauline corpus and places special emphasis on the Spirit's agency in enabling believers to experience God's salvation personally and in transforming their moral and devotional lives accordingly. Similarly, one of Phoebe Palmer's most important contributions to Wesleyan theology was in underscoring the pneumatological basis of the signature doctrine of "entire sanctification." Because of this contribution, Palmer played in nineteenth-century American Christianity a role analogous to that played by the Pastoral Epistles in the Pauline canon. The first part of this study is a thumbnail sketch of Palmer's life and thought, with special attention to her own experience of sanctification. The second part shows how her life and thought illustrate what Paul says in Titus about the Holy Spirit and its role in the transformation of the Christian believer.

I

Phoebe Palmer was a "cradle Methodist," steeped in and committed to Wesleyan theology and piety. Her father, Henry Worrall, was an Englishman who, as a boy, had heard John Wesley preach and had even received his membership ticket into a Methodist society from the hand of the patriarch himself. Worrall later emigrated to America, where he met and married Dorothea Wade, a girl of "pious [Methodist?] parentage." The couple joined the Duane Street Methodist Episcopal Church in New York City and raised their large family — they had sixteen children, eight of whom reached maturity — in that congregation. Phoebe, the fourth child in this large brood, was born on December 18, 1807. Her sister Sarah, who also comes into this story, was born two years earlier. Phoebe and Sarah were much alike and very close: both were deeply pious, morally scrupulous, and intellectually gifted, though Phoebe was more emotionally and socially reserved than Sarah, a fact whose importance will become clear in what follows.

On September 28, 1827, Phoebe married Walter Palmer, a young physician and, like herself, a devout Methodist. Their marriage was solid and happy, but in the early years was repeatedly stricken by tragedy. Their first two children, both sons, died of natural causes in infancy — in 1829 and 1830, respectively — and their fourth, a daughter, was killed in 1836 at the age of eleven months in a crib fire caused by a careless nurse. (The Palmers' other three children would all grow to adulthood and become active Methodists and supporters of their parents' evangelistic work.) In "praying through" her grief, Palmer came to believe that her maternal love was "idolatrous" and that God had taken her children to enable her to give herself unreservedly to him. She was also worried that her devotion to Walter eclipsed her devotion to God and that she had never undergone a "conversion experience" or felt the religious fervor that Methodism idealized. Thus, she seemed to herself both too emotional with respect to her family life and insufficiently emotional with respect to her religious life.

Meanwhile, much was happening in the life of her sister Sarah. In 1831, she had married Thomas Lankford of New York City, and four years later she experienced what all Methodists were taught to pray for and expect: the experience of entire sanctification. She promptly assumed the leadership of two Methodist women's prayer groups. In February 1836, shortly after she and her husband had moved in with Walter and Phoebe, she combined these prayer groups into one and invited the members — which now included Phoebe — to meet weekly in the Palmer-Lankford home. This was the genesis of what would later be known as the Tuesday Meetings for the Promotion of Holiness. Sarah also began praying that Phoebe too would experience entire sanctification — and made no secret of it to Phoebe. Her prayers were soon answered.

On July 26, 1837, Phoebe underwent what she came to call her "day of days." In her diary account of this experience she reports the almost immediate resolution of the emotional issues that had been troubling her, and she hints at several key themes in her mature theology:

> The Lord reigns unrivaled in my heart; He has my supreme affections: for some days past I have experienced such a heartfelt want of the assurance of being cleansed from all unrighteousness, to know that the motives influencing every thought, word, and action, originate from a pure fountain, that I last evening resolved I could no longer do without it. Between the hours of eight and nine — while pleading at the throne of grace for the fulfillment of the exceeding great and precious promises; pleading also the fullness and freeness of the atonement, its unbounded efficacy, and making an entire surrender of body, soul, and spirit; time, talents, and influence; and also of the dearest ties of nature, my beloved husband and child; in a world, my earthly all — I received the assurance that God the Father, through the atoning Lamb, accepted the sacrifice; my heart was emptied of self, and cleansed of all idols, from all filthiness of the flesh and spirit, and I realized that I dwelt in God, and felt that He had become the portion of my soul, my All in All.[1]

To unpack the significance of this passage, we must pause to recall John Wesley's understanding of salvation, which it presumes. Wesley tells us that it consists in "two general parts, justification and sanctification." The former is "another word for pardon . . . the forgiveness of all our sins and (what is necessarily implied therein) our acceptance with God." The latter is spiritual rebirth by the power of the Holy Spirit. The regenerate person feels "love to all mankind, and more especially to the children of God," and is freed from "the love of the world, the love of pleasure, of ease, of honor, of money; together with pride, anger, self-will, and every other evil temper. . . ." Justification is thus a "relative change," that is, a change in a person's relationship with God, while sanctification is a "real change," a total transformation of her inward character and outward conduct.[2] Justification occurs the moment one places her faith in Christ, and this new status before God lasts as long as one's faith in Christ lasts. But Wesley is less clear about sanctification. It certainly *begins* at the moment one places her faith in Christ, and it would be *lost* if she ever lost faith. But whether her sanctification is *completed* at the moment it *begins* or at some subsequent moment (perhaps just before death, after a lifetime of faithful living) is a point on which Wesley expressed different views at differ-

---

1. Palmer, *The Way of Holiness with Notes by the Way* (1843; reprint, Salem: Schmul, 1988), 81-82.

2. John Wesley, *The Scripture Way of Salvation* (1765), WJW 2:155-56.

ent times. Phoebe Palmer, who knew Wesley's writings intimately,[3] understood him to assert that, whatever spiritual growth might take place in a believer's life as a result of justification ("the first blessing" or "first work of grace"), a moment would come when that growth reached its culmination in sanctification ("the second blessing" or "second work of grace"). And the believer should assiduously pray that it will come sooner rather than later.

Palmer experienced the second blessing on her "day of days." The spiritual crisis through which she had been passing for some months was not due to any doubt that God had pardoned her sins, but to her unmet desire for God to purify her heart. And this crisis was resolved not by some cataclysmic emotional experience, but by her reasoned decision to sacrifice all her "redeemed powers" to God, an action taken in full reliance on God's promise to accept her sacrifice for Christ's sake. She "laid her all upon the altar," and was assured that her self-offering was accepted, not because of the intrinsic worth of her gift, but because the One to whom it was given, the crucified Christ, purifies whatever is freely and unreservedly given to him and maintains it in a state of purity as long as the believer keeps it consecrated to his service. Thus, she came to realize that the only thing required for instantaneous and entire sanctification was wholehearted self-surrender to God. It was this act which delivered her from what she took to be her idolatrous emotional attachments to her family and from her worries that her faith was at best lukewarm.

It is tempting to think that in an age when American industrial capitalism was burgeoning, Palmer had translated Wesley's understanding of sanctification into something like a business transaction between the believer and God, complete with a formal covenant document, spelling out all that she had surrendered in exchange for the assurance that she was now free from the demonic control that earthly goods have over human life. But we must add two important qualifications to this assessment. First, there is something more to Palmer's "altar covenant" than a cold, calculated property exchange. The distinctively Wesleyan emphasis on the centrality of the "holy tempers" in the life of Christian faith is still present, though in muted form, in her affirmation that God had her "supreme affections." That is, this is a personal interaction, not merely a legal transaction. Second, the divine initiative in this interaction is not forgotten. For the promise that the Christian's act of self-surrender will be accepted by the Lord is attested in the written Word of God,

---

3. She was also familiar with the works of John Fletcher and the renowned British Methodist Bible scholar Adam Clarke and modeled her own piety on the spiritual autobiographies of such early Methodist saints such as Mary Bosanquet Fletcher, Hester Ann Rogers, and William Carvasso.

Case Study

and any impulse to make this act of self-surrender is ascribed to the indwelling Spirit. Both of these points are made clear in the account she later gave of her "day of days." Speaking of herself in the third person, she wrote:

> And now, realizing that she was engaged in a transaction eternal in its consequences, she here, in the strength and as in the presence of the Father, Son, and Holy Spirit, and those spirits that minister to the heirs of salvation, said, "O Lord, I call heaven and earth to witness that *I now lay body, soul, and spirit, with all these redeemed powers, upon thine altar, to be forever* Thine! 'Tis done! Thou hast promised to receive me! *Thou canst not be unfaithful! Thou dost receive me now!* From this time henceforth I am thine — wholly thine!" The enemy suggested, "'Tis but the work of your own understanding — the effort of your own will." But . . . the Spirit helped her infirmities: "Do not your perceptions of right — even your *own understanding* — assure you that it is matter of *thanksgiving to God* that you have been thus enabled to present your all to him?" "Yes," responded her whole heart, "it has all been the work of the Spirit." . . . The Spirit now bore full testimony to her spirit, of the Truth of the Word! She felt in experimental verity that it was not in vain that she had believed; her very existence seemed lost and swallowed up in God. . . .[4]

This experience not only seems to have resolved her spiritual and emotional crisis, it also launched her on a remarkable career as an evangelist.

Four aspects of her work deserve mention. First, the Tuesday Meetings quickly began to grow. As noted above, these were originally for women only, but men began to be admitted in December 1839. Phoebe took over leadership of these meetings in 1840 when the Lankfords moved to upstate New York, and she presided over the meetings whenever she was at home for the rest of her life. At times, as many as three hundred were present, and to accommodate such numbers the Palmers had to add a wing to their home and later to move into a much larger one. Those who attended included many of the most prominent Christians of that era, and many of these reported that the meetings had a transformative effect on their spiritual lives and professional careers.

Second, Palmer soon became one of the most sought-after evangelists of her time. Between 1838 and her death in 1874, she preached at well over three hundred camp meetings and holiness revivals in the United States, Canada, and Great Britain.[5] Yet she avoided the histrionics that many other reviv-

---

4. See Palmer, *The Way of Holiness*, 30-31 (original orthography).
5. For a chronological listing of her engagements, see Charles Edward White, *The Beauty*

alists displayed. One of hearers reported that "her intellect and action reveal discipline and self-control," that "she is calm and free from vociferation, and is rarely vehement," and that "in her communications there is more of logic than rhetoric." Apparently the great effect her preaching had on her hearers was due to the evident concern she demonstrated for their spiritual welfare, to the "intense earnestness" of her manner, and to the clarity and simplicity of her messages.[6] Careful records were kept of the number of persons who reported that they had been converted or sanctified at her services, and although we must allow for the effects of peer pressure, crowd psychology, and spiritual self-deception in reckoning her effectiveness as an evangelist, it is undeniable that she was gladly heard by hundreds of thousands of people.

Third, although "soul-saving" was always Palmer's chief objective, she also made important contributions to social welfare. In 1848, she helped found the Five Points Mission in New York, which addressed the problems of alcoholism, unemployment, prostitution, and unsanitary living conditions in the urban slums. She supported missionary work in China and among American Jews, a scheme to return freed slaves to Africa, and the temperance crusade. Also noteworthy were Palmer's contributions to women's rights, especially in the church. Her books *Promise of the Father* (1859) and *Tongue of Fire on Daughters of the Lord* (1869) argue, on pneumatological grounds and with great hermeneutical and church-historical sophistication, that women should be allowed to "prophesy" and testify publicly. And although she herself did not advocate women's ordination, several of the "holiness churches" which sprang from her work were among the earliest Christian denominations to break the gender barrier in the pulpit.

Finally, Palmer was a prolific writer. She wrote or edited sixteen books, the most popular of which, *The Way of Holiness,* went through over fifty editions and sold some one hundred thousand copies worldwide. She was a regular contributor to *The Guide to Holiness* from its founding in 1839. And when, in 1864, she and Walter purchased the journal and she became its editor, its circulation promptly rose from thirteen thousand to over thirty thousand. Finally, she carried on an immense correspondence with people throughout the world, many of whom she never met but who sought her spiritual counsel after hearing her preach or reading her books.

Phoebe Palmer's extraordinary career as an evangelist and reformer

---

of Holiness: Phoebe Palmer as Theologian, Revivalist, Feminist, and Humanitarian (Grand Rapids: Zondervan, 1986), 237-44.

6. Quoted in Harold E. Raser, *Phoebe Palmer, Her Life and Thought* (Lewiston: Edwin Mellen, 1987), 117.

compares favorably, both in its immediate impact and in its enduring effects, with the careers of her contemporaries Charles Grandison Finney and Dwight L. Moody. That fact that she was largely neglected by American church historians in the century after her death is highly regrettable, and the recent resurgence of interest in her life and work is well warranted and very welcome.[7]

II

We have seen that Phoebe Palmer stood quite self-consciously within the tradition of Wesleyan theology and spirituality. Yet, as we shall now show, she, following the lead of Fletcher and Clarke,[8] subtly adapts that tradition by highlighting the role of the Holy Spirit in the sanctification of believers, or more precisely by mapping out a *method* by which the Spirit's power could effectively be tapped. Her distinctive take on this issue makes her story very illuminating for readers of Paul's letter to Titus, in which this same issue is central.

On her "day of days," Palmer found resolution for several issues that had plagued her as a young adult: the excessiveness of her grief over the deaths of three of her children, the excessiveness of her affection for her husband, the deficiencies of her religious zeal, and the "filthiness of the flesh and spirit." We may wonder whether her familial emotions were as idolatrously excessive and her flesh and spirit as "filthy" as she supposed, and we may disagree that intense religious emotions are as accurate an index of spiritual sincerity as she and many other Methodists of that time believed. What matters here is that she equated entire sanctification with emotional integration and moral transformation and understood the experience as a kind of personal Pentecost, as "the baptism of the Holy Spirit."[9] Put differently, what entire

---

7. For a succinct summary of Palmer's own accomplishments, as well as those of her contemporaries who report having been directly and deeply affected by her ministry, see Thomas C. Oden, ed., *Phoebe Palmer: Selected Writings* (New York and Mahwah: Paulist, 1988), 1-8. Oden rightly underscores how strange it is, given the impressiveness of these accomplishments, that Palmer was all but forgotten from a few decades after her death until the 1980s, when she was rediscovered. Such neglect was probably due both to her gender and to the fact that the denominations which trace their origins to her teachings are often regarded by scholars who represent the "mainline" churches as sectarian fringe groups.

8. For details on Palmer's use of Fletcher, Clarke, and other second- and third-generation Methodist writers, see White, *Beauty of Holiness*, 120-59; Raser, *Phoebe Palmer*, 230-54.

9. For details on how the pneumatology of early Methodism and the Holiness Movement

sanctification came to mean for her personally, and what she taught her hearers to understand by it, was the Spirit-empowered reorientation (or suppression) of one's natural loves, and the Spirit-empowered amendment of one's inner motives and outward conduct, brought about by a deliberate, voluntary, and irrevocable act of self-surrender. This "altar covenant" is conceptualized as a formal property exchange or business transaction. As noted above, we should not be misled by the commercial imagery she uses to describe this covenant into overlooking its genuinely relational aspects, but neither should we overlook the fact this imagery expressed well what she believed was the comforting definitiveness and reasonableness of the act of self-surrender. Nor should we be surprised that her use of this imagery in her evangelistic campaigns spoke so powerfully to her hearers throughout the United States, Canada, and Great Britain, given that these nations were all engaged at that time, though in different ways and to different extents, in rapid territorial or imperial expansion and economic growth. Thus, although Palmer embraced Wesley's hallmark doctrine of entire sanctification, she also subtly modified it by insisting that a person can receive the "second blessing" in its entirety and in an instant of time by cutting a contract with God. And in modifying the doctrine she also hit on an extraordinarily effective way of "selling" it.

Palmer did not suppose that simply *making* the altar covenant automatically guaranteed that one would *keep* the blessing of sanctification that the Holy Spirit conferred through it. The prolongation of the effect of making the covenant depended on several things: disciplined practice of the means of grace and other spiritual disciplines, scrupulous observance of the standard "Victorian" moral strictures (no tobacco, alcohol, dancing, card-playing, fancy dress, or jewelry, etc.), and willingness to testify publicly to the continuing activity of the Holy Spirit in one's life.[10] Here again, Palmer both adopts and subtly modifies her tradition. For the accountability groups of primitive Methodism had a decidedly centripetal quality: the members were expected to search their hearts for whatever traces of sin might still lurk there, to acknowledge these in the privacy of a small group of trusted friends, and to accept the group's advice, reproof, and encouragement in making spiritual progress — or, in the relatively rare case of persons who might plausibly claim to have achieved sanctification, in maintaining it. But early Methodist bands and classes were kept small, intimate, and confidential precisely be-

---

in particular influenced early Pentecostalism, see Donald W. Dayton, *Theological Roots of Pentecostalism* (Peabody: Hendrickson, 1987), chapters 3-5.

10. For a summary of the moral disciplines and devotional practices she espoused, see White, *Beauty of Holiness*, 146-54.

cause for most members entire sanctification was still a goal to be attained, or, if it had been achieved, a state to be painstakingly preserved in the face of the world's temptations. For Palmer, in contrast, entire sanctification could be achieved by a "shorter way" than primitive Methodism had presumed,[11] simply by making the altar covenant. Thus, while her revival services were designed, like Wesley's, to bring sinners into the state of justification, they were also intended, unlike Wesley's, to bring the justified into the state of entire sanctification. Moreover, her Tuesday Meetings were designed, like early Methodist bands and classes, to bring the justified into the state of entire sanctification and to keep the entirely sanctified in that state. But because the "shorter way" was presumed to be open, right away, to anyone willing to take it, the format of the Tuesday Meetings (and similar prayer groups organized throughout the world in accordance with the same principles) was centrifugal, and thus quite different from that of the early Methodist accountability groups. These Meetings were more like solemn pep rallies, with numbers in the hundreds and with the program dominated by testimonies to spiritual victories already achieved and by earnest exhortations to the not-yet-sanctified to make the necessary act of consecration without further delay.

In fairness to her, we must carefully distinguish Palmer's "perfectionism" from all kinds of Pelagian self-salvation. True again to her Arminian-Wesleyan roots, she was a synergist, insisting both on ascribing salvation entirely to the operation of God's grace in the human soul and on emphasizing the responsibility of the human person to accept it freely and cooperate with it industriously.[12] She resolutely insisted that the impulse to "lay one's all upon the altar," the power to overcome one's natural resistance to doing so, and the transformative effects on one's character and conduct that result from doing so are all to be credited not to oneself but to the Holy Spirit. But she just as resolutely insisted that although the Holy Spirit *empowers,* it does not *coerce,* the human act of self-consecration and that the day-to-day living of the sanctified life involves voluntary practice of the prescribed devotional exercises and disciplined cultivation of healthy moral habits. Conversely, one is always "free" to take something of one's own off the altar, with the result that one loses her sanctification — at least until she makes a fresh act of consecration. Thus, holiness is both a gift that we undeservedly receive through faith in Christ and a task that we dutifully perform, day by day, through the power of the Holy Spirit. Moreover, in calling the altar covenant "irrevoca-

---

11. On "the shorter way" to sanctification, see Palmer, *The Way of Holiness,* 15-37.
12. See, e.g., Phoebe Palmer, *Entire Devotion to God* (1845; reprint, Salem: Schmul, 1979), 17; *The Way of Holiness,* 34-36.

ble," Palmer does not mean that one cannot revoke it, but that one must not revoke it, or, to put the point more positively, that one must depend constantly on the Spirit's empowerment in keeping true to one's promises and in performing one's devotional exercises and moral duties. One can rely on God, but one must not presume on him. It is noteworthy, for our purposes, that Palmer strikes the delicate balance between these poles by quoting Paul's letter to Titus:

> Did the resolution to be a Bible Christian — the determination to consecrate all to God by laying all upon the altar of sacrifice — or the act of entering into the bonds of an everlasting covenant to be wholly the Lord's — bring about this entrance into the new and living way? How could these purposes, however well intentioned, result in having the heart sprinkled from an evil conscience, and the body washed with pure water? Can aught but the blood of Christ do this? Perhaps few with more conscious poverty of spirit would respond in the negative to these inquiries, than that traveler in the king's highway, whose experience has been alluded to [i.e., herself]. "Jesus, my Lord, thy blood alone / Hath power sufficient to atone" were the confirmed sentiments of her heart. "Not by works of righteousness which we have done, but according to his mercy he saveth us; by the washing of regeneration and renewing of the Holy Ghost" [Tit 3:5] was the response ever uppermost in her heart in answer to such inquiries. Yet she conceived that it was by these pious resolves she was enabled thus to be a worker together with God.[13]

Wall notes the intertextual relationship between Titus 3 and Acts 2 and observes the subtle pneumatological differences between them, with the former emphasizing the Spirit's work of engendering personal transformation in the believer and the latter its power to motivate believers for mission in the world. It is the former conception that Palmer presses into service here and that predominates throughout her lengthy analysis of the religious experiences of other Holiness folk in *Faith and Its Effects*.[14]

This brings us to a final point: in assessing Phoebe Palmer's contribution to American Christianity, Charles White has argued that she furnished a

---

13. Palmer, *The Way of Holiness*, 42.
14. Of course, just as these two pneumatologies may be regarded in canonical context as compatible and correlative rather than mutually exclusive, so too there is no question that Palmer happily embraced both views of the Spirit's work — using the Pauline "transformational" conception when the justification or sanctification of individual believers was under consideration and the Lukan "vocational" conception when accounting for the phenomenal success of her own evangelistic labors and the Holiness Movement as a whole.

valuable corrective to the overemphasis that many previous evangelists had placed on justification. A century earlier Wesley had sought to strike a "well-balanced synthesis" between justification and sanctification, "avoiding the extremes of both antinomianism and Pelagianism."[15] But in the ongoing debate with the Calvinists, whose solafideism led them to suspect that such a "synthesis" represented a new form of semi-Pelagianism at best, Wesley, along with Fletcher and Clarke, sometimes tilted toward perfectionism. Palmer was faced with a similar "sanctification gap," due not only to the dominance of Reformed theology in earlier American revivalism but also to the fact that even among the Methodists, whose influence on American Christianity was certainly on the rise, the stress on holy living was waning.[16] And as a good Wesleyan, she responded accordingly, anchoring the doctrine of sanctification in pneumatology, as Fletcher and Clarke had done, and providing a simple how-to manual for securing and maintaining the Spirit's empowerment.

There is, therefore, a curious way in which the role that Phoebe Palmer played in the religious life of North America (and to a lesser extent Great Britain) in the mid-nineteenth century is analogous to the role played by the Pastoral Epistles in the thirteen-letter Pauline canon and in the NT as a whole. The analogy must not be pressed too far, of course. Palmer does not, for example, emphasize ecclesiology or missiology as forcefully as the Pastoral Epistles. But her work does illustrate two points made in Wall's commentary on all three Pastorals and particularly in his Rule-of-Faith reading of Titus: First, Palmer shows that a robust pneumatology is the key to a healthy resolution of the grace-works paradox. The early church understood this when it canonized the Pastoral Epistles. These three letters round off the Pauline corpus and protect it from charges of antinomianism that might otherwise have been lodged against it (cf. Jas 2:14-26; 2 Pet 3:14-18). The Pastoral Epistles affirm that the Holy Spirit transforms the character and conduct of those believers who freely open themselves to its freeing power, while preventing them from indulging in the kinds of spiritual pride and works-righteousness that Paul attacks in his other letters. Second, Palmer shows that holy living, in accordance with Christ's example and empowered by the indwelling Holy Spirit, is both the daunting obligation and the high privilege of all Christians in all times and places. The social, religious, political, and cultural differences between Wesley's London and Palmer's New York, as between Timothy's Ephe-

---

15. White, *Beauty of Holiness*, 178-85.
16. White, *Beauty of Holiness*, 178-85. White suggests that both "the roughness of frontier life and the richness of urban life militated against the doctrine [of sanctification]." He borrows the term "sanctification gap" from Richard F. Lovelace, *Dynamics of Spiritual Life: An Evangelical Theology of Renewal* (Downers Grove: InterVarsity, 1979), 232-35.

sus and Titus's Crete, may have required adjustments in congregational structure and missionary strategy, but they did not warrant any diminishment in the performance of "the works of moral rectitude" (Tit 2:4), works that certainly do not save us by themselves but that do express our gratitude to the God who has saved us by Christ through the Holy Spirit.

Index of Authors

Aageson, James W., 15, 36, 47
Adam, A. K. M., 52
Albin, Thomas R., 202, 204, 205
Allan, J. A., 47
Allison, Dale C., 365
Arichea, Daniel C., 46
Aune, David Edward, 57
Auwers, J. M., 18

Baker, Frank, 202, 203
Barrett, C. K., 46, 250
Barton, John, 3, 18, 41, 52
Bassler, Jouette M., x, 4, 29, 31, 46, 47, 107, 110, 180, 218, 226, 234, 236, 240, 241, 246, 250, 256, 265, 288, 340, 349, 361
Bauckham, Richard, 74
Beale, G. K., 51
Belleville, Linda L., 47, 91
Bernhard, J. H., 46
Blackburn, Barry L., 48
Bleich, David, 52
Bockmuehl, Markus N. A., 271
Boring, M. Eugene, 92
Breytenbach, Cilliers, 4
Brock, Ann G., 97
Brox, Norbert, 46
Bruce, F. F., 17, 48
Brueggemann, Walter, 367

Calvin, John, x, 46, 48, 68, 113, 121, 196, 200, 306, 336, 363, 386
Campbell, Douglas A., 362, 366, 380
Campbell, R. Alastair, 48
Carson, D. A., 51
Childs, Brevard S., x, 4, 29, 41, 48, 59, 126, 152, 216, 231, 243, 269, 271, 274, 279, 280, 313, 369
Clark, Richard, 49
Clarke, Adam, 393, 396, 400
Clarke, Andrew D., 37
Collins, Raymond F., x, 4, 46, 48, 66, 73, 95, 106, 109, 114, 116, 121, 133, 144, 153, 178, 219, 220, 232, 233, 234, 237, 247, 269, 282, 332, 355, 360, 379
Conzelmann, Hans, 11, 46, 156, 265
Critchley, S., 266
Crites, S., 52

D'Angelo, Mary R., 48, 114
Davies, Margaret, 46, 48
Davies, Rupert, 202
Davies, W. D., 365
Dayton, Donald W., 397
Decter, Midge, 350
DeSilva, David A., 226
Dibelius, Martin, 11, 46, 156, 265
Donelson, Lewis R., 23, 48, 351, 385
Duff, Jeremy, 48
Dunderberg, Ismo, 20, 21, 22

Index of Authors

Dunn, James D. G., 49, 72, 236, 362
Durken, D., 51

Easton, Burton Scott, 46
Eichrodt, Walther, 67
Ellicott, C. J., 46
Ellingworth, Paul, 48
Elliott, J. K., 48
Enns, Peter, 311

Farmer, William Reuben, 17, 57
Fee, Gordon D., 46
Fiore, Benjamin, 46, 48, 60, 224, 234, 265
Fitzmyer, Joseph A., 48, 99
Flett, John G., 84, 177
Forsaith, Peter S., 322, 323
Fowl, Stephen E., xi, 4, 41, 52, 220
Fretheim, Terence E., 96
Frey, Jorg, 4
Fuller, J. W., 48
Funk, Robert W., 16, 17, 57, 112

Gamble, Harry Y., 16, 18
Gasque, W. Ward, 37, 48
Gilligan, Carol, 189, 190
Gladwell, Malcolm, 192, 193
Goodwin, Mark J., 48
Gorman, Michael J., 52, 296, 313
Grayston, K., 48
Green, Joel B., xi, 1, 2, 40, 53
Gregory, Andrew F., 37, 53
Grieb, A. K., 253
Gundry, Robert H., 48
Gunter, W. Stephen, 207
Guthrie, Donald, 46

Hagner, Donald A., 48, 354
Hahneman, Geoffrey M., 22
Hanson, Anthony Tyrrell, 46, 48, 114
Harding, Mark, 4, 48
Harrington, Daniel J., 46, 224, 234, 265
Harris, Murray J., 48, 354
Harrison, P. N., 48
Hatton, Howard A., 46
Haykin, Michael A. G., 48

Hays, Richard B., 221, 222, 253
Hendriksen, William, 46
Herdan, G., 48
Highet, Gilbert, 60
Holland, Norman Norwood, 52
Holmes, J. M., 49
Horsley, Richard A., 11
Houlden, John L., 46
Hultgren, Arland J., 47, 49, 72

Jaeger, Werner W., 60
Jenson, Robert W., 41, 42, 52, 169, 270
Johnson, Luke T., x, 4, 7, 9, 11, 12, 28, 47, 49, 53, 57, 65, 80, 88, 93, 99, 102, 105, 112, 125, 140, 141, 142, 143, 182, 220, 226, 240, 253, 256, 262
Jonge, H. J., 18

Karris, Robert J., 47, 49, 141
Käsemann, Ernst, 171
Keck, Leander E., 268-69
Kee, Howard Clark, 99
Kelly, J. N. D., 47, 241, 265
Kidd, Reggie M., 49
Knight, George W., III, 4, 47, 49, 91, 107, 226, 236, 261, 281, 342, 345, 349, 354, 361, 362
Knowles, G. W. S., 321
Knox, John, 19
Köstenberger, Andreas J., 49, 91
Kovacs, Judith L., 21
Kroeger, Catherine, 49

Lane, William L., 49
Lau, Andrew Y., 49
Lemcio, Eugene E., xi, 37, 56, 62
Levenson, Jon D., 3
Levison, John R., 124, 173, 223, 276, 362, 369, 370
Lincoln, Andrew T., 7
Lindemann, A., 18
Livingstone, Elizabeth A., 51
Lock, Walter, 47
Lovelace, Richard F., 400

Index of Authors

MacDonald, Dennis R., 49
MacDonald, M. Y., 49
Malherbe, Abraham J., 11, 30, 49, 53, 68, 149
March, W. Eugene, 49
Marshall, I. Howard, x, 4, 30, 47, 49, 76, 91, 93, 95, 96, 104, 107, 108, 110, 117, 130, 139, 149, 151, 228, 237, 252, 254, 268, 278, 309, 354, 358, 362
Martin, Ralph P., 47, 48, 50, 369
Matthews, Shelly, 97
McDonald, Lee Martin, 53
McEleney, Neil J., 50
McKnight, Scot, 62
Meade, David G., 53
Meier, John P., 50
Merk, Otto, 50
Metzger, Bruce M., 53
Miller, James D., 50
Mitchell, Margaret M., 35, 53, 222
Mitton, C. Leslie, 24
Moore, Charles E., ix
Moore, Henry, 326
Morgan, Robert, 4
Mott, Stephen Charles, 50
Moule, C. F. D., 17, 50, 57, 256, 369
Mounce, William D., 4, 47, 94, 287, 365
Mount, Christopher N., 37
Moxness, Halvor, 53
Murphy-O'Connor, Jerome, 50

Neumann, Kenneth J., 50
Ngewa, Samuel, 4, 8, 47
Niebuhr, Karl-Wilhelm, 50
Niebuhr, Richard R., 17, 57
Nielson, Charles Merritt, 23, 50
Nienhuis, David, 43, 50

Oden, Thomas C., 396
Osburn, Carroll D., 48, 50

Padgett, Alan, 50
Page, Sydney, 50
Parry, R. St. John, 47
Patsch, Hermann, 50

Patzia, Arthur G., 53
Payne, Philip Burton, 50, 91
Perkins, Pheme, 97
Pervo, Richard I., 22, 34, 38, 50
Petersen, William L., 50
Phillips, Thomas E., 285
Pierce, Ronald W., 4, 91
Porter, Stanley E., 2, 4, 15, 47, 50, 51, 170, 231
Prior, Michael, 50

Quash, Ben, 70
Quinn, Jerome D., 22, 47, 50

Rack, Henry D., 202
Radner, Ephraim, 355
Raser, Harold E., 395, 396
Ratheiser, Gershom M. H., 66
Rawson, John, 203
Robinson, Anthony B., 259
Robinson, James M., 252
Robinson, T. A., 51
Rohrbaugh, Richard L., 53
Rowe, C. Kavin, 12, 37, 53, 174, 253
Runyon, Theodore, 201
Rupp, Gordon, 202

Sanders, James A., x, 53, 268
Scholer, D. M., 51
Schreiner, Thomas R., 49, 91
Schüssler Fiorenza, Elisabeth, 97
Schwarz, Roland, 51
Scott, Ernest Findlay, 47
Seitz, Christopher, 26, 53
Semmel, Bernard, 203
Simon, John S., 202
Simpson, Edmund Kidley, 47
Skeat, T. C., 51
Smith, David Raymond, 77
Smith, Richard, 252
Stanley, David Michael, 132
Steele, Richard B., 44, 201
Stettler, Hanna, 51
Stott, John R. W., 47
Strange, W. A., 38

Streiff, Patrick Philipp, 321, 322, 323
Sumney, Jerry L., 61
Sundberg, Albert C., 22

Talbert, Charles H., 50
Taylor, Charles, 8
Thiselton, Anthony C., 51
Tipei, John F., 224
Torrance, Alan J., 271
Towner, Philip H., x, 4, 20, 47, 51, 74, 87, 99, 100, 101, 121, 123, 139, 147, 240, 241, 257, 268, 270, 286, 342, 354, 358, 359, 362, 365, 371, 377, 379, 381, 386
Treier, Daniel J., 53, 312
Trembath, Kern R., 275
Trobisch, David, 17, 18, 38, 53, 231, 269
Turner, Max, 2, 40, 53
Tweedy, J., 46
Twomey, Jay, 47, 77, 138, 239, 282
Tyson, Joseph B., 38

Vanhoozer, Kevin J., 53
Verheyden, Joseph, 52
Verner, David C., 51
Viviano, Benedict Thomas, 51
von Campenhausen, Hans, 28-29

Wacker, William C., 47

Wagner, J. Ross, 253, 271-74
Wall, Robert W., 37, 43, 50, 52, 53, 55, 56, 62, 85, 187, 269, 294
Walton, Steve, 36
Watson, Francis, 53, 252-53
Webster, John, 40, 53, 84, 177, 311
Wells, Samuel, 70
Wenham, David, 37
Westerholm, Stephen, 52
White, Charles Edward, 396, 399, 400
Wilder, Terry L., 6
Wilhite, David E., 368
Wilson, S. G., 52, 369
Winter, Bruce W., 37, 52, 96, 128
Wire, Antoinette Clark, 52
Witherington, Ben, III, 47, 52, 256, 258
Wolter, Michael, 52
Wolterstorff, Nicholas, 26
Wood, Charles M., 19, 53
Wright, D. F., 52
Wright, N. T., 362, 366

Yarbrough, Mark M., 36, 52
Young, Frances M., 52, 90, 183, 184, 295, 334, 385

Zamfir, Korinna, 52, 87

Index of Subjects

Acts of the Apostles, 224, 230, 234, 244, 267, 272-73, 285-88, 301, 363-65
　canonical context/setting, 13, 18, 20, 21, 22, 36-40, 55-56, 58, 69, 70, 74, 81, 86, 95, 98-99, 102-3, 118, 124, 150, 156, 220, 234, 243, 287, 367
　Paul of Acts, 10-15, 36-40, 58, 67, 72, 84, 103, 112, 135, 156, 166, 171-73, 215, 219, 267, 286-87, 294, 314, 332, 338, 340
Administrators (bishops), 28, 65, 98-112, 177-82, 339-42, 375, 382
Apostle, apostleship, 5-7, 9-11, 14, 32-33, 38-39, 55-59, 63, 76, 84-85, 92, 102, 112, 133, 151, 171, 173-75, 177, 195, 216-17, 224-25, 227, 236-38, 243, 264, 268, 302, 313, 335-36, 358
Authority, 28-30, 37, 56, 58, 76, 79-80, 89-93, 101-5, 124, 178-79, 184, 192-93, 224, 25, 358-60
　of Scripture, 310-14
Authorship, ix-x, 4-7, 15-16, 21-22, 25, 36-38, 60, 72, 86-87, 152, 310

Bible. *See* Scripture
Bishops. *See* Administrators

Calling, 32, 58, 71, 84-85, 98, 103, 122, 143, 155, 177, 193, 199, 217-20, 291, 305-6, 335
Canon (biblical, Pauline), 1-2, 8-9, 15-27, 40-43, 72, 81-84, 100, 102, 125-26, 152-53, 167, 185, 193, 231, 251, 253, 269, 277, 297, 311, 331, 335, 369
　canonical approach, 1-4, 15, 21, 24, 37, 86, 112, 173, 185, 331, 369
　canonical context, 2, 16, 55, 72, 81, 92, 135, 143, 186, 215, 223, 252, 285, 334, 354, 399
　canonical (final) form, 1, 6, 9-11, 15, 19, 22-27, 36, 62, 185, 351, 367
　canonical process (canonization), 1-2, 15-24, 25, 34-38, 40, 42-43, 62, 146, 153, 167, 178, 193, 243, 251, 269, 273, 299, 303, 313, 331, 335, 369
Catechesis, 33, 36, 41, 63, 65, 67, 73, 90, 92, 99, 114-15, 123, 138, 140, 183, 192, 235-37, 247, 250-51, 265-70, 279, 304, 347, 353, 376, 383
Christ Jesus, 11, 14, 33, 42, 55, 58, 59, 64, 66, 70, 73-74, 79-85, 114-16, 117, 133-35, 140-41, 145-47, 219, 229-30, 242-43, 248, 253, 263, 278-82, 353-54, 365. *See also* Rule of faith reading: Christ Jesus
Church, 1-2, 11-15, 27-30, 42. *See also* Rule of faith reading: community of the Spirit
Conversion, 33, 35, 58, 65, 67, 71-74, 79, 81, 83, 118, 164-66, 175, 184, 187-88, 222, 258, 263, 270, 336, 348, 353, 359-60, 385

Deacon, 28, 101, 107-10, 321, 324

Devil. *See* Satan
Discipleship, 31, 108. *See also* Rule of faith reading: Christian life and discipleship

Elder, 76, 98-103, 108-10, 113, 124, 128, 132-34, 145-46, 161, 181-82, 225, 339-42
Emperor, 80-83, 147, 156, 175, 185
Ephesus, 12, 39, 56, 62-63, 92-93, 129
Epiphany, 14, 147, 293, 294-95, 332, 352-57, 357-67, 374-89
Eschatology, 33, 73, 115, 121, 125, 143, 150, 247, 260, 265, 282-83, 290, 297, 315-18. *See also* Rule of faith reading: consummation
Ethics, 11, 66, 89, 171-72, 185, 189-90, 196, 305, 307, 340-41, 385-86. *See also* Rule of faith reading: Christian life and discipleship; Virtues; Vices

Gnostic, Gnosticism, 20-21, 97, 118, 152, 166, 252
Good works, 14, 25, 30-32, 80, 85, 89, 135, 149-50, 163, 176, 194, 199-200, 253, 308-12, 357, 359, 362, 376-77

Heresy, heretics, 19, 22, 43, 167, 169, 180, 232-33, 236
Holiness, 25, 121, 160, 167-68, 196, 312
Hospitality, 107, 194, 288, 301, 307
House, household, 8, 12-15, 27-30, 34, 62, 65-66, 78-82, 117-20, 127-31, 136-38, 148, 155-56, 171, 176-81, 186, 192, 195, 220, 226, 233, 255-56, 261-62, 288, 299, 301-2, 314, 331, 334, 340-43, 346-53, 375, 382-89
  household codes, management, 13, 65, 98-114, 127, 132, 136-37, 156, 161, 177-81, 184, 305, 331-32, 343, 347, 349, 351-53, 358, 376, 383-84
  household of God, 12-13, 27-30, 57, 65-66, 69, 79-81, 89, 98, 101-2, 105, 111, 119, 127-32, 158, 170, 177-81, 234, 255-56, 267, 288, 347, 375
  oikonomia theou, 44, 64-65, 75, 80, 82, 99, 101, 118, 127, 131, 134, 155, 161-62, 171, 172, 178, 181, 185, 197, 199, 202, 220-21, 234, 261, 269, 278, 288, 302, 343, 375, 383

Imitation. *See* Paul, imitation of
Imperial cult. *See* Emperor
Intertext, intertextuality, 37, 62, 71, 77, 87, 90, 104, 146, 219, 221, 223, 228, 240, 254, 266, 271, 273, 275, 282-87, 362, 364, 399
Irenaeus, 19, 20, 24, 34, 118

Jesus. *See* Christ Jesus
Judaism, 12, 14, 28, 39, 62, 72, 80, 90, 92, 98-99, 121, 125, 129, 157, 165, 183, 224, 243, 245, 267, 272-73, 294, 303, 334

Kingdom of God, 83, 279, 345, 359, 370
Knowledge of the truth, 33, 55, 73, 78, 81-84, 115, 146, 158-60, 166, 174, 191, 202, 257-58, 263, 301, 336-37, 353, 375-76, 380, 382

Law. *See* Torah
Laying on of hands, 103, 124, 173, 223-24, 300, 306
Love, 66-70, 80, 97, 109, 118, 123, 138, 155-56, 161, 171-73, 220-23, 261-62, 283, 348, 361
LXX. *See* Septuagint

Marcion, Marcionism, 18-24, 34, 152, 197-98, 227
Missio Dei (mission of God), 84, 94, 175, 184
Money (wealth, possessions), 89, 131, 141-43, 148-51, 162-63, 168, 177, 186, 195, 200

Opponents, 5-6, 7, 15, 19, 29, 35, 40, 61, 69, 73, 75-78, 119-20, 130, 152, 172, 197, 222, 239, 250-59, 260-63, 267, 279-80, 287, 300-301, 307-8, 331-33, 338, 342, 343-46, 356, 388

Paul. *See also* Apostle; Authorship
  absence, 7-8, 11, 17, 33, 55-57, 59, 61-62,

Index of Subjects

65, 71, 83, 111-12, 162, 195, 215, 217, 224, 251, 291, 303, 331-34, 338, 386
biography, 16, 58, 155, 165, 173, 194, 233, 265
canonical Paul, 5, 16, 21-23, 32-33, 34, 35, 37, 39, 59, 62, 70, 72, 93, 135, 165, 183, 187, 193, 219, 267, 304, 318, 332
imitation of, 5, 60, 92, 216, 220, 226-29, 237, 264-67, 280-81, 293-94, 308-9, 315
memories of historical Paul, 5, 16, 20, 29, 30, 34, 35, 58, 135, 215-16, 220, 230-31, 237, 239, 251, 290, 304, 388
mission of, 11-15, 31, 39, 62, 84-85, 156, 219, 293, 344, 350-51
Pauline tradition/witness/legacy, 20-21, 39, 56, 98, 151-52, 160, 168-69, 171, 193, 215-16, 221, 227-31, 237-38, 253-54, 267, 300, 301, 335, 369-70
teaching of, 108, 137, 149, 216, 251-52, 292, 297, 368
Philo, 63, 67, 205, 238, 245, 276, 280, 347-48
Piety *(eusebeia)*, 31, 114, 121, 140, 144, 160, 167, 169, 191-92, 261, 337
Prayer, 71, 78-82, 87-88, 119, 159, 175-76, 243-45
Pseudonymity. *See* Authorship

Resurrection, 73, 116-17, 241-48, 249-57, 275-76, 294, 297-98, 316-17, 365
Rome, 14, 37, 56, 83, 129, 147-48, 181, 234, 243, 285, 359-60
Rule of faith reading, 25, 29, 35, 40-43, 63, 109
  Christ Jesus, 163-69, 293-99, 378-84
  Christian life and discipleship, 186-95, 304-14, 383-88
  community of the Spirit, 169-86, 299-304, 381-84
  consummation, 195-200, 363-70, 388-89
  Creator God, 154-63, 289-93, 374-78
Salvation, 14, 33, 59-60, 73, 76, 79, 82-84, 95-98, 122-23, 125, 154-58, 162-63, 165, 166-67, 182, 183, 187, 190, 198, 242, 244-47, 269-70, 293-94, 316, 338, 352-55, 361-67, 368-70, 380, 384, 386-88
Satan, devil(s), 76-77, 130, 173, 197, 247, 256-58, 263, 293, 307, 317, 349
Scripture, x-xi, 1-4, 16, 19, 24-27, 40-41, 84, 167, 183, 251, 267-79, 298, 302-3, 310-14, 369
Septuagint (LXX), 268, 270, 271-74, 277, 376
Servants, slaves, 28, 99-104, 110, 131, 137-38, 151, 179-81, 184, 262, 347, 351. *See also* Deacons
Spirit, divine, x, 24-27, 30, 42, 44, 66, 76, 115-16, 124, 152, 170-71, 172-73, 180-82, 197, 222-25, 228, 230, 261, 275-76, 290, 300-301, 302, 303, 310-12, 359-70, 377-78, 381-84, 387-88. *See also* Rule of faith reading: community of the Spirit
Spirit, human, 17, 93, 222-23, 252-53, 275-76, 288, 300, 306, 324, 387
Stoics, Stoicism, 89, 105, 125, 142, 337, 359
Succession, successor/trident, 7-8, 9-11, 12, 29-32, 34-36, 56, 60, 62-63, 92, 120, 124, 152, 160-61, 182, 216, 217, 219-21, 224-25, 227-31, 232-34, 235-38, 244-45, 248, 250, 251, 260, 264-69, 281-83, 288, 292, 308-9, 314

Synagogue. *See* Judaism

Teach, teaching, teacher, 5, 8, 17-18, 29-30, 33, 56, 64, 73, 84, 89-94, 123-26, 136-39, 140-43, 144-47, 169, 172, 182, 192, 193, 216, 230, 237, 249-59, 265-66, 276, 279, 312-15, 351
Tertullian, 19, 22-24, 34, 41-43, 156, 163, 166, 167, 170, 252-53, 305, 367-68, 379, 384, 388
Theological interpretation, 1-2, 9, 27, 40-41, 44, 72. *See also* Canon; Rule of faith reading
Torah, 64, 66, 68-69, 72, 79, 128, 139, 162, 166, 171-72, 231, 273, 276, 333, 338, 356, 364, 372

Index of Subjects

Tradition. *See* Paul: Pauline tradition/witness/legacy; Succession
Truth. *See* Knowledge of the truth

Valentinus, 19-23, 34, 227, 252
Vices, 31, 68-69, 141, 209, 238, 260-61, 302, 305, 307-8, 310, 331, 344, 353, 357, 360-61, 364, 366, 385
Virtues, 8, 31, 66, 68-69, 97, 98, 101, 102, 105, 107-10, 112, 123, 130, 144, 168, 179, 223, 238, 264-68, 278, 288, 305-6, 309, 310, 317, 344, 347-50, 353, 359, 360, 382, 385-86

Widow/widowers, 13, 102, 106, 127-31, 161, 168, 184, 199
Women, 85-98, 106, 109-10, 120, 128-30, 150, 161, 174, 181, 184, 188-90, 262, 348-51, 383
Works. *See* Good works
Worship, 67, 73, 76, 79-90, 100, 114-15, 124, 146, 157, 170-71, 175-76, 178, 300

Index of Scripture References

OLD TESTAMENT AND APOCRYPHA

Genesis
1–3	189
1:2	376, 378
1:26	159
1:26-31	197
1:27-28	97, 375
1:28	96, 119
1:29-30	119
1:29-31	379
1:31	119, 158, 376
2:7	275-76
2:7-8	95
2:13-15	93
2:18-25	95
3:13	95
3:16	96
3:17	94
4:1	95-96
4:1-2	95
12:1-3	122
17	338

Exodus
1:15	263
6:6	286, 356, 380
8:15-16	266
12:27	286
13:13-15	356
14:30	286
15	92
15:13	356
19:3-6	356
19:5	381
19:5-6	380
19:10-15	356
19:16-20	356
20:14	69
21:8-11	341
22:22	128
29:10	76
30:9	281
32:1	273
33:2-3	376
33:20–34:8	75

Leviticus
1:3-4	82
4:15	76
16:21	72
17:4	82
18:22	69
20:13	69
22:14	72

Numbers
8:10	224
12:6-8	113
15:29-30	113
16:8-11	254
18:31	132
27:18-23	124
28:7	281

Deuteronomy
1:13	179
4–6	113
6	177
6:4	75, 82
6:4-5	67
7:8	356
14:29	128
19:15	134
21:15	341
23:2-4	113
25:4	132-33
25:5-10	341
31:30	113
32:15	339
32:36	84
34:9	124, 224

Joshua
24:1	99

1 Samuel
12:23	80
23:10-11	336

Index of Scripture References

2 Samuel
7:25	268
7:27	336

1 Kings
1:36	268
8:26	268
8:28	336

2 Kings
2:2	224
2:4	224
2:6	224
2:15	224
2:16-18	224

Ezra
6	80

Job
2:6	76-77
36:10	254

Psalms
21:21-22	286
21:28	286
21:30	287
21:31-32	287
37:37	326
92:5	268
109:8	101
117:27-28	376
134:2	88

Proverbs
2:6	241
3:6	251
11:5	251

Isaiah
1:24	137
2:2	260
10:33	137
12:2	339
26:13	254
42:19	336
44	75
44:3	365
53:11	116
66:18-23	355

Ezekiel
36–37	276
36:25	363, 381
36:28	381
36:29	381
36:33	381
37:1-14	275
37:9	276
37:23	381

Hosea
3:5	260
9:4	281

Joel (LXX)
3:1	317, 363
3:1-2	362
3:1-4	363
3:1-5	260
3:5	363
3:6	363

Zephaniah
1:14	282

Zechariah
7:9-10	128

2 Maccabees
4:16	265
6:8	265
7:24	268
7:37-38	84
11:24	265
12:25	268

3 Maccabees
4:10	265

4 Maccabees
6:29	84
17:21-22	84

Sirach
2:1	235
3:1	235
3:14	128
4:1	235
17:26	254
27:27	268
29:3	268
35:3	254
35:12	134

2 Esdras
14:38-41	275

NEW TESTAMENT

Matthew
1:1-17	243
5:17-18	219
5:17-20	267
5:17-48	66
6:1-21	66
6:2	117
6:16	117
7:5	117
7:13	143
7:24-27	150
18:15-17	134
19:12	119
19:28	365
22:18	117
22:34-40	66
22:38	66
23:13-29	117
24	117
24:9-14	197
24:51	117
28:5-7	116
28:16-20	116
28:19-20	85, 169
28:20	314, 365

Mark
7:19	119
9:35	108
10:43	108

Index of Scripture References

10:45	84, 166	2:36	116	13:22-23	243
13	117	2:42-47	38, 178, 186	13:38-39	171
13:5-27	263	3:17	72	13:47	33, 171
		4:19-20	359	14:15-17	154
Luke		4:24	137	14:22	266
1:1-2	140	4:32-35	130	14:23	92, 99, 340
1:1-4	2	4:32–5:11	186	15	38
2:29	137	4:37	102	15:1-3	92
2:36-38	130	5:2	102	15:1-29	38
3:16	368	5:27-32	81	15:4-21	67, 333
3:23-38	372	5:29-32	359	15:5-11	67
5:17	64	5:34	64	15:6-11	74
6:20-26	150	5:42	178	15:9	118
6:27-36	307	6	103-4	15:13-29	55
6:31-36	107	6:1-6	129	15:16-18	178
6:45-49	150	6:1-7	102-3, 128, 186, 272	15:20	118
7:11-17	129			15:36-41	285
10:7	133	6:3	103	15:37-38	286
19:44	101	6:6	124	16–20	265
21	117	8:17	224	16	234
22:19-20	380	8:18-20	225	16:1	221, 265
24:51-54	117	9	165, 173	16:1-3	341
		9:1-9	71	16:1-5	55, 124, 210
John		9:1-21	248	16:4	99
1:18	75	9:15	84	16:10-16	285
3:3	370, 378	9:15-16	38, 58, 71, 103, 155, 156, 172, 217, 244, 336	16:14-15	181
3:3-8	370			16:15	107, 178
3:5	370			16:34	178
13:33	55	9:16	85, 309	16:35	107
16:7	368, 381	9:17-18	124	16:40	100, 178
		9:22	56	17:1-5	67, 267
Acts		9:39	129	17:3	72
1:1-2	364	10–11	343	17:3-5	267
1:3-8	301	10:45	343, 363	17:5-15	81
1:3-10	117	11:1-18	38	17:16-34	112
1:4-5	363	11:2	343	17:18-31	89
1:6-7	147	11:13-14	178	17:22-29	154
1:7	282	12:12	285	17:22-31	158
1:20	107, 243	12:17	38	17:23	367
1:21-22	58, 74	12:25	286	17:24-25	117
2	364, 369, 399	13–14	365-66	18	288, 372
2:17	317, 363	13:1-3	76, 103, 124, 145	18:5	56
2:17-18	363	13:1-4	172	18:5-6	99
2:21	363	13:3	124	18:5-8	39
2:29	74	13:11-41	294	18:7	178
2:32	74	13:13	285	18:8	178
2:33	363, 368, 381	13:14-52	267	18:26	188

Index of Scripture References

19–20	63	28:17-31	37, 56, 314	5:12–6:23	94
19	62, 106, 174	28:23-28	267	5:15	376
19:1-7	370	28:30-31	234, 286, 314	6	187, 249, 253, 257, 296, 297, 307, 385
19:9	62	**Romans**		6:1-14	246
19:10	62	1–4	366	6:3-11	164
19:17	62	1	173, 191, 228	6:4	303, 365
19:21-22	63	1:1	173	6:4-11	318
19:22	56	1:1-5	375	6:12	253, 307
19:23-30	81	1:1-15	56	6:16-20	257
19:23-40	65	1:3-4	114, 242	6:22	364, 367
19:25	250	1:4	116	6:22-23	318
19:34	62	1:5	225	7:6	365
20	282	1:10	57	7:7-12	64, 209
20:1-6	63	1:10-11	15, 62, 112	7:11	94
20:3	373	1:13-15	314	7:12-13	372
20:4	373	1:15	37	7:13–8:2	94
20:5-16	285	1:16	228	8	154, 300, 337, 368, 382, 387
20:7-12	100, 178	1:16-18	221	8:9-17	368
20:17	99	1:17	283	8:16-17	176
20:17-35	9, 39, 58, 192, 215, 243, 285, 309	1:19–2:5	302	8:18	253
20:18-21	264	1:28-31	184, 350	8:18-25	378
20:18-35	58, 63, 266	2:1-11	362	8:18-27	376
20:23-24	266	2:1-16	364	8:23-24	176
20:24	266	2:5-6	318	8:24	247
20:28-30	197	2:5-11	146	8:27	176
20:29-35	227	2:6-11	125	8:28-30	230
21:1-18	285	2:11	134, 318	8:29-33	301
21:8	281	2:16	230, 294, 367	8:33	336
21:17-26	38	3:21	165	8:35	66
21:18-26	287	3:21-26	169, 229	9–11	157, 199, 219, 293
21:21-26	67	3:21-31	361, 366	9:20-23	256
21:25	118-19	3:22	270	9:25-26	158
21:26	135	3:22-26	380	9:30–10:13	361
22–28	80	3:24	164, 166	10:4	171
22–26	287	4:1-5	361	10:9	73, 297
22:1-21	285	4:7-8	355	10:9-13	365
23:29	109	4:13-20	122	10:13	363
24:21	243	4:13-25	217	11:11-24	365
25:16	109	4:17	122	11:17-24	334
26:15-18	71	4:20-21	337	11:36	74
26:19-23	243	4:23-25	337	12–13	386
26:25	88	5–8	366, 380	12	180, 221, 382
27	33, 233	5:3	247	12:1	32
27:1–28:16	285	5:5	66, 362, 368	12:1-2	284, 377
27:27-44	77	5:6	380	12:2	80, 365, 368
28:17-22	285	5:12	94		

413

Index of Scripture References

12:3	223	7	35, 87, 106, 131, 185, 197, 198	16:10-11	15, 123
12:6	206			16:16	122
12:12	247	7:8-9	131		
13:1-4	80	7:31	197	**2 Corinthians**	
13:1-7	80, 184, 358	8-11	119	1:1	173
13:1-10	383	8-10	197, 345	3:6	107
13:9	66	9	133	4:1-15	335, 338
13:12	230	9:1	58	4:4	284
14	119	9:2	133	4:7	2
14:17	345	9:7	240	4:7-18	286
15:20	254	9:9	133	5:1-5	378
15:24	286	9:9-11	368	5:10	125, 364
15:25	108	9:10	240	5:16-17	378
15:31	173	9:11	221	5:17	365
16:1	28	9:15	133	5:18	108, 173
16:3	288	9:18-23	184	6:1	376
16:6	122	9:19-23	100	6:18	329
16:13	336	9:22	125	7:1	88
		9:24-25	240	7:3	246
1 Corinthians		9:27	125, 160	8:1	376
1-4	372, 382	10:32-33	125	8:19-20	108
1:1	173	11-14	170, 382	9:7	251
1:2	363	11	87	9:8	32, 142, 309
1:8	109, 230	11:1	227	10:2-6	76
1:10-12	222	11:1-16	87	11:3	94
1:16	234	11:4-5	87	13:1-2	112
1:18-25	229	11:8-9	94	13:5	125
1:18—2:5	229	11:17	63		
2-4	346	11:17-34	87	**Galatians**	
2:4-5	222	11:27-32	125	1:1	58, 173
2:6-16	368	12-14	170, 180, 183, 221, 223, 300, 382	1:4	166, 284, 380
2:7	230			1:5	74
2:13	30, 221	12	124	1:11	58
3:10-13	254	12:1-3	221, 223	1:11-17	71
3:11-12	200	12:4-11	221	1:16-17	74
3:30	371	12:11	180	2	343
4:16-17	15	13	222	2:1-3	333
4:19-20	222	13:1-2	222	2:1-10	333, 343
5-12	119	13:7	247	2:7	113
5-7	119	13:13	348	2:7-9	333
5	77, 173	14	87	2:9	113
5:5	76, 77	14:33	170	2:10	333, 373
5:9-13	77	15	233, 253, 254	2:16	270
6:9-11	295, 360, 370	15:3-7	114	2:21	376
6:11	88, 116, 255	15:10	376	3:4-29	122
7-10	191	15:12	252	3:19-20	166
		16:3-7	112	3:19-29	209

414

Index of Scripture References

3:28	13, 87, 131, 137
4:1-2	65
5:16-26	66, 366
5:21	295
6:1-10	28, 107
6:10	89, 204
6:12-16	165
6:15	365
6:16	100

Ephesians

1:1	173
1:4	230
1:9	108
1:13	251
1:21	284
2:1-10	360
2:2	284
2:8-9	227
2:8-10	32
2:15	305
2:19-22	113
2:20	200, 254
3:3-4	2, 114
3:4	108
3:20-21	74
4–6	386
4	180, 382
4:28	365
5:3	59
5:5	295
5:26	357, 364
6:10-20	76

Philippians

1:1	28, 102
1:12-18	55
1:12-30	286
2:1-2	220
2:3-9	165
2:5-8	229, 380
2:5-11	116, 169, 248, 282
2:6-8	83
2:6-11	114
2:8	242
2:9-11	116
2:12-13	126
2:17	281
3:4-11	165
3:12-14	240
3:19-20	143
3:20	59, 229, 283
4	233
4:2-3	15

Colossians

1:1	173
1:5	251
1:6	376
1:10	309
1:15-20	114
1:22-23	109
1:24	244
1:27	59
1:29	122
2	345
2:9	311
3–4	386
3:1-8	360
3:10	365
3:11	13, 131
4:13	239
4:14	284

1 Thessalonians

1:3	348
1:9	158
2:12	295
2:17–3:5	112
3–4	386
3:2	15
3:13	146
4:3-6	119
4:11	63
4:17	246
5:1	282
5:3	143
5:4	230
5:12	122
5:23	146

2 Thessalonians

1:10	230
2:3	143
2:4-12	63
2:8	146
2:17	309

1-2 Timothy, Titus

For the page numbers of treatments of each textual unit in the Pastoral Epistles, see the Table of Contents.

Hebrews

4:12-13	135
8–10	82
10:22	364
10:26	72
13:1	329

James

1:13-16	143
1:26-27	129
1:27	128
2:14-26	400
3	349
3:1	125
3:1-2	160
3:6	254
3:13	179
4:1-2	143
4:1–5:6	149
5:4	250
5:7	240
5:19-20	77

1 Peter

1:17	134
2:11-17	358
2:12	101
2:16	336
3:13-17	80

2 Peter

1:16–2:1	74
2–3	143
3:1-7	260
3:2-7	196
3:11-13	196

Index of Scripture References

3:14-18	400	2:28–3:3	370	**3 John**	
3:15	17	2:29	370, 378	5-8	107
3:15-16	18, 35, 126, 269, 277, 328	3:9	378		
		3:11	174, 222	**Revelation**	
3:16	17, 269	4:7-8	66	1:1-4	2
		4:9	361	5:9-10	313
1 John		4:12	361	12:5-12	116
1:1	174	4:19	361	12:10-12	197
1:1-3	236, 243	5:6	370	13	80
1:1-4	58			13:11-18	260
1:1-5	74, 174, 313	**2 John**		17:8-11	143
1:3	59, 307, 338	8-11	307	19:16	147
1:5	355				

www.ingramcontent.com/pod-product-compliance
Lightning Source LLC
Chambersburg PA
CBHW020118240426
43673CB00038B/527